FUZZY CONTROLLERS – RECENT ADVANCES IN THEORY AND APPLICATIONS

Edited by **Sohail Iqbal, Nora Boumella** and **Juan Carlos Figueroa-García**

Fuzzy Controllers – Recent Advances in Theory and Applications
http://dx.doi.org/10.5772/2622
Edited by Sohail Iqbal, Nora Boumella and Juan Carlos Figueroa-García

Contributors

Teodor Lucian Grigorie, Ruxandra Mihaela Botez, Andrei Vladimir Popov, Stela Rusu-Anghel, Lucian Gherman, Omer Aydogdu, Ramazan Akkaya, M.H. Fazel Zarandi, Fereidoon Moghadas Nejad, H. Zakeri, Xin Wang, Edwin E. Yaz, James Long, Tim Miller, S. Bouallègue, J. Haggège, M. Benrejeb, Meriem Nachidi, Ahmed El Hajjaji, Ying-Shieh Kung, Chung-Chun Huang, Liang-Chiao Huang, Ping Zhang, Guodong Gao, Maguid H. M. Hassan, M. Chadli, A. El Hajjaji, Pedro Ponce, Arturo Molina, Rafael Mendoza, Kwanchai Sinthipsomboon, Issaree Hunsacharoonroj, Josept Khedari, Watcharin Po-ngaen, Pornjit Pratumsuwan, Yousif I. Al Mashhadany, Carlos André Guerra Fonseca, Fábio Meneghetti Ugulino de Araújo, Marconi Câmara Rodrigues, Nora Boumella, Juan Carlos Figueroa, Sohail Iqbal, Muhammad M.A.S. Mahmoud, Morteza Seidi, Marzieh Hajiaghamemar, Bruce Segee, Wudhichai Assawinchaichote, Yassine Manai, Mohamed Benrejeb, Mavungu Masiala, Mohsen Ghribi, Azeddine Kaddouri, Georgios A. Tsengenes, Georgios A. Adamidis, B. S. K. K. Ibrahim, M. O. Tokhi, M. S. Huq, S. C. Gharooni, José Luis Azcue, Alfeu J. Sguarezi Filho, Ernesto Ruppert

Published by InTech
Janeza Trdine 9, 51000 Rijeka, Croatia

Publishing Process Manager Iva Simcic
Technical Editor InTech Prepress, Novi Sad
Cover InTech Design team

Additional hard copies can be obtained from orders@intechopen.com

Fuzzy Controllers – Recent Advances in Theory and Applications,
Edited by Sohail Iqbal, Nora Boumella and Juan Carlos Figueroa-García
p. cm.
ISBN 978-953-51-0759-0

For EU product safety concerns:
IN TECH d.o.o., Prolaz Marije Krucifikse Kozulić 3, 51000 Rijeka, Croatia,
info@intechopen.com or visit our website at intechopen.com.

Meet the editors

Sohail Iqbal received the M.Sc. and M.Phil degrees in mathematics from Quaid-i-Azam University, Pakistan in 2002 and 2004, respectively, and Ph.D. degree in surgical robotics from University of Paris-Est, France in 2010. He was a scientific advisor under French ministry of higher education from 2008 to 2010. He is currently an assistant professor at National University of Science and Technology, Pakistan. His main research interest is to apply mathematical techniques to different areas of computer science and engineering with special focus on surgical robotics. His research interest includes robot modeling and control, interval analysis, and fuzzy controllers.

Nora Boumella received a B.S. and M S. in electronics in 1997 and 2002 from Institute of Electronics, Batna University, Algeria. She is Ph.D. student at Batna University and at the University of Paris Est-UPEC, France. Actually, she is assistant professor at Batna University and research assistant at ETRHB, Algeria. She is with the research team of the LSSI laboratory, Algeria and also with SCTIC team of the LISSI laboratory, France. Her research interests include fuzzy logic and its application to control and networks. She is student member of IEEE society and the National Research task Group (GDR-MACS).

Juan Carlos Figueroa-García is Assistant professor at the Universidad Distrital Francisco José de Caldas in Bogotá - Colombia. He obtained a Bachelor degree on Industrial Engineering and a Master degree in Industrial Engineering at the same University. He is finishing his Doctoral studies on fuzzy optimization at the National University of Colombia, Campus Bogotá. He served as co-editor of multiple international Journals. He participated in various international conferences as the North American Fuzzy Information Processing Society (NAFIPS), the International Conference on Intelligent Computing (ICIC), IEEE Symposium Series on Computational Intelligence (SSCI), the IEEE World Congress on Computational Intelligence (WCCI), among others as chair and/or reviewer. He wrote more than 30 technical papers in different Journals and Conference proceedings, and participated in different books. He was awarded in NAFIPS'10 with the "Outstanding Paper Award", ICIC'11 with the "Best Paper Award" and FEDCSIS'12 with the IFSA's "Young Scientist Award" for his advances on Type-2 fuzzy markov chains and Type-2 fuzzy sets theory. His particular interests are Type-2 fuzzy sets theory, fuzzy optimization, fuzzy statistics, fuzzy markov chains, evolutionary algorithms applied to missing data problems, linear programming, and time series analysis.

Contents

Preface

At the core of many engineering problems is the problem of control of different systems. These systems range all the way from classical inverted pendulum to auto-focusing system of a digital camera. Fuzzy control systems have demonstrated their enhanced performance in all these areas. Although initially fuzzy systems were associated only to the artificial intelligence that has refrained to the development of theoretical fuzzy systems, in 1985 Japanese researchers Seiji Yasunobu and Soji Miyamoto demonstrated the superiority of fuzzy control systems for the Sendai railway. From that moment on, many applications have taken the advantage of the inherent potential offered by fuzzy controllers. Some notable works on the applications of fuzzy controllers are inverted pendulum balancing by Takeshi Yamakawa, improved vacuum cleaners by Panasonic corporation, stable CCD development by Canon Inc., energy efficient air conditioners by Mitsubishi Companies and fuel efficient automatic space docking by NASA.

Since fuzzy controllers have proven their performance in many domains of science and technology, it has led to further development of the theory of fuzzy systems to solve even more intricate problems. In this book, our purpose is to present the recent developments both in theory and applications of fuzzy controllers. The book is a collection of chapters which are the result of the coordinated work of scholars worldwide. Each chapter presents a different application of fuzzy controllers along with the necessary development of the theory. Any reader can study every chapter of this book as a self-contained research work. Moreover, this book can be recommended to students who have done the basics of fuzzy set theory earlier on and now they want to apply it. Reading of the entire book will provide you with a variety of ideas to develop theory and apply it to fuzzy control problems.

This book starts with theory development and its application to solve an aerospace engineering problem, then a fuzzy controller is used in electric railway transportation. In the subsequent chapters, further theory and its applications to solve a variety of problems are presented. These problems include the fault tolerant control of a vehicle, integral wheelchair control, and hierarchical fuzzy control among others. Book concludes with a chapter on describing the new areas in fuzzy controllers.

Reviewing all the received chapters, proposing improvements, and all the tasks of book editing within few months were not possible without the dedicated efforts of my colleagues and co-editors of the book Nora Boumella and Juan Carlos Figueroa García. I am thankful to both for their commitment to excellence.

During the review of the book chapters and book editing Iva Simcic, publishing process manager of INTECH, provided fast and efficient feedback and guidance. I would like to thank her for her professionalism.

Special thanks to my teachers Sarmad Abbasi and Yacine Amirat for guiding me to understand the techniques of scientific research. I would also like to express my gratitude to Arshad Ali, principal NUST School of Electrical Engineering and Computer Science who always encourage faculty to take initiatives to promote a culture of scientific investigation.

I am highly indebted to Higher Education Commission of Pakistan for revolutionizing the science and technology. Moreover, I am also thankful to National University of Sciences and Technology, Pakistan for providing an idea environment for research and development.

Sohail Iqbal
National University of Science and Technology,
Pakistan

Nora Boumella
University of Batna, Batna,
Algeria

Juan Carlos Figueroa-García,
Universidad Distrital Francisco Jose de Caldas, Bogota,
Colombia

Chapter 1

Fuzzy Logic Control of a Smart Actuation System in a Morphing Wing

Teodor Lucian Grigorie, Ruxandra Mihaela Botez and Andrei Vladimir Popov

Additional information is available at the end of the chapter

http://dx.doi.org/10.5772/48778

1. Introduction

The actual trends in aerospace engineering are related to the green aircrafts development and to theirs' constructive parts optimization in order to obtain important fuel and energy savings. A lot of these studies refer to the aircrafts' shape optimization, taking into account that the aircraft drag force influences directly the fuel consumption. In this way, a very interesting and provocative concept was launched on the market, i.e. "morphing aircraft". Considering the drag reduction, fuel consumption economy and flight envelope increasing promising benefits, many universities, R&D institutions and industry initiated and developed morphing aircrafts studies in the last decade (Munday and Jacob, 2002; Sanders, 2003; Manzo et al., 2004; Skillen and Crossley, 2005; Bornengo et al., 2005; Moorhouse et al., 2006; Namgoong et al., 2006; Namgoong et al., 2007; Seigler et al., 2007; Obradovic and Subbarao, 2011 a; Obradovic and Subbarao, 2011 b; Gamboa et al., 2009; Baldelli at al., 2008; Inoyama et al., 2008; Thill et al., 2008; Perera and Guo, 2009; Bilgen et al., 2009; Bilgen et al., 2010; Thill et al., 2010; Seber and Sakarya, 2010; Wildschek et al., 2010; Ahmed et al., 2011). The multidisciplinary aspects involved by such studies, bring together research teams in many fields of the science: aerodynamics and aeroelasticity, automation, electrical engineering, materials engineering, control and software engineering. Categorized as a part of the "Smart structures" engineering field, the general concept of morphing aircrafts includes some particular elements, as a function by the complexity of the developed morphing application. Recent researches in smart materials and adaptive structures fields have led to a new way to obtain a morphing aircraft by changing the shape of its wings through the control of the airfoils cambers; the concept was called "morphing wing". Therefore, a lot of architecture were and are still imagined, designed, studied and developed, for this new concept application. One of these is our team project including the numerical simulations and experimental multidisciplinary studies using the wind tunnel for a morphing wing equipped with a flexible skin, smart material actuators and pressure sensors. The aim of these studies is to develop an automatic system that, based on the information related to the pressure distribution along the wing chord, moves the transition point from the laminar to the turbulent regime closer to the trailing edge in order to obtain a larger laminar flow region, and, as a consequence, a drag reduction.

The objective of the research presented here is to develop a new morphing mechanism using smart materials such as Shape Memory Alloy (SMA) as actuators and fuzzy logic techniques. These smart actuators deform the upper wing surface, made of a flexible skin, so that the laminar-to-turbulent transition point moves closer to the wing trailing edge. The ultimate goal of this research project is to achieve drag reduction as a function of flow condition by changing the wing shape. The transition location detection is based on pressure signals measured by optical and Kulite sensors installed on the upper wing flexible surface. Depending on the project evolution phase, two architectures are considered for the morphing system: open loop and closed loop. The difference between these two architectures is their use of the transition point as a feedback signal. This research work was a part of a morphing wing project developed by the Ecole de Technologie Supérieure in Montréal, Canada, in collaboration with the Ecole Polytechnique in Montréal and the Institute for Aerospace Research at the National Research Council Canada (IAR-NRC) (Brailovski et al., 2008; Coutu et al., 2007; Coutu et al., 2009; Georges et al., 2009; Grigorie & Botez, 2009; Grigorie & Botez, 2010; Grigorie et al., 2010 a; Grigorie et al., 2010 b; Grigorie et al., 2010 c; Popov et al., 2008 a; Popov et al., 2008 b; Popov et al., 2009 a; Popov et al., 2009 b; Popov et al., 2010 a; Popov et al., 2010 b; Popov et al., 2010 c; Sainmont et. al., 2009), initiated and financially supported by the following government and industry associations: the Consortium for Research and Innovation in Aerospace in Quebec (CRIAQ), the National Sciences and Engineering Research Council of Canada (NSERC), Bombardier Aerospace, Thales Avionics, and the National Research Council Canada Institute for Aerospace Research (NRC-IAR).

2. Architecture of the controlled structure

To achieve the aerodynamic imposed purpose in the project, a first phase of the studies involved the determination of some optimized airfoils available for 35 different flow conditions (five Mach numbers and seven angles of attack combinations). The optimized airfoils were derived from a laminar WTEA-TE1 reference airfoil (Khalid & Jones, 1993 a; Khalid & Jones, 1993 b), and were used as a starting point for the actuation system design.

The chosen wing model was a rectangular one, with a chord of 0.5 m and a span of 0.9 m. The model was equipped with a flexible skin made of composite materials (layers of carbon and Kevlar fibers in a resin matrix) morphed by two actuation lines (Fig. 1). Each of our actuation lines uses three shape memory alloys wires (1.8 m in length) as actuators, connected to a current controllable power supply. Also, each line contains a cam, which moves in translation relative to the structure. The cam causes the movement of a rod related on the roller and on the skin. The recall used is a gas spring. So, when the SMA is heating the actuator contracts and the cam moves to the right, resulting in the rise of the roller and the displacement of the skin upwards. In contrast, the cooling of the SMA results in a movement of the cam to the left, and thus a movement of the skin down. The horizontal displacement of each actuator is converted into a vertical displacement at a rate 3:1 (results a cam factor c_f=1/3). From the optimized airfoils, an approximately 8 mm maximum vertical displacement was obtained for the rods, so, a 24 mm maximum horizontal displacement should be actuated.

In the same time, 32 pressure sensors (16 optical sensors and 16 Kulite sensors), were disposed on the flexible skin in different positions along of the chord. The sensors are positioned on two diagonal lines at an angle of 15 degrees from centreline (Fig. 2). The rigid lower structure was made from Aluminium, and was designed to allow space for the actuation system and wiring (Fig. 3).

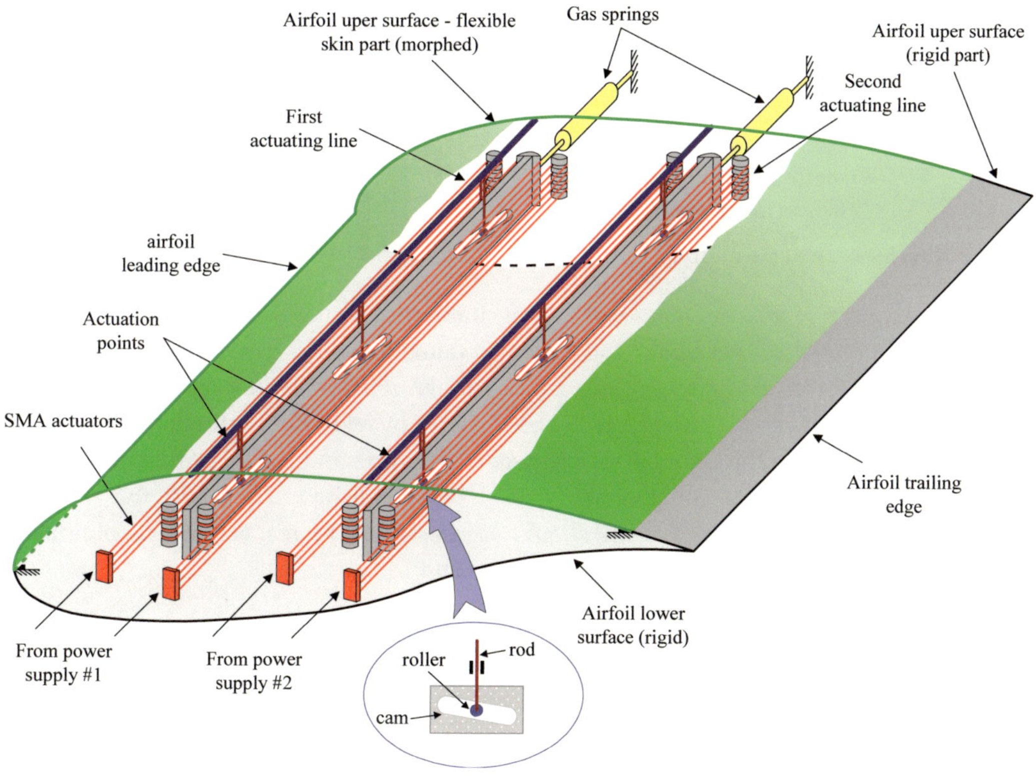

Figure 1. Model of the flexible structure.

Starting from the reference airfoil, depending on different flow conditions, 35 optimized airfoils were calculated for the desired morphed positions of the airfoil. The flow conditions were established as combinations of seven incidence angles (-1˚, -0.5˚, 0˚, 0.5˚, 1˚, 1.5˚, 2˚) and five Mach numbers (0.2, 0.225, 0.25, 0.275, 0.3). Each of the calculated optimized airfoils should be able to keep the transition point as much as possible near the trailing edge.

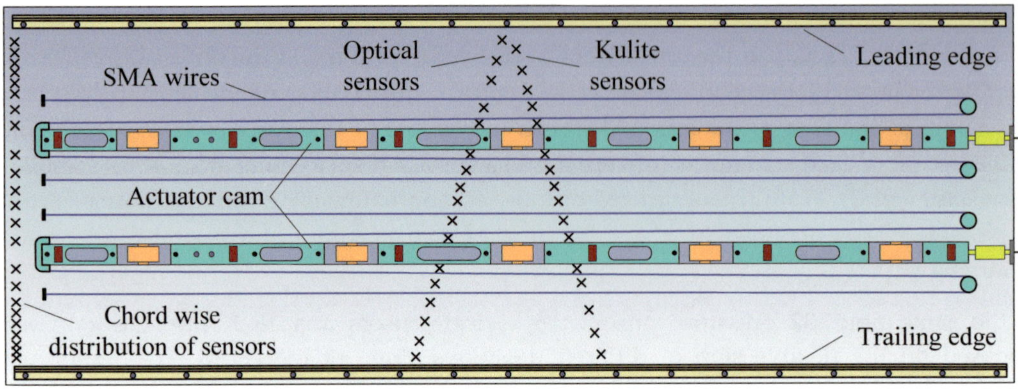

Figure 2. Pressure sensors distribution on the flexible skin

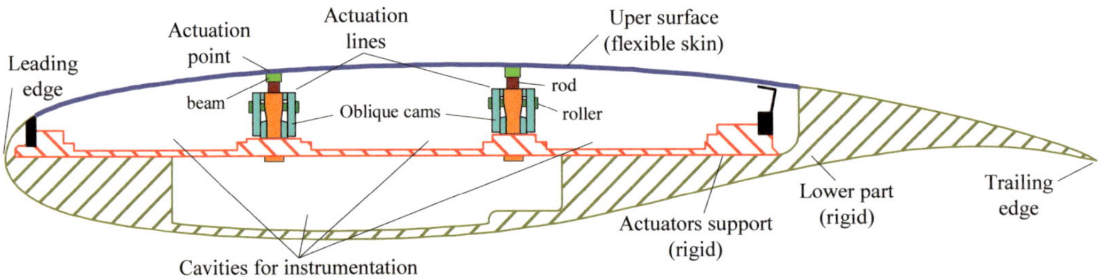

Figure 3. Cross section of the morphing wing model.

The SMA actuator wires are made of nickel-titanium, and contract like muscles when electrically driven. Also, these have the ability to personalize the association of deflections with the applied forces, providing in this way a variety of shapes and sizes extremely useful to achieve actuation system goals. How the SMA wires provide high forces with the price of small strains, to achieve the right balance between the forces and the deformations, required by the actuation system, a compromise should be established. Therefore, the structural components of the actuation system should be designed to respect the capabilities of actuators to accommodate the required deflections and forces.

3. Open loop control of the morphing wing

For each of the two actuation lines the open loop control architecture used a controller which took as a reference value the required displacement of the actuators from a database stored in the computer memory to obtain the morphing wing optimized airfoil shape (Fig. 4); because the actuation lines' structure was identical, both of them used the same controller. As feedback signal the position signal from a linear variable differential transducer (LVDT) connected to the oblique cam sliding rod of each actuator was used. This method was called "open-loop control" due to the fact that this control method does not take direct information from the pressure sensors concerning the wind flow characteristics.

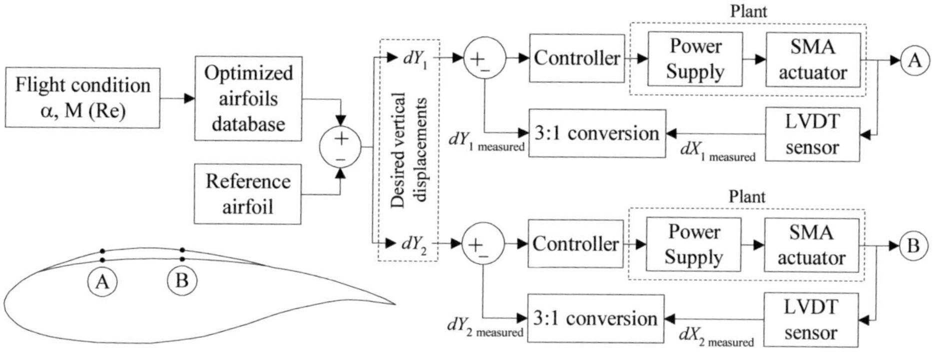

Figure 4. Open loop control architecture.

The SMA actuator control can be achieved using any method for position control. However, the specific properties of SMA actuators such as hysteresis, the first cycle effect and the impact of long-term changes must be considered.

Based on the 35 studied flight conditions, a database of the 35 optimized airfoils was built. For each flight condition, a pair of optimal vertical deflections (dY_{1opt}, dY_{2opt}) for the two actuation lines is apparent. The SMA actuators morphed the airfoil until the vertical deflections of the two actuation lines (dY_{1real}, dY_{2real}) became equal to the required deflections (dY_{1opt}, dY_{2opt}). The vertical deflections of the real airfoil at the actuation points were measured using two position transducers. The controller's role is to send a command to supply an electrical current signal to the SMA actuators, based on the error signals (e) between the required vertical displacements and the obtained displacements. The designed controller was valid for both actuation lines, which are practically identical.

From the point of view of the controller, the literature provides a lot of control techniques for automatic systems. The global technology evolution has triggered an ever-increasing complexity of applications, both in industry and in the scientific research fields. Many researchers have concentrated their efforts on providing simple control algorithms to cope with the increasing complexity of the controlled systems (Al-Odienat & Al-Lawama, 2008). The main challenge of a control designer is to find a formal way to convert the knowledge and experience of a system operator into a well-designed control algorithm (Kovacic & Bogdan, 2006). From another point of view, a control design method should allow full flexibility in the adjustment of the control surface, as the systems involved in practice are, generally, complex, strongly nonlinear and often with poorly defined dynamics (Al-Odienat & Al-Lawama, 2008). If a conventional control methodology, based on linear system theory, is to be used, a linearized model of the nonlinear system should have been developed beforehand. Because the validity of a linearized model is limited to a range around the operating point, no guarantee of good performance can be provided by the obtained controller. Therefore, to achieve satisfactory control of a complex nonlinear system, a nonlinear controller should be developed (Al-Odienat & Al-Lawama, 2008; Hampel et al., 2000; Kovacic & Bogdan, 2006; Verbruggen & Bruijn, 1997). From another perspective, if it would be difficult to precisely describe the controlled system by conventional mathematical relations, the design of a controller using classical analytical methods would be totally impractical (Hampel et al., 2000; Kovacic & Bogdan, 2006). Such systems have been the motivation for developing a control system designed by a skilled operator, based on their multi-year experience and knowledge of the static and dynamic characteristics of a system; known as a Fuzzy Logic Controller (FLC) (Hampel et al., 2000). FLCs are based on fuzzy logic theory, developed by L. Zadeh (Zadeh, 1965). By using multivalent fuzzy logic, linguistic expressions in antecedent and consequent parts of IF-THEN rules describing the operator's actions can be efficiently converted into a fully-structured control algorithm suitable for microcomputer implementation or implementation with specially-designed fuzzy processors (Kovacic & Bogdan, 2006). In contrast to traditional linear and nonlinear control theory, an FLC is not based on a mathematical model, and it does provide a certain level of artificial intelligence compared to conventional PID controllers (Al-Odienat & Al-Lawama, 2008).

Due to the strong non-linear character of the smart materials actuators used in our application, one variant for the controller was developed by using the fuzzy logic techniques. We tried to counterbalance the existence of a rigorous mathematical model, a prior developed for system, avoiding in this way the loss of precision from linearization and uncertainties in the system's parameters, which negatively influences the quality of the resulting control. In the same time, we used the intuitive handling, simplicity and flexibility capabilities offered by the fuzzy logic techniques and due to their closeness to human perception and reasoning; fuzzy logic is an interface between logic an human reasoning, providing an intuitive method for describing systems in human terms and automates the conversion of those system specifications into effective models (Castellano et al., 2003; Kovacic & Bogdan, 2006; Prasad Reddy et al., 2011; Zadeh, 1965).

The controller chosen structure was a PD fuzzy logic one, having as inputs the error (difference between the desired and measured vertical displacement) and the change in error (the derivative of the error), and as output the voltage controlling the Power Supply output current (Fig. 5) (Kovacic & Bogdan, 2006). Widely accepted for capturing expert knowledge, a Mamdani controller type was used, due to its simple structure of "min-max" operations (Castellano et al., 2003).

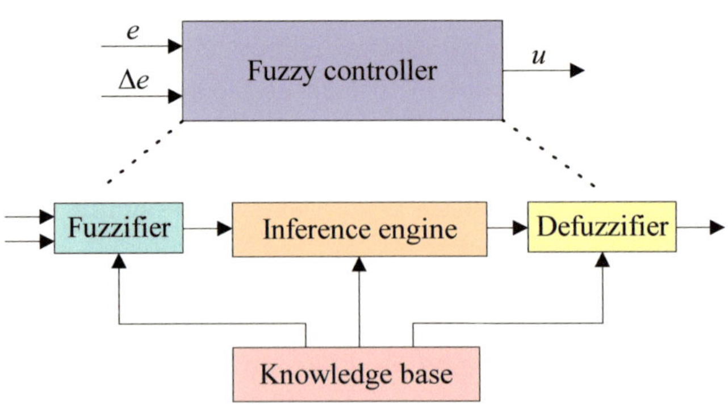

Figure 5. Fuzzy controller architecture.

The fuzzy controller internal mechanism during operation was relatively simple. On the base of the membership functions (Fig. 6), stored in the knowledge base, the fuzzifier converted the crisp inputs in linguistic variables. For our system, three membership functions were chosen for both of the two inputs (N-negative, Z-zero, P-positive), while five membership functions were considered for output (ZE-zero, PS-positive small, PM-positive medium, PB-positive big, PVB-positive very big)(Fig. 6 and Table 1); the used shape was the triangular one, defined by a lower limit a, an upper limit b, and a value m $(a \le m \le b)$:

$$\mu_A(x) = \begin{cases} 0, & \text{if } x \le a \\ \dfrac{x-a}{m-a}, & \text{if } a < x \le m \\ \dfrac{b-x}{b-m}, & \text{if } m < x < b \\ 0, & \text{if } x \ge b \end{cases} \tag{1}$$

[-1, 1] interval was considered as universe of discourse for the two inputs, while for the outputs was used [0, 1] interval.

Further, the inference engine converted the fuzzy inputs to the fuzzy output, based on the "If-Then" type fuzzy rules in Table 2.

The fuzzified inputs were applied to the antecedents of the fuzzy rules by using the fuzzy operator "AND"; in this way was obtained a single number, representing the result of the antecedent evaluation. To obtain the output of each rule, the antecedent evaluation was applied to the membership function of the consequent and the clipping (alpha-cut) method was used; each consequent membership function was cut at the level of the antecedent truth. Unifying the outputs of all eight rules, the aggregation process was performed and a fuzzy set resulted for the output variable.

mf/	Input 1 (e)			Input 2 (Δe)			Output (u)				
parameter	*mf1*	*mf2*	*mf3*	*mf1*	*mf2*	*mf3*	*mf1*	*mf2*	*mf3*	*mf4*	*mf5*
a	-1	-1	0	-1	-0.5	0	0	0.1	0.3	0.6	0.8
m	-1	0	1	-1	0	1	0	0.25	0.5	0.75	1
b	0	1	1	0	0.5	1	0.1	0.4	0.7	0.9	1

Table 1. Parameters of the input-output membership functions

e/Δe	N	Z	P
N	ZE	ZE	ZE
Z	PS	ZE	ZE
P	PM	PVB	PB

Table 2. Inference rules

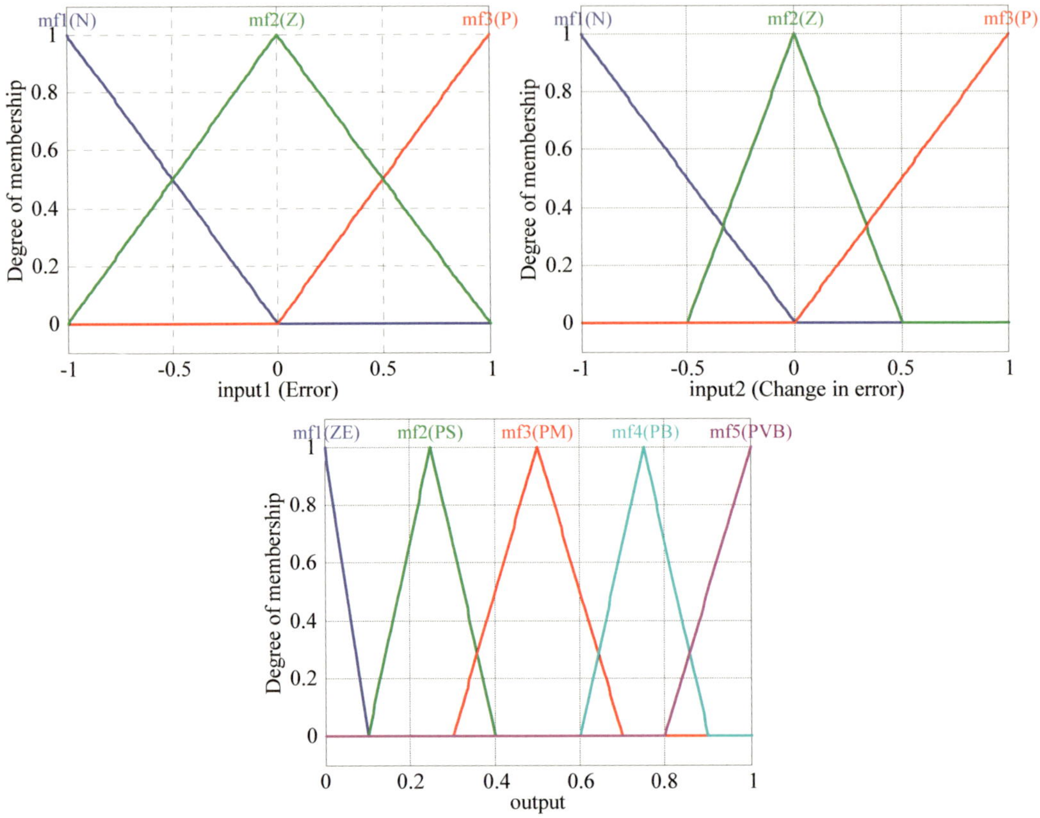

Figure 6. Membership functions

Because the output of the fuzzy system should be a crisp number, finally a defuzzification process was realized (Fig. 7); the Centroid of area (COA) method was used. The control surface resulted as in Fig. 8.

The fuzzy control surface was chosen in this way because it is normal that in the SMA cooling phase the actuators would not be powered. Therefore, the fuzzy controller was chosen to work in tandem with a bi-positional controller (particularly an on-off one). The cooling phase may occur not only when controlling a long-term phase, when a switch between two values of the actuator displacements is commended, but also in a short-lived phase, which happens when the real value of the deformation exceeds its desired value and the actuator wires need to be cooled. As a consequence, the final controller should behave as a switch between the SMA cooling and heating phases, in which the output current is 0 A, or is controlled by the fuzzy logic controller.

As a consequence, the resulted controller operational scheme can be organised as in Fig. 9.

To optimize all coefficients in the control scheme, the open loop of the morphing wing system was implemented in Matlab-Simulink model as in Fig. 10.

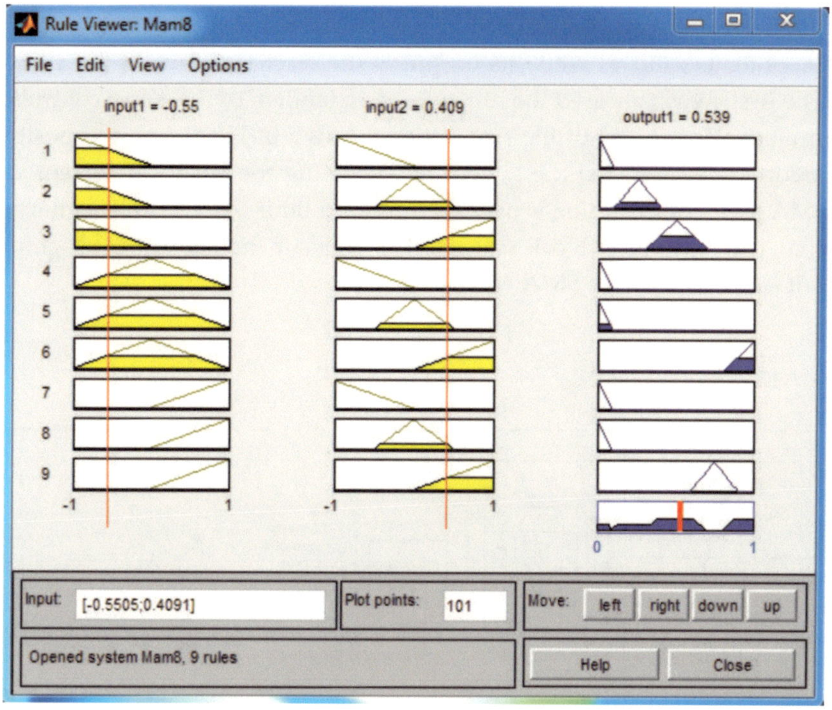

Figure 7. Fuzzy system operating mechanism.

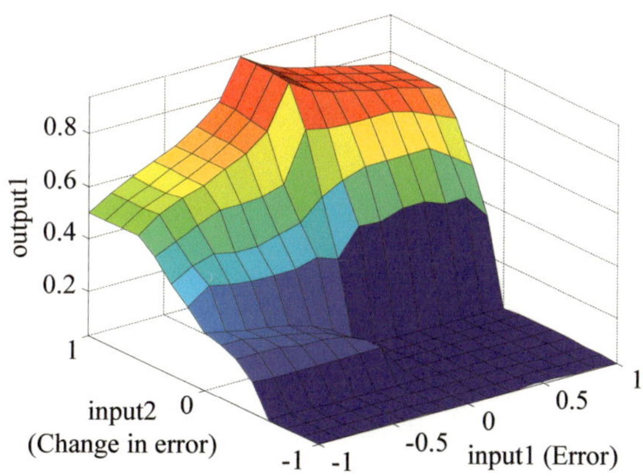

Figure 8. Control surface.

The "Mechanical system" block implements all the forces influencing the SMA load force: the aerodynamic force F_{aero}, the skin force F_{skin}, and the gas spring force F_{spring}; in the initialization phase, the actuators are preloaded by the gas springs even when there is no aerodynamic load applied on the flexible skin.

The "Fuzzy controller" block models the controller presented in Fig. 9. Also, SMA actuators' physical limitations in terms of temperature and supplying currents were considered in this block. Its detailed Simulink scheme is shown in Fig. 11. The block inputs are the control error (the difference between the desired and the obtained displacements – see Fig. 9) and the SMA wires temperatures, while its output is the electrical current used to control the actuators. The first switch assured the functioning in tandem of the fuzzy controller with the on-off controller selecting one of the two options shown in Fig. 9 (error is positive or not), while the second one protected the system by switching the electrical current value to 0A when the SMA temperature value is over the imposed limit. As a supplementary protection measure, a current saturation block was used to prevent the current from going over the physical limit supported by the SMA wires.

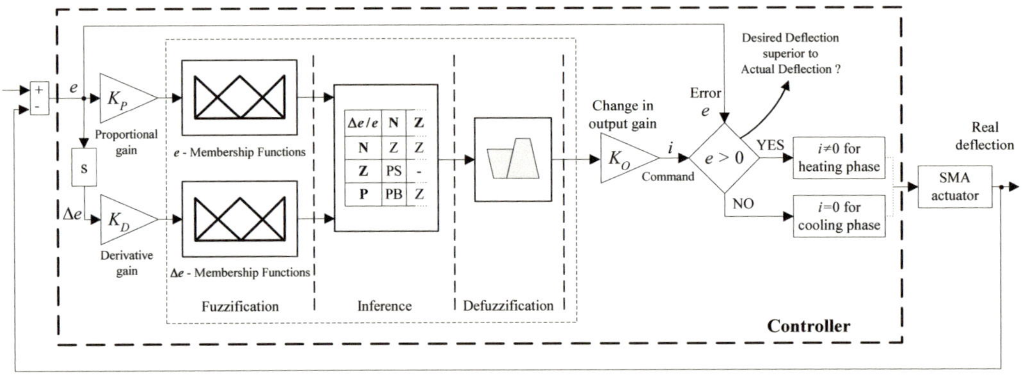

Figure 9. Operational scheme of the controller.

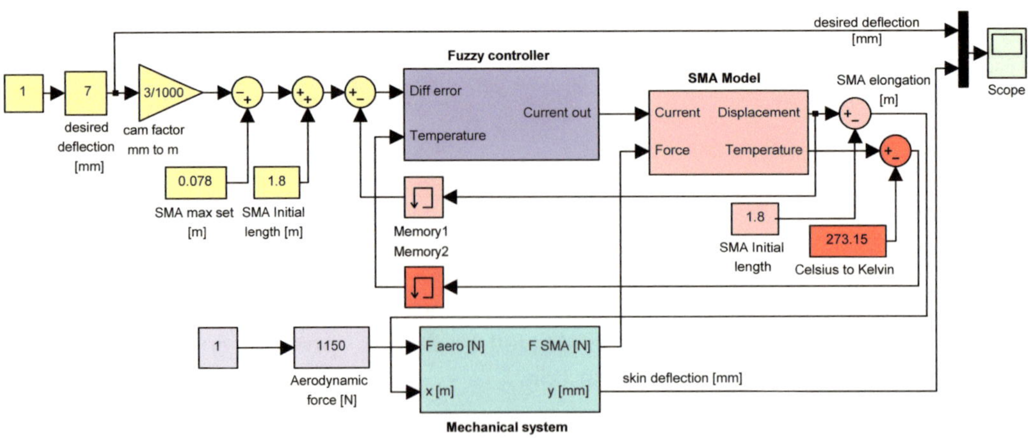

Figure 10. Simulation model of the morphing wing system open loop.

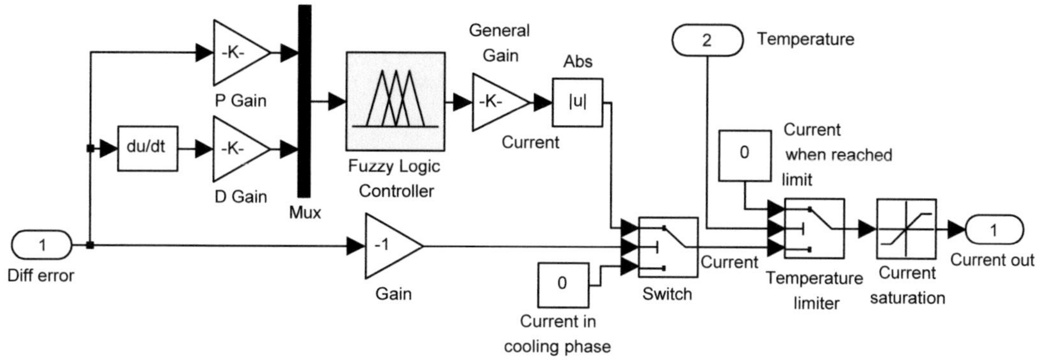

Figure 11. "Fuzzy controller" block.

Another important block in the scheme in Fig. 10 is the „SMA model" block. This block implemented a non-linear model for the SMA actuators using a Matlab S-function. The model was built in the Shape Memory Alloys and Intelligent Systems Laboratory (LAMSI) at ETS, using Lickhatchev's theoretical model (Terriault et al., 2006).

After a tuning operation the optimum values of the gains in the scheme were established. Further, the controller was tested through numerical simulation to ensure that it works well. Fig. 12 shows the response of the actuator relative to the desired vertical displacement, the SMA actuator envelope (obtained vertical displacement vs. temperature), the SMA temperature in time, and the SMA loading force vs. temperature. Using a preliminary estimation of the forces loading the mechanical system, the next values were considered in simulations: 1150 N for aerodynamic force; 1250 N for gas spring pretension force; and the linear elastic coefficients of 2.95 N/mm and 100 N/mm, for the gas spring and for the flexible skin, respectively.

The relative allure of the obtained and desired displacements, proved the good functioning of the controller; the system's response is a critically damped one, an easier latency being observed in the cooling phase of the SMA wires in comparison with theirs heating phase. The SMAs temperature oscillations in the steady-state of the actuation position are due to theirs thermal inertia, and do not affect significantly the SMA elongation. The shape of the "displacement vs. temperature" and "loading force vs. temperature" envelopes highlights the strong nonlinear behavior of the SMA actuators.

To validate the control some experimental tests in wind tunnel were performed; all tests were performed in the IAR-NRC wind tunnel at Ottawa. The open loop experimental model is presented in Fig. 13.

According to the architecture presented in Fig. 13, the controller acted on the SMA lines by using a data acquisition card and two power supplies. The controller had also a feedback from the SMA lines behavior by using the information from two position sensors. As power supplies were chosen two Programmable Switching Power Supplies AMREL SPS100-33, while a Quanser Q8 data acquisition card was used to interface them with the control software. The card was connected to a PC and programmed via Matlab/Simulink R2006b and WinCon 5.2. The Matlab/Simulink implemented controller received the feedback signals from two Linear Variable Differential Transformer (LVDT) potentiometers, used as position sensors to monitor the SMA wires elongations. Also, as a safety feature for the experimental model, the SMA wires temperatures were monitored and limited by the control system. Therefore, as acquisition card inputs were considered the signals from the two LVDT potentiometers and the six signals from the thermocouples installed on each of the SMA wires' components, while as outputs were considered 4 channels, used to initialize and to control each power supply through theirs analog/external control features by means of a DB-15 I/O connector.

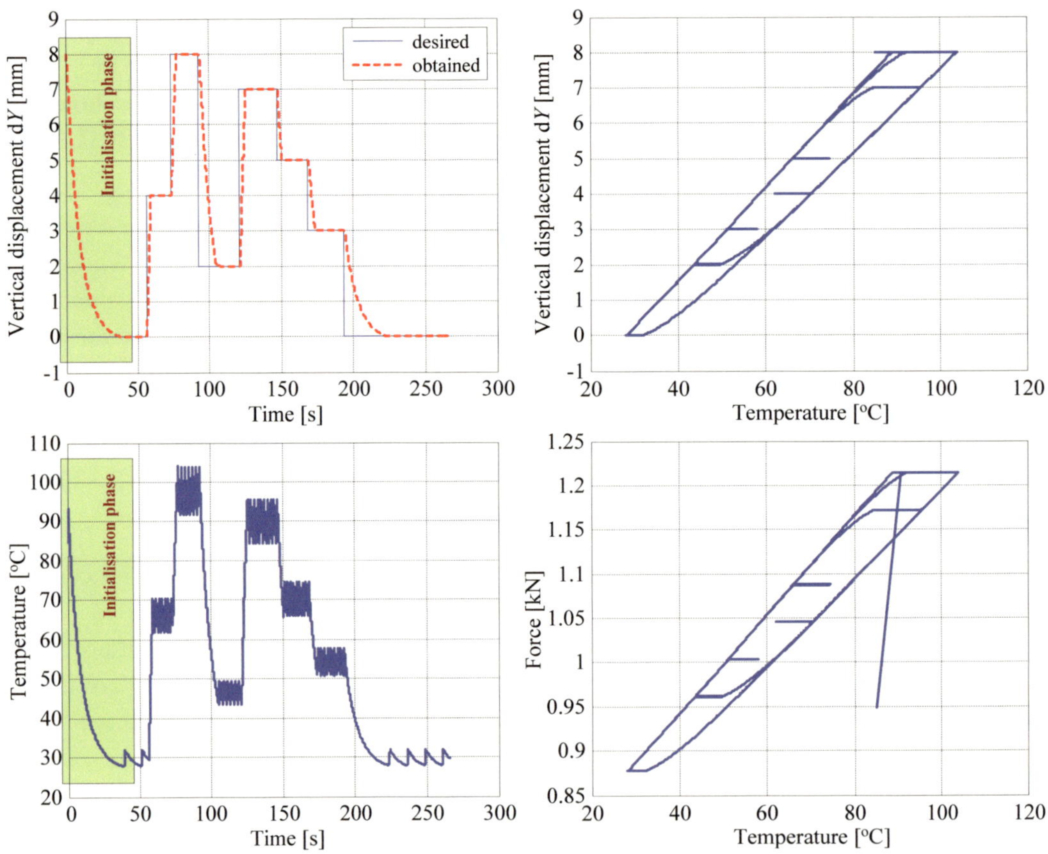

Figure 12. Numerical simulation results

In the open loop wind tunnel tests, simultaneously with the controller validation, the real-time detection and visualization of the transition point position were performed (Fig. 13), for all the thirty-five optimized airfoils; a comparative study was realized based on the transition point position estimation for the reference airfoil and for each optimized airfoil, with the aim to validate the aerodynamic part of the project. In this way, the pressure data signals obtained from the Kulite pressure sensors were used; these data were acquired using the IAR-NRC analog data acquisition system, which was connected to the sensors. The sampling rate of each channel was at 15 kHz, which allowed a pressure fluctuation FFT spectral decomposition of up to 7.5 kHz for all channels. The signals were processed in real time using Simulink. The pressure signals were analyzed using Fast Fourier Transforms (FFT) decomposition to detect the magnitude of the noise in the surface air flow. Subsequently, the data was filtered by means of high-pass filters and processed by calculating the Root Mean Square (RMS) of the signal to obtain a plot diagram of the pressure fluctuations in the flow boundary layer. This signal processing was necessary to disparate the inherent electronically induced noise, by the Tollmien-Schlichting waves that are responsible for triggering the transition from laminar to turbulent flow. The measurements analysis revealed that the transition appeared at frequencies between 3÷5kHz and the magnitude of the pressure variations in the laminar flow boundary layer were on the order of 5e-4 Pa. The transition from the laminar flow to turbulent flow was shown by an increase in the pressure fluctuation, which was indicated by a drastic variation of the pressure signal RMS.

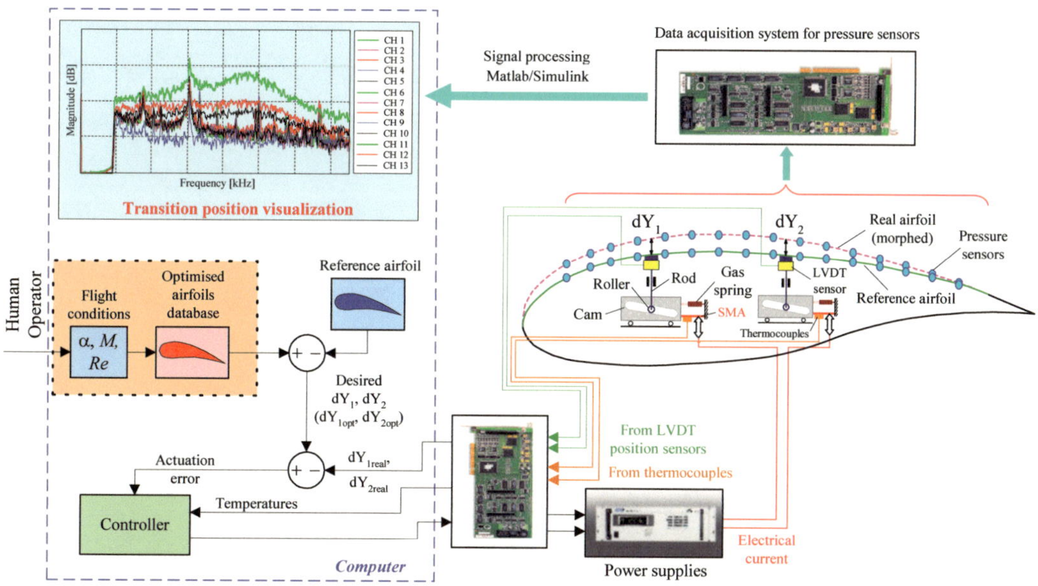

Figure 13. Architecture of the open loop morphing wing model.

In Fig. 14 are presented the results obtained for the open loop controller testing in the flow case characterized by M=0.275 and α=1.5 deg (run test 51); can be easily observed that, because of the gas springs pretension forces, the controller worked even the required vertical displacements for the actuation lines were zero millimeters. Also, some noise parasitizing the LVDT sensors measurements appeared in this test due to the wind tunnel electrical power sources and its instrumentation equipment. The transition monitoring revealed that this noise level did not influence significantly the transition point position; the positioning resolution was determined by the density of the chord-disposed pressure sensors.

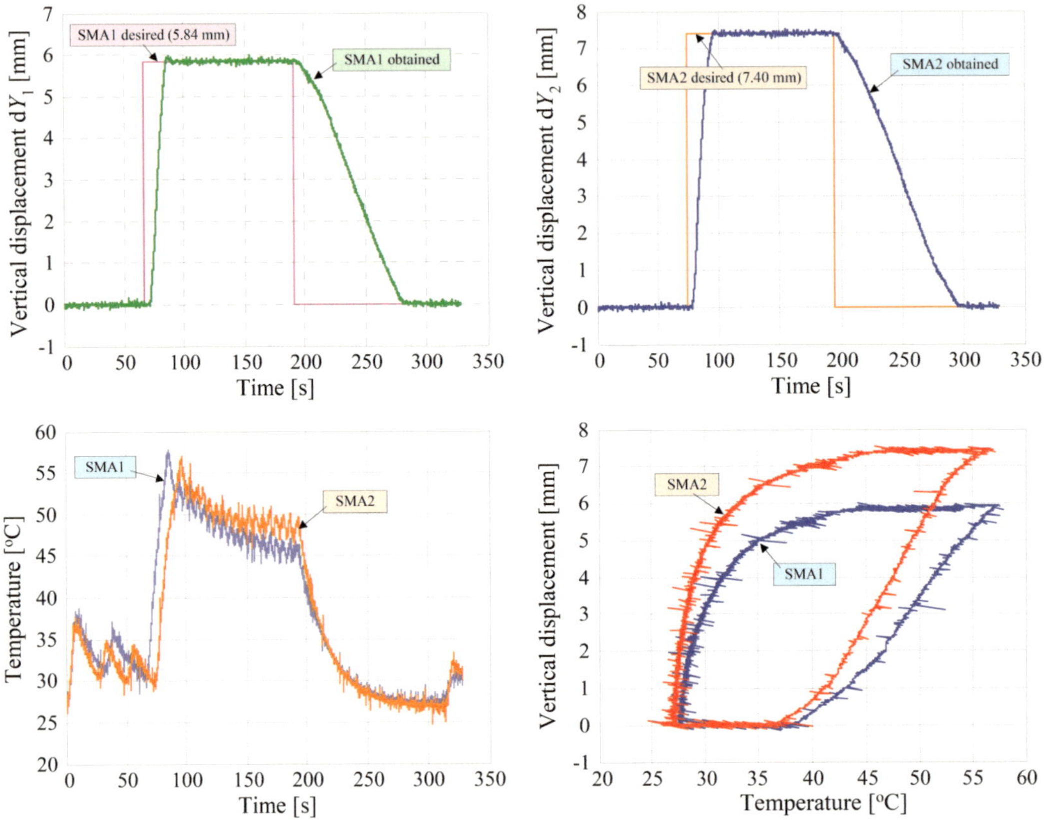

Figure 14. Wind tunnel test results for M=0.275 and α=1.5 deg flow condition.

Fig. 15 depicts the results obtained by the transition monitoring for the run test 51 (M=0.275 and α=1.5 deg); shown are the instant plots of the RMS's and spectrum for the pressure signals channels with un-morphed and morphed airfoil.

From 16 Kulite pressure sensors initially mounted on the flexible skin, only 13 channels were available (CH1 to CH13): sensor #1 was broken before the wind tunnel test, while the sensors #12 and #13 were removed from plots due to the bad dynamic signals which show electrical failure of the sensors. The left hand column presents the results for the reference (un-morphed) airfoil, and the right hand side column display the results for the optimized (morphed) airfoil. The spike of the RMS and the highest noise band on the spectral plots (CH 11 cian spectra on the right low plot) for the morphed airfoil case suggested that the flow was already turned turbulent on sensor on the channel 11 (eleventh available Kulite sensor), near the trailing edge; therefore, the transition point position was somewhere near the CH 11. For un-morphed airfoil the transition was localized by the sensor on the channel 8, with maximum RMS and the highest noise band on the spectral plots (CH 8 black spectra on the left middle plot).

The results obtained from the wind tunnel tests of open loop architecture showed that the controller performed very well in enhancing the wind aerodynamic performance.

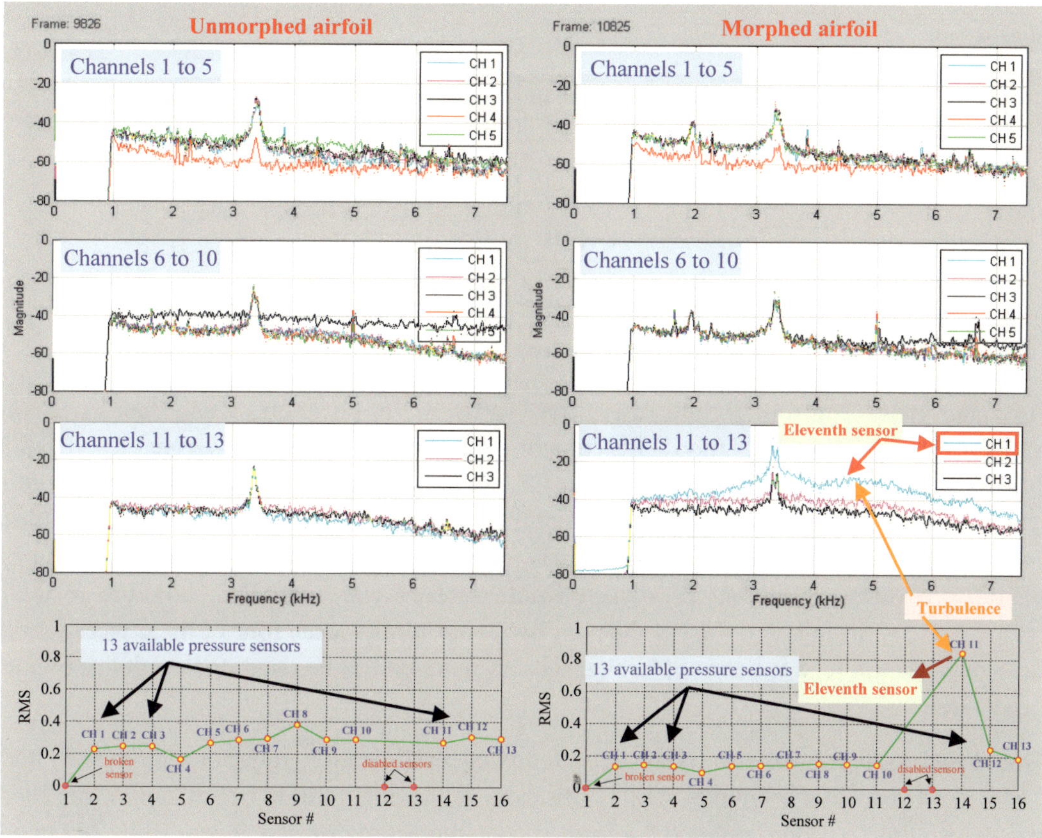

Figure 15. Transition monitoring in wind tunnel test for M=0.275 and α=1.5 deg.

4. Closed loop control of the morphing wing

The next step of the work on the morphing wing project supposed the development of the closed loop control, based on the pressure information received from the sensors and on the transition point position estimation. The closed loop control included, as inner loop, the actuation lines previous presented controller (Popov et al., 2010 a; Popov et al., 2010 b; Popov et al., 2010 c).

The closed loop architecture was developed in order to generate real time optimized airfoils starting from the information received from the pressure sensors and targeting the morphing wing main goal: the improvement of the laminar flow over the wing upper surface (Fig. 16); the previously calculated optimized airfoils database was by-passed in this control strategy, and were used just to see if the closed loop real time optimizer conducted to similar results for morphed airfoil in a flow case. To achieve the control, a mixed optimization method was used, between „the gradient ascent" or „hill climbing" method and the „simulated annealing" method. Two variants were tested for the starting point on the optimization map control: 1) dY_1=4 mm, dY_2=4 mm (Fig. 16), and 2) dY_{1opt}, dY_{2opt} of the theoretically obtained optimized airfoil (Popov et al., 2010 a; Popov et al., 2010 b; Popov et al., 2010 c).

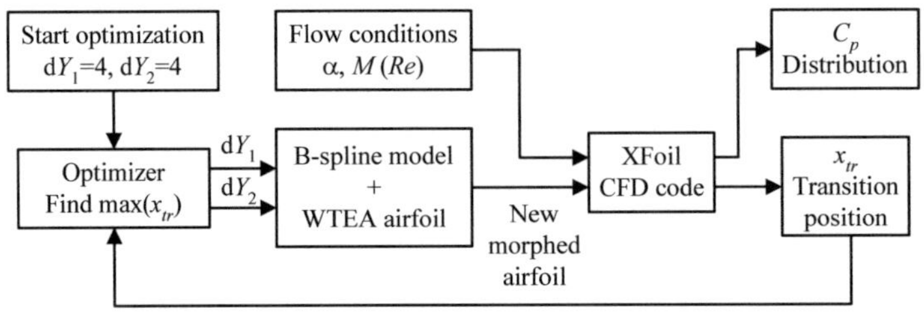

Figure 16. Optimization logic scheme for closed loop.

For the new control architecture, the software application was developed in Matlab/Simulink and two National Instruments Data Acquisition Cards were used: NI-DAQ USB 6210 and NI-DAQ USB 6229 (Quanser Q8 data acquisition card was removed from this configuration). As feedback signal for control was used the transition point position estimated starting from the pressure signals from the Kulite sensors. In the beginning of wind-tunnel tests, a number of sixteen Kulite sensors were installed, but due to their removal and re-installation during the next two wind tunnel tests, four of them were found defective. Therefore, a number of twelve sensors remained to be used during the last wind tunnel tests.

The closed loop control results and the followed optimization trajectory for α=0.5° and M=0.3 flow case are shown in Fig. 17. In this case, as starting point in optimization was used the point with the coordinates dY_{1opt} and dY_{2opt}, characterizing the theoretically obtained optimized airfoil: dY_{1opt}=4.81 mm, and dY_{2opt}=7.45 mm. The obtained rezults validated the theoretical optimized airfoil obtained by Ecole Polytechnique in Montreal for this flow case, taking into account that optimization method implemented in the closed loop conducted to a morphed airfoil almost identical with the first one (dY_{1opt_cl}=4.66 mm, and dY_{2opt_cl} =7.28 mm), and the transition was detected on the same pressure sensor with the open loop case (the tenth sensor in the array).

In Figs 18 and 19 are presented the FFTs of the Kulite pressure sensors data, and the pressure data RMSs for un-morphed (reference) and closed loop real time optimized airfoils, in this flow case. In Fig. 19 can be also observed the N factor (for transition positioning) distribution for reference airfoil and optimized airfoil. The distribution was estimated by using the XFoil computational fluid dynamics; XFoil code is free licensed software in which the e^n transition criterion is used (Drela, 2003; Drela and Giles, 1987). In these graphs, the N values calculated by XFoil for various sensors are defined by circles. In the morphed-to-optimized airfoil case, the RMS plot displayed in Fig. 19 with star symbols, showed that the sensor with the maximum RMS has become the tenth sensor plotted

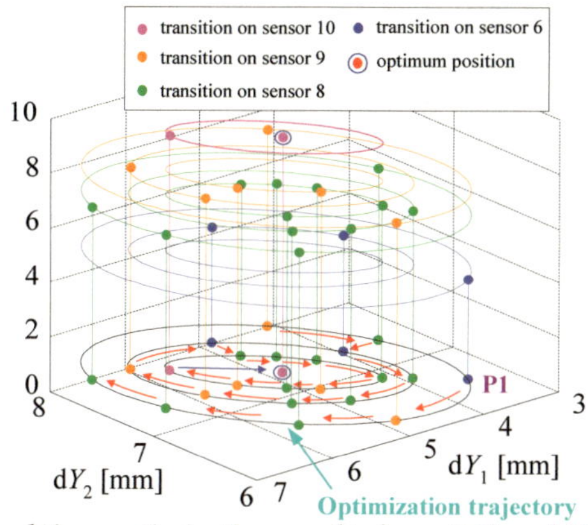

Figure 17. The closed loop real time optimization results for α=0.5° and M=0.3 flow case.

The spectral decomposition of the pressure signals in Fig. 18 confirmed the Tollmien–Schlichting wave's occurrence in the tenth sensor, visible in the highest power spectra (twelfth channel in the right hand side plots) in the frequency band of 2–5 kHz.

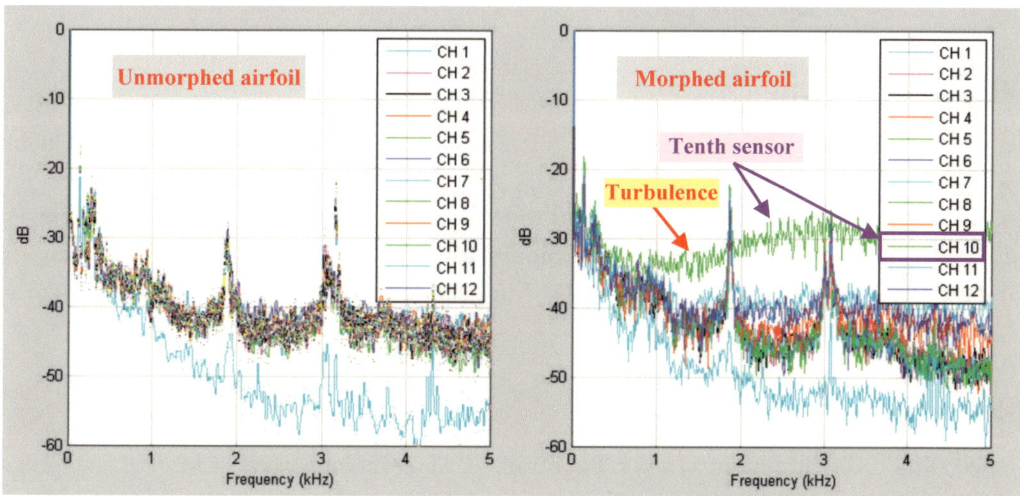

Figure 18. Pressure signals FFT for un-morphed and real time optimized airfoils, for α= 0.5° and M=0.3.

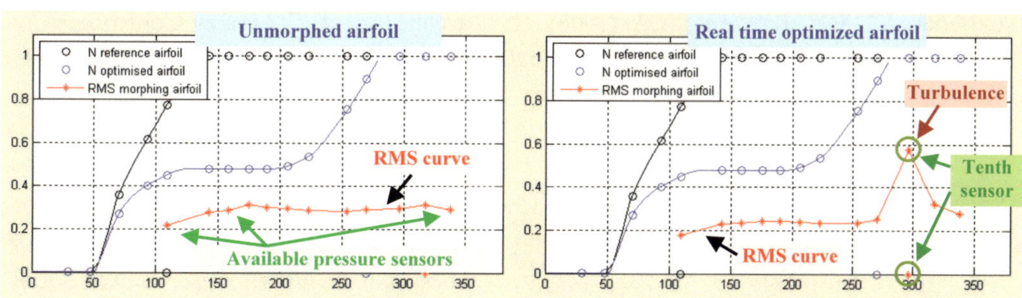

Figure 19. The pressure data RMSs and the N factor distribution

5. Conclusions

The design and validation results for an actuation system of a morphing wing were exposed. The developed morphing mechanism used smart materials such as Shape Memory Alloy (SMA) in the actuation mechanism. Two architectures were developed for the used control system: an open loop, and a closed loop one. The open loop architecture of the controller was used as an inner loop of the closed loop structure, and included a PD fuzzy logic controler in tandem with an on-off clasical controller. Both of the control architectures were validated in wind tunnel tests in parallel with the transition point real time position detection and visualization. In the closed loop controller architecture, the information about the external airflow state received from the pressure sensors system was considered and the decisions have been taken based on the transition point position estimation.

Author details

Teodor Lucian Grigorie, Ruxandra Mihaela Botez and Andrei Vladimir Popov
École de Technologie Supérieure, Canada

Acknowledgement

We would like to thank the Consortium of Research in the Aerospatial Industry in Quebec (CRIAQ), Thales Avionics, Bombardier Aerospace, and the National Sciences and Engineering Research Council (NSERC) for the support that made this research possible. We would also like to thank George Henri Simon for initiating the CRIAQ 7.1 project, and Philippe Molaret from Thales Avionics and Eric Laurendeau from Bombardier Aeronautics for their collaboration on this work.

6. References

Ahmed, M.R.; Abdelrahman, M.M.; ElBayoumi, G. M. & ElNomrossy, M.M. (2011). Optimal wing twist distribution for roll control of MAVs, *The Aeronautical Journal*, Royal Aeronautical Society, vol. 115, 2011, pp. 641-649, ISSN: 0001-9240

Al-Odienat, A.I. & Al-Lawama, A.A. (2008). The Advantages of PID Fuzzy Controllers Over The Conventional Types, *American Journal of Applied Sciences,* Vol. 5, No. 6, pp. 653-658, June 2008, ISSN: 1546-9239

Baldelli, D.H.; Lee, D.H.; Sanchez Pena R.S. & Cannon, B. (2008). Modeling and Control of an Aeroelastic Morphing Vehicle, *Journal of Guidance, Control, and Dynamics*, Vol. 31, No. 6, November–December 2008, pp. 1687-1699, ISSN: 0731-5090

Bilgen, O.; Kochersberger, K.B. & Inman, D.J. (2009). Macro-Fiber Composite Actuators for a Swept Wing Unmanned Aircraft, *The Aeronautical Journal*, Royal Aeronautical Society, Vol. 113, 2009, pp. 385-395, ISSN: 0001-9240

Bilgen, O.; Kochersberger, K.B.; Inman, D.J. & Ohanian, O.J. (2010). Novel, Bidirectional, Variable-Camber Airfoil via Macro-Fiber Composite Actuators, *Journal of Aircraft*, Vol. 47, No. 1, January–February 2010, pp. 303-314, ISSN: 0021-8669

Bornengo, D.; Scarpa, F. & Remillat, C. (2005). Evaluation of hexagonal chiral structure for morphing airfoil concept, *Proceedings of the Institution of Mechanical Engineers, Part G: Journal of Aerospace Engineering*, 2005, vol. 219, 3, pp. 185-192, ISSN: 0954-4100

Brailovski, V.; Terriault, P.; Coutu, D.; Georges, T.; Morellon, E.; Fischer, C. & Berube, S. (2008). Morphing laminar wing with flexible extrados powered by shape memory alloy actuators, Proceedings of ASME 2008 Conference on Smart Materials, Adaptive Structures and Intelligent Systems (SMASIS2008), pp. 615-623, ISBN: 978-0-7918-4331-4, Maryland, USA, October 28–30, 2008, Publisher ASME, Ellicott City

Castellano, G.; Fanelli, A. M. & Mencar, C. (2003). Design of transparent mamdani fuzzy inference systems. In *Design and application of hybrid intelligent systems* book, IOS Print, Amsterdam, pp. 468–476, ISBN:1-58603-394-8

Coutu, D.; Brailovski, V.; Terriault, P. & Fischer, C. (2007). Experimental validation of the 3D numerical model for an adaptive laminar wing with flexible extrados, Proceedings of the 18th International Conference of Adaptive Structures and Technologies, 10 pages, Ottawa, Ontario, Canada, 3-5 October, 2007

Coutu, D.; Brailovski, V. & Terriault, P. (2009). Promising benefits of an active-extrados morphing laminar wing, *AIAA Journal of Aircraft*, Vol. 46, No. 2, pp. 730-731, March-April 2009, ISSN: 0021-8669

Drela, M. (2003). Implicit Implementation of the Full en Transition Criterion, 21st Applied Aerodynamics Conference, Orlando, Florida, 23–26 June 2003, pp. 1–8.

Drela, M. & Giles, M.B. (1987). Viscous-Inviscid Analysis of Transonic and Low Reynolds Number Airfoils, *Journal of Aircraft*, Vol. 25, No. 10, 1987, pp. 1347–1355, ISSN: 0021-8669

Gamboa, P.; Vale, J.; Lau, F. J. P. & Suleman, A. (2009). Optimization of a Morphing Wing Based on Coupled Aerodynamic and Structural Constraints, *AIAA Journal*, Vol. 47, No. 9, September 2009, pp. 2087-2104, ISSN: 0001-1452

Georges, T.; Brailovski, V.; Morellon, E.; Coutu, D. & Terriault, P. (2009). Design of Shape Memory Alloy Actuators for Morphing Laminar Wing With Flexible Extrados, *Journal of Mechanical Design*, Vol. 131, No. 9, 9 pages, 091006, September 2009, ISSN: 1050-0472

Grigorie, T.L. & Botez, R.M. (2009). Adaptive neuro-fuzzy inference system based controllers for Smart Material Actuator modeling, *Proceedings of the Institution of Mechanical Engineers, Part G: Journal of Aerospace Engineering*, Vol. 223, No. 6, pp. 655-668, June 2009, ISSN: 0954-4100

Grigorie, T.L. & Botez, R.M. (2010). New adaptive controller method for SMA hysteresis modeling of a morphing wing, *The Aeronautical Journal*, Vol. 114, No. 1151, pp. 1-13, January 2010, ISSN: 0001-9240

Grigorie, T.L.; Popov, A.V.; Botez, R.M.; Mébarki, Y. & Mamou, M. (2010 a). Modeling and testing of a morphing wing in open-loop architecture, *AIAA Journal of Aircraft*, Vol. 47, No. 3, pp. 917-923, May–June 2010, ISSN: 0021-8669

Grigorie, T. L.; Popov, A.V.; Botez, R.M.; Mamou, M. & Mebarki, Y. (2010 b). A morphing wing used shape memory alloy actuators new control technique with bi-positional and PI laws optimum combination. Part 1: design phase, Proceedings of the 7th International Conference on Informatics in Control, Automation and Robotics ICINCO 2010, pp. 5-12, ISBN: 978-989-8425-00-3, Madeira, Portugal, 15-18 June, 2010, SciTePress – Science and Technology Publications, Funchal

Grigorie, T. L.; Popov, A.V.; Botez, R.M.; Mamou, M. & Mebarki, Y. (2010 c). A morphing wing used shape memory alloy actuators new control technique with bi-positional and PI laws optimum combination. Part 2: experimental validation, Proceedings of the 7th International Conference on Informatics in Control, Automation and Robotics ICINCO 2010, pp. 13-19, ISBN: 978-989-8425-00-3, Madeira, Portugal, 15-18 June, 2010, SciTePress – Science and Technology Publications, Funchal

Hampel, R.; Wagenknecht, M. & Chaker, N. (2000). *Fuzzy Control – Theory and Practice*, Physica-Verlag, ISBN-13: 978-3790813272, USA

Inoyama, D.; Sanders, B.P. & Joo, J.J. (2008). Topology Optimization Approach for the Determination of the Multiple-Configuration Morphing Wing Structure, *Journal of Aircraft*, Vol. 45, No. 6, November–December 2008, pp. 1853-1863, ISSN: 0021-8669

Khalid, M. & Jones, D.J. (1993). Navier Stokes Investigation of Blunt Trailing Edge Airfoils using O-Grids, *AIAA Journal of Aircraft*, vol.30, no.5, pp. 797-800, 1993, ISSN: 0021-8669

Khalid, M. & Jones, D.J. (1993). A CFD Investigation of the Blunt Trailing Edge Airfoils in Transonic Flow, Inaugural Conference of the CFD Society of Canada

Kovacic, Z. & Bogdan, S. (2006). *Fuzzy Controller Design – Theory and applications*, Taylor and Francis Group, ISBN: 978-0849337475, USA

Manzo, J.; Garcia, E. & Wickenheiser, A.M. (2004) Adaptive Structural Systems and Compliant Skin Technology of Morphing Aircraft Structures, Proceedings of SPIE: The International Society for Optical Engineering, Vol. 5390, 2004, pp. 225–234

Moorhouse D.J.; Sanders B.; von Spakovsky, M.R. & Butt, J. (2006). Benefits and Design Challenges of Adaptive Structures for Morphing Aircraft, *The Aeronautical Journal*, Royal Aeronautical Society, vol. 110, 2006, pp. 157-162, ISSN: 0001-9240

Munday, D. & Jacob, J.D. (2002). Active Control of Separation on a Wing with Conformal Camber, *AIAA Journal of Aircraft*, 39, No. 1, ISSN: 0021-8669

Namgoong, H.; Crossley, W.A. & Lyrintzis, A.S. (2006). Morphing Airfoil Design for Minimum Aerodynamic Drag and Actuation Energy Including Aerodynamic Work, AIAA Paper 2006-2041, 2006, pp. 5407–5421

Namgoong, H.; Crossley, W.A. & and Lyrintzis, A.S. (2007). Aerodynamic Optimization of a Morphing Airfoil Using Energy as an Objective, *AIAA Journal*, Vol. 45, No. 9, September 2007, pp. 2113-2124, ISSN: 0001-1452

Obradovic, B. & Subbarao, K. (2011 a). Modeling of Dynamic Loading of Morphing-Wing Aircraft, *Journal of Aircraft*, Vol. 48, No. 2, March–April 2011, pp. 424-435, ISSN: 0021-8669

Obradovic, B. & Subbarao, K. (2011 b). Modeling of Flight Dynamics of Morphing-Wing Aircraft, *Journal of Aircraft*, Vol. 48, No. 2, March–April 2011, pp. 391-402, ISSN: 0021-8669

Perera, M. & Guo, S. (2009). Optimal design of an aeroelastic wing structure with seamless control surfaces, *Proceedings of the Institution of Mechanical Engineers, Part G: Journal of Aerospace Engineering*, August 1, 2009, vol. 223, 8, pp. 1141-1151, ISSN: 0954-4100

Popov, A.V.; Botez, R.M. & Labib, M. (2008 a). Transition point detection from the surface pressure distribution for controller design, *AIAA Journal of Aircraft*, Vol. 45, No. 1, pp. 23-28, January-February 2008, ISSN: 0021-8669

Popov, A.V.; Labib, M.; Fays, J. & Botez, R.M. (2008 b). Closed loop control simulations on a morphing laminar airfoil using shape memory alloys actuators, *AIAA Journal of Aircraft*, Vol. 45, No. 5, pp. 1794-1803, September-October 2008, ISSN: 0021-8669

Popov, A.V.; Botez, R.M.; Mamou, M.; Mebarki, Y.; Jahrhaus, B.; Khalid. M. & Grigorie, T.L. (2009 a). Drag reduction by improving laminar flows past morphing configurations, AVT-168 NATO Symposium on the Morphing Vehicles, 12 pages, 20-23 April, 2009, Published by NATO, Evora, Portugal

Popov, A.V.; Botez, R. M.; Mamou, M. & Grigorie, T.L. (2009 b). Optical sensor pressure measurements variations with temperature in wind tunnel testing, *AIAA Journal of Aircraft*, Vol. 46, No. 4, pp. 1314-1318, July-August 2009, ISSN: 0021-8669

Popov, A.V.; Grigorie, T. L.; Botez, R.M.; Mamou, M. & Mebarki, Y. (2010 a). Morphing wing real time optimization in wind tunnel tests, Proceedings of the 7th International Conference on Informatics in Control, Automation and Robotics ICINCO 2010, pp. 114-124, ISBN: 978-989-8425-00-3, Madeira, Portugal, 15-18 June, 2010, SciTePress – Science and Technology Publications, Funchal

Popov, A.V.; Grigorie, T. L.; Botez, R.M.; Mamou, M. & Mebarki, Y. (2010 b). Closed-Loop Control Validation of a Morphing Wing Using Wind Tunnel Tests, *AIAA Journal of Aircraft*, Vol. 47, No. 4, pp. 1309-1317, July–August 2010, ISSN: 0021-8669

Popov, A.V.; Grigorie, T. L.; Botez, R.M.; Mamou, M. & Mebarki, Y. (2010 c). Real Time Morphing Wing Optimization Validation Using Wind-Tunnel Tests, *AIAA Journal of Aircraft*, Vol. 47, No. 4, pp. 1346-1355, July–August 2010, ISSN: 0021-8669

Prasad Reddy, P.V.G.D. & Hari, Gh.V.M.K. (2011). Fuzzy Based PSO for Software Effort Estimation, International Conference on Information Technology and Mobile Communication (AIM 2011), Nagpur, India, Volume 147, Part 2, April 2011, pp. 227-232, ISSN: 1865-0929

Sainmont, C.; Paraschivoiu, I. & Coutu, D. (2009). Multidisciplinary Approach for the Optimization of a Laminar Airfoil Equipped with a Morphing Upper Surface, AVT-168 NATO Symposium on the Morphing Vehicles, 20-23 April, 2009, Published by NATO, Evora, Portugal

Sanders, B. (2003). Aerodynamic and Aeroelastic Characteristics of Wings with Conformal Control Surfaces for Morphing Aircraft, *Journal of Aircraft*, Vol. 40, No. 1, 2003, pp. 94–99, ISSN: 0021-8669

Seber, G. & Sakarya, E. (2010). Nonlinear Modeling and Aeroelastic Analysis of an Adaptive Camber Wing, *AIAA Journal of Aircraft*, Vol. 47, No. 6, November–December 2010, pp. 2067-2074, ISSN: 0021-8669

Seigler, T.M.; Neal, D.A.; Bae, J.S. & Inman, D.J. (2007). Modeling and Flight Control of Large-Scale Morphing Aircraft, *Journal of Aircraft*, Vol. 44, No. 4, July–August 2007, pp. 1077-1087, ISSN: 0021-8669

Skillen, M.D. & Crossley, W.A. (2005). Developing Response Surface Based Wing Weight Equations for Conceptual Morphing Aircraft Sizing, AIAA Paper 2005-1960, 2005, pp. 2007–2019

Terriault, P.; Viens, F. & Brailovski, V. (2006). Non-isothermal Finite Element Modeling of a Shape Memory Alloy Actuator Using ANSYS, *Computational Materials Science*, Vol. 36, No. 4, July 2006, pp. 397-410, ISSN: 0927-0256

Thill, C.; Etches, J.; Bond, I.P.; Potter, K.D. & Weaver, P.M. (2008). Morphing skins – review, *The Aeronautical Journal*, Royal Aeronautical Society, Vol. 112, 2008, pp. 117-139, ISSN: 0001-9240

Thill, C.; Downsborough, J.D.; Lai, J.S.; Bond, I.P. & Jones, D.P. (2010). Aerodynamic study of corrugated skins for morphing wing applications, *The Aeronautical Journal*, Royal Aeronautical Society, vol. 114, 2010, pp. 237-244, ISSN: 0001-9240

Verbruggen, H.B. & Bruijn, P.M. (1997). Fuzzy control and conventional control: What is (and can be) the real contribution of Fuzzy Systems?, *Fuzzy Sets Systems*, Vol. 90, No. 2, pp. 151–160, September 1997, ISSN: 0165-0114

Wildschek, A.; Havar, T. & Plötner, K. (2010). An all-composite, all-electric, morphing trailing edge device for flight control on a blended-wing-body airliner", *Proceedings of the Institution of Mechanical Engineers, Part G: Journal of Aerospace Engineering*, January 2010, vol. 224, 1, pp. 1-9, ISSN: 0954-4100

Zadeh, L.A. (1965). Fuzzy sets, *Information and Control*, Vol. 8, No. 3, pp. 339-353, June 1965, ISSN: 00199958

Chapter 2

Embedded Fuzzy Logic Controllers in Electric Railway Transportation Systems

Stela Rusu-Anghel and Lucian Gherman

Additional information is available at the end of the chapter

http://dx.doi.org/10.5772/48588

1. Introduction

A. Power system harmonic pollution limitation using Fuzzy Logic controlled active filters

1.1. Introduction

Nonlinear loads system has been grooving on influence in electric power due to the advance of power electronics technologies. As a result, the harmonic pollution in the power system deteriorates the power quality significantly. One effect of the harmonic pollution is the harmonic resonance which may result in major voltage distortion in the power system.

1.1.1. Harmonic effect

The current harmonic components could cause the following problems:

- resonance effect with overvoltage and overcurrent consequences,
- additional losses,
- psophomentic disturbance of the telecommunication systems,
- disturbance in the remote control systems,
- malfunction of protection devices,
- misoperation of semiconductor-controllers.

The harmonic disturbance basically could be characterized by the individual (1) and total (2) harmonic distortion factors:

$$D_k = \frac{X_k}{X_1} \tag{1}$$

$$THD_X = \frac{\sqrt{\sum_{k=2}^{\infty} X^2{}_k}}{X_1} \tag{2}$$

where:

$k = \frac{f}{50Hz}$: the harmonic order;

X_k : k^{th} harmonic component of *I* or *V*;

X_1 : fundamental frequency component of *I* or *V*

1.1.2. Psophometric interference

The high power lines could influence the neighbouring telecommunication networks by the following ways:

- Capacitive coupling: The voltage of the power line causes charging current ;
- Inductive coupling: The line current induces longitudinal emf.

The most dominant part of the psophometric noise is the inducing effect caused by the zero sequence components of the current. The power balance of the three-phase is near symmetrical during normal operation, thus the coupling is measurable only if the distance between the two systems is comparable with the phase distance of one system. However electric traction is a single-phase system with ground return and in consequence it is a natural zero sequence system. That is why it is important to calculate the psophometric noise. [1]

By telecommunication lines the rate of the disturbance could be characterized by the so called psophometric voltage. It could be calculated by this formula:

$$V_p = \sqrt{\sum_f \left(\frac{p_f}{p_{800}} \cdot V_f \right)^2} \tag{3}$$

where: V_f : voltage component by f frequency; P_f : psophometric weigh by f frequency; $P_{800} = 1000$.

The psophometric weight has been determined after human tests; it could be seen on Fig. 1. It could be concluded that the main part of the noise disturbance is caused by the 800 Hz and surrounding harmonics. The psophometric weighting could be applied for the current components, too, the formula is the same like in (3), however, this value is characteristic to the zero sequence current of power line regarding its possible disturbing effect. This is the so called disturbing current [1].

1.1.3. Active filtering

Several researchers propose the installation of active filter in order to damp the harmonic resonance effect. The magnitude of damping provided by the active filter, the level of harmonic distortion, may become worse in certain locations along the radial line. One solution is to use multiple active filters located in the proximity of nonlinear load element. In case of railway transportation, the power system pollution is mainly originated by the use of DC locomotives equipped with rectifier units (fig. 2).

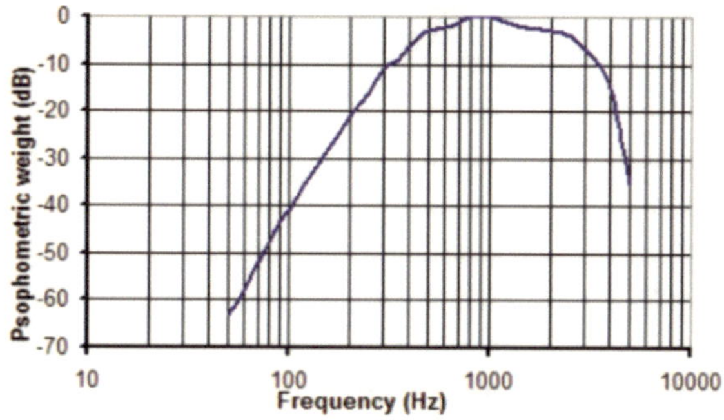

Figure 1. The psophometric weight

The harmonic filters are mandatory to limit the harmonic currents flowing into upstream network and to decrease the resonance effect causing current amplification along the 25 kV supply line. The combination of power factor correction capacitors, parasitic capacitance of contact line and the system inductance (power cables, transformers, etc.) often result in resonant frequency in the 600 – 800 Hz range.

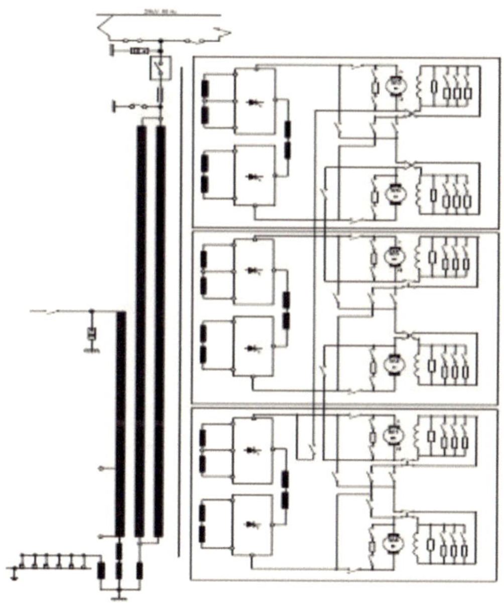

Figure 2. Electrical diagram of the EA – 060 locomotive used in Romania

Most active filter technologies, which focus on compensating harmonic current of nonlinear loads, can not adequately address this issue.

We propose the application of active filters in order to limit the harmonic currents produced by the traction system. The active filter could be located in locomotive or on the substation, or both. Coordination of harmonic of multiple filter units may become a problem since the railway transportation system is characterized by the presence of different types of locomotive from different ages of technology (DC motor with rectifier unit, thyristor). However, in differently from the type of locomotive, the harmonic production needs to be eliminated or limited to a acceptable value imposed by international standards.

In [2] a solution for the coordination of multiple active filters is proposed. The active filter units which are placed on different locations can perform the harmonic filtering without a direct communication using the droop characteristic. We implement the same solution using a fuzzy logic control system.

1.2. Power quality in railway transportation

Power distribution system in electric railway transportation is presented in fig. 3.

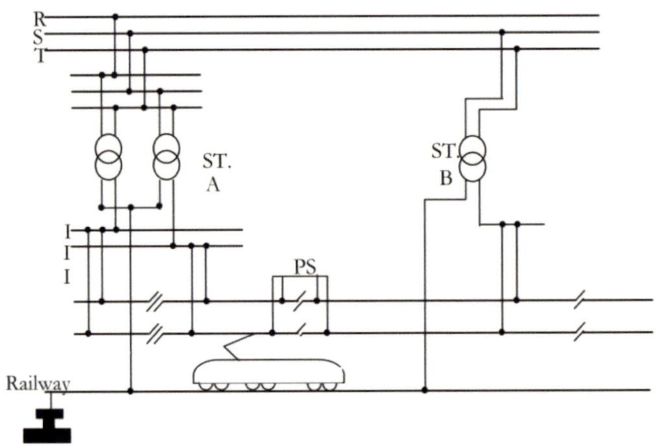

Figure 3. Power distribution system

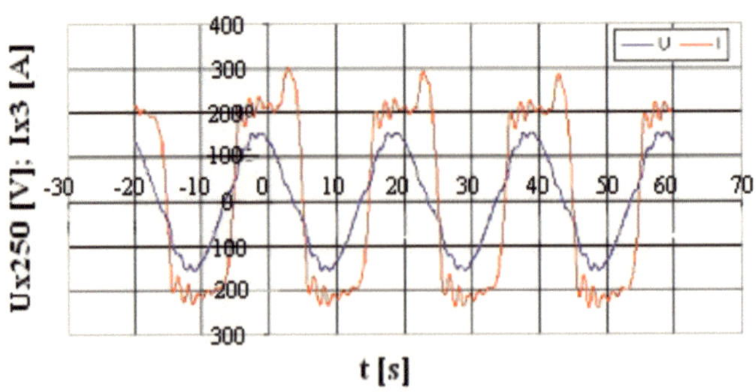

Figure 4. ST load current and voltage waveform in power substation

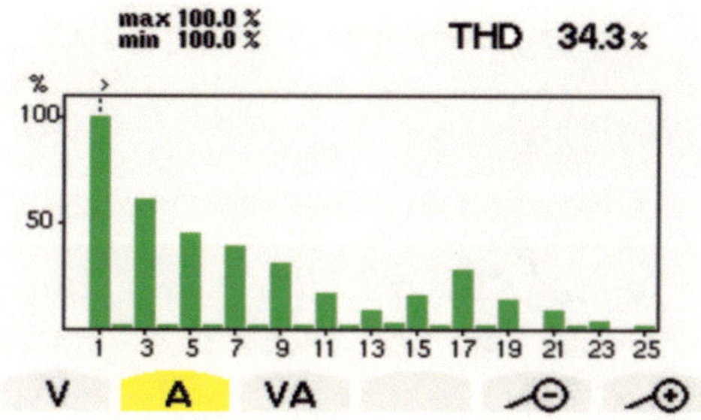

Figure 5. Harmonic spectrum of load current in power substation

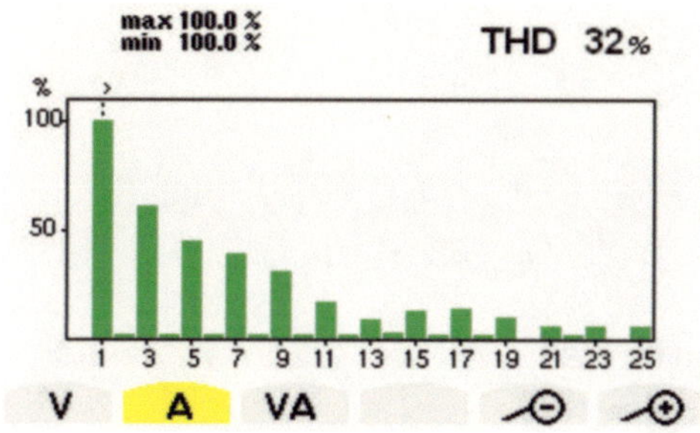

Figure 6. Harmonic spectrum of load current in locomotive

In fig. 4, we present the waveforms for a work regime recorded in a real substation. In fig.s 5 and 6, is presented the harmonic spectrum for the load current in power substation and in locomotive. Comparing these two different spectrums, it could be concluded that the resonance effect is the highest at the 15th and 17th harmonics. Over the 25th harmonics the supply system is decreasing the harmonic current. THD becomes to 34%, far exceeding the admissible values. The resonance phenomenon increase psophometric interference.

1.3. Active filtering solutions for railway power systems

For harmonic compensations in case of railway applications the best choice is the single phase bridge inverter with PWM controlled current control. In order to perform the harmonic compensations it is necessary to present the control structure of the active power filter. The control method is based on instantaneous power theory [3], [4] and [5].

The single phase power system can be defined using:

$$u(t) = U\cos(\omega t) \qquad i(t) = I\cos(\omega t - \varphi) \tag{4}$$

In order to perform the orthogonal transformation of the single phase system to a synchronous reference frame a fictitious imaginary phase defined as is introduced:

$$u_i(t) = U_i\sin(\omega t) \qquad i_i(t) = I_i\sin(\omega t - \varphi) \tag{5}$$

we obtain an orthogonal coordinate system with:

$$u_{\alpha} = u(t) \text{ and } u_{\beta} = u_i(t) \tag{6}$$

The active power P_{AV} and Pi_{AV} is given by:

$$P_{AV} = \frac{P_{\alpha\beta AV}}{2} = \left(\frac{2}{T}\right)\int_{0}^{\frac{T}{4}}\left[u_{\alpha}i_{\alpha} + u_{\beta}i_{\beta}\right]dt \tag{7}$$

$$P_{i_{AV}} = \frac{P_{i_{\alpha\beta AV}}}{2} = \left(\frac{2}{T}\right)\int_{0}^{\frac{T}{4}}\left[u_{\alpha}i_{\alpha} + u_{\beta}i_{\beta}\right]dt \tag{8}$$

The instantaneous power is:

$$\begin{aligned} p_{\alpha\beta} &= u_{\alpha}i_{\alpha} + u_{\beta}i_{\beta} \quad (a) \\ q_{\alpha\beta} &= u_{\alpha}i_{\alpha} - u_{\beta}i_{\beta} \quad (b) \end{aligned} \tag{9}$$

And the power factor is given by:

$$\varphi = arctg\left(\frac{q_{\alpha\beta}}{p_{\alpha\beta}}\right) \tag{10}$$

Using p-q-r power theory introduced by Kim and Akagi, allows to present the power situation in synchronous rotation frame. In case we have:

$$u_{\alpha\beta} = \sqrt{{u_{\alpha}}^2 + {u_{\beta}}^2} \tag{11}$$

and

$$\theta = \tan^{-1}\left(\frac{u_{\beta}}{u_{\alpha}}\right) \tag{12}$$

$$\begin{bmatrix} u_p \\ u_q \\ u_r \end{bmatrix} = \frac{1}{u_{\alpha\beta}}\begin{bmatrix} u_{\alpha} & u_{\beta} & 0 \\ 0 & 0 & 0 \\ 0 & 0 & u_{\alpha\beta} \end{bmatrix}\begin{bmatrix} u_{\alpha} \\ u_{\beta} \\ 0 \end{bmatrix} = \begin{bmatrix} u_{\alpha\beta} \\ 0 \\ 0 \end{bmatrix} \tag{13}$$

and similarly

$$\begin{bmatrix} i_p \\ i_q \\ i_r \end{bmatrix} = \frac{1}{u_{\alpha\beta}}\begin{bmatrix} u_{\alpha} & u_{\beta} & 0 \\ 0 & 0 & 0 \\ 0 & 0 & u_{\alpha\beta} \end{bmatrix}\begin{bmatrix} i_{\alpha} \\ i_{\beta} \\ 0 \end{bmatrix} = \begin{bmatrix} i_{\alpha\beta} \\ 0 \\ 0 \end{bmatrix} \tag{14}$$

where:

$$i_{\alpha\beta} = \frac{p_{\alpha\beta}}{u_{\alpha\beta}} \tag{15}$$

where as:

$$p_{\alpha\beta} = u_{\alpha} i_{\alpha} + u_{\alpha} i_{\alpha} = p \tag{16}$$

Finally we can state:

$$\begin{aligned} u_p &= u_{\alpha\beta} && (a) \\ i_p &= i_{\alpha\beta} && (b) \\ u_q &= u_r \equiv i_q = i_r = 0 && (c) \\ p &= u_p i_p && (d) \end{aligned} \tag{17}$$

From (9a,b) can be obtain

$$\begin{matrix} i_{\alpha} \\ i_{\beta} \end{matrix} = \frac{1}{u^2_{\alpha\beta}} \begin{bmatrix} u_{\alpha} & -u_{\beta} \\ u_{\beta} & u_{\alpha} \end{bmatrix} \begin{bmatrix} P_{AV} + p_{\sim} \\ Q_{AV} + q_{\sim} \end{bmatrix} \tag{18}$$

In order to realize the compensation of whole reactive and distortion powers is necessary to compensate Q_{AV} – component as well as to filter $q_{\sim}$ and $p_{\sim}$ components. The reference current is:

$$i_{REF} = \frac{1}{u^2_{\alpha\beta}} \left[u_{\alpha} (p - P_{AV}) - u_{\beta} (Q_{AV} + q_{\sim}) \right] \tag{19}$$

In fig. 7 we present the active power filter operation considered in two cases: substation placed AF and locomotive placed AF.

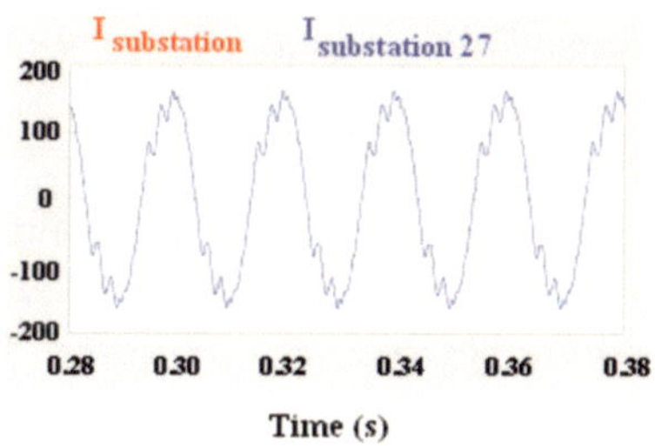

Figure 7. Substation current without filtering at 25 kV and the current in 110 kV network

As it can be observed the placement of active filters in only one place can not provide the necessary filtering in the power line feeding the substation simultaneously to the contact line filtering.

Due to this fact it is necessary to adopt different control strategy and solutions.

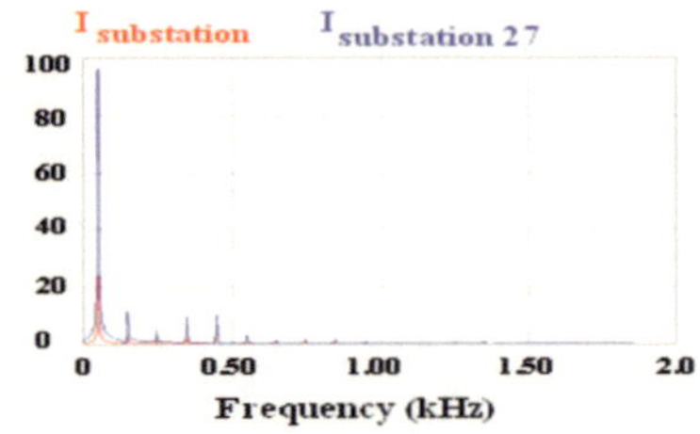

Figure 8. Substation Harmonics without filtering

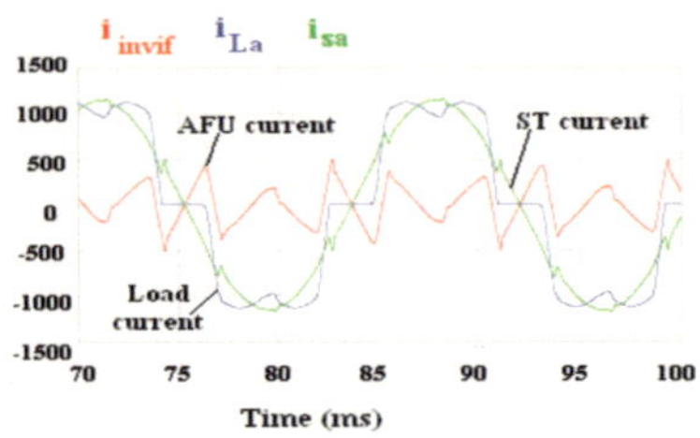

Figure 9. Substation AFU waveforms in substation and in locomotive unit

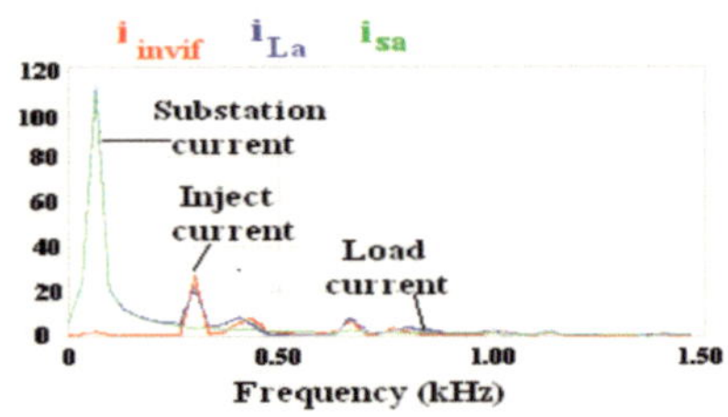

Figure 10. Harmonic components for active filter placed

1.3.1. Coordination of multiple active filters in railway power systems

We propose a solution which has the advantage to share the workload of harmonic filtering between several active filter units. This solution was presented in [2] for the situation of industrial power lines. In our situation we consider the case when the railway system is equipped with active filter unit placed in the substation and locomotive has also an active filter unit integrated. In this case using the existing control algorithms, the harmonic filtering is not coordinated between the locomotive and substation because this would required a real time communication between the AF unit of the locomotive and AF in the substation. This impossible task can be performed using the distributed active filter solution presented in [2] which has been proved to be valid in industrial power systems equipped with distributed active filters (DAFS).

Using this method, several active filter units are installed along the electric power line. All the active filter units operate as a harmonic conductance to reduce voltage harmonics. The active filter unit acts as given:

$$i_x = G_x \cdot U_{x,h} \tag{20}$$

where $U_{x,h}$ represents the harmonic components of the line voltage U_x.

The line voltage U_x is measured and transformed into U^e_{xq} and U^e_{xd} using high pass filters (HPF), the ripples of U^e_{xq} and U^e_{xd} are extracted. The voltage harmonics U^e_{xq} and U^e_{xd} are then multiplied by the conductance command of the active filter. Based on the current command and the measured current, the current regulator calculate the voltage command

$$v_x^* = \frac{L_x}{\Delta T}\left(i_x^* - i_x\right) + U_x \tag{21}$$

In order to share the harmonic workload among the active filter units, it is necessary to use the droop relationship between the conductance command and the volt-ampere of the active filter unit.

$$G_x = G_{x0} + b_x(S_x - S_{x0}) \tag{22}$$

where: G_x are the conductance command for the active filter units; G_0 and S_0 are the rated operation point of each active filter unit.

The conductance command G_x of active filter unit (AFU_x) is determinate by the volt-ampere consumption of this active filter unit. To obtain the volt-ampere S_x of AFU_x, the RMS values of voltage and current associated with AFU_x are calculated:

$$\begin{aligned} U_{xRMS} &= \sqrt{\left\{\left(U^s_{xq}\right)^2 + \left(U^s_{xd}\right)^2\right\}dc} \\ i_{xRMS} &= \sqrt{\left\{\left(i^s_{xq}\right)^2 + \left(i^s_{xd}\right)^2\right\}dc} \\ S_x &= U_{xRMS} \cdot i_{xRMS} \end{aligned} \tag{23}$$

where the dc values are extracted by low-pass filters. E_x is the stationary frame value of the current i_x. We consider the case of coordination between the substation active filter AFUx and railway locomotive filter AFU_y. The volt-ampere associated with AFUx and AFU_y can be expressed as following:

$$\begin{aligned} S_x &= \left|U_x\right| \cdot G_x \left|U_{x,h}\right| \approx \left|U_{x,f}\right| \cdot G_x \left|U_{x,h}\right| \\ S_y &= \left|U_y\right| \cdot G_y \left|U_{y,h}\right| \approx \left|U_{y,f}\right| \cdot G_y \left|U_{y,h}\right| \end{aligned} \tag{24}$$

The droop characteristics of both active filter units are given:

$$\begin{aligned} G_x &= G_{x0} + b_x(S_x - S_{x0}) \\ G_y &= G_{y0} + b_y(S_y - S_{y0}) \end{aligned} \tag{25}$$

Based on (24) and (25), the relationship between S_x and B_x can be derived:

$$S_x = \frac{b_x S_{x0} - G_{x0}}{b_x} \quad S_y = \frac{b_y S_{y0} - G_{y0}}{b_y} \tag{26}$$

If the droop characteristics of the active filter units are assigned as follows:

$$G_{x0} - b_x S_{x0} = G_{y0} - b_y S_{y0} \tag{27}$$

$$b_x S_x \approx b_y S_y \tag{28}$$

The slope of the droop should be set in inverse-proportion to the volt-ampere rating of each *AFUs* to achieve the desired load distribution. This can be extended to the case of multiple installations of active filter units.

$$b_x S_{x0} = b_y S_{y0} \tag{29}$$

The above droop settings allow harmonic filtering workload being shared in proportion to the volt-ampere rating of the active filter units. The control structure of the proposed system is presented in fig. 11. In our case since the system has a rather variable structure (due to the traffic variability and locomotive distribution) we propose a fuzzy logic conductance calculator.

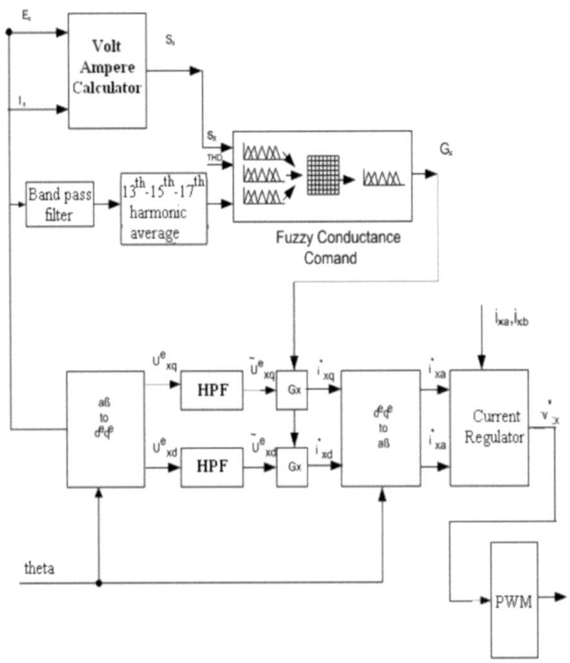

Figure 11. Fuzzy logic control for the active filter distribution

This calculator identifies the appropriate value of the Gx according to the actual load and load capability of the filter and the harmonic spectrum characteristic. Considering the case when the active filter AF1 is located in substation and we have also an active filter operating at locomotive level we can coordinate them using a load sharing algorithm which is implemented by the fuzzy logic conductance command block.

The phase line voltage is measured and transformed into Uxq and Uxd in synchronous reference frame. Using high pass filters (HPF), the voltage line harmonics are extracted and multiplied by the conductance command Gx computed by the fuzzy logic conductance controller. The current commands Ixs and Ixd of the active filter computed by the Clark transformation block are transformed to the current commands I_x. Based on the current command, the current regulator calculates the voltage command Vx as given:

$$v_x^* = \frac{L_x}{\Delta T}(i_x^* - i_x) + U_x \tag{30}$$

The fuzzy logic command can be tuned according to the capability of each unit in order to have a different response for each situation.

The principle of operation of the fuzzy logic conductance command block is based on the analysis of three parameters : the volt ampere S_x for the corresponding active filter, the total THD of the current measured in active filter location and the averaged value of the sensitive harmonics (in our case the 13th-17th harmonic).

1.4. Fuzzy logic conductance command block

The fuzzy logic conductance block is designed in order to reduce the harmonic distortion components considering the distribution of the active filters. The distortion components bare reduced using the fuzzy inference, the fuzzy logic conductance reacts differently in function of filter volt-ampere, THD value and in order to avoid resonance, the average value of 15th-17th-19th harmonics.

The variables of the inference system were represented as membership functions and the normalization of the each input variable was made in order to match the value of the inputs 0 ÷ 1 range.

In fig.s 12, 13 and 14 are presented the membership functions for the input magnitudes, and in fig. 15 is presented the membership functions for the output magnitude.

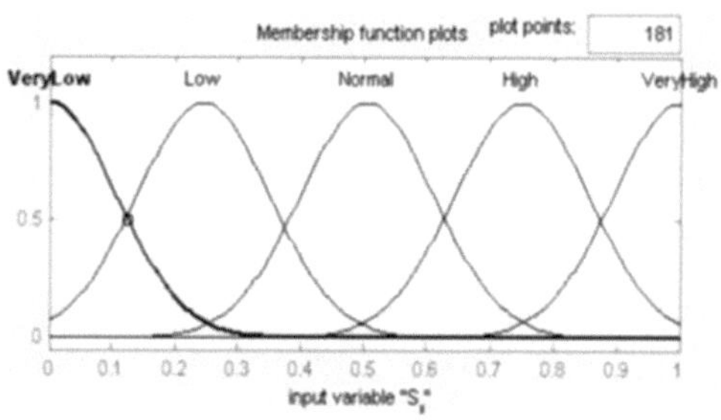

Figure 12. Membership functions for S_x

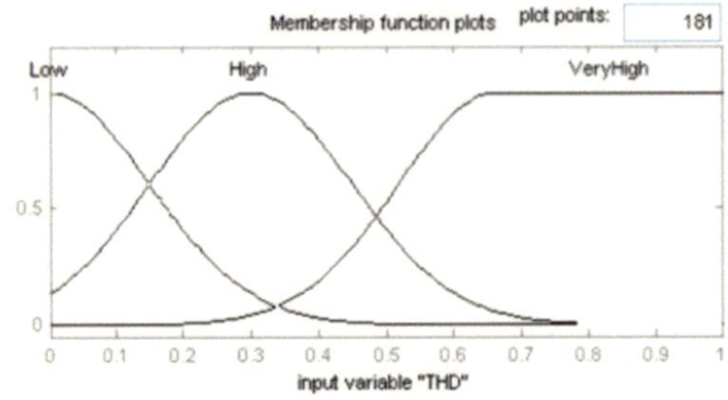

Figure 13. Membership functions for THD

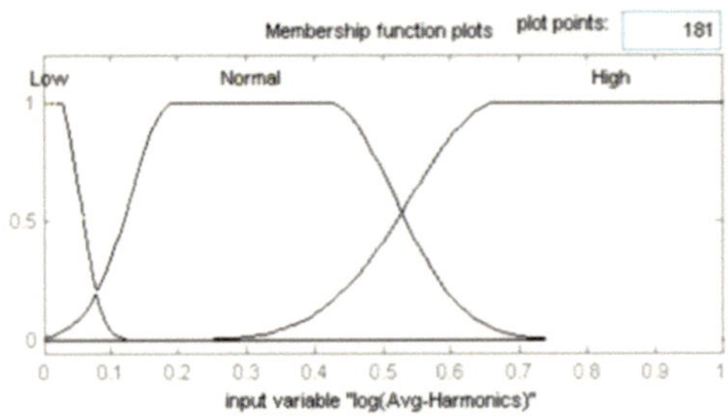

Figure 14. Membership functions for Avg Harmonics

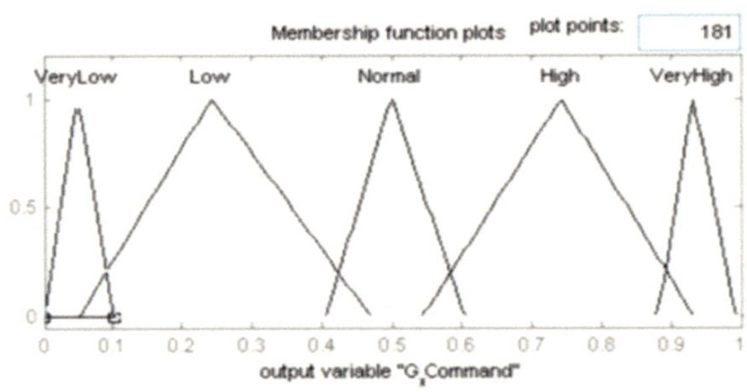

Figure 15. Membership functions for G_x Command

The most important element of the fuzzy systems is the base of rules which implements the relationship between the inputs and the output of the system. The response surfaces of the system are presented in fig.s 16 and 17.

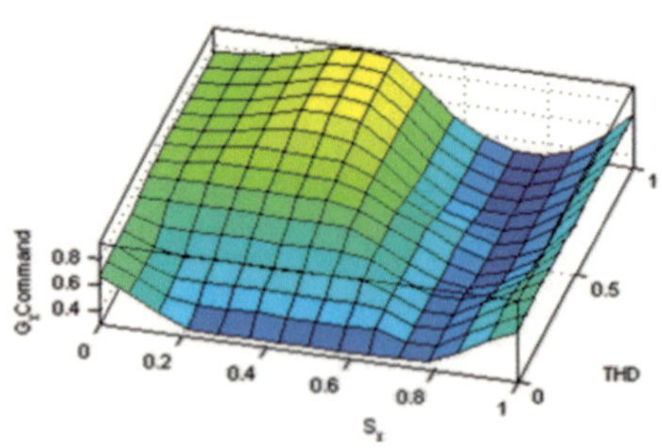

Figure 16. Surface G_x vs. THD and S_x

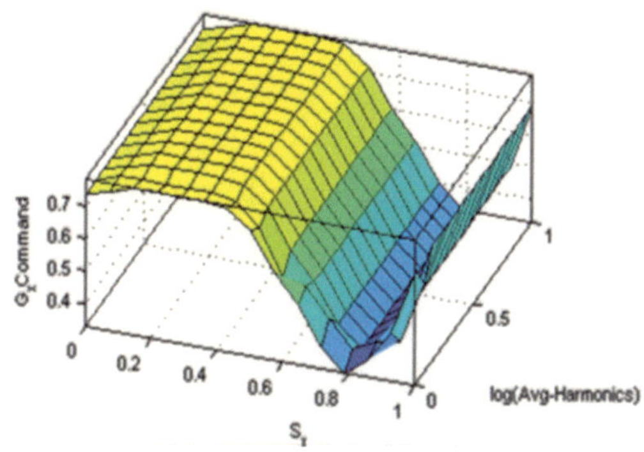

Figure 17. Surface G_x vs. THD and log(Avg-Harmonic)

1.5. Simulation results

The control algorithm is implemented in PSIM and the control in Matlab Simulink and fuzzy logic toolbox (fig. 18). The proposed solution is applied for the railway power distribution system in order to demonstrate its capability to share the harmonic filter among the various active filter units.

The current and voltage component on the filtered harmonic orders are reduced dramatically and the typical effect of the 3rd and 5th harmonics have been neglected, but the significant high frequency components (mainly 17th and 19th harmonics).

The circuit model of the railway is illustrated in fig. 19. Two active filter units are placed, one in substation location and the 2nd at the locomotive level. The locomotive represents a nonlinear load comprising several rectifier units. The parameters of the simulation are given as follows: power system (27kV, 50Hz); line parameters usual values in railway transportation 0,47Ω/km.

The control structure is similar for each unit but the filters characteristics need to be tuned according to their location.

Fig. 9 contains the wave forms when both active filter are working. The harmonic distortion is improved as the THD are reduce by the filter in action of the AF_1 and AF_2.

The active filter units of the DAFS adjust the conductance command G_1 and G_2 based on their own droop characteristics for the volt-ampere consumption for AF_1 and AF_2, which indicates that the filtering workload is evenly shared between the active filter units of the system (fig. 20 and 21).

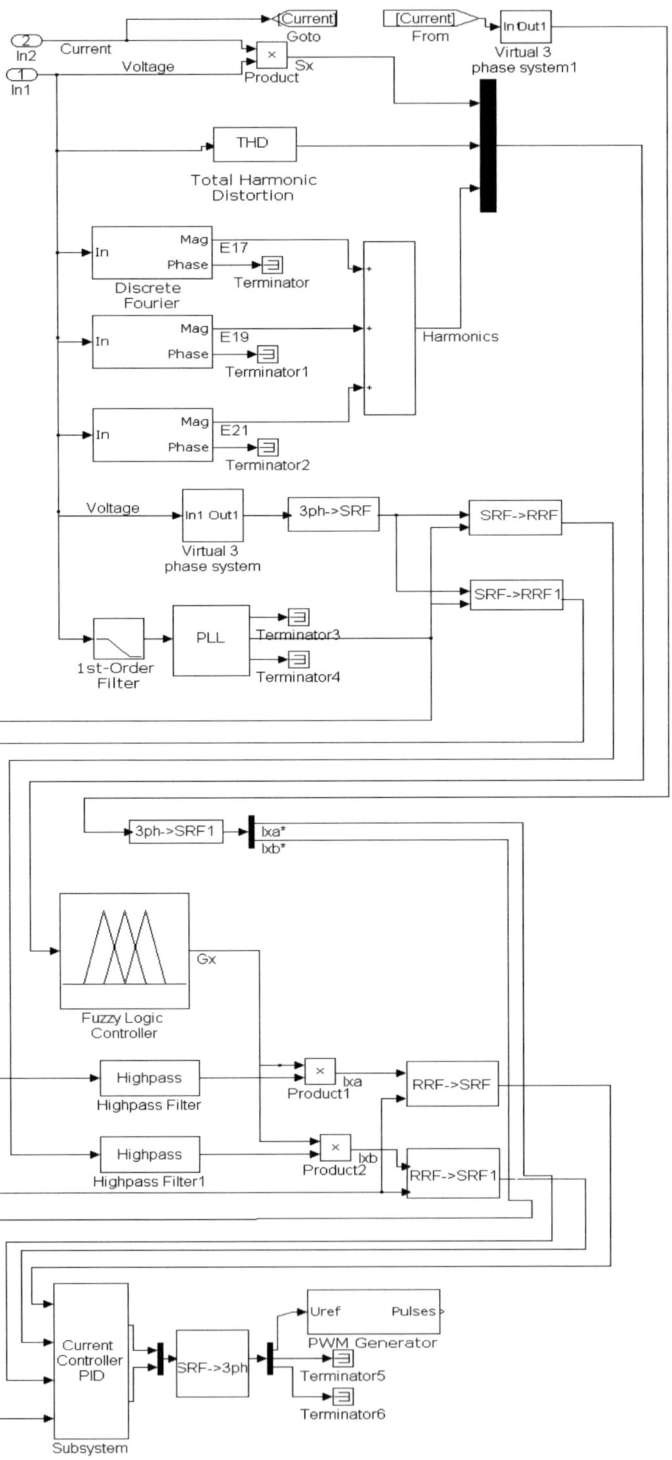

Figure 18. Fuzzy logic control for the distributed active filter

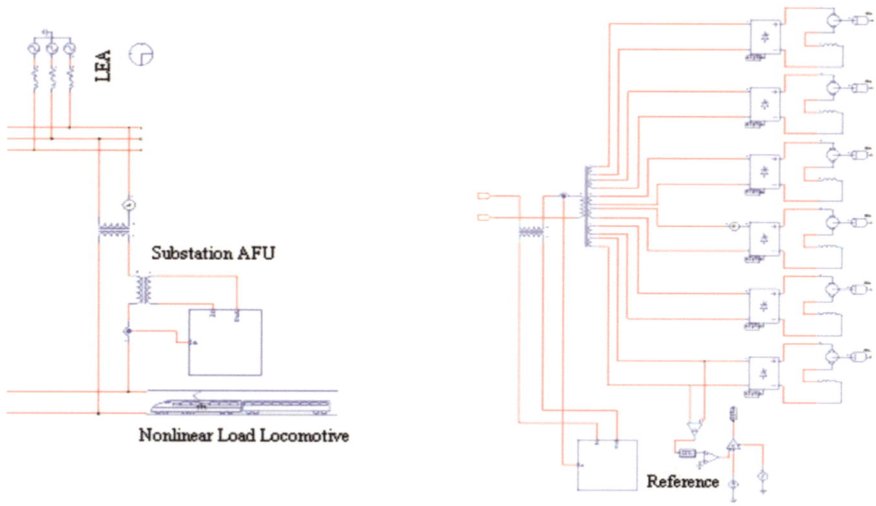

(a) Substation model (b) Locomotive model

Figure 19. a) and b). Railway power system simulation

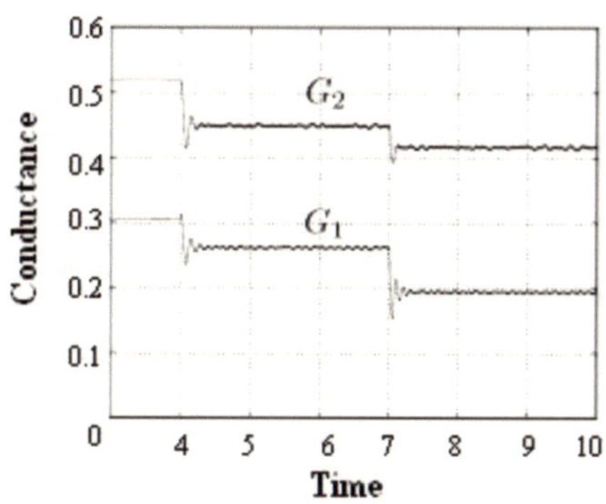

Figure 20. Variation of G_1 and G_2.

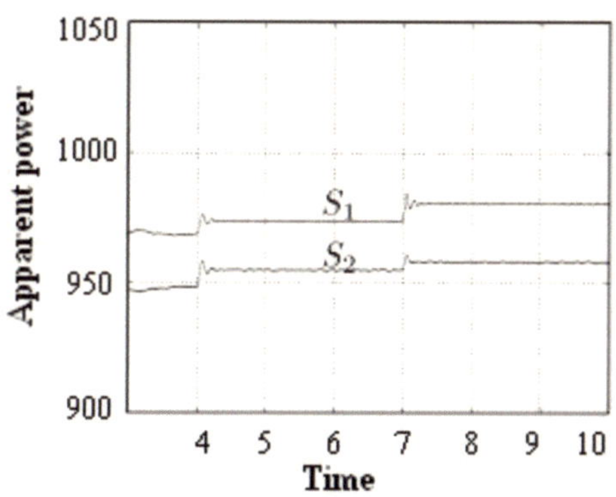

Figure 21. Variation of S_1 and S_2

2. B. Advanced system for the control of work regime of railway electric drive equipment

2.1. Introduction

Although the contact line in electric railway transport (and not only) can be regarded as a line of electric power distribution, it has several (mechanical and electric) characteristics that differ from the usual power systems. Thus, the most common failure regimes are the short circuit in the contact line (L.C.), sub-sectioning (P.S.) or in traction sub-stations (ST), produced by dielectric breakdown of insulators or mechanical failures caused by the pantograph of the electric engine (fig. 22).

The sudden growth of currents in the case of short circuits has negative consequences both upon the fixed installations of electric traction (thermal and dynamic effects) and upon other nearby installations (dangerous inductions in the phone networks, in the low voltage grids on pipelines, etc., which can endanger the life of the personnel in the vicinity of the railways.

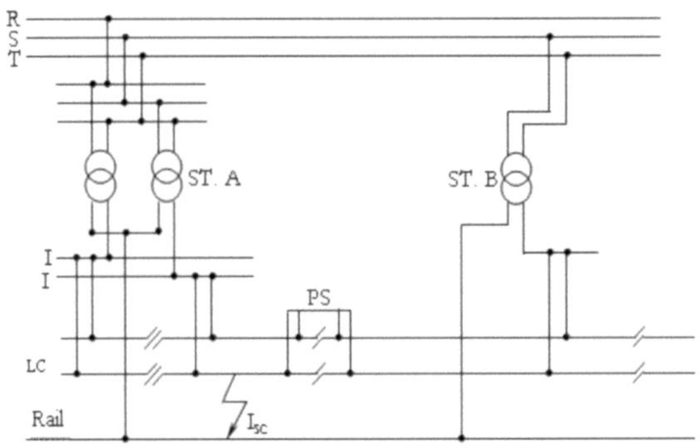

Figure 22. Electric power feeding of railway traction

In the case of single-phase electric railways with the frequency of 50 Hz, the distance between two ST is 50 ÷ 60 km, depending on the profile of the line. For the simple lines, the high value of characteristic impedance (0,47 Ω/km), leads to minimal short circuit currents (at the end of the line), below the maximal load currents.

In the case of short circuits in the vicinity of the ST, the currents reach up to eight times the charge current, and this is why they have to be cut off as quickly as possible. Neither the low current short circuits must be maintained for too long, as they have negative effects upon the installation.

Because of the elements mentioned above, protecting the contact line feeders by maximal current protection is not efficient enough. At present, distance protection is being used, either by di/dt relays or by impedance ones.

The di/dt relays function on the basis of the existing deforming regime existing in the contact line, current regime which should be diminished as much as possible in the future. The elimination of the deforming regime will make the di/dt relay inefficient.

Impedance relays, which are widely used in all power systems, can distinguish between an overload and a short circuit [11]. Because of the configuration of the contact line, the shape of the RX characteristic of the relay in the complex plane should be modified for each traction substation separately, which is difficult to achieve in practice. In order that RX characteristic meets the requirements imposed to the protection system, the complexity and cost increase [12].

2.2. The structure of the protection device

In order to secure protection against the abnormal work regimes of the contact lines and transformers, we designed a complex device meant to replace both the maximal current, low voltage relays etc., and the impedance relay. The block diagram of the device is given in fig. 23 [10].

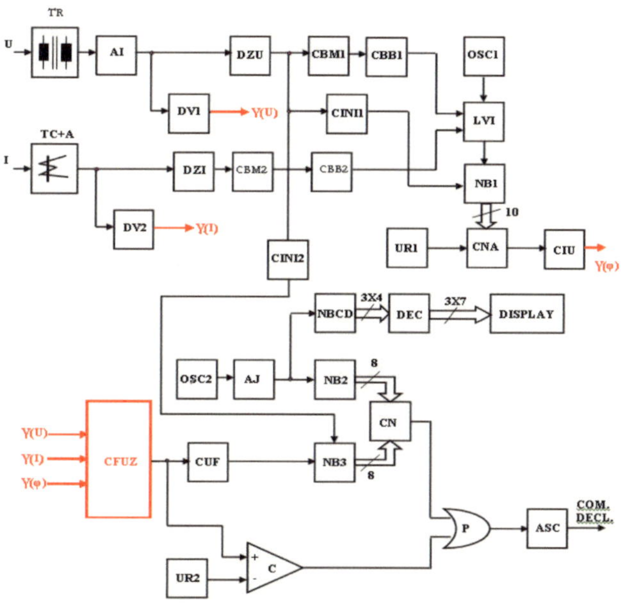

Figure 23. The block diagram of the protection device

The voltage of the power circuit is converted to a reduced value, accepted by the electronic circuit, by means of a group of instrument transformers TR, thus achieving, at the same time, galvanic separation of the power circuit using the insulation amplifier AI, which works with unitary amplification factor. At the output of the insulation amplifier AI we obtained an alternating voltage with a maximal amplitude of 10 V, fed both to a peak detector DV1 and to a device meant to detect the passage through zero of the voltage wave, DZU .

At the output of the peak detector DV1 we obtained signal V(U), whose value is proportional to the value of the voltage in the power circuit. Signal V(U) is fed to one of the analogue inputs of the fuzzy microcontroller. The voltage wave zero passage detector, marked DZU, is meant to generate an impulse at each such passage. The impulse obtained at the output of this block is fed on the one hand to a monostable switch circuit CBM1, in order to obtain a square impulse with a well determined shape and duration, and on the other hand, to an initialization circuit, CINI1. The signal at the output of the monostable switch circuit CBM1 is fed to the bistable switch circuit CBB1, triggering the switch of its output at each impulse received. The bistable switch circuit CBB1 is meant to trigger the determination the phase shift between the voltage and the current in the power circuit by means of a validation/inhibition logic (block LVI) of the access of some square impulses generated by the oscillator OSC 1 and fed to the asynchronous binary counter NB1.

The value of the current in the power circuit is converted by the ensemble current translator – amplifier TC+A into a voltage signal V(I) whose amplitude is 10V, which is fed to the peak detector DV2. At the output of the peak detector we obtain signal V(I), which is fed to one of the analogue inputs of the fuzzy controller. The current signal is also fed to a zero passage detector of the signal corresponding to the current, DZI, which commands a monostable switch circuit, CBM2, and a bistable switch circuit CBB2, both having similar functions with those on the branch corresponding to the voltage wave. The bistable switch circuit CBB2 is meant to stop the phase shift determination process, and it acts in this sense through the validation/inhibition logic.

As shown before, we input to the fuzzy microcontroller three analogue signals V(U), V(I) and V(ϕ), having values ranging between (0…5) V, whose values depend on the voltage, current and phase shift in the power grid. According to the value of the three signals and using the original processing program implemented on the fuzzy controller under the form of processing rules, at its analogue output we obtained a continuous voltage ranging in the domain (0…5)V. Its value is higher when the regime on the contact line approaches the failure regime, respectively when it is under failure regime and it is directly proportional to the seriousness of the failure.

What has to be done is to disconnect the contact line in a time interval that is inversely proportional to the seriousness of the failure. At the same time, it is necessary to keep on feeding the contact line in the situation of short term failures (caused for instance by atmospheric overcharges).

Meeting these requirements can be achieved by a programmable time delay circuit. This is made of a voltage – frequency converter connected to the output of the fuzzy controller, where a square signal is obtained, whose frequency is directly proportional to the voltage given by the fuzzy controller. These square impulses are then fed to a binary counter NB3, which shows – during one counting period – a value which is directly proportional to the voltage at the output of the fuzzy microcontroller. Counter NB3 is set on 8 binary ranks. Its outputs are fed to the input of a numeric comparator , CN. At the other inputs of the numeric comparator we apply the outputs of another binary comparator NB2, that is meant to memorize a value pre-established by the user. This value is input to the counter by means of the adjusting block AJ, respectively of the tact oscillator OSC2. The impulses fed to binary counter NB2 are simultaneously fed to a decimal code counter NBCD, whose outputs are connected to a decoding system DEC and then to a 7-segment display, marked DISPLAY. In this way, the user has a permanent control over the value given by binary counter NB2. This value represents the very threshold that triggers the main contact line feeding interrupter. Numeric comparator CN signals the situation when the numeric value in counter NB3 becomes equal to the threshold value in counter NB2. It is necessary to enable the modification of the threshold value for the main interrupter, according to the various normal functioning regimes established by the concrete practical situation and which have to be dealt with accordingly. The threshold is established by the users, according to the experience accumulated in time.

It is obvious that the triggering of the contact line main feeding interrupter is done in a time interval that is directly proportional to the threshold value in binary counter NB2, and inversely proportional to the voltage at the analogue output of the fuzzy microcontroller. The main interrupter can be triggered almost instantaneously, if the fuzzy microcontroller outputs a 5V voltage, which corresponds to highly dangerous failure. This value is sensed by comparator C, which permanently compares the output value of the fuzzy controller to a 5V reference voltage, fed by reference source UR2.

In case of reaching a regime that triggers the main interrupter, at the output of port P we have logic 1. This signal is power amplified by means of command signal amplifier ASC, which outputs a high enough signal to command the main interrupter.

For a correct functioning, binary counter NB3 has to be periodically reset, so that its value should not reach the threshold value memorized by binary counter NB2, even under a normal functioning regime. This condition is met during each period of the voltage in the grid, by initialization circuit CINI2. This circuit too, uses as time reference the zero passage impulse of the grid voltage. It is preferable to initialize counter NB3 just once during one period, as in this case, the value of counter NB3 depends on two operations of phase determination – corresponding to the two semiperiods – which achieves in this way a high immunity to very short perturbations or incorrect work regimes along the contact line.

All the circuits presented above have been designed built and tested and they worked correctly.

2.3. The Fuzzy Controller

As mentioned before, in order to offer a complex protection of the contact line in railway electric transport, using mono-phase AC (27,5 [kV], 50 [Hz]) we designed a Fuzzy relay, starting from the practical case of a railway electric traction sub-station [10]. This relay allows a maximal current, overcharge, distance and minimal voltage protection. Although initially we did not take into consideration directional protection (the inverse current circulation between two traction substations), its introduction is not a problem and we consider that the Fuzzy relay can achieve that too.

a. Information on the input magnitudes

We considered the following usual regimes:

Variable		Linguistic values	Variation domain	Universe of discourse [%]
Input	Current	normal	50 ÷ 600 [A]	0÷30,8
		overcharge	600÷800 [A]	25,6÷41
		short-circuit	800÷2000 [A]	35,9÷100
	Voltage	short-circuit	16 ÷ 20 [kV]	0÷43,5
		overcharge	20 ÷ 25 [kV]	26,1÷87
		normal	25 ÷ 27,5 [kV]	69,6÷100
	Phase shift	normal	0÷30 [grad]	0÷43,8
		overcharge	30÷60 [grad]	31,3÷81,3
		short-circuit	60÷80 [grad]	68,8÷100
Output	Command	blocked	0 [V]	0
		high delay	1,66 [V]	33,3
		low delay	3,33 [V]	66,6
		instant	5 [V]	100

Table 1. Input and Output Magnitudes

In figure 24 we present the recorded values for the current in one ST with high traffic protected with usual distance relay. One may notice a rather high frequency of critical work regimes transitory (three short-circuits at long distance, without disconnection due to a mechanical failure: 1, 2, 4; and three overloads: 3, 5 and 6 all in a period of twenty minutes). The waveforms for three cases: normal, overload and short-circuit are presented in figures 25, 26 and 27. The phase shift between current and voltage for three situations are clearly different which justify the selection of phase as an important factor in identification of critical regimes. Another interesting characteristic is the smoothing of the current waveform during the short-circuit situation (even in the case of long distance short-circuit) and the phase shift increase which is produced by the change of the complex impedance of the system.

As the scale representing the transfer functions that correspond to the processed magnitudes is a percentage one (0 - 100%), we needed to norm the discussion universe, by means of a 1st degree polynomial function.

In fig. 28, 29, 30 are presented the membership functions for the input magnitudes, and in fig. 31 is present the output magnitude.

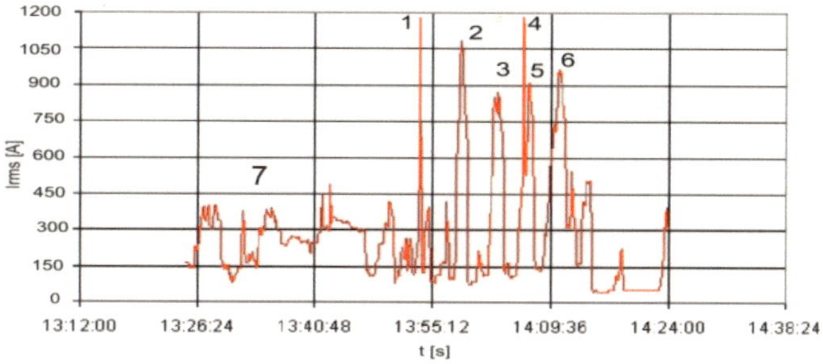

Figure 24. ST load current in different work conditions: 1,2,4 – long distance short-circuit; 3,5,6 – overload; 7 – normal load

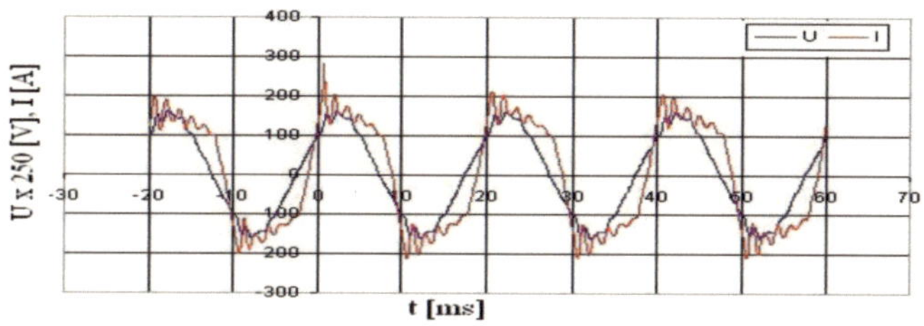

Figure 25. ST load current and voltage wave in normal regime

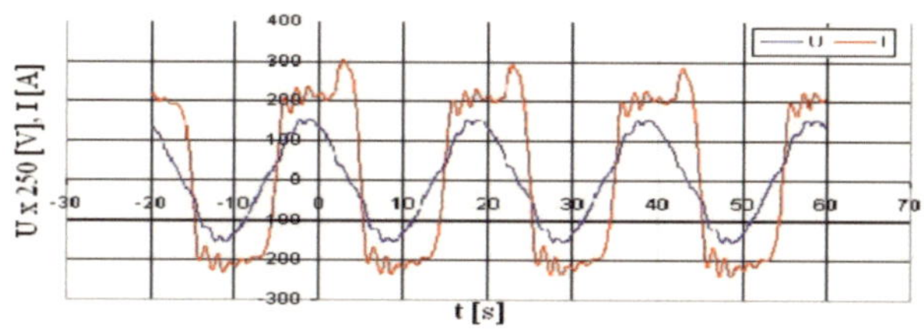

Figure 26. ST load current and voltage wave form in overload regime

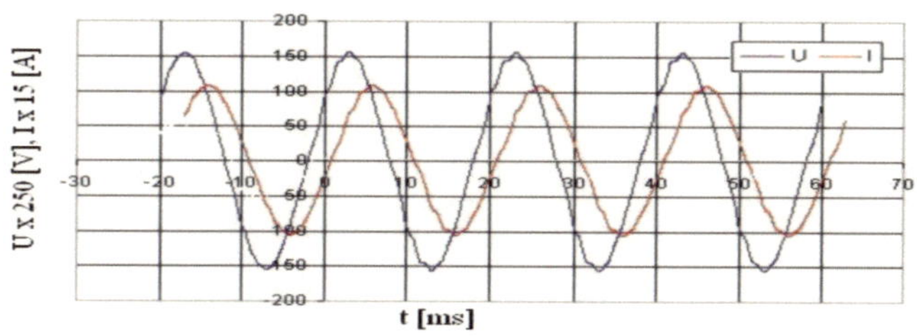

Figure 27. ST load current and voltage in short-circuit regime

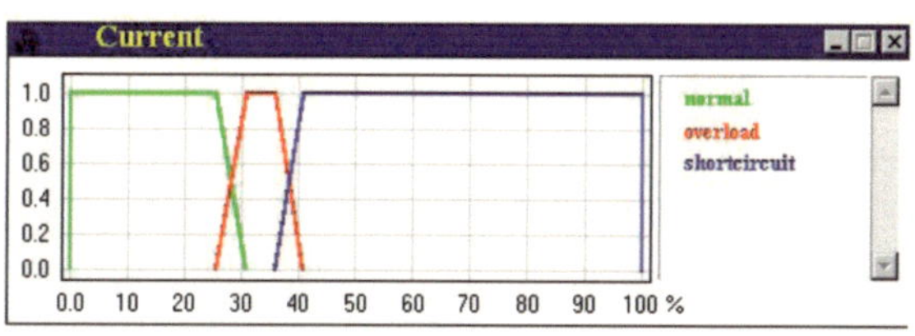

Figure 28. Representation of membership functions for the input magnitude "current"

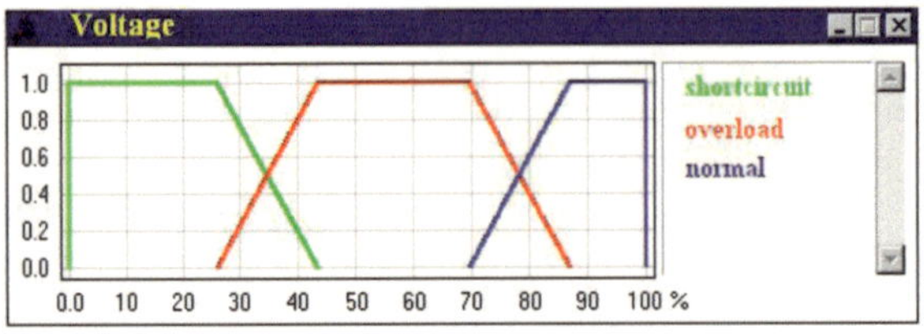

Figure 29. Representation of membership functions for the input magnitude "voltage"

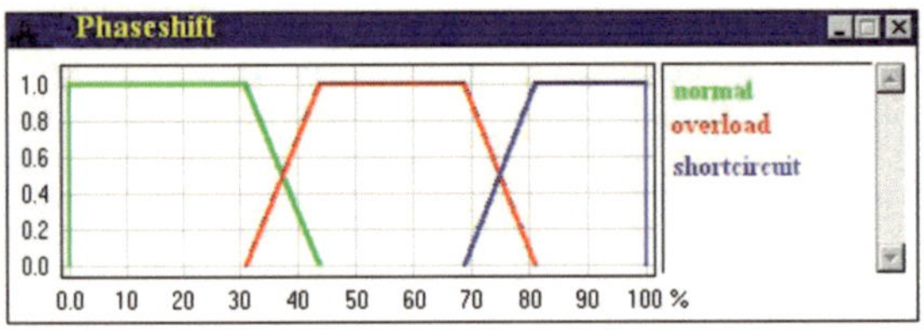

Figure 30. Representation of membership functions for the input magnitude "phase shift"

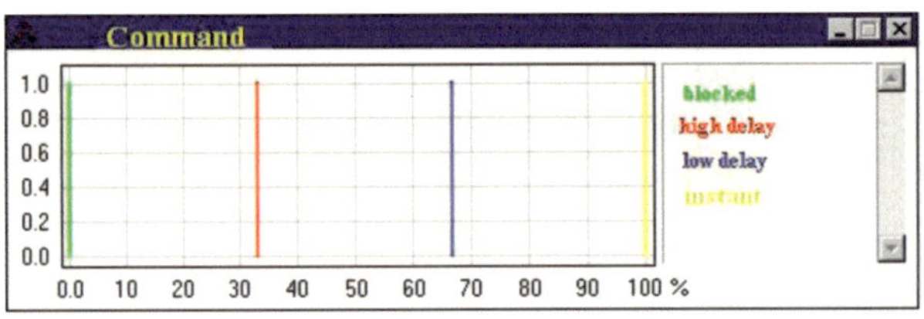

Figure 31. Representation of membership functions for the output magnitude "command"

b. Command rules (inference)

The rules have been established for practical reasons after having checked the reference literature and consulted experts in electric traction and protection installations for electrical systems.

Fig. 32 shows the rules base which connecting the fuzzy input variables to the fuzzy output variable, by means of the inference method (max/min). For deffuzification we chose the Singleton weight centers method due to its major advantage, namely the short processing time, a stringent condition for the real time functioning of the Fuzzy controller with a function of relay. For this reason, for the practical application under analysis we established Singleton-type membership functions corresponding to the linguistic term "command" of the output magnitude. Using the max-min inference method alongside with the defuzzification method is widely spread in practice and has lead to outstanding performances of the regulation systems.

Fig. 33 shows the command surface for three constant values voltage corresponding to the cases described above (normal, overload and short-circuit).

TABLE	If			then	
	current	voltage	phaseshift	command	weight
1. Rule	normal	normal	normal	blocked	1.0
2. Rule	normal	normal	overload	high delay	1.0
3. Rule	normal	normal	short-circuit	instant	1.0
4. Rule	normal	overload	normal	low delay	1.0
5. Rule	normal	overload	overload	high delay	1.0
6. Rule	normal	overload	short-circuit	instant	1.0
7. Rule	normal	short-circuit	normal	instant	1.0
8. Rule	normal	short-circuit	overload	instant	1.0
9. Rule	normal	short-circuit	short-circuit	instant	1.0
10. Rule	overload	normal	normal	blocked	1.0
11. Rule	overload	normal	overload	high delay	1.0
12. Rule	overload	normal	short-circuit	instant	1.0
13. Rule	overload	overload	normal	high delay	1.0
14. Rule	overload	overload	overload	low delay	1.0
15. Rule	overload	overload	short-circuit	instant	1.0
16. Rule	overload	short-circuit	normal	high delay	1.0
17. Rule	overload	short-circuit	overload	instant	1.0
18. Rule	overload	short-circuit	short-circuit	instant	1.0
19. Rule	short-circuit	normal	normal	low delay	1.0
20. Rule	short-circuit	normal	overload	low delay	1.0
21. Rule	short-circuit	normal	short-circuit	instant	1.0
22. Rule	short-circuit	overload	normal	low delay	1.0
23. Rule	short-circuit	overload	overload	instant	1.0
24. Rule	short-circuit	overload	short-circuit	instant	1.0
25. Rule	short-circuit	short-circuit	normal	instant	1.0
26. Rule	short-circuit	short-circuit	overload	instant	1.0
27. Rule	short-circuit	short-circuit	short-circuit	instant	1.0

Figure 32. Rules base

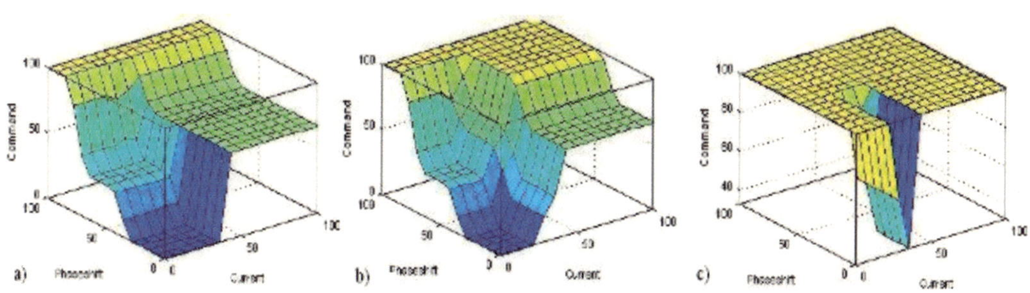

Figure 33. Command surfaces for three voltage values

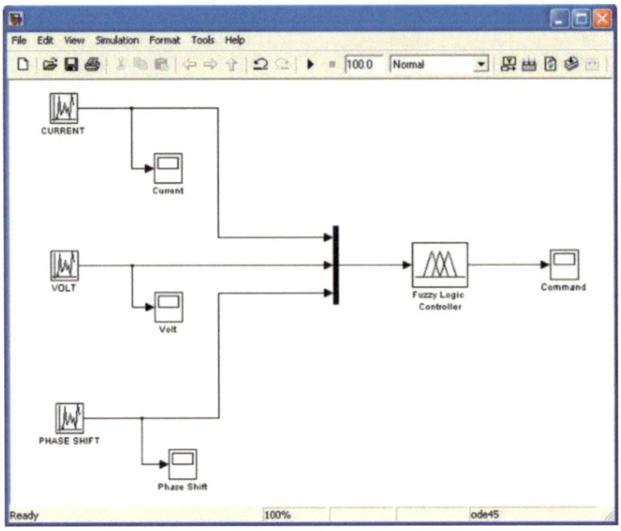

Figure 34. Simulation diagram

Fuzzy controller simulation is realized in Matlab – Simulink (fig. 34). We randomly generated several combinations of input variables (fig. 35, 36 and 37), and the analysis of the response (fig. 38) proved the correct functioning of the fuzzy system, according to the rules base established.

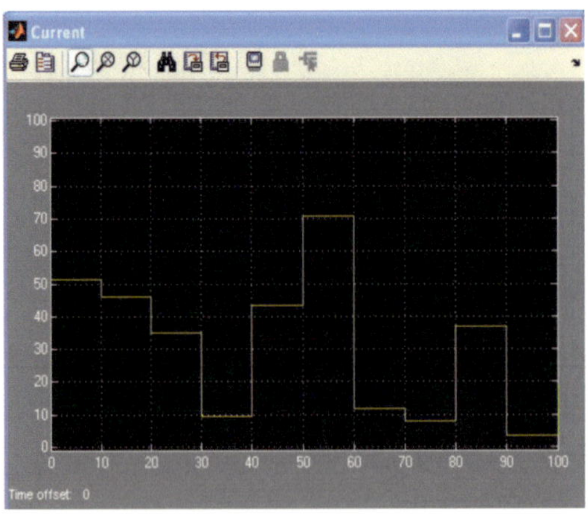

Figure 35. Input magnitude CURRENT

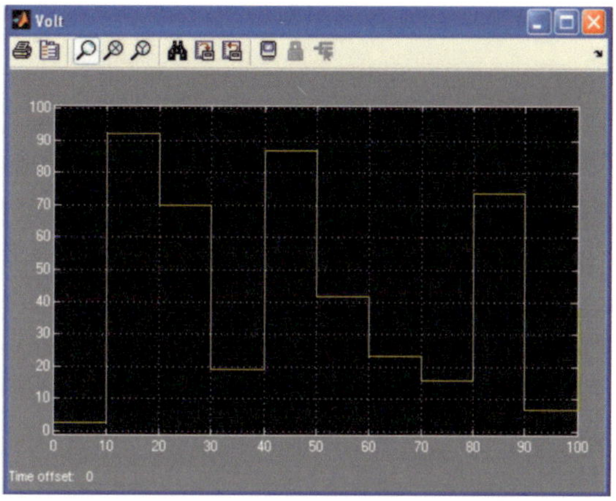

Figure 36. Input magnitude VOLTAGE

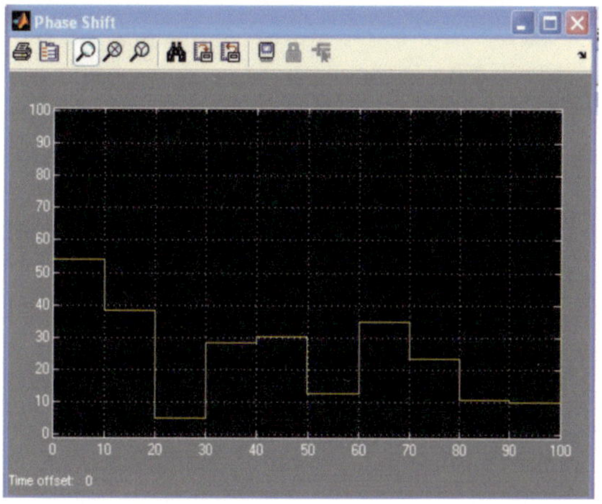

Figure 37. Input magnitude PHASE SHIFT

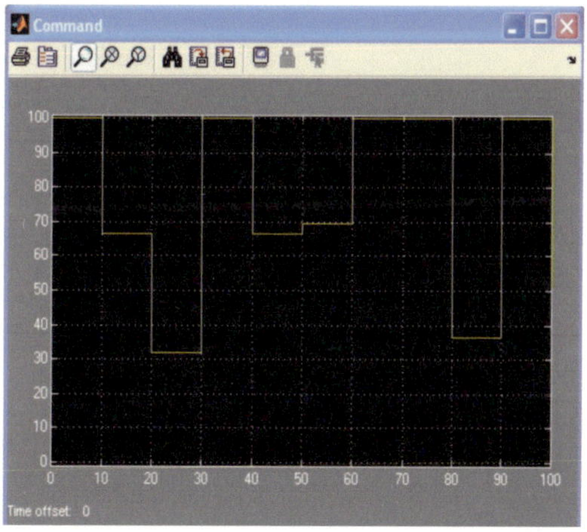

Figure 38. Output magnitude COMMAND

The fuzzy system has been implemented on an eZdsp TMS320F2812 development board produced by Spectrum Digital.

2.4. Hardware implementation and testing for the Fuzzy Logic relay for railway protection

The development cycle is based on three stages: first the fuzzy logic relay is designed and tuned on Matlab – Simulink using a Simpower System model of the railway ST because the testing in the real system would have been extremely expensive and dangerous. This allows the simulation, parameters tuning and optimization of rules data base.

In the second stage, the final structure of the fuzzy logic operations are prepared for hardware implementation. In order to achieve a high speed operation some hardware specific features of the DSP are employed to reduce the computation resources for the application. One operation which requires intensive computation is the deffuzification which need complex instruction. Each input (voltage, current and phase shift) is sampled using an 8 bit ADC. The input variables are quantified in order to obtain the degree of membership of each point of the input for each fuzzy set. For each point is associated an index value corresponding to the membership function. The rule base in coded using the same index system in order to have the correspondence between the index of active membership functions with the corresponding part of the rule base.

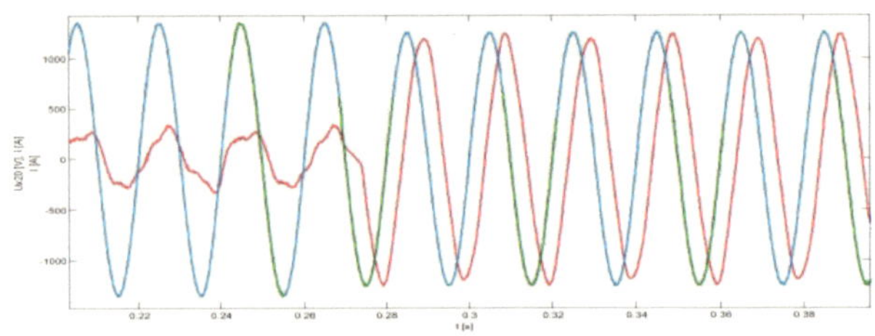

a) long distance short circuit

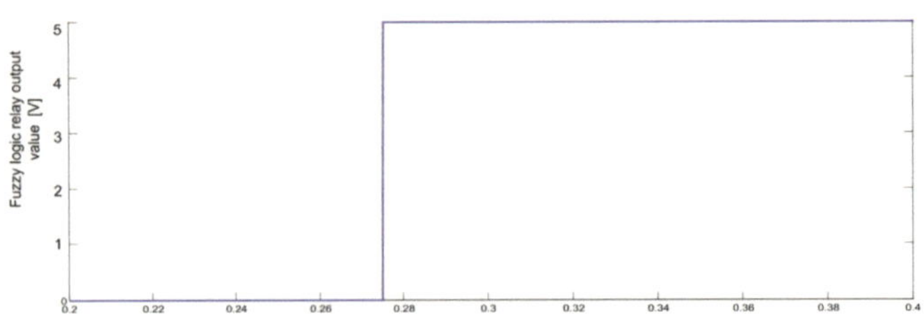

b) relay response

Figure 39. Fault processing by the fuzzy logic relay

Finally, the structure of the system operation is coded using Code Composer Studio development environment in C. The resulting assembly code is optimized for speed in order to have the shortest cycle time. For the hardware implementation we have considered a Spectrum Digital DSP development board with TMS320F2812 processor.

From the point of computation resources this can offer sufficient processing speed in order to meet the application requirement at a reasonable development time (since no assembly coding was necessary). This hardware solution used to implement the fuzzy logic relay structure is simple and provide good performance/price output.

After manual verification of the correct functioning of the DSP fuzzy processor the entire system was put under test in a real ST (in parallel with the existing protective system). In figure 10 a one long distance short circuit it has been identified and the actual response of the relay is presented in fig 10 b. One may notice the extremely fast response of the proposed fuzzy relay system (the short circuit was not identified by the usual impedance relay due to the misclassification of the fault).

The existing protection system obviously has considered the event as an overload and it disconnected the main switch about one minute after.

3. C. Control system for catenary – Pantograph dynamic interaction force

3.1. Introduction

An issue of great importance in railway electric transportation is the quality of the sliding contact „pantograph- catenary suspension".

An improper contact produces electric arcs with unfavorable consequences on energy loss, reliability and wear of the subassemblies subjected to the arc, electromagnetic pollution, etc.

Of main interest is the behavior of the dynamic response of the two mechanical subsystems coupled by the contact force (pantograph- catenary suspension), each of them having totally different structures and dynamic properties.

The aims of the numerical simulation analysis were to obtain conclusive information for kineto-static and dynamic characterization of the „pantograph - catenary suspension" assembly's behavior.

Based on the simulations performed in this work, using an original program, was found that the dynamic response of the studied assembly produces variation of the contact force in very large ranges, depending on the train's travel speed and other parameters, being the one which leads to detachments, thus to electric arcs.

Currently, there are several world-wide used models for pantograph–catenary interaction, which apply especially at high speeds (over 350km/h) and rely on different principles [19], [20], [21]. These models have different degrees of complexity. Most of them consider simplifications, as taking into account all the factors (i.e. aerodynamic forces, friction, proper oscillation of the locomotive, etc.) leads to a very difficult problem. The traffic at speeds above 350km/h is made on the specific lines, namely the railways, catenary suspensions and locomotives are especially built and designed for these conditions. However, in Romania and the neighboring countries this traffic runs on normal lines, which through modernization can be improved to support speeds from 140km/h up to 220km/h. In this case the railway, the catenary suspension and the locomotives are just the upgraded classical ones. The current paper refers to this part of this problem, which has not been extensively treated in the literature.

The conclusions presented in this work have a special importance, based on which following to be achieved an intelligent management system of the pantograph's pressure force regime, taking into account the speed, its momentary position and the coupled dynamic model of the two subassemblies: pantograph- catenary suspension.

3.2. Analysis of the "Catenary-Pantograph" assembly's dynamic behavior by numerical simulation

The purpose of the numerical simulation, by results interpretation, was the possibility to test the validity of the issued hypothesis upon the real systems' behavior, being in operation, as *dynamically coupled subassemblies*.

The analysis was made using the *TENSI-CABLE* calculation program, specially conceived by one of this work's authors for the dynamic behavior's study of some strength structures composed by flexible elements.

The program's essence consists in the possibility to determine the structure's response to a dynamic stimulus, of „excitation force" or „imposed motion" type, into a section required by the user. From space and paternity considerate of the calculation program, in this work are presented and commented only the results of some of the performed simulations.

The study of the „catenary suspension–pantograph" assembly's dynamic behavior, conducted by numerical simulation, was made considering a catenary suspension with standard configuration in Romania, having the parameters written in table 2.

Material: Contact wire Carrier cable Articulated pendulum	- copper, section 100 mm^2 - galvanized steel, section 70mm^2 - galvanized wire, section 28 mm^2
Suspension's total length	- 196 m
Distance between the supporting pillars	- 3 spans of 60,0m each
Distance between the articulated pendulums	- 6 m / 8m (9 pendulums per span)
Mechanical stress: Upper wire Lower wire	 - 12.000N - 12.000N
Specific mass: Upper wire Lower wire	 - 0,89 kg/m - 0,61 kg/m
Axial rigidity Upper wire Lower wire	- 10500 kN - 5000 kN

Table 2. Standard's catenary parameters

The catenary simulated is a simple style catenary, which was chosen because it has all the characteristic dynamic effects. A diagram of the model is given in fig. 40, where:

Tower stiffness: S; Dropper stiffness: K; Distance to the i-th tower: W_j; Distance to the i-th dropper: X_j; Stiffness of the two wires: EI_A; EI_B; Density of the two wires: ρ_A; ρ_B; Tension in the two wires: T_A; T_B.

The contact force, as excitation force considered in simulation, is the one afferent to a basic pantograph of which designing parameters are typical to EP3 pantographs, being in current operation at Romanian Railways, (fig. 40).

For the study made on the simulation model, it was built the input data block comprising the determinant geometrical and mechanical parameters for the component elements of the studied assembly.

In simulation were considered three spans of catenary (fig. 41), having a number of 70 nodes and 103 elements.

The equations governing the response of the catenary are obtained through the displacement of the contact wire and messenger wire, expressed as Fourier sine series expansions. The displacement shapes of the contact wire and messenger wire from equilibrium are each expressed as Fourier sine series expansions, and a good approximation of the shape is possible if enough terms are used the series expansions are given below:

$$y_A(x,t) = \sum A_m(t) \sin\left(\frac{m\pi x}{L}\right) \text{ - messenger wire} \tag{31}$$

$$y_B(x,t) = \sum B_m(t) \sin\left(\frac{m\pi x}{L}\right) \text{ - contact wire} \tag{32}$$

where: y – the wire displacement; A_m – the amplitude of the m-th sine term for the messenger wire; B_m - the amplitude of the m-th sine term for the contact wire; x – the displacement along the catenary; L – the total length of the catenary; m – an integer, designates the harmonic number.

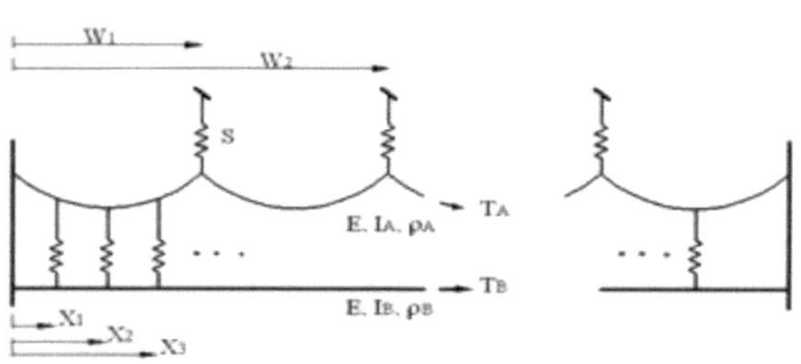

Figure 40. Catenary model

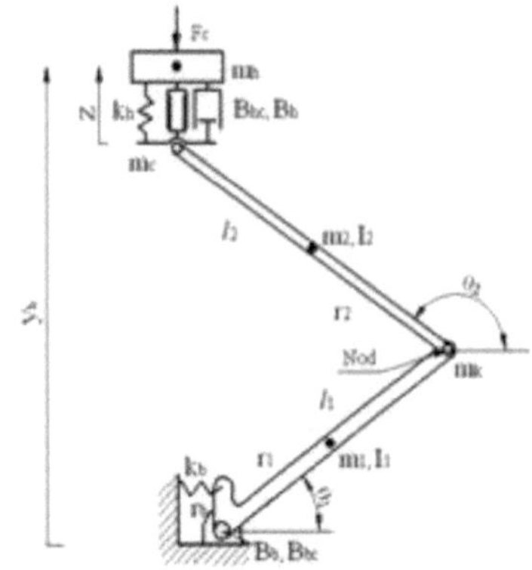

Figure 41. Pantograph model

The equations of motion contain displacement and acceleration terms ($A, \ddot{A}, B, \ddot{B}$). When the system is excited, the catenary's response is harmonic so the acceleration terms are:

$$\ddot{A}_m = -\omega^2 A_m \tag{33}$$

$$\ddot{B}_m = -\omega^2 B_m \tag{34}$$

where: ω - the natural frequency of vibration

The orthogonal modes of the catenary can be considered separately and the result from modal analysis gives the equation for each mode:

$$M_i \ddot{z}_i + 2\xi_i \omega_i M_i \dot{z}_i + \omega_i^2 M_i Z_i = Q_i \tag{35}$$

where: $z_i(t)$ – the i-th model response; m_i – the i-th modal mass; ξ_i - the damping ratio; ω_i – the i-th natural frequency; Q_i – the i-th modal forcing function.

Simulation started at time t=0 seconds with the pantograph at pillar zero, on the contact wire acting the pantograph's lifting force, becoming contact force starting with this moment.

By pantograph's forwarding along the running track, it moves successively the catenary's sections upwards and, thus, induces a vibrating motion of the wire of which oscillations, after pantograph's passing, propagate along the contact wire.

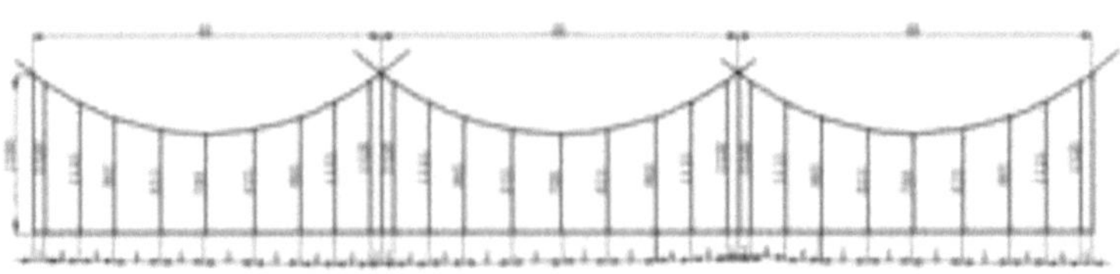

Figure 42. The three spans of the catenary

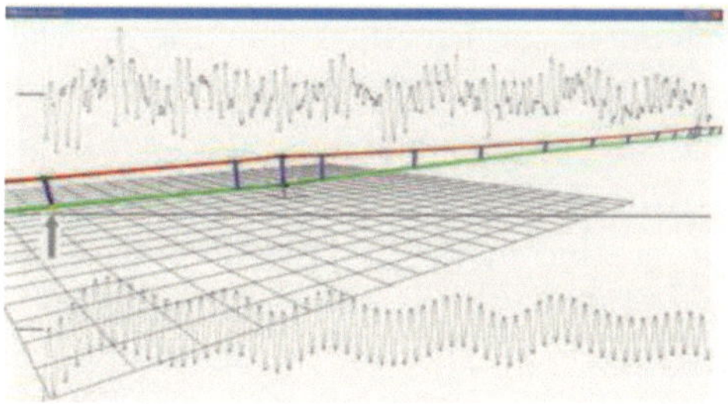

Figure 43. Propagation of the oscillating motion induced by the pantograph's excitation force and catenary's deformation, after t=8,98s

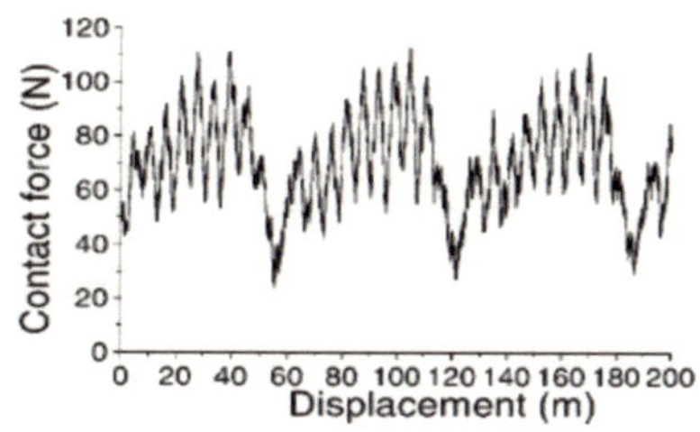

(a) 140 km/h

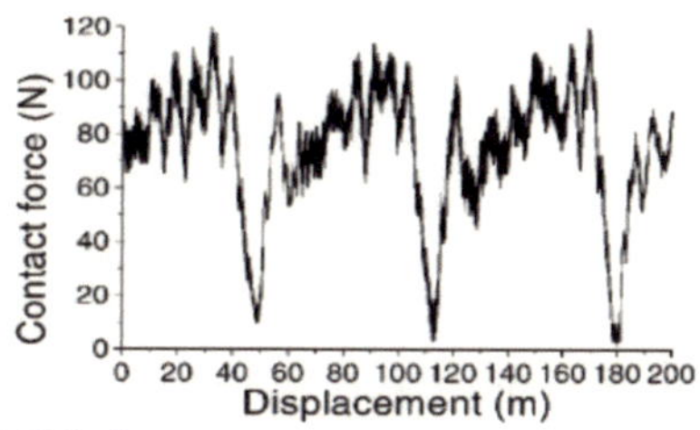

(b) 160 km/h

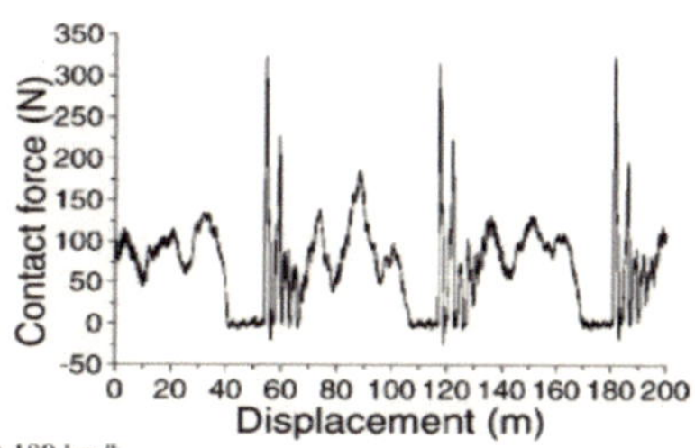

(c) 180 km/h

Figure 44. Contact force at different speed

Exemplifying of this phenomenon is shown in fig. 43 that includes also the deformed shape of the catenary suspension, afferent to the pantograph's position right at a node located in the last third of the first span.

The shape shifting of the catenary's distortion right at the pillars (from a steep descent to a slope less pronounced) has the most pronounced effect on the pantograph's performances, the operation data confirming also that in these areas are noticed also the most frequent contact losses. This conclusion is confirmed also in the specialty literature, the authors finding that at speeds over 150km/h, even the pantograph's crosshead shoe could keep the contact (because the upper suspension, being lighter, could accommodate to a greater movement between the crosshead shoe and the frame), the pantograph's frame responds slower (because, having a greater mass and inertia forces are higher) and, while the pantograph passes the area in the right of a supporting pillar, it sub-vibrates, the result being a smaller contact force.

Table 3 shows the characteristics of contact force at a different speed. It can be seen that with the increasing of speed the characteristics of contact force are getting worse. The speed of 160 km/h is a critical point. At this speed, the contact force approaches to zero. It means that the slipper-shoe of the pantograph lost contact with the overhead line.

Speed (km/h)	100	120	140	160	170	180
Max. contact force (N)	99	103	105	117	119	367
Max. contact force (N)	42	40	24	2	0	0

Table 3. The contact force at different speed

When the running speed is less than this speed, the contact force is larger than zero and the pantograph – catenary system works well. But when the running speed is larger than 160 km/h, loss of contact occurs and becomes more frequent with the increasing of the speed. Considering the minimum contact force should be larger than 20 ~ 30 N in order to keep good contact, we can see from the result that the EP3 pantograph together with the tested catenary, is only suitable for running speed less than 140 km/h. Figure 44 shows the contact force under a speed of 140, 160 and 180 km/h. At a speed of 180 km/h, the contact is lost, and the impact causes large maximum contact force.

3.3. Active control strategies

Studying the previously presented problem, one can observe that the contact force between the pantograph and the catenary is variable, due to a different dynamical behavior of the two parts, with maxima and minima which occur at a frequency of 0.5÷2 [Hz].

For flow speeds over 350km/h, on special lines built and equipped for this purpose, one can find in the literature active control solutions of contact force through "classical" methods [22] [23] [24] [25] [26] or advanced methods [27], [28], [29].

These are quite expensive and not profitable when used at lower speeds (160km/h÷ 220km/h). For this case, we propose a contact force control system of the pantograph-catenary based on the fuzzy logic.

Our aim is to reduce variations in the contact force, by eliminating the pantograph detachment and the appearance of excessive peaks (Table 3), which lead to a premature wear of the contact wire. The structure of the contact force control system is shown in Figure 45.

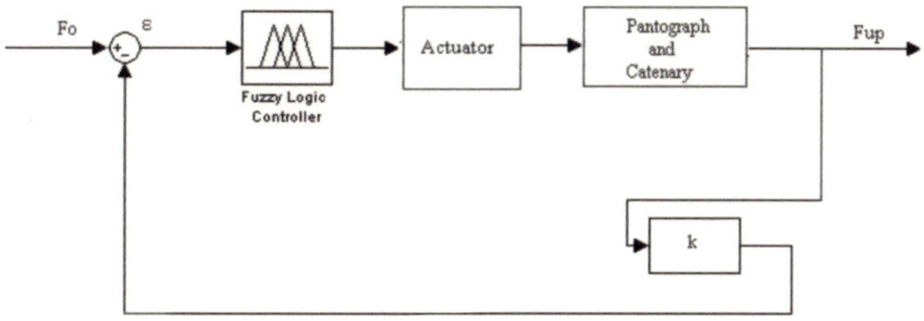

Figure 45. System structure

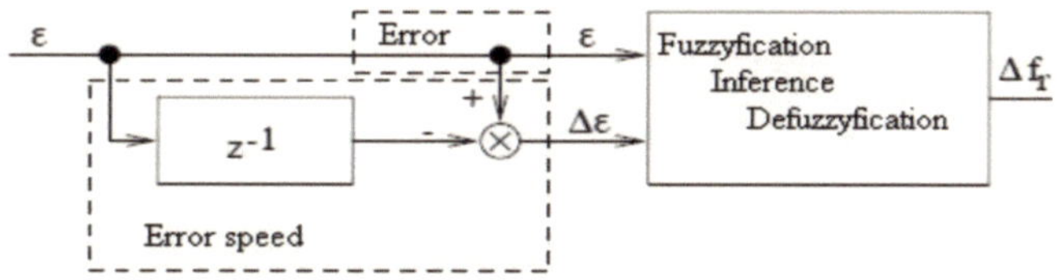

Figure 46. Fuzzy controller

The proposed fuzzy controller presented in Figure 46, will determine the correction through which the contact force will be closer to the desired value, using the information given by the error (ε) and rate of change of the error (Δε).

The variables (ε) and (Δε) are converted into fuzzy variables, using membership functions and the discussion universes in Figures 47, 48 and 49.

The variables (ε) and (Δε) are processed using the inference of the 49 rules (Table 4) through the method of min/max. Output defuzification is made by the centroid method.

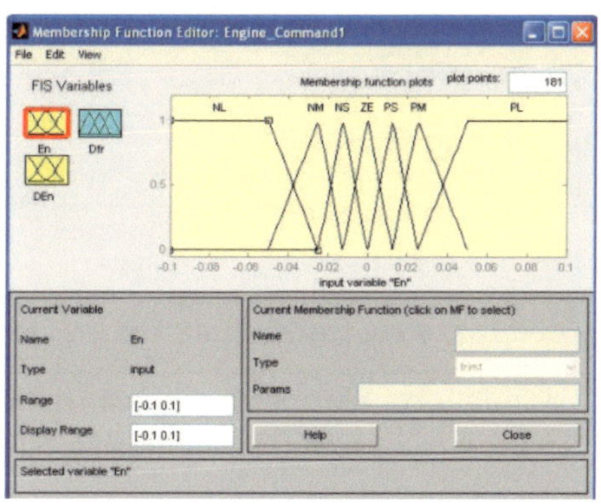

Figure 47. Membership functions for error

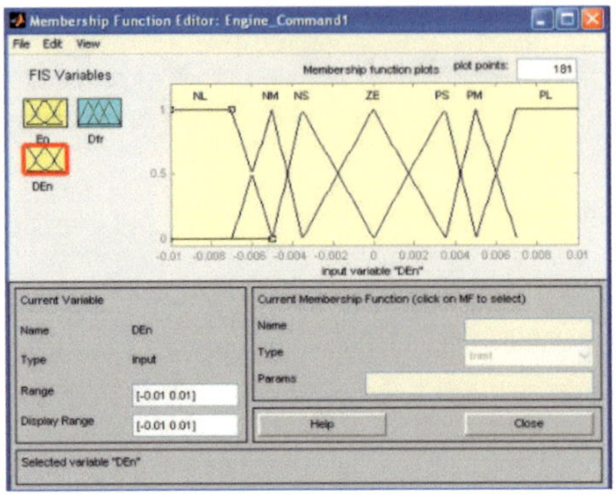

Figure 48. Membership functions for speed error

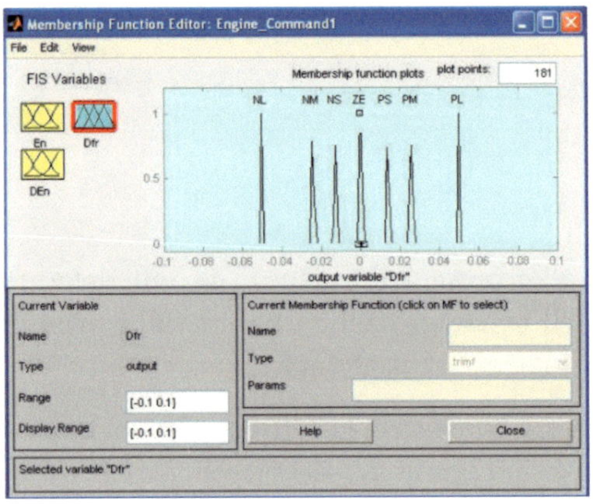

Figure 49. Membership functions for command

Δf_r (ε_n \\ $\Delta\varepsilon_n$)	NL	NM	NS	ZE	PS	PM	PL
NL	NL	NL	NL	NL	NM	NS	ZE
NM	NL	NL	NL	NM	NS	ZE	PS
NS	NL	NL	NM	NS	ZE	PS	PM
ZE	NL	NM	NS	ZE	PS	PM	PL
PS	NM	NS	ZE	PS	PM	PL	PL
PM	NS	ZE	PS	PM	PL	PL	PL
PL	ZE	PS	PM	PL	PL	PL	PL

Table 4. Rule base

The control area of the proposed fuzzy controller is shown in Figure 50.

Using a Matlab-Simulink simulation, we performed a fuzzy controller functionality simulation. The simulation results are presented in Figures 51, 52 and 53.

For the signal error, a triangular variation was chosen, which went through all of the conversation universe (with a linear increase error from -0.1 to +0.1, followed by a linear decrease to the initial value). The derivative of the error has constant maximum positive values within the first ten seconds and minimum negative values in the next ten seconds.

The command variable follows the base of rules, namely while the error grows, the correction of contact force gets stronger, as there is a non-linear relationship between the two variables, which is in agreement with the experiment.

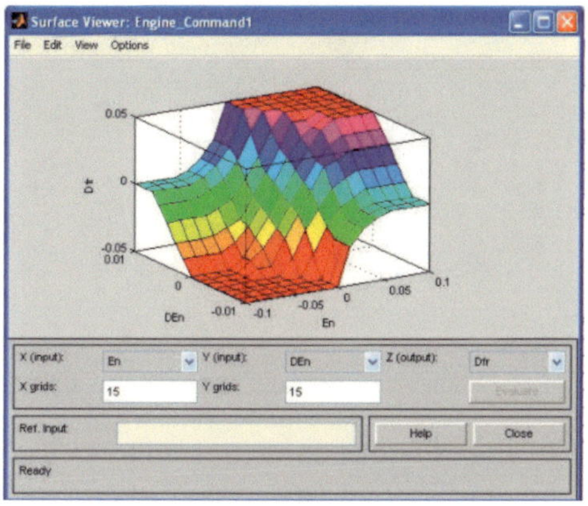

Figure 50. Control surface

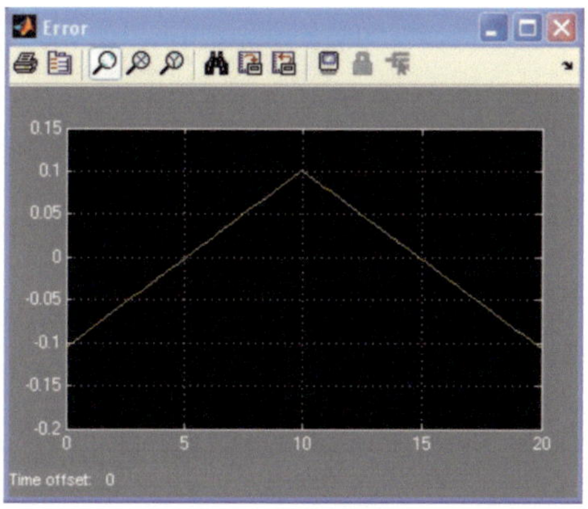

Figure 51. Input signal for error

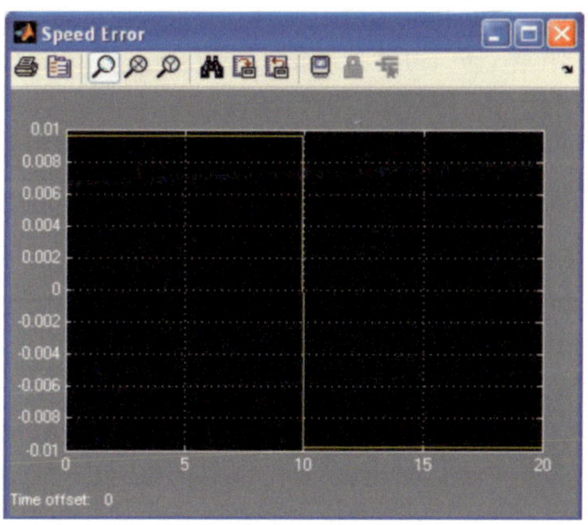

Figure 52. Input signal for speed error

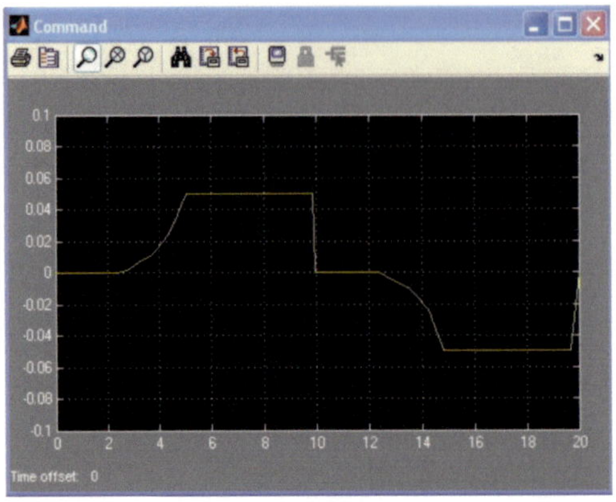

Figure 53. Output signal

When the error changes sign, the strength correction follows the same principle, but in the opposite direction. One concludes that the established rules lead to contact force stabilization. Using the original TENSI-CABLE model and applying the corrections established by the fuzzy system over the dynamic contact force, we were able to estimate the new variation form of the force between the pantograph and the catenary.

Note the small variations ±10N around the value of 75N, which was considered to be the optimal value of the contact force in order to achieve a correct transfer of energy.

The above mentioned variations may be reduced even more in the real implementation phase of the controller, by using a correction of the base of rules.

The speed of response of the control system is very high: only the upper arms have to be moved, reducing the mass to be moved with respect to the case of the force acting of the linkage frame and moving the mass of the whole pantograph. A brushless DC motor with low inertia and small electro-mechanical time constant could be the simplest choice for the electrical actuator.

An important observation must be considered, independently upon the chosen control strategy. In order to overcome the first drawback, the uplift contact force can be subdivised into two terms: a mean term given by a constant force, provided by the traditional passive mechanism (usually a spring or pneumatic cylinder) as in standard pantographs and an additional oscillating term provided by a closed-loop active actuator. In such a way the current collection capability can be maintained even in a case of a failure in the active control apparatus.

A crucial problem to be overcome for a practical implementation of closed-loops active pantograph is the measurement of the contact force. The force sensor must be reliable and lasting in a harsh environment. The traditional solution is to measure the contact force at the support points of the contact strips and to compensate for the inertia of the contact strip by an accelerometer. The required instrumentation is expensive and its life-time is short due to the high temperature and to the vibrational phenomene. Ref [23] presents other methods of simulation for the contact force, which eliminate the previously mentioned disadvantages.

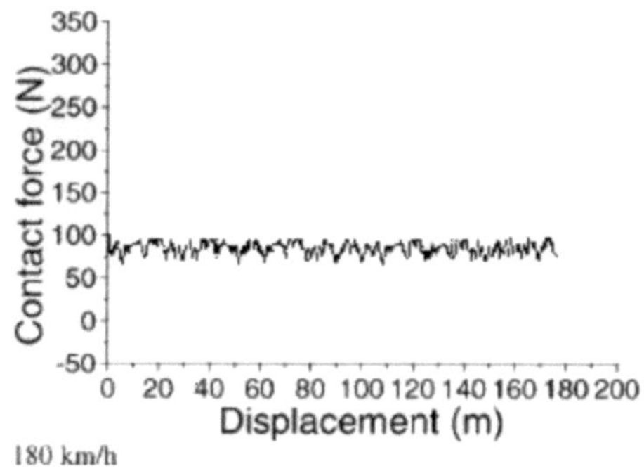

Figure 54. Contact force corrected

4. Conclusion

It can be concluded that usual active harmonic filtering the network side harmonic distortion is reduced very effectively, but the psophometric effect caused by the current along the traction system basically did not change [9]. This situation cannot be tolerated since the effects of induced currents due to the harmonic components and resonance can produce catastrophic effects upon the various equipments placed in the vicinity of the railway power lines.

The proposed Fuzzy DAFS can deploy several small-rated active filter units at various locations within the facility to damp the harmonic resonance. Compared to a centralized, large – rated active filter, the distributed, small-rated active filters with fuzzy logic controlled DAFS can reduce harmonics in the railway power system with improved effectiveness.

The advantage of the presented system based on fuzzy logic is the fact the use of a rather distributed system which is capable to adapt to the railway configuration. Using several filter units, the system has the capability to eliminate harmonic pollution and to avoid harmonic resonance in railway systems. By means using simulation results, we have validating the system considering the coordination of two active filters: one placed in substation area, and the 2nd placed at the end of the line (locomotive level).

Part (B) introduces a complex for the protection of the contact line and of the railway electric transport installations, based on the fuzzy logic. The system we presented has been built in practice and its experimental implementation has shown a series of advantages with respect to the actual systems, such as: low cost; adaptability to any real situation by the appropriate modification of the rules base; very short response time (5μs) of the fuzzy controller; it functionally replaces several protection systems, taking over all their functions. The system has the great advantage over other fuzzy logic relay systems that is designed considering the specific railway power system behavior.

Based on an original numerical model for the dynamical interaction pantograph-catenary, part (C) analyzes the evolution of the contact force between them, concluding that control could be lost at speeds above 170km/h, with multiple disadvantages. The mathematical model is complex, nonlinear and can not be used directly in managing online the contact force regime. This paper proposes a simple solution based on the fuzzy logic, which eliminates excessive variations, therefore enabling a good electrical contact between the pantograph and the catenary. The system was designed for the traffic of electric locomotives on classical lines, with speeds up to 220 km/h.

Author details

Stela Rusu-Anghel and Lucian Gherman
Politehnica University of Timisoara, Romania

5. References

[1] P. Kiss[1], A. Balogh[2], A. Dan[1], I. Varjasi[2], The Application of Active Filter Supported by Pulse Width Modulated Inverters in the Harmonic Simulation of the High Power Electric Traction , *Proceedings of ICREPQ 2008 – Canary Islands,* pp. 231-236.

[2] Po-Tai Cheng, Zhung-Lin Lee, Distributed Active Filter Systems (DAFS): A new approach to power system harmonics, *The 39th IEEE Conference IAS 2004,* Seattle, USA, pp. 94 – 101.

[3] H. Akagi, Modern active filters and traditional passive filters, *Bulletin of the Polish Academy of Sciences Technical Sciences,* Vol. 54, No. 3, 2006, Warsaw , pp. 255 – 269.

[4] B. Dobrucky, M. Pokorny, V. Racek, R. Havrila, A New Method of the Instantaneous Reactive Power Determination for Single-Phase Power Electronics Systems, *Proceedings EPE 2003 Lausanne* , pp. 1 – 9.

[5] Juraj Altus[1)], Jan Michalik[1)], Branislav Dobrucky[1)], L.H. Viet[2)], Single-Phase Power Active Filter Using Instantaneous Reactive Power Theory – Theoretical and Practical Approach, *Journal of Electrical Power Quality and Utilization,* Vol. 11, No. 1, 2005, pp. 33 – 38.

[6] Ahmed A. Helal, Nahla E. Zakzouk, and Yasser G. Desouky, Fuzzy Logic Controlled Shunt Active Power Filter for Three-phase Four-wire Systems with Balanced and Unbalanced Loads, *Proceedings World Academy of science, Engineering and Technology 58 2009,* ISSN 2070 - 3740, pp. 621 – 627.

[7] Soumia Kerrouche, Fateh Krim, Three-phase Active Filter Based on Fuzzy Logic Controller, *International Journal of Sciences and Techniques of Automatic Control & computer engineering IJ-STA,* Vol. 3, No. 1, 2009, pp. 942 – 955.

[8] Victor M. Moreno[1], Alberto Pigazo[1], Improved Injection Current Controller in Single-Phase Shunt Active Power Filters, *International Conference on Renewable Energy and Power Quality ICREPQ 2005,* Saragossa, Spain

[9] Hideaki Fujita, Takahiro Yamasaki, Hirofumi Akagi, A Hybrid Active Filter for Damping of Harmonic resonance in Industrial Power Systems, *Proceedings IEEE Transactionson Power Electronics,* Vol.15, No.2, March 2000, Japan, pp. 215 – 222.

[10] S. Rusu – Anghel and others, "Advanced System for the Control of Work Regime of Railway Electric Drive Equipment", Contract research no. 53/2009, Politehnica University of Timisoara – SC. SOFTRONIC S.A. Craiova, Romania, 2009.

[11] Popovic, T. Kuhn, M. "Automated fault analysis: From requirements to implementation", Power & energy Society General Meeting, 2009. PES '09. IEEE, pp 1 – 6, 2009, Calgary, AB.

[12] Saleem, A.Z. ; Khan, Z.A. ; Imran, A. "Algorithms and hardware design of modern numeric overcurrent and distance relays", Electrical Engineering, 2008. ICEE 2008. Second International Conference on IEEE, pp 1 – 5, 2008, Lahore.

[13] Soliman, W.M. ; Soudy, B.E.-D.H. ; Wahab, M.A.A. ; Mansour, M.M. "Power generation station faults diagnosis based on fuzzy relations using information of protective relays and circuit breakers", Electric Power and Energy Conversion Systems, 2009. EPECS '09. International Conference on IEEE, pp 1 – 6, 2010, Sharjah.

[14] Farzad Zhalefar, Majid Sanaye-Pasand, "A new Fuzzy-logic-based Extendet Blocking Scheme for Differential Protection of power Transformers", Control and Intelligent Processing Center of Excellence, School of Electrical and Computer Engineering, University of Tehran, Tehran, Iran, Eds. Taylor & Francis, vol 38, pp 675-694, 2010.

[15] Hubertus, J ; Mooney, J ; Alexander, G. "Application Considerations for Distance Relays on Impedance-Grounded Systems", Protective Relay Engineers, 2008 61st Annual Conference for IEEE, pp 196-203, 2008, College Station, TX.

[16] Youssef, O.A.S. "Applications of fuzzy inference mechanisms to power system relaying" Power Systems Conference and Exposition, 2004. IEEE PES, vol 1, pp 560 – 567, 2005.

[17] Spectrum Digital Inc, Application Note The Design and Development of Fuzzy Logic Controllers, 2009.

[18] N. Rusu, J. Averseng, C. Miklos, C. Alic, S. Anghel "Dynamic Modeling of Pantograph – Catenary System for Energy Loss Control" Conference on Automation, Quality and Testing, Proceedings of AQTR-IEEE, vol III pp 11 – 14, Cluj-Napoca, Romania, 2006.

[19] A. Carnicero, J. Simenez, A. Ramos, C. Sanchez "Simulation Models of the Catenary – Pantograph Dynamic Interaction: Validations and Applications " , Proceedings of Power Transmissions in High Speed Railways Systems Seminar, pp 13 – 26, ESIEE – Awiens, France, 2009.

[20] J. Bennet et al, "Advanced Algorithm to Calculate Mechanical Forces on a Catenary", Computers in Railways IX, pp 857 – 868, Germany, 05.2009.

[21] Weihua Zhang et al, "Hybrid Simulation of Dynamics for the Pantograph - Catenary System", Vehicle System Dynamics, Volume 38, Issue 6, Pp 393 – 414, 2002.

[22] M. A. Abdullah, Y. Michitsuji, M. Nagai, N. Miyajima, "Integrated Simulation between Flexible Body of Catenary and Active Control Pantograph for Contact force Variation Control", Journal of Mechanical Systems for Transportation and Logistics, Vol 3, No. 1, 2010 pp 166 – 177 .

[23] G. Diana, F. Fossati, F. Resta, "High Speed Railway: Collecting Pantographs Active control and Overhead Lines Diagnostic Solutions", Vehicle System Dynamics, Volume 30, Issue 1, pp 69 – 84, 1998.

[24] D.N. O'Connor, S.D. Eppinger, W.P. Seering, D.N. Wormley, "Active Control of a High-Speed Pantograph", Journal of Dynamic Systems, Measurement, and Control, Vol 119, pp 1 - 4, March 1997

[25] A. Balestrino, O. Bruno, A. Landi, L. Sani, "Innovative Solutions for Overhead Catenary-Pantograph System : Wire Actuated control and Observed Contact Force", Vehicle System Dynamics, Volume 33, Issue 2, pp 69 – 89, 2000.

[26] A. Levant, A. Pisano, E. Usai, "Output-Feedback Control of the Contact Force in High-Speed-Train Pantographs", Proceedings of the 40th IEEE Conference on Decision and Control, pp 1831 – 1836, Orlando, Florida USA, December 2001.

[27] B. Allotta, A. Pisano, L. Pugi, E. Usai, "VSC of servo-actuated ATR90-type pantograph", Proceedings of the 44th IEEE Conference on Decision and the european Control Conference 2005, pp 590 - 595, Seville, Spain, December 2005.

[28] Y. J. Huang, "Discrete fuzzy variable structure control for pantograph position control", Electrical Engineering 2004, No 86, pp 171 – 177.

[29] Y. J. Huang, T. C. Kuo, "Discrete Pantograph Position Control for the High Speed Transportation Systems", Proceedings of the 2004 IEEE International Conference on Networking, Sensing & Control Taipei, Taiwan, pp 21 – 23, March, 2004.

Chapter 3

Design of a Real Coded GA Based Fuzzy Controller for Speed Control of a Brushless DC Motor

Omer Aydogdu and Ramazan Akkaya

Additional information is available at the end of the chapter

http://dx.doi.org/10.5772/49972

1. Introduction

Fuzzy controllers are nonlinear elements used in the control of linguistically defined systems, which can not be modeled accurately. Besides, they are an effective approach for various complex and ill-defined systems [1,2]. In design of fuzzy controllers, there is not well defined approach. The sophisticated and tedious design process is usually implemented by an expert. The success of the controller depends on the knowledge and skill of the expert. In some cases, even a very experienced and skillful expert's extensive efforts may not yield optimal solution for fuzzy controller design. The optimal design of fuzzy controller has a critical role for their more widespread and effective use. The design inherently requires the determination of a great deal of features and parameters. For this reason, fuzzy controller design problem has a number of local values in a large solution space in the direction of a number of objectives. The conventional trial-and-error based method makes the solution of the problem very difficult [3].

Genetic algorithms (GAs) are optimization strategies performing a stochastic search by iteratively processing 'populations' of solutions according to their fitness, i.e. a predefined scalar index of satisfaction of the design objectives. In control applications, the fitness is usually related to performance measures such as integral error, settling time, and so on. Fitness function may contain more than one objective like the minimization of settling time, steady state error and maximum overshoot. Thus, fitness function can be addressed as a multi objective function. GAs are effective in solving multi-objective optimization problems [4,5].

Most of the GA approaches in use represent the constraint variable using binary form of coding. One of the major disadvantages of using binary coding is the slow convergence speed of the fitness function. Binary coding is also not at all efficient to be used in computer memory. Therefore, the use of real coded genetic algorithm can overcome the inefficient use of computer memory and can contribute the performance. This contribution becomes clear when a lot of parameters are needed to be adjusted in the same problem and higher precision is required for the final result. In literature, for real valued numerical optimization problem, floating point representations were proven to outperform binary representations because they are more consistent, more precise and they lead to faster execution. Also, real coded GA is inherently faster than the binary code GA, because the chromosomes do not have to be decoded prior to the evaluation of the objective function [6].

Brushless DC (BLDC) motors are one of the motor types rapidly gaining popularity. Due to their favorable electrical and mechanical properties like high starting torque, high efficiency and noiseless operation, the BLDC motors are widely used in various consumer and industrial systems such as actuation, robotics, machine tools, servo motor drives, home appliances, computer peripherals, and automotive applications [5,7]. Operation of the BLDC motors requires non-linear control due to their non-linear characteristics and presence of sensors to estimate rotor position. Moreover, owing to some drawbacks of position sensors such as cost, space requirement and instability, sensorless speed control has recently gained importance [8]. It is possible to determine when to commutate the motor drive voltages by sensing the back emf voltage on an undriven motor terminal during one of the drive phases. Use of fuzzy controllers that have non-linear processes such as fuzzification, defuzzification and fuzzy inference is suitable for BLDC motor control.

In this study, sensorless speed control of the BLDC motor with real coded GA based fuzzy controller has been designed, simulated and practically implemented. ADSP-21992 digital signal processor (DSP) is used to realize the conventional and optimal fuzzy controller algorithms and sensorless speed control of the BLDC motor has been experimentally implemented successfully.

2. Real coded GA based fuzzy controller

The realized control system general diagram is shown in Figure 1. As shown in the figure, the control system includes two closed loops. The inner loop is the fuzzy controller loop that accomplishes speed control of BLDC motor. The outer loop, which processes the fuzzy controller and system operations in background, is the genetic algorithm loop that tunes the controller parameters in regard to performance index of the control system.

2.1. Fuzzy controller

In this study, Mamdani type fuzzy controller, which has five blocks namely normalization, fuzzifier, inference mechanism, defuzzifier and denormalization, has been used [8]. Block diagram of the real coded GA based fuzzy controller consisting two inputs (e_1, e_2) and one output (u) is shown in Figure 2.

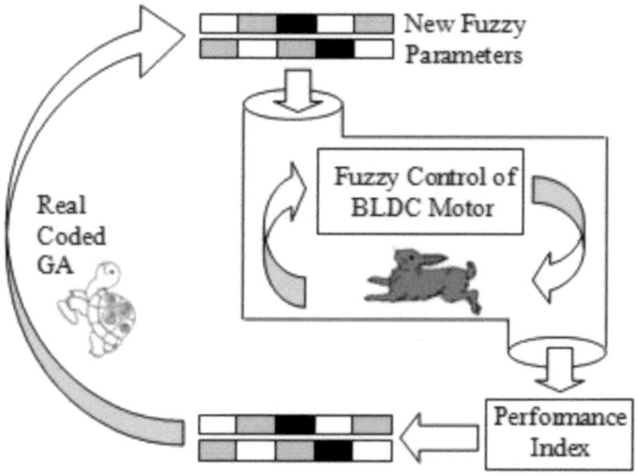

Figure 1. Real Coded GA based fuzzy control of the BLDC motor

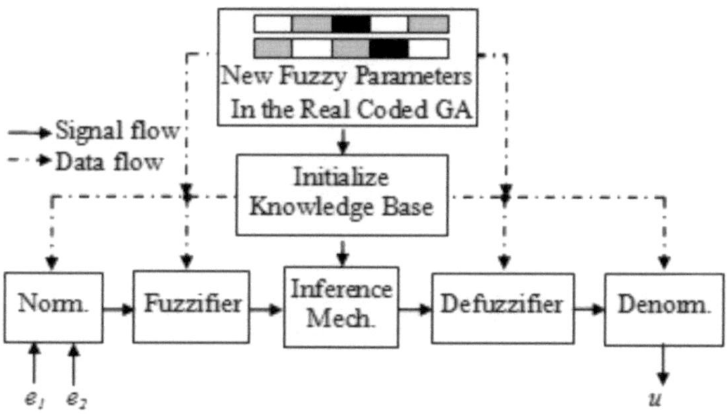

Figure 2. Block diagram of the Real Coded GA based fuzzy controller

In closed-loop control systems, the use of error (e_1) and the change in error (e_2) as controller input is a universal approach. In the implemented fuzzy controller, error and change in error have been used as inputs. As given in Eq. (1), the error is the difference between the reference speed and the actual rotor speed.

$$e_1(t) = \omega^*(t) - \omega(t) \tag{1}$$

Here, $e_1(t)$ is the speed error, $\omega^*(t)$ is the reference speed and $\omega(t)$ is the actual motor speed. The change in error $e_2(t)$ is determined by Eq. (2) [9,10].

$$e_2(t) = \frac{d}{dt}e_1(t) \tag{2}$$

In a fuzzy control system as shown in Figure 2, two normalization parameters (n_1, n_2) for inputs (e_1, e_2) and one denormalization parameter (n_3) for output (u) is defined. In normalization process, the input values are scaled in the range [-1,+1] and in denormalization process the output values of fuzzy controller are converted to a value depending on the terminal control element. Obtaining the normalization and denormalization parameters of fuzzy controller is important for system stability.

In the fuzzifier process, the crisp input values (e_1, e_2) are converted into fuzzy values. Also, the fuzzy values obtained in fuzzy inference mechanism must be converted to crisp output value (u) by defuzzifier process. For this purpose, triangular fuzzy membership function is defined for each input and output values by seven clusters. Figure 3, illustrates the membership function used to fuzzify two input values (e_1, e_2) and defuziffy output (u) of the realized fuzzy controller. For seven clusters in the membership functions as shown in Figure 3, seven linguistic variables are defined as; Negative Big (*NB*), Negative Medium (*NM*), Negative Small (*NS*), Zero (*Z*), Positive Small (*PS*), Positive Medium (*PM*) and Positive Big (*PB*). Initially, the overlap rates of membership functions are 50%. As illustrated in Figure 3, peak or bottom points of membership functions to be tuned are defined as a_1 and a_2 for e_1, b_1 and b_2 for e_2, c_1 and c_2 for u. Therefore, the design of optimal fuzzy controller requires optimization of at least six parameters (a_1, a_2, b_1, b_2, c_1, c_2) by using real coded GA for fuzzification and defuzzification processes that are both nonlinear.

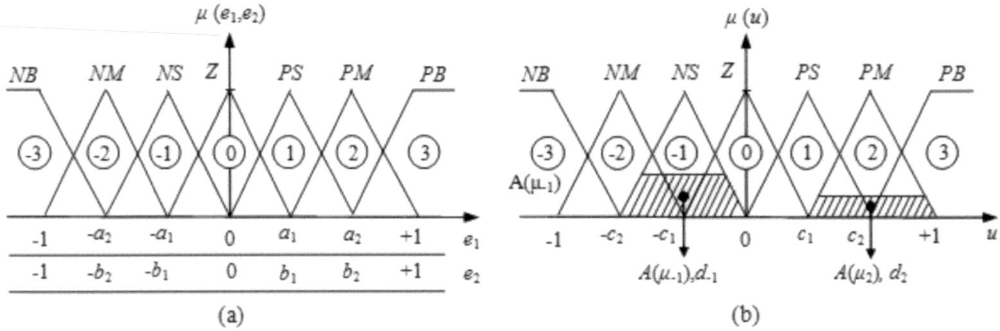

Figure 3. Membership functions of (a) input (e_1,e_2), (b) output (u)

In this study, the center-of-gravity method given by Eq. (3) has been used in defuzzifier process for simulation and real time DSP application.

$$u = \frac{\sum_{i=1}^{m} d_i A(\mu_i)}{\sum_{i=1}^{m} A(\mu_i)} \tag{3}$$

Here, u is the fuzzy controller output, d_i is the distance between i^{th} fuzzy set and the center, $A(\mu i)$ is the area value of ith fuzzy set.

The rule definition is subjective and based on the expert's knowledge and experience. For the system with two inputs and seven membership functions in each range, it leads to a 7x7 decision table and 49 fuzzy rules. For example, two fuzzy rules are decribed as;

if e_1 is *NB* **and** e_2 is *NB* **then** u is R_1,
if e_1 is *NB* **and** e_2 is *NM* **then** u is R_2,

Sliding mode rule base table used by fuzzy controller is given in Table 1. In the sliding mode rule base, when an assumption is made such that $R_1= -R_{13}$, $R_2= -R_{12}$, $R_3= -R_{11}$, $R_4= -R_{10}$, $R_5= -R_9$, $R_6= -R_8$, it is required to determine a minimum of seven parameters (R_1-R_7) by using real coded GA.

Input-e_1	Input-e_2						
	NB	*NM*	*NS*	*Z*	*PS*	*PM*	*PB*
NB	R_1	R_2	R_3	R_4	R_5	R_6	R_7
NM	R_2	R_3	R_4	R_5	R_6	R_7	R_8
NS	R_3	R_4	R_5	R_6	R_7	R_8	R_9
Z	R_4	R_5	R_6	R_7	R_8	R_9	R_{10}
PS	R_5	R_6	R_7	R_8	R_9	R_{10}	R_{11}
PM	R_6	R_7	R_8	R_9	R_{10}	R_{11}	R_{12}
PB	R_7	R_8	R_9	R_{10}	R_{11}	R_{12}	R_{13}

Table 1. Sliding mode rule base

The developed fuzzy logic uses the min-max compositional rule of inference. The inference mechanism of fuzzy controller is implemented in regard to the rule base given by Eq. (4).

$$\mu_i(u) = min\,(\mu_i(e_1), \mu_i(e_2)) \tag{4}$$

Fuzzy controllers are nonlinear tools because of the nonlinearity of logical inference, fuzzifier and defuzzifier processes. As mentioned earlier, design of fuzzy controller requires determination of a minimum of 16 parameters comprised of three normalization parameters, six membership function parameters and seven sliding mode rule base parameters. The parameters are decided in regard to the symetrical properties of the controller and that imposes limitations for the controller. The reduction of the number of parameters gives acceptable results and it can be preferred in design process to simplify the sophisticated optimization process.

2.2. Optimization of fuzzy controller by means of real coded GA

In problem solving, the precision of the numbers is crucial. In binary coded GA, the accuracy is limited by the size of the chromosomes. However, the use of real coded GA, which can be coded by real numbers, is advantageous. Real coded GA is more accurate and occupies less space in memory. In literature, it has been reported that, real coded GAs operate faster than binary coded GAs and they can converge to global optimum faster [11]. Also, in the optimization of systems consisting a great deal of parameters to be optimized as in fuzzy controllers, the chromosomes in the binary coded GA becomes too long and the parameter accuracy can not be handled. However, in the developed algorithm, the parameters are coded by integer number set and the parameter accuracy can be determined arbitrarily. Also, in the developed algorithm, binary coding can be accomplished in the limited valued parameters for the optimization of sliding mode rule base table (R_1, R_2, R_3, R_4, R_5, R_6, R_7).

In Figure 4, the flowchart of real coded GA used in the study is shown. Some of the GA parameters such as the possible lower and upper limit values of parameters, the precision of parameters, the termination criterion or loop number, the mutation probability, the crossover probability, the population number and elitism property is required to be initialized.

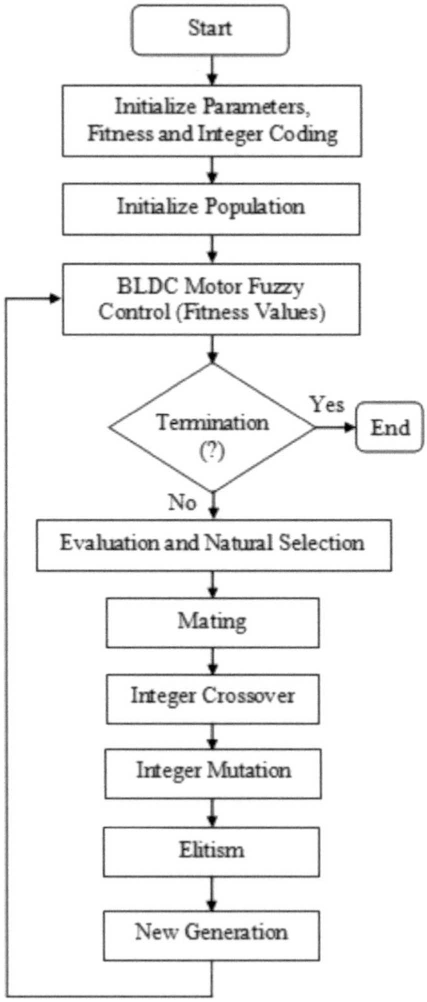

Figure 4. Flowchart of the Real Coded GA based fuzzy controller

In the proposed algorithm, the normalization parameters (n_1, n_2) and de-normalization parameter (n_3), the membership function parameters (a_1, a_2, b_1, b_2, c_1, c_2) and rule base (R_1, R_2, R_3, R_4, R_5, R_6, R_7) of the fuzzy controller have been optimized. Two approaches have been used in determination of parameters in optimal design of fuzzy controller by using real coded GA. In the first approach, the parameters for optimal fuzzy controller have been determined sequentially. This approach is similar to the self-tuning adaptive system employed in adaptive control systems. The second approach is a method based on the simultaneous optimization of normalization factors, membership functions and rules. Fuzzy controller parameters are not fully independent of each other [12]. For this reason, simultaneously tuning of all the parameters is the optimum solution. However, the large number of fuzzy control parameters makes the second approach more difficult to implement.

The performance index defined for the fuzzy controller is given in Eq.(5) [3]. This equation has also been used as multiple objective function employed in optimization process for real coded GA.

$$J_{in} = \int_0^{t_1} |\, e_1 \,|\, dt + \int_{t_1}^{t} |\, e_1 \,|\, t\, dt + 6 \int_0^{t} \delta \left(\frac{d\omega}{dt} \right) |\, e_1 \,|\, dt \tag{5}$$

In Eq.(5), J_{in} is the performance index used as fitness value in real coded GA, e_1 is the error value and t_1 is the settling time of the reference speed in BLDC motor fuzzy control system.

In Figure 5 (a), the coding of three normalization parameters in six digit number string in real coded GA is depicted. Here, in six digit number string, two of it is assigned for integer part and four of it is for the fractional part. As shown in Figure 5 (b), a total of six coding has been implemented for three membership functions. Here, a_1 and a_2 are the membership function parameters defined for input (e_1); b_1 and b_2 are the membership function parameters defined for input (e_2); and c_1 and c_2 are the membership function parameters defined for output (u). All obtained membership function parameters are less than one. In Figure 5 (c), the sliding mode rule base parameters presented in Table 1 are shown. These parameters take integer values in the range [1,2,3]. Therefore, each parameter is denoted by one digit. As shown in Figure 5, a total of 63 digits have been used for all of the codes. Additionally, the precision of parameters can be increased by increasing the number of digits. In coding structure shown in Figure 5, the precision of membership functions is 0.0001.

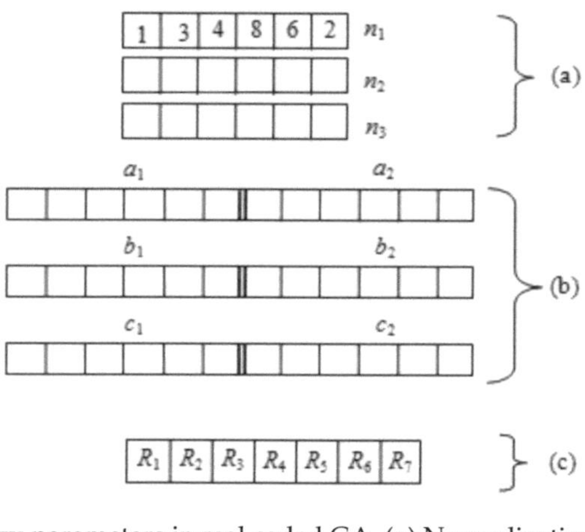

Figure 5. Coding of the fuzzy parameters in real coded GA, (a) Normalization, (b) Membership functions, and (c) Sliding mode rule table

In the implemented algorithm, the initial population can be preferably set by the user or can be randomly appointed a value in regard to Eq.(6). An important feature of random generator is that in each execution of the algorithm different values are initialized.

$$N_{ipop} = (P_h - P_\ell)\ Random\ (P_{pop}) + P_\ell \tag{6}$$

Here, N_{ipop} is the initial population, P_h and P_ℓ are the minimum and maximum values the parameter can have and P_{pop} is the random number generated between zero and one. Fitness value of each chromosome in initial population is determined by using performance index which is given by Eq.(5). As shown in the Figure 4, if the termination criterion is met, real coded GA loop ends but optimal fuzzy control system keeps operating. Else, next step in real coded GA is executed. In this study, Roulette wheel method is employed in natural selection process. In binary coded GA, the crossover operation can be implemented by using methods like single-point or two-point crossover. However, in real coded GA, the mixing methods give better results in crossover operation. In mixing method, the values of two parameter are compared and new generations are produced using Eq. (7).

$$P_{new} = \beta P_{an} + (1-\beta)P_{bn} \tag{7}$$

where β is a number randomly generated between 0 and 1, P_{an} is the nth parameter of mother chromosome, P_{bn} is the nth parameter of father chromosome [13,14].

Genetic algorithms sometimes converge prematurely. In order to prevent convergence to a local point, new solutions are obtained by means of mutation. In this study, the number of parameters to be applied to the mutation operation has been determined by multiplying the total number of parameters with mutation rate. The elements to apply mutation operation are determined and they are replaced by randomly generated numbers.

In the developed algorithm, the elitism, a mechanism in which the individuals with the best fitness values in previous population are guaranteed their place in the next population, is implemented by selecting. Later, new fitness value is determined again for new population. Optimization process goes on until the termination criterion is met.

3. Sensorless control of BLDC motor

The BLDC control drive system is based on the feedback of rotor position, which is obtained at fixed points typically every 60 electrical degrees for six-step commutations of the phase currents. So, the operation of BLDC motor requires a control system and position sensors to estimate rotor position. Rotor position is sensed using Hall effect sensors embedded into the stator frequently. However, sensorless speed control has recently gained importance owing to the elimination of some drawbacks of sensors such as cost, space requirement and instability. Figure 6 shows basic block diagram of sensorless control of BLDC motor with real coded GA based fuzzy controller.

In Figure 6, ω^* is the reference speed (rad/sec), ω is the actual rotor speed (rad/sec), θ is the rotor position (degree), u is the control signal used to reference moment (N-m), i_a, i_b, i_c are the actual phase currents (Amper), i_a^*, i_b^*, i_c^* are the reference phase currents (Amper), S_1-S_6 are switches of the inverter and V_{dc} is the supply voltage of the inverter (Volt).

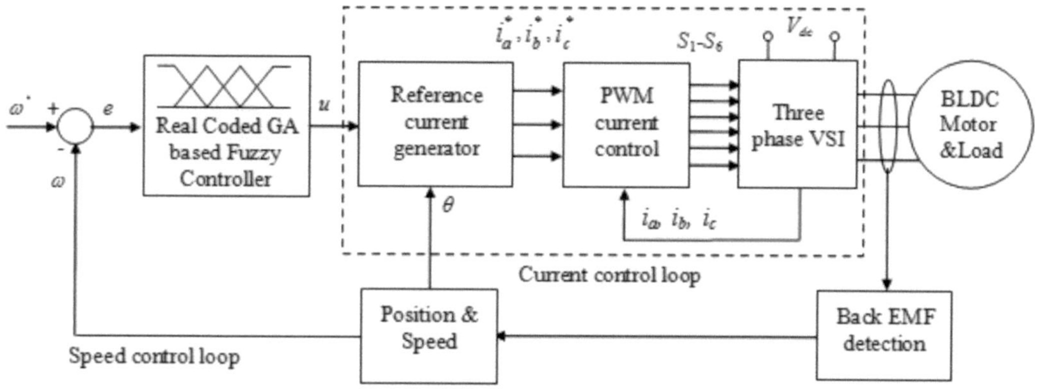

Figure 6. Block diagram of sensorless control of the BLDC motor drive system

In speed control loop as shown in the block digram, the reference speed and the actual motor speed is compared and the error signal is obtained. These signals (e_1, e_2) are employed in fuzzy controller and reference current (I^*) is produced for control system. The current control loop regulates the BLDC motor current to the reference current value generated by the speed controller. The current control loop consists of reference current generator, PWM current control unit and a three phase voltage source inverter (VSI). Position of the BLDC motor is obtained by employing zero crossing back emf detection method eliminating position sensor requirement.

3.1. Modeling of the BLDC motor

Figure 7 describes the basic building blocks of the BLDC motor and inverter that results in a system producing a linear speed-torque characteristic similar to the conventional DC motor. BLDC motor has three phase windings on the stator similar to three phase squirrel cage induction motor and magnets are placed on the rotor to provide air gap flux resulting in brushless rotor construction. When the motor is operated at a certain speed, trapezoidal emfs are induced in stator phase windings. The quasi-square wave AC current is fed to stator phase windings through electronic commutator using current controlled voltage source inverter and rotor position sensor resulting in constant torque development by the motor.

At any instant, two out of three phase stator windings of the motor carry currents synchronized with developed electromagnetic torque as shown in Figure 8. Active switching states for three phase inverter operation, three phase back-emf waveforms and torques of all phases are illustrated in Figure 8. Here, three phase PWM inverter operation can be divided into six modes according to the current conduction states.

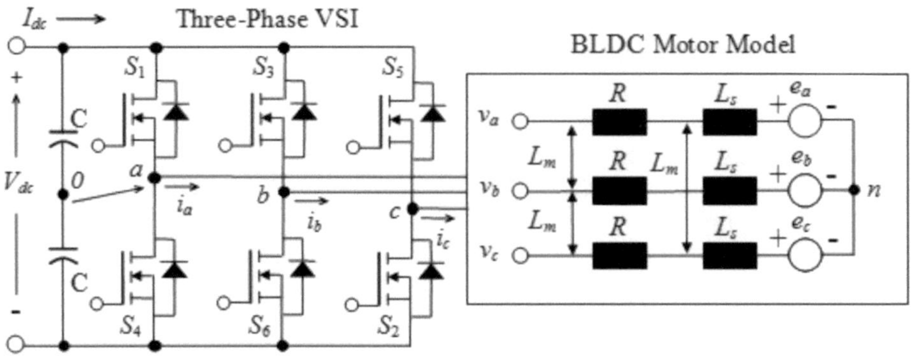

Figure 7. Configuration of the BLDC motor and inverter system

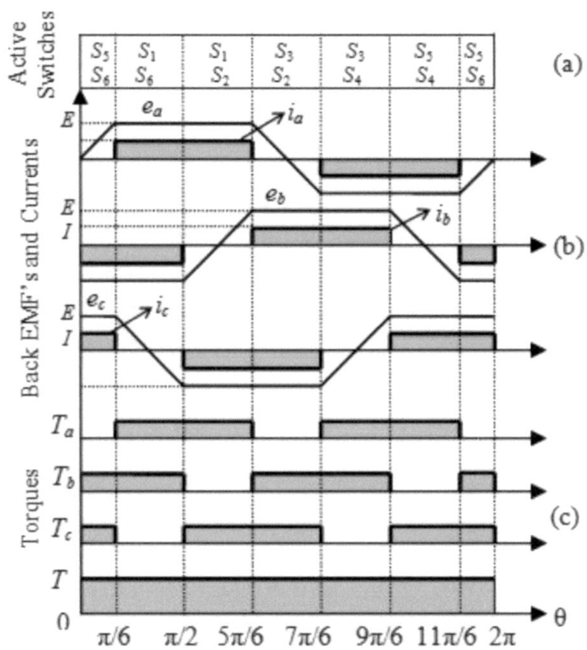

Figure 8. (a) Active switches, (b) Back emf and phase current waveforms, and (c) Three phase torques of the BLDC motor drive system

Analysis of the BLDC motor is based on the following assumptions for simplicity and accuracy [3,10,15,16].

1. The BLDC motor is not saturated.
2. Stator resistances of all the windings are equal, self and mutual inductances are constant.
3. Semiconductor devices in the inverter are ideal.
4. Iron losses are negligible.

Back-emf waveforms of all phases are equal under above assumptions. A BLDC motor model can be represented as;

$$\frac{d}{dt}\begin{bmatrix} i_a \\ i_b \\ i_c \end{bmatrix} = \begin{bmatrix} 1/L & 0 & 0 \\ 0 & 1/L & 0 \\ 0 & 0 & 1/L \end{bmatrix}\begin{bmatrix} v_a \\ v_b \\ v_c \end{bmatrix} - \begin{bmatrix} R/L & 0 & 0 \\ 0 & R/L & 0 \\ 0 & 0 & R/L \end{bmatrix}\begin{bmatrix} i_a \\ i_b \\ i_c \end{bmatrix} - \begin{bmatrix} 1/L & 0 & 0 \\ 0 & 1/L & 0 \\ 0 & 0 & 1/L \end{bmatrix}\begin{bmatrix} e_a \\ e_b \\ e_c \end{bmatrix}, \quad (L = L_s - L_m) \tag{8}$$

where v_a, v_b, and v_c are the phase voltages, i_a, i_b, and i_c are the phase currents, R and L_s are the stator resistance and inductance, L_m is the mutual inductance, e_a, e_b, and e_c are the trapezoidal back-emfs.

The motion equation is expressed as;

$$\frac{d}{dt}\omega = \frac{1}{J}(T_e - T_\ell - B\omega) \tag{9}$$

$$\frac{d}{dt}\theta = \omega \tag{10}$$

where T_ℓ is the load torque in Nm, J is the moment of inertia in kgm², B is the frictional coefficient in Nms/rad, and ω is the rotor speed in electrical rad/sec. The output torque is redefined by Eq.(11) using back-emfs.

$$T_e = (e_a\, i_a + e_b\, i_b + e_c\, i_c) \,/\, \omega \tag{11}$$

This torque expression causes a computational difficulty at zero speed as the induced emf is zero. In this study, the trapezoidal back-emf waveforms are modeled as a function of rotor position to be able to estimate position actively according to the operation speed.

3.2. Modeling of trapezoidal back-emf

The back-emfs can be expressed as a function of rotor position (θ) [17];

$$\begin{bmatrix} e_a \\ e_b \\ e_c \end{bmatrix} = E\begin{bmatrix} f_a(\theta) \\ f_b(\theta) \\ f_c(\theta) \end{bmatrix}, \quad (E = k_e\omega) \tag{12}$$

where k_e is back-emf constant, $f_a(\theta)$, $f_b(\theta)$, and $f_c(\theta)$ are the functions of rotor position as shown in Figure 8. In this study, $f_a(\theta)$ trapezoidal function with limit values between +1 and -1 expressed by Eq.(13) has been employed.

$$f_a(\theta)=\begin{cases}(6/\pi)\theta & (0<\theta\leq\pi/6)\\ 1 & (\pi/6<\theta\leq 5\pi/6)\\ -(6/\pi)\theta+6 & (5\pi/6<\theta\leq 7\pi/6)\\ -1 & (7\pi/6<\theta\leq 11\pi/6)\\ (6/\pi)\theta-12 & (11\pi/6<\theta\leq 2\pi)\end{cases} \tag{13}$$

f_b (θ) and f_c (θ) can be determined in a similar way considering Figure 8. Substituting equations (12)-(13) into equation (11), the output torque expression becomes,

$$T_e = k_e\,(f_a(\theta)\,i_a + f_b(\theta)\,i_b + f_c(\theta)\,i_c) \tag{14}$$

3.3. Advanced simulation model of BLDC motor by using Runge-Kutta numerical integration method

Runge-Kutta method is a frequently used method for solving differential equations numerically. In engineering solutions, fourth order Runge-Kutta method is the most widely used one [18]. For BLDC motor simulations, i_a, i_b, i_c, ω and θ parameters, which have been given by Eqs. (8), (9) and (10) are calculated by using fourth order Runge-Kutta method. For example, the current associated with the a-phase (i_a) is calculated using Eq. (15). Other parameters are calculated in the similar way.

$$\begin{aligned}
k_1 &= \frac{1}{L}(v_a - R\,i_a(kT) - e_a)\\
k_2 &= \frac{1}{L}(v_a - R\,(\,i_a(kT) + \frac{k_1}{2}) - e_a)\\
k_3 &= \frac{1}{L}(v_a - R\,(\,i_a(kT) + \frac{k_2}{2}) - e_a)\\
k_4 &= \frac{1}{L}(v_a - R\,(\,i_a(kT) + k_3) - e_a)\\
i_a((k+1)T) &= i_a(kT) + \frac{T}{6}(k_1 + 2\,k_2 + 2\,k_3 + k_4)
\end{aligned} \tag{15}$$

where k is the sample and T is the sampling period.

3.4. Reference current generator

Reference current generator determines reference phase currents (i_a^*, i_b^*, i_c^*) of the motor in regard to reference current amplitude (I^*), which is calculated using rotor position (θ). Reference current amplitude (I^*) can be obtained from Eq.(16).

$$I^* = u / k_t \tag{16}$$

where u is the control signal and k_t is the torque constant. Phase currents given in Table 2 can be attained from Figure 8. These currents are input to PWM current control block [19].

Rotor position (θ-Degree)	Reference currents (A)		
	i_a^*	i_b^*	i_c^*
0-30	0	$-I^*$	I^*
30-90	I^*	$-I^*$	0
90-150	I^*	0	$-I^*$
150-210	0	I^*	$-I^*$
210-270	$-I^*$	I^*	0
270-330	$-I^*$	0	I^*
330-360	0	$-I^*$	I^*

Table 2. Reference currents of the BLDC motor

3.5. Current control block

In PWM current control block, reference phase currents (i_a^*, i_b^*, i_c^*) acquired from reference current generator is compared with actual phase currents of the motor (i_a, i_b, i_c). These current error values (e_{ia}, e_{ib}, e_{ic}) obtained using Eq. (17) are applied to inverter hysteresis band ($\pm h_b$) and in regard to the switching states shown in Figure 8 (a), switching signals of three-phase PWM inverter are generated [15,16].

$$\begin{aligned} e_{ia} &= i_a^* - i_a \\ e_{ib} &= i_b^* - i_b \\ e_{ic} &= i_c^* - i_c \end{aligned} \tag{17}$$

Inverter phase voltages (v_{ao}, v_{bo}, v_{co}) in reference to midpoint of DC supply voltage (V_{dc}) are obtained using Eq. (18) by using current error values.

$$\begin{aligned} v_{ao} &= \begin{bmatrix} V_{dc}/2 & e_{ia} \geq h_b \\ -V_{dc}/2 & e_{ia} \leq h_b \end{bmatrix} \\ v_{bo} &= \begin{bmatrix} V_{dc}/2 & e_{ib} \geq h_b \\ -V_{dc}/2 & e_{ib} \leq h_b \end{bmatrix} \\ v_{co} &= \begin{bmatrix} V_{dc}/2 & e_{ic} \geq h_b \\ -V_{dc}/2 & e_{ic} \leq h_b \end{bmatrix} \end{aligned} \tag{18}$$

BLDC motor phase voltages (v_a, v_b, v_c) are given in Eq. (19) related to inverter phase voltages determined from Eq. (18).

$$\begin{aligned} v_a &= \frac{1}{3}(2v_{ao} - v_{bo} - v_{co}) \\ v_b &= \frac{1}{3}(2v_{bo} - v_{ao} - v_{co}) \\ v_c &= \frac{1}{3}(2v_{co} - v_{ao} - v_{bo}) \end{aligned} \tag{19}$$

4. Simulation results

An algorithm has been developed to simulate the proposed real coded GA based fuzzy controller in BLDC motor drive. In all simulations and practical applications, the BLDC motor and inverter having the parameters listed in Table 3 have been used.

BLDC motor type	**Ametek 119003-01**
Rating (*P*)	106 watt
Number of Phase (Connection)	3 (Star)
Rated speed	4228 rpm.
Rated current	6.8 A
Stator equivalent resistance (*R*)	0.348 Ω
Stator equivalent inductance (*L*)	0.314 mH
Moment of inertia (*J*)	0.0019 Ncm-s^2
Number of Pole (*p*)	8
Voltage constant (k_e)	0.0419 V/rad/s
Torque constant (k_t)	4.19 Ncm/A
PWM frequency (f_{PWM})	20 kHz
Inverter DC supply (V_{dc})	24 volt
Inverter hysteresis limits (h_b)	± 0.5
Inverter current limiter (I_{base})	20 A

Table 3. Parameters of the BLDC motor and Inverter

First of all, conventional fuzzy controller is designed based on trial-error method and simulation. The parameters of conventional fuzzy controller are obtained as; n_1=10, n_2=1, n_3=2.2, a_1=0.33, a_2=0.66, b_1=0.33, b_2=0.66, c_1=0.33, c_2=0.66, R_1=*NB*, R_2=*NB*, R_3=*NM*, R_4=*NM*, R_5=*NS*, R_6=*NS*, R_7=*Z*, R_8=*PS*, R_9=*PS*, R_{10}=*PM*, R_{11}=*PM*, R_{12}=*PB*, R_{13}=*PB*.

During simulation of sequential approach, normalization parameters, then rule base and the membership functions have been optimized sequentially. In this approach, the chosen values for mutation probability is 0.05, crossover probability is 0.8, population number is 20, the reference speed for the BLDC motor is set at 2000 rpm, and the motor operates in full load. In the second approach which uses simultaneous optimization, the process is implemented by coding all fuzzy controller parameters in GA simultaneously. In this approach, the chosen values for mutation probability is 0.1, crossover probability is 1, population number is 20, the reference speed for the BLDC motor is set at 2000 rpm and the motor operates in full load. The obtained design parameters of optimal fuzzy controllers using sequential and simultaneous real coded GA are given in Table 4.

For a reference speed of 2000 rpm and operating the BLDC motor in full load, the speed responses and error variations of conventional fuzzy control, sequential GA based fuzzy control and simultaneous GA based fuzzy control are shown in Figure 9 (a) and 9 (b), respectively.

Fuzzy Controller	Sequential Real Coded GA	Simultaneous Real Coded GA
Norm. Parameters	n_1=642.348, n_2=29.895, n_3=3.144	n_1=369.102, n_2=8.448, n_3=9.849
Parameters of Membership Func.	a_1=0.8488, b_1=1.1002, c_1=1.1309 a_2=1.6005, b_2=2.1, c_2=1.5	a_1=1.3035, b_1=1.0762, c_1=0.2051 a_2=1.5191, b_2=2.9, c_2=1.62
Rule Base	R_1=NM, R_2=PM, R_3=NB, R_4=NM, R_5=Z, R_6=NM, R_7=Z, R_8=PM, R_9=Z, R_{10}=PM, R_{11}=PB, R_{12}=NM, R_{13}=PM	R_1=NB, R_2=PM, R_3=NS, R_4=NB, R_5=NB, R_6=NM, R_7=NS, R_8=PM, R_9=PB, R_{10}=PB, R_{11}=PS, R_{12}=NM, R_{13}=PB
Performance Index	J_{in}= 3.2349 (For 150 generations)	J_{in}= 3.2327 (For 850 generations)

Table 4. Optimal design parameters of Real Coded GA based fuzzy controllers

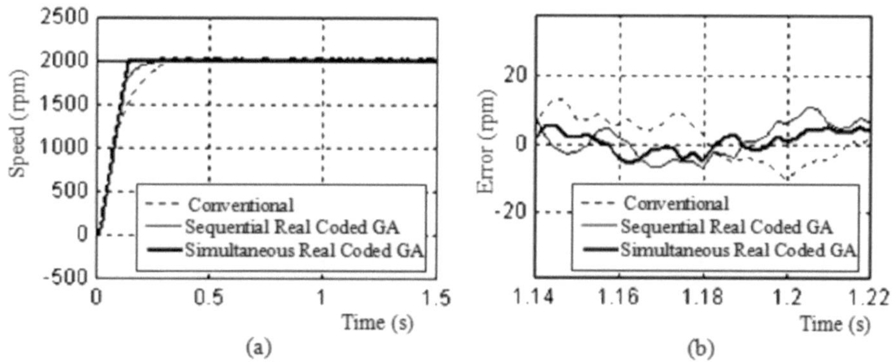

Figure 9. (a) Speed responses and, (b) Errors of conventional and GA based fuzzy controllers

The convergence of performance index (J_{in}) for sequential and simultaneous real coded GA based fuzzy control system are shown in Figure 10 (a) and 10 (b), respectively.

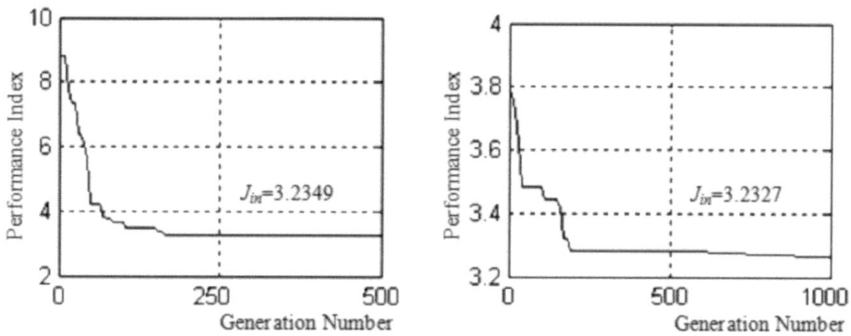

Figure 10. Performance index of the (a) sequential, (b) simultaneous real coded GA based fuzzy control system

In the sequential optimization method, the performance index (J_{in}) of the control system reduces to 3.2349 and this process completes in 150 generations using real coded GA. In the simultaneous optimization method, the performance index of the system (J_{in}) has been reduced to 3.2327. This is the best optimization value obtained in this study. The optimization process with simultaneous GA completes in 850 generations. Also, the performance index value indicates that simultaneous optimization process gives better results than the sequential optimization process. However, while the overall controller is optimized in 150 generations in sequential optimization method, the optimization is completed in 850 generations in simultaneous approach, in which all parameters are optimized simultaneously.

5. Experimental results

Block diagram of the configuration of DSP based experimental system is shown in Figure 11. The experimental system consist of a brushless DC motor, a voltage source inverter, a current detector for hysteresis current control loop, back-emf detector for sensorless speed control loop, ADSP-21992 Ez-Kit Lite evaluation board, interface devices between ADSP and driver board, a PC and VisualDSP++ software for emulating and programming the DSP.

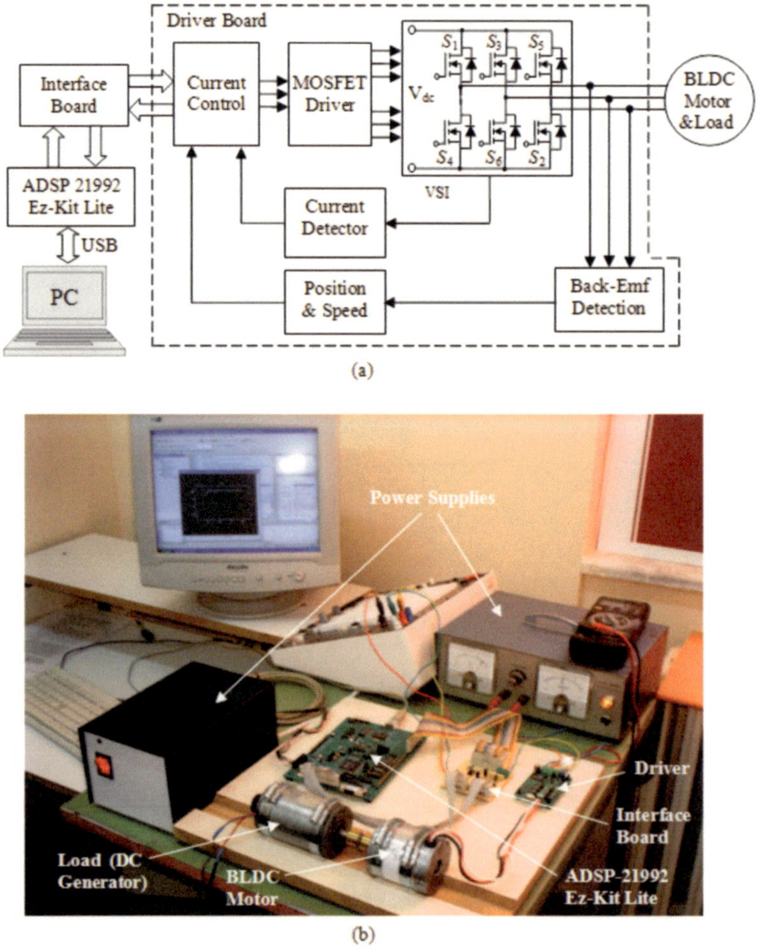

Figure 11. (a) Block diagram, (b) an overview picture of experimental setup of BLDC motor control systems

In the experimental study, sensorless control of the BLDC motor was implemented successfully using conventional fuzzy controller, sequential and simultaneous real coded GA based fuzzy controller, which have parameters obtained by simulation and given in Table 4. Optimal fuzzy controller was implemented in high level C programming language; the program was compiled by VisualDSP++ C compiler and downloaded to the ADSP-21992 DSP controller board. The block diagram of the configuration of closed loop speed control of BLDC motor executed without position and speed sensors is illustrated in Fig 11(a). The experimental setup implemented in the laboratory is shown in Fig 11(b). The reference speed for BLDC motor is set at 2000 rpm, and the motor operates in full load similar with the simulations.

In Figure 12, phase to phase voltage and phase current waveforms of BLDC motor are shown. The responses of both conventional and sequential real coded GA based fuzzy controller are shown in Figure 13, conventional fuzzy and simultaneous real coded GA based fuzzy controller are shown in Figure 14, sequential real coded GA based fuzzy and simultaneous real coded GA based fuzzy controller are shown in Figure 15, respectively.

The experimental results illustrated in these figures prove that the BLDC motor control system was implemented successfully and it operates stably. Also, it is indicated that simulation results show agreement with experimental results.

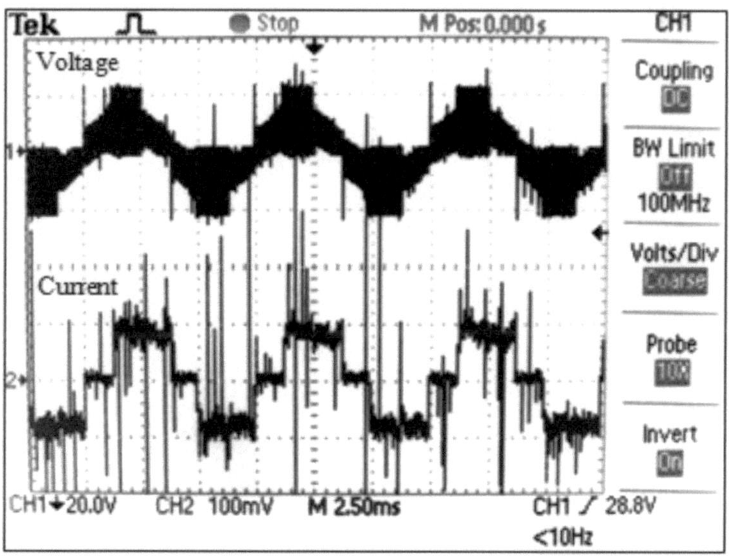

Figure 12. Phase to phase voltage and phase current of the BLDC motor. Time/Div:2.50msec, Volt/Div:20.0V(CH1), Amper/Div:2.00A(CH2)

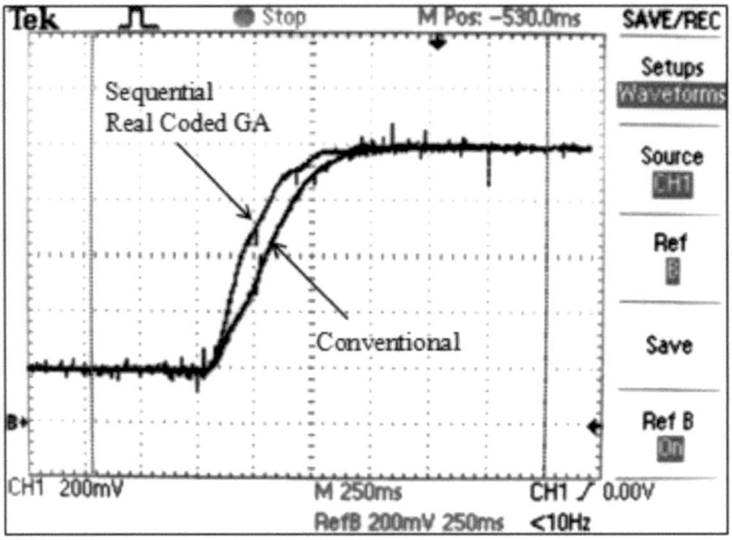

Figure 13. Speed responses of sequential and conventional fuzzy control of the BLDC motor. Time/Div:250 msec, Volt/Div:400 rpm.

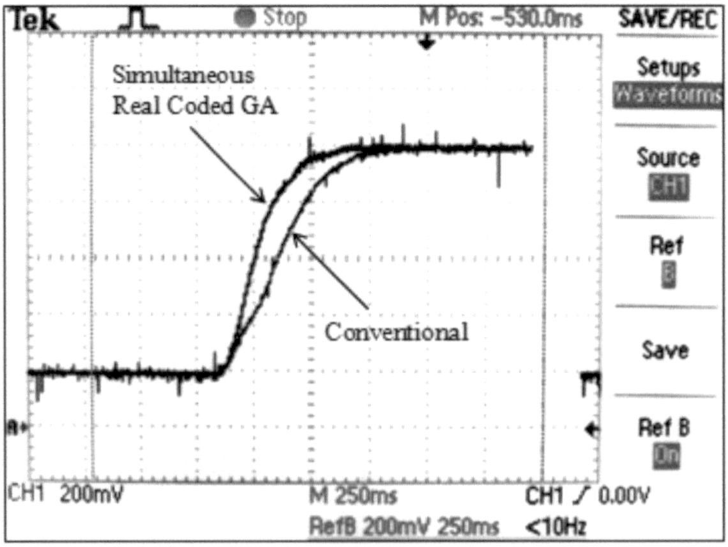

Figure 14. Speed responses of simultaneous and conventional fuzzy control of the BLDC motor. Time/Div:2.50 msec, Volt/Div:400 rpm.

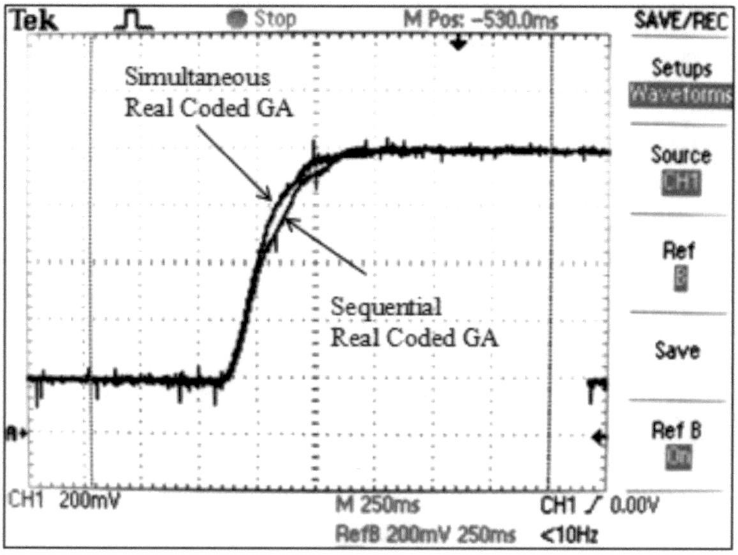

Figure 15. Speed responses of sequential and simultaneous Real Coded GA based fuzzy controller. Time/Div:250 msec, Volt/Div:400 rpm.

6. Limitations of the proposed methods

Although real coded genetic algorithm based fuzzy controller has shown a good behaviour for sensorless speed control of a Brushless DC Motor, we think that there are some limitations and disadvantages as follows in proposed method.

- Like other artificial intelligence techniques, the genetic algorithm cannot assure constant optimisation response times. Even more, the difference between the shortest and the longest optimisation response time is much larger than with conventional gradient methods. This unfortunate genetic algorithm property limits the genetic algorithms' use in real time applications.
- Genetic algorithm applications in controls which are performed in real time are limited because of random solutions and convergence, in other words this means that the entire population is improving, but this could not be said for an individual within this population. Therefore, it is unreasonable to use genetic algorithms for on-line controls in real time systems without testing them first on a simulation model.
- For the design of an effective controller, simulation model of the system is necessary to obtain the most accurately. However, even if the best controller have been designed in

simulation environment, fine tuning may be require in order to use the same controller in on-line system.

- Micro genetic algorithm which can produce near optimal solution may be used in on-line system for fine tuning.
- It is not possible to show the stability of the fuzzy controlled system, since the model is not known. If the system model is obtained exactly, the use of tradional gradient descent methods may give better result for optimal control in on-line systems.
- In fuzzy control systems, computing time could be long, because of the complex operations such as fuzzifications and particularly defuzzification. So, the fuzzy controller hardware requires high-speed processors, such as DSP, FPGA.
- The advantage of sensorless BLDC motor control is that the sensing part can be omitted, and thus overall costs can be considerably reduced. In addition, the disadvantages of sensorless control are higher requirements for control algorithms and more complicated electronics.

7. Conclusions

As a result of the study, optimal fuzzy controller has been designed off-line by using real coded GA and the obtained fuzzy controller has been used on-line for DSP-based BLDC motor control system. Modeling of the BLDC motor was performed more accurately to take account of trapezoidal back-emf waveforms and furthermore, fourth order Runge-Kutta numerical integration method was used to decrease the truncation error and numerical instabilities in simulation. Also, the results of our research indicate that an improvement in the transient state and steady state responses of the system has been obtained by means of optimization process using real coded GA. It is clear that, sequential optimization takes less time. Also, observing the system speed response and error curves, it can be deduced that the sequential method gives satisfactory results and that it can be preferred in applications. It was observed that the use of real coded GA makes it possible to adjust system parameters more precisely. Also, the size of chromosomes, in which a great deal of parameters is coded, is reduced. Besides, the proposed method limits the process time to minutes.

Author details

Omer Aydogdu and Ramazan Akkaya
Department of Electrical and Electronics Engineering,
Faculty of Engineering and Architecture, Selcuk University, Konya, Turkey

Acknowledgement

This study was supported by Selcuk University Scientific Research Projects (BAP) Support Fund under contract number 2003/051.

8. References

[1] F. Cupetino, V. Giordano, D. Naso, B. Turchiano, L. Salvatore (2003) On-Line Genetic Design of Fuzzy Controllers for DC Drives with Variable Load. IEE Electronics Letters, Vol. 39 (5), pp. 479-480.

[2] G. Acosta, E. Todorovich (2003) Genetic Algorithm and Fuzzy Control: A Practical Synergism for Industrial Applications. Elsevier Science Direct, Computer in Industry, Vol. 52, pp. 183-195.

[3] O. Aydogdu (2006) Sensorless Control of Brushless DC Machines by means of Genetic Based Fuzzy Controller. PhD. Thesis, Selcuk University, Turkey.

[4] F. Ashrafzadeh, E.P. Nowicki, M. Mohammadian, J.S. Salmon (1996) An Effective Approach for Optimal Design of Fuzzy Controllers. IEEE Canadian Conference on Electrical and Computer Engineering, pp. 542-545, Alberta, Canada.

[5] C. Xia, P. Guo, T. Shi, M. Wang (2004) Speed control of brushless dc motor using genetic algorithm based fuzzy controller. Proc. of Int. Conf. on Intelligent Mechatronics and Automation, pp. 460-464, Chengdu, Chine.

[6] H.P. Stpathy (2003) Real Coded for Parameters Optimization in Short-Term Load Forecasting. Springer-Verlag Berlin Heidelberg IWANN, pp. 417-124.

[7] N. Hemati, M.C. Leu (1992) A complete model characterization of brushless dc motors. IEEE Transactions on Industry Applications, Vol. 28 (1), pp. 172-180.

[8] O. Aydogdu, R. Akkaya (2005) DSP Based Fuzzy Control of a Brushless DC Motor Without Position and Speed Sensors. Proceedings of 4th International Advanced Technologies Symposium, pp. 182-187, Konya, Turkey.

[9] C.K Lee, W.H. Pang (1994) A Brushless DC Motor Speed Control System Using Fuzzy Rules. IEE Power Electronics and Variable Speed Drives, pp. 101-106.

[10] V. Donescu, D.O. Neacsu, G. Griva, F. Profumo (1996) A Systematic Design Method for Fuzzy Controller for Brushless DC Motor Drives. Proc. of the 27th. IEEE Annual Power Electronics Specialists Conference, pp. 689-694, Baveno, İtaly.

[11] M. Çunkaş, R. Akkaya (2002) Compare with Binary and Real Coded Genetic Algorithms. Selcuk University The Journal of Engineering, Vol. 7 (2), pp. 11-17.

[12] C.J. Wu, G.Y. Liu (200) A Genetic Approach for Simultaneous Design of Membership Functions and Fuzzy Control Rules. Kluwer Academic Pub. Journal of Intelligent and Robotic Systems, Vol. 28, pp. 195-211.

[13] N.J. Radcliff (1991) Formal Analysis and Random Respectful Recombination. In Proc. of Fourth International Conference on Genetic Algorithms, San Diego, CA, USA.

[14] R.L. Haupt, S. Haupt (1998) Practical Genetic Algorithms, A Willey-Interscience Publication, USA.

[15] B. Lee, M. Ehsani (2003) Advanced Simulation Model for Brushless DC Motor Drives. Taylor & Francis Inc. Electric Power Component and Systems, Vol. 31, pp. 841-868.

[16] H.A. Toliyat, T. Gopalarathnam (2002) AC Machines Controlled as DC Machines (Brushless DC Machines/Electronics). In: L.S. Timothyl, (eds) The Power Electronic Handbook. CRC Press LLC, New York, pp. 78-100.

[17] B. Sing, K. Jain (2003) Implementation of DSP based digital speed controller for permanent magnet brushless dc motor. IE(I) Journal-EL., Vol. 84, pp. 16-21.
[18] J.R. Rice (1983) Numerical Methods, Software, and Analysis. McGraw-Hill, New York.
[19] T. Kim (2003) Sensorless Control of the BLDC Motors from Near-Zero to Full Speed. PhD. Thesis, Texas A&M University, Texas, USA.

Chapter 4

A Type-2 Fuzzy Model Based on Three Dimensional Membership Functions for Smart Thresholding in Control Systems

M.H. Fazel Zarandi, Fereidoon Moghadas Nejad and H. Zakeri

Additional information is available at the end of the chapter

http://dx.doi.org/10.5772/47798

1. Introduction

This chapter focuses on the basic concepts of novel fuzzy sets, three dimensional (3D) memberships and how they are applied in the design of type-1 and type-2 fuzzy thresholding in control systems. Automatic fuzzification and membership functions shape selection play a crucial role in fuzzy thresholding design and finally determination of outputs via defuzzification. The related methodology and theoretical base will be discussed in depth, using real examples in automatic control (Pavement distress detection and classification). In spatial domain, selection of membership functions is a difficult task. It should be noted that selection of a supper membership function is a golden key. This is one of the major aims of this chapter to introduce a robust method to consider the uncertainty of membership values by using flexible thresholding for controller problems.

In direct approach to fuzzy modeling, deep knowledge of expert plays a key role for membership functions generation. In application, ambiguity of membership function assignment is the main problem with fuzzy sets and systems. So, different fuzzy membership functions may have various impacts on the systems and, then, different thresholds in control problems.

To solve this problem, type II fuzzy thresholding is recommended. The upper and lower membership functions promote this dilemma; however the figure of uncertainty (FOU) has a fixed value that is equal to one, in upper and lower membership function. So, Type-2 fuzzy logic can effectively improve the control characteristics using FOU of the membership functions.

In this chapter, a smart thresholding technique with its application will be presented, which processes threshold as flexible type-2 fuzzy sets. The concept of ultra-fuzziness aims at capturing/eliminating the uncertainties within fuzzy systems using regular (type I) fuzzy sets. A measure of 3D ultra-fuzziness is also presented. Several Experimental results are provided in order to demonstrate the usefulness of the proposed approach.

We start with a real problem in control. The simplest method is to visually inspect the pavements and evaluate them by subjective human experts. This approach, however, involves high labor costs and produces unreliable and inconsistent results. Furthermore, it exposes the inspectors to dangerous working conditions on highways. Destructive Testing (DT) and Non Destructive Testing (NDT) are both costly and time consuming. To overcome the limitations of the subjective visual evaluation process; several attempts have been made to develop an automatic procedure (Moghadas Nejad and Zakeri, 2011,a,b,c) and (Daqi et al, 2009).

Most current systems use computer vision and image processing technologies to automate the process. However, due to the irregularities of pavement surfaces, there has been a limited success inaccurately detecting cracks and classifying crack types. In addition, most systems require complex algorithm with high levels of computing power. While many attempts have been made to automatically collect pavement crack data, better approaches are needed to evaluate these automated crack measurement systems (Moghadas Nejad and Zakeri, 2011,a,b,c) and (Daqi et al,2009)

A Hybrid Automatic Expert System (HAES) for automatic distress detection developed, based on complex AI methods (Expert system, Polar Fuzzy Logic) and image processing methods (Wavelet Transform, Inverse Wavelet Transform, 3D Radon Transform, Fast Fourier transform, EH, etc). Fuzzy logic methods are one among favorite and overwhelming architect that used for uncertainty simulations. Type-1 fuzzy sets (T1 FSs) have been successfully used many area such as image processing, pattern recognition, machin learning. (Choi and Rhee, 2009), (Hagras,2004), (Hwang. Rhee, 2004), (Hwang. Rhee, 2007), (John, 2000), (Karnik, J. Mendel, 1999), (Liang et al. 2000), (Liang, J. Mendel, 2001), (Makrehchi, et al. 2003), (Rhee, 2007), (Rhee, Choi, 2007), (Rhee, Hwang, 2001), (Rhee, Hwang, 2002) and (Rhee, Hwang, 2003). Automatic generation of T1 FMFs classified as a interesting and hot research area. many T1 FMF generation models have been tested and various degree of successes achieved (Choi and Rhee, 2009), (Makrehchi, et al.2003), (Medasani et al,1998), (Rhee, and Krishnapuram, 1993), (Wang, 1994) and (Yang and Bose, 2006). Heuristics, histograms, probability, and entropy are good tools to automate the T1 FMFs generation. Several methods under title of AI have been implemented to data sets to generate T1 FMFs. A good classification proposed for T1 FMFs by Choi and Rhee, (2009). Based on this classification, algorithms based on the fuzzy nearest neighbor, back-propagation neural network, fuzzy C-means (FCM), robust agglomerative Gaussian mixture decomposition (RAGMD), and self-organizing feature map (SOFM) were used to generate T1 FMFs must be a considered as FMFs generator. (Choi and Rhee, 2009).

Uncertain meaning, uncertain measurement and noisy data are main causes that we cannot obtain satisfactory results using T1 FSs, therefore in this mode employment of type-2 fuzzy sets (T2 FSs) for managing uncertainty solved the problems (Ensafi & Tizhoosh, 2005), (Choi and Rhee, 2009). Choi and Rhee (2009) stated that, because of the extra degree of freedom (DOF), T2 FSs can control the blurring better than T1 FSs. However, undesirable amount of computations stand in front of extension T2 FSs in vast scale applications. Interval type-2 fuzzy sets (IT2 FSs) are proposed to reduce the complexity (Choi and Rhee, 2009). Many algorithms based on the T2 FMF have been proposed. (Choi and Rhee, 2009), (Hagras,2004), (Hwang. Rhee, 2004), (Hwang. Rhee, 2007), (John, 2000), (Karnik, J. Mendel, 1999), (Liang et al. 2000), (Liang, J. Mendel, 2001), (Makrehchi, et al. 2003), (Rhee, 2007), (Rhee, Choi, 2007), (Rhee, Hwang, 2001), (Rhee, Hwang, 2002) and (Rhee, Hwang, 2003).

In this chapter, we focus on the generation of 3D Polar fuzzy Memberships functions to use in hybrid expert system for systematic pavement distress detection and classification. In particular, we consider 3D polar type-1 fuzzy membership functions (3D T1 PMFs) that are generated from sample images and then developed to 3D polar type-2 fuzzy membership functions (3D T2 PMFs). First, we review three methods based on heuristics, histograms, and interval type-1 fuzzy C-means (IT1 FCM). For each method, the footprint of uncertainty (FOU) is only required to be obtained, since the FOU can completely describe a T1 PMF. We proposed two methods based on 3D domain and then 3D polar under the theory of type 2 fuzzy sets.

This paper is organized as follows.

In Section 2, we briefly review basic concepts and existing methods and background. In Section 3, we managed the IT2 FMF generation methods. In Section 4, concepts of polar fuzzy are discussed and we explain how our proposed IT2 PMF generation methods can be implemented. Section 5 approximate reasoning and fuzzy inference discussed. Finally, Section 6 gives the summary and conclusions.

2. Background

The extension of T1 FSs to T2 FSs can be used to effectively describe uncertainties in situations where the available information is uncertain. T2 FSs consider as a blurred membership function. The blurring used to model the uncertainty of crisp T1 FSs. A T2 FS can be formulated as follow:

$$\overset{=}{A} = \int_{x \in X} \frac{\mu_{\overset{=}{A}(x)}}{x} = \int_{x \in X} \frac{\left[\int_{x \in X} \frac{f_x(u)}{u} \right]}{XJ_x}, XJ_x \subseteq [0,1] \tag{1}$$

where $f_x(u)$ is the blurred membership function and J_x is the original membership (Mendel, 2001). Footprint of uncertainty (FOU) is a region between the blurred membership function. The FOU of $\check{A}$ can be expressed by as

$$FOU\left(\overset{=}{A}\right) = \bigcup_{\forall x \epsilon X} J_x = \left\{(x,u) : u \epsilon J_x \subseteq [0,1]\right\} \overline{\mu_{\tilde{A}}} = \overline{FOU}\left(\overset{=}{A}\right) and\,by\, \underline{\mu_{\tilde{A}}} = \underline{FOU}\left(\overset{=}{A}\right) \tag{2}$$

FOU constructed form upper membership function (UMF) and lower membership function (LMF). (Choi and Rhee, 2009)

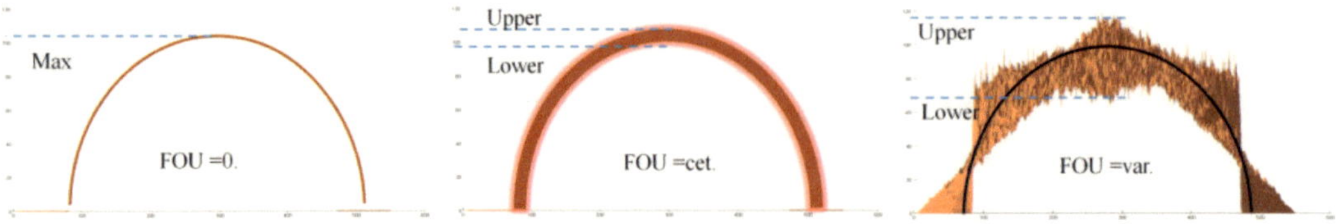

Figure 1. A possible way to construct type II fuzzy sets. The interval between lower and upper membership values (shaded region) should capture the footprint of uncertainty (FOU).

Although T2 FSs may be useful in modeling uncertainty, where T1 FSs cannot, the operations of T2 FSs involve numerous embedded T2 FSs which consider all possible combinations of secondary membership values. Therefore, undesirably large amount of computations may be required. An effectively method to reduce the computational complexity is interval type-2 fuzzy sets (IT2 FSs).

In General, FOU ($\overset{=}{A}$) can be expressed as: (Choi and Rhee, 2009)

$$\mathrm{FOU}\left(\overset{=}{A}\right)=\bigcup\left[\underline{FOU}\left(\overset{=}{A}\right),\overline{FOU}\left(\overset{=}{A}\right)\right]_{\forall x\epsilon X} \tag{3}$$

As a result, IT2 FSs requires only simple interval arithmetic for computing.

3. Automatic MF generators (AMFG)

In this section, we introduce a method for effectively crating IPT-1 FMF automatically from images data. Several methods such as heuristics, histograms, and interval type-2 fuzzy C-means (IT2 FCM) are proposed by (Choi & Rhee, 2009) for generating IT2 FMF automatically from pattern data. Using scaling factor and heuristic T1 FMFs, IT2 FMF simply can be generating. The histogram based method uses suitable parameterized functions chosen to model the smoothed histogram for each class and feature extracted from sample data (Choi and Rhee, 2009),(Hagras,2004), (Hwang and Rhee, 2004), (Hwang and Rhee, 2007), (John, 2000), (Karnik, J. Mendel, 1999), (Liang et al. 2000), (Liang, J. Mendel, 2001), (Makrehchi, et al. 2003), (Rhee, 2007), (Rhee and Choi, 2007), (Hwang and Rhee, 2001), (Rhee, Hwang, 2002) and (Rhee and Hwang, 2003). The IT2 FCM based method uses the derived formulas of the IT2 FMFs in the IT2 FCM algorithm (Hwang and Rhee, 2002). A detailed description of each method is discussed. The heuristic method simply uses an appropriate predefined T1 FMF function, such as triangular, trapezoidal, Gaussian, S, or p function, to name a few, to initially represent the distribution of the pattern data. The following are some frequently used heuristic membership functions. (Choi and Rhee, 2009) Membership functions for fuzzy sets can be constructed by any method exact, heuristic and Meta heuristic, such as triangular, trapezoidal, Gaussian, S, or p function in the domain. Two most important constraints must be considered for selecting a membership functions first, A membership function must be restricted between [0 1] and the next $\mu_A(x)$ must be unique. Four possible membership functions are presented in Fig.2. Where type III and polar are new generation of fuzzy membership function that can be used in several application in the control and classification domains. In the field of pavement management system this new generation of MF play a powerful link between several tools such as multi-resolution methods (wavelet and beyond the wavelet methods), image processing, NN and expert system.

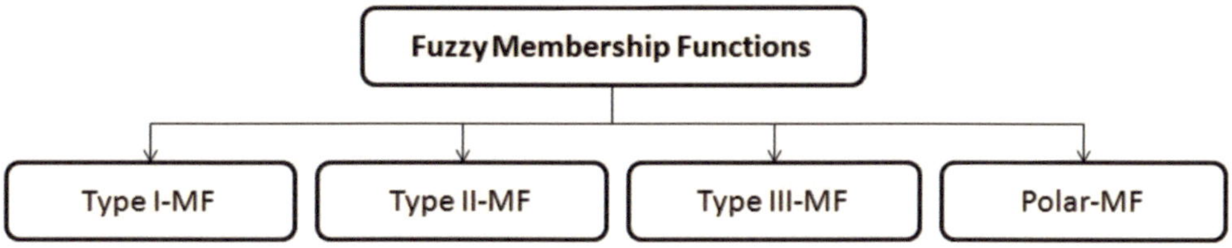

Figure 2. Possible membership functions

A possible membership function can be defined for every category by expert with any tools. For example using image processing techniques and Radon transform, several membership function generated and shows in Fig.3 for pavement cracking distress.

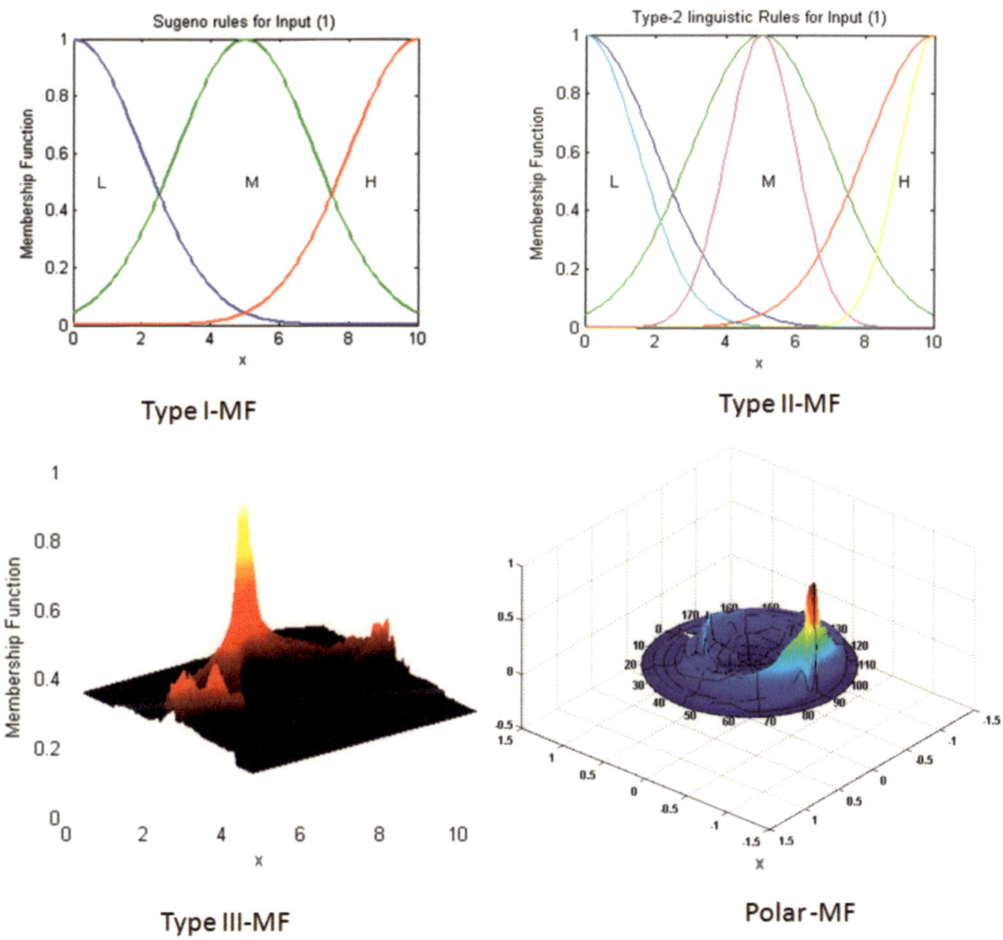

Figure 3. Variety of membership functions

More simple and complex functions can be used under the form of discrete and continues. Generally the ordinary functions categorized in Triangular, Trapezoidal, Γ-membership, S-membership, Logistic, Exponential-like and Gaussian function. Additionally several more advanced membership function which generate by automatic generator introduced. More applications in image processing frequently used heuristic membership functions that can be generally categorized in Table.1.

• Triangular function	$IF\ x \le a, then\ \mu = 0$ $IF\ a \le x \le b, Then\ \mu = (x-a)/(b-a)$ $IF\ a \le x \le b, Then\ \mu = (c-x)/(c-b)$ $IF\ x \ge c, then\ \mu = 0$
• Trapezoidal function	$IF\ x \le a, then\ \mu = 0$ $IF\ a \le x \le b, Then\ \mu = (x-a)/(b-a)$ $IF\ b \le x \le c, Then\ \mu = 1$ $IF\ c \le x \le d, Then\ \mu = (c-x)/(d-c)$ $IF\ x \ge d, then\ \mu = 0$
• Gaussian function	$\mu(x) = \left(e^{-(x-c)^2/2\sigma^2}\right)$
• S-function • $b = (a+b)/2$	$IF\ x \le a, then\ \mu = 0$ $IF\ a \le x \le b, Then\ \mu = 2 \times \left((x-a)/(b-a)\right)^2$ $IF\ a \le x \le b, Then\ \mu = 1 - 2 \times \left((x-a)/(c-a)\right)^2$ $IF\ x \ge c, then\ \mu = 1$
• P-function	$IF\ x \le c, then\ \pi(x) = s(x; c-b, c-\frac{b}{2}, c)$ $IF\ x > c, then\ \pi(x) = s(x; c-b, c-\frac{b}{2}, c)$

Table 1. Heuristic membership functions, (Choi & Rhee,2009)

By control parameters, one can select a various interval pattern. Theses parameters usually trained and learned by experts. Under the title of Control Parameter (α), the UMF of the IT2 FMF and LMF can be designed. The LMF and UMF determined by scaling α *and* β between 0 and 1, which can be also tuned in supervised and unsupervised manner or provided by an expert. Choi & Rhee, (2009) proposed a simple definition for FOU, which categorized in heuristic methods. For feature i

$$\begin{aligned} \mathrm{FOU}\left(\overset{=}{A}\right) &= \bigcup \left[\underline{FOU}\left(\overset{=}{A}\right), \overline{FOU}\left(\overset{=}{A}\right) \right]_{\forall x \epsilon X} \\ &= \bigcup \left[\underline{FOU}\left(\overset{=}{A}\right), \alpha.\underline{FOU}\left(\overset{=}{A}\right) \right]_{\forall x \epsilon X} \quad or \bigcup \left[\beta.\overline{FOU}\left(\overset{=}{A}\right), \overline{FOU}\left(\overset{=}{A}\right) \right]_{\forall x \epsilon X} \end{aligned} \tag{4}$$

$$0 < \alpha , \beta < 1$$

to generalization, Choi & Rhee, (2009) choose the min operation as intersection for obtain the overall FOU by taking intersections of all upper and lower memberships.

$$\begin{aligned} \mathrm{FOU}\left(\overset{=}{A}\right) &= \bigcup \left[\underline{FOU}\left(\overset{=}{A}\right), \overline{FOU}\left(\overset{=}{A}\right) \right]_{\forall x \epsilon X} \\ &= \bigcup \left[\underline{\min\left\{ FOU\left(\overset{=}{A}\right)\right\}}, \min\left\{ \alpha.\underline{FOU}\left(\overset{=}{A}\right)\right\} \right]_{\forall x \epsilon X} \quad or \bigcup \left[min\left\{ \beta.\overline{FOU}\left(\overset{=}{A}\right)\right\}, \min\left\{ \overline{FOU}\left(\overset{=}{A}\right)\right\} \right]_{\forall x \epsilon X} \end{aligned} \tag{5}$$

where $\overline{FOU}\left(\overset{=}{A}\right)$ and $\underline{FOU}\left(\overset{=}{A}\right)$ are the minimum UMF and LMF among all UMFs and LMFs, respectively. Heuristic method which proposed Choi & Rhee (2009) is summarized in Fig.4.

Histogram based method (HBM) for membership function generation is another method which is more flexible than heuristic methods. In HBM, distribution of the feature values, have a crucial role in T1 FMF determination elements. Choi & Rhee, (2009) clearly stated that,"membership functions generated from HBM may be considered more suitable for arbitrary distributed data than from heuristics". Based on this theory Choi & Rhee (2009) propose a new method for generation IT2 FMFs. Using smoothed histograms which generated by hyper-cube or triangular window and then normalized, the upper and lower membership function flourished and mapped to real data. Selection a well trained parameters function to model the smoothed histograms has a tangible ramification on performances of MF generator system. To avoid over fitting lowest, the suitable degree of the polynomial function (PF) is stood out as the knee point of error. As a result, HBM FSs requires good estimation of PF.

In our case, as a real example in control, Type, severity and extents of cracking in pavement surface transform in a transform realm to generate a simple features. Simple features can use for generation of T1 FMF. Approximate parameter values such as the number, height, and location of peaks which related to cracking used to determine the optimal parameter values of the function.

Choi & Rhee (2009) considered Gaussian functions as suitable to model the IT2 FMFs (Rhee and Krishnapuram, 1993). They used a heuristic approach (Choi & Rhee, 2009) to obtain the initial parameters. Choi & Rhee (2009) ignored the ones that have small peaks. This means that we have a threshold that it considers as a crisp threshold. The $\underline{FOU}\left(\overset{=}{A}\right)$ and $\overline{FOU}\left(\overset{=}{A}\right)$ are obtained by again fitting PFs to the smoothed histograms. New again histograms crystallized upper and lower MFs fitted to PF. As dimensional parameters or overall size of problem increase, undesirably become more and more. These complexities arise due to the high process in smoothing and fitting. This is a challenging point that set in motion to

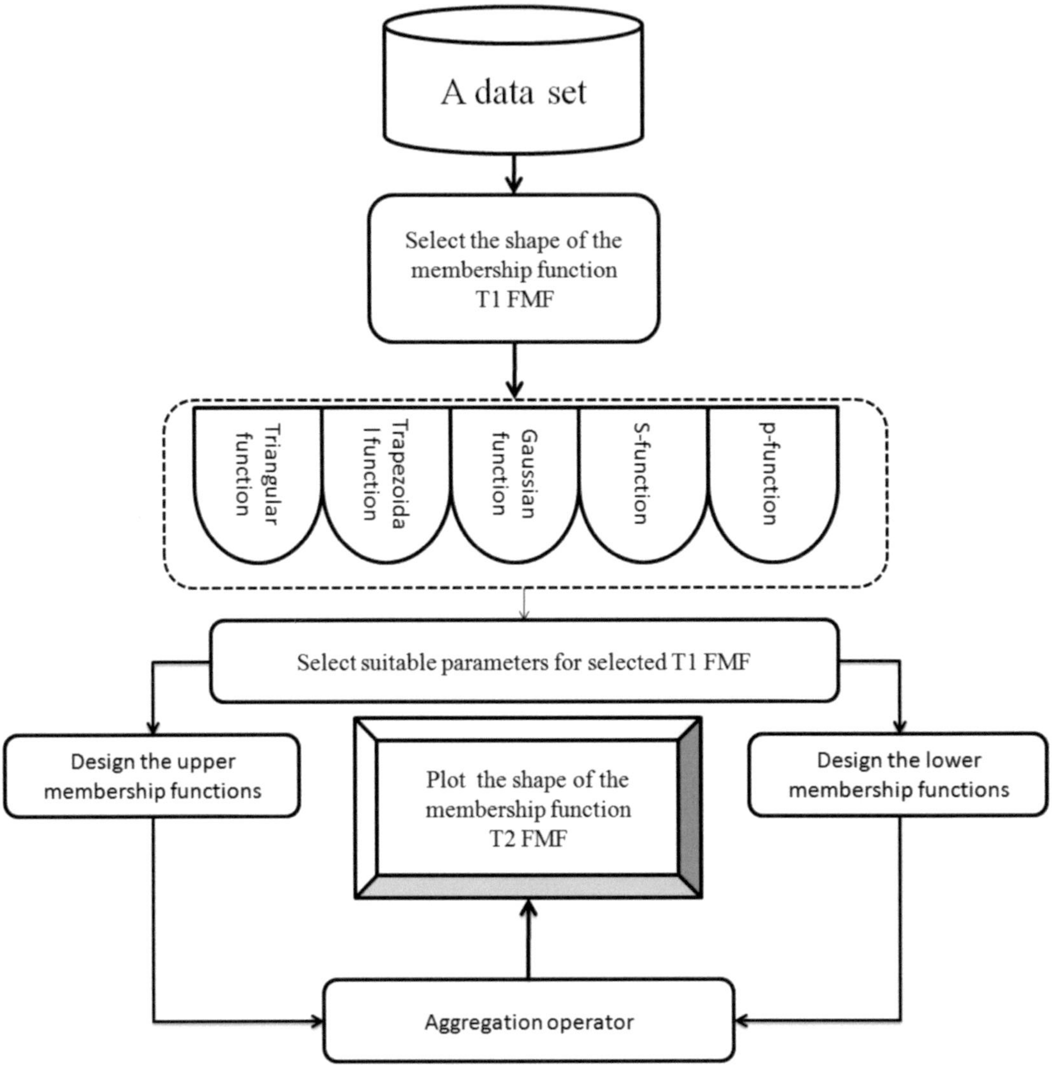

Figure 4. Heuristic based IT2 FMF generation method

product a new heuristic to handle computational load. Choi & Rhee (2009) proposed two steep methods **1)** calculate one-dimensional 1DUMF and 1DLMF for HBM. **2)** Obtain the overall $\underline{FOU}\left(\bar{\bar{A}}\right)$ and $\overline{FOU}\left(\bar{\bar{A}}\right)$ by Intersections operation. Intersections operation which proposed for this aggregation expressed as

$$\mathrm{FOU}\left(\bar{\bar{A}}\right) = \bigcup\left[\underline{FOU}\left(\bar{\bar{A}}\right), \overline{FOU}\left(\bar{\bar{A}}\right)\right]_{\forall x \epsilon X} = \left[\underline{min_i\left\{FOU\left(\bar{\bar{A}}\right)\right\}}, min_i\left\{\overline{FOU}\left(\bar{\bar{A}}\right)\right\}\right]_{\forall x \epsilon X} \quad (6)$$

where $\overline{FOU}\left(\overset{=}{A}\right)$ is the UMF, $\underline{FOU\left(\overset{=}{A}\right)}$ is the LMF, and i is the feature's number. From our points of view, the main contributions of Choi & Rhee's methods are developing in membership's generation. These methods enable them to transfer the knowledge when expert facing with N dimensional features. These methods are applicable for images realm. We assert that this contribution is valuable. Nevertheless we would like to highlight that high process in discrete smoothing and fitting(first 1DUMF and 1DLMF calculation and then aggregation) faced us to problem to products an effective MF generator. Heuristic method to generate T2 FMF's, which proposed Choi & Rhee (2009) is summarized in Fig.5.

Choi & Rhee (2009) considered **fuzzy C-means (FCM)** functions to model the IT2 FMFs (Hwang and Rhee, 2007) (Choi & Rhee, 2009). The fuzzifier m in FCM, can be fired as a membership generator. IT2 FCM based method proposed by Choi & Rhee (2009). They stated that, *"Due to the constraint on the memberships we cannot design this region with any particular single value of fuzzifier m to be used in the FCM"*. IT2 FCM algorithm was proposed to solving this problem (Hwang and Rhee, 2007). Indeed they products a simple dynamic fuzzifuyer AMFG to generating the Membership function. According to IT2 FCM, two fuzzifier m_1, m_2 are employed to control the blurring area in fuzzy domain. The proposed IT2 FMF in IT2 FCM expressed as (Choi & Rhee, 2009).

$$J_x = \left\{ \left(x,u\right) : u\epsilon[\underline{FOU}\left(\overset{=}{A}\right), \overline{FOU}\left(\overset{=}{A}\right)] \right\} \tag{7}$$

$$\overline{FOU}\left(\overset{=}{A}\right) = \left\{ \begin{array}{l} IF \dfrac{1}{\sum_{K=1}^{C}\left(\dfrac{d_{ij}}{d_{ik}}\right)^{\frac{2}{(m_1-1)}}} > \dfrac{1}{\sum_{K=1}^{C}\left(\dfrac{d_{ij}}{d_{ik}}\right)^{\frac{2}{(m_2-1)}}} \\ THEN\ \overline{FOU}\left(\overset{=}{A}\right) = \dfrac{1}{\sum_{K=1}^{C}\left(\dfrac{d_{ij}}{d_{ik}}\right)^{\frac{2}{(m_1-1)}}} \\ ELSE\ \overline{FOU}\left(\overset{=}{A}\right) = \dfrac{1}{\sum_{K=1}^{C}\left(\dfrac{d_{ij}}{d_{ik}}\right)^{\frac{2}{(m_2-1)}}} \end{array} \right\}, \tag{8}$$

and

$$\underline{FOU}\left(\overset{=}{A}\right)=\begin{cases} IF\dfrac{1}{\sum_{K=1}^{C}\left(\dfrac{d_{ij}}{d_{ik}}\right)^{\frac{2}{(m_1-1)}}}\leq\dfrac{1}{\sum_{K=1}^{C}\left(\dfrac{d_{ij}}{d_{ik}}\right)^{\frac{2}{(m_2-1)}}} \\ THEN\ \overline{FOU}\left(\overset{=}{A}\right)=\dfrac{1}{\sum_{K=1}^{C}\left(\dfrac{d_{ij}}{d_{ik}}\right)^{\frac{2}{(m_1-1)}}} \\ ELSE\ \overline{FOU}\left(\overset{=}{A}\right)=\dfrac{1}{\sum_{K=1}^{C}\left(\dfrac{d_{ij}}{d_{ik}}\right)^{\frac{2}{(m_2-1)}}} \end{cases} \tag{9}$$

However IT2 FCM for updating cluster prototypes requires type-reduction. Using type-2 fuzzy operations therefore is essential. The crisp center obtained mean of centers of defuzzification as the centroid obtained by the type-reduction according Eq.10

$$V_{\tilde{x}}=\left[\underline{C},\bar{C}\right]=\frac{\sum_{\overline{FOU}\left(\overset{=}{A}\right)\in J_{x1}}\cdots\sum_{\overline{FOU}\left(\overset{=}{A}\right)\in J_{x1}}1}{\dfrac{\sum_{i=1}^{N}x_i\overline{FOU}\left(\overset{=}{A}\right)_i^m}{\sum_{i=1}^{N}\overline{FOU}\left(\overset{=}{A}\right)_i^m}} \tag{10}$$

The UMF and LMF for class k and input pattern xj can be expressed by modifying

$$d_{kj}^{*}=min_p\left\{d(x_j,V_{\tilde{x}}^{\ k})\right\},p\epsilon\left\{n_k\right\} \tag{11}$$

Based on Choi & Rhee's (2009) method the membership values for the UMFs and LMFs are based on m_1 and m_2 and they are highly dependent on value selection of threshold which is itself considered crisp. Choi & Rhee's (2009) stated that IT2 FCM can desirably control the uncertainty that is quite simple handle all features of high dimensional problems. Their heuristic method summarized in Fig 6.

The accuracy of IT2 FCM highly dependent on fuzzifiers selection. These parameters have significant role in designing the FOU for a data set. In general, select unsuitable fuzzifier worth poor clustering. (Choi & Rhee's, 2009)

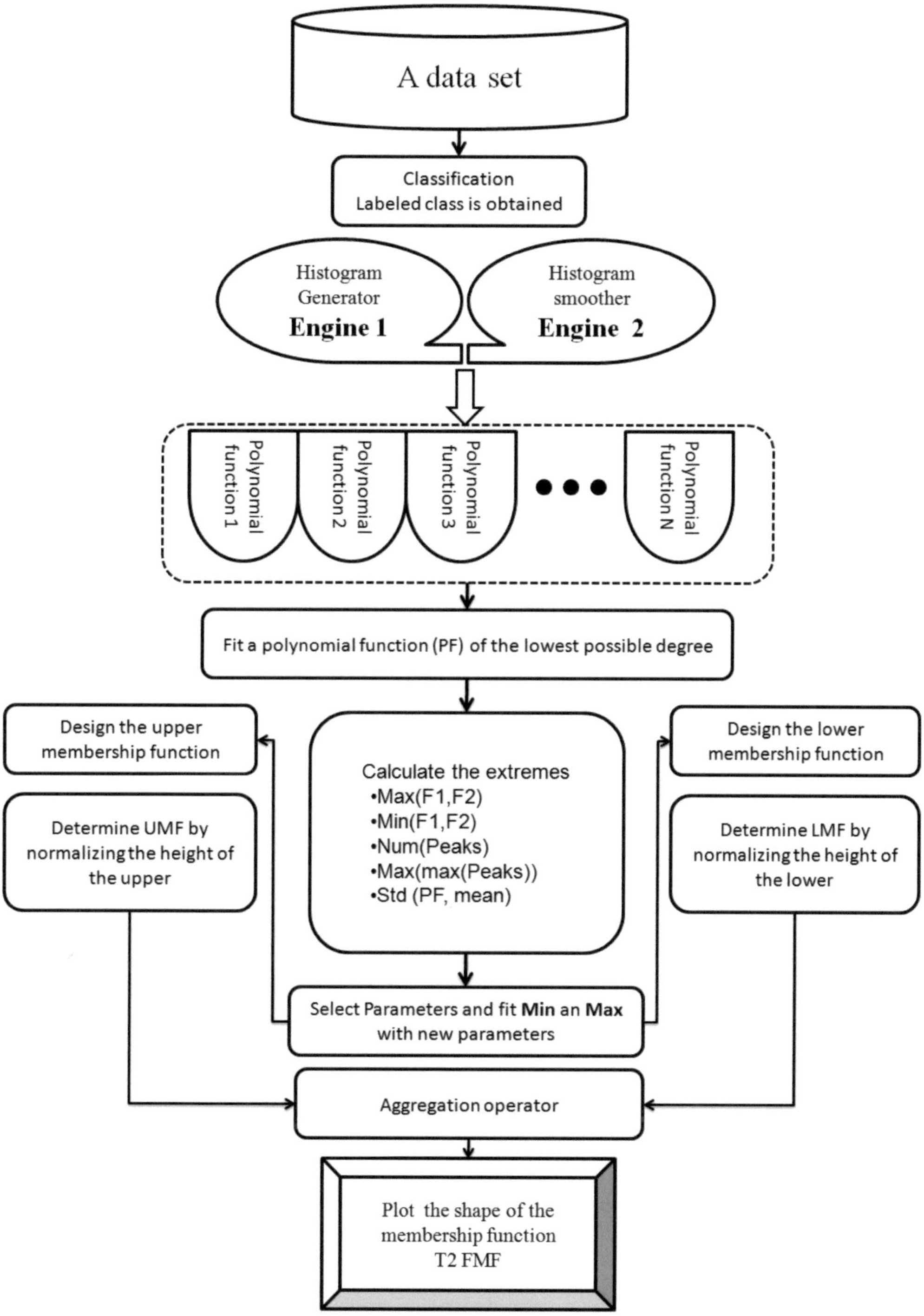

Figure 5. Heuristic based IT2 FMF generation method

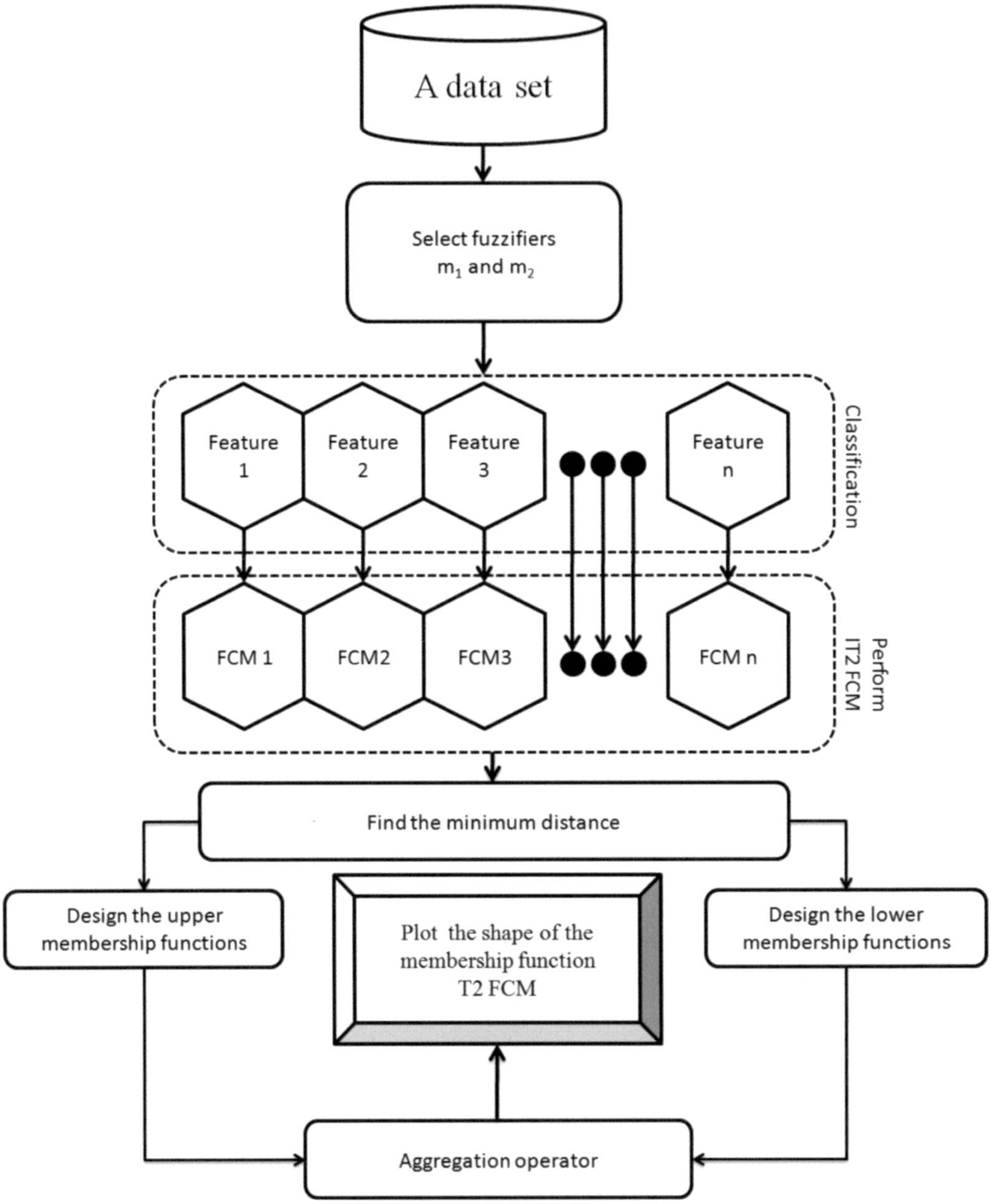

Figure 6. Heuristic based IT2 FCM generation method

4. Interval type-2 Polar Fuzzy Method (IT2 PFM)

4.1. Type III-MF

The Interval type-2 Polar Fuzzy Method (IT2 PFM) algorithm was proposed to automatically control the uncertainty. In this section, we proposed an intelligent IT2 FMF generator agent. First, the IT2 FMF algorithm introduced, and then our IT2 FPM based method are described. We selected Cubic Smoothing Spline (CSS) for generate the upper and lower membership functions because of non-uniform illumination of the Three Dimensional Memebership Functions (3DMFs). In the Type-2 domain, the estimation of the $3DMF_u$ and $3DMF_L$ are exanimate from the fitting of a cubic smoothing Spline,(Mora et al.,2011) to the 3DMF*(x,y)*. The select CSS is a special class of Spline that can capture the low 3DMF value that limited the non-uniformity of the 3DMF (Culpin, 1986). The fitting objective is to minimize the equation.

$$M = P.\sum_{y=1}^{m}\sum_{x=1}^{n}(f(x,y) - s(x,y))^2 + (1-p)\iint(D^2S(x,y))^2dxdy, \tag{12}$$

where, this equation include two parts:

- *Compactness:* measures how close the spline is to the data that reflect to the summation term which weighed by the smoothing factor p,
- *Smoothness:* measures the spline smoothness using its second derivative that reflect to the integral term weighed by (1 - p).

The smoothing factor p, controls the balance between being an interpolating spline crossing all data points (with p = 1) and being a strictly smooth Spline (with p = 0). The smoothing spline *f* minimizes when

$$\left[\left[P\sum_{j=1}^{n}\left(\omega(j)\left|y(:,j) - f(x(j))\right|^2\right)\right] + \left[(1-p)\int\lambda(t)\left|D^2f(t)\right|^2 dt.\right]\right] \tag{13}$$

where, $|z|_2$ represent for the sum of the squares of all the entries of *n*, N and M is the number of entries of x and y, and the integral is over the smallest interval containing all the entries of x and y. The default value for the weight vector w in the error measure is ones (size(x)). The default value for the piecewise constant weight function λ in the roughness measure is the constant function 1. Further, D_2f denotes the second derivative of the function f. The default value for the smoothing parameter, p, is chosen in dependence on the given data sites x and y (Pal and Bezdek, 1994). The smoothing parameter determines the relative weight to place on the contradictory demands of having f be smooth vs having f be close to the data. For p = 0, f is the least-squares straight line fit to the data, while, at the other extreme, i.e., for p = 1, f is the variational, or 'natural' cubic spline interpolant. As p moves from 0 to 1, the smoothing spline changes from one extreme to the other. (See Fig. 7)

The interesting range for p is often near $1/\left(1 + \left(min(N,M)\right)^3/600\right)$, with *h* the average spacing of the data sites, and it is in this range that the default value for *p* is chosen. For uniformly spaced data, one would expect a close following of the data for $p = 1/(1 + (min(N,M))^3/6000)$ and some satisfactory smoothing for

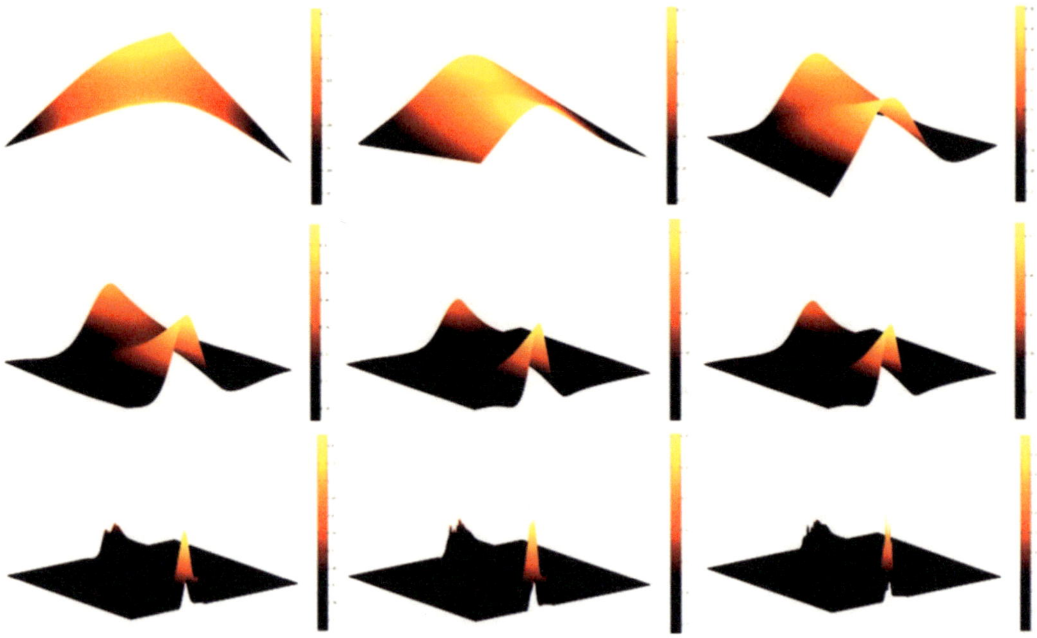

Figure 7. As p moves from 0 to 1, the smoothing spline changes from one extreme to the other.

$$p = 1/\left(1 + \left(min\left(N,M\right)\right)^3 / 60\right).p > 1 \tag{14}$$

can be input, but this leads to a smoothing spline even rougher than the variational cubic spline interpolate (Pal and Bezdek,1994).

$$p = \left(\frac{1}{1+\frac{(min(N,M))^3}{600}}\right), p_U = \left(\frac{1}{1+\frac{(min(N,M))^3}{\alpha\times 600}}\right)_U, p_L = \left(\frac{1}{1+\frac{(min(N,M))^3}{\beta\times 600}}\right)_L \tag{15}$$

A reference smoothing factor $\left(p = 1e-4\right)$ was obtained empirically for constructed MF in upper bound and $\left(p = 0.93e-5\right)$ for constructed MF in lower bound. For example, in the case of image thresholding, After testing several thresholds, the general rule can be extract from 3DRT thresholds for upper and lower bounds by good selection of α and β.

4.1.1. *A measure of ultrafuzziness*

Using a simple method, we turned ultrafuzzy to the 3DRT fuzzy set. According a type II membership function, MF must be in [0,1]. One can be taking out the normalization form 3DMF using division every point by max 3DRT.

$$RTMF_{(i,j)} = \left(\left[v_{(3DRT)(i,j)}^{h} \right] \Big/ \max\left[v_{(3DRT)(i,j)}^{h} \right] \right)^{\frac{1}{h}}, \tag{16}$$

$$\mu_{(i,j)} = \left(\left[v_{(3DRT)(i,j)}^{h} \right] \Big/ \max\left[v_{(3DRT)(i,j)}^{h} \right] \right)^{\frac{1}{h}} + H, \tag{17}$$

and

$$GR_{(i,j)} = \frac{1}{(MN)^{h}} \sum_{j=1}^{N} \sum_{i=1}^{M} \left(\left[v_{(3DRT)(i,j)}^{h} \right] \Big/ \max\left[v_{(3DRT)(i,j)}^{h} \right] \right)^{\frac{1}{h}}, \tag{18}$$

where, M and N denotes the size of 3DMF platform,H is high platform, $h\epsilon(1,\infty)$ and $v_{(3DRT)(i,j)}^{h}$ is 3DRT value in the position *i* and *j*. Select a bigger h is worth a more enhanced distress for example in pavement distress detection and classification problem and smoother noisy background (see Fig.8). In order to define a type II fuzzy set, one can define a type I fuzzy set and assign upper and lower membership degrees to each element to (re)construct the footprint of uncertainty (Fig. 9) (Tizhoosh,2005). For example, when Radon Transform is applied to wavelet modulus, a distress (crack) is transformed into a peak in radon domain. Originally, every distress reflects to RT and has different intensity in 3DMF histograms. For example mean of 3DRT have variety range. According to the above Eq. 18 the max GR must be equal 1. To extend the fuzzy membership to type II fuzzy sets, ultrafuzziness should be zero, if the MF can be selected without any ambiguous such as type I. The amount of ultrafuzziness will increase by rising uncertainly bound.

The extreme case of maximal ultrafuzziness, equal 1, is worth to completely vagueness. pal and bezdek (1994) had extensive reviewed well known fuzziness index, two general classes proposed by them was additive and multiplicative class (Pal and Bezdek,1994). Based on kufmann's Index of fuzziness for a set $A \in r_n(x)$,

$$H_{ka}(A) = \left(\frac{2}{n^{k}} \right) d(A, A^{near}) \tag{19}$$

Where, $k \in R^{+}$, d is a metric, and A^{near} is the crisp set close to the A. generally, based on *d*, weigh of k determined. The $d(A, A^{near})$ and linear or quadratic $H_{ka}(A)$ cab be determined by q-norms,

$$d(A,A^{near}) = \left(\sum_{i=1}^{n}\left|\mu_i - \mu_{A^{near},i}\right|^q\right)^{1/q} \quad H_{ka}(q,A) = \left(\frac{2}{n^{\frac{1}{q}}}\right)\left(\sum_{i=1}^{n}\left|\mu_i - \mu_{A^{near},i}\right|^q\right)^{1/q} \tag{20}$$

Where $q \in [1,\infty)$. On the other side, Tizhoosh developed a simple ultrafuzziness index for the special case as fallow (Tizhoosh, 2005),

$$\tilde{\gamma}(\tilde{A}) = \frac{1}{MN}\sum_{i=1}^{M-1}\sum_{j=1}^{N-1}\left[\mu_U(g_{ij}) - \mu_L(g_{ij})\right] \tag{21}$$

where $\mu_U(g) = \left[\mu_A(g)\right]^{1/\alpha}$ and $\mu_U(g) = \left[\mu_A(g)\right]^{1/\alpha}$, $\alpha \in (1,2]$. and in general term it present as follow,

$$\tilde{\gamma}(\tilde{A}) = \frac{1}{MN}\sum_{g=0}^{L-1}\left[\mu_U(g_{ij}) - \mu_L(g_{ij})\right]\times h(g) \tag{22}$$

Based on these theory and with respect to Tizhoosh's method (Tizhoosh, 2005),for developing ultrafuzziness on 2D data, a measure of ultrafuzziness $\tilde{\gamma}$ for a platform 3DMF with M*N sets, surf 3DMF and the membership function $\mu_{\tilde{A}(i,j)}$ can be developed as follows:

$$\tilde{\gamma}(A) = \left(\frac{1}{(MN)^{\frac{1}{q}}}\right)\left[\sum_{j=1}^{M-1}\sum_{i=1}^{N-1}\left|\mu_{u(i,j)} - \mu_{L(i,j)}\right|^q\right]^{1/q}$$

$$\frac{\partial}{\partial T}\tilde{\gamma}\left(RT_{(i,j)}\right) = \frac{\partial}{\partial T}\left(\frac{1}{(MN)^{\frac{1}{q}}}\right)\left[\sum_{j=1}^{M-1}\sum_{i=1}^{N-1}\left|\mu_{u((i,j),T)} - \mu_{L((i,j),T)}\right|^q\right]^{1/q} = 0 \tag{23}$$

This basic definition relies on the assumption that the singletons sitting on the FOU are all equal in height (which is the reason why the interval-based type II is used), (Tizhoosh, 2005). The variation in the space can be measured by this method, therefore the new Index introduced in three dimensional domain of FOU for 3D fuzzy sets, (3DFOU). This method can resolve the problems about the ultrafuzziness index -"uncertainty (FOU) has a constant value, that equals one, in all the intervals of the universe of discourse" (Ioannis et al., 2008) - using introducing flexible membership function across the intervals path (see Fig 9, 10).

Similarly, We are evaluated, proposed method, based four conditions *Minimum ultrafuzziness, Maximum ultrafuzziness, Equal ultrafuzziness* and *Reduced ultrafuzziness* that every measure of fuzziness should satisfy, which introduced by Kaufmann (Kaufmann, 1975). In a similar way, we established that the new index is qualified for measure of ultrafuzziness in 3D domain with these conditions.

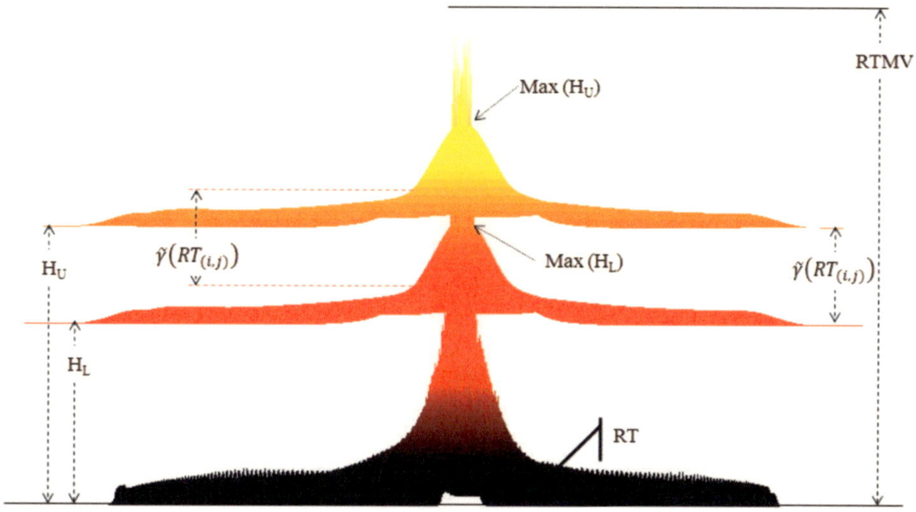

Figure 8. Basic rules for construction 3D fuzzy type II memebership function.

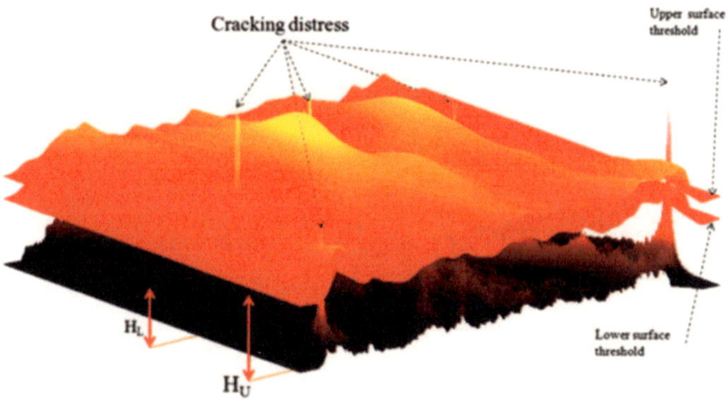

Figure 9. Three dimensional domain of FOU for 3D fuzzy sets, (3DFOU)

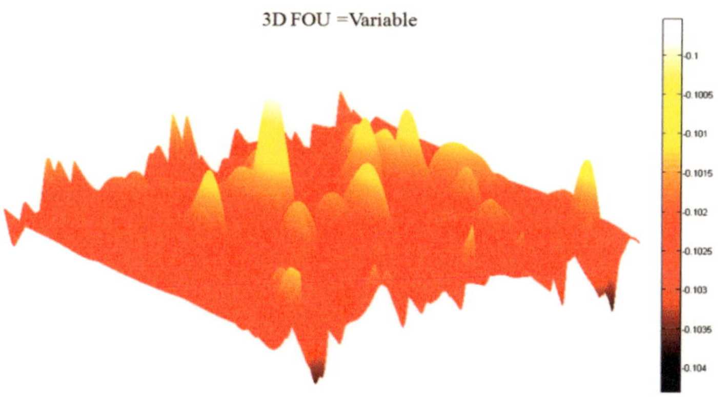

Figure 10. Example of Three FOU for 3D fuzzy sets, (3DFOU) using proposed algorithm

1. ***IF*** $\mu_{(i,j)}$ consider as a type I fuzzy set ***Then*** $\mu_{u(i,j)} = \mu_{L(i,j)}$ ***AND*** $\tilde{\gamma}(A) = 0$

$$\tilde{\gamma}(A) = \left(\frac{1}{(MN)^{\frac{1}{q}}}\right)\left[\sum_{j=1}^{M-1}\sum_{i=1}^{N-1}\left|\mu_{u(i,j)} - \mu_{U(i,j)}\right|^{q}\right]^{1/q} = 0 \ for\, q \in [1,\infty). \tag{24}$$

2. ***IF*** $\left|\mu_{u(i,j)} - \mu_{L(i,j)}\right| = 1$ (high ambiguity) ***Then*** $\tilde{\gamma}(\tilde{A}) = 1$.

$$\tilde{\gamma}(A) = \left(\frac{1}{(MN)^{\frac{1}{q}}}\right)\left[\sum_{j=1}^{M-1}\sum_{i=1}^{N-1}\left|\mu_{u(i,j)} - \mu_{U(i,j)}\right|^{q}\right]^{1/q} = 1 \ for\, q \in [1,\infty). \tag{25}$$

3. $\tilde{\gamma}(\tilde{A}) = \tilde{\gamma}(\tilde{\tilde{A}})$ Where $(\tilde{\tilde{A}})$is type II fuzzy set and it's complement set can be determined by 1- $\mu_{u(i,j)}$ and 1- $\mu_{L(i,j)}$, therefore complement set defined as follow

   For the complement set, the ultrafuzziness $\tilde{\gamma}$ is equal:

$$\tilde{\gamma}(\tilde{\tilde{A}}) = \left(\frac{1}{(MN)^{\frac{1}{q}}}\right)\left[\sum_{j=1}^{M-1}\sum_{i=1}^{N-1}\left|1 - \mu_{u(i,j)} - 1 - \mu_{L(i,j)}\right|^{q}\right]^{1/q} = \tilde{\gamma}(\tilde{A}) \ for\, q \in [1,\infty) \tag{26}$$

4. ***IF*** $3DFOU_{(i,j)} < 3DFOU_{(d,c)}$ ***Then*** $\tilde{\gamma}(\tilde{A}_{(i,j)}) < \tilde{\gamma}(\tilde{A}_{(d,c)})$.

4.1.2. Finding the optimum interval 3DMF

The general approach for 3DMF based on upper and lower MF is equal:

$$\xi = \left[1 - \frac{\min \tilde{\gamma}(i,j)}{\max \tilde{\gamma}(i,j)}\right], SURF(i,j) = \mu_L(g_{ij})[\xi + 1], OR\, \mu_U(g_{ij})[1 - \xi] \tag{27}$$

Where (ξ) is ultra fuzzy coefficient and $\tilde{\gamma}(i,j)$ *is* ultra fuzzy value for $\mu_{u(i,j)}$ and $\mu_{L(i,j)}$, in upper and lower threshold.

4.2. Interval type-2 polar based method

Image processing is one among interesting applications of 3DMF. Instead of type reduce from Type-2 to type-1, we used a polar transform to make uniformity by same scale in [0,2π]. The RT of a two-dimensional function $f(x,y)$ in (r,θ) plane is defined as:

$$P(r,\theta) = R(r,\theta)[f(x,y)] = \int_{-\infty}^{+\infty}\int_{-\infty}^{+\infty} f(x,y)\delta(r - x\cos\theta - y\sin\theta)\,dx\,dy, \tag{28}$$

where $f(x, y)$ represents an image, $P(r, \theta)$ is the radon transform of $f(x, y)$, θ represents the line direction, and r is the distance away from the origin of coordinates. (Radon, 1919), (Miao et al., 2012) Where $\delta(\cdot)$ is the Dirac function, $r\in[-\infty,\infty]$ is the perpendicular distance of a line from the origin and $\theta\in[0,\pi]$ is the angle formed by the distance vector. For the spatial case such as 3DMF, the fuzziness can be calculated as follows (Tizhoosh, 2005);

$$\gamma_l(A)=\left(\frac{2}{(MN)}\right)\left[\sum_{j=1}^{M-1}\sum_{i=1}^{N-1}min\left[\mu_{A(r_{i,j})},1-\mu_{A(r_{i,j})}\right]\right], \tag{29}$$

where $M\times N$ is subset $A\subseteq X$ with L radon transform value, $r\in[0,L-1]$, the histogram $h(RT)$ and the membership function $\mu x(RT)$, the linear index of fuzziness γ_l can be defined as follows (see Fig.6):

$$\gamma_l(A)=\left(\frac{2}{(MN)}\right)\left[\sum_{r=0}^{L-1}h(r)\times min\left[\mu_{A(r)},1-\mu_{A(r)}\right]\right], \tag{30}$$

To quantify the object fuzziness, a suitable membership function $\mu_A(r)$ should be determined. Tizhoosh present different functions, such as the standard S-function, the Huang and Wang function, LR-type fuzzy number (Tizhoosh et al, 1998; Huang and Wang, 1995; Pal and Bezdek, 1994; Pal and Murthy, 1990). Similar 3DMF presented in section 4.1, to generation of polar MF, CSS is used. The estimation of the MF also exanimate from the fitting of a cubic smoothing Spline, (Mora et al.,2011) to the 3DPMF(r,θ). The fitting objective is to minimize the equation.

$$M=P.\sum_{y=1}^{m}\sum_{x=1}^{n}(f(r,\theta)-s(r,\theta))^2+(1-p)\iint(D^2s(r,\theta))^2drd\theta, \tag{31}$$

where, this equation include two parts: *Compactness* and *Smoothness*. The smoothing factor p, controls the balance between being an interpolating spline crossing all data points (with p = 1) and being a strictly smooth Spline (with p = 0). In the polar transform, as p moves from 0 to 1, the smoothing spline changes from one extreme to the other. (See Fig. 11)

Using Radon transform for MF generation have several benefits such as Translation, Rotation and Scaling in IT2 FPM. (Miao et al., 2012).

$$R(\rho,\theta)\{f(x-x_0,y-y_0\}=P(r-r_0,\theta), \tag{32}$$

$$R(\rho,\theta)\{f(xcos\varphi+ysin\varphi,-xcos\varphi+ysin\varphi\}=P(\rho,\theta+\varphi) \tag{33}$$

$$R(\rho,\theta)\left\{f\left(x/\gamma,y/\gamma\right)\right\}=\gamma P\left(r/\gamma,\theta\right),\gamma\neq 0 \tag{34}$$

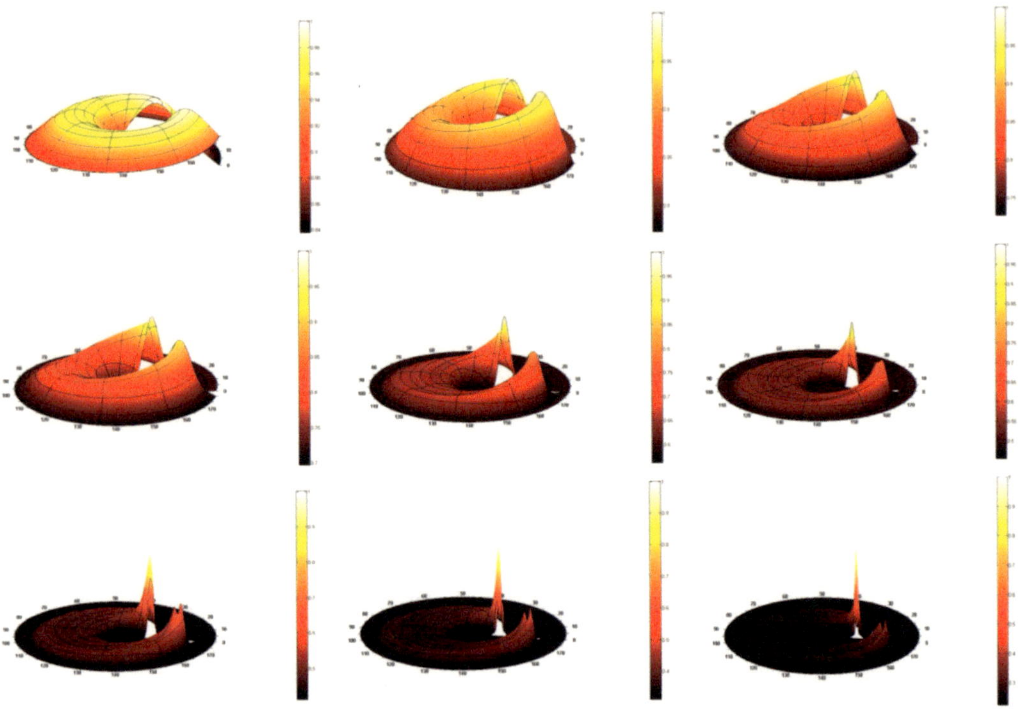

Figure 11. A sample of polar memberships function, As p moves from 0 to 1, the smoothing spline changes from one extreme to the other.

Where $r_0 = x_0 \cos\theta + y_0 \sin\ \theta$, γ is the scaling factor and φ is the rotation angle. A rotation of $f(x, y)$ by angle φ leads to a translation of $P(\rho,\theta)$ in the variable θ. A scaling of $f(x, y)$ results in a scaling in the ρ coordinate, as well as an intensity scaling of $P(\rho,\theta)$. (Miao et al., 2012). For the Fuzzy Polar based Method, we proposed use the following heuristic approach. This method consists of seven steps to obtain the 3D membership function in the polar domain.

Step 1. Three Dimensional Surface **(3D Data)**, Using Radon transform generate the 3D surface from image and construct 3D data surface.

Step 2. Three Dimensional Polar Surface (**3D Polar**), Transfer data to the polar domain and uniform data in multi-scale.

Step 3. Polar Histogram Generator **(PHG)**, generates polar histogram in all direction using polar histogram generator.

Step 4. Approximate Smoother fitting parameters (**SF**), Perform SF parameter to obtain the approximate parameter value (p).

Step 5. Polar Smooth Generator (**PSG)** smooths the histogram of the overall polar surface.

Step 6. Perform **PSG** fitting for the upper and lower histogram values.

Step 7. Determine PFMF, by normalizing the height of the upper PSG and LMF by the lower PSG.

On advantages of T2 PFM method is decrease on computational load in comparison with histogram based IT2 FMF. According our proposed method computational load can decrease, due to the stimulatory dimension in muli-scale surface and decrease computational load because of modified histogram smoothing process and fitting. Instead finding the one-dimensional UMF and LMF for each class label and feature which used by histogram based method, we fired all points in polar system with a cubic-spline. Next, we obtain the overall UMF and LMF Simultaneously. To obtain the generated IT2 PMF, it essential the three polar FOU (3D PFOU) be calculated. The UMF and LMF are designed by refitting cubic-spline. According proposed method the smoothed histograms have values that are above or below the mother fitted surface. Fig. 12a shows the one example constructed by polar upper and lower cubic-spline functions.

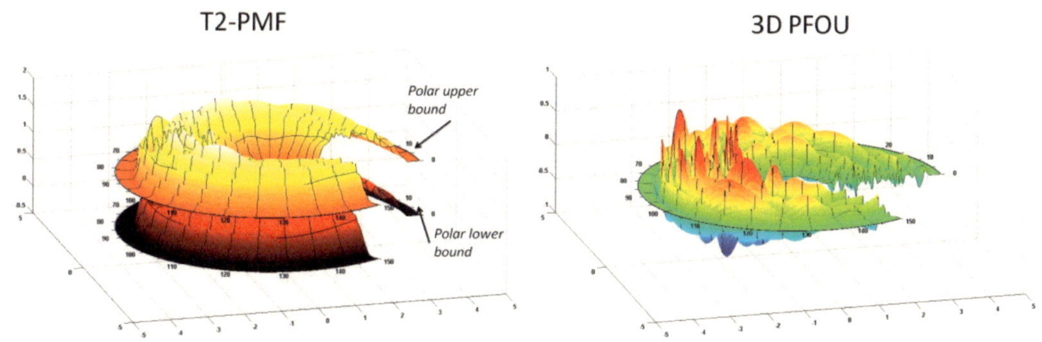

Figure 12. A)Three dimensional domain polar upper bound and lower bound, b) FOU for 3D polar fuzzy sets, (3D PFOU)

Using the upper and lower mother surface, to obtain the 3D PFOU, the PUMFs and PLMFs surface are designed. The UMF and LMFs surface normalized. Fig. 12,b. shows the IT2 PMF obtained by our proposed method. The shaded region between the 3D UMF and 3D LMF indicates the 3D PFOU. As shown in the Fig.13, our proposed method can effectively design IT2 FMFs based on the distribution of the input 3D data. The 3D PFOU can be expressed as

$$\mathrm{PFOU}\left(\overset{=}{A}\right)=\bigcup\left[\underline{PFOU}\left(\overset{=}{A}\right),\overline{PFOU}\left(\overset{=}{A}\right)\right]_{\forall x\epsilon X}=\bigcup\left[\underline{\min\left\{PFOU\left(\overset{=}{A}\right)\right\}},\min\left\{\underline{PFOU}\left(\overset{=}{A}\right)\right\}\right]_{\forall x\epsilon X} \tag{35}$$

where $\overline{PFOU}\left(\overset{=}{A}\right)$ is the UMF, $\underline{PFOU}\left(\overset{=}{A}\right)$ s the LMF, and i is the feature number.

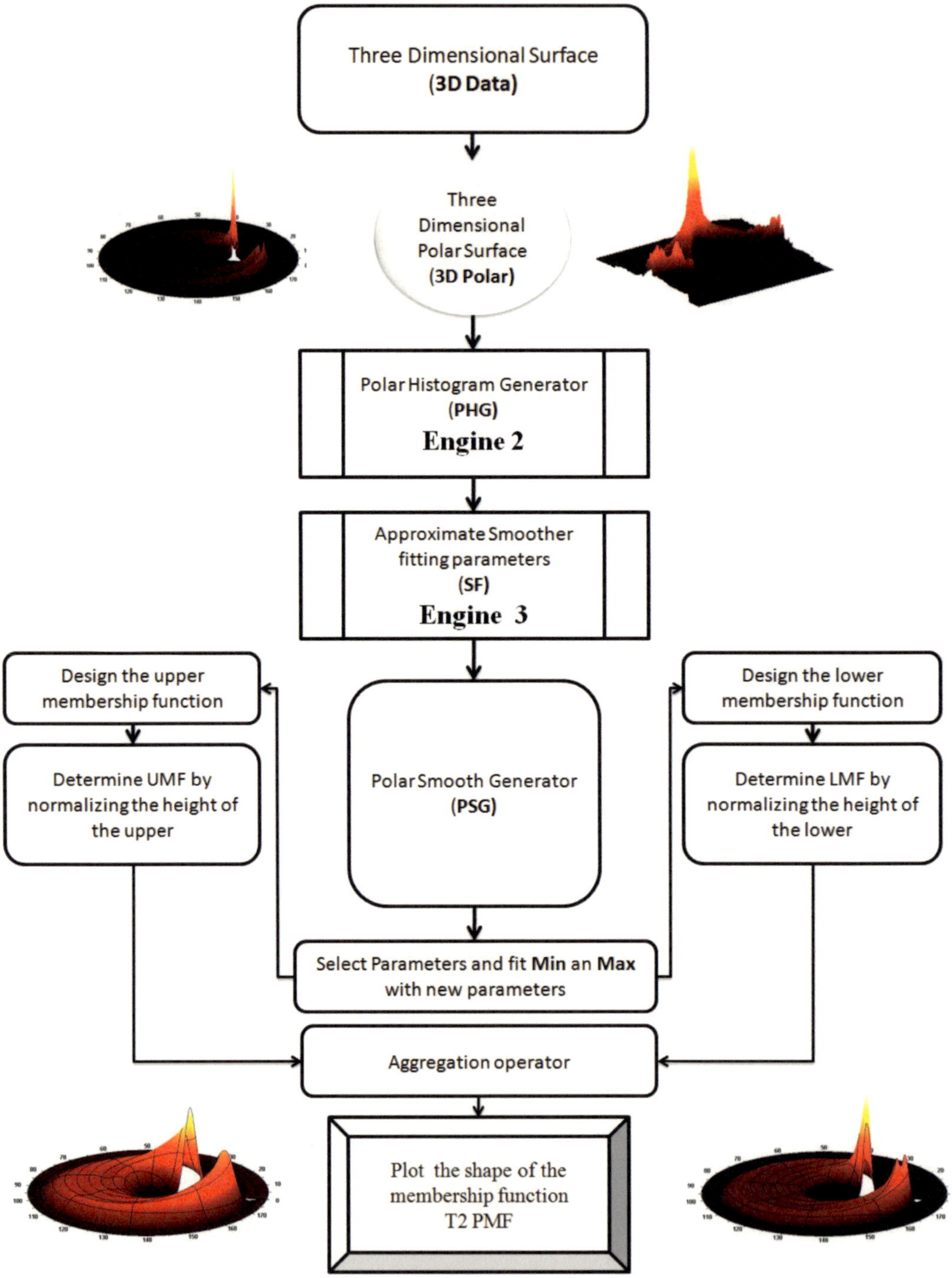

Figure 13. Heuristic based IT2 FPM generation method

4.2.1. *A measure of polar ultrafuzziness*

Polar ultrafuzzy can be calculated based on 3DMF fuzzy set. Such as defuzzifcation method proposed in measure of surface ultrafuzziness in section 4.1.1., type II membership function must be in [0,1]. Similaraway, normalization must be used for 3D PMF generation by division every point at (ρ, θ) by max 3D PRT.

$$PN_{(\rho,\theta)} = \left(\left[v_{(3D\,PMF)(\rho,\theta)}^{h} \right] \Big/ max\left[v_{(3D\,PMF)(\rho,\theta)}^{h} \right] \right)^{\frac{1}{h}}, \tag{36}$$

$$\mu_{(\rho,\theta)} = \left(\left[v_{(3D\,MF)(\rho,\theta)}^{h} \right] \Big/ max\left[v_{(3DRT)(\rho,\theta)}^{h} \right] \right)^{\frac{1}{h}} + H \tag{37}$$

and

$$GR_{(i,j)} = \frac{1}{2(2\pi r)^{h}} \int_{0}^{2\pi}\int_{0}^{r} \left(\left[v_{(3DMF)(\rho,\theta)}^{h} \right] \Big/ max\left[v_{(3DRT)(\rho,\theta)}^{h} \right] \right)^{\frac{1}{h}} d\rho d\theta, \tag{38}$$

where, $2\pi r$ denotes the size of 3DPMF platform,H is high polar platform $H\epsilon[0,1]$, $h\epsilon(1,\infty)$ and $v_{(3DRT)(\rho,\theta)}^{h}$ is 3DMF value in the position ρ and θ. In thresholding, selection H controller can use for select an optimum threshold based on type II fuzzy. Select a bigger H is worth a more enhanced maximum value. In order to define a type II fuzzy set in polar domain, first we develop a type I fuzzy set and assign upper and lower membership degrees to each element to (re)construct the footprint of uncertainty in polar system (Fig. 14). Hear we select H=0 to calculate the real 3D PMF. In polar system the definition for uncertainty is slightly deferent 3D FMF. Uncertainty can present in ring and height which reflect to polar memberships function. (Fig. 16) For example, when Radon Transform is applied to wavelet modulus, a distress (crack) is transformed into a peak in radon domain. Originally, every distress reflects to RT and has different intensity in 3DMF histograms. For example mean of 3D PRT have variety range. According to the above Eq. 38 the max GR must be equal 1. Similaty 3D FMF method, in 3D PMF, the amount of ultrafuzziness will increase by rising uncertainly bound.

The extreme case of maximal ultrafuzziness in polar system, equal 1, is worth to completely vagueness. Based on Pal and Bezdek (1994) research on several fuzziness index, two general classes proposed by them was additive and multiplicative class (Pal and Bezdek, 1994). Based on Kufmann's Index of fuzziness for a set $P \in r_n(x)$,

$$H_{ka}(A)=\left(\frac{2}{n^k}\right)d(P,P^{near}) \tag{39}$$

Where, $k\in R^+$,d is a metric, and A^{near} is the crisp set close to the P. generally, based on d,weigh of k determined. The $d(P,P^{near})$ and linear or quadratic $H_{ka}(P)$ can be determined by q-norms such as 3D FMF,

$$d(P,P^{near})=\left(\sum_{i=1}^{n}\left|\mu_{(\rho,\theta)}-\mu_{A^{near},(\rho,\theta)}\right|^q\right)^{1/q},H_{ka}(q,P)=\left(\frac{2}{n^{\frac{1}{q}}}\right)\left(\sum_{i=1}^{n}\left|\mu_i-\mu_{P^{near},i}\right|^q\right)^{1/q} \tag{40}$$

Where $q\in\left[1,\infty\right)$. Based on Tizhoosh ultrafuzziness index, we developed a new index in continues polar domain (Tizhoosh, 2005),

$$\tilde{\gamma}\left(\tilde{P}\right)=\frac{1}{4\pi\rho^2}\int_0^{2\pi}\int_0^{r}\left(\mu_U(g_{(\rho,\theta)})-\mu_L(g_{(\rho,\theta)})\right)d\rho d\theta, \tag{41}$$

Where $\mu_U(g)=\left[\mu_A(g)\right]^{1/\alpha}$ and $\mu_L(g)=\left[\mu_A(g)\right]^{1/\beta}$, and in general term it present as follow,

$$\tilde{\gamma}\left(\tilde{P}\right)=\frac{1}{4\pi\rho^2}\int_0^{2\pi}\int_0^{r}\int_0^{1}\left(\mu_U(g_{(\rho,\theta)})-\mu_L(g_{(\rho,\theta)})\right)\times h(g)\,d\rho.d\theta.dh \tag{42}$$

A measure of ultrafuzziness $\tilde{\gamma}$ for a polar 3D FMF in $4\pi\rho^2$, polar 3D FMF and the membership function $\mu_{\tilde{P}(\rho,\theta)}$ can be developed as follows:

$$\tilde{\gamma}(P)=\left(\frac{1}{(Area)^{\frac{1}{q}}}\right)\left[\int_0^{2\pi}\int_0^{r}\left|\mu_U(g_{(\rho,\theta)})-\mu_L(g_{(\rho,\theta)})\right|^q\right]^{1/q},$$

$$\frac{\partial}{\partial T}\tilde{\gamma}\left(PMF_{(\rho,\theta)}\right)=\frac{\partial}{\partial T}\left(\frac{1}{(Area)^{\frac{1}{q}}}\right)\left[\int_0^{2\pi}\int_0^{r}\left|\mu_U(g_{(\rho,\theta)})-\mu_L(g_{(\rho,\theta)})\right|^q\right]^{1/q}d\rho d\theta=0 \tag{43}$$

The variation in the polar space can be measured by this method, therefore the new Index introduced in polar dimensional domain of FOU for 3D polar fuzzy sets, (3D PFOU). This method can resolve the problems about the discontinues domain and in a same time reduce on dimension by using polar transform. (see Fig 15, 16).

Similarly, Kaufmann conditions consists of *Minimum ultrafuzziness, Maximum ultrafuzziness, Equal ultrafuzziness* and *Reduced ultrafuzziness* evaluated for polar method (Kaufmann, 1975). Polar Index is qualified for measure of ultrafuzziness in 3D polar domain with these conditions.

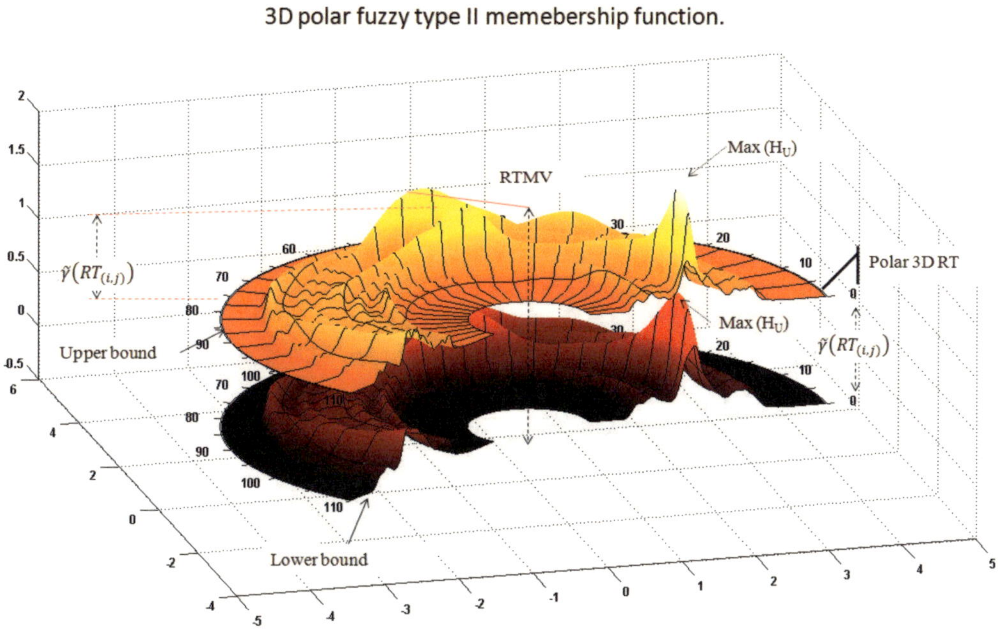

Figure 14. Basic rules for construction 3D polar fuzzy type II memebership function.

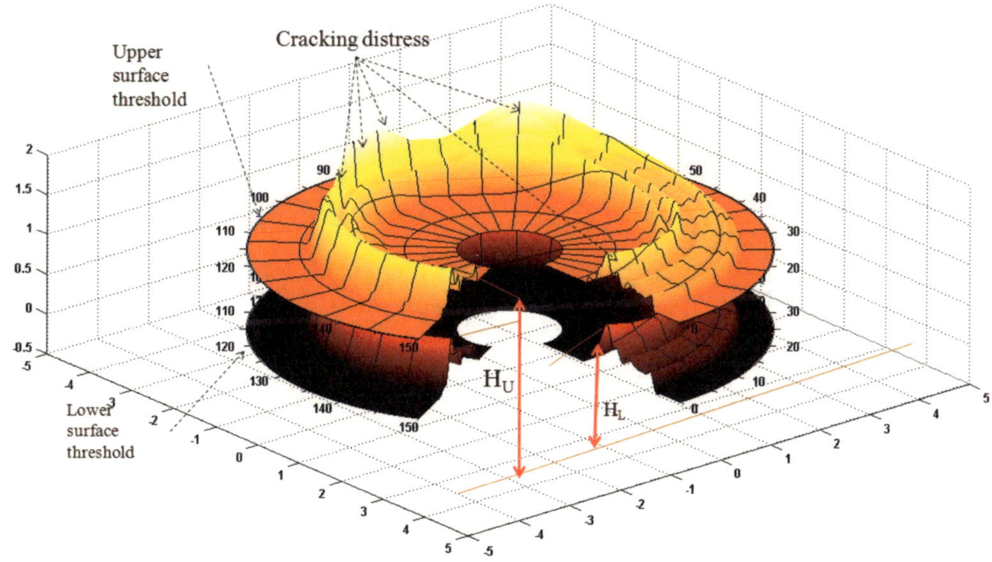

Figure 15. Three dimensional polar domain of FOU for 3D fuzzy sets, (3D PFOU)

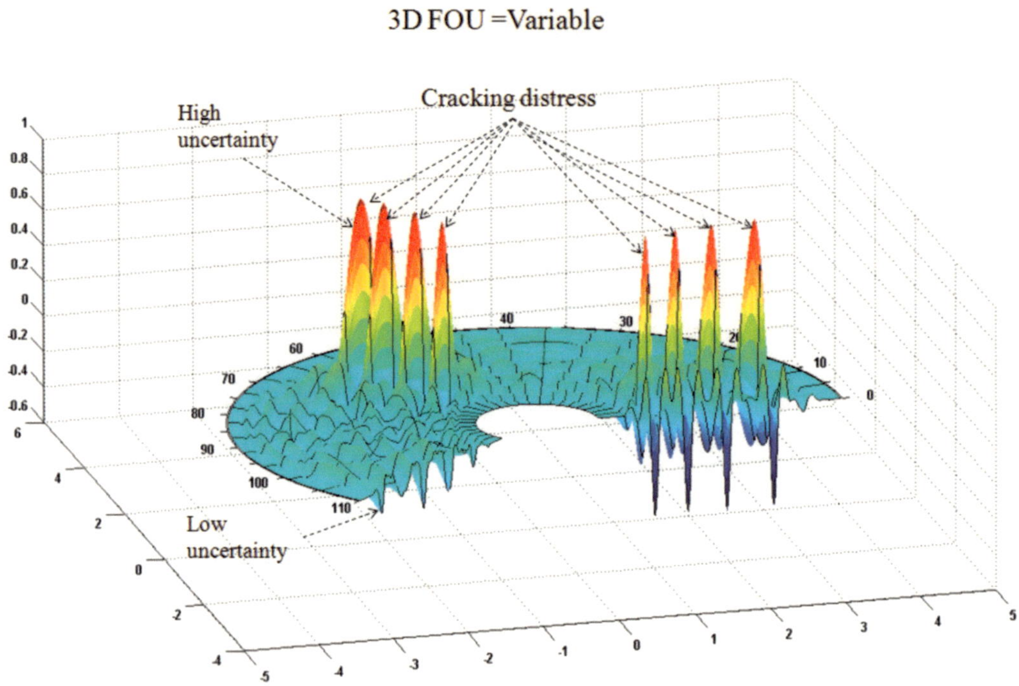

Figure 16. Example of Three polar FOU for 3D fuzzy sets, (3D PFOU) using proposed algorithm

1. **IF** $\mu_{(\rho,\theta)}$ consider as a type I polar fuzzy set **Then** $\mu_{u(\rho,\theta)} = \mu_{L(\rho,\theta)}$ **AND** $\tilde{\gamma}(P) = 0$

$$\tilde{\gamma}(P) = \left(\frac{1}{(Area)^{\frac{1}{q}}} \right) \left[\int_0^{2\pi} \int_0^{r} \left| \mu_U(g_{(\rho,\theta)}) - \mu_L(g_{(\rho,\theta)}) \right|^q \right]^{1/q} = 0 \; for \, q \in [1,\infty). \tag{44}$$

2. ***IF*** $\left| \mu_{u(\rho,\theta)} - \mu_{L(\rho,\theta)} \right| = 1$ (high ambiguity) ***Then*** $\tilde{\gamma}(\tilde{P}) = 1$

$$\tilde{\gamma}(P) = \left(\frac{1}{(Area)^{\frac{1}{q}}} \right) \left[\int_0^{2\pi} \int_0^{r} \left| \mu_U(g_{(\rho,\theta)}) - \mu_L(g_{(\rho,\theta)}) \right|^q \right]^{1/q} = 1 \; for \, q \in [1,\infty). \tag{45}$$

3. $\tilde{\gamma}(\tilde{P}) = \tilde{\gamma}(\tilde{\bar{P}})$. Where $(\tilde{\bar{P}})$ is type II fuzzy set and it's complement set can be determined by 1- $\mu_{u(\rho,\theta)}$ and 1- $\mu_{L(\rho,\theta)}$, therefore complement set defined as follow

$$\tilde{\tilde{P}} = \left\{ x, \mu_{u(\rho,\theta)}, \mu_{u(\rho,\theta)} \middle| \begin{array}{c} 1 - \left(\left[v_{(3DPRT)(\rho,\theta)}^{h} \right] \Big/ \max\left[v_{(3DPRT)(\rho,\theta)}^{h} \right] \right)^{\frac{1}{h}} + H_U \\ , \\ 1 - \left(\left[v_{(3DPRT)(\rho,\theta)}^{h} \right] \Big/ \max\left[v_{(3DPRT)(\rho,\theta)}^{h} \right] \right)^{\frac{1}{h}} + H_L \end{array} \right\} \tag{46}$$

Where $H_U = H_L = 0$, for the complement set, the ultrafuzziness $\tilde{\gamma}$ is equal:

$$\tilde{\gamma}\left(\tilde{\tilde{P}}\right) = \left(\frac{1}{(Area)^{\frac{1}{q}}} \right) \left[\int_0^{2\pi} \int_0^{r} \left| 1 - \mu_U(g_{(\rho,\theta)}) - 1 + \mu_L(g_{(\rho,\theta)}) \right|^q \right]^{1/q} = \tilde{\gamma}\left(\tilde{P}\right) for\, q \in [1, \infty) \tag{47}$$

4. ***IF*** $3DPFOU_{(\rho,\theta)} < 3DPFOU_{(d,c)}$ ***Then*** $\tilde{\gamma}\left(\tilde{P}_{(\rho,\theta)}\right) < \tilde{\gamma}\left(\tilde{P}_{(d,c)}\right)$.

4.2.2. Finding the optimum interval 3D PMF

The general approach for 3DMF based on upper and lower MF is equal:

$$\xi_P = \left[-\frac{\tilde{\gamma}(\rho,\theta)}{2} \right], IT2\,PMF(\rho,\theta) = \left[\mu_L\left(g_{\rho,\theta}\right) - \xi_P \right], OR \left[\mu_U\left(g_{\rho,\theta}\right) + \xi_P \right] \tag{48}$$

Where (ξ_P) is polar ultra fuzzy coefficient and $\tilde{\gamma}(\rho,\theta)$ *is* ultra fuzzy value for $\mu_{u(\rho,\theta)}$ and $\mu_{L(\rho,\theta)}$, in upper and lower bound. For example, Fig.16 presents the principle polar memberships function of the interval type 2 polar fuzzy sets in position (ρ,θ).

5. Polar fuzzy type-2 approximate reasoning

In this part, basic theory of fuzzy polar rule interpolation in fuzzy rule based will be presented for polar membership's function of type -2 fuzzy sets. Lets us show polar fuzzy rules with multiple antecedent and single consequent based on T2 PMF rules, Multi Input Single Output (MISO):

***Rule 1*:** **If** X_1 is $(\overset{=}{PA})_{11}$ & X_2 is $(\overset{=}{PA})_{12}$ & … & X_m is $(\overset{=}{PA})_{1m}$ **Then** Y is $(\overset{=}{PC})_1$

***Rule 2*:** **If** X_1 is $(\overset{=}{PA})_{21}$ & X_2 is $(\overset{=}{PA})_{22}$ & … & X_m is $(\overline{\overline{PA}})_{2m}$ **Then** Y is $(\overset{=}{PC})_2$

***Rule n*:** **If** X_1 is $(\overset{=}{PA})_{n1}$ & X_2 is $(\overset{=}{PA})_{n2}$ & … & X_m is $(\overset{=}{PA})_{nm}$ **Then** Y is $(\overset{=}{PC})_n$

Where X_p denotes the pth T2-PFM antecedent and Y denote the T2- PFM consequence. $(\overset{=}{PA})_{nm}$ is the n,m th consequence of T2-PFM fuzzy set of Rule n. According polar MISO method, fuzzy interpolative polar reasoning result which denoted by $\left(\overset{=}{P}\right)$ can be extracted based on observation polar fuzzy set $\left(\overset{=}{O}\right)$.

***Observation*:** **If** X_1 is $(\overset{=}{O})_1$ & X_2 is $(\overset{=}{O})_2$ & … & X_m is $(\overset{=}{O})_m$

***Conclusions*:** $\overset{=}{O}$ is $\overset{=}{P}$.

This method at the first glance, is similar to method which proposed by Chen & Chang (2011) under the title of "fuzzy rule interpolation based on principle membership functions and uncertainty grad function of interval type-2 fuzzy sets"; however, the main difference between our proposed method with their method relay in type decreasing (Chen & Chang, 2011). Based on Chen & Chang (2011) method first type -2 reduced by type-1, then MISO applied, but in our method first MISO applied separately on upper and lower. After that the type-2 polar reasoning result which denoted by $\left(\overset{=}{P}\right)$ extracted and interval 3D PMF calculated based on section 4.2 theories. This method can be expanded for Multi Input Multi Output (MIMO) systems based on polar T2 PMF's. For example lets us show polar fuzzy rules with multiple antecedents and multiple consequent based on T2 PMF rules, Multi Input Multi Output (MIMO):

***Rule 1*:** **If** X_1 is $(\overset{=}{PA})_{11}$ & … & X_m is $(\overset{=}{PA})_{1m}$ **Then** Y is $(\overset{=}{PC})_{11}$ & $(\overset{=}{PC})_{12}$ & …& $(\overset{=}{PC})_{1r}$

***Rule 2*:** **If** X_1 is $(\overset{=}{PA})_{21}$ & … & X_m is $(\overset{=}{PA})_{2m}$ **Then** Y is $(\overset{=}{PC})_{21}$ & $(\overset{=}{PC})_{22}$ & …& $(\overset{=}{PC})_{2r}$

***Rule n*:** **If** X_1 is $(\overset{=}{PA})_{n1}$ & … & X_m is $(\overset{=}{PA})_{nm}$ **Then** Y is $(\overset{=}{PC})_{n1}$ & $(\overset{=}{PC})_{n2}$ & …& $(\overset{=}{PC})_{nr}$

***Observation*:** **If** X_1 is $(\overset{=}{O})_1$ & … & X_m is $(\overset{=}{O})_r$

***Conclusions*:** $\overset{=}{O}$ is $\overset{=}{P}_1$ & $\overset{=}{P}_2$ & …& $\overset{=}{P}_r$.

where, such as polar MISO, X_p denotes the pth T2-PFM antecedent and Y denote the T2- PFM consequence which expanded in $(\overset{=}{PC})_{nr}$, r denote the number of consequence in rule n.

$(\overset{=}{PA})_{nm}$ is the n,m th consequence of T2-PFM fuzzy set of Rule n. According polar MIMO method, fuzzy interpolative polar reasoning result which denoted by $\left(\overset{=}{P_r}\right)$ can be extracted based on observation polar fuzzy set $\left(\overset{=}{O}\right)$ in window r for conscience r.

Logical and Mamdani, in the linguistic models considered as prepositions. The general form of these linguistic rules shows as:

Mamdani:

$$\textbf{If } X_1 \text{ is } \left(\overset{=}{PA}\right)_{n1} \ \& \ldots \& \ X_m \text{ is } \left(\overset{=}{PA}\right)_{nm} \quad \textbf{Then } \text{Y is } \left(\overset{=}{PC}\right)_{n1} \ \& \left(\overset{=}{PC}\right)_{n2} \ \& \ldots \& \left(\overset{=}{PC}\right)_{nr}$$

Logical:

$$\textbf{If } X_1 \text{ is } \left\| \overline{\left(\overline{\overline{PA}}\right)_{n1}} \right\| \ \& \ldots \& \ X_m \text{ is } \left\| \overline{\left(\overline{\overline{PA}}\right)_{nm}} \right\| \textbf{Then } \text{Y is } \left(\overset{=}{PC}\right)_{n1} \ \& \left(\overset{=}{PC}\right)_{n2} \ \& \ldots \& \left(\overset{=}{PC}\right)_{nr}$$

Where $\left(\overset{=}{PA}\right)_{nm}$ is the T2 PFM as an antecedent variable in polar system $\left(\overset{=}{PC}\right)_{nr}$ is the consequent variable, n denotes to number of rule and r denoted to r denote the number of consequences and $\left\| \overline{\left(\overline{\overline{PA}}\right)_{n1}} \right\|$ is complement of the T2 PFM as an antecedent variable in polar system. Concrete effective model proposed by Yager, is a complex method for combination of these two models, presented as follow:

$$\overset{=}{P_y} = \beta(\overset{=}{P_L}) + (1-\beta)(\overset{=}{P_M}) \tag{49}$$

Where $\overset{=}{P_y}$ is the Yager result(complex model), $(\overset{=}{P_L})$ is result of polar type-2 fuzzy under logical model, $\overset{=}{P_M}$ is consequents of mamdani model and β is control factor which move from 0 to 1. (Fazel et al. 2009). The defuzzication method for every θ must be computed based on theory which presented in section 4.2. Defuzzification agent in polar system constructed as three steps,

Step 1. Calculate the center of area inθ, in which θ defined from 0, to 2π (Gold Veins Root)
Step 2. Plot the fuzzy Gold veins determined from first step.
Step 3. Calculate the center of Gold veins and consider it as defuzzify conclusion result.

In step 1, center of area or center of gravity can be calculated in polar system using eq.38, which is a most common model used :

$$C(\theta)=\left(\frac{1}{Area(\theta)}\right)\left[\int_0^r \left|\mu_U\left(g_{(\rho,\theta)}\right).\rho-\mu_L\left(g_{(\rho,\theta)}\right).\rho\right| d\rho.\right] \tag{50}$$

and

$$C(\theta)_m=\left(\frac{1}{Area(\theta)^q}\right)\left[\int_0^r \left|\left(\mu_U\left(g_{(\rho,\theta)}\right)\right)^q.\rho-\left(\mu_L\left(g_{(\rho,\theta)}\right)\right)^q.\rho\right| d\rho\right] \tag{51}$$

Gold Veins Root is a vector consist of paired $(\theta,C(\theta))$, which is shows the direction center of gravity and it present a useful information from membership function variance and crisp result without type reduction. $C(\theta)_m$ is a modified Gold Veins Root that can be control the final defuzzication result, in which q play a defuzzifer role. An example of Gold Veins Root extracted from polar T2 PMF is depicted in Fig.17. Two result from original and modified center of gravity by q=3, present in Fig 17.

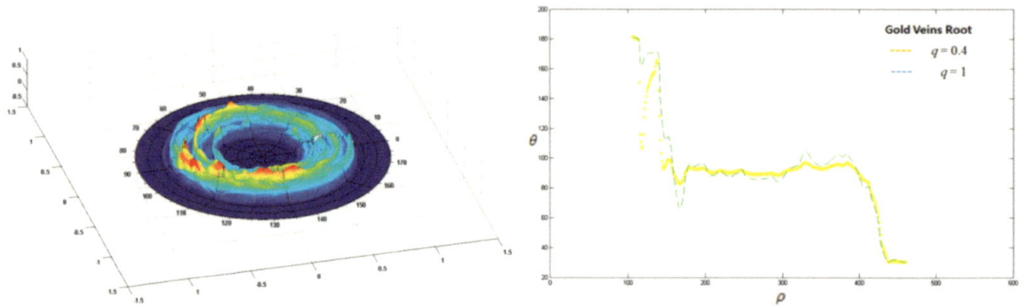

Figure 17. Gold Veins Root in T2 PMF

In order to effectively implementation and test proposed model in some applications such as prediction problem and pattern recognition, such as the other models in fuzzy, we need set in motion to product a crisp result. We chose a heuristic function to generate a best crisp defuuzy value from Gold Veins Root, based on Eq.51

$$C=\left[\frac{\max(GVR)-\min(GVR)}{2}\right] \tag{52}$$

For the case Fig.18, C=96.33 worth in blurred section from $\rho=200,400$, provided good prediction orientation and radios for extension of T2 PFM. Now we present a logical method for type -2 in 3D techniques. Remove type reduction; turn T2 PMF as faster than existing techniques and to be more accurate model for type-2 inference techniques because of combination Logical & Mamdani models.

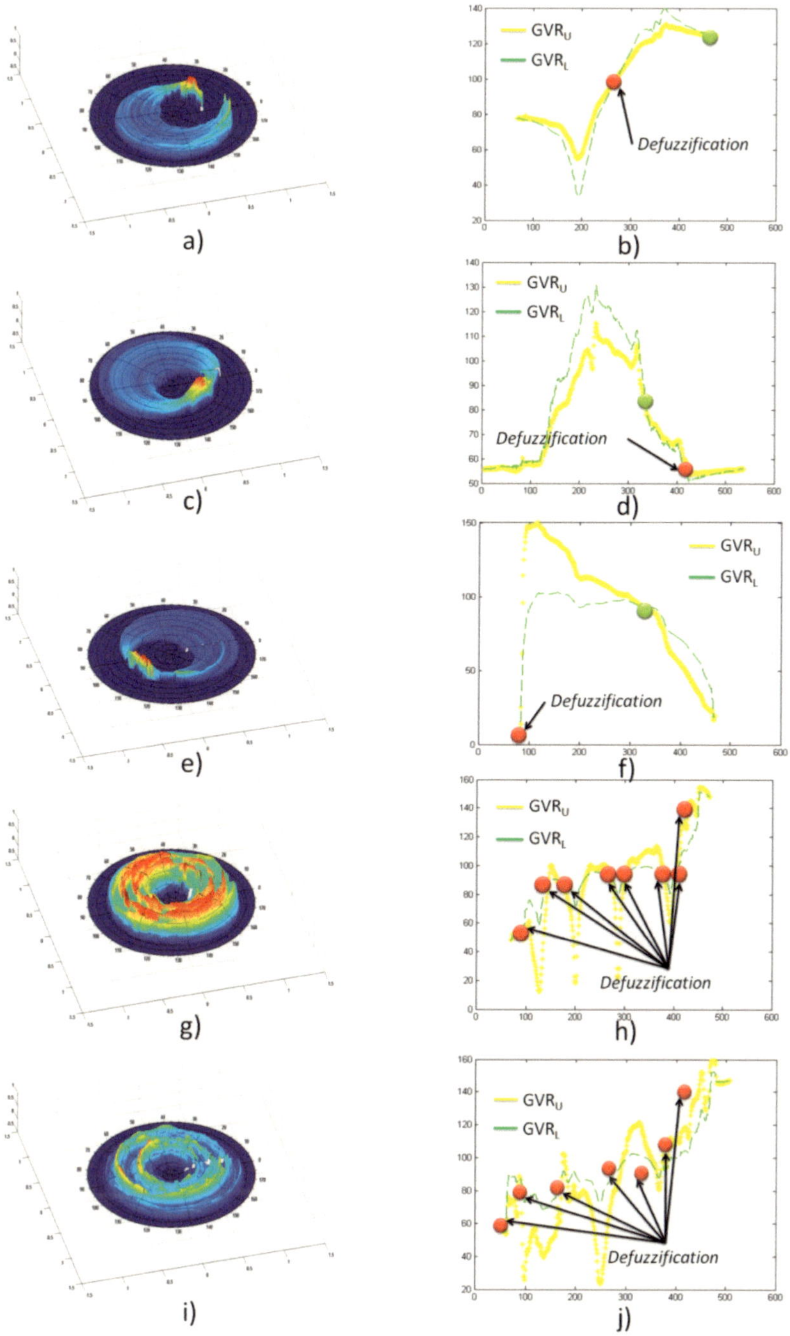

Figure 18. a) Input T2 PMF longitudinal cracking, b)Final difuzzification points longitudinal Cracking, c) Input T2 PMF transverse cracking, d)Final difuzzification points transverse Cracking, e) Input T2PMF diagonal cracking, f)Final difuzzification points diagonal Cracking, g) Input T2 PMF block cracking, h)Final difuzzification points block Cracking, i) Input T2 PMF aligator cracking, j)Final difuzzification points alligator Cracking.

6. Conclusions

In this chapter the basic concepts of new fuzzy sets, three dimensional (3D) memberships and how they are applied in the design of type-1 and type-2 fuzzy thresholding in control systems are presented. The robustness of a system highly depends on automatic fuzzification and membership functions shape and defuzzification. The related methodology and theoretical base are discussed, using real examples in automatic control in civil engineering. Selection of a supper membership function is a golden key in fuzzy controls. A robust method to consider the uncertainty of membership values by using flexible thresholding for controller problems proposed in the special a polar domain presented in this chapter. Different fuzzy membership functions may have various impacts on the systems and, then, different thresholds in control problems. To solve this problem, type II fuzzy thresholding is recommended. The upper and lower membership functions promote this dilemma; however the figure of uncertainty (FOU) has a fixed value that is equal to one, in all the upper and lower membership function. Type-2 fuzzy logic can effectively improve the control characteristic by using FOU of the membership functions.

A new fuzzy thresholding (flexible thresholding) technique developed, which processes threshold as a flexible type-2 fuzzy sets. Experimental results are provided in order to demonstrate the usefulness of the proposed approach. A review of types of fuzzy threshold methods in control problems provided and their algorithms presented. In type-2 thresholding method, measurement of fuzziness gives a quantitative index to vagueness. To quantify the object fuzziness, a suitable membership function based on thresholding for control problems introduced. A measure for ultra-fuzziness in 3D fuzzy model is proposed. A new method for thresholding algorithm based on 3D type-2 fuzzy and selection the optimum thresholding in 3D surface are addressed. By an example the validity of novel fuzzy algorithm in control systems, based on three dimensional membership functions demonstrated.

This paper presents a new type of fuzzy membership functions and uncertainly grade in the frame of polar systems. The proposed method can be used and generalized for several problems; however in this paper we present implementation of polar fuzzy type-2(PFT2) as a part of Hybrid expert system for pavement distress detection and classification.

Vast applications are predicted this fuzzy reasoning. The central idea of this work was to introduce the application of polar type II fuzzy sets.

The most important aspect of the proposed model is the ability of self-organization of the membership function and initial height platform without requiring programming.

Additional experiments reinforced this conclusion. More extensive investigations on other measures of ultrafuzziness and the effect of parameters influencing the width/length of FOU should certainly be conducted.

Author details

M.H. Fazel Zarandi
Department of Industrial Engineering, Amirkabir University of Technology, Tehran, Iran

Fereidoon Moghadas Nejad and Hamzeh Zakeri
Department of Civil and Environmental Engineering, Amirkabir University of Technology, Tehran, Iran

7. References

A Mora, P.M.Vieira, Manivannan.A and Fonseca.J.M, Automated Drusen Detection in Retinal Images using Analytical Modelling Algorithms, *BioMedical Engineering OnLine* 2011,

A.Kaufmann, *Introduction to the Theory of Fuzzy Subsets—Fundamental Theoretical Elements* vol. 1, Academic Press, New York (1975).

C. Hwang, F. Rhee, An interval type-2 fuzzy C spherical shells algorithm, in: Proceedings of the 2004 IEEE International Conference on Fuzzy Systems, 2004, pp. 1117–1122.

C. Hwang, F. Rhee, Uncertain fuzzy clustering: interval type-2 fuzzy approach to C-means, IEEE Transactions on Fuzzy Systems 15 (1) (2007) 107–120.

C. Yang, N. Bose, Generating fuzzy membership function with self-organizing feature map, Pattern Recognition Letters 27 (5) (2006) 356–365.

Choi, B.I., Rhee,C.H. Interval type-2 fuzzy membership function generation methods for pattern recognition, Information Sciences 179 (2009) 2102–2122.

D.Culpin: Calculation of cubic smoothing splines for equally spaced data. Numerische Mathematik 1986, 48:627-638.

F. Rhee, B. Choi, Interval type-2 fuzzy membership function design and its application to radial basis function neural networks, in: Proceedings of the 2007 IEEE International Conference on Fuzzy Systems, 2007, pp. 2047–2052.

F. Rhee, C. Hwang, A type-2 fuzzy C-means clustering algorithm, in: Proceedings of the 2001 Joint Conference IFSA/NAFIPS, 2001, pp. 1919–1926.

F. Rhee, C. Hwang, An interval type-2 fuzzy K-nearest neighbor, in: Proceedings of the 2003 IEEE International Conference on Fuzzy Systems, 2003, pp.802–807.

F. Rhee, C. Hwang, An interval type-2 fuzzy perceptron, in: Proceedings of the 2002 IEEE International Conference on Fuzzy Systems, 2002, pp. 1331–1335.

F. Rhee, Uncertain fuzzy clustering: insights and recommendations, IEEE Computational Intelligence Magazine 2 (1) (2007) 44–56.

F.Moghadas Nejad, , H.Zakeri, , 2011b. An optimum feature extraction method based on wavelet radon transform and dynamic neural network for pavement distress classification. Expert Syst. Appl. 38, 9442 9460.

F.Moghadas Nejad, H.Zakeri, 2011c. A comparison of multiresolution methods for detection and isolation of pavement distress. Expert Syst.Appl.38,2857-2872.

F.Moghadas Nejad, H.Zakeri, 2011a. An expert system based on wavelet transform and radon neural network for pavement distress classification .Expert Syst. Appl. 38,7088 7101.

H. Hagras, A hierarchical type-2 fuzzy logic control architecture for autonomous mobile robots, IEEE Transactions on Fuzzy Systems 12 (4) (2004) 524–539.

H.R Tizhoosh., previous Image thresholdingnext using type-2 fuzzy sets, Pattern Recognition 38 (2005), pp. 2363–2372.

H.R.Tizhoosh, G. Krell, T. Lilienblum, C.J. Moore and B. Michaelis, Enhancement and associative restoration of electronic portal images in radiotherapy, *Int. J. Med. Informatics* 49 (1998) (2), pp. 157–171.

Ioannis K. Vlachos, George D. Sergiadis, Comment on: "Image thresholding using type II fuzzy sets", Pattern Recognition, Volume 41, Issue 5, May 2008, Pages 1810-1811.

J.M.Mendel, Uncertain Rule-Based Fuzzy Logic Systems, Prentice-Hall, Englewood Cliffs, NJ (2001).

M. Makrehchi, O. Basir, M. Karnel, Generation of fuzzy membership function using information theory measures and genetic algorithm, Lecture Notes in Computer Science 275 (2003) 603–610.

M.H.Fazel Zarandi, M.Zarinbal, I.B.Türksen: Type-II Fuzzy Possibilistic C-Mean Clustering. IFSA/EUSFLAT Conf. 2009: 30-35.

M.Qiguang, L.Juan, L.Weisheng, S.Junjie, W.Yiding, Three novel invariant moments based on radon and polar harmonic transforms, Optics Communications 285 (2012) 1044–1048.

N. Karnik, J. Mendel, Applications of type-2 fuzzy logic systems to forecasting of time series, Information Sciences 120 (1999) 89–111

P.Ensafi, , H.R.Tizhoosh, Type-2 Fuzzy image enhancement International Conference on Image Analysis and Recognition- ICIAR2005, Springer Lecture Notes in Computer Science series (Springer LCNS), Toronto, Canada, Sep. 28-30 (2005).

Q. Liang, J. Mendel, Interval type-2 fuzzy logic systems: Theory and Design, IEEE Transactions on Fuzzy Systems 8 (5) (2000) 535–550.

Q. Liang, J. Mendel, Overcoming time-varying co-channel interference using type-2 fuzzy adaptive filter, IEEE Transactions on Circuits and Systems-II:Analog and Digital Signal Processing 47 (2000) 1419–1428.

R. John, Embedded interval valued type-2 fuzzy sets, in: Proceedings of the 2002 IEEE International Conference on Fuzzy Systems, (2002), pp. 1316–1320.

R.N Pal and .C Bezdek., measuring fuzzy uncertainty, IEEE , transactions on fuzzy systems, , 1994,vol. 2, no. 2, PP.107–118.

S. Medasani, J. Kim, R. Krishnapuram, An overview of membership function generation techniques for pattern recognition, International Journalof Approximate Reasoning 19 (3–4) (1998) 391–417.

S. Wang, Generating fuzzy membership functions: a monotonic neural network, Fuzzy Sets and Systems 61 (1) (1994) 71–81.

S.K. Pal and C.A. Murthy, Fuzzy thresholding: mathematical framework bound functions and weighted moving average technique, *Pattern Recognition Lett.* 11 (1990), pp. 197–206.

Z.Daqi, S,Qu. L,He. and S.Sh. Automatic Ridgelet image enhancement algorithm for road crack image based on fuzzy entropy and fuzzy divergence. (2009),*In press, Optics and Lasers in Engineering.*

Chapter 5

Fuzzy Control of Nonlinear Systems with General Performance Criteria

Xin Wang, Edwin E. Yaz, James Long and Tim Miller

Additional information is available at the end of the chapter

http://dx.doi.org/10.5772/48298

1. Introduction

Research on control of non-linear systems over the years has produced many results: control based on linearization, global feedback linearization, non-linear H_∞ control, sliding mode control, variable structure control, state dependent Riccati equation control, etc [5]. This chapter will focus on fuzzy control techniques. Fuzzy control systems have recently shown growing popularity in non-linear system control applications. A fuzzy control system is essentially an effective way to decompose the task of non-linear system control into a group of local linear controls based on a set of design-specific model rules. Fuzzy control also provides a mechanism to blend these local linear control problems all together to achieve overall control of the original non-linear system. In this regard, fuzzy control technique has its unique advantage over other kinds of non-linear control techniques. Latest research on fuzzy control systems design is aimed to improve the optimality and robustness of the controller performance by combining the advantage of modern control theory with the Takagi-Sugeno fuzzy model [7–10, 13, 14].

In this chapter, we address the non-linear state feedback control design of both continuous-time and discrete-time non-linear fuzzy control systems using the Linear Matrix Inequality (LMI) approach. We characterize the solution of the non-linear control problem with the LMI, which provides a sufficient condition for satisfying various performance criteria. A preliminary investigation into the LMI approach to non-linear fuzzy control systems can be found in [7, 8, 13]. The purpose behind this novel approach is to convert a non-linear system control problem into a convex optimization problem which is solved by a LMI at each time. The recent development in convex optimization provides efficient algorithms for solving LMIs. If a solution can be expressed in a LMI form, then there exist optimization algorithms providing efficient global numerical solutions [3]. Therefore if the LMI is feasible, then LMI control technique provides globally stable solutions satisfying the corresponding mixed performance criteria [4, 6, 15–20]. We further propose to employ mixed performance criteria to design the controller guaranteeing the quadratic sub-optimality with inherent stability property in combination with dissipative type of disturbance attenuation.

In the following sections, we first introduce the Takagi-Sugeno fuzzy modelling for non-linear systems in both continuous time and discrete time. We then propose the general performance criteria in section 3. Then, the LMI control solutions are derived to characterize the optimal and robust fuzzy control of continuous time and discrete time non-linear systems, respectively. The inverted pendulum system control is used as an illustrative example to demonstrate the effectiveness and robustness of our proposed approaches.

The following notation is used in this work: $x \in \mathcal{R}^n$ denotes n-dimensional real vector with norm $\|x\| = (x^T x)^{1/2}$ where $(.)^T$ indicates transpose. $A \geq 0$ for a symmetric matrix denotes a positive semi-definite matrix. $\mathcal{L}_2$ and l_2 denotes the space of infinite sequences of finite dimensional random vectors with finite energy, i.e. $\int_0^\infty \|x_t\|^2 < \infty$ in continuous-time, and $\Sigma_{k=0}^{\infty}\|x_k\|^2 < \infty$ in discrete-time, respectively.

2. Takagi-Sugeno system model

The importance of the Takagi-Sugeno fuzzy system model is that it provides an effective way to decompose a complicated non-linear system into local dynamical relations and express those local dynamics of each fuzzy implication rule by a linear system model. The overall fuzzy non-linear system model is achieved by fuzzy "blending" of the linear system models, so that the overall non-linear control performance is achieved. Both of the continuous-time and the discrete-time system models are summarized below.

2.1. Continuous-time Takagi-Sugeno system model

The ith rule of the Takagi-Sugeno fuzzy model can be expressed by the following forms:

Model Rule i:
If $\varphi_1(t)$ is M_{i1},$\varphi_2(t)$ is M_{i2},... and $\varphi_p(t)$ is M_{ip},
Then the input-affine continuous-time fuzzy system equation is:

$$\begin{aligned} \dot{x}(t) &= A_i x(t) + B_i u(t) + F_i w(t) \\ y(t) &= C_i x(t) + D_i u(t) + Z_i w(t) \\ & i = 1,2,3,...,r \end{aligned} \tag{1}$$

where $x(t) \in \mathcal{R}^n$ is the state vector, $u(t) \in \mathcal{R}^m$ is the control input vector, $y(t) \in \mathcal{R}^q$ is the performance output vector, $w(t) \in \mathcal{R}^s$ is $\mathcal{L}_2$ type of disturbance, r is the total number of model rules, M_{ij} is the fuzzy set. The coefficient matrices are $A_i \in \mathcal{R}^{n\times n}, B_i \in \mathcal{R}^{n\times m}, F_i \in \mathcal{R}^{n\times s}, C_i \in \mathcal{R}^{q\times n}, D_i \in \mathcal{R}^{q\times m}, Z_i \in \mathcal{R}^{q\times s}$. And $\varphi_1, ..., \varphi_p$ are known premise variables, which can be functions of state variables, external disturbance and time.

It is assumed that the premises are not the function of the input vector $u(t)$, which is needed to avoid the defuzzification process of fuzzy controller. If we use $\varphi(t)$ to denote the vector containing all the individual elements $\varphi_1(t), \varphi_2(t), ..., \varphi_p(t)$, then the overall fuzzy system is

$$\begin{aligned} \dot{x}(t) &= \frac{\sum_{i=1}^r g_i(\varphi(t))[A_i x(t) + B_i u(t) + F_i w(t)]}{\sum_{i=1}^r g_i(\varphi(t))} = \sum_{i=1}^r h_i(\varphi(t))[A_i x(t) + B_i u(t) + F_i w(t)] \\ y(t) &= \frac{\sum_{i=1}^r g_i(\varphi(t))[C_i x(t) + D_i u(t) + Z_i w(t)]}{\sum_{i=1}^r g_i(\varphi(t))} = \sum_{i=1}^r h_i(\varphi(t))[C_i x(t) + D_i u(t) + Z_i w(t)] \end{aligned} \tag{2}$$

where

$$\varphi(t) = [\varphi_1(t), \varphi_2(t), ..., \varphi_p(t)] \tag{3}$$

$$g_i(\varphi(t)) = \prod_{j=1}^{p} M_{ij}(\varphi_j(t)) \tag{4}$$

$$h_i(\varphi(t)) = \frac{g_i(\varphi(t))}{\sum_{i=1}^{r} g_i(\varphi(t))} \tag{5}$$

for all time t. The term $M_{ij}(\varphi_j(t))$ is the grade membership function of $\phi_j(t)$ in M_{ij}.

Since, the following properties hold

$$\begin{aligned} &\sum_{i=1}^{r} g_i(\varphi(t)) > 0 \\ &g_i(\varphi(t)) \geq 0, i = 1, 2, 3, ..., r \end{aligned} \tag{6}$$

We have

$$\begin{aligned} &\sum_{i=1}^{r} h_i(\varphi(t)) = 1 \\ &h_i(\varphi(t)) \geq 0, i = 1, 2, 3, ..., r \end{aligned} \tag{7}$$

for all time t.

It is assumed that the state feedback is available and the non-linear state feedback control input is given by

$$u(t) = -\sum_{i=1}^{r} h_i(\varphi(t))K_i x(t) \tag{8}$$

Substituting this into the system and performance output equation, we have

$$\begin{aligned} \dot{x}(t) &= \sum_{i=1}^{r}\sum_{j=1}^{r} h_i(\varphi(t))h_j(\varphi(t))(A_i - B_i K_j)x(t) + \sum_{i=1}^{r} h_i(\varphi(t))F_i w(t) \\ y(t) &= \sum_{i=1}^{r}\sum_{j=1}^{r} h_i(\varphi(t))h_j(\varphi(t))(C_i - D_i K_j)x(k) + \sum_{i=1}^{r} h_i(\varphi(t))Z_i w(t) \end{aligned} \tag{9}$$

Using the notation

$$\begin{aligned} G_{ij} &= A_i - B_i K_j \\ H_{ij} &= C_i - D_i K_j \end{aligned} \tag{10}$$

then the system equation becomes

$$\begin{aligned} \dot{x}(t) &= \sum_{i=1}^{r}\sum_{j=1}^{r} h_i(\varphi(t))h_j(\varphi(t))G_{ij}x(t) + \sum_{i=1}^{r} h_i(\varphi(t))F_i w(t) \\ y(t) &= \sum_{i=1}^{r}\sum_{j=1}^{r} h_i(\varphi(t))h_j(\varphi(t))H_{ij}x(t) + \sum_{i=1}^{r} h_i(\varphi(t))Z_i w(t) \end{aligned} \tag{11}$$

2.2. Discrete-time Takagi-Sugeno system model

At time step k, the ith rule of the Takagi-Sugeno fuzzy model can be expressed by the following forms:

Model Rule i:
If $\varphi_1(k)$ is M_{i1},$\varphi_2(k)$ is M_{i2},... and $\varphi_p(k)$ is M_{ip},
Then the input-affine discrete-time fuzzy system equation is:

$$\begin{aligned} x(k+1) &= A_i x(k) + B_i u(k) + F_i w(k) \\ y(k) &= C_i x(k) + D_i u(k) + Z_i w(k) \\ i &= 1,2,3,...,r \end{aligned} \tag{12}$$

where $x(k) \in \mathcal{R}^n$ is the state vector, $u(k) \in \mathcal{R}^m$ is the control input vector, $y(k) \in \mathcal{R}^q$ is the performance output vector, $w(k) \in \mathcal{R}^s$ is l_2 type of disturbance, r is the total number of model rules, M_{ij} is the fuzzy set. The coefficient matrices are $A_i \in \mathcal{R}^{n\times n}, B_i \in \mathcal{R}^{n\times m}, F_i \in \mathcal{R}^{n\times s}, C_i \in \mathcal{R}^{q\times n}, D_i \in \mathcal{R}^{q\times m}, Z_i \in \mathcal{R}^{q\times s}$. And $\varphi_1, ..., \varphi_p$ are known premise variables which can be functions of state variables, external disturbance and time.

It is assumed that the premises are not the function of the input vector $u(k)$, which is needed to avoid the defuzzification process of fuzzy controller. If we use $\varphi(k)$ to denote the vector containing all the individual elements $\varphi_1(k), \varphi_2(k), ..., \varphi_p(k)$, then the overall fuzzy system is

$$\begin{aligned} x(k+1) &= \frac{\sum_{i=1}^{r} g_i(\varphi(k))A_i x(k)+B_i u(k)+F_i w(k)}{\sum_{i=1}^{r} g_i(\varphi(k))} = \sum_{i=1}^{r} h_i(\varphi(k))A_i x(k)+B_i u(k)+F_i w(k) \\ y(k) &= \frac{\sum_{i=1}^{r} g_i(\varphi(k))C_i x(k)+D_i u(k)+Z_i w(k)}{\sum_{i=1}^{r} g_i(\varphi(k))} = \sum_{i=1}^{r} h_i(\varphi(k))C_i x(k)+D_i u(k)+Z_i w(k) \end{aligned} \tag{13}$$

where

$$\varphi(k) = [\varphi_1(k), \varphi_2(k), ..., \varphi_p(k)] \tag{14}$$

$$g_i(\varphi(k)) = \prod_{j=1}^{p} M_{ij}(\varphi_j(k)) \tag{15}$$

$$h_i(\varphi(k)) = \frac{g_i(\varphi(k))}{\sum_{i=1}^{r} g_i(\varphi(k))} \tag{16}$$

for all k. The term $M_{ij}(\varphi_j(k))$ is the grade membership function of $\phi_j(k)$ in M_{ij}.

Since, the following properties hold

$$\begin{aligned} \sum_{i=1}^{r} g_i(\varphi(k)) &> 0 \\ g_i(\varphi(k)) &\geq 0, i = 1,2,3,...,r \end{aligned} \tag{17}$$

We have

$$\begin{aligned} \sum_{i=1}^{r} h_i(\varphi(k)) &= 1 \\ h_i(\varphi(k)) &\geq 0, i = 1,2,3,...,r \end{aligned} \tag{18}$$

for all k.

It is assumed that the state feedback is available and the non-linear state feedback control input is given by

$$u(k) = -\sum_{i=1}^{r} h_i(\varphi(k))K_i x(k) \tag{19}$$

Substituting this into the system and performance output equation, we have

$$\begin{aligned} x(k+1) &= \sum_{i=1}^{r}\sum_{j=1}^{r} h_i(\varphi(k))h_j(\varphi(k))(A_i - B_iK_j)x(k) + \sum_{i=1}^{r} h_i(\varphi(k))F_i w(k) \\ y(k) &= \sum_{i=1}^{r}\sum_{j=1}^{r} h_i(\varphi(k))h_j(\varphi(k))(C_i - D_iK_j)x(k) + \sum_{i=1}^{r} h_i(\varphi(k))Z_i w(k) \end{aligned} \tag{20}$$

Using the notation

$$\begin{aligned} G_{ij} &= A_i - B_iK_j \\ H_{ij} &= C_i - D_iK_j \end{aligned} \tag{21}$$

then the system equation becomes

$$\begin{aligned} x(k+1) &= \sum_{i=1}^{r}\sum_{j=1}^{r} h_i(\varphi(k))h_j(\varphi(k))G_{ij}x(k) + \sum_{i=1}^{r} h_i(\varphi(k))F_i w(k) \\ y(k) &= \sum_{i=1}^{r}\sum_{j=1}^{r} h_i(\varphi(k))h_j(\varphi(k))H_{ij}x(k) + \sum_{i=1}^{r} h_i(\varphi(k))Z_i w(k) \end{aligned} \tag{22}$$

3. General performance criteria

In this section, we propose the general performance criteria for non-linear control design, which yields a mixed Non-Linear Quadratic Regular (NLQR) in combination with $\mathcal{H}_\infty$ or dissipative performance index. The commonly used system performance criteria, including bounded-realness, positive-realness, sector boundedness and quadratic cost criterion, become special cases of the general performance criteria. Both the continuous-time and discrete-time general performance criteria are given below:

3.1. Continuous-time general performance criteria

Consider the quadratic Lyapunov function

$$V(t) = x^T(t)Px(t) > 0 \tag{23}$$

for the following difference inequality

$$\dot{V}(t) + x^T(t)Qx(t) + u^T(t)Ru(t) + \alpha y^T(t)y(t) - \beta y^T(t)w(t) + \gamma w^T(t)w(t) \leq 0 \tag{24}$$

with $Q > 0, R > 0$ functions of $x(t)$.

Note that upon integration over time from 0 to T_f, (24) yields

$$V(T_f) + \int_0^{T_f} [(x^T(t)Qx(t) + u^T(t)Ru(t)]dt +$$
$$\int_0^{T_f} [\alpha y^T(t)y(t) - \beta y^T(t)w(t) + \gamma w^T(t)w(t)]dt \leq V(0) \tag{25}$$

By properly specifying the value of weighing matrices Q, R, C_i, D_i, Z_i and α, β, γ, mixed performance criteria can be used in non-linear control design, which yields a mixed Non-linear Quadratic Regulator (NLQR) in combination with dissipative type performance index with disturbance reduction capability. For example, if we take $\alpha = 1, \beta = 0, \gamma < 0$, (25) yields

$$V(T_f) + \int_0^{T_f} [(x^T(t)Qx(t) + u^T(t)Ru(t) + y^T(t)y(t)]dt +$$
$$\leq V(0) - \gamma \int_0^{T_f} [w^T(t)w(t)]dt \tag{26}$$

which is a mixed $NLQR - H_\infty$ Design [16–18].

Other possible performance criteria which can be used in this framework with various design parameters α, β, γ are given in Table.1. Design coefficients α and γ can be maximized or minimized to optimize the controller behavior. It should also be noted that the satisfaction of any of the criteria in Table 1 will also guarantee asymptotic stability of the controlled system.

3.2. Discrete-time general performance criteria

Consider the quadratic Lyapunov function

$$V(k) = x^T(k)Px(k) \tag{27}$$

for the following difference inequality

$$V(k+1) - V(k) + x^T(k)Qx(k) + u^T(k)Ru(k) + \alpha y^T(k)y(k) - \beta y^T(k)w(k) + \gamma w^T(k)w(k) \leq 0 \tag{28}$$

with $Q > 0, R > 0$ functions of $x(k)$.

Note that upon summation over k, (28) yields

$$V(N) + \sum_{k=0}^{N-1} (x^T(k)Qx(k) + u^T(k)Ru(k) + \alpha y^T(k)y(k) - \beta y^T(k)w(k) + \gamma w^T(k)w(k)) \leq V(0) \tag{29}$$

By properly specifying the value of weighing matrices Q, R, C_i, D_i, Z_i and α, β, γ, mixed performance criteria can be used in non-linear control design, which yields a mixed Non-linear Quadratic Regulator (NLQR) in combination with dissipative type performance index with disturbance reduction capability. For example, if we take $\alpha = 1, \beta = 0, \gamma < 0$, (29) yields

$$V(N) + \sum_{k=0}^{N-1} (x^T(k)Qx(k) + u^T(k)Ru(k) + \alpha y^T(k)y(k)) \leq V(0) - \gamma \sum_{k=0}^{N-1} w^T(k)w(k) \tag{30}$$

which is a mixed $NLQR - H_\infty$ Design [16–18]. In (19), γ can be minimized to achieve a smaller $l_2 - l_2$ or H_∞ gain for the closed loop system.

Other possible performance criteria which can be used in this framework with various design parameters α, β, γ are given in Table.1. Design coefficients α and γ can be maximized or minimized to optimize the controller behavior. It should also be noted that the satisfaction of any of the criteria in Table 1 will also guarantee asymptotic stability of the controlled system.

α	β	γ	Performance Criteria
1	0	<0	$NLQR - \mathcal{H}_\infty$ *Design*
0	1	0	$NLQR$ – *Passivity Design*
0	1	>0	$NLQR$ – *Input Strict Passivity Design*
>0	1	0	$NLQR$ – *Output Strict Passivity Design*
>0	1	>0	$NLQR$ – *Very Strict Passivity*

Table 1. Various performance criteria in a general framework

4. Fuzzy LMI control of continuous time non-linear systems with general performance criteria

The main results of this chapter are summarized in section 4 and section 5. The following theorem provides the fuzzy LMI control to the continuous time non-linear systems with general performance criteria.

Theorem 1 Given the system model and performance output (2) and control input (8), if there exist matrices $S = P^{-1} > 0$ for all $t \geq 0$, such that the following LMI holds:

$$\begin{bmatrix} \Lambda_{11} & \Lambda_{12} & \Lambda_{13} & \Lambda_{14} & \Lambda_{15} \\ * & \Lambda_{22} & \Lambda_{23} & 0 & 0 \\ * & * & I & 0 & 0 \\ * & * & * & R^{-1} & 0 \\ * & * & * & * & I \end{bmatrix} \geq 0 \tag{31}$$

where

$$\begin{aligned} \Lambda_{11} &= -\frac{1}{2}[SA_i^T - M_jB_i^T + SA_j^T - M_i^TB_j^T + A_iS - B_iM_j + A_jS - B_jM_i] \\ \Lambda_{12} &= -\frac{1}{2}(F_i + F_j) + \frac{\beta}{4}[SC_i^T - M_jD_i^T + SC_j^T - M_i^TD_j^T] \\ \Lambda_{13} &= \frac{1}{2}\alpha^{1/2}[SC_i^T - M_jD_i^T + SC_j^T - M_i^TD_j^T] \\ \Lambda_{14} &= \frac{1}{2}(M_i^T + M_j^T) \\ \Lambda_{15} &= SQ^{T/2} \\ \Lambda_{22} &= -\gamma I + \frac{1}{2}\beta(Z_i + Z_j)^T \\ \Lambda_{23} &= \frac{1}{2}\alpha^{1/2}[Z_i + Z_j]^T \end{aligned} \tag{32}$$

using the notation

$$M_i = K_i P^{-1} = K_i S \tag{33}$$

then inequality (24) is satisfied.

Proof

By applying system model and performance output (2)(11), and state feedback input (8), the performance index inequality (24) becomes

$$\begin{aligned}
&[\sum_{i=1}^{r}\sum_{j=1}^{r} h_i(\varphi(t))h_j(\varphi(t))G_{ij}x(t) + \sum_{i=1}^{r} h_i(\varphi(t))F_i w(t)]^T P x(t) + \\
&x^T(t)P[\sum_{i=1}^{r}\sum_{j=1}^{r} h_i(\varphi(t))h_j(\varphi(t))G_{ij}x(t) + \sum_{i=1}^{r} h_i(\varphi(t))F_i w(t)] + \\
&x^T(t)Qx(t) + [-\sum_{i=1}^{r} h_i\varphi(t)K_i x(t)]^T R[-\sum_{i=1}^{r} h_i\varphi(t)K_i x(t)] \\
&\alpha[\sum_{i=1}^{r}\sum_{j=1}^{r} h_i(\varphi(t))h_j(\varphi(t))H_{ij}x(t) + \sum_{i=1}^{r} h_i(\varphi(t))Z_i w(t)]^T \\
&\times[\sum_{i=1}^{r}\sum_{j=1}^{r} h_i(\varphi(t))h_j(\varphi(t))H_{ij}x(t) + \sum_{i=1}^{r} h_i(\varphi(t))Z_i w(t)] \\
&-\beta[\sum_{i=1}^{r}\sum_{j=1}^{r} h_i(\varphi(t))h_j(\varphi(t))H_{ij}x(t) + \sum_{i=1}^{r} h_i(\varphi(t))Z_i w(t)]^T \times w(t) \\
&+\gamma w^T(t)w(t) \leq 0
\end{aligned} \tag{34}$$

Inequality (34) is equivalent to

$$\begin{bmatrix} x^T(t) & w^T(t) \end{bmatrix} \times \begin{bmatrix} \Delta_{11} & \Delta_{12} \\ * & \Delta_{22} \end{bmatrix} \times \begin{bmatrix} x(t) \\ w(t) \end{bmatrix} \leq 0 \tag{35}$$

where

$$\begin{aligned}
\Delta_{11} &= (\sum_i\sum_j h_i h_j G_{ij})^T P + P(\sum_i\sum_j h_i h_j G_{ij}) + Q + [\sum_i h_i K_i]^T R[\sum_i h_i K_i] + \\
&\quad \alpha[\sum_i\sum_j h_i h_j H_{ij}]^T[\sum_i\sum_j h_i h_j H_{ij}] \\
\Delta_{12} &= P(\sum_i h_i F_i) + \alpha[\sum_i\sum_j h_i h_j H_{ij}]^T[\sum_i h_i Z_i] - \frac{\beta}{2}[\sum_i\sum_j h_i h_j H_{ij}]^T \\
\Delta_{22} &= \gamma I + \alpha[\sum_i h_i Z_i]^T[\sum_i h_i Z_i] - \beta[\sum_i h_i Z_i]^T
\end{aligned} \tag{36}$$

Inequality (35) can be rewritten as

$$\begin{bmatrix} \Theta_{11} & \Theta_{12} \\ * & \Theta_{22} \end{bmatrix} - \alpha \begin{bmatrix} [\sum_i\sum_j h_i h_j H_{ij}]^T \\ [\sum_i h_i Z_i]^T \end{bmatrix} \times [[\sum_i\sum_j h_i h_j H_{ij}]\ [\sum_i h_i Z_i]] \geq 0 \tag{37}$$

where

$$\Theta_{11} = -(\sum_i \sum_j h_i h_j G_{ij})^T P - P(\sum_i \sum_j h_i h_j G_{ij}) - Q - [\sum_i h_i K_i]^T R [\sum_i h_i K_i]$$

$$\Theta_{12} = -P(\sum_i h_i F_i) + \frac{\beta}{2}[\sum_i \sum_j h_i h_j H_{ij}]^T$$

$$\Theta_{22} = -\gamma I + \beta[\sum_i h_i Z_i]^T \tag{38}$$

By applying Schur complement to inequality (37), we have

$$\begin{bmatrix} \Theta_{11} & \Theta_{12} & \alpha^{1/2}[\sum_i \sum_j h_i h_j H_{ij}]^T \\ * & \Theta_{22} & \alpha^{1/2}[\sum_i h_i Z_i]^T \\ * & * & I \end{bmatrix} \geq 0 \tag{39}$$

Similarly, inequality (39) can also be written as

$$\begin{bmatrix} \Phi_{11} & \Phi_{12} & \alpha^{1/2}[\sum_i \sum_j h_i h_j H_{ij}]^T \\ * & \Phi_{22} & \alpha^{1/2}[\sum_i h_i Z_i]^T \\ * & * & I \end{bmatrix} - \begin{bmatrix} [\sum_i h_i K_i]^T \\ 0 \\ 0 \end{bmatrix} R \left[[\sum_i h_i K_i] \; 0 \; 0 \right] \geq 0 \tag{40}$$

where

$$\Phi_{11} = -(\sum_i \sum_j h_i h_j G_{ij})^T P - P(\sum_i \sum_j h_i h_j G_{ij}) - Q$$

$$\Phi_{12} = -P(\sum_i h_i F_i) + \frac{\beta}{2}[\sum_i \sum_j h_i h_j H_{ij}]^T$$

$$\Phi_{22} = -\gamma I + \beta[\sum_i h_i Z_i]^T \tag{41}$$

By applying Schur complement again to (40), we have

$$\begin{bmatrix} \Phi_{11} & \Phi_{12} & \alpha^{1/2}[\sum_i \sum_j h_i h_j H_{ij}]^T & [\sum_i h_i K_i]^T \\ * & \Phi_{22} & \alpha^{1/2}[\sum_i h_i Z_i]^T & 0 \\ * & * & I & 0 \\ * & * & * & R^{-1} \end{bmatrix} \geq 0 \tag{42}$$

Equivalently, we have

$$\sum_i \sum_j h_i h_j \times \begin{bmatrix} \Gamma_{11} & \Gamma_{12} & \Gamma_{13} & \Gamma_{14} \\ * & \Gamma_{22} & \Gamma_{23} & 0 \\ * & * & I & 0 \\ * & * & * & R^{-1} \end{bmatrix} \geq 0 \tag{43}$$

where

$$\Gamma_{11} = -\frac{1}{2}[(A_i - B_iK_j) + (A_j - B_jK_i)]^T P - \frac{1}{2}P[(A_i - B_iK_j) + (A_j - B_jK_i)] - Q$$
$$\Gamma_{12} = -\frac{1}{2}P(F_i + F_j) + \frac{\beta}{4}[(C_i - D_iK_j) + (C_j - D_jK_i)]^T$$
$$\Gamma_{13} = -\frac{1}{2}\alpha^{1/2}[(C_i - D_iK_j) + (C_j - D_jK_i)]^T$$
$$\Gamma_{14} = -\frac{1}{2}(K_i + K_j)^T$$
$$\Gamma_{22} = -\gamma I + \frac{1}{2}\beta(Z_i + Z_j)^T$$
$$\Gamma_{23} = \frac{1}{2}\alpha^{1/2}(Z_i + Z_j)^T \quad (44)$$

Therefore, we have the following LMI

$$\begin{bmatrix} \Gamma_{11} & \Gamma_{12} & \Gamma_{13} & \Gamma_{14} \\ * & \Gamma_{22} & \Gamma_{23} & 0 \\ * & * & I & 0 \\ * & * & * & R^{-1} \end{bmatrix} \geq 0 \quad (45)$$

By multiplying both sides of the LMI above by the block diagonal matrix $diag\{S, I, I, I\}$, where $S = P^{-1}$, and using the notation

$$M_i = K_i P^{-1} = K_i S \quad (46)$$

we obtain

$$\begin{bmatrix} X_{11} & X_{12} & X_{13} & X_{14} \\ * & X_{22} & X_{23} & 0 \\ * & * & I & 0 \\ * & * & * & R^{-1} \end{bmatrix} \geq 0 \quad (47)$$

where

$$X_{11} = -\frac{1}{2}[SA_i^T - M_jB_i^T + SA_j^T - M_i^TB_j^T + A_iS - B_iM_j + A_jS - B_jM_i] - SQS$$
$$X_{12} = -\frac{1}{2}(F_i + F_j) + \frac{\beta}{4}[SC_i^T - M_j^TD_i^T + SC_j^T - M_i^TD_j^T]$$
$$X_{13} = \frac{1}{2}\alpha^{1/2}[SC_i^T - M_j^TD_i^T + SC_j^T - M_i^TD_j^T]$$
$$X_{14} = \frac{1}{2}(M_i^T + M_j^T)$$
$$X_{22} = -\gamma I + \frac{1}{2}\beta(Z_i + Z_j)^T$$
$$X_{23} = \frac{1}{2}\alpha^{1/2}(Z_i + Z_j)^T \quad (48)$$

By applying Schur complement again, the final LMI is derived

$$\begin{bmatrix} \Lambda_{11} & \Lambda_{12} & \Lambda_{13} & \Lambda_{14} & \Lambda_{15} \\ * & \Lambda_{22} & \Lambda_{23} & 0 & 0 \\ * & * & I & 0 & 0 \\ * & * & * & R^{-1} & 0 \\ * & * & * & * & I \end{bmatrix} \geq 0 \tag{49}$$

where

$$\Lambda_{11} = -\frac{1}{2}[SA_i^T - M_jB_i^T + SA_j^T - M_i^TB_j^T + A_iS - B_iM_j + A_jS - B_jM_i]$$

$$\Lambda_{12} = -\frac{1}{2}(F_i + F_j) + \frac{\beta}{4}[SC_i^T - M_jD_i^T + SC_j^T - M_i^TD_j^T]$$

$$\Lambda_{13} = \frac{1}{2}\alpha^{1/2}[SC_i^T - M_jD_i^T + SC_j^T - M_i^TD_j^T]$$

$$\Lambda_{14} = \frac{1}{2}(M_i^T + M_j^T)$$

$$\Lambda_{15} = SQ^{T/2}$$

$$\Lambda_{22} = -\gamma I + \frac{1}{2}\beta(Z_i + Z_j)^T$$

$$\Lambda_{23} = \frac{1}{2}\alpha^{1/2}[Z_i + Z_j]^T \tag{50}$$

Hence, if the LMI (49) holds, inequality (24) is satisfied. This concludes the proof of the theorem.

Remark 1: For the chosen performance criterion, the LMI (49) need to be solved at each time to find matrices S, M, by using relation (33), we can find the feedback control gain, therefore, the feedback control can be found to satisfy the chosen criterion.

5. Fuzzy LMI control of discrete time non-linear systems with general performance criteria

This section summarizes the main results for fuzzy LMI control of discrete time non-linear systems with general performance criteria:

Theorem 2: Given the closed loop system and performance output (13), and control input (19), if there exist matrices $S = P^{-1} > 0$ for all $k \geq 0$, such that the following LMI holds:

$$\begin{bmatrix} \Xi_{11} & \Xi_{12} & \Xi_{13} & \Xi_{14} & \Xi_{15} & \Xi_{16} \\ * & \Xi_{22} & \Xi_{23} & \Xi_{24} & 0 & 0 \\ * & * & S & 0 & 0 & 0 \\ * & * & * & I & 0 & 0 \\ * & * & * & * & R^{-1} & 0 \\ * & * & * & * & * & I \end{bmatrix} \geq 0 \tag{51}$$

where

$$\begin{aligned}
\Xi_{11} &= S \\
\Xi_{12} &= \frac{\beta}{4}(C_iS - D_iY_j + C_jS - D_jY_i)^T \\
\Xi_{13} &= \frac{1}{2}(A_iS - B_iY_j + A_jS - B_jY_i)^T \\
\Xi_{14} &= \frac{1}{2}\alpha^{1/2}(C_iS - D_iY_j + C_jS - D_jY_i)^T \\
\Xi_{15} &= \frac{1}{2}(Y_i + Y_j)^T \\
\Xi_{16} &= SQ^{T/2} \\
\Xi_{22} &= -\gamma I + \frac{\beta}{2}(Z_i + Z_j)^T \\
\Xi_{23} &= \frac{1}{2}\alpha^{1/2}(F_i + F_j)^T \\
\Xi_{24} &= \frac{1}{2}\alpha^{1/2}(Z_i + Z_j)^T
\end{aligned} \tag{52}$$

and

$$S(k+1) > S(k) \tag{53}$$

where $S(k) = P^{-1}(k)$, then (28) is satisfied with the feedback control gain being found by

$$K(k) = Y(k)P(k) \tag{54}$$

Proof

The performance index inequality (28) can be explicitly written as

$$\begin{aligned}
&[\sum_{i=1}^{r}\sum_{j=1}^{r} h_i(\varphi(k))h_j(\varphi(k))G_{ij}x(k) + \sum_{i=1}^{r} h_i(\varphi(k))F_iw(k)]^T \\
&\times P \times [\sum_{i=1}^{r}\sum_{j=1}^{r} h_i(\varphi(k))h_j(\varphi(k))G_{ij}x(k) + \sum_{i=1}^{r} h_i(\varphi(k))F_iw(k)] \\
&-x^T(k)Px(k) + x^T(k)Qx(k) + [-\sum_{i=1}^{r} h_i(\varphi(k))K_ix(k)]^T R[-\sum_{i=1}^{r} h_i(\varphi(k))K_ix(k)] + \\
&\alpha[\sum_{i=1}^{r}\sum_{j=1}^{r} h_i(\varphi(k))h_j(\varphi(k))H_{ij}x(k) + \sum_{i=1}^{r} h_i(\varphi(k))Z_iw(k)]^T \\
&\times[\sum_{i=1}^{r}\sum_{j=1}^{r} h_i(\varphi(k))h_j(\varphi(k))H_{ij}x(k) + \sum_{i=1}^{r} h_i(\varphi(k))Z_iw(k)] \\
&-\beta[\sum_{i=1}^{r}\sum_{j=1}^{r} h_i(\varphi(k))h_j(\varphi(k))H_{ij}x(k) + \sum_{i=1}^{r} h_i(\varphi(k))Z_iw(k)]^T \times w(k) \\
&+\gamma w^T(k)w(k) \leq 0
\end{aligned} \tag{55}$$

Equivalently,

$$[x^T(k)\ w^T(k)]\begin{bmatrix}-P+Q & 0\\ 0 & \gamma I\end{bmatrix}\begin{bmatrix}x(k)\\ w(k)\end{bmatrix}+$$
$$[x^T(k)\ w^T(k)]\left[(\sum_i\sum_j h_ih_jG_{ij})\ (\sum_i h_iF_i)\right]^T\times P\times\left[(\sum_i\sum_j h_ih_jG_{ij})\ (\sum_i h_iF_i)\right]\begin{bmatrix}x(k)\\ w(k)\end{bmatrix}+$$
$$+x^T(k)[\sum_i h_iK_i]^TR[\sum_i h_iK_i]x(k)+$$
$$\alpha\left[x^T(k)\ w^T(k)\right]\left[(\sum_i\sum_j h_ih_jH_{ij})\ (\sum_i h_iZ_i)\right]^T\times\left[(\sum_i\sum_j h_ih_jH_{ij})\ (\sum_i h_iZ_i)\right]\begin{bmatrix}x(k)\\ w(k)\end{bmatrix}+$$
$$-\beta\left[x^T(k)\ w^T(k)\right]\left[(\sum_i\sum_j h_ih_jH_{ij})\ (\sum_i h_iZ_i)\right]^T w(k)\le 0 \tag{56}$$

which can be written, after collecting terms, as

$$[x^T(k)\ w^T(k)]\begin{bmatrix}\Upsilon_{11} & \Upsilon_{12}\\ * & \Upsilon_{22}\end{bmatrix}\begin{bmatrix}x(k)\\ w(k)\end{bmatrix}+$$
$$[x^T(k)\ w^T(k)]\left[(\sum_i\sum_j h_ih_jG_{ij})\ (\sum_i h_iF_i)\right]^T\times P\times\left[(\sum_i\sum_j h_ih_jG_{ij})\ (\sum_i h_iF_i)\right]\begin{bmatrix}x(k)\\ w(k)\end{bmatrix}+$$
$$\alpha\left[x^T(k)\ w^T(k)\right]\left[(\sum_i\sum_j h_ih_jH_{ij})\ (\sum_i h_iZ_i)\right]^T\times\left[(\sum_i\sum_j h_ih_jH_{ij})\ (\sum_i h_iZ_i)\right]\begin{bmatrix}x(k)\\ w(k)\end{bmatrix}\ge 0 \tag{57}$$

where

$$\begin{aligned}\Upsilon_{11} &= P-Q-[\sum_i h_iK_i]^TR[\sum_i h_iK_i]\\ \Upsilon_{12} &= \frac{\beta}{2}[\sum_i\sum_j h_ih_jH_{ij}]^T\\ \Upsilon_{22} &= -\gamma I+\beta[\sum_i h_iZ_i]^T\end{aligned} \tag{58}$$

Equivalently, we have

$$\begin{bmatrix}\Upsilon_{11} & \Upsilon_{12}\\ * & \Upsilon_{22}\end{bmatrix}-\left[(\sum_i\sum_j h_ih_jG_{ij})\ (\sum_i h_iF_i)\right]^T\times P\times\left[(\sum_i\sum_j h_ih_jG_{ij})\ (\sum_i h_iF_i)\right]-$$
$$\alpha\left[(\sum_i\sum_j h_ih_jH_{ij})\ (\sum_i h_iZ_i)\right]^T\times\left[(\sum_i\sum_j h_ih_jH_{ij})\ (\sum_i h_iZ_i)\right]\ge 0 \tag{59}$$

By applying Schur complement, we obtain

$$\begin{bmatrix}\Upsilon_{11} & \Upsilon_{12} & (\sum_i\sum_j h_ih_jG_{ij}))^T\\ * & \Upsilon_{22} & (\sum_i h_iF_i)^T\\ * & * & P^{-1}\end{bmatrix}-\alpha\left[(\sum_i\sum_j h_ih_jH_{ij})\ (\sum_i h_iZ_i)\right]^T\times\left[(\sum_i\sum_j h_ih_jH_{ij})\ (\sum_i h_iZ_i)\right]\ge 0 \tag{60}$$

By applying Schur complement again, we obtain

$$\begin{bmatrix} \Upsilon_{11} & \Upsilon_{12} & (\sum_i \sum_j h_i h_j G_{ij}))^T & \alpha^{1/2}(\sum_i \sum_j h_i h_j H_{ij})^T \\ * & \Upsilon_{22} & (\sum_i h_i F_i)^T & \alpha^{1/2}(\sum_i h_i Z_i)^T \\ * & * & P^{-1} & 0 \\ * & * & * & I \end{bmatrix} \geq 0 \tag{61}$$

Equivalently, the following inequality holds

$$\begin{bmatrix} \Psi_{11} & \Psi_{12} & (\sum_i \sum_j h_i h_j G_{ij}))^T & \alpha^{1/2}(\sum_i \sum_j h_i h_j H_{ij})^T \\ * & \Psi_{22} & (\sum_i h_i F_i)^T & \alpha^{1/2}(\sum_i h_i Z_i)^T \\ * & * & P^{-1} & 0 \\ * & * & * & I \end{bmatrix} - \begin{bmatrix} (\sum_i h_i K_i)^T \\ 0 \\ 0 \\ 0 \end{bmatrix} \times R \times \left[(\sum_i h_i K_i)\ 0\ 0\ 0\right] \geq 0 \tag{62}$$

where

$$\Psi_{11} = P - Q$$
$$\Psi_{12} = \frac{\beta}{2}[\sum_i \sum_j h_i h_j H_{ij}]^T$$
$$\Psi_{22} = -\gamma I + \beta[\sum_i h_i Z_i]^T \tag{63}$$

By applying Schur complement one more time, we have

$$\begin{bmatrix} \Psi_{11} & \Psi_{12} & (\sum_i \sum_j h_i h_j G_{ij}))^T & \alpha^{1/2}(\sum_i \sum_j h_i h_j H_{ij})^T & (\sum_i h_i K_i)^T \\ * & \Psi_{22} & (\sum_i h_i F_i)^T & \alpha^{1/2}(\sum_i h_i Z_i)^T & 0 \\ * & * & P^{-1} & 0 & 0 \\ * & * & * & I & 0 \\ * & * & * & * & R^{-1} \end{bmatrix} \geq 0 \tag{64}$$

By factoring out the $\sum_i \sum_j h_i(\varphi_k) h_j(\varphi_k)$ term, we have

$$\begin{bmatrix} \Omega_{11} & \Omega_{12} & \Omega_{13} & \Omega_{14} & \Omega_{15} \\ * & \Omega_{22} & \Omega_{23} & \Omega_{24} & 0 \\ * & * & P^{-1} & 0 & 0 \\ * & * & * & I & 0 \\ * & * & * & * & R^{-1} \end{bmatrix} \geq 0 \tag{65}$$

where

$$\begin{aligned}
\Omega_{11} &= P - Q \\
\Omega_{12} &= \frac{\beta}{4}[H_{ji} + H_{ij}]^T \\
\Omega_{13} &= \frac{1}{2}(G_{ji} + G_{ij}))^T \\
\Omega_{14} &= \frac{1}{2}\alpha^{1/2}(H_{ij} + H_{ji})^T \\
\Omega_{15} &= \frac{1}{2}(K_i + K_j)^T \\
\Omega_{22} &= -\gamma I + \frac{\beta}{2}(Z_i + Z_j)^T \\
\Omega_{23} &= \frac{1}{2}(F_i + F_j)^T \\
\Omega_{24} &= \frac{1}{2}\alpha^{1/2}(Z_i + Z_j)^T
\end{aligned} \tag{66}$$

By pre-multiplying and post-multiplying the matrix with the block diagonal matrix $diag(S, I, I, I, I)$, where $S = P^{-1}$, and applying Schur complement again, the following LMI result is obtained

$$\begin{bmatrix} \Xi_{11} & \Xi_{12} & \Xi_{13} & \Xi_{14} & \Xi_{15} & \Xi_{16} \\ * & \Xi_{22} & \Xi_{23} & \Xi_{24} & 0 & 0 \\ * & * & S & 0 & 0 & 0 \\ * & * & * & I & 0 & 0 \\ * & * & * & * & R^{-1} & 0 \\ * & * & * & * & * & I \end{bmatrix} \geq 0 \tag{67}$$

where

$$\begin{aligned}
\Xi_{11} &= S \\
\Xi_{12} &= \frac{\beta}{4}(C_i S - D_i Y_j + C_j S - D_j Y_i)^T \\
\Xi_{13} &= \frac{1}{2}(A_i S - B_i Y_j + A_j S - B_j Y_i)^T \\
\Xi_{14} &= \frac{1}{2}\alpha^{1/2}(C_i S - D_i Y_j + C_j S - D_j Y_i)^T \\
\Xi_{15} &= \frac{1}{2}(Y_i + Y_j)^T \\
\Xi_{16} &= S Q^{T/2} \\
\Xi_{22} &= -\gamma I + \frac{\beta}{2}(Z_i + Z_j)^T \\
\Xi_{23} &= \frac{1}{2}\alpha^{1/2}(F_i + F_j)^T \\
\Xi_{24} &= \frac{1}{2}\alpha^{1/2}(Z_i + Z_j)^T
\end{aligned} \tag{68}$$

where $S(k) = P^{-1}(k)$, then (28) is satisfied with the feedback control gain being found by

$$K(k) = Y(k)P(k) \tag{69}$$

6. Application to the inverted pendulum system

The inverted pendulum on a cart problem is a benchmark control problem used widely to test control algorithms. A pendulum beam attached at one end can rotate freely in the vertical 2-dimensional plane. The angle of the beam with respect to the vertical direction is denoted at angle θ. The external force u is desired to set angle of the beam θ (x_1) and angular velocity $\dot{\theta}$ (x_2) to zero while satisfying the mixed performance criteria. A model of the inverted pendulum on a cart problem is given by [1, 9]:

$$\begin{aligned} \dot{x}_1 &= x_2 + \epsilon_1 w \\ \dot{x}_2 &= \frac{gsin(x_1) - amLx_2^2 sin(2x_1)/2 - acos(x_1)u}{4L/3 - amLcos^2(x_1)} + \epsilon_2 w \end{aligned} \tag{70}$$

where x_1 is the angle of the pendulum from vertical direction, x_2 is the angular velocity of the pendulum, g is the gravity constant, m is the mass of the pendulum, M is the mass of the cart, L is the length of the center of mass (the entire length of the pendulum beam equals $2L$), u is the external force, control input to the system, w is the $\mathcal{L}_2$ type of disturbance, $a = \frac{1}{m+M}$ is a constant, and $\epsilon_1.\epsilon_2$ is the weighing coefficients of disturbance.

Due to the system non-linearity, we approximate the system using the following two-rule fuzzy model:

continuous-time fuzzy model

Rule 1: If $|x_1(t)|$ is close to zero,
Then $\dot{x}(t) = A_1x(t) + B_1u(t) + F_1w(t)$

Rule 2: If $|x_1(t)|$ is close to $\pi/2$,
Then $\dot{x}(t) = A_2x(t) + B_2u(t) + F_2w(t)$

where

$$A_1 = \begin{bmatrix} 0 & 1 \\ \frac{g}{4L/3 - amL} & 0 \end{bmatrix} B_1 = \begin{bmatrix} 0 \\ -\frac{a}{4L/3 - amL} \end{bmatrix} F_1 = \begin{bmatrix} \epsilon_1 \\ \epsilon_2 \end{bmatrix}$$
$$A_2 = \begin{bmatrix} 0 & 1 \\ \frac{2g}{\pi(4L/3 - amL\delta^2)} & 0 \end{bmatrix} B_1 = \begin{bmatrix} 0 \\ -\frac{a\delta}{4L/3 - amL\delta^2} \end{bmatrix} F_1 = \begin{bmatrix} \epsilon_1 \\ \epsilon_2 \end{bmatrix} with\ \delta = cos(80^o) \tag{71}$$

discrete-time fuzzy model

Rule 1: If $|x_1(k)|$ is close to zero,
Then $x(k+1) = \mathcal{A}_1x(k) + \mathcal{B}_1u(k) + \mathcal{F}_1w(k)$

Rule 2: If $|x_1(k)|$ is close to $\pi/2$,
Then $x(k+1) = \mathcal{A}_2x(k) + \mathcal{B}_2u(k) + \mathcal{F}_2w(k)$

where

$$\mathcal{A}_1 = \begin{bmatrix} 1 & T \\ \frac{gT}{4L/3-amL} & 1 \end{bmatrix} \mathcal{B}_1 = \begin{bmatrix} 0 \\ -\frac{aT}{4L/3-amL} \end{bmatrix} \mathcal{F}_1 = \begin{bmatrix} \epsilon_1 T \\ \epsilon_2 T \end{bmatrix}$$

$$\mathcal{A}_2 = \begin{bmatrix} 1 & T \\ \frac{2gT}{\pi(4L/3-amL\delta^2)} & 1 \end{bmatrix} \mathcal{B}_2 = \begin{bmatrix} 0 \\ -\frac{a\delta T}{4L/3-amL\delta^2} \end{bmatrix} \mathcal{F}_2 = \begin{bmatrix} \epsilon_1 T \\ \epsilon_2 T \end{bmatrix}$$

$$with\ \delta = cos(80^o), Sampling\ time\ T = 0.001 \tag{72}$$

The following values are used in our simulation:

$$M = 8kg, m = 2kg, L = 0.5m, g = 9.8m/s^2, \epsilon_1 = 1, \epsilon_2 = 0$$

and the initial condition of $x_1(0) = \pi/6, x_2(0) = -\pi/6$. The membership function of Rule 1 and Rule 2 is shown below in Fig.1.

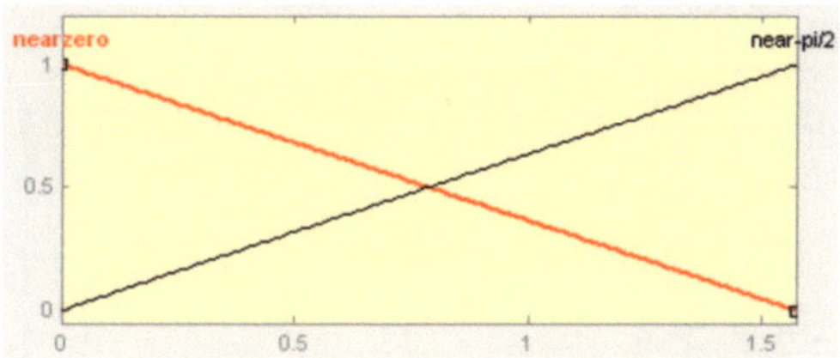

Figure 1. Membership functions of Rule 1 and Rule 2.

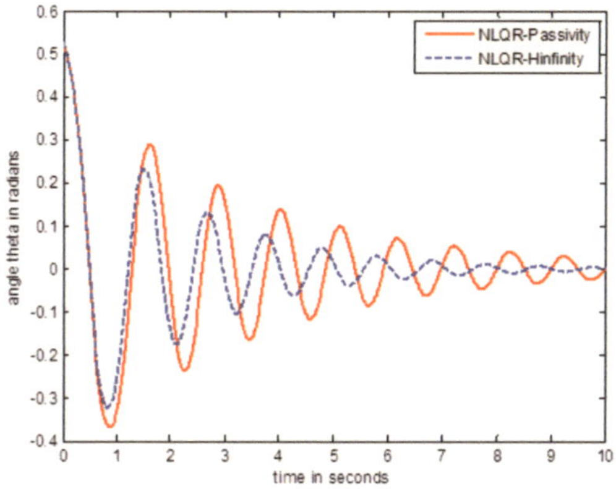

Figure 2. Angle trajectory of the inverted pendulum.

The feedback control gain can be found from (31)(51) by solving the LMI at each time. The following design parameters are chosen to satisfy:

Mixed $NLQR - \mathcal{H}_\infty$ criteria:

$$C = [1 \quad 1], D = [1], Q = diag[1001], R = 1, \alpha = 1, \beta = 0, \gamma = -5$$

Mixed $NLQR - passivity$ criteria:

$$C = [1 \quad 1], D = [1], Q = diag[1001], R = 1, \alpha = 1, \beta = 5, \gamma = 0$$

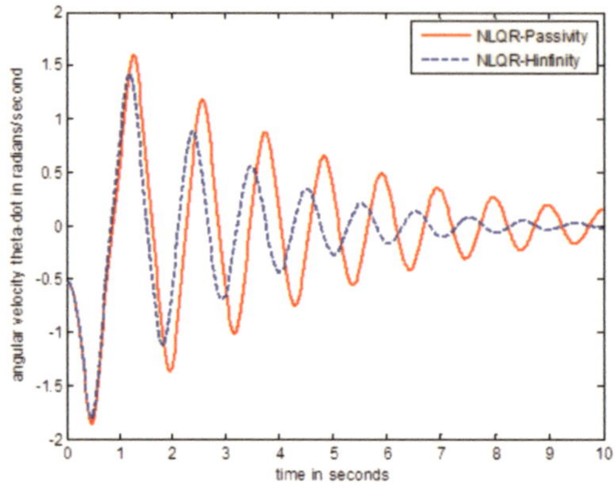

Figure 3. Angular velocity trajectory of the inverted pendulum.

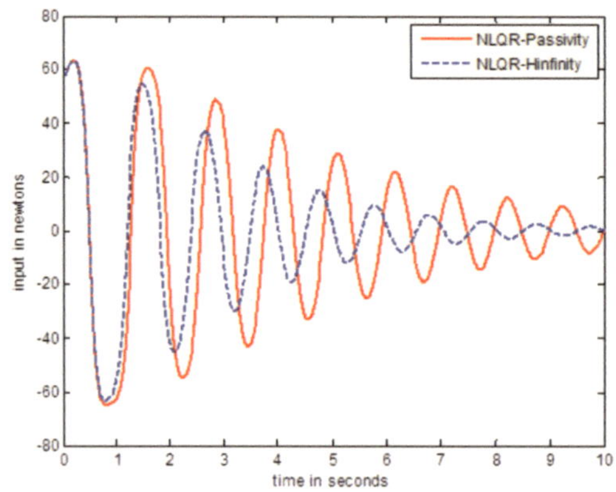

Figure 4. Control input applied to the inverted pendulum.

The mixed criteria control performance results are shown in the Figs.2-4. From these figures, we find that the novel fuzzy LMI control has satisfactory performance. The mixed $NLQR - H_\infty$ criteria control has a smaller overshoot and a faster response than the one with passivity property. The new technique controls the inverted pendulum very well under the effect of finite energy disturbance. It should also be noted that the LMI fuzzy control with mixed performance criteria satisfies global asymptotic stability.

7. Summary

This chapter presents a novel fuzzy control approach for both of continuous time and discrete time non-linear systems based on the LMI solutions. The Takagi-Sugeno fuzzy model is applied to decompose the non-linear system. Multiple performance criteria are used to design the controller and the relative weighting matrices of these criteria can be achieved by choosing different coefficient matrices. The optimal control can be obtained by solving LMI at each time. The inverted pendulum is used as an example to demonstrate its effectiveness. The simulation studies show that the proposed method provides a satisfactory alternative to the existing non-linear control approaches.

Author details

Xin Wang
Oregon Institute of Technology, Department of Electrical and Renewable Energy Engineering, Klamath Falls, Oregon, USA

Edwin E. Yaz
Marquette University, Department of Electrical and Computer Engineering, Haggerty Hall of Engineering, Milwaukee, Wisconsin, USA

James Long
Oregon Institute of Technology, Department of Computer Systems Engineering Technology, Klamath Falls, Oregon, USA

Tim Miller
Green Lite Motors Corporation, Portland, OR, USA

8. References

[1] Baumann W.T, Rugh W.J (1986) Feedback Control of Non-linear Systems by Extended Linearization. IEEE Trans. Automatic Control. Vol. AC-31, No.1, pp.40-46.
[2] Basar T and Bernhard P (1995) H-infinity Optimal Control and Related Minimax Design Problems, A Dynamic Game Approach, 2nd Ed.,Birkhauser, 1995.
[3] Boyd S, Ghaoui L E, Feron E, Balakrishnan V (1994) Linear Matrix Inequalities in System and Control Theory, SIAM Studies in Applied Mathematics, SIAM, Philadelphia.
[4] Huang Y, Lu W-M (1996) Non-linear Optimal Control: Alternatives to Hamilton-Jacobi Equation, Proc. of 35th Conf. on Decision and Control, Kobe, Japan, pp. 3942-3947.
[5] Khalil H.K (2002) Non-linear Systems, 3rd Ed., Prentice Hall, N.J.
[6] Mohseni J, Yaz E, Olejniczak K (1998) State Dependent LMI Control of Discrete-Time Non-linear Systems, Proc. of the 37th IEEE Conference on Decision and Control, Tampa, FL, pp. 4626-4627.
[7] Takagi T, Sugeno M (1985) Fuzzy Identification of Systems and Its Applications to Model and Control, IEEE Trans. Syst. Man. Cyber., Vol. 15, pp.116-132.
[8] Tanaka K, Sugeno M (1990) Stability Analysis of Fuzzy Systems Using Lyapunov's Direct Method, Proc. NAFIPS90, pp. 133-136.
[9] Tanaka K, Ikeda T, Wang H.O (1996) Design of Fuzzy Control Systems Based on Relaxed LMI Stability Conditions, the 35th IEEE Conference on Decision and Control, Kobe, Vol.1, pp. 598-603.
[10] Tanaka K, Wang H.O (2001) Fuzzy Control Systems Design and Analysis, A Linear Matrix Inequality Approach, Wiley.
[11] Van der Shaft A.J (1993) Non-linear State Space H1 control Theory, in Perspectives in control, H. J. Trentelman and J. C. Willems, Eds. Birkhauser.
[12] Vidyasagar M (2002) Non-linear System Analysis, 2nd Ed., SIAM.
[13] Wang L.X (1994) Adaptive Fuzzy Systems and Control: Design and Stability Analysis, Prentice Hall, Englewood Cliffs, NJ.

[14] Wang H.O, Tanaka K, Griffin M (1996) An Approach to Fuzzy Control of Non-linear Systems: Stability and Design Issues, IEEE Trans. Fuzzy Syst., Vol. 4, No. 1, pp.14-23.
[15] Wang X, Yaz E.E (2009) The State Dependent Control of Continuous-Time Non-linear Systems with Mixed Performance Criteria, Proc. of IASTED Int. Conf. on Identi cation Control and Applications, Honolulu, HI, pp. 98-102.
[16] Wang X, Yaz E.E (2010) Robust multi-criteria optimal fuzzy control of continuous-time non-linear systems, Proc. of the 2010 American Control Conference, Baltimore, MD, USA, pp. 6460-6465.
[17] Wang X, Yaz E.E, Jeong C.S (2010) Robust non-linear feedback control of discrete-time non-linear systems with mixed performance criteria, Proc. of the 2010 American Control Conference, Baltimore, MD, USA,pp. 6357-6362.
[18] Wang X, Yaz E.E (2010) Robust multi-criteria optimal fuzzy control of discrete-time non-linear systems, Proc. of the 49th IEEE Conference on Decision and Control, Atlanta, Georgia, USA, pp. 4269-4274.
[19] Wang X, Yaz E.E, Yaz Y.I (2010) Robust and resilient state dependent control of continuous-time non-linear systems with general performance criteria, Proc. of the 49th IEEE Conference on Decision and Control, Atlanta, Georgia, USA, pp. 603-608.
[20] Wang X, Yaz E.E, Yaz Y.I, Robust and resilient state dependent control of discrete time non-linear systems with general performance criteria, Proc. of the 18th IFAC Congress, Milano, Italy, pp. 10904-10909.

Chapter 6

A New Method for Tuning PID-Type Fuzzy Controllers Using Particle Swarm Optimization

S. Bouallègue, J. Haggège and M. Benrejeb

Additional information is available at the end of the chapter

http://dx.doi.org/10.5772/47139

1. Introduction

The complexity of dynamic system, especially when only qualitative knowledge about the process is available, makes it generally difficult to elaborate an analytic model which is sufficiently precise enough for the control. Thus, it is interesting to use, for this kind of systems, non conventional control techniques, such as fuzzy logic, in order to achieve high performances and robustness [8, 15, 20–22, 24, 33, 34]. Fuzzy logic control approach has been widely used in many successful industrial applications which have demonstrated high robustness and effectiveness properties.

In the literature, various Fuzzy Controller (FC) structures are proposed and extensively studied. The particular structure given by Qiao and Mizumoto in [26], namely PID-type FC, is especially established and improved within the practical framework in [11, 16, 31]. Such a FC structure, which retains the characteristics similar to the conventional PID controller, can be decomposed into the equivalent proportional, integral and derivative control components as shown in [26]. In order to improve further the performance of the transient and steady state responses of this kind of fuzzy controller, various strategies and methods are proposed to tune the PID-type fuzzy controller parameters.

Indeed, Qiao and Mizumoto [26] designed a parameter adaptive PID-type FC based on a peak observer mechanism. This self-tuning mechanism decreases the equivalent integral control component of the fuzzy controller gradually with the system response process time. On the other hand, Woo et al. [31] developed a method to tune the scaling factors related to integral and derivative components of the PID-type FC structure via two empirical functions and based on the system's error information. In [12, 16], the authors proposed a technique that adjusts the scaling factors, corresponding to the derivative and integral components of the PID-type FC, using a fuzzy inference mechanism. However, the major drawback of all these PID-type FC structures is the difficult choice of their relative scaling factors. Indeed, the fuzzy controller dynamic behaviour depends on this adequate choice. The tuning procedure depends on the control experience and knowledge of the human operator, and it is generally achieved based on a classical trials-errors procedure. Up to now, there is neither clear mor systematic method to guide such a choice. So, this tuning problem becomes more delicate and harder as the complexity of the controlled plant increases. Hence, the proposition of a systematic approach to tune the scaling factors of these particular PID-type FC structures is interesting.

In this study, a new approach based on the Particle Swarm Optimization (PSO) meta-heuristic technique is proposed for systematically tuning the scaling factors of the PID-type FC, both with and without self-tuning mechanisms. This work can be considered as an extension of the results given in [11, 12, 16, 26, 31]. The fuzzy control design is formulated as a constrained optimization problem which is efficiently solved based on a developed PSO algorithm. In order to specify more robustness and performance control objectives of the proposed PSO-tuned PID-type FC, different optimization criteria are considered and compared subject to several various control constraints defined in the time-domain framework.

The remainder of this chapter is organized as follows. In Section 2, the proposed fuzzy PID-type FC structures, both with and without self-tuning scaling factors mechanisms, are presented and discussed within the discrete-time framework. Two adaptive mechanisms for scaling factors tuning are especially adopted. The optimization-based problems of the PID-type FC scaling factors tuning are formulated in Section 3. The developed constrained PSO algorithm, used in solving the formulated problems, is also described. An external static penalty technique is used to deal with optimization constraints. Theoretical conditions for convergence algorithm and parameters choice are established, based on the stability theory of dynamic systems. Section 4 is dedicated to apply the proposed fuzzy control approaches on an electrical DC drive benchmark and a thermal process within an experimental real-time framework based on an Advantech PCI-1710 multi-functions board associated with a PC computer and MATLAB/Simulink environment. Performances on convergence properties of the proposed PSO and the used GAO algorithm, are compared for the known Integral Absolute Error (IAE) and the Integral Square Error (ISE) criterion cases. The real-time fuzzy controllers are developed through the compilation and linking stage, in a form of a Dynamic Link Library (DLL) which is, then, loaded in memory and started-up.

2. PID-type fuzzy control design

In this section, the considered PID-type FC structures are briefly described within the discrete-time framework based on [11, 12, 16, 26, 31].

2.1. Discrete-time PID-type FLC

Proposed by Qiao and Mizumoto in [26] within continuous-time formalism, this particular fuzzy controller structure, called PID-type FC, retains the characteristics similar to the conventional PID controller. This result remains valid while using a type of FC with triangular and uniformly distributed membership functions for the fuzzy inputs and a crisp output, a product-sum inference and a center of gravity defuzzification methods.

Under these conditions, the equivalent proportional, integral and derivative control components of such a PID-type FC are given by $\alpha K_e \mathcal{P} + \beta K_d \mathcal{D}$, $\beta K_e \mathcal{P}$, and $\alpha K_d \mathcal{D}$, respectively, as shown in [16, 26, 31]. In these expressions, $\mathcal{P}$ and $\mathcal{D}$ represent relative coefficients, K_e, K_d,

α and β denote the scaling factors associated to the inputs and output of the FC, as shown in Figure 1. The proof of this computation is shown with more details in [26].

When approximating the integral and derivative terms within the discrete-time framework, we can consider the closed-loop control structure for a discrete-time PID-type FC, as shown in Figure 1.

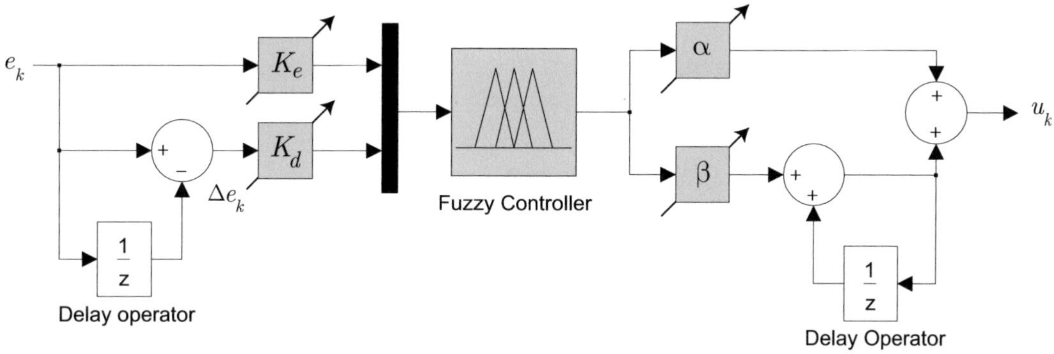

Figure 1. The proposed discrete-time PID-type FC structure.

As shown in [11, 16, 26, 31], the dynamic behaviour of this PID-type FC structure is strongly dependent on the scaling factors K_e, K_d, α and β, difficult and delicate to tune.

2.2. PID-type FC with self-tuning mechanisms

In order to improve the performances of the considered PID-type FC structure, various self-tuning mechanisms for scaling factors have been proposed in the literature. Two methods are especially adopted in this chapter.

2.2.1. *Self-tuning via Empirical Functions Tuner Method EFTM*

In this self-tuning method [31], the PID-type FC integral and derivative components updating are achieved based on scaling factors β and K_d, using the information on system's error as follows:

$$\begin{aligned} \beta_k &= \beta_0 \Phi(e_k) \\ K_{dk} &= K_{d0} \Psi(e_k) \end{aligned} \quad (1)$$

where β_0 and K_{d0} are the initial values of β and K_d, respectively, $\Phi(.)$ and $\Psi(.)$ are the empirical tuner functions defined, respectively, by:

$$\begin{aligned} \Phi(e_k) &= \phi_1 |e_k| + \phi_2 \\ \Psi(e_k) &= \psi_1 (1 - |e_k|) + \psi_2 \end{aligned} \quad (2)$$

In these equations, the parameters to be tuned ϕ_1, ϕ_2, ψ_1 and ψ_2 are all positive. The empirical function related to integral component decreases as the error decreases while the function related to derivative factor increases. Indeed, the objective of the function is to decrease the parameter with the change of error. However, the function has an inverse objective to make constant the proportional effect. Hence, the system may not always keep quick reaction against the error as demonstrated by Woo et al. in [31].

2.2.2. *Self-tuning via Relative Rate Observer Method RROM*

In this self-tuning method [12, 16], the PID-type FC integral and derivative components updating are achieved as follows:

$$\begin{aligned} \beta_k &= \frac{\beta_0}{K_f \delta_k} \\ K_{dk} &= K_{d0} K_{fd} K_f \delta_k \end{aligned} \tag{3}$$

where δ_k is the output of the fuzzy Relative Rate Observer (RRO) K_f is the output scaling factor for δ_k and K_{fd} is the additional parameter that affects only the derivative factor of the FC.

The rule-base for δ_k, as used by Eksin et al. [12] and Güzelkaya et al. [16], is considered for the fuzzy RRO. This fuzzy RRO block has as inputs the absolute values of error $|e_k|$ and the variable r_k, defined subsequently, as shown in Table 1.

$\|e_k\|/r_k$	S	M	F
S	M	M	L
SM	SM	M	L
M	S	SM	M
L	S	S	SM

Table 1. Fuzzy rule-base for the variable δ_k.

The linguistic levels assigned to the input $|e_k|$ and the output variable δ_k are as follows: L (Large), M (Medium), SM (Small Medium) and S (Small). For the input variable r_k, the following linguistic levels are assigned: F (Fast), M (Moderate) and S (Slow).

The variable r_k, defined in [12, 16] and called normalized acceleration, gives "relative rate" information about the fastness or slowness of the system response as shown in Table 2. It is defined as follows [16]:

$$r_k = \frac{\Delta e_k - \Delta e_{k-1}}{\Delta e^*} = \frac{\Delta\left(\Delta e_k\right)}{\Delta e^*} \tag{4}$$

where Δe_k and $\Delta\left(\Delta e_k\right)$ are the incremental change in error and the so-called acceleration in error given respectively by:

$$\Delta e_k = e_k - e_{k-1} \tag{5}$$

$$\Delta\left(\Delta e_k\right) = \Delta e_k - \Delta e_{k-1} \tag{6}$$

In equation (4), the variable Δe^* is chosen as follows:

$$\Delta e^* = \begin{cases} \Delta e_k & if \ \ |\Delta e_k| \geq |\Delta e_{k-1}| \\ \Delta e_{k-1} & if \ \ |\Delta e_k| < |\Delta e_{k-1}| \end{cases} \tag{7}$$

Δe^*	$\Delta\left(\Delta e_k\right)$	System response
Positive	Positive	Fast
Positive	Negative	Slow
Negative	Positive	Slow
Negative	Negative	Fast

Table 2. Nature of the system response depending on the variable r_k.

For this RROM self-tuning approach, the uniformly distributed triangular and the symmetrical membership functions, as shown in Figures 2, 3, 4, are assigned for the fuzzy inputs r_k and $|e_k|$, and fuzzy output variable δ_k. The view of the above fuzzy rule-base is illustrated in Figure 5.

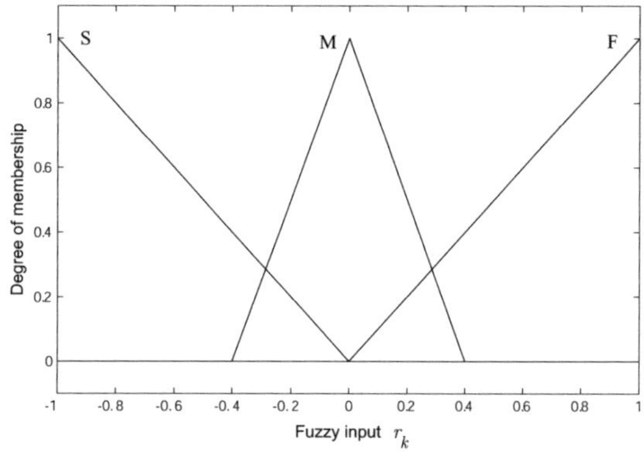

Figure 2. Membership functions for r_k.

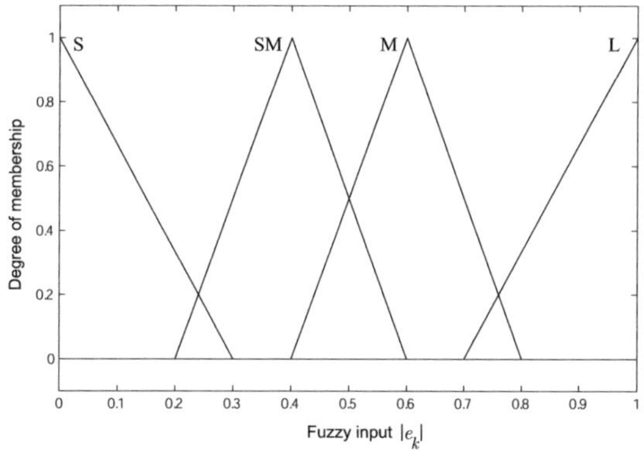

Figure 3. Membership functions for $|e_k|$.

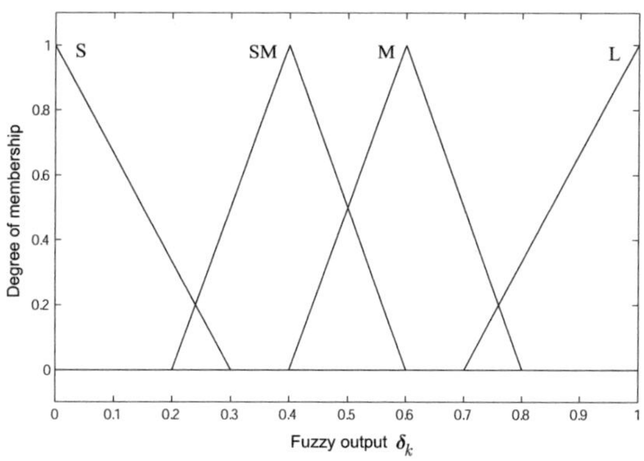

Figure 4. Membership functions for δ_k.

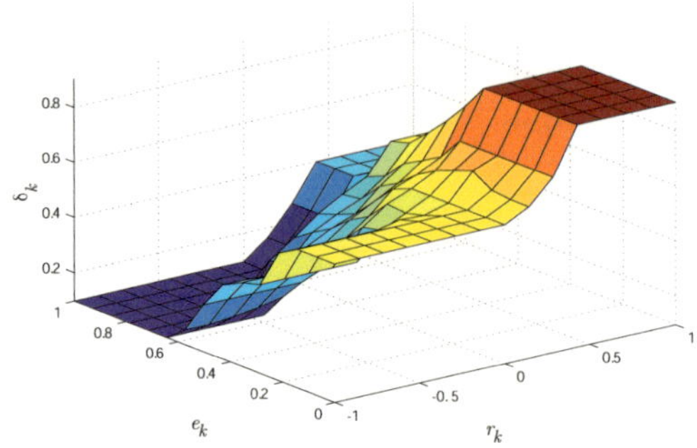

Figure 5. View of the fuzzy rule-base for δ_k.

3. The proposed PSO-based approach

In this section, the problem of scaling factors tuning, for all defined PID-type FC structures, is formulated as a constrained optimization problem which is solved using the proposed PSO-based approach.

3.1. PID-type FC tuning problem formulation

The choice of the adequate values for the scaling factors of each PID-type FC structure is often done by a trials-errors hard procedure. This tuning problem becomes difficult and delicate without a systematic design method. To deal with these difficulties, the optimization of these scaling factors is proposed like a promising solution. This tuning problem can be formulated as the following constrained optimization problem:

$$\begin{cases} \underset{\boldsymbol{x}\in\mathbb{D}}{minimize} f(\boldsymbol{x}) \\ subjectto \\ g_l(\boldsymbol{x}) \leq 0; \quad \forall l = 1, \ldots, n_{con} \end{cases} \tag{8}$$

where $f : \mathbb{R}^m \to \mathbb{R}$ the cost function, $\mathbb{D} = \{\boldsymbol{x} \in \mathbb{D}^m; \boldsymbol{x}_{\min} \leq \boldsymbol{x} \leq \boldsymbol{x}_{\max}\}$ the initial search space, which is supposed containing the desired design parameters, and $g_l : \mathbb{R}^m \to \mathbb{R}$ the problem's constraints.

The optimization-based tuning problem consists in finding the optimal decision variables $\boldsymbol{x}^* = \left(x_1^*, x_2^*, \ldots, x_m^*\right)^T$, representing the scaling factors of a given PID-type FC structure, which minimize the defined cost function, chosen as the ISE and IAE performance criteria. These cost functions are minimized, using the proposed constrained PSO algorithm, under various time-domain control constraints such as overshoot D, steady state error E_{ss}, rise time t_r and settling time t_s of the system's step response, as shown in the equations (9), (10) and (11).

Hence, in the case of the PID-type FC structure without self-tuning mechanisms, the scaling factors to be optimized are K_e, K_d, α and β. The formulated optimization problem is defined as follows:

$$\begin{cases} \underset{\boldsymbol{x}=(K_e,K_d,\alpha,\beta)^T\in\mathbb{R}_+^4}{minimize} \quad f(\boldsymbol{x}) \\ subjectto \\ D \leq D^{\max}; t_s \leq t_s^{\max}; t_r \leq t_r^{\max}; E_{ss} \leq E_{ss}^{\max} \end{cases} \tag{9}$$

where $D^{\max}$, $E_{ss}^{\max}$, $t_r^{\max}$ and $t_s^{\max}$ are the specified overshoot, steady state, rise and settling times respectively, that constraint the step response of the PSO-tuned PID-type FC controlled system, and can define some time-domain templates.

In the case of the PID-type FC structure with the EFTM self-tuning mechanism, the scaling factors to be optimized are φ_1, φ_2, ψ_1 and ψ_2. The formulated optimization problem is defined as follows:

$$\begin{cases} \underset{\boldsymbol{x}=(\varphi_1,\varphi_2,\psi_1,\psi_2)^T \in \mathbb{R}_+^4}{minimize} \quad f(\boldsymbol{x}) \\ subject to \\ D \leq D^{\max}; t_s \leq t_s^{\max}; t_r \leq t_r^{\max}; E_{ss} \leq E_{ss}^{\max} \end{cases} \tag{10}$$

For the PID-type FC structure with the RROM self-tuning mechanism, the scaling factors to be optimized are K_f and K_{fd}. The formulated optimization problem is defined as follows:

$$\begin{cases} \underset{\boldsymbol{x}=\left(K_f,K_{fd}\right)^T \in \mathbb{R}_+^2}{minimiser} \quad f(\boldsymbol{x}) \\ subject to \\ D \leq D^{\max}; t_s \leq t_s^{\max}; t_r \leq t_r^{\max}; E_{ss} \leq E_{ss}^{\max} \end{cases} \tag{11}$$

3.2. Particle Swarm Optimization technique

In this study, the proposed PSO approach is presented and a constrained PSO algorithm is also developed. The convergence conditions of such an algorithm are analyzed and established.

3.2.1. Overview

The PSO technique is an evolutionary computation method developed by Kennedy and Eberhart [9]. This recent meta-heuristic technique is inspired by the swarming or collaborative behaviour of biological populations. The cooperation and the exchange of information between population individuals allow solving various complex optimization problems [10, 25, 27, 28, 30].

Without any regularity on the cost function to be optimized, the recourse to this stochastic and global optimization technique is justified by the empirical evidence of its superiority in solving a variety of non-linear, non-convex and non-smooth problems. In comparison with other meta-heuristics, this optimization technique is a simple concept, easy to implement, and a computationally efficient algorithm [10, 27, 30]. The convergence and parameters selection of the PSO algorithm are proved using several advanced theoretical analysis proposed by Ruben and Kamran in [27] and Van den Bergh in [30]. Its stochastic behaviour allows overcoming the local minima problem.

Particle swarm optimisation has been enormously successful in several and various industrial domains [18, 19]. It has been used across a wide range of engineering applications. These applications can be summarized around domains of robotics, image and signal processing, electronic circuits design, communication networks, but more especially the domain of plant control design, as shown in [2–6].

3.2.2. Basic PSO algorithm

The basic PSO algorithm uses a swarm consisting of n_p particles (i.e. $\boldsymbol{x}^1, \boldsymbol{x}^2, \ldots, \boldsymbol{x}^{n_p}$), randomly distributed in the considered initial search space, to find an optimal solution $\boldsymbol{x}^* = \arg\min f(\boldsymbol{x}) \in \mathbb{R}^m$ of a generic optimization problem (8). Each particle, that represents a potential solution, is characterised by a position and a velocity given by $\boldsymbol{x}_k^i := \left(x_k^{i,1}, x_k^{i,2}, \ldots, x_k^{i,m}\right)^T$ and $\boldsymbol{v}_k^i := \left(v_k^{i,1}, v_k^{i,2}, \ldots, v_k^{i,m}\right)^T$ where $(i,k) \in [[1, n_p]] \times [\![1, k_{\max}]\!]$.

At each algorithm iteration, the ith particle position, $\boldsymbol{x}^i \in \mathbb{R}^m$, evolves based on the following update rules:

$$\boldsymbol{x}_{k+1}^i = \boldsymbol{x}_k^i + \boldsymbol{v}_{k+1}^i \tag{12}$$

$$\boldsymbol{v}_{k+1}^i = w_{k+1}\boldsymbol{v}_k^i + c_1 r_{1,k}^i \left(\boldsymbol{p}_k^i - x_k^i\right) + c_2 r_{2,k}^i \left(\boldsymbol{p}_k^g - x_k^i\right) \tag{13}$$

where

w_{k+1}: the inertia factor,

c_1, c_2: the cognitive and the social scaling factors respectively,

$r_{1,k}^i, r_{2,k}^i$: random numbers uniformly distributed in the interval $[\![0,1]\!]$,

$\boldsymbol{p}_k^i$: the best previously obtained position of the ith particle,

$\boldsymbol{p}_k^g$: the best obtained position in the entire swarm at the current iteration k.

Hence, the principle of a particle displacement in the swarm is graphically shown in the Figure 6, for a two dimensional design space.

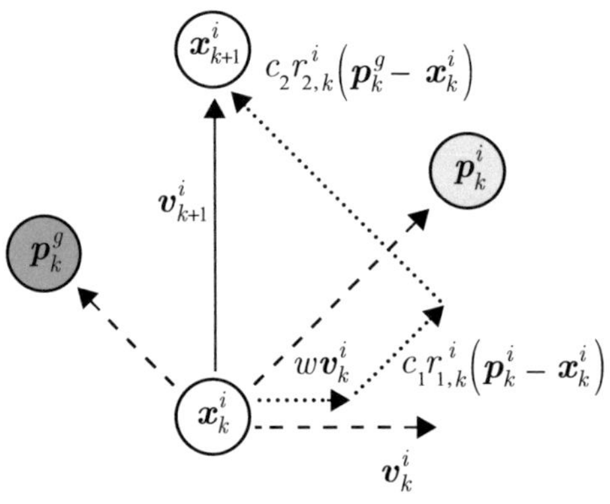

Figure 6. Particle position and velocity updates.

In order to improve the exploration and exploitation capacities of the proposed PSO algorithm, we choose for the inertia factor a linear evolution with respect to the algorithm iteration as given by Shi and Eberhart in [28]:

$$w_{k+1} = w_{\max} - \left(\frac{w_{\max} - w_{\min}}{k_{\max}}\right) k \tag{14}$$

where $w_{\max} = 0.9$ and $w_{\min} = 0.4$ represent the maximum and minimum inertia factor values, respectively, $k_{\max}$ is the maximum iteration number.

Similarly to other meta-heuristic methods, the PSO algorithm is originally formulated as an unconstrained optimizer. Several techniques have been proposed to deal with constraints. One useful approach is by augmenting the cost function of problem (8) with penalties proportional to the degree of constraint infeasibility. In this paper, the following external static penalty technique is used:

$$\varphi(\boldsymbol{x}) = f(\boldsymbol{x}) + \sum_{l=1}^{n_{con}} \chi_l \max\left[0, g_l(\boldsymbol{x})^2\right] \tag{15}$$

where χ_l is a prescribed scaling penalty parameters and n_{con} is the number of problem constraints $g_l(\boldsymbol{x})$.

Finally, the basic proposed PSO algorithm can be summarized by the following steps:

1. Define all PSO algorithm parameters such as swarm size n_p, maximum and minimum inertia factor values, cognitive c_1 and social c_2 scaling factors, etc.
2. Initialize the n_p particles with randomly chosen positions $\boldsymbol{x}_0^i$ and velocities $\boldsymbol{v}_0^i$ in the search space $\mathbb{D}$. Evaluate the initial population and determine $\boldsymbol{p}_0^i$ and $\boldsymbol{p}_0^g$.
3. Increment the iteration number k. For each particle apply the update equations (12) and (13), and evaluate the corresponding fitness values $\varphi_k^i = \varphi\left(\boldsymbol{x}_k^i\right)$:
   - if $\varphi_k^i \leq pbest_k^i$ then $pbest_k^i = \varphi_k^i$ and $\boldsymbol{p}_k^i = \boldsymbol{x}_k^i$;
   - if $\varphi_k^i \leq gbest_k$ then $gbest_k = \varphi_k^i$ and $\boldsymbol{p}_k^g = \boldsymbol{x}_k^i$;

   where $pbest_k^i$ and $gbest_k$ represent the best previously fitness of the ith particle and the entire swarm, respectively.
4. If the termination criterion is satisfied, the algorithm terminates with the solution $\boldsymbol{x}^* = \arg\min_{\boldsymbol{x}_k^i} \left\{f\left(\boldsymbol{x}_k^i\right), \forall i, k\right\}$. Otherwise, go to step 3.

3.2.3. The convergence of PSO algorithm analysis

In this part, the proposed PSO algorithm is analysed based on results in [27, 30]. Theoretical conditions for convergence algorithm and parameters choice are established.

Let us replace the velocity update equation (13) into the position update equation (12) to get the following expression:

$$\boldsymbol{x}_{k+1}^i = \left(1 - c_1 r_{1,k}^i - c_2 r_{2,k}^i\right)\boldsymbol{x}_k^i + w\boldsymbol{v}_k^i + c_1 r_{1,k}^i \boldsymbol{p}_k^i + c_2 r_{2,k}^i \boldsymbol{p}_k^g \tag{16}$$

A similar re-arrangement of the velocity term (13) leads to:

$$\boldsymbol{v}_{k+1}^i = -\left(c_1 r_{1,k}^i + c_2 r_{2,k}^i\right)\boldsymbol{x}_k^i + w\boldsymbol{v}_k^i + c_1 r_{1,k}^i \boldsymbol{p}_k^i + c_2 r_{2,k}^i \boldsymbol{p}_k^g \tag{17}$$

The obtained equations (16) and (17) can be combined and written in matrix form as:

$$\begin{bmatrix} \boldsymbol{x}_{k+1}^i \\ \boldsymbol{v}_{k+1}^i \end{bmatrix} = \begin{bmatrix} 1 - \left(c_1 r_{1,k}^i + c_2 r_{2,k}^i\right) & w \\ -\left(c_1 r_{1,k}^i + c_2 r_{2,k}^i\right) & w \end{bmatrix} \begin{bmatrix} \boldsymbol{x}_k^i \\ \boldsymbol{v}_k^i \end{bmatrix} + \begin{bmatrix} c_1 r_{1,k}^i & c_2 r_{2,k}^i \\ c_1 r_{1,k}^i & c_2 r_{2,k}^i \end{bmatrix} \begin{bmatrix} \boldsymbol{p}_k^i \\ \boldsymbol{p}_k^g \end{bmatrix} \tag{18}$$

This above expression can be considered as a state-space representation of a discrete-time dynamic linear system, given by:

$$\hat{y}_{k+1} = \mathcal{M}\hat{y}_k + \mathcal{N}\hat{u}_k \tag{19}$$

where $\hat{y}_k$ is the state vector, $\hat{u}_k$ the external input system, $\mathcal{M}$ and $\mathcal{N}$ the dynamic and input matrices respectively, defined as:

$$\hat{y}_k = \begin{bmatrix} \boldsymbol{x}_k^i \\ \boldsymbol{v}_k^i \end{bmatrix}; \hat{u}_k = \begin{bmatrix} \boldsymbol{p}_k^i \\ \boldsymbol{p}_k^g \end{bmatrix}; \mathcal{M} = \begin{bmatrix} 1 - \left(c_1 r_{1,k}^i + c_2 r_{2,k}^i\right) & w \\ -\left(c_1 r_{1,k}^i + c_2 r_{2,k}^i\right) & w \end{bmatrix}; \mathcal{N} = \begin{bmatrix} c_1 r_{1,k}^i & c_2 r_{2,k}^i \\ c_1 r_{1,k}^i & c_2 r_{2,k}^i \end{bmatrix} \tag{20}$$

For a given particle, the convergent behaviour can be maintained while assuming that the external input is constant, as there is no external excitation in the dynamic system. In such a case, as the iterations go to infinity the updated positions and velocities become constants from the kth to the $(k+1)^{th}$ iteration, given the following equilibrium state:

$$\hat{y}_{k+1} - \hat{y}_k = \begin{bmatrix} -\left(c_1 r_{1,k}^i + c_2 r_{2,k}^i\right) & w \\ -\left(c_1 r_{1,k}^i + c_2 r_{2,k}^i\right) & w-1 \end{bmatrix} \begin{bmatrix} \boldsymbol{x}_k^i \\ \boldsymbol{v}_k^i \end{bmatrix} + \begin{bmatrix} c_1 r_{1,k}^i & c_2 r_{2,k}^i \\ c_1 r_{1,k}^i & c_2 r_{2,k}^i \end{bmatrix} \begin{bmatrix} \boldsymbol{p}_k^i \\ \boldsymbol{p}_k^g \end{bmatrix} = \begin{bmatrix} 0 \\ 0 \end{bmatrix} \tag{21}$$

which is true only when:

$$\begin{aligned} &\boldsymbol{x}_k^i = \boldsymbol{p}_k^i = \boldsymbol{p}_k^g, \\ &\boldsymbol{v}_k^i = 0 \end{aligned} \tag{22}$$

Therefore, we obtain an equilibrium point, for which all particles tend to converge as algorithm iteration progresses, given by:

$$\hat{y}_{eq} = \left[\boldsymbol{p}_k^g, 0\right]^T \tag{23}$$

So, the dynamic behaviour of the ith particle can be analysed using the eigenvalues derived from the dynamic matrix formulation (19) and (20), solutions of the following characteristic polynomial:

$$\lambda^2 - \left(1 + w - c_1 r_{1,k}^i - c_2 r_{2,k}^i\right)\lambda + w = 0 \tag{24}$$

The following necessary and sufficient conditions for stability of the considered discrete-time dynamic system (20) are obtained while applying the classical Jury criterion:

$$\begin{aligned} &|w| < 1 \\ &c_1 r_{1,k}^i + c_2 r_{2,k}^i > 0 \\ &w + 1 - \tfrac{c_1 r_{1,k}^i + c_2 r_{2,k}^i}{2} > 0 \end{aligned} \tag{25}$$

Knowing that $r_{1,k}^i, r_{2,k}^i \in [\![0,1]\!]$, the above stability conditions are equivalents to the following set of parameter selection heuristics which guarantee convergence for the PSO algorithm:

$$\begin{aligned} &0 < c_1 + c_2 < 4 \\ &\tfrac{c_1 + c_2}{2} - 1 < w < 1 \end{aligned} \tag{26}$$

While these heuristics provide useful selection parameter bounds, an analysis of the effect of the different parameter settings is achieved and verified by some numerical simulations to determine the effect of such parameters in the PSO algorithm convergence performances.

In order to illustrate the efficiency of the proposed PSO algorithm in the resolution of problems (9), (10) and (11), several comparisons with the Genetic Algorithms Optimization GAO-based method [14, 29] are considered. The next section is dedicated to the application of the proposed PSO-tuned PID-FC approaches to an electrical DC drive and a thermal process within a developed real-time framework.

4. Real-time control approach implementation

In this section, all designed PSO-tuned PID-type FC structures are applied to two different systems such as an electrical DC drive and a thermal PT-326 Process Trainer benchmarks. Real-time implementations and experimental results of these control laws are presented and discussed.

4.1. Control of an electrical DC drive benchmark

4.1.1. Plant model description

The considered benchmark is a 250 watts electrical DC drive, as shown in Figure 15. The machine's speed rotation is 3000 rpm at 180 volts DC armature voltage. The motor is supplied by an AC-DC power converter. The developed real-time application acquires input data (speed of the DC drive) and generates control signal for thyristors of AC-DC power converter (PWM signal). This is achieved using a data acquisition and control system based on a PC computer and a multi-functions data acquisition PCI-1710 board which is compatible with MATLAB/Simulink [1, 17].

The considered electrical DC drive can be described by the following model that is used in the design setup:

$$G(s) = \frac{k_m}{(1 + \tau_m s)(1 + \tau_e s)} \tag{27}$$

The model's parameters are obtained by an experimental identification procedure and they are summarized in Table 3 with their associated uncertainty bounds. Also, this model is sampled with 10 ms sampling time for simulation and experimental setups.

Parameters	Nominal values	Uncertainty bounds
k_m	0.05	75 %
τ_m	300 ms	75 %
τ_e	14 ms	75 %

Table 3. Identified DC drive model parameters.

4.1.2. Simulation results

For all proposed PSO-tuned PID-type FC structures, product-sum inference and center of gravity defuzzification methods are adopted for the FC block. Uniformly distributed and symmetrical membership functions, are assigned for the fuzzy input and output variables. The associated fuzzy rule-base is given in Table 4.

e_k / Δe_k	N	Z	P
N	NB	N	Z
Z	N	Z	P
P	Z	P	PB

Table 4. Fuzzy rule-base for the output u_{fz}.

The linguistic levels assigned to the input variables e_k and Δe_k, and the output variable u_{fz} are given as follows: N (Negative), Z (Zero), P (Positive), N (Negative), NB (Negative Big) and PB (Positive Big). The view of this rule-base is illustrated in Figure 7.

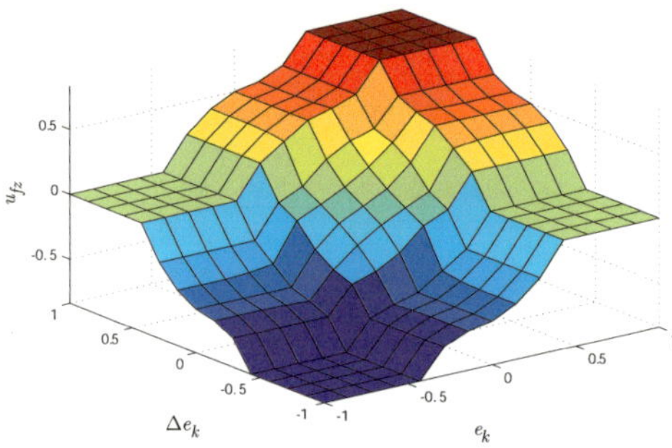

Figure 7. View of fuzzy rule-base for the fuzzy output u_{fz}.

The swarm size algorithm's choice is generally a problem-dependent in PSO framework. However, Eberhart and Shi [10] as well as Poli et al. [25] show that this parameter is often set empirically in relation to the dimensionality and perceived difficulty of a considered optimization problem. They suggest that swarm size values in the range 20-50 are quite common. For this purpose, we have tested the proposed PSO algorithm with different values in this range for the case of PID-type FC structure without self-tuning mechanisms. Globally, all the found results are close to each other. But, best values of the fitness are obtained while using a swarm size equal to 30. Henceforth, this value will be adopted for our following works.

In the PSO framework, it is necessary to run the algorithm several times in order to get some statistical data on the quality of results and so to validate the proposed approach. We run the proposed algorithm 20 times and feasible solutions are found in 98 % of trials and within an acceptable CPU computation time for the IAE and ISE criterion cases. The obtained optimization results are summarized in Tables 5, 6 and 7. Besides, the fact that the algorithm's convergence always takes place in the same region of the design space, whatever is the initial population, indicates that the algorithm succeeds in finding a region of the interesting research space to explore. The performances comparison of PSO- and GAO-based approaches is achieved in the same conditions.

Cost function	Algorithm	Best	Mean	Worst	St. dev.
ISE	PSO	0.0193	0.0304	0.0511	0.018
ISE	GAO	0.1200	0.1780	0.2410	0.050
IAE	PSO	0.0162	0.0261	0.0497	0.016
IAE	GAO	0.1892	0.2835	0.3227	0.066

Table 5. Optimization results from 20 trials of problem (9).

Cost function	Algorithm	Best	Mean	Worst	St. dev.
ISE	PSO	0.0660	0.0765	0.1030	0.015
ISE	GAO	0.0820	0.0912	0.1330	0.012
IAE	PSO	0.0659	0.0838	0.0946	0.014
IAE	GAO	0.0718	0.0814	0.0973	0.013

Table 6. Optimization results from 20 trials of problem (10).

Cost function	Algorithm	Best	Mean	Worst	St. dev.
ISE	PSO	0.0559	0.0792	0.0840	0.013
ISE	GAO	0.0822	0.0936	0.1120	0.015
IAE	PSO	0.0673	0.0861	0.0993	0.016
IAE	GAO	0.0855	0.0905	0.1009	0.008

Table 7. Optimization results from 20 trials of problem (11).

Indeed, the population size, used in the GAO algorithm, is set as 30 individuals and the maximum generation number is 50. However, the GA parameters, used for MATLAB simulations, are chosen as the Stochastic Uniform selection and the Gaussian mutation methods. The Elite Count is set as 2 and the Crossover Fraction as 0.8. The algorithm stops when the number of generations reaches the specified value for the maximum generation.

According to the statistical analysis of Tables 5,6 and 7, we can conclude that the proposed PSO-based approach produces better results in comparison with the standard GAO-based one. Also, while using a Pentium IV, 1.73 GHz and MATLAB 7.7.0, the CPU computation times are about 358 and 364 seconds for ISE and IAE criteria, respectively, for the considered PID-type FC without self-tuning mechanisms structure.

On the other hand, performances on convergence properties of the proposed PSO and the used GAO algorithm, in term of iterations number's required to find the best solution, are compared for the IAE criterion case, as shown in Figures 8 and 9. While using the proposed PSO-based method, we succeed to obtain the optimal solution within only about 28 iterations. However, the GAO-based method finds the same result after 40 iterations. All these observations can show the superiority of the proposed PSO-based method in comparison with the GAO-based one. Indeed, the quality of the obtained optimal solution, the fastness convergence as well as the simple software implementation is better than those of the GAO-based approach.

In a typical optimization procedure, the scaling parameters χ_l, given in equation (15), will be linearly increased at each iteration step so constraints are gradually enforced. Generally, the quality of the solution will directly depend on the value of the specified scaling parameters. In this paper and in order to make the proposed approach simple, great and constant scaling penalty parameters, equal to 10^3, are used for simulations. Indeed, simulation results show that with a great values of χ_l, the control system performances are weakly degraded and the effects on the tuning parameters are less meaningful. The PSO algorithm convergence is faster than the case with linearly variable scaling parameters.

The robustness of the proposed PSO algorithm convergence, under variation of the cognitive, social and inertia factor parameters, is analysed based on numerical simulations as shown

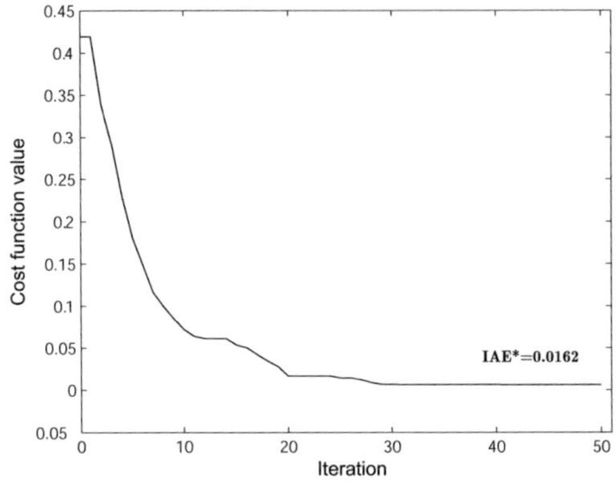

Figure 8. Convergence properties of the proposed PSO algorithm: IAE criterion case.

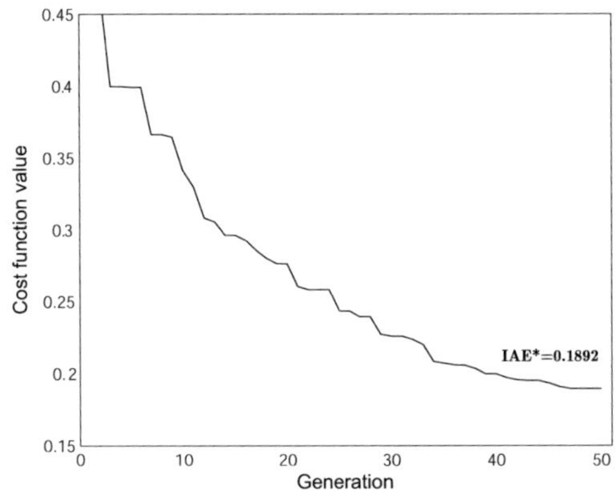

Figure 9. Convergence properties of the standard GAO algorithm: IAE criterion case.

in Figure 10 and Figure 11. The PSO algorithm's convergence is guaranteed within the established domain given by the equation (26).

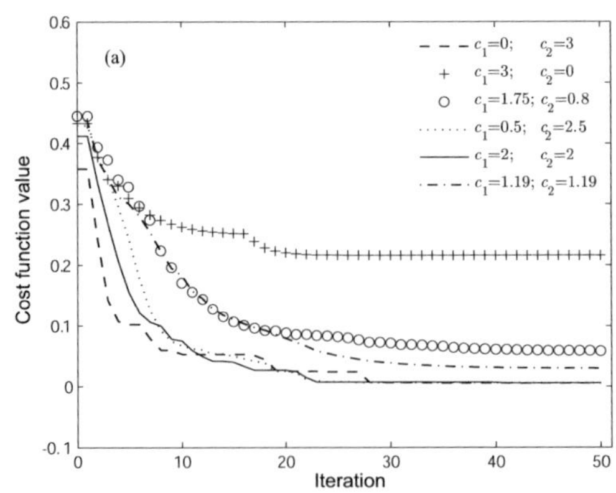

Figure 10. Robustness of the proposed PSO algorithm under variations of the cognitive and social parameters: IAE criterion case.

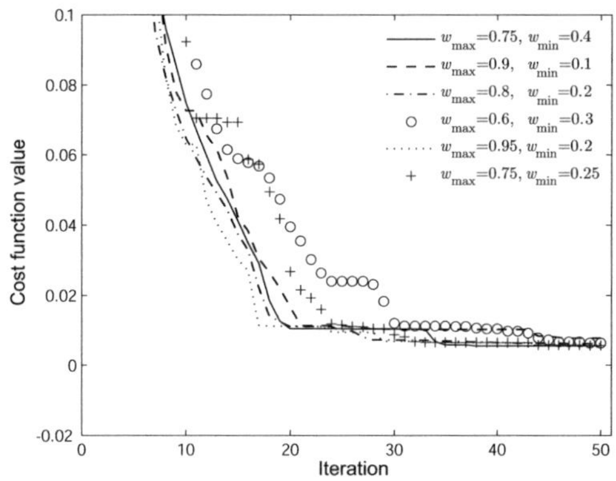

Figure 11. Robustness of the proposed PSO algorithm under variations of the inertia factor: IAE criterion case.

The robust stability of the proposed PSO-tuned PID-type FC approach is analysed while considering external disturbances and model uncertainties. According to uncertain bounds on nominal plant parameters, given in Table 1, we are going to consider the following family of continuous-time transfer functions supposed including the real studied plant:

$$\mathcal{G} = \left\{ \hat{G}(s) = \frac{k_m}{(1+\tau_m s)(1+\tau_e s)}; k_m \in \left[k_m^{\min}, k_m^{\max}\right], \tau_e \in \left[\tau_e^{\min}, \tau_e^{\max}\right], \tau_m \in \left[\tau_m^{\min}, \tau_m^{\max}\right] \right\} \tag{28}$$

Figure 12 shows the step responses of a family of 5 random generated closed-loop uncertain models. The stability robustness of the uncertain plants, under the above considered uncertainty types, is guaranteed for all designed PID-type FC structures.

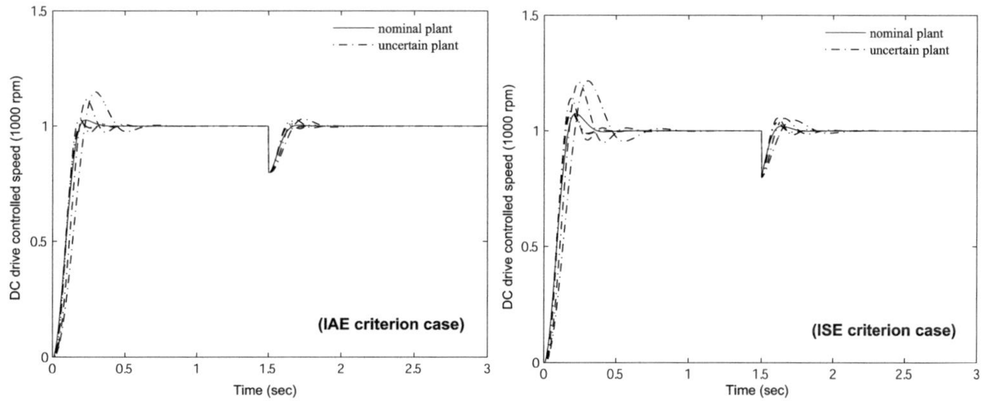

Figure 12. Stability robustness of the PSO-tuned PID-type fuzzy controlled system under model parameters uncertainties and external disturbances.

Finally, the time-domain performances of all proposed PID-type FC structures, are compared for the PSO- and GAO-based design cases as shown in Figure 13.

Besides, Table 8 shows the superiorities of the self-tuning EFTM and RROM PID-type FC structures in relation to the one without self-tuning mechanisms as verified in [16]. Remember that the considered time-domain constraints for the PID-type FC tuning problems (9), 10)

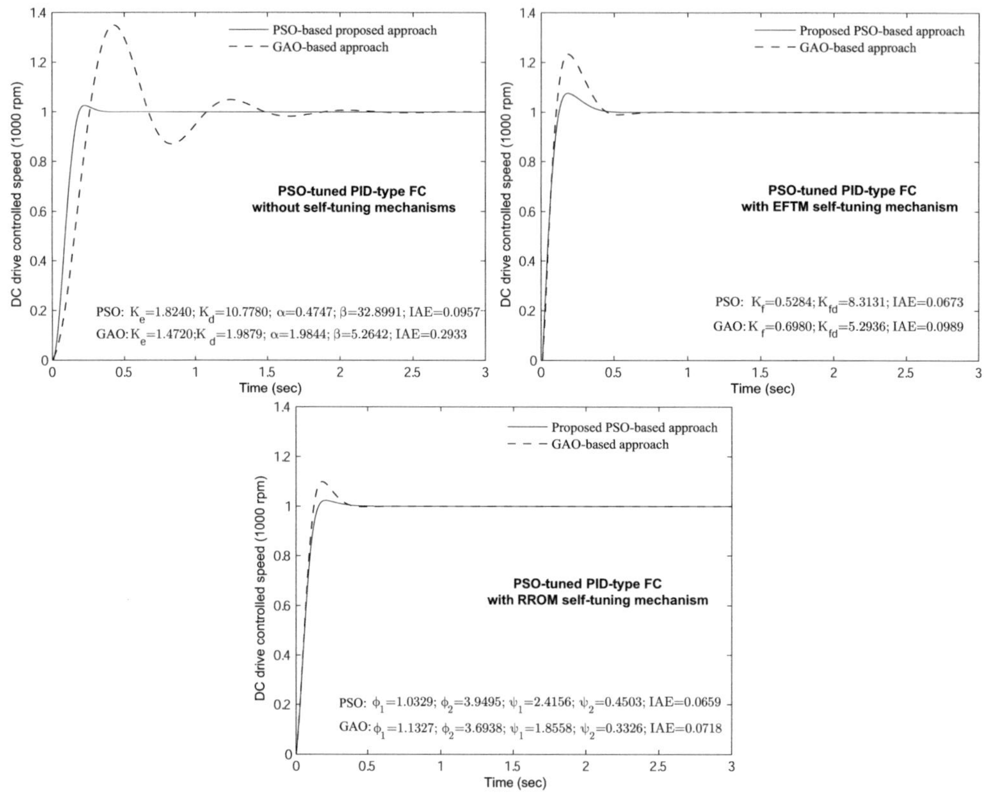

Figure 13. Time-domain performances comparison of all designed PSO- and GAO-tuned PID-type FC structures: IAE criterion case.

and (11) problems, defined in terms of overshoot, steady state, rise and settling times, have been specified as $D^{max} = 20\%$, $E_{ss}^{max} = 0$, $t_r^{max} = 0.25$ sec and $t_s^{max} = 0.75$ sec.

PSO-tuned PID-type FC structure	$D(\%)$	t_r(sec)	t_s (sec)	E_{ss}	CPU computation time (sec)
without self-tuning mechanisms	17.5	0.23	0.49	0	364
with EFTM self-tuning mechanism	15	0.21	0.64	0	370
with RROM self-tuning mechanism	7	0.20	0.68	0	392

Table 8. Performances of the PSO-tuned PID-type FC structures: IAE criterion case.

4.1.3. Experimental setup and results

In order to illustrate the efficiency of the proposed PSO-tuned fuzzy control structures within a real-time framework, the example of the PID-type FC without self-tuning mechanism is considered. The same principle of implementation remains valid for the other PID-type FC structures.

The controlled process is constituted by the single-phase AC-DC power converter and the independent excitation DC motor. A schematic diagram of the experimental setup prepared for testing of the designed controller is shown in Figure 14. The developed experimental benchmark is given by Figure 15. The designed real-time application acquires input data (speed of the DC drive) and generates control signals for the AC-DC power converter through a thyristors gate drive circuit. This is achieved using a data acquisition and control system based on PC and a multi-function data acquisition PCI-1710 board with 12-bit resolution of A/D converter and up to 100 KHz sampling rate. A thyristors gate drive circuit, based on a multivibrator, is used to generate a triggering burst of high-frequency impulses. A pulse transformer is used to assure the galvanic insulation between the control and power circuits. The acquired speed measure, obtained from tachometer sensor, must be adapted to be applied to the used multi-function PCI-1710 board. The complete electronic circuit diagram of the designed control system is given in [1, 17].

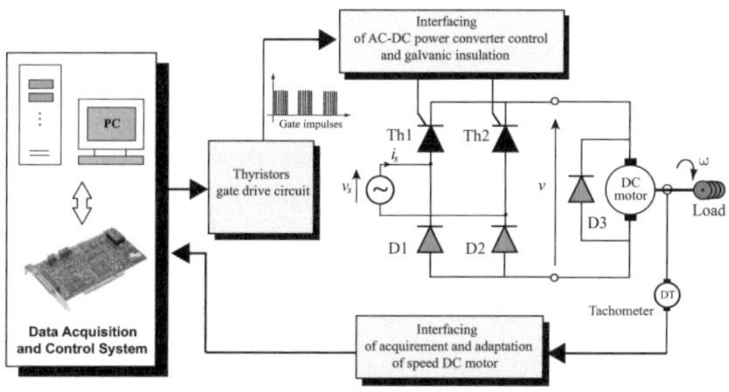

Figure 14. The proposed experimental setup schematic.

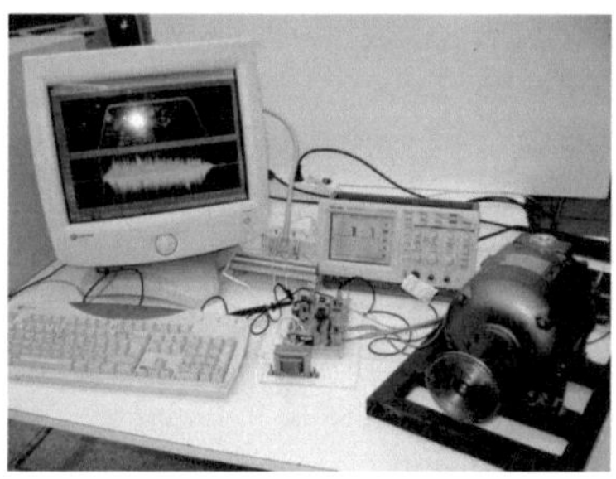

Figure 15. The developed experimental DC drive benchmark.

The multi-function data acquisition PCI-1710 board allows achieving measurement and controlling functions. This target is used to create a real-time application to let the implemented controller system run while synchronized to a real-time clock. The model of the plant was removed from the simulation model, and instead of it, the input device driver (Analog Input) and the output device driver (Analog Output) were introduced as shown in Figure 17. These device drivers close the feedback loop when moving from simulations to experiments. Device driver's blocks include procedures to access the inputs-outputs board. The real-time controller is developed through the compilation and linking stage, in a form of a Dynamic Link Library (DLL) which is then loaded in memory and started-up

The practical implementation of the PSO-tuned PID-type FC approach leads to the experimental results of Figure 17 and Figure 18. The obtained results are satisfactory for a simple, systematic and non-conventional control approach and point out the controller's viability and validate the proposed control approach. The measured speed tracking error of the controlled DC drive is very small (less than 10 % of set point) showing the high performances of the proposed control especially in terms of tracking. On the other hand,

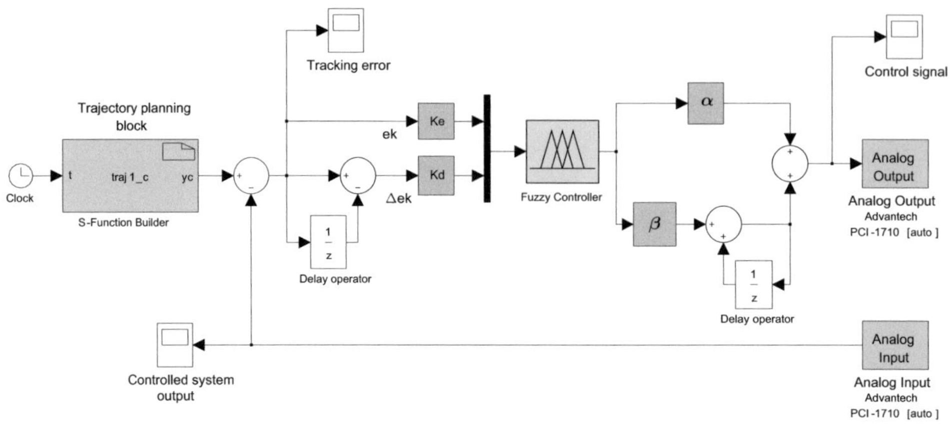

Figure 16. PCI-1710 board based real-time implementation of the proposed PSO-tuned PID-type FC structure.

Figure 18 shows the robustness of the proposed PSO-tuned PID-type FC in rejection of an external load disturbance applied on the controlled system. The dynamic of the disturbance rejection is fast and guaranteed.

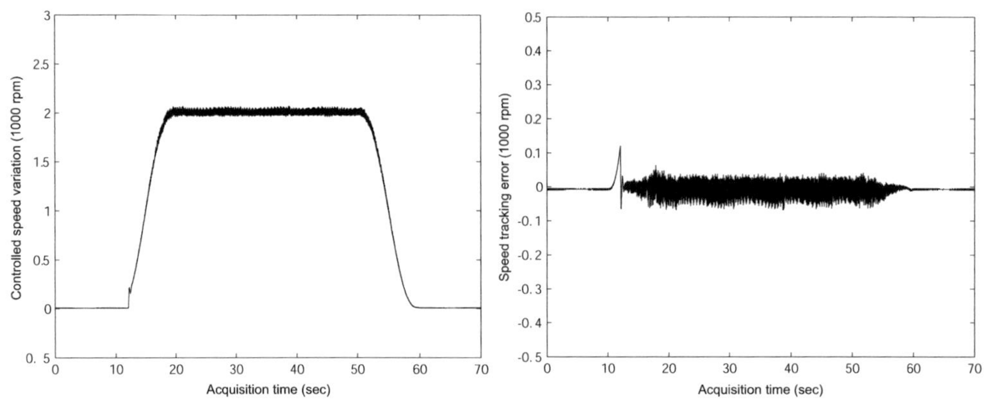

Figure 17. Experimental results of PSO-tuned PID-type FC implementation: fuzzy controller tracking performances.

4.2. Control of a thermal process benchmark

4.2.1. Plant model description

The thermal process to be controlled, shown in the photography of Figure 20, is based on a known PT-326 Process trainer [13], initially developed with an analog control system and modified in order to be digitally controlled. To power the heating resistor, a single-phase AC-AC converter, is developed [7].

In this prototype, the air drawn from atmosphere by a centrifugal blower is injected, through a heating element, in a polypropylene pipe, and rejected in the atmosphere. The amount of air

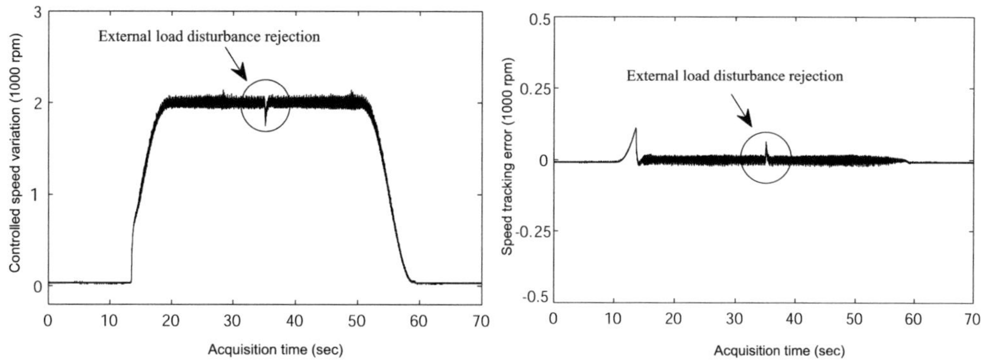

Figure 18. Experimental results of PSO-tuned PID-type FC implementation: fuzzy controller robustness under external load disturbance.

flowing in the pipe can be adjusted by the mean of an inlet throttle attached to the blower. The process consists of heating the air flowing in the pipe to the desired temperature level. The digital control system generates a 40W signal which determines the amount of electrical power supplied to heating resistor made of $10K\Omega/7W$ power resistors. According to these settings, the experimental trials show that the controlled air temperature can be varied up to 20°C from the ambient temperature. The assigned control objective is to regulate the temperature of the air at a desired level, with high tracking performance and under internal disturbances, like model parameters variation, and output disturbances. The temperature sensor can be placed at three different locations on the path of the air flow. A variation in the temperature makes a voltage variation at the sensor's output. The amount of air trough the pipe, adjusted by setting the opening of the throttle, can also be used to generate an output disturbance, in order to test the efficiency of the proposed control system.

The controlled system input is the voltage applied to the AC-AC power electronic circuit feeding the heating resistor, and the output is the air flow temperature in the pipe, expressed by a 50 mV/°C voltage, obtained after amplification of the LM35 temperature sensor's output signal. As shown in [23, 32], this process can be characterized as a non-linear system with a pure time delay. The pure time delay depends on the position of the temperature sensor element inserted into the air stream at any one of the three positions along the tube. When the temperature in the air volume inside the tube is assumed uniform a linear model can be obtained. To identify a numerical model of the considered plant, some experimental trials lead to consider the following transfer function, between the heater input voltage and the sensor's output voltage:

$$G(s) = \frac{k_m}{1+\tau s} e^{-\tau_d s} \tag{29}$$

where k_m is the DC gain system, τ is the time constant system, and τ_d is the time delay system.

This obtained plant model is assumed to be the nominal one and will be adopted in PSO-tuned PID-type FC synthesis step. These model's parameters are obtained by an experimental identification procedure and they are summarized in Table 9 with their associated uncertainty bounds. Also, this model is sampled with 2 sec sampling time for simulation and experimental setups.

Parameters	Nominal values	Uncertainty bounds
k_m	20	50 %
τ	65 sec	50 %
τ_d	1 sec	50 %

Table 9. Identified Thermal Process model parameters.

For this PSO-tuned PID-type fuzzy control example, we represent only the obtained experimental results. For the numerical simulations step, both IAE and ISE criterion, used for the electrical DC drive control, are investigated for this thermal process example. Same problems (9), (10) and (11) are considered and resolved by the developed constrained PSO algorithm.

4.2.2. Experimental setup and results

The developed real-time application acquires air temperature measure and generates control signals for the triac of AC-AC power converter through a gate drive circuit, as shown in Figure 19. This is achieved using a control system based on PC and the used multi-function data acquisition PCI-1710 board. A triac gate drive circuit is used to generate a Pulse Width Modulation (PWM) control signal synchronized with the zero-crossing of the AC voltage. The acquired air temperature measure is scaled before being applied to the used multi-function PCI-1710 board used to create a real-time application to let the implemented controller system run while synchronized to a real-time clock. This leads to experimental results shown in Figure 21 and Figure 22.

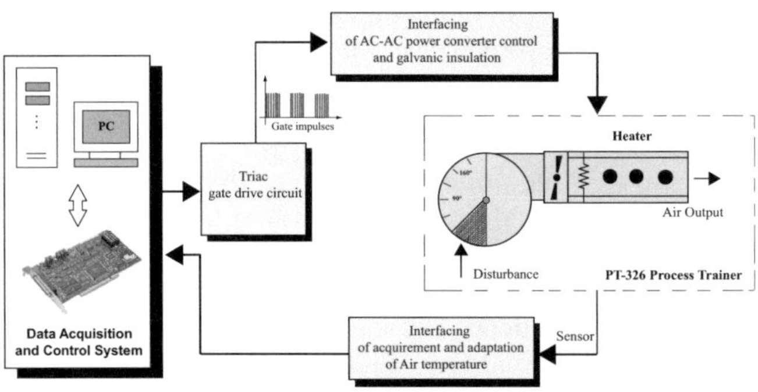

Figure 19. The proposed thermal process experimental setup schematic.

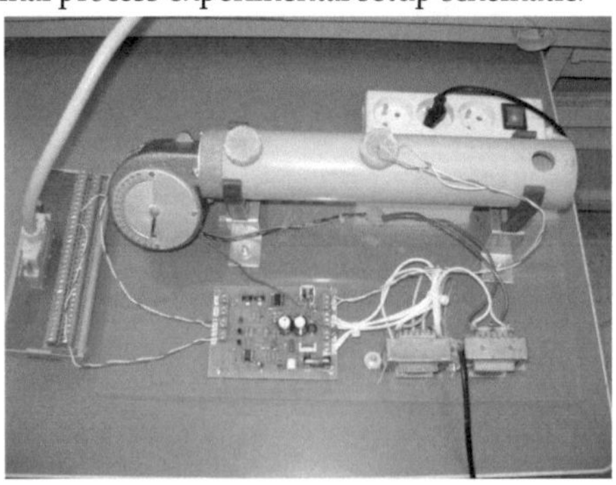

Figure 20. Developed experimental benchmark of the PT-326 Process Trainer.

As shown in Figure 21 and Figure 22, the controlled air temperature of the considered thermal process tracks the desired trajectory with high performance in terms of response speed and precision in the two considered cases. The robustness of the proposed control strategy in term of output static disturbance rejection, which caused by the throttle opening, is improved.

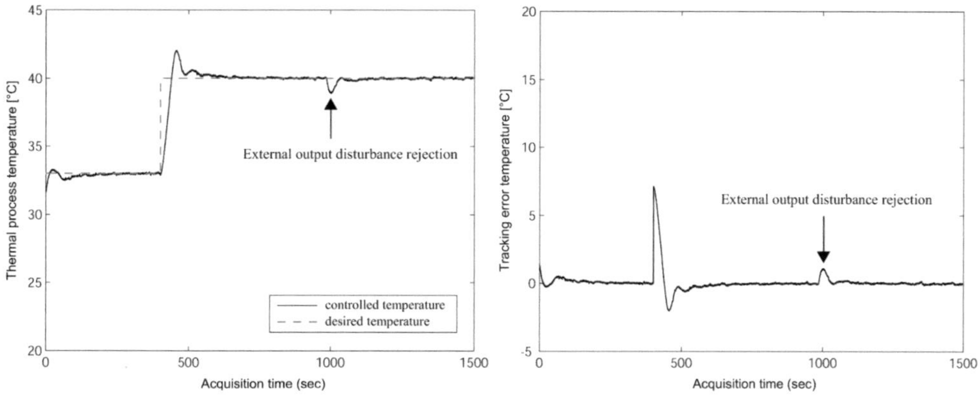

Figure 21. Experimental result of PSO-tuned fuzzy controlled PT-326 Process Trainer: IAE criterion case.

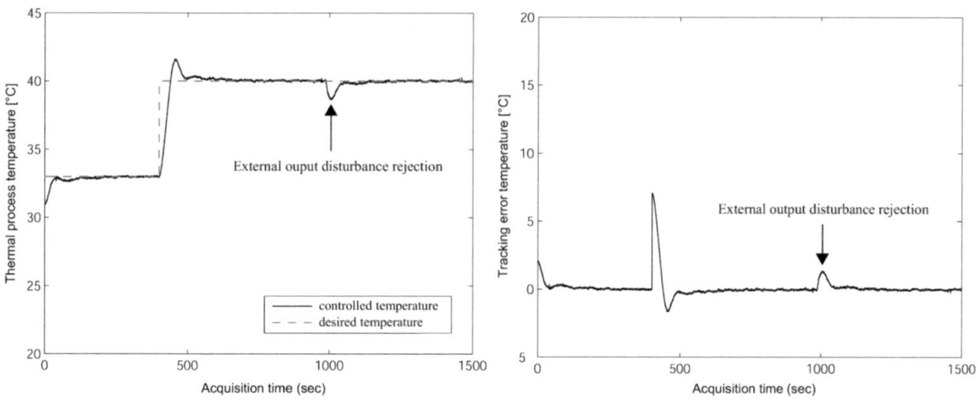

Figure 22. Experimental result of PSO-tuned fuzzy controlled PT-326 Process Trainer: ISE criterion case.

5. Conclusion

In this study, a new method for tuning PID-type FC structures, using a constrained PSO-based technique, is proposed and successfully applied to an electrical DC drive and thermal process within a real-time framework. This efficient tool leads to a robust and systematic fuzzy control design approach. The performances comparison, with the standard GAO-based method, shows the efficiency and superiority of the proposed PSO-based approach in terms of the obtained solution qualities, the convergence speed and the simple software implementation of its algorithm.

The practical implementation of the PSO-tuned PID-type FC approach, for the considered electrical DC drive and the thermal PT-326 Process Trainer benchmarks, leads to several satisfactory experimental results showing the high performances of the proposed control especially in terms of tracking and robustness.

The PSO-tuned PID-type FC structures robustness, under external influences such as the output static disturbances and parametric uncertainties, are proven. The control design methodology is systematic, practical and simple without need to exact analytic plant model description. The obtained simulation and experimental results show the efficiency in terms of performance and robustness of the proposed fuzzy control approach which can be applied in industrial motor control field.

Author details

S. Bouallègue
Higher Insitute of Industrial Systems of Gabes (ISSIG), Salaheddine Elayoubi Street, 6032 Gabes, Tunisia

J. Haggège and M. Benrejeb
National Engineering School of Tunis (ENIT), BP 37, le Belvédère, 1002 Tunis, Tunisia

All authors are with the Research Laboratory in Automatic Control (LA.R.A) of ENIT.

6. References

[1] Bouallègue, S., Haggège, J., Benrejeb, M., (2012). On a robust real-time $\mathcal{H}_\infty$ controller design for an electrical drive, International Journal of Modelling, Identification and Control, 15 (2), pp. 89-96.

[2] Bouallègue, S., Haggège, J., Ayadi, M., Benrejeb, M., (2012). PID-type fuzzy logic controller tuning based on particle swarm optimization, Engineering Applications of Artificial Intelligence, 25 (3), pp. 484-493.

[3] Bouallègue, S., (2011). Optimisation par essaim particulaire de lois de commande robuste : théorie et mise en œuvre pratique, Editions Universitaires Européennes, ISBN : 978-613-1-59335-2, Saarbrücken, Germany.

[4] Bouallègue, S., Haggège, J., Benrejeb, M., (2010). Structured Loop-Shaping $\mathcal{H}_\infty$ Controller Design using Particle Swarm Optimization. Proceedings of the 2010 IEEE International Conference on Systems, Man, and Cybernetics SMC'10, Istanbul.

[5] Bouallègue, S., Haggège, J., Benrejeb, M., (2010). Structured Mixed-Sensitivity $\mathcal{H}_\infty$ Design using Particle Swarm Optimization. Proceedings of the 7th IEEE International Multi-Conference on Systems, Signals and Devices SSD'10, Amman.

[6] Bouallègue, S., Haggège, J., Benrejeb, M., (2011). Particle Swarm Optimization-Based Fixed-Structure $\mathcal{H}_\infty$ Control Design. International Journal of Control, Automation, and Systems 9 (2), pp. 258-266.

[7] Bouallègue, S., Haggège,J., and Benrejeb, M., (2009). Real-Time $\mathcal{H}_\infty$ Control Design for a Thermal Process, Proceedings of the 10th International conference on Sciences and Techniques of Automatic control & computer engineering STA'2009-ACS, pp. 949-958, Hammamet, Tunisia.

[8] Bühler, H., (1994). Réglage par logique floue, Presses polytechniques et universitaires romandes, Lausanne.

[9] Eberhart, R.C., Kennedy, J., (1995). A New Optimizer Using Particle Swarm Theory. Proceedings of the 6th International Symposium on Micro Machine and Human Science, Nagoya, pp. 39-43.
[10] Eberhart, R.C., Shi, Y., (2001). Particle Swarm Optimization: Developments, Applications and Resources. Proceedings of the IEEE Congress on Evolutionary Computation, Seoul, Korea, pp. 81-86.
[11] Eker, I., Torun, Y., (2006). Fuzzy logic control to be conventional method. Energy Conversion and Management 47, pp. 377-394.
[12] Eksin, I., Güzelkaya, M., Gürleyen, F., (2001). A new methodology for deriving the rule-base of a fuzzy logic controller with a new internal structure. Engineering Applications of Artificial Intelligence 14, pp. 617-628.
[13] Feedback, (1980). Process Trainer PT326, Feedback Instruments Limited, Crowborough, United Kingdom.
[14] Goldberg, D.E., (1989). Genetic Algorithms in Search, Optimization, and Machine Learning. Addison-Wesley.
[15] Grigorie, L. (editor), (2011). Fuzzy Controllers, Theory and Applications, ISBN 978-953-307-543-3, InTech, Croatia.
[16] Güzelkaya, M., Eksin, I., Yesil, E., (2003). Self-tuning of PID-type fuzzy logic controller coefficients via relative rate observer. Engineering Applications of Artificial Intelligence 16, pp. 227-236.
[17] Haggège, J., Ayadi, M., Bouallègue, S., Benrejeb, M., (2010). Design of Fuzzy Flatness-based Controller for a DC Drive. Control and Intelligent Systems 38 (3), pp. 164-172.
[18] Korosec, P., (editor), (2010). New Achievements in Evolutionary Computation, ISBN 978-953-307-053-7, 2010, InTech, Croatia.
[19] Lazinica, A. (editor), (2009). Particle Swarm Optimization, ISBN 978-953-7619-48-0, InTech, Croatia.
[20] Lee, C.C., (1990). Fuzzy Logic in Control Systems: Fuzzy Logic Controller. Part I. IEEE Transactions on Systems, Man, and Cybernetics 20 (2), pp. 404-418.
[21] Lee, C.C., (1990). Fuzzy Logic in Control Systems: Fuzzy Logic Controller. Part II. IEEE Transactions on Systems, Man, and Cybernetics 20 (2), pp. 419-435.
[22] Mamdani, E.H., (1974). Application of fuzzy logic algorithms for control of simple dynamic plant, Proceedings of the Institute of Electrical Engineering (IEE), 121 (12), pp.1585-1588
[23] Mohd, R., Yeoh Keat, H., Sahnius, U., Norhaliza, A.W., (2007). Modelling of PT326 Hot Air Blower Trainer Kit Using PRBS Signal and Cross-Correlation Technique, Jurnal Teknologi, vol. 42, pp. 9-22.
[24] Passino, K.M., Yurkovich, S., (1998). Fuzzy Control. Addison Wesley Longman, Menlo Park, California.
[25] Poli, R., Kennedy, J., Blackwell, T., (2007). Particle Swarm Optimization: An Overview. Swarm Intelligence, Springer 1, pp. 33-57.
[26] Qiao, W.Z., Mizumoto, M., (1996). PID type fuzzy controller and parameters adaptive method. Fuzzy Sets and Systems 78, pp. 23-35.
[27] Ruben, E.P., Kamran, B., (2007). Particle Swarm Optimization in Structural Design, in: Chan, F.T.S., Tiwari, M.K. (Eds.), Swarm Intelligence: Focus on Ant and Particle Swarm Optimization. In-Tech Education and Publishing, Vienna, pp. 373-394.

[28] Shi, Y., Eberhart, R., (1999). Empirical study of particle swarm optimization. Proceedings of the 1999 Congress on Evolutionary Computation, Washington, pp. 1945-1950.
[29] The MathWorks Inc., (2009). Genetic Algorithm and Direct Search ToolboxTM: User's Guide. Natick.
[30] Van den Bergh, F., (2006). An Analysis of Particle Swarm Optimizers. PhD Thesis, University of Pretoria, Pretoria, South Africa.
[31] Woo, Z-W., Chung, H-Y., Lin, J-J., (2000). A PID type fuzzy controller with self-tuning scaling factors. Fuzzy Sets and Systems 115, pp. 321-326.
[32] Yesil, E., Güzelkaya, M., Eksin, I., Tekin, O.A., (2008). Online Tuning of Set-point Regulator with a Blending Mechanism Using PI Controller, Turk J Elec Engin, 16 (2), pp. 143-157.
[33] Zadeh, L.A., (1994). Soft computing and fuzzy logic, IEEE Software, 11 (6), pp. 48-56.
[34] Zadeh, L.A., (1965). Fuzzy Sets, Information and Control, 8, pp. 338-353.

Chapter 7

Output Tracking Control for Fuzzy Systems via Static-Output Feedback Design

Meriem Nachidi and Ahmed El Hajjaji

Additional information is available at the end of the chapter

http://dx.doi.org/10.5772/47138

1. Introduction

Over the past decades, many advances have been made in the field of control theory which rely on state-space theory. The control design methodology that has been most investigated for the state-feedback control, see for example [1, 2] and the references therein. The state-feedback control design supposes that all the system states are available, which is not always possible in realistic applications. Instead, one has to deal with the absence of full-state information by using observers. From the control point of view, observers can be used as part of dynamical controllers. This observer-based design has been extensively studied in the literature [3, 4]. However, it leads to high-order controllers. As a matter of fact, one has to solve a large problem, which increases numerical computations for large scale systems. Other difficulties may arise, if we consider additional performances, such as disturbance rejection, time delays, uncertainties, etc. Hence, it is more suitable to develop methodologies which involve a design with a low dimensionality. In this context, intensive efforts have been devoted to design low-order controllers [3, 5–7]. In particular, it has been shown that designing reduced order stabilizing controllers can be cast as a static output-feedback stabilization problem. Also, it is recognized that, in general, the static output-feedback control design may not exist for certain systems. Note that an important advantage of these controllers is that they are easy to implement without significant numerical burden.

In general, the synthesis of static output-feedback stabilizing controllers is known to be a hard task [5–7]. The main difficulty rises from its nonconvexity. In the literature, some convexification techniques and iterative algorithms have been proposed to handle this problem [3, 5, 7]. A comprehensive survey on static output-feedback stabilization can be found in [6]. The authors show that despite the considerable efforts devoted to solve this problem, there is yet no methodology that can solve it exactly, so it is still an important open topic. However, it has been shown that for SISO (Single-Input Single-Output) systems, this problem can be solved exactly based on an algebraic characterization [8, 9]. Unfortunately, these approaches are valid only for SISO case and cannot be used to take into account additional constraints on the system. In any case, the investigation of this topic within the field of fuzzy control is continuously increasing and leading to many approaches. A most efficient approach is based on the Linear Matrix Inequality (LMI) technique: see for example [10–12]. Indeed, since the developed interior-point methods [13], LMIs can be solved in polynomial-time, using numerical algorithms [14]. Recently, other approach, based on a projective algorithm has been proposed [15]. Notice that the existing LMI tools have opened an important research area in system and control theory and tackled numerous unsolved problems [14]. Therefore, our main focus in this chapter is the design of static output-feedback controllers using LMI theory for a class of nonlinear systems described by Takagi-Sugeno (T-S) fuzzy models.

Recently, the study of T-S fuzzy models has attracted the attention of many of researchers: see [16] and references therein. Fuzzy models have local dynamics (i.e., dynamics in different state space regions), that are represented by local linear systems. The overall model of a fuzzy system is then obtained by interpolating these linear models through nonlinear fuzzy membership functions. Unlike conventional modeling techniques, which use a single model to describe the global behavior of a nonlinear system, fuzzy modeling is essentially a multi-model approach, in which simple local linear submodels are designed in the form of a convex combination of local models in order to describe the global behavior of the nonlinear system. This kind of models has proved to be a good representation for a certain class of nonlinear dynamic systems.

Since the work by [17] on stability analysis and state feedback stabilization for fuzzy systems, the Parallel Distributed Compensation (PDC) procedure has extensively been used for the control of such systems: for more details see [16]. The basic idea of this procedure is to design a feedback gain for each local model, and then to construct a global controller from these local gains, so that the global stability of the overall fuzzy system can be guaranteed. The most interesting of this concept is that the obtained stability conditions do not depend on the nonlinearities (membership functions), so that this makes possible to use linear system techniques for nonlinear control design.

Up to now, the stabilization control design for T-S systems is successfully investigated based on state-feedback or static/dynamic output-feedback [18, 19]. However, the design of a controller which guarantees an adequate tracking performance for finite-dimensional systems is more general problem than the stabilization one, and is still attract considerable attentions due to demand from practical dynamical processes in electric, mechanics, agriculture, ... One of our main interest in this chapter is solving the static output-feedback tracking problem. Due to the fact that the T-S fuzzy models aggregate a set of local linear subsystems, blended together through nonlinear scalar functions, the static output-feedback control problem can be very complicated to solve. With regard to the literature of fuzzy control, a few recent approaches have dealt with the tracking control design problem for nonlinear systems described by T-S fuzzy model. Generally speaking, the incorporation of linearization techniques and adaptive schemes usually needs system's perfect knowledge and leads to complicated adaptation control laws. In [20], the author has been shown that the use of the feedback linearization strategy [21] may lead to unbounded controllers, since their stability is not guaranteed. To overcome these drawbacks, LMI-based methodologies have been developed for tracking control problem, using observer-based fuzzy controller to deal with the absence of full-state information [22].

In this context, this chapter will tackle the static output-feedback fuzzy tracking control problem, focusing on an H_∞ tracking performance, related to an output tracking error for all bounded references inputs. The presented results are an extension of already published works for the stabilization case [12, 23]. In fact, to solve the nonconvexity problem, inherent to static output-feedback control synthesis, a cone complementarity formulation [7] for T-S fuzzy systems is used combined with an iterative algorithm. This algorithm has to optimize a linear objective function subject to a set of LMIs in each iteration. Thus, controllers are derived that not only ensure stability of the closed-loop system, but also provide a prescribed level of output tracking error attenuation.

The main contribution of this chapter is the purpose of a simple procedure reflected by an efficient LMI-based iterative algorithm to solve the fuzzy tracking control problem for nonlinear systems described by discrete-time T-S models. Therefore, since the proposed fuzzy tracking controllers have a low-order character, they are suitable for industrial application. Furthermore, this chapter shows an application to a relevant practical problem, in power engineering and drives field, of the proposed design procedure: guaranteeing a good tracking of the output voltage of DC-DC buck converter [24–26].

2. Problem formulation and preliminaries

Consider a nonlinear system which is approximated by a T-S fuzzy model of the following form:

$i^{th}\mathcal{R}ule$: IF $z_1(k)$ is μ_1^i and ... and $z_p(k)$ is μ_p^i,

$$\text{THEN} \begin{cases} x(k+1) = (A_i + \Delta A_i(k))x(k) + (B_i + \Delta B_i(k))u(k) + E_i w(k), \\ y(k) = C_i x(k), i = 1, \ldots, N, \end{cases} \tag{1}$$

where $x(k) \in \Re^n$ is the state vector, $u(k) \in \Re^{n_u}$ is the input vector, $w(k) \in \Re^{n_w}$ comprises the bounded external disturbances and $y(k) \in \Re^{n_y}$ is the system output. N is the number of IF-THEN rules. $z_1(k), \ldots z_p(k)$ are the premise variables (that comprises states and/or inputs) and μ_j^i $(i = 1, \ldots, N, j = 1, \ldots, p)$ are the fuzzy sets. A_i, B_i, C_i and E_i are known constant matrices of appropriate size, $\Delta A_i(k)$, $\Delta B_i(k)$ are unknown matrices representing time-varying parameter uncertainties, and are assumed to be as follows:

$$[\Delta A_i(k)\ \Delta B_i(k)] = [M_1 F(k) N_{1i}\ M_2 F(k) N_{2i}], \quad i = 1, 2, \ldots, N, \tag{2}$$

where M_i, N_{1i} and N_{2i} are known real constant matrices. $F(k)$ is the uncertainty function that satisfies the classical bounded condition:

$$F(k)^T F(k) \leq I, \quad \forall k. \tag{3}$$

Thus, the global T-S model is an interpolation of all uncertain subsystems through nonlinear functions [16]:

$$\begin{aligned} x(k+1) &= \frac{\sum_{i=1}^{N} \theta_i(z) \left[(A_i + \Delta A_i(k))x(k) + (B_i + \Delta B_i(k))u(k) + E_i w(k)\right]}{\sum_{i=1}^{N} \theta_i(z)}, \\ &= \sum_{i=1}^{N} \alpha_i(z) \left[(A_i + \Delta A_i(k))x(k) + (B_i + \Delta B_i(k))u(k) + E_i w(k)\right], \\ y(k) &= \sum_{i=1}^{N} \alpha_i(z) C_i x(k), \end{aligned} \tag{4}$$

where $\theta_i, i = 1, \ldots, N$, is the membership function corresponding to system rule i, and $\alpha_i(z) = \theta_i(z)/\sum_{i=1}^{N}\theta_i(z)$, fulfills the convex property: $0 \leq \alpha_i(z) \leq 1$ and $\sum_{i=1}^{N}\alpha_i(z) = 1$.

Note that using the so-called sector of nonlinearity approach, a wide number of nonlinear systems can be represented exactly by T-S models in a compact set of the state space. However, with the growing complexity of nonlinear systems, it is useful to take into account the approximations in the dynamical process. Thus, the main objective of the next paragraph is to provide stability conditions that ensure the tracking performance for the uncertain T-S model (4).

3. H_∞ output tracking performance analysis

This section gives sufficient stability conditions which ensure an H_∞ output tracking performance of the uncertain system (4) using a fuzzy Lyapunov function. We recall the following lemma which will be used in this section.

Lemma 3.1. *[27] Let $\mathcal{A}, \mathcal{D}, \mathcal{S}, \mathcal{W}$ and $\mathcal{F}$ be real matrices of appropriate dimension such that $\mathcal{W} > 0$ and $\mathcal{F}\mathcal{F}^T \leq I$. Then, for any scalar $\epsilon > 0$ such that $\mathcal{W} - \epsilon\mathcal{D}\mathcal{D}^T > 0$, we have $(\mathcal{A} + \mathcal{D}\mathcal{F}\mathcal{S})^T\mathcal{W}^{-1}(\mathcal{A} + \mathcal{D}\mathcal{F}\mathcal{S}) \leq \mathcal{A}^T(\mathcal{W} - \epsilon\mathcal{D}\mathcal{D}^T)^{-1}\mathcal{A} + \epsilon^{-1}\mathcal{S}^T\mathcal{S}$.*

Suppose that the desired trajectory can be generated by the following reference model as follows:

$$\begin{cases} x_d(k+1) = \mathbb{A}x_d(k) + \mathbb{B}r(k), \\ y_d(k) = \mathbb{C}x_d(k), \end{cases} \tag{5}$$

where, $y_d(k)$ has the same dimension as $y(k)$, $x_d(k)$ and $r(k) \in \Re^{n_r}$ are respectively the reference state and the bounded reference input, $\mathbb{A}$, $\mathbb{B}$ and $\mathbb{C}$ are appropriately dimensional constant matrices with $\mathbb{A}$ Hurwitz.

Since we deal with the static output-feedback control design problem, the fuzzy controller can incorporates information from $y(k)$ and $y_d(k)$. Thus, the control law which is based on the classical structure of the Parallel Distributed Compensation (PDC) concept [17, 28] shares the same fuzzy sets as the T-S system and can be given as follows:

$$\begin{aligned} &i^{th}\mathcal{R}ule\text{: IF } \; z_1(k) \text{ is } \mu_1^i \text{ and } \ldots \text{ and } z_p(k) \text{ is } \mu_p^i, \\ &\text{THEN} \quad u(k) = K_i(y(k) - y_d(k)), \end{aligned} \tag{6}$$

where the the controller gain K_i is to be chosen. The overall static output-feedback control law is thus inferred as:

$$u(k) = \sum_{i=1}^{N}\alpha_i(z)K_i(y(k) - y_d(k)). \tag{7}$$

The advantages of the static output-feedback controller (7), is well discussed in the literature [3], [6]. This fact motivates us to use such type of control law avoiding the complex control schemes with an additional observer.

Combining (4), (5) and (7), the following augmented closed-loop system is obtained

$$\tilde{x}(k+1) = \sum_{i,j,s=1}^{N} \alpha_i(z)\alpha_j(z)\alpha_s(z) \left[(G_{1ijs} + G_{2ijs}(k))\tilde{x}(k) + W_i\tilde{w}(k) \right], \tag{8}$$

where

$$G_{1ijs} = \begin{bmatrix} A_i + B_i K_j C_s & -B_i K_j \mathbb{C} \\ 0 & \mathbb{A} \end{bmatrix},$$

$$G_{2ijs}(k) = \begin{bmatrix} \Delta A_i(k) + \Delta B_i(k) K_j C_s & -\Delta B_i(k) K_j \mathbb{C} \\ 0 & 0 \end{bmatrix}, \tag{9}$$

$$W_i = \begin{bmatrix} E_i & 0 \\ 0 & \mathbb{B} \end{bmatrix}, \tilde{x} = \begin{bmatrix} x(k) \\ x_d(k) \end{bmatrix}, \tilde{w} = \begin{bmatrix} w(k) \\ r(k) \end{bmatrix},$$

Hence, to meet the required tracking performance, the effect of $\tilde{w}(k)$ on the tracking error $y(k) - y_d(k)$ should be attenuated below a desired level in the sense of [29]:

$$\sum_{k=0}^{k_f} (y(k) - y_d(k))^T (y(k) - y_d(k)) \leq \gamma^2 \sum_{k=0}^{k_f} \tilde{w}(k)^T \tilde{w}(k), \tag{10}$$

$\forall k_f \neq 0$, and $\forall \tilde{w}(k) \in l_2$, k_f is the control final time.

The following theorem shows that H_∞ output tracking performances can be guaranteed if there exist some matrices satisfying certain conditions.

Theorem 3.1. *The augmented closed-loop system in (8) achieves the H_∞ output tracking performance γ, if there exists matrices $P_1 > 0, \ldots, P_N > 0$ and controller gains $K_1, \ldots, K_N$ such that the following conditions hold:*

$$\begin{bmatrix} -P_r^{-1} & 0 & 0 & G_{1ijs} & W_i & \tilde{M} \\ 0 & -\epsilon I & 0 & \tilde{N}_{ijs} & 0 & 0 \\ 0 & 0 & -I & H_i & 0 & 0 \\ G_{1ijs}^T & \tilde{N}_{ijs}^T & H_i^T & -P_i & 0 & 0 \\ W_i^T & 0 & 0 & 0 & -\gamma^2 I & 0 \\ \tilde{M}^T & 0 & 0 & 0 & 0 & -\epsilon^{-1} I \end{bmatrix} < 0, \quad 1 \leq i,j,s,r \leq N, \tag{11}$$

where

G_{1ijs} *and* W_i *are defined in (9),* $H_i = [C_i \quad -\mathbb{C}]$, $\tilde{M} = \begin{bmatrix} M_1 & M_2 \\ 0 & 0 \end{bmatrix}$ *and* $\tilde{N}_{ijs} = \begin{bmatrix} N_{1i} & 0 \\ N_{2i}K_jC_s & -N_{2i}K_j\mathbb{C} \end{bmatrix}$.

Proof. Consider the following fuzzy Lyapunov function $V(\tilde{x},k)$ given by

$$V(\tilde{x},k) = \tilde{x}(k)^T \sum_{i=1}^{N} \alpha_i(z) P_i \tilde{x}(k).$$

The stability of (8) is ensured, under zero initial condition, with guaranteed H_∞ performance (10) if [29]:

$$\Delta V(\tilde{x},k) + (y(k) - y_d(k))^T (y(k) - y_d(k)) - \gamma^2 \tilde{\varpi}(k)^T \tilde{\varpi}(k) < 0 \tag{12}$$

where $\Delta V(\tilde{x},k)$ is the rate of V along the trajectory:

$$\Delta V(\tilde{x},k) = V(\tilde{x}(k+1)) - V(\tilde{x}(k)). \tag{13}$$

By substituting (13) in(12), we have:

$$\tilde{x}(k+1)^T P^+ \tilde{x}(k+1) - \tilde{x}(k)^T P_z \tilde{x}(k) + (y(k) - y_d(k))^T (y(k) - y_d(k)) - \gamma^2 \tilde{\varpi}(k)^T \tilde{\varpi}(k) < 0 \tag{14}$$

where

$$P_z = \sum_{i=1}^{N} \alpha_i(z) P_i \text{ and } P^+ = \sum_{i=1}^{N} \alpha_i(z(k+1)) P_i.$$

Now, let

$$\begin{aligned} G_z(k) &= \sum_{i,j,s=1}^{N} \alpha_i(z)\alpha_j(z)\alpha_s(z) G_{1ijs} + \sum_{i,j,s=1}^{N} \alpha_i(z)\alpha_j(z)\alpha_s(z) G_{2ijs}(k), \\ W_z &= \sum_{i=1}^{N} \alpha_i(z) W_i. \end{aligned} \tag{15}$$

Then, the inequality (14) can be rewritten as follows

$$\begin{aligned} &[G_z(k)\tilde{x}(k) + W_z\tilde{\varpi}(k)]^T P^+ [G_z(k)\tilde{x}(k) + W_z\tilde{\varpi}(k)] - \tilde{x}(k)^T P_z \tilde{x}(k) - \gamma^2 \tilde{\varpi}(k)^T \tilde{\varpi}(k) + \\ &(y(k) - y_d(k))^T (y(k) - y_d(k)) < 0. \end{aligned} \tag{16}$$

By consequence, (16) leads to:

$$\begin{bmatrix} \tilde{x}(k) \\ \tilde{\varpi}(k) \end{bmatrix}^T (\mathcal{M}_1 - \mathcal{M}_2) \begin{bmatrix} \tilde{x}(k) \\ \tilde{\varpi}(k) \end{bmatrix} < 0, \tag{17}$$

where

$$\mathcal{M}_1 = \begin{bmatrix} G_z(k)^T P^+ G_z(k) & G_z(k)^T P^+ W_z \\ W_z^T P^+ G_z(k) & W_z^T P^+ W_z \end{bmatrix},$$

$$\mathcal{M}_2 = \begin{bmatrix} P_z - H_z^T H_z & 0 \\ 0 & \gamma^2 \end{bmatrix}, \tag{18}$$

$$H_z = \sum_{i=1}^{N} \alpha_i(z) H_i.$$

Thus, to proof (12), it is sufficient to show that

$$\mathcal{M}_1 - \mathcal{M}_2 < 0. \tag{19}$$

The first part of (19) can also be rewritten as

$$\mathcal{M}_1 - \mathcal{M}_2 = (\tilde{G}_z + \tilde{M}F(k)\mathcal{N}_z)^T P^+ (\tilde{G}_z + \tilde{M}F(k)\mathcal{N}_z), \tag{20}$$

where

$$\tilde{G}_z = \left[G_{1z} \; W_z \right], G_{1z} = \sum_{i,j,s=1}^{N} \alpha_i(z)\alpha_j(z)\alpha_s(z) G_{1ijs},$$

$$\textit{and} \quad \mathcal{N}_z = \left[\sum_{i,j,s=1}^{N} \alpha_i(z)\alpha_j(z)\alpha_s(z)\tilde{N}_{1ijs} \; 0 \right]. \tag{21}$$

On the other hand, pre- and post-multiplying (11) by $diag\{P_r, I, I, I, I, I\}$ gives

$$\Gamma_{ijs}^r \equiv \begin{bmatrix} -P_r & 0 & 0 & P_r G_{1ijs} & P_r W_i & P_r \tilde{M} \\ 0 & -\epsilon I & 0 & \tilde{N}_{ijs} & 0 & 0 \\ 0 & 0 & -I & H_i & 0 & 0 \\ G_{1ijs}^T P_r & \tilde{N}_{ijs}^T & H_i^T & -P_i & 0 & 0 \\ W_i^T P_r & 0 & 0 & 0 & -\gamma^2 I & 0 \\ \tilde{M}^T P_r & 0 & 0 & 0 & 0 & -\epsilon^{-1} I \end{bmatrix} < 0, \quad 1 \le i, j, s, r \le N. \tag{22}$$

Since $\sum_{i=1}^{N} \alpha_i(z) = \sum_{r=1}^{N} \alpha_r(k+1) = 1$, (22) can be written as

$$\sum_{r=1}^{N} \alpha_r(k+1) \sum_{i,j,s=1}^{N} \alpha_i(z)\alpha_j(z)\alpha_s(z)\Gamma^r_{ijs} \equiv \begin{bmatrix} -P^+ & 0 & 0 & P^+G_{1z} & P^+W_z & P^+\tilde{M} \\ 0 & -\epsilon I & 0 & \tilde{N}_z & 0 & 0 \\ 0 & 0 & -I & H_z & 0 & 0 \\ G_{1z}^T P^+ & \tilde{N}_z^T & H_z^T & -P_z & 0 & 0 \\ W_z^T P^+ & 0 & 0 & 0 & -\gamma^2 I & 0 \\ \tilde{M}^T P^+ & 0 & 0 & 0 & 0 & -\epsilon^{-1} I \end{bmatrix} < 0, \quad (23)$$

Applying Schur complement on (23), it is straightforward to verify that the condition (23) is equivalent to the following inequalities:

$$\begin{aligned} &(P^+\tilde{G}_z)^T \left(P^+ - \epsilon P^+\tilde{M}\tilde{M}^T P^+\right)^{-1} P^+\tilde{G}_z + \epsilon^{-1}\mathcal{N}_z^T\mathcal{N}_z - \mathcal{M}_2 < 0 \ \text{ and} \\ &P^+ - \epsilon P^+\tilde{M}\tilde{M}^T P^+ > 0. \end{aligned} \quad (24)$$

Using (20), (24) and Lemma 3.1, we have

$$\begin{aligned} \mathcal{M}_1 - \mathcal{M}_2 &= (\tilde{G}_z + \tilde{M}F(k)\mathcal{N}_z)^T P^+ (\tilde{G}_z + \tilde{M}F(k)\mathcal{N}_z) \\ &\leq (P^+\tilde{G}_z)^T \left(P^+ - \epsilon P^+\tilde{M}\tilde{M}^T P^+\right)^{-1} P^+\tilde{G}_z + \epsilon^{-1}\mathcal{N}_z^T\mathcal{N}_z - \mathcal{M}_2 \\ &< 0. \end{aligned} \quad (25)$$

By consequence

$$\sum_{k=0}^{k_f} (y(k) - y_d(k))^T (y(k) - y_d(k)) < \gamma^2 \sum_{k=0}^{k_f} \tilde{w}(k)^T \tilde{w}(k).$$

Hence, H_∞ output tracking performance is achieved with the prescribed attenuation level γ. On the other hand, it follows from (11) and (25) that $\Delta V(\tilde{x}) < 0$ for $\tilde{w}(k) = 0$, which leads that the uncertain system (8) with $\tilde{w}(k) = 0$ is robustly asymptotically stable. □

4. H_∞ fuzzy tracking controller synthesis

In this section, a cone complementarity formulation [7] is used to solve the bilinearity involved in (11). The idea is based on converting the conditions (11) to convex and nonconvex parts and then casting them into an optimization problem subject to some LMIs. For this, first recall the following lemma, which generalizes the result of [7].

Lemma 4.1. *[12] Let $P_i \in \Re^{n\times n}$, $Q_i \in \Re^{n\times n}$, $i = 1, \ldots, N$ be any symmetric positive definite matrices, then the following statements are equivalent:*

(a): $P_i Q_i = I,\ i = 1, \ldots, N.$

$$(b): \begin{cases} \sum_{i=1}^{N} \mathbf{Tr}(P_i Q_i) = N \times n, \\ \begin{bmatrix} P_i & I \\ I & Q_i \end{bmatrix} \geq 0,\ 1 \leq i \leq N. \end{cases}$$

Using $P_r = Q_r^{-1}$, the stability condition (11) can be rewritten as follows:

$$\Omega_{ijs}^r \equiv \begin{bmatrix} -Q_r & 0 & 0 & G_{1ijs} & W_i & \tilde{M} \\ 0 & -\epsilon I & 0 & \tilde{N}_{ijs} & 0 & 0 \\ 0 & 0 & -I & H_i & 0 & 0 \\ G_{1ijs}^T & \tilde{N}_{ijs}^T & H_i^T & -P_i & 0 & 0 \\ W_i^T & 0 & 0 & 0 & -\gamma^2 I & 0 \\ \tilde{M}^T & 0 & 0 & 0 & 0 & -\epsilon^{-1} I \end{bmatrix} < 0, \quad 1 \leq i,j,s,r \leq N, \tag{26}$$

$$P_r Q_r = I,\ 1 \leq r \leq N. \tag{27}$$

Before giving the final formulation of the problem in hand, we suggest to relax the LMIs (26) from the point of view number of LMIs to be satisfied, for this, we suggest to use the following lemma.

Lemma 4.2. *[12] Consider the following matrix* $\bar{\mathbf{A}} = \sum_{i,j,s=1}^{N} \alpha_{ijs} \mathbf{A}_{ijs}$, *where* $\alpha_{ijs} = \alpha_i \alpha_j \alpha_s$ *and* $\sum_{i=1}^{N} \alpha_i = 1$. *Then,* $\bar{\mathbf{A}}$ *can be expressed as follows*

$$\bar{\mathbf{A}} = \sum_{i=1}^{N} \alpha_i^3 \mathbf{A}_{iii} + \sum_{s>j\geq i}^{N} \alpha_{ijs}(\mathbf{A}_{ijs} + \mathbf{A}_{jsi} + \mathbf{A}_{sij}) + \sum_{s\geq j>i}^{N} \alpha_{ijs}(\mathbf{A}_{sji} + \mathbf{A}_{isj} + \mathbf{A}_{jis}),$$

Moreover,

$$\sum_{ijs=1}^{N} \alpha_{ijs} = \sum_{i=1}^{N} \alpha_i^3 + 3 \sum_{s>j\geq i}^{N} \alpha_{ijs} + 3 \sum_{s\geq j>i}^{N} \alpha_{ijs} = 1.$$

Hence, using Lemma 4.2, (26) can be rewritten as follows:

$$\begin{aligned} &\Upsilon_{iii}^r < 0,\ 1 \leq i,r \leq N, \\ &\Phi_{ijs}^r \leq 0,\ 1 \leq i \leq j < s \leq N,\ 1 \leq r \leq N, \\ &\Psi_{ijs}^r \leq 0,\ 1 \leq i < j \leq s \leq N,\ 1 \leq r \leq N, \end{aligned} \tag{28}$$

where,

$$\Upsilon^r_{iii} \equiv \begin{bmatrix} -Q_r & 0 & 0 & G_{1iii} & W_i & \tilde{M} \\ 0 & -\epsilon I & 0 & \tilde{N}_{iii} & 0 & 0 \\ 0 & 0 & -I & H_i & 0 & 0 \\ G^T_{1iii} & \tilde{N}^T_{iii} & H_i^T & -P_i & 0 & 0 \\ W_i^T & 0 & 0 & 0 & -\gamma^2 I & 0 \\ \tilde{M}^T & 0 & 0 & 0 & 0 & -\epsilon^{-1} I \end{bmatrix},$$

$$\Phi^r_{ijs} \equiv \begin{bmatrix} -3Q_r & 0 & 0 & G_{ijs}+G_{jsi}+G_{sij} & \mathcal{W} & 3\tilde{M} \\ 0 & -3\epsilon I & 0 & \tilde{N}_{ijs}+\tilde{N}_{jsi}+\tilde{N}_{sij} & 0 & 0 \\ 0 & 0 & -3I & H_i+H_j+H_s & 0 & 0 \\ * & * & * & -(P_i+P_j+P_s) & 0 & 0 \\ * & 0 & 0 & 0 & -3\gamma^2 I & 0 \\ * & 0 & 0 & 0 & 0 & -3\epsilon^{-1} I \end{bmatrix},$$

$$\Psi^r_{ijs} \equiv \begin{bmatrix} -3Q_r & 0 & 0 & G_{sji}+G_{isj}+G_{jis} & \mathcal{W} & 3\tilde{M} \\ 0 & -3\epsilon I & 0 & \tilde{N}_{sji}+\tilde{N}_{isj}+\tilde{N}_{jis} & 0 & 0 \\ 0 & 0 & -3I & H_i+H_j+H_s & 0 & 0 \\ * & * & * & -(P_i+P_j+P_s) & 0 & 0 \\ * & 0 & 0 & 0 & -3\gamma^2 I & 0 \\ * & 0 & 0 & 0 & 0 & -3\epsilon^{-1} I \end{bmatrix},$$

where $\mathcal{W} = W_i + W_j + W_s$.
From Lemma 4.2, It is only sufficient to see that [12]

$$\sum_{i=1}^{N} \alpha_i(z)\Omega^r_{ijs} = \sum_{i=1}^{N} \alpha_i^3(k)\Upsilon^r_{iii} + \sum_{i\le j<s}^{N} \alpha_i(z)\alpha_j(z)\alpha_s(z)\Phi^r_{ijs} + \sum_{i<j\le s}^{N} \alpha_i(z)\alpha_j(z)\alpha_s(z)\Psi^r_{ijs}.$$

It should be noted that, Lemma 4.2 is very useful in reducing the number of LMIs to be satisfied. Indeed, (26) leads to N^4 LMIs to be satisfied. In contrast, by using Lemma 4.2, this number decreases to $(N^2(N^2+2))/3$.

Now, back to our main problem. We suggest to use Lemma 4.1 to handle the nonconvexity involved in (27), as it is clearly shown by the following theorem:

Theorem 4.1. *Given a weight $\beta > 0$ and $\epsilon > 0$. The augmented closed-loop system in (8) achieves the H_∞ output tracking performance γ, if there exists positive definite matrices $P_1 > 0, \ldots, P_N > 0$, $Q_1 > 0, \ldots, Q_N > 0$ and controller gains $K_1, \ldots, K_N$ such that the following optimization problem is solvable and equal to $n_{\tilde{x}} \times N$:*

$$\begin{cases} \underset{K_i, P_i, Q_i, \gamma}{\text{minimize}} \ \beta \sum_{i=1}^{N} \mathbf{Tr}(P_i Q_i) + (1-\beta)\gamma \\ \\ \text{subject to:} \\ \\ (28) \ \text{and} \ \begin{bmatrix} P_i & I \\ I & Q_i \end{bmatrix} \geq 0, \ 1 \leq i \leq N. \end{cases} \tag{29}$$

The following iterative algorithm [7, 12] can be used to linearize the objective function of the optimization problem (29).

Algorithm 4.1

give a weight β, fix a tolerance ε (for example $\varepsilon = 10^{-6}$) and execute the following steps:

- Step 1: Set $P_i^0 = I$ and $Q_i^0 = I$, for $i = 1, \ldots, N$.
- Step 2: Solve the following LMI optimization:

$$\underset{K_i, P_i, Q_i, \gamma}{\text{minimize}} \ \beta \sum_{i=1}^{N} \mathbf{Tr}(P_i^* Q_i + Q_i^* P_i) + (1-\beta)\gamma$$
subject to :
$$(28) \text{ and } \begin{bmatrix} P_i & I \\ I & Q_i \end{bmatrix} \geq 0, 1 \leq i \leq N.$$

- Step 3: If $\|P_i - Q_i^{-1}\| \leq \varepsilon$.
  While $\|P_i - Q_i^{-1}\| \leq \varepsilon$,
  Select $\beta = \beta - 0.01$ and repeat from step 1. Else
  Set $P_i^* \longleftarrow P_i$, $Q_i^* \longleftarrow Q_i$ and repeat from step 2.

Remark 4.1. *In the optimization problem (29), the attenuation level γ is also included in the optimization function. Thus, a multi-objective optimization problem is solved by the Algorithm 4.1.*

5. Illustrative example

In this section, the proposed tracking control scheme is applied to regulate the output voltage of DC-DC converter. The model of a buck converter is described in Fig. 1. Using the Kirchoff laws, the converter of Fig. 1 can be represented by the following discrete-time nonlinear model [24]:

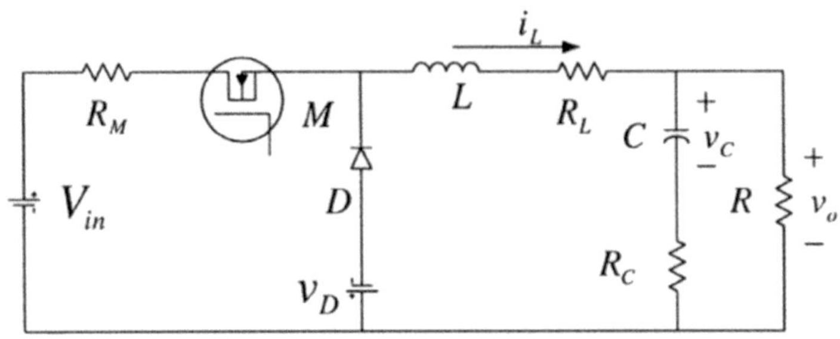

Figure 1. Buck converter circuit.

$$x(k+1) = \begin{bmatrix} \frac{-T_s}{L}(R_L + \frac{R(k)R_c}{R(k)+R_c}) + 1 & \frac{-T_s R(k)}{L(R(k)+R_c)} \\ \frac{T_s R(k)}{C(R(k)+R_c)} & \frac{-T_s}{C(R(k)+R_c)} + 1 \end{bmatrix} x(k) +$$

$$\begin{bmatrix} \frac{-T_s}{L}(R_M i_L(k) - V_{in}(k) - V_D) \\ 0 \end{bmatrix} u(k) + \begin{bmatrix} \frac{-T_s V_D}{L} \\ 0 \end{bmatrix}, \tag{30}$$

$$y(k) = \begin{bmatrix} \frac{R(k)R_c}{(R(k)+R_c)} & \frac{R(k)}{(R(k)+R_c)} \end{bmatrix} x(k),$$

where $x(k) = [i_L(k)\ v_c(k)]^T$ is the state vector, $u(k)$ is the control vector i.e. the duty cycle of the switched **M**, $y(k)$ is the output vector i.e. the output voltage and T_s is the sampling period $T_s = 0.001 \times 1/f_0$, with f_0 is the resonance frequency of the buck converter (30). $R(k)$ and $V_{in}(k)$ are uncertain parameters satisfying $R(k) \in [\underline{R}(k), \overline{R}(k)]$, $V_{in}(k) \in [\underline{V_{in}}(k), \overline{V_{in}}(k)]$. Table (1) gives the parameter values of the buck converter (Fig. 1). Similar to [24], we assume that the inductor current belongs in a compact set: $i_L(k) \in [\underline{i}_L, \overline{i}_L]$, and select the membership functions as follows

$$\alpha_1(k) = \frac{-i_L(k) + \overline{i}_L}{\overline{i}_L - \underline{i}_L}, \quad \alpha_2(k) = 1 - \alpha_1(k). \tag{31}$$

The nonlinear system (30) can be represented by the following uncertain T-S model:

$\mathcal{R}ule^i$ If $i_L(k)$ is μ_i

$$\text{Then} \begin{cases} x(k+1) = (A_{noi} + \Delta A_i(k))x(k) + (B_{noi} + \Delta B_i(k))u(k) + E_i w(k), \\ y(k) = C_i x(k), \quad i = 1,2, \end{cases} \tag{32}$$

where
$A_{no1} = A_{no2} = \frac{\overline{A}_1+\underline{A}_1}{2}, B_{no1} = \frac{\overline{B}_1+\underline{B}_1}{2}, B_{no2} = \frac{\overline{B}_2+\underline{B}_2}{2}$, with

$$\overline{A}_1 = \overline{A}_2 = \begin{bmatrix} -\frac{T_s}{L}(R_L + \frac{\overline{R}R_c}{(\overline{R}+R_c)}) + 1 & -\frac{T_s\overline{R}}{L(\overline{R}+R_C)} \\ \frac{T_s\overline{R}}{C(\overline{R}+R_C)} & -\frac{T_s}{C(\overline{R}+R_c)} + 1 \end{bmatrix},$$

$$\underline{A}_1 = \underline{A}_2 = \begin{bmatrix} -\frac{T_s}{L}(R_L + \frac{\underline{R}R_c}{(\underline{R}+R_c)}) + 1 & -\frac{T_s\underline{R}}{L(\underline{R}+R_C)} \\ \frac{T_s\underline{R}}{C(\underline{R}+R_C)} & -\frac{T_s}{C(\underline{R}+R_c)} + 1 \end{bmatrix},$$

$$\overline{B}_1 = \begin{bmatrix} -\frac{T_s}{L}(R_M\underline{i}_L - \overline{V_{in}} - V_D) \\ 0 \end{bmatrix}, \quad \overline{B}_2 = \begin{bmatrix} -\frac{T_s}{L}(R_M\bar{i}_L - \overline{V_{in}} - V_D) \\ 0 \end{bmatrix},$$

$$\underline{B}_1 = \begin{bmatrix} -\frac{T_s}{L}(R_M\underline{i}_L - \underline{V_{in}} - V_D) \\ 0 \end{bmatrix}, \quad \underline{B}_2 = \begin{bmatrix} -\frac{T_s}{L}(R_M\bar{i}_L - \underline{V_{in}} - V_D) \\ 0 \end{bmatrix},$$

$$C_1 = C_2 = \begin{bmatrix} \frac{RR_c}{R+R_c} & \frac{R}{R+R_c} \end{bmatrix}, \text{ and } E_1 = E_2 = \begin{bmatrix} 1 \\ 0 \end{bmatrix}.$$

$\Delta A_1(k)$, $\Delta A_2(k)$, $\Delta B_1(k)$ and $\Delta B_2(k)$ can be represented in the form of (2) with $M_1 = 0.1$, $M_2 = \begin{bmatrix} 1\,0 \\ 0\,0 \end{bmatrix}$, $N_{11} = 10\frac{\overline{A}_1-\underline{A}_1}{2}, N_{12} = N_{11}$, $N_{21} = \frac{\overline{B}_1-\underline{B}_1}{2}$, $N_{22} = \frac{\overline{B}_2-\underline{B}_2}{2}$.

In this example, the objective is to make the output voltage of the buck converter, i.e. v_o follow a desired signal to meet the H_∞ tracking performance of the uncertain system (30).
The reference system matrices of (5) is selected as follows

$$\mathbb{A} = \begin{bmatrix} 0.5 & 0 \\ 0 & 0.5 \end{bmatrix}, \mathbb{B} = \begin{bmatrix} 0 \\ 1 \end{bmatrix}, \mathbb{C} = \begin{bmatrix} 0 & 1 \end{bmatrix}. \tag{33}$$

Let $\beta = 0.99$ and $\epsilon = 1$, using the Algorithm 4.1, the following feasible solution is obtained after only 41 iterations:

$$P_1 = \begin{bmatrix} 0.122328 & 0.72818 & 0 & -0.070451 \\ 0.72818 & 7.378511 & 0 & -0.550637 \\ 0 & 0 & 1 & 0 \\ -0.070451 & -0.550637 & 0 & 2.846761 \end{bmatrix},$$

$$P_2 = \begin{bmatrix} 0.124832 & 0.7441565 & 0 & -0.09171 \\ 0.7441565 & 7.455168 & 0 & -0.661751 \\ 0 & 0 & 1.116002 & 0 \\ -0.09171 & -0.661751 & 0 & 3.00123 \end{bmatrix},$$

$$Q_1 = \begin{bmatrix} 19.852249 & -1.950697 & 0 & 0.113988 \\ -1.950697 & 0.329190 & 0 & 0.015398 \\ 0 & 0 & 1 & 0 \\ 0.113988 & 0.015398 & 0 & 0.357075 \end{bmatrix},$$

$$Q_2 = \begin{bmatrix} 19.869471 & -1.967944 & 0 & 0.173243 \\ -1.967944 & 0.3317250 & 0 & 0.013007 \\ 0 & 0 & 0.896056 & 0 \\ 0.173243 & 0.013007 & 0 & 0.341358 \end{bmatrix},$$

$$K_1 = -6.0943; \quad K_2 = -7.1963,$$

and the H_∞ output tracking performance index: $\gamma = 2.52$. Hence, according to (7), the static output-feedback control law that ensures the desired trajectory tracking for (30) is given as follows:

$$u(k) = (\alpha_1(k)K_1 + \alpha_2(k)K_2)(y(k) - y_d(k)). \tag{34}$$

Fig. 2 shows the evolution of the output signal of the nonlinear system (30), using the fuzzy controller, with an external disturbance input $w(k)$ defined as $w(k) = \frac{r_o}{1+15(k+1)} - T_s V_D / L$, where, r_o is a random number taken from a uniform distribution over $[0,\ 2]$, the uncertain parameters are as follow

$$\begin{aligned} R(k) &= \tfrac{\overline{R}+\underline{R}}{2} + \tfrac{\overline{R}-\underline{R}}{2} cos(k\pi/T_s), \\ V_{in}(k) &= \tfrac{\overline{V_{in}}+\underline{V_{in}}}{2} + \tfrac{\overline{V_{in}}-\underline{V_{in}}}{2} cos(k\pi/T_s), \end{aligned} \tag{35}$$

and the reference signal $r(k)$, are supposed to be

$$\begin{cases} r(k) = 12V & \text{for} \quad 0 \le k \le 0.005s, \\ r(k) = 6V & \text{for} \quad 0.005 < k \le 0.01s, \\ r(k) = 24V & \text{for} \quad k > 0.01s, \end{cases} \tag{36}$$

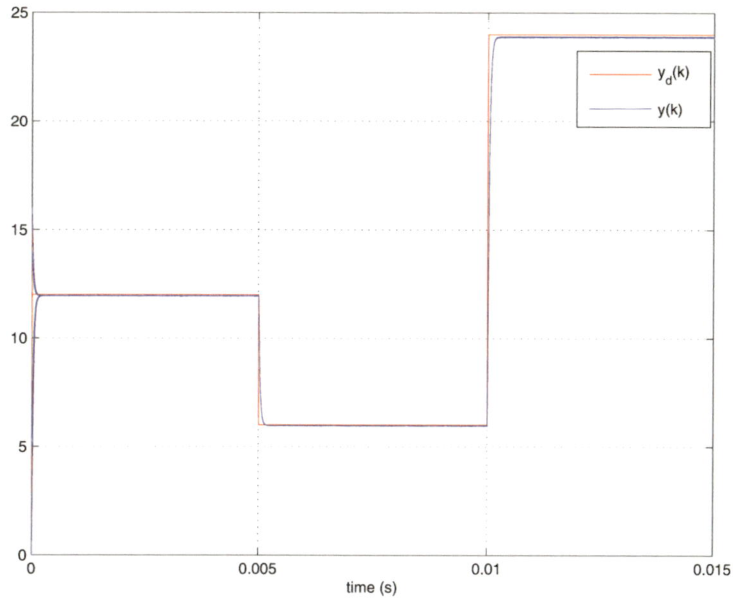

Figure 2. Response of $y(k)$ and $y_d(k)$.

Fig. 3 and Fig. 4 depict a zoom of Fig. 2 at 0 s and between 5 ms and 10 ms respectively. It can be seen that the designed fuzzy static output-feedback controller ensures the robust stability of the nonlinear system (30) and guarantees an acceptable H_∞ trajectory tracking performance level.

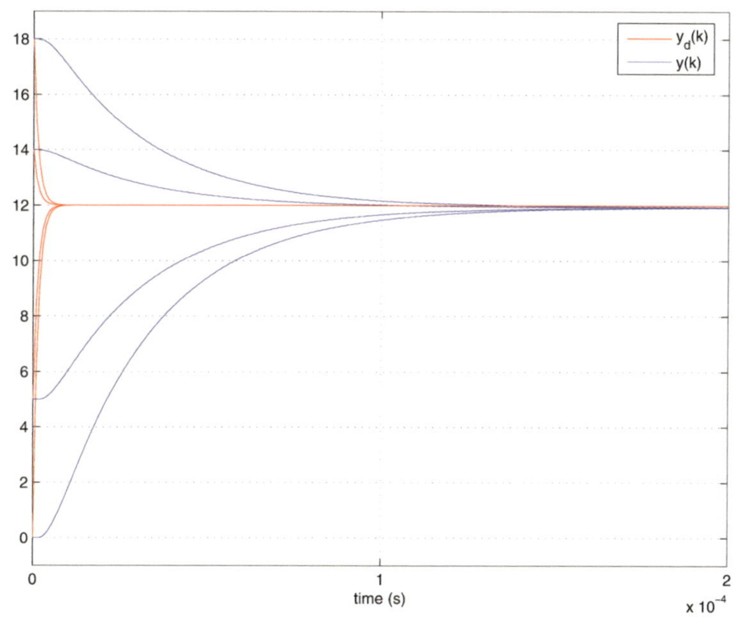

Figure 3. Zoom on Fig. 2 at 0 sec.

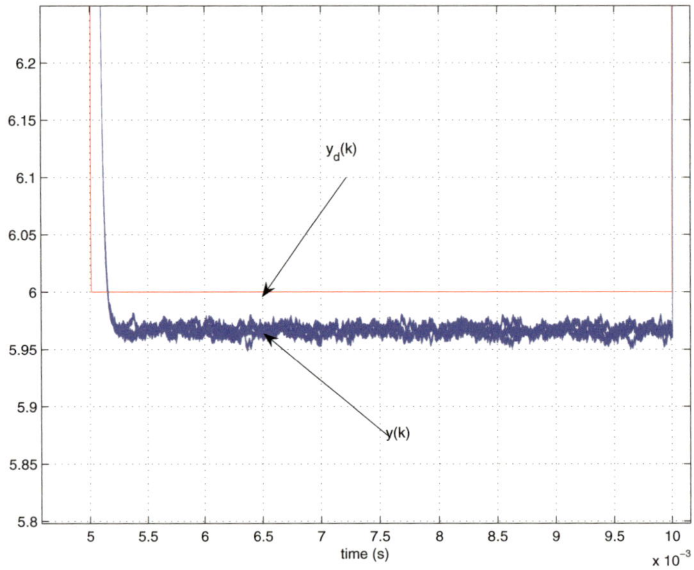

Figure 4. Zoom on Fig. 2 between 5 msec and 10 msec.

Parameter	Value	Unity
Input voltage, $V_{in}(k)$	$V_{in}(k) \in [10,\ 30]$	V
Current in the inductance , i_L	-8 - 8	A
Inductance, L	98.58	μH
Parasitic resistance of L, R_L	48.5	$m\Omega$
Capacitor, C	202.5	μF
Parasitic resistance of C, R_c	162	$m\Omega$
Resistance of Switch, R_M	0.27	Ω
Diode voltage, V_D	0.82	V
Load resistance, $R(k)$	$R(k) \in [2,\ 10]$	Ω

Table 1. Parameter values of the buck converter.

6. Conclusion

In this chapter, the problem of model reference tracking control with a guaranteed H_∞ performance is solved for uncertain discrete-time fuzzy systems. Based on the fuzzy Lyapunov function and cone complementary formulation, a fuzzy static output controller is calculated to make small as possible as the tracking output error and reject disturbances.

Author details

Meriem Nachidi
Departamento de Ingeneriía de Sistemas y Automática, University of Carlos III, Madrid, Spain.

Ahmed El Hajjaji
Laboratoire Modélisation, Information et Systèmes, University of Picardie Jules Verne, Amiens, France.

7. References

[1] B.D.O. Anderson and J.B. Moore. *Linear Optimal Control*. Prentice-Hall, Englewood Cliffs, 1971.

[2] H. Khalil. *Nonlinear Systems*. Pearson Higher Education, 2002.

[3] J. C. Geromel, C. C. de Souza, and R. E. Skelton. Static output feedback controllers: Stability and convexity. *IEEE Transactions on Automatic Control*, 43, 1998.

[4] R. Johansson and A. Robertsson. Observer-based strict positive real (spr)feedback control system design. *Automatica*, 38, 2002.

[5] T. Iwasaki and R.E. Skelton. The xy-centring algorithm for the dual lmi problem: a new approach to fixed-order control design. *Int. J. Control*, 62(6):1257–1272, 1995.

[6] V.L. Syrmos, C.T. Abdallah, P. Dorato, and K. Grigoriadis. Static output feedbackŮa survey. *Automatica*, 33(2):125–137, 1997.

[7] L. El Ghaoui, F. Oustry, and M. Ait Rami. A cone complementarity linearisation algorithm for static output-feedback and related problems. *IEEE Trans. Automat. Contr.*, 42:11–71, 1997.

[8] D. Mustafa. LQG optimal scalar static output feedback. *Systems and Control Letters*, 27(1):9–19, 1996.

[9] D. Henrion, M. Sebek, and V. Kucera. An algorithm for static output feedback simultaneous stabilization of scalar plants. In *Proceedings of the IFAC World Congress on Automatic Control, Barcelona, Spain*, 2001.

[10] S.-S. Chen, Y.-C. Chang, S.-F. Su, S.-L. Chung, and T.-T. Lee. Robust static output-feedback stabilization for nonlinear discrete-time systems with time delay via fuzzy control approach. *IEEE Transactions on Fuzzy Systems*, 13(2):263–272, 2005.

[11] D. Huang and S. K. Nguang. Robust H_∞ static output feedback control of fuzzy systems: an ilmi approach. *IEEE Transactions on Systems, Man, and Cybernetics, Part-B*, 36(1):216–222, 2006.

[12] M. Nachidi, A. Benzaouia, F. Tadeo, and M. Ait Rami. LMI-based approach for output-feedback stabilization for discrete time Takagi-Sugeno systems. *IEEE Transactions on Fuzzy Systems*, 16(5):1188–1196, 2008.

[13] Yu. Nesterov and A. Nemirovsky. *Interior-Point Polynomial Methods in Convex Programming*. Philadelphia, PA: SIAM, 1994.

[14] S. Boyd, L. El Ghaoui, E. Feron, and V. Balakrishnan. *Linear matrix inequalities in system and control theory*. Philadelphia, PA: SIAM, 1994.

[15] M. Ait Rami, U. Helmeke, and J. B. Moore. A finite steps algorithm for solving convex feasability problems. *Journal of Global Optimization*, 38:143–160, 2007.

[16] K. Tanaka and H. O. Wang. *Fuzzy Control Systems Design and Analysis: A Linear Matrix Inequality Approach*. New York: Wiley , New York: Wiley, 2001.

[17] K. Tanaka and M. Sugeno. Stability analysis and design of fuzzy control systems. *Fuzzy Sets and Syst.*, 45:135–156, 1992.

[18] T. M. Guerra and L. Vermeiren. LMI-based relaxed nonquadratic stabilization conditions for nonlinear systems in the takagi-sugeno's form. *Automatica*, 40(5):823–829, 2004.

[19] S. Xu and J. Lam. Robust H_∞ control for uncertain discrete-time-delay fuzzy systems via output feedback controllers. *IEEE Trans. Fuzzy Syst.*, 13:82–93, 2005.

[20] H. Ying. Analytical analysis and feedback linearization tracking control of the general takagi-sugeno fuzzy dynamic systems. *IEEE Transactions Systems, Man, Cybern.*, 29:290–298, 1999.

[21] C. C. Kung and H. Li. Tracking control of nonlinear systems by fuzzy model-based controller. In *6th IEEE International Conference*, page 623–628, 1997.

[22] C. S. Tseng, B. S. Chen, and H. J. Uang. Fuzzy tracking control design for nonlinear dynamic systems via T-S fuzzy model. *IEEE Transaction on fuzzy systems*, 8(2):200–211, 2001.

[23] M. Nachidi, F. Tadeo, A. Benzaouia and M. Ait Rami. Static output-feedback for Takagi-Sugeno systems with delays. *International Journal of Adaptive Control and Signal Processing*, 25:295–312, 2011.

[24] K.-Y. Lian, J.-J. Liou, and C.-Y Huang. LMI-based integral fuzzy control of DC-DC converters. *IEEE Transactions on Fuzzy systems*, 14:71–80, 2006.

[25] A. Balestrino, A. Landi, and L. Sani. Cuk converter global control via fuzzy logic and scaling factors. *IEEE Trans. Indusriel Applications*, 38:406–413, 2002.

[26] G. Papafotiou, T. Geyer, and M. Morari. Hybrid modelling and optimal control of swich-mode dc-dc converters. In *IEEE Workshop on Computers in Power Electronics, Champaign, IL, USA*, 2004.

[27] Y. Wang, L. Xie, and C. E. de Souza. Robust control of a class of uncertain nonlinear systems. *Syst. Control Lett.*, 19, 1999.

[28] H. O. Wang, K. Tanaka, and M. F. Griffin. An approach to fuzzy control of nonlinear systems: Stability and design issues. *IEEE Trans. Fuzzy syst.*, 4(1):14–23, 1996.

[29] B.-S. Chen, C.-S. Tseng, and H.-J. Uang. Robustness design of nonlinear dynamic systems via fuzzy linear control. *IEEE Trans. Fuzzy Syst.*, 7:571–585, 1999.

Chapter 8

FPGA-Based Motion Control IC for Linear Motor Drive X-Y Table Using Adaptive Fuzzy Control

Ying-Shieh Kung, Chung-Chun Huang and Liang-Chiao Huang

Additional information is available at the end of the chapter

http://dx.doi.org/10.5772/48457

1. Introduction

The development of a compact and high performance motion controller for the X-Y table of a CNC machine has been an important field in literatures (Groove, 1996; Goto et al., 1996; Hanafi et al., 2003). The typical architecture of the conventional motion control system for X-Y table is shown in Fig. 1, which consists of a central controller, two sets of servo drivers and an X-Y table. The central controller, which usually adopts a float-pointed processor, performs the function of motion trajectory and data communication with servo drivers and with external device. Each servo driver usually use a fixed-pointed processor, some specific ICs and an inverter to perform the functions of position/speed/current control at each single axis of X-Y table and to do the data communication with the central controller. Data communication between two devices uses an analog signal, a bus signal or a serial asynchronous signal. However, the motion control system in Fig.1 has some drawbacks, such as large volume, easy effect by the noise, expensive cost, inflexible, etc. In addition, data communication and handshake protocol between the central controller and servo drivers slow down the system executing speed.

In recent years, the FPGA has been widely applied in implementing the digital control system (Cho, 2009; Monmasson et al. 2011; Sanchez-Solano et al. 2007). Besides, an embedded processor IP and an application IP can be developed and downloaded into FPGA to construct a SoPC environment (Altera, 2004; Hall and Hamblem, 2004), allowing the users to design a SoPC module by mixing hardware and software in one FPGA chip (Kung et al. 2004; Kung and Tsai, 2007; Kung and Chen, 2008). Therefore, based on the FPGA technology, we improve the aforementioned drawbacks and integrate the central controller and the controller part of two servo drivers in Fig. 1 into a motion control IC in this study, which is shown in Fig. 2. Our proposed motion control IC has two IPs (Intellectual Properties). One IP performs the functions of the motion trajectory by software. The other IP performs the functions of two axes' position/speed/current controllers by hardware. As the results, this two IP will parallel processing in FPGA, and the hardware/software co-design technology in FPGA can make the motion controller of X-Y more compact, flexible, better performance and less cost. Further, the X-Y table usually leads to the existence of unmodelled dynamics and disturbances which often significantly deteriorate the system performance during a machining process. Many studies attempt to improve the tracking performance in a machining process (Lin et al., 2006; Wang and Lee, 1999). Lin et al. (2006) adopts a recurrent-neural-network sliding-mode controller to improve the motion tracking performance of the X-Y table. Wang and Lee (1999) integrate the cross-coupled control and neural network techniques to achieve a high accuracy of the motion tracking in the linear motor X-Y table. However, due to the complicate computation of the neural-network, the algorithms of above two studies are realized in the PC-based control system.

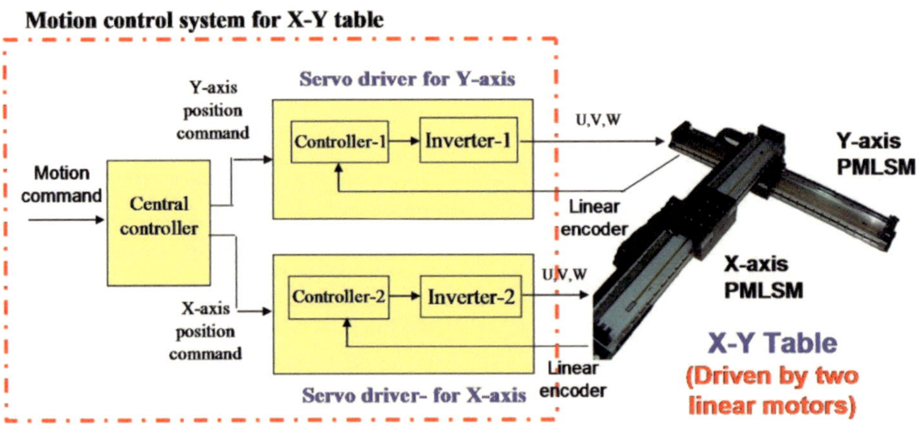

Figure 1. Conventional motion control system for X-Y table

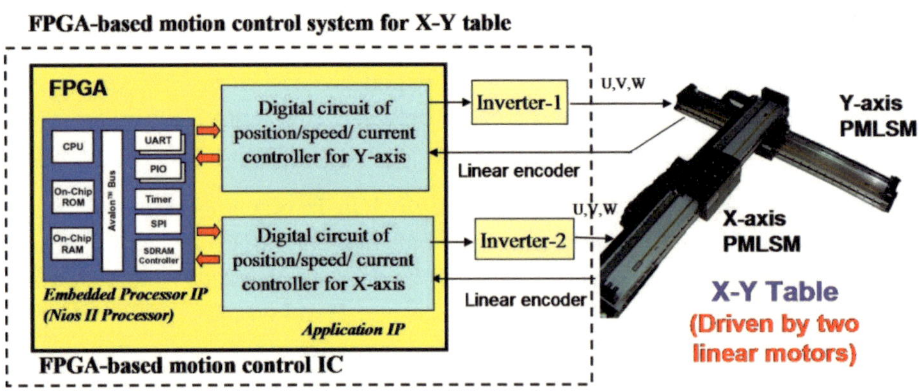

Figure 2. Proposed FPGA-based motion control system for X-Y table

In this chapter, a motion control IC for linear motor drive X-Y table based on FPGA (Field programmable gate array) technology is presented and shown in Fig.3. Firstly, the mathematical model of the X-Y table is defined. Secondly, an adaptive fuzzy controller

(AFC) is introduced and adopted in position loop of X-Y table to improve the motion tracking performance under unmodelled uncertainty condition. Thirdly, in implementation, an FPGA embedded by a Nios II processor is used to design the overall circuits of the motion control IC which the scheme of position/speed/current control for two PMLSMs (permanent magnetic linear synchronous motors) is realized by hardware in FPGA and the motion trajectory algorithm for X-Y table is implemented by software using Nios II embedded processor. To reduce the FPGA resource usage, an FSM (Finite state machine) joined by a multiplier, an adder, a LUT (Look-up table), some comparators and registers is used to model the overall AFC algorithm. And VHDL (VHSIC hardware description language) is adopted to describe the FSM. Herein, Altera Stratix II EP2S60, which has 48,352 ALUTs (Adaptive Look-Up Tables), total 2,544,192 RAM bits, and a Nios II embedded processor which has a 32-bit configurable CPU core, 16 M byte Flash memory, 1 M byte SRAM and 16 M byte SDRAM, is used. Therefore, a fully digital motion controller can be implemented by an FPGA using hardware/software co-design technology which will make the motion controller of the X-Y table more compact, flexible and better performance. Finally, an experimental system is set up to verify the performance of the proposed motion control IC for linear motor drive X-Y table.

2. System description of X-Y table and motion controller design

The internal architecture of the proposed FPGA-based controller system for a linear motor drive X-Y table is shown in Fig. 3, in which the motion trajectory is implemented by software using Nios II embedded processor; the position, speed and current vector controller for two PMLSMs are implemented by hardware in FPGA chip. The mathematical modeling of PMLSM, AFC algorithm and motion trajectory planning are introduced as follows:

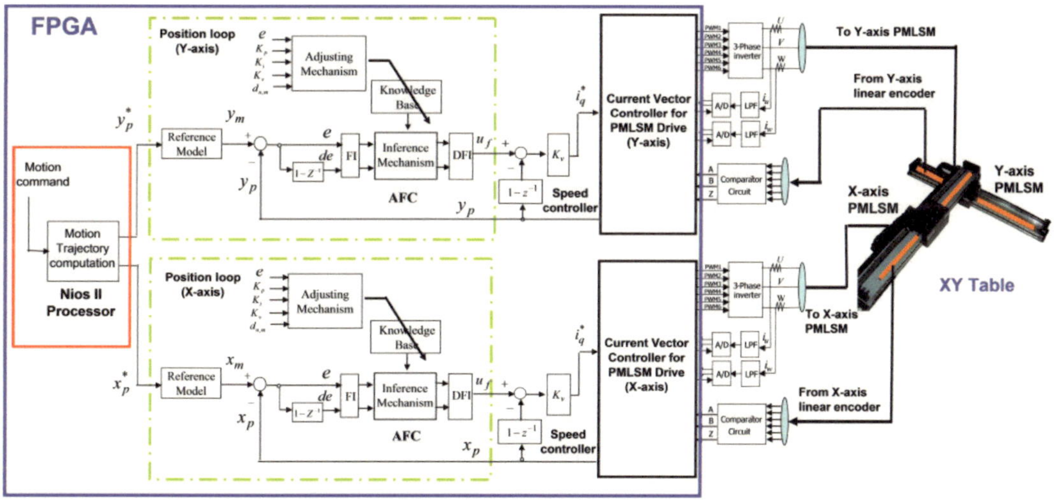

Figure 3. The architecture of a motion controller system for linear motor drive X-Y table

2.1. Mathematical model of the PMLSM drive

The dynamic model of a typical PMLSM can be described in the synchronous rotating reference frame, as follows

$$\frac{di_d}{dt} = -\frac{R_s}{L_d} i_d + \frac{\pi}{\tau} \frac{L_q}{L_d} \dot{x}_p i_q + \frac{1}{L_d} v_d \tag{1}$$

$$\frac{di_q}{dt} = -\frac{\pi}{\tau} \frac{L_d}{L_q} \dot{x}_p i_d - \frac{R_s}{L_q} i_q - \frac{\pi}{\tau} \frac{\lambda_f}{L_q} \dot{x}_p + \frac{1}{L_q} v_q \tag{2}$$

where v_d, v_q are the d and q axis voltages; i_d, i_q, are the d and q axis currents, R_s is the phase winding resistance; L_d, L_q are the d and q axis inductance; $\dot{x}_p$ is the translator speed; λ_f is the permanent magnet flux linkage; τ is the pole pitch. The developed electromagnetic thrust force is given by

$$F_e = \frac{3\pi}{2\tau}((L_d - L_q)i_d + \lambda_f)i_q \tag{3}$$

The current control of a PMLSM drive is based on a vector control approach. That is, if we control i_d to 0 in Fig.3, the PMLSM will be decoupled, so that control a PMLSM will become easy as to control a DC linear motor. After simplification and considering the mechanical load, the model of a PMLSM can be written as the following equations,

$$F_e = \frac{3}{2} \frac{\pi}{\tau} \lambda_f i_q \triangleq K_t i_q \tag{4}$$

with

$$K_t = \frac{3}{2} \frac{\pi}{\tau} \lambda_f \tag{5}$$

and the mechanical dynamic equation of PMLSM in x-axis table is

$$F_e - F_L = M_m \frac{d^2 x_p}{dt^2} + B_m \frac{dx_p}{dt} \tag{6}$$

where F_e, K_t, M_m, B_m and F_L represent the motor thrust force, the force constant, the total mass of the moving element, the viscous friction coefficient and the external force, respectively. In addition, the current loop of the PMLSM drive in Fig.3 includes PI controller, coordinate transformations of Clark, Modified inverse Clark, Park, inverse Park, SVPWM (Space Vector Pulse Width Muldulation), pulse signal detection of the encoder etc. The coordination transformation of the PMLSM in Fig. 3 can be described in synchronous rotating reference frame. Figure 4 is the coordination system in rotating motor which includes stationary *a-b-c* frame, stationary α-β frame and synchronously rotating *d-q* frame. Further, the formulations among three coordination systems are presented as follows.

1. *Clarke* : stationary *a-b-c* frame to stationary α-β frame.

$$\begin{bmatrix} i_\alpha \\ i_\beta \end{bmatrix} = \begin{bmatrix} \frac{2}{3} & \frac{-1}{3} & \frac{-1}{3} \\ 0 & \frac{1}{\sqrt{3}} & \frac{-1}{\sqrt{3}} \end{bmatrix} \begin{bmatrix} i_a \\ i_b \\ i_c \end{bmatrix} \tag{7}$$

2. Modified $Clarke^{-1}$: stationary α-β frame to stationary *a-b-c* frame.

$$\begin{bmatrix} v_a \\ v_b \\ v_c \end{bmatrix} = \begin{bmatrix} 1 & 0 \\ \frac{-1}{2} & \frac{\sqrt{3}}{2} \\ \frac{-1}{2} & \frac{-\sqrt{3}}{2} \end{bmatrix} \begin{bmatrix} v_\beta \\ v_\alpha \end{bmatrix} \tag{8}$$

3. *Park* : stationary α-β frame to rotating *d-q* frame.

$$\begin{bmatrix} i_d \\ i_q \end{bmatrix} = \begin{bmatrix} \cos\theta_e & \sin\theta_e \\ -\sin\theta_e & \cos\theta_e \end{bmatrix} \begin{bmatrix} i_\alpha \\ i_\beta \end{bmatrix} \tag{9}$$

4. $Park^{-1}$: rotating *d-q* frame to stationary α-β frame.

$$\begin{bmatrix} v_\alpha \\ v_\beta \end{bmatrix} = \begin{bmatrix} \cos\theta_e & -\sin\theta_e \\ \sin\theta_e & \cos\theta_e \end{bmatrix} \begin{bmatrix} v_d \\ v_q \end{bmatrix} \tag{10}$$

where θ_e is the electrical angle.

In Fig. 3, two digital *PI* controllers are presented in the current loop of PMLSM. For the example in *d* frame, the formulation is shown as follows.

$$e_d(k) = i_d^*(k) - i_d(k) \tag{11}$$

$$v_{p\_d}(k) = k_{p\_d}\, e_d(k) \tag{12}$$

$$v_{i\_d}(k) = v_{i\_d}(k-1) + k_{i\_d}\, e_d(k-1) \tag{13}$$

$$v_d(k) = v_{p\_d}(k) + v_{i\_d}(k) \tag{14}$$

the e_d is the error between current command and measured current. The k_{p_d}, k_{i_d} are *P* controller gain and *I* controller gain, respectively. The $v_{p\_d}(k)$, $v_{i\_d}(k)$, $v_d(k)$ are the output of *P* controller only, *I* controller only and the *PI* controller, respectively. Similarity, the formulation of *PI* controller in *q* frame is the same.

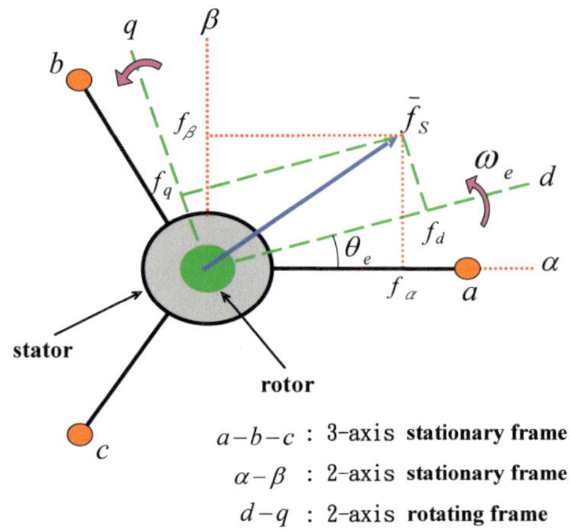

Figure 4. Transformation between stationary axes and rotating axes

2.2. Adaptive fuzzy controller (AFC) in position control loop

The green dash rectangular area in Fig. 3 presents the architecture of an AFC. It consists of a fuzzy controller, a reference model and a parameter adjusting mechanism. Detailed description of these is as follows.

1. Fuzzy controller (FC):

In Fig.3, the tracking error and the change of the error, *e*, *de* are defined as

$$e(k) = \psi_m(k) - \psi_p(k) \tag{15}$$

$$de(k) = e(k) - e(k-1) \tag{16}$$

and *e*, *de* and u_f are input and output variables of FC, respectively. Besides ψ_m represents x_m or y_m, and ψ_p represents x_p or y_p. The design procedure of the FC is as follows:

a. Take the *e* and *de* as the input variables of the FC, and define their linguist variables as *E* and *dE*. The linguist value of *E* and *dE* are {A_0, A_1, A_2, A_3, A_4, A_5, A_6} and {B_0, B_1, B_2, B_3, B_4, B_5, B_6}, respectively. Each linguist value of *E* and *dE* is based on the symmetrical triangular membership function which is shown in Fig.5. The symmetrical triangular membership function are determined uniquely by three real numbers $\xi_1 \le \xi_2 \le \xi_3$, if one fixes $f(\xi_1) = f(\xi_3) = 0$ and $f(\xi_2) = 1$. With respect to the universe of discourse of [-6.6], the numbers for these linguistic values are selected as follows:

$$\begin{aligned} &A_0 = B_0 : \{-6,-6,-4\}, A_1 = B_1 : \{-6,-4,-2\}, A_2 = B_2 : \{-4,-2,0\}, \\ &A_3 = B_3 : \{-2,0,2\}, A_4 = B_4 : \{0,2,4\}, A_5 = B_5 : \{2,4,6\}, A_6 = B_6 : \{4,6,6\} \end{aligned} \tag{17}$$

b. Compute the membership degree of the *e* and *de*. Figure 5 shows that the only two linguistic values are excited (resulting in a non-zero membership) in any input value, and the membership degree is obtained by

$$\mu_{A_i}(e) = \frac{e_{i+1} - e}{2} \text{and } \mu_{A_{i+1}}(e) = 1 - \mu_{A_i}(e) \tag{18}$$

where $e_{i+1} \triangleq -6 + 2*(i+1)$. Similar results can be obtained in computing the membership degree $\mu_{B_j}(de)$.

c. Select the initial fuzzy control rules, such as,

$$\text{IF } e \text{ is } \mathrm{A_i} \text{ and } \Delta\mathrm{e} \text{ is } \mathrm{B_j} \text{ THEN } u_f \text{ is } \mathrm{c_{j,i}} \tag{19}$$

where i *and* j = 0~6, A_i and B_j are fuzzy number, and $c_{j,i}$ is a real number. The graph of the fuzzy rule table and the fuzzification are shown in Fig. 5.

d. Construct the output of the fuzzy system $u_f(e,de)$ by using the singleton fuzzifier, product-inference rule, and central average defuzzifier method. Although there are total 49 fuzzy rules in Fig. 5 will be inferred, actually only 4 fuzzy rules can be effectively excited to generate a non-zero output. Therefore, if an error e is located between e_i and e_{i+1}, and an error change de is located between de_j and de_{j+1}, only four linguistic values A_i, A_{i+1}, B_j, B_{j+1} and corresponding consequent values $c_{j,i}$, $c_{j+1,i}$, $c_{j,i+1}$, $c_{j+1,i+1}$ can be excited, and the output of the fuzzy system can be inferred by the following expression:

$$u_f(e,de) = \frac{\sum_{n=i}^{i+1}\sum_{m=j}^{j+1} c_{m,n}[\mu_{A_n}(e) * \mu_{B_m}(de)]}{\sum_{n=i}^{i+1}\sum_{m=j}^{j+1} \mu_{A_n}(e) * \mu_{B_m}(de)} \triangleq \sum_{n=i}^{i+1}\sum_{m=j}^{j+1} c_{m,n} * d_{n,m} \tag{20}$$

where $d_{n,m} \triangleq \mu_{A_n}(e) * \mu_{B_m}(de)$. And those $c_{i,j}$ are adjustable parameters. In addition, by using (18), it is straightforward to obtain $\sum_{n=i}^{i+1}\sum_{m=j}^{j+1} d_{n,m} = 1$ in (20).

2. Reference model (RM):

Second order system is usually as the RM in the adaptive control system. Therefore, the transfer function of the RM in Fig.3 can be expressed as

$$\frac{\psi_m(s)}{\psi_p^*(s)} = \frac{\omega_n^2}{s^2 + 2\varsigma\omega_n s + \omega_n^2} \tag{21}$$

where ω_n is natural frequency and ς is damping ratio. Furthermore, because the characteristics of no overshoot, fast response and zero steady-state error are the important factors in the design of a PMLSM servo system; therefore, it can be considered as the selective criterion of ω_n and ς. The design methodology is described as follows: Firstly, the (21) matches the requirement of a zero steady-state error condition. Secondly, if we choose $\varsigma \geq 1$, it can guarantee no overshoot condition. Especially, the critical damp value $\varsigma = 1$ has a fastest step response. Hence, the relation between the rising time t_r and the natural frequency ω_n for a step input response in (21) can be derived and shown as follows.

$$(1+\omega_n t_r)e^{-\omega_n t_r} = 0.1 \tag{22}$$

Once the t_r is chosen, the natural frequency ω_n can be obtained. Furthermore, applying the bilinear transformation, (21) can be transformed to a discrete model by

$$\frac{\psi_m(z^{-1})}{\psi_p^*(z^{-1})} = \frac{a_0 + a_1 z^{-1} + a_2 z^{-2}}{1 + b_1 z^{-1} + b_2 z^{-2}} \tag{23}$$

and the difference equation is written as.

$$\psi_m(k) = -b_1\psi_m(k-1) - b_2\psi_m(k-2) + a_0\psi_p^*(k) + a_1\psi_p^*(k-1) + a_2\psi_p^*(k-2) \tag{24}$$

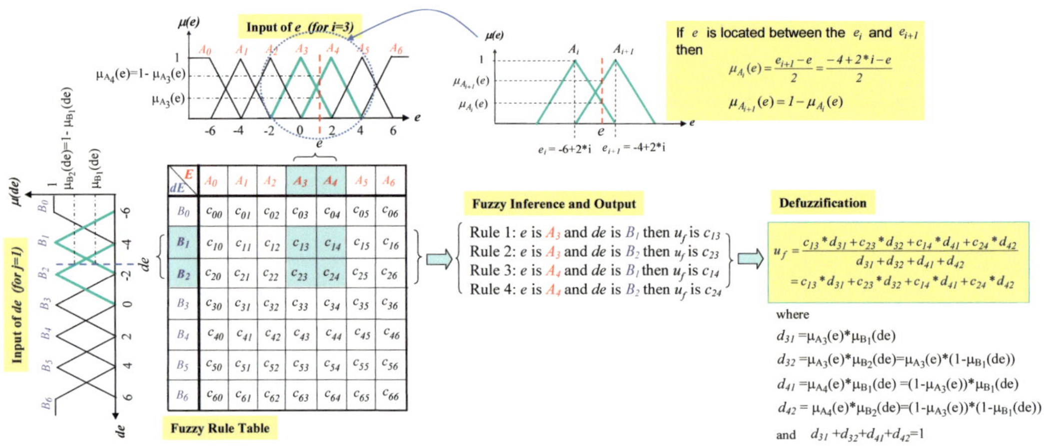

Figure 5. The symmetrical triangular membership function of *e* and *de*, fuzzy rule table, fuzzy inference and fuzzification

3. Parameter adjusting mechanism:

The gradient descent method is used to derive the AFC control law in Fig. 3. The objective of the parameters adjustment in FC is to minimize the square error between the mover position and the output of the RM. The instantaneous cost function is defined by

$$J(k+1) = \frac{1}{2}e_m(k+1)^2 = \frac{1}{2}\left[\psi_m(k+1) - \psi_p(k+1)\right]^2 \tag{25}$$

and the four defuzzifier parameters of $c_{j,i}$, $c_{j+1,i}$, $c_{j,i+1}$, $c_{j+1,i+1}$ are adjusted according to

$$\Delta c_{m,n}(k+1) \propto -\frac{\partial J(k+1)}{\partial c_{m,n}(k)} = -\alpha\frac{\partial J(k+1)}{\partial c_{m,n}(k)} \tag{26}$$

with $m = j$, j+1, $n = i$,i+1 and where α represents learning rate. However, following the similar derivation with (Kung & Tsai, 2007), the $\Delta c_{m,n}$ can be obtained as

$$\Delta c_{m,n}(k) \quad \approx \alpha(K_p + K_i)K_v e(k)d_{n,m} \tag{27}$$

with $m = j$, $j+1$ and $n = i$,$i+1$.

2.3. Motion trajectory planning of X-Y table

The circular, window and star motion trajectories are typical used as the performance evaluation of the motion controller for X-Y table.

a. In circular motion trajectory, it is computed by

$$x_i = r \ \sin(\theta_i) \tag{28}$$

$$y_i = r \ \cos(\theta_i) \tag{29}$$

with $\theta_i = \theta_{i-1} + \Delta\theta$. Where $\Delta\theta$, r, x_i, y_i are angle increment, radius, X-axis trajectory command and Y-axis trajectory command, respectively.

b. The window motion trajectory is shown in Fig.6. The formulation is derived as follows:

a-trajectory:

$$x_i = x_{i-1}, y_i = S + y_{i-1} \tag{30}$$

b-trajectory:

$$(\theta_i : \frac{6}{4}\pi \rightarrow 2\pi, \text{ and } \theta_i = \theta_{i-1} + \Delta\theta)$$

$$x_i = O_{x1} + r\cos(\theta_i), y_i = O_{y1} + r\sin(\theta_i) \tag{31}$$

c-trajectory:

$$x_i = S + x_{i-1}, y_i = y_{i-1} \tag{32}$$

d-trajectory:

$$(\theta_i : \pi \rightarrow \frac{6}{4}\pi, \text{ and } \theta_i = \theta_{i-1} + \Delta\theta)$$

$$x_i = O_{x2} + r\cos(\theta_i), y_i = O_{y2} + r\sin(\theta_i) \tag{33}$$

e-trajectory:

$$x_i = x_{i-1}, y_i = -S + y_{i-1} \tag{34}$$

f-trajectory:

$$(\theta_i : \frac{1}{2}\pi \to \pi, \text{ and } \theta_i = \theta_{i-1} + \Delta\theta)$$

$$x_i = O_{x3} + r\cos(\theta_i), y_i = O_{y3} + r\sin(\theta_i) \tag{35}$$

g-trajectory:

$$x_i = -S + x_{i-1}, y_i = y_{i-1} \tag{36}$$

h-trajectory:

$$(\theta_i : 0 \to \frac{1}{2}\pi, \text{ and } \theta_i = \theta_{i-1} + \Delta\theta)$$

$$x_i = O_{x4} + r\cos(\theta_i), y_i = O_{y4} + r\sin(\theta_i) \tag{37}$$

i-trajectory:

$$x_i = x_{i-1}, y_i = S + y_{i-1} \tag{38}$$

where $S, \Delta\theta, x_i, y_i$ are position increment, angle increment, X-axis trajectory command and Y-axis trajectory command, respectively. In addition, the (O_{x1}, O_{y1}), (O_{x2}, O_{y2}), (O_{x3}, O_{y3}), (O_{x4}, O_{y4}) are arc center of b-, d-, f-, and h-trajectory in the Fig. 6 and r is the radius. The motion speed of the table is determined by $\Delta\theta$.

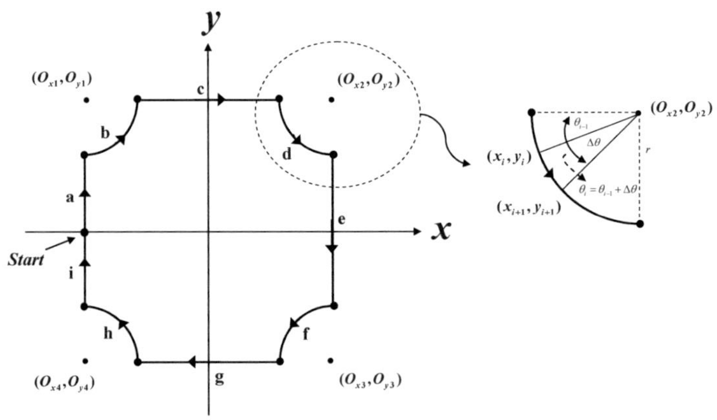

Figure 6. Window motion trajectory

c. Star motion trajectory is shown in Fig.7. The formulation is derived as follows:

a-trajectory :

$$x_i = S + x_{i-1}, \qquad y_i = y_{i-1} \tag{39}$$

b-trajectory :

$$x_i = -S * \sin 54^o + x_{i-1}, \qquad y_i = -S * \sin 36^o + y_{i-1} \tag{40}$$

c-trajectory :

$$x_i = S * \sin 18^o + x_{i-1}, \qquad y_i = S * \sin 72^o + y_{i-1} \tag{41}$$

d-trajectory :

$$x_i = S * \sin 18^o + x_{i-1}, \qquad y_i = -S * \sin 72^o + y_{i-1} \tag{42}$$

e-trajectory :

$$x_i = -S * \sin 54^o + x_{i-1}, \qquad y_i = S * \sin 36^o + y_{i-1} \tag{43}$$

Where S, x_i, y_i are position increment, X-axis trajectory command and Y-axis trajectory command, respectively. The motion speed of the table is determined by S.

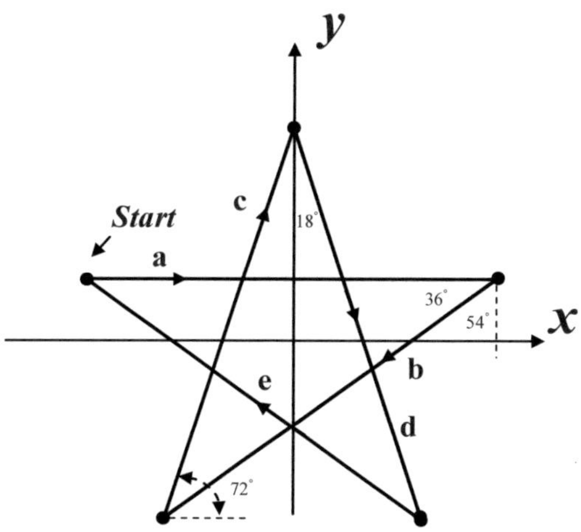

Figure 7. Star motion trajectory

3. The design of a motion control IC for linear motor drive X-Y table

Figure 8 illustrates the internal architecture of the proposed FPGA-based motion control IC for linear motor drive X-Y table. The FPGA uses Altera Stratix II EP2S60, which has 48,352 ALUTs (Adaptive Look-Up Tables), 36 DSP blocks, 144 embedded multipliers, 718 maximum user I/O pins, total 2,544,192 RAM bits, and a Nios II embedded processor which has a 32-bit configurable CPU core, 16 M byte flash memory, 1 M byte SRAM and 16 M byte SDRAM. The Nios II processor can be downloaded into FPGA to construct a SoPC environment. The internal circuit in Fig. 8 comprises a Nios II embedded processor IP (Intellectual Properties) and an application IP. The Nios II processor is depicted to both generate the motion trajectory and collect the response data. The application IP includes the circuits of two position AFC and speed P controllers as well as two current vector controllers for X-axis and Y-axis table. The sampling frequency of position control loop is designed with 2kHz. The operating clock rate of the designed FPGA controller is 50MHz and the frequency divider generates 50 Mhz (*Clk*), 25 MHz (*Clk-step*), 2 kHz (*Clk-sp*) and 16 kHz (*Clk-cur*) clock to supply all module circuits of application IP in Fig. 8.

An FSM is also employed to model the AFC of the position loop and P controller of the speed loop in X-axis table and shown in Fig. 9, which uses one adder, one multiplier, a look-up table, comparators, registers, etc. and manipulates 35 steps machine to carry out the overall computation. With exception of the data type in reference model are 24-bits, others data type are designed with 12-bits length, 2's complement and Q11 format. Although the algorithm of AFC is highly complexity, the FSM can give a very adequate modeling and easily be described by VHDL. Furthermore, steps s_0~s_6 execute the computation of reference model output; steps s_6~s_9 are for the computation of mover velocity, position error and error change; steps s_9~s_{12} execute the function of the fuzzification; s_{13} describe the look-up table and s_{14}~s_{22} defuzzification; and steps s_{23}~s_{34} execute the computation of velocity and current command output, and the tuning of fuzzy rule parameters. The SD is the section determination of *e* and *de* and the RS,1 represents the right shift function with one bit. The operation of each step in Fig.9 can be completed within 40ns (25 MHz clock) in FPGA; therefore total 35 steps need a 1.4μs operation time. It doesn't loss any control performance for the overall system because the operation time with 1.4μs is much less than the sampling interval, 500 μs (2 kHz), of the position control loop in Fig.3. In Fig. 8, the QEP circuit and circuit for current vector control refer to (Kung & Tsai, 2007). Further, the Nios II embedded processor IP is depicted to perform the function of the motion trajectory and two-axis position/speed loop controller for X-Y table in software. Figure 10 illustrates the flow charts of the main program and the interrupt service routine (ISR), where the interrupt interval is designed with 2ms. All programs are coded in the C programming language. Then, through the complier and linker operation in the Nios II IDE (Integrated Development Environment), the execution code is produced and can be downloaded to the external Flash or SDRAM via JTAG interface.

Under the proposed design method, the overall resource usage of the proposed motion control IC is listed in Table 1 which the two AFC circuits need 16,110 ALUTs, the Nios II embedded processor IP needs 8,275 ALUTs and 46,848 RAM bits and the application IP needs 22,928 ALUTs and 595,968 RAM bits in FPGA. Therefore, the motion control IC uses 64.5% ALUTs resource and 25.2% RAM resource of Stratix II EP2S60.

IP	Module circuit	ALUTs	Memory (bits)
Nios II Embedded Processor IP		8,275	46,848
Application IP	2 x Adaptive fuzzy controller (AFC)	16,110	0
	2 x Current loop controller (Current vector control, SVPWM,ADC,QEP)	6,818	595,968
Total		31,203	642,816

Table 1. The resource usage of a motion control IC in FPGA

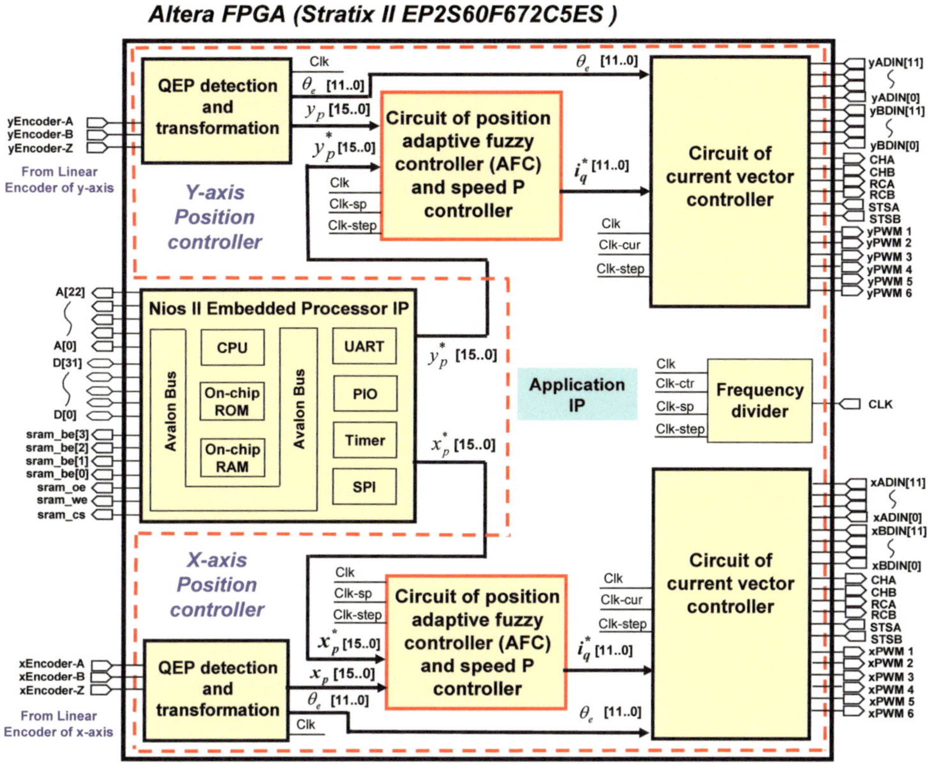

Figure 8. The internal architecture of a motion control IC for linear motor drive X-Y table

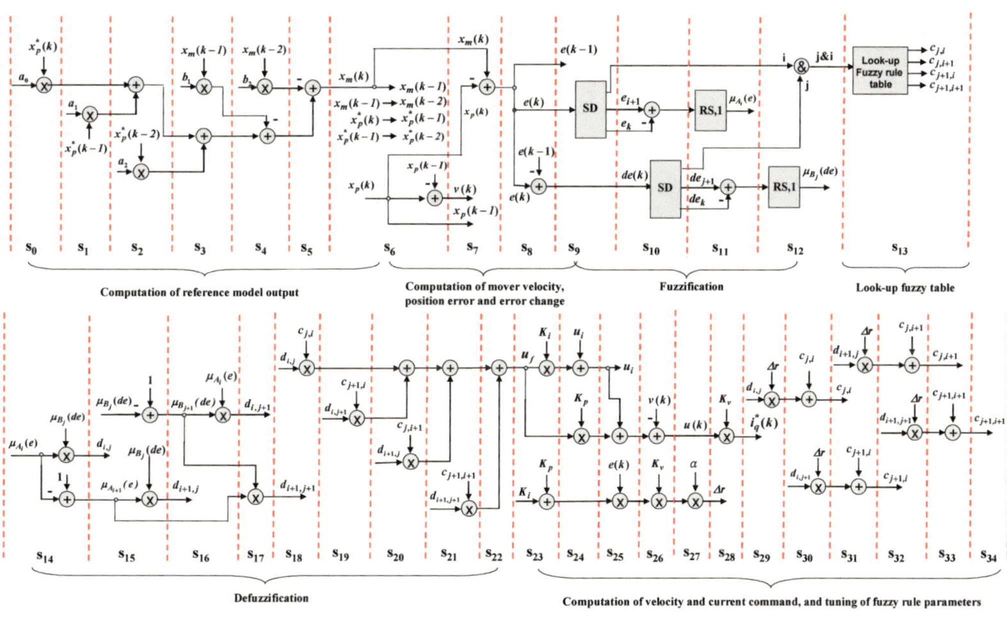

Figure 9. State diagram of an FSM for describing the AFC in position loop and P controller in speed loop (for X-axis Table)

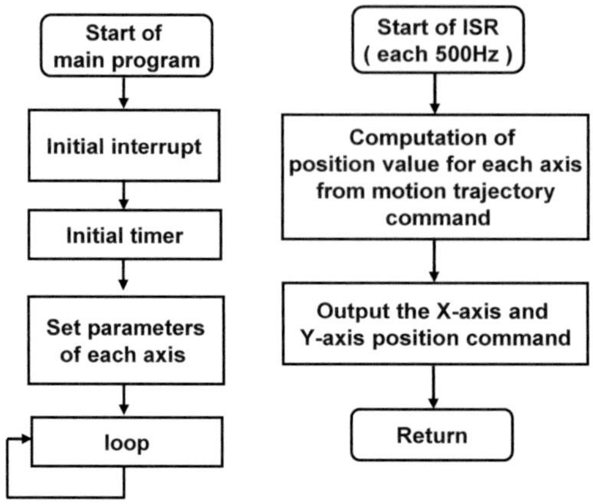

Figure 10. Flow chart of the main and ISR program in Nios II embedded processor

4. Experimental results

The overall experimental system depicted in Fig.3 includes an FPGA (Stratix II EP2S60F672C5) experimental board, two voltage source IGBT inverters and an X-Y table which is driven by two PMLSMs. The PMLSM was manufactured by the BALDOR electric company; and it is a single-axis stage with a cog-free linear motor and a stroke length with 600mm. The parameters of the motor are: $R_s = 27\,\Omega$, $L_d = L_q = 23.3$ mH, $K_t = 79.9$N/A. The input voltage, continuous current, peak current (10% duty) and continuous power of the PMLSM are 220V, 1.6A, 4.8A and 54W, respectively. The maximum speed and acceleration are 4m/s and 4 g but depend on external load. The moving mass is 2.5Kg, the maximum payload is 22.5Kg and the maximum thrust force is 73N under continuous operating conditions. A linear encoder with a resolution of 5μm is mounted on the PMLSM as the position sensor, and the pole pitch is 30.5mm (about 6100 pulses). The inverter has three sets of IGBT power transistors. The collector-emitter voltage of the IGBT is rated 600V; the gate-emitter voltage is rated ±20V, and the DC collector current is rated 25A and in short time (1ms) is 50A. The photo-IC, Toshiba TLP250, is used in the gate driving circuit of IGBT. Input signals of the inverter are PWM signals from the FPGA device.

To confirm the effectiveness of the proposed AFC in linear drive X-Y table, a realization of position controller based on the FPGA in Fig.3 is constructed and some experiments are evaluated. The control sampling frequency of the current, speed and position loops are designed as 16kHz, 2kHz and 2kHz, respectively. In the motion control IC, two position/speed/current controllers are all realized by hardware in FPGA, and the motion trajectory algorithm is implemented by software using the Nios II embedded processor. The speed controller adopts a P controller and the AFC is used in the position loop. The transfer function of the reference model is selected by a second order system with the natural frequency of 30 rad/s and damping ratio of 1. The step response is first tested to evaluate the performance of the proposed controller. Figures 11 and 12 respectively show the position step responses for X-axis and Y-axis table using the FC (learning rate=0) and AFC (learning rate=0.1). The position command is a 4/3Hz square wave signal with 10mm amplitude. In Figs. 11(a) and 12(a), when an 11 kg load is added upon the mover of the X-Y table and the fuzzy control by using a fixed rule table, the position dynamic response in X-axis and Y-axis table exhibits a 12.8% and 23.1% overshoot and severe oscillation, respectively. Accordingly, an AFC is adopted in Fig.3. When the proposed AFC is used with learning rate being 0.1, the tracking results are highly improved and presented in Figs. 11(c) and 12(c). Initially, the position response in X-axis or Y-axis table tracks the output of the reference model with oscillation. After one or two square wave commands, the $c_{i,j}$ parameters in fuzzy rule table are tuned to adequate values, and the position response in X-axis or Y-axis table can closely follow the output of the reference model. Further, the tracking motion about circular, window and star trajectory by using FC and AFC are experimented. To evaluate the tracking performance, the indices are firstly defined as follows.

$$T(k) = \sqrt{(x_m(k) - x_p(x))^2 + (y_m(k) - y_p(x))^2} \tag{44}$$

$$m = \sum_{k=1}^{n} T(k) / n \tag{45}$$

$$\sigma = \sqrt{\sum_{k=1}^{n} (T(k) - m)^2 / n} \tag{46}$$

Where $T(k)$, m and σ respectively represent instantaneous value, mean and variance of tracking error. In the circular tracking motion, the circle command is with center (25, 25) cm and radius 10cm and its experimental results are shown in Figs. 13~14. In the window tracking motion, the trajectory is designed as Fig.6 and its experimental results are shown in Figs. 15~16. In the star tracking motion, the trajectory is designed as Fig.7 and its experimental results are shown in Figs. 17~18. Further, the tracking performance in Figs 13~18 by using FC and AFC control algorithm are evaluated according to the indices of (44)~(46), and its results are listed in Table 2. Compared with FC, the mean of tracking errors

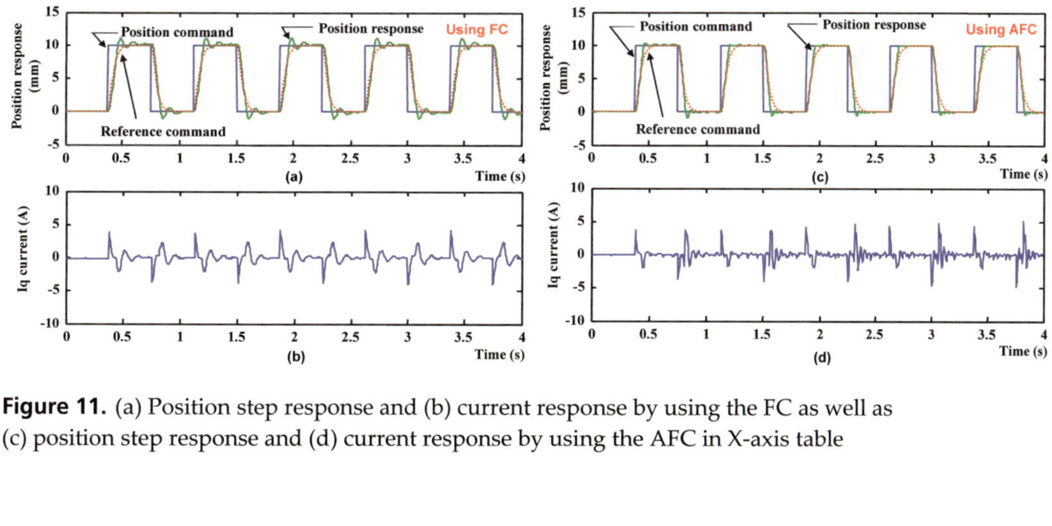

Figure 11. (a) Position step response and (b) current response by using the FC as well as (c) position step response and (d) current response by using the AFC in X-axis table

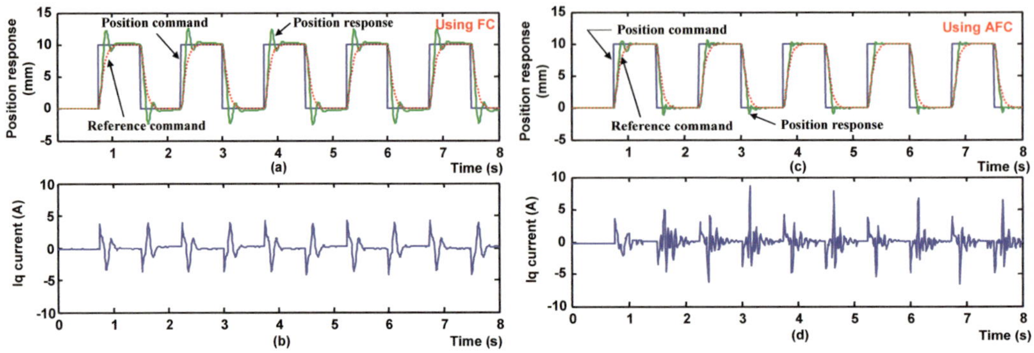

Figure 12. (a) Position step response and (b) current response by using the FC as well as (c) position step response and (d) current response by using the AFC in Y-axis table

in circular, winddow and star motion trajectory are significantly reduced about 41.6%, 14.6% and 12.8% and the variance of tracking errors reduced about 33.3%, 64.6% and 47.4% after using AFC. Therefore, it shows that the AFC has a better tracking performance than FC in motion control of linear motor drive X-Y table. Finally, from the experimental results of Figs.11~18, it demonstrates that the proposed AFC and the FPGA-based motion control IC used for the linear motor drive X-Y table is effective and correct.

5. Conclusion

This study successfully presents a motion control IC for linear motor drive X-Y table based on FPGA technology. The works herein are summarized as follows.

1. The functionalities required to build a fully digital motion controller of linear motor drive X-Y table, such as the two current vector controllers, two speed P controllers, and two position AFCs and one motion trajectory planning, have been integrated in one FPGA chip.
2. An FSM joined by one multiplier, one adder, one LUT, or some comparators and registers has been employed to model the overall AFC algorithm, such that it not only is easily implemented by VHDL but also the resources usage can be reduced in the FPGA.
3. The software/hardware co-design technology under SoPC environment has been successfully applied to the motion controller of linear motor drive X-Y table.

However, the experimental results by step response as well as the circular, window and star motion trajectory tracking, has been revealed that the software/hardware co-design technology with the parallel processing well in the motion control system of linear motor drive X-Y table.

Control algorithm	Fuzzy controller (FC)			Adaptive fuzzy controller (AFC)		
Tracking error (mm)	Circular motion	Window motion	Star motion	Circular motion	Window motion	Star motion
Mean	3.51	1.43	1.64	2.05	1.22	1.43
Variance	0.60	2.12	3.52	0.40	0.75	1.85

Table 2. Evaluation of tracking performance using FC and AFC

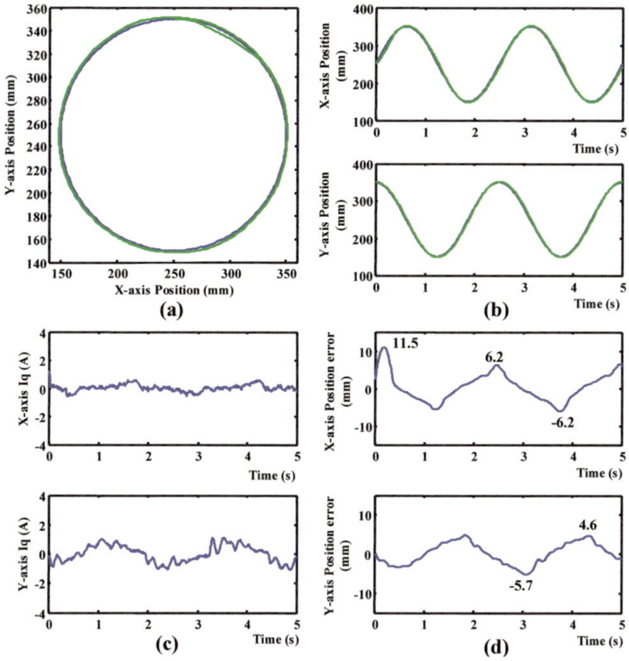

Figure 13. Circular trajectory response by using the FC (a) Star trajectory tracking (b) Position tracking in X- and Y-axis table (c) Control efforts in X- and Y-axis table (d) Tracking errors in X- and Y-axis table

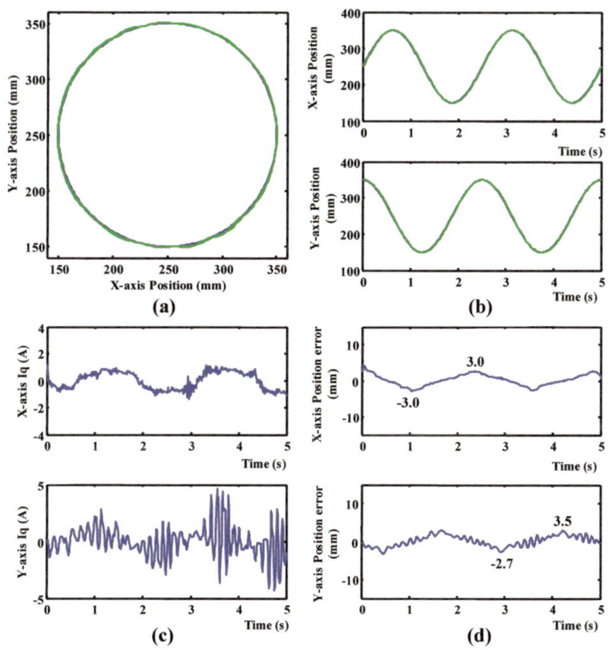

Figure 14. Circular trajectory response by using the AFC (a) Star trajectory tracking (b) Position tracking in X- and Y-axis table (c) Control efforts in X- and Y-axis table (d) Tracking errors in X- and Y-axis table

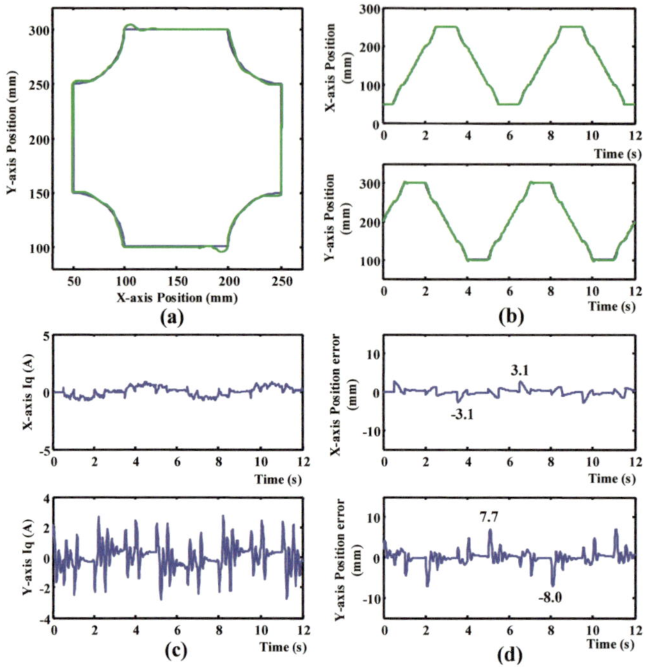

Figure 15. Window trajectory response by using the FC (a) Star trajectory tracking (b) Position tracking in X- and Y-axis table (c) Control efforts in X- and Y-axis table (d) Tracking errors in X- and Y-axis table

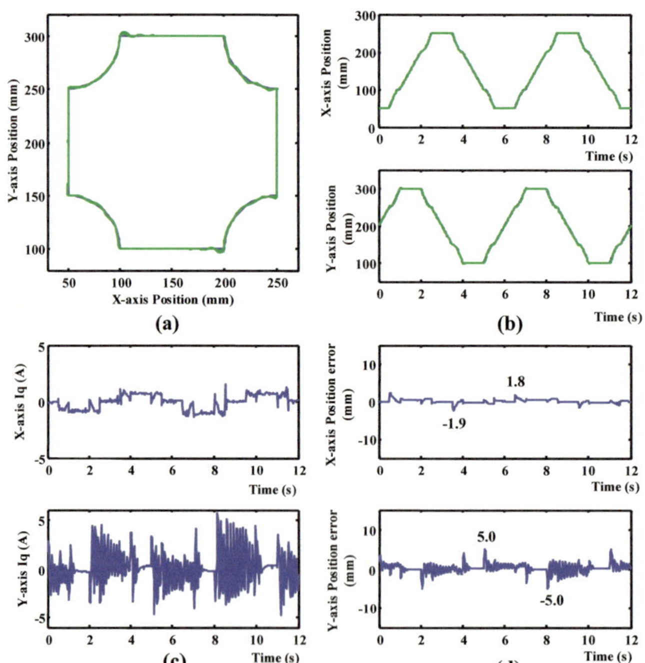

Figure 16. Window trajectory response by using the AFC (a) Star trajectory tracking (b) Position tracking in X- and Y-axis table (c) Control efforts in X- and Y-axis table (d) Tracking errors in X- and Y-axis table

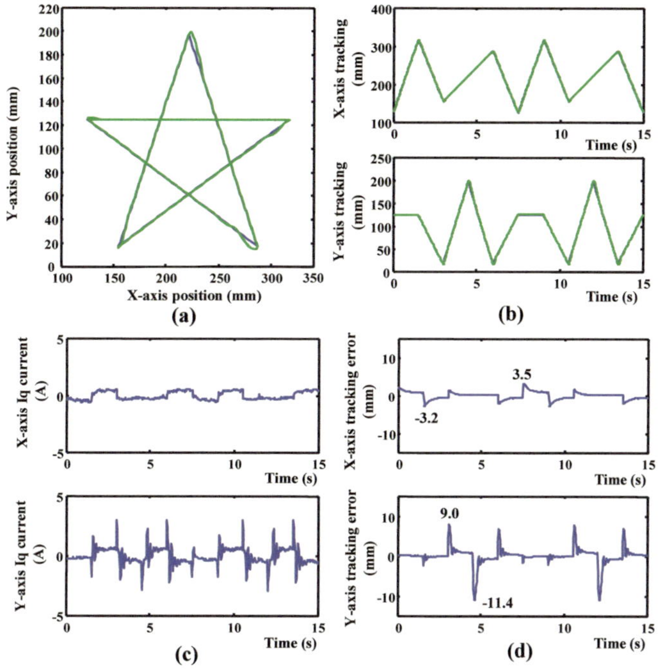

Figure 17. Star trajectory response by using the FC (a) Star trajectory tracking (b) Position tracking in X- and Y-axis table (c) Control efforts in X- and Y-axis table (d) Tracking errors in X- and Y-axis table

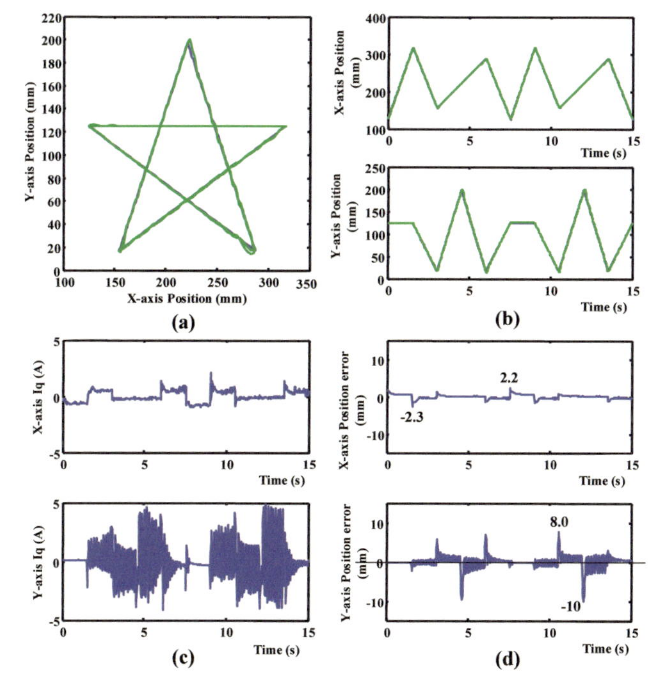

Figure 18. Star trajectory response by using the AFC (a) Star trajectory tracking (b) Position tracking in X- and Y-axis table (c) Control efforts in X- and Y-axis table (d) Tracking errors in X- and Y-axis table

Author details

Ying-Shieh Kung
Department of Electrical Engineering, Southern Taiwan University, Taiwan

Chung-Chun Huang and Liang-Chiao Huang
Green Energy and Environment Research Laboratories, Industrial Technology Research Institute, Taiwan

Acknowledgement

The financial support provided by Bureau of Energy is gratefully acknowledged.

6. References

Cho, J. U., Le, Q. N. and Jeon, J. W. (2009) An FPGA-based multiple-axis motion control chip, *IEEE Trans. Ind. Electron.*, vol. 56, no.3, pp.856-870.

Groove, M.P. (1996) *Fundamentals of modern manufacturing: materials, process, and systems.* Prentice Hall, Upper Saddle River, NJ.

Goto, S., Nakamura, M. and Kyura, N. (1996) Accurate contour control of mechatronic servo systems using gaussian networks. *IEEE Trans. Ind. Electron.*, vol.43, no. 4, pp. 469-476.

Hanafi, D., Tordon, M. and Katupitiya, J. (2003) An active axis control system for a conventional CNC machine. *Proceedings of IEEE/ASME International Conference on Advanced Intelligent Mechatronics*, pp. 1188-1193.

Hall, T.S., Hamblen, J.O. (2004) System-on-a-programmable -chip development platforms in the classroom. *IEEE Trans. on Education*, vol.47, no.4, pp.502-507.

Lin, F.J., SHieh, P.H. and Shen, P.H. (2006) Robust recurrent-neural-network sliding-mode control for the X-Y table of a CNC machine. *IEE Proc. Control Theory Application*, vol. 153, no. 1, pp. 111-123.

Monmasson, E., Idkhajine L. and Naouar, M.W. (2011) FPGA-based Controllers. *IEEE Trans. Electron. Magaz.*, vol. 5, no.1, pp.14-26.

Kung, Y.S., Huang P.G. and Chen, C.W. (2004) Development of a SOPC for PMSM drives. *Proceedings of the IEEE International Midwest Symposium on Circuits and Systems*, vol. II, pp. II-329~II-332.

Kung, Y.S. and Tsai, M.H. (2007) FPGA-based speed control IC for PMSM drive with adaptive fuzzy control. *IEEE Trans. on Power Electronics*, vol. 22, no. 6, pp. 2476-2486.

Kung, Y.S. and Chen, C.S. (2008). Realization of a motion control IC for robot manipulator based on novel FPGA technology. *Robot manipulators, programming, design and control.* pp.291~312, I-Tech, Vienna.

Sanchez-Solano, S., Cabrera, A. J., Baturone, I., Moreno-Velo, F.J., Brox, M. (2007) FPGA implementation of embedded fuzzy controllers for robotic applications. *IEEE Trans. Ind. Electron.*, vol. 54, no. 4, pp. 1937-1945.

SOPC World, (2004) Altera Corporation.

Wang, G.J. and Lee, T.J. (1999) Neural-network cross-coupled control system with application on circular tracking of linear motor X-Y table. *International Joint Conference on Neural Networks*, pp. 2194-2199.

Chapter 9

Novel Yinger Learning Variable Universe Fuzzy Controller

Ping Zhang and Guodong Gao

Additional information is available at the end of the chapter

http://dx.doi.org/10.5772/48266

1. Introduction

Fuzzy control is a practical alternative for a variety of challenging of challenging control applications because it provides a convenient method for constructing nonlinear controllers via the use of heuristic information. The heuristic information may come from an operator who has acted as a human controller for a process. In the fuzzy control design methodology, a set of rules are written down by the operator on how to control the process, then make these into a fuzzy controller that emulates the decision-making process of the human. In some cases, the heuristic information may come from other novel intelligent applications. In other cases, the heuristic information may come from a control engineer who has performed extensive mathematical modeling, analysis, and development of control algorithms for a particular process. Regardless of where the heuristic control knowledge comes from, fuzzy control provides a user-friendly formalism for representing and implementing the ideas.

Over the past few decades, fuzzy logic theory is widely used: process control, management and decision making, operations research, economies. Dealing with simple 'yes' and 'no' answers is no longer satisfactory enough; a degree of membership (Zadeh, 1965) became a new way of solving problems. Fuzzy logic derives from the truth that the human common sense reasoning mode is approximate in nature.

In this chapter we provide a control engineering perspective on novel fuzzy controller. We take a pragmatic engineering approach to the design, analysis, performance evaluation, and implement of fuzzy control system. The chapter is basically broken into five parts. In section 2, we provide an overview of conventional control system design. In section 3 the basic theories of variable universe fuzzy control are been introduced. In section 4, we cover the novel fuzzy controller based on Yinger algorithm. In section 5, we use some examples to show how to design, simulate, and implement these controllers. Finally, in section 6, we explain how to write a computer program to simulate the novel fuzzy control system, using either a high-level language or Matlab.

2. Conventional control system design

2.1. Introduction

A control system is a device, or set of devices to manage, command, direct or regulate the behavior of other devices or system. There are two common classes of control systems, with many variations and combinations: logic or sequential controls, and feedback or linear controls. There is also fuzzy logic, which attempts to combine some of the design simplicity of logic with the utility of linear control. Some devices or systems are inherently not controllable. A basic control system is shown in figure 1. The plant is object to be controlled. Its inputs are $u(t)$, its outputs are $y(t)$, and reference input is $r(t)$.

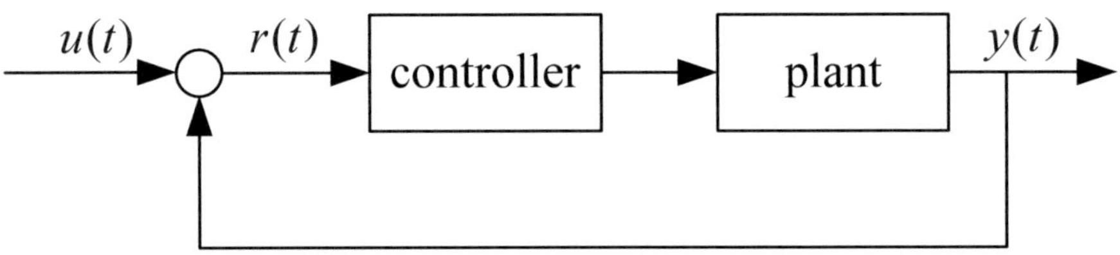

Figure 1. Control system

2.2. Mathematical modeling

The mathematical model is a description of a system using mathematical concepts and language. The process of developing a mathematical model is termed mathematical modeling. Mathematical models are used not only in the natural sciences (such as physics, biology, earth science, meteorology) and engineering disciplines (such as computer science, artificial intelligence), but also in the social sciences (such as economics, psychology, sociology and political science),physicists, engineers, statisticians, operations research analysts and economists use mathematical models most extensively. A model may help to explain a system and to study the effects of different components, and to make predictions about behaviour.

Mathematical models can take many forms, including but not limited to dynamical systems, statistical models, differential equations, or game theoretic models. These and other types of models can overlap, with a given model involving a variety of abstract structures. In general, mathematical models may include logical models, as far as logic is taken as a part of mathematics. In many cases, the quality of a scientific field depends on how well the mathematical models developed on the theoretical side agree with results of repeatable experiments. Lack of agreement between theoretical mathematical models and experimental measurements often leads to important advances as better theories are developed.

When a control engineer is given a control problem, often one of the first tasks is the development of a mathematical model of the process to be controlled, in order to gain a clear understanding of the problem. Basically, there are only a few ways to actually generate the model. We can use first principles of physics to write down a model. Another way is to perform "system identification" via the use of real plant data to produce a model of the system. Sometimes a combined approach is used where we use physics to write down a general different equation that we believe represent the plant behavior, and then we perform experiments on the plant to determine certain model parameters or functions.

Often, more than one mathematical model is produced. A "truth model" is one that is developed to be as accurate as possible so that it can be used in simulation-based evaluations of control systems. It must be understood, however, that there is never a perfect mathematical model for the plant. The mathematical model is an abstraction and hence cannot perfectly represent all possible dynamics of any physical process. This is not to say that we cannot produce models that are "accurate enough" to closely represent the behavior of a physical system. Usually, control engineer to be able to design a controller that will work. Then, they often also need a very accurate model to test the controller in simulation before it is tested in an experimental setting. Hence, lower-order "design model" are also often developed that may satisfy certain assumption yet still capture the essential plant behavior. Indeed, it is quite an art to produce good low-order model that satisfy these constraints. We emphasize that the reason we often need simpler models is that the synthesis techniques for controller often require that the model of the plant satisfy certain assumptions or there methods generally cannot be used.

Linear models such as the one in Equation (1) have been used extensively in the past and the control theory for linear system is quite mature.

$$\begin{aligned} \dot{x} &= Ax + Bu \\ y &= Cx + Du \end{aligned} \tag{1}$$

In this case u is the m-dimensional input; x is the n-dimensional state; y is the p-dimensional output; and A,B,C and D are matrices of appropriate dimension. Such models are appropriate for use with frequency domain design techniques, the root-locus method, state-space methods, and so on. Sometimes it is assumed that the parameters of the linear model are constant but unknown, or can be perturbed form their nominal values.

Much of the current focus in control is on the development of controllers using nonlinear models of the plant of the form

$$\begin{aligned} \dot{x} &= f(x,u) \\ y &= g(x,u) \end{aligned} \tag{2}$$

Where the variables are defined as for the linear model and f and g are nonlinear functions of their arguments. One form of the nonlinear model that has received significant attention is

$$\dot{x} = f(x) + g(x)u \tag{3}$$

Since it is possible to exploit the structure of this model to construct nonlinear controllers. Of particular with both of the above nonlinear models is the case where f and g are not completely known and subsequent research focuses on robust control of nonlinear system.

Discrete time versions of the above models are also used, and stochastic effect are often taken into account via the addition of a input or other stochastic effects. Under certain assumptions you can linearize the nonlinear model in Equation(2) to obtain a linear one. In this case we sometimes think of the nonlinear model as the truth model, and the linear model that are generated form it as control design model.

There are certain properties of the plant that the control engineer often seeks to identify early in the design process. For instance, the stability of the plant may be analyzed. The effects of certain nonlinearities are also studied. The engineer may want to determine if the plant is controllable to see, for example, if the control input will be able to properly affect the plant; and observable to see, for example, if the chosen sensors will allow the controller observe the critical plant behavior so that it can be compensated Overall, this analysis of the plant's behavior gives the control engineer a fundamental understanding of the plant dynamics.

2.3. Performance objectives and design constrains

Controller design entails constructing a controller to meet the specifications. Often the first issue to address is whether to use open or closed-loop control. Often, need to pay for a sensor for the feedback information and there need to justification for this cost. Moreover, feedback can destabilize the system. Do not develop a feedback controller just because you are used to developing feedback controllers; you may want to consider an open-loop controllers since it may provide adequate performance. Assuming you use feedback control, the closed-loop specifications can involve the following factors: Disturbance rejection properties; Insensitivity to plant parameter variations; Stability; Rise-time.

2.4. Controller design

Conventional control has provided numerous methods for controllers for dynamic system. Some of there are listed below:

1. Proportional-integral-derivative(PID) control:Over 90% of the controllers in operation today are PID controllers. This approach is often viewed as simple, reliable,and easy to understand. Often, like fuzzy controller, heuristics are used to tune PID controllers.
2. State-space methods: State feedback,observers,and so on.
3. Optimal control: Linear quadratic regulator,use of Pontryagin's minimum principle or dynamic programming,an so on.
4. Nonlinear methods: Feedback linearization, Lyapunov redesign, sliding mode control, backstepping, and so on.
5. Adaptive control; model reference adaptive control,self-tuning regulators, nonlinear adaptive control,and so on.

Basically,there conventional approaches to control system design offer a variety of ways to utilize information from mathematical model on how to do good control. Sometimes they do not take into account certain heuristic information early in the design process, but use heuristics when the controller is implemented to tune it(tuning is invariably needed since the model used for the controller development is not perfectly accurate).Unfortunately, when using some approaches to conventional control, some engineers become somewhat removed from the control problem, and sometimes this leads to the development of unrealistic control laws. Sometimes in conventional control, useful heuristics are ignored because they do not fit into the proper mathematical framework, and this can cause problem.

2.5. Performance evaluation

The next step in the design process is to perform analysis and performance evaluation. Basically, we need performance evaluation to test that we design does in fact meet the closed-loop specifications. This can be particularly important in safety-critical applications such as the control of a washing machine or an electric shaver, it may not be as important in the sense that failures will not imply the loss of life, so some of the rigorous evaluation methods can sometimes be ignored. Basically, there are three general ways to verify that a control system is operating properly: (1) mathematical analysis based on the use of formal models, (2) simulation-based analysis that most often uses formal models, and (3) experimental investigations on the real system.

3. Variable fuzzy control system design

The fuzzy controller block diagram is given in figure 2. The plant outputs are denoted by $y(t)$, its input is denoted by $u(t)$, and the reference input to the fuzzy controller is denoted by $r(t)$.

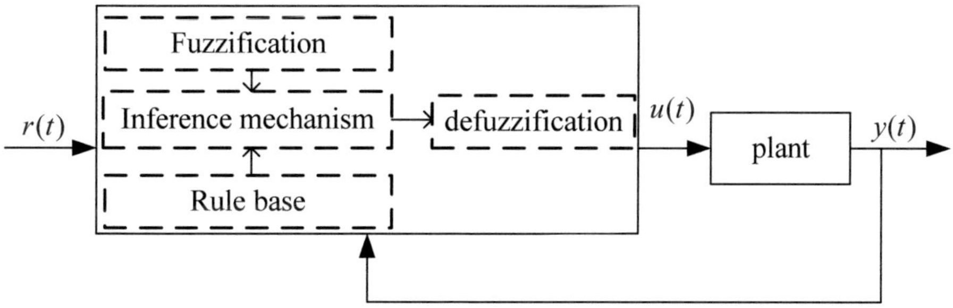

Figure 2. Fuzzy controller architecture

3.1. Fuzzy controller

Basically, the difficult task of modeling and simulating complex real-world systems for controller systems development, especially when implementation issues are considered, is well documented. Even if a relatively accurate model of a dynamic system can be developed, it is often too complex to use require restrictive assumptions for the plant. It is for this reason that in practice conventional controllers are often developed via simple models of the plant behavior that satisfy the necessary assumptions, and via the ad hoc tuning of relatively simple linear or nonlinear controllers. Regardless, it is well understood.

Fuzzy control provides a formal methodology for representing, manipulating, and implementing a human's heuristic knowledge about how to control a system.

The fuzzy controller block diagram is given in Figure 2, where we show a fuzzy controller embedded in a closed-loop control system. The plant outputs are denoted by y(t), its inputs are denoted by u(t), and the reference input to the fuzzy controller is denoted by r(t).

The fuzzy controller has four main components: (1) The" rule-base" holds the knowledge, in the form of a set of rules are relevant at the current time and then decides what the input to the plant should be, (3) The fuzzification interface simply modifies the inputs so that they can be interpreted and compared to the rules in the rule-base. And (4) the defuzzification interface converts the conclusions reached by the inference mechanism into the inputs to the plant.

To design the fuzzy controller, the control engineer must gather information on how the artificial decision maker should act in the closed-loop system. Sometimes this information can come from a human decision maker who performs the control task, while at other times the control engineer can come to understand the plant dynamics and write down a set of rules about how to control the system without outside help. These "rules" basically say, "If should be some value." A whole set of such "If-Then" rules is loaded into the rule-base, and specifications are met.

3.2. Structure of variable adaptive fuzzy controller

Let $X_i = \left[-E, E\right](i = 1,2,\cdots,n)$ be the universe of input variable $x_i(i = 1,2,\cdots,n)$, and $Y = [-U,U]$ be the universe of output variable y . $\mu_i = \{A_{ij}\}_{(1\le j\le m)}$ stands for a fuzzy partition on X_i ,and $\mathrm{B} = \{B_j\}_{(1\le j\le m)}$ defines a fuzzy partition on Y . A group of fuzzy inference rules is formed as follow:

If x_1 is A_{1j} and x_2 is A_{2j} and…and x_n is A_{nj} then y is B_j , $j = 1,2,\cdots,m$

The fuzzy logic system can be represented as an n-dimension piecewise interpolation function $F(x, x_2, \cdots, x_n)$:

$$F(x,x_2,\cdots,x_n) = y(x,x_2,\cdots,x_n) = \sum_{j=1}^{m} \prod_{i=1}^{n} A_{ij}(x_i) y_j \tag{4}$$

Generally speaking, a function $\alpha : X \to [0,1], x \to \alpha(x)$ can be called a contraction-expansion factor on $X_i = \left[-E, E\right]$. The so-called variable universe means X_i and Y can change with changing variable x_i and y expressed by:

$$X_i(x_i) = [-\alpha(x_i)E_i, \alpha(x_i)E_i] \tag{5}$$

$$Y(y) = [-\beta(y)U, \beta(y)U] \tag{6}$$

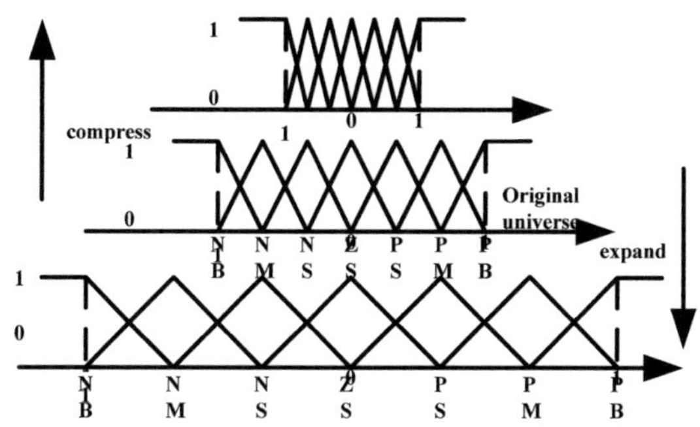

Figure 3. Universe compress and expand

4. Novel fuzzy controller based on Yinger algorithm

Novel fuzzy controller is composed of three parts. Firstly, new kind of contraction-expansion factor is established, then local space is optimized, finally novel controller dynamically adjust output by rules.

4.1. Optimal local spaces

Many real-world environments in which learning systems have to operate are time-varying. Several aspects of the learning problem can vary, including the mapping to be learned, and the sampling distribution that governs the input-space location of exemplars that make up the input information. In this section, K-Vector Nearest Neighbors (K-VNN) is proposed to this problem.

Define 1. Lets Ω_k is input sets which can be defined to local space as:

$$\Omega_k \equiv \{X_1, \cdots, X_K\} = \{X_i | D(X_i, X_m) < h\} \tag{7}$$

Where h is radius of local space (Ω_k), and data-window is changed by adjusting it. $D(A,B)$ is the distance function which is defined by (8), $X_1, \cdots, X_K$ are messages to input.

Define 2. Lets $A = [A_1, \cdots, A_n]$ and $B = [B_1, \cdots, B_n]$,in the Euclidean space, gets distance and intersection angle:

$$\begin{cases} d(A,B) = \sqrt{\|A-B\|_2} \\ \theta(A,B) = \arccos A^T B \big/ \|A\|_2 \bullet \|B\|_2 \end{cases} \tag{8}$$

According to (7), we can get the distance and intersection angle of X_i and X_d, from input-output specimen choice similar message to Ω_k.

If intersection angle of X_i and X_d .greater than 90°, thinking X_i stray from X_d ,and define as follows:

$$D(X_i, X_d) = ae^{\left[-d(X_i, X_d)\right]} + b\sin\left[\varphi(X_i, X_d)\right] \\ (0 \le a \le 1/2, 0 \le b \le 1/2) \tag{9}$$

From (9), we can see, if X_i is more similar to X_d, $e^{\left[-d(X_i, X_d)\right]}$ and $\sin\left[\varphi(X_i, X_d)\right]$ are more similar to 1, use this method and get the new input set

$$\Omega_k = \left\{(X_1, Y_1), \cdots, (X_K, Y_K) \middle| D(X_1, X_d) > \cdots > D(X_k, X_d)\right\} \tag{10}$$

From this section, some noise can be deleted by this section.

4.2. Contraction-expansion factor

Now the popular contraction-expansion factor is $\alpha(x) = 1 - ce^{(-kx^2)}$ ($c \in (0\ 1)$ $k \ge 0$), but the algorithm module can not be realized easily by C++ which support some methods by using VC++ accomplish control system. So building up a kind of contraction-expansion factor to nonlinear system is very important.

1. Establish differential equation

Firstly, $\alpha(e(t))$ is strictly monotonously increasing on [0 1] and monotonously decreasing on [-1 0].

Secondly, $e(t) \to 0$ Then $\alpha(e(t)) \to \varepsilon = 0.0001$ and $|e(t)| \to 1$ then $\alpha(e(t)) \to 1$.

Thirdly, $\Delta\alpha(e(t)) = k\Delta e(t)$, and to the same $\Delta e(t)$, $e(t)$ is larger and $\Delta\alpha(e(t))$ is larger too. From those conditions the differential equation can be build as follow:

$$\Delta\alpha(e(t)) = ke(t)\Delta e(t)(E - e^2(t)) \tag{11}$$

get hold of:

$$\alpha(x) = -\frac{1}{4}kx^4 + \frac{E}{2}kx^2 + c \tag{12}$$

and initialized condition:

when $e(t) = 0$ then $\alpha(e(t)) = D(X_i, X_d)$,and $|\ e(t)\ |$=E $\alpha(e(t)) = 1$

get hold of:

$$\alpha(x) = -\frac{1}{4}kx^4 + \frac{E}{2}kx^2 + D(X_{i,}X_d) \tag{13}$$

2. Analyze and verify characters

1. Duality $\forall e(t) \in E \ \alpha(e(t)) = \alpha(-e(t))$
2. Near zero $\alpha(0) = D(X_{i,}X_d) > 0$
3. Monotonicity: $\forall e(t_1), e(t_2) \in [0, E]$ if $e(t_1) \geq e(t_2)$ then $\alpha(e(t_1)) \geq \alpha(e(t_2))$
4. Normality $\alpha(E) = \alpha(-E) = 1$

$$\alpha(x) = -\frac{1}{4}kx^4 + \frac{E}{2}kx^2 + D(X_{i,}X_d)$$

is the primary function can easily realize in nonlinear system. So the new kind of contraction-expansion factor is satisfied with the requests.

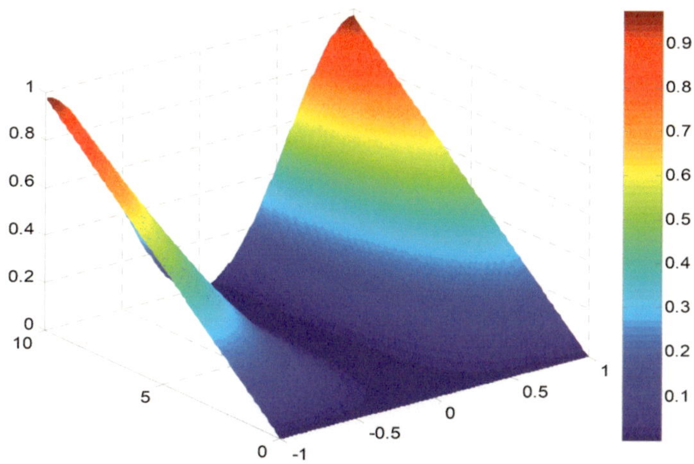

Figure 4. Function cluster surface (k>0)

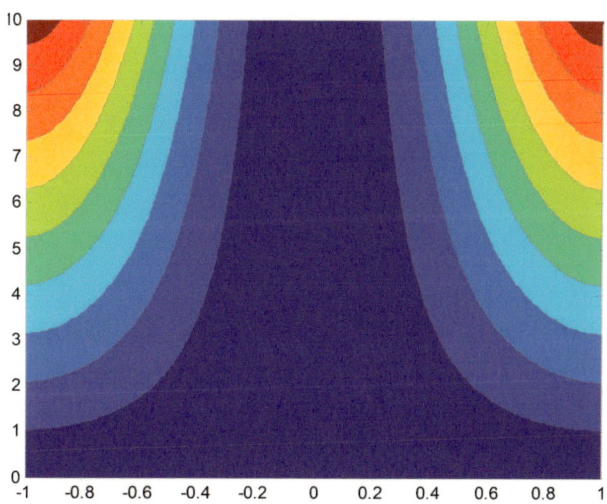

Figure 5. Function cluster surface contour(k>0)

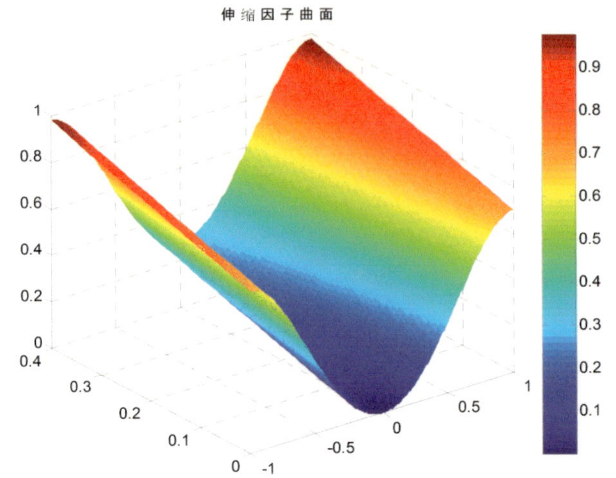

Figure 6. Function cluster surface (c<1)

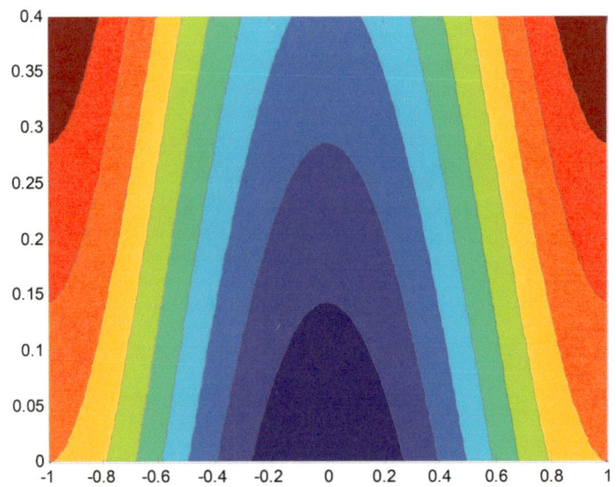

Figure 7. Function cluster surface contour (c<1)

5. Examples

Choose the typical non-linear system to the new algorithm.

$$\text{Plant: } \dot{x}(t) = \frac{1-e^{-x(t)}}{1+e^{-x(t)}} + u(t) \qquad (14)$$
$$y(t) = x(t)$$

$$\lim_{t\to\infty}\|e(t)\| = \lim_{t\to\infty}\|r(t)-y(t)\| = 0 \qquad (15)$$

$$\text{And } u(t) = u_c(t)$$

$$U[-1,1]$$

We can get the rules as follows:

$$if \;\; e \;\; is \;\; Nb \;\; then \;\; u \;\; is \;\; NB, \; if \;\; e \;\; is \;\; Nm \;\; then \;\; u \;\; is \;\; NM$$

$$if \;\; e \;\; is \;\; Ns \;\; then \;\; u \;\; is \;\; NS, \; if \;\; e \;\; is \;\; Pb \;\; then \;\; u \;\; is \;\; PB$$

$$if \;\; e \;\; is \;\; Pm \;\; then \;\; u \;\; is \;\; PM, \; if \;\; e \;\; is \;\; Ps \;\; then \;\; u \;\; is \;\; PS$$

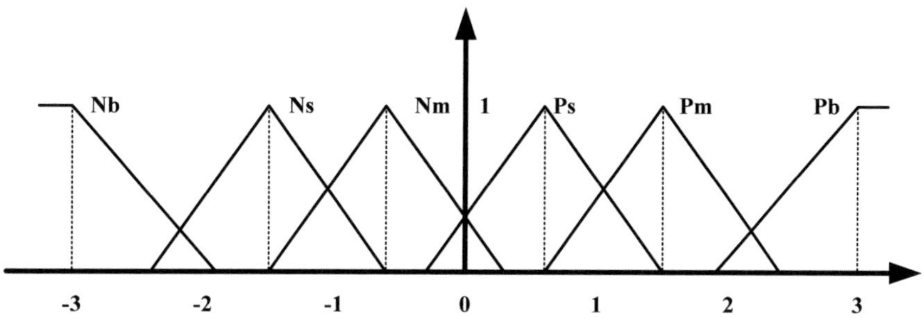

Figure 8. Function

$$Nb(e)=\begin{cases}1\,, & e\le -3\\ \dfrac{e+1.9}{-1.1}, & -3\le e\le -1.9\\ 0\,, & etc\end{cases} \quad Nm(e)=\begin{cases}\dfrac{e+2.4}{0.9}, & -2.4\le e\le -1.5\\ \dfrac{e+0.6}{-0.9}, & -1.5\le e\le -0.6\\ 0\,, & etc\end{cases}$$

$$Ns(e)=\begin{cases}\dfrac{e+1.5}{0.9}, & -1.5\le e\le -0.6\\ \dfrac{e}{-0.6}, & -0.6\le e\le 0\\ 0\,, & etc\end{cases} \quad Ps(e)=\begin{cases}\dfrac{e}{0.6}, & 0\le e\le 0.6\\ \dfrac{e-1.5}{-0.9}, & 0.6\le e\le 1.5\\ 0\,, & etc\end{cases}$$

$$Pm(e)=\begin{cases}\dfrac{e-0.6}{0.9}, & 0.6\le e\le -1.5\\ \dfrac{e-2.4}{-0.9}, & 1.5\le e\le 2.4\\ 0\,, & etc\end{cases} \quad Nb(e)=\begin{cases}1\,, & e\ge -3\\ \dfrac{e-1.9}{1.1}, & 1.9\le e\le 3\\ 0\,, & etc\end{cases}$$

$$y_1 = -1, y_2 = -0.5, y_3 = -0.2, y_4 = 0.2, y_5 = 0.5, y_6 = 1$$

$$u_c(t) = \beta(t)U\sum_{j=1}^{m}\prod_{i=1}^{n} A_{ij}(\frac{e(t)}{\alpha(e(t))})y_j$$

$$\text{make } \alpha(e(t)) = -\frac{1}{81}e(t)^4 + \frac{2}{9}e(t)^2 + 0.0001$$

$$\text{and } \lim_{t\to\infty}\|e(t)\| = 0,\ P_n = (p_1, p_2, \cdots p_n)^\tau$$

$$\text{then } \beta'(t) = K\sum_{i=1}^{n} p_i e_i(t)$$

$$\beta(0) = 1,\ P_n\big|_{n=1} = p_1 = 1,\ k = 2,\ U = 3$$

$$u_c(t) = \beta(t)U\sum_{j=1}^{m}\prod_{i=1}^{n} A_{ij}(\frac{e(t)}{\alpha(e(t))})y_j$$

$$u_c(t) = \beta(t)U\sum_{j=1}^{m}\prod_{i=1}^{n} A_{ij}(\frac{e(t)}{\alpha(e(t))})y_j$$

$$= (k\int_0^t e^\tau(t)P_n dt + \beta(0))U\sum_{j=1}^{m}\prod_{i=1}^{n} A_{ij}(\frac{e(t)}{\alpha(e(t))})y_j$$

$$= 6(\int_0^t e(t)dt + 1)[-Nb(e'(t)) - 0.5Nm(e'(t)) - 0.2Ns(e'(t)) \quad +0.2Ps(e'(t)) + 0.5Pm(e'(t)) + Pb(e'(t))]$$

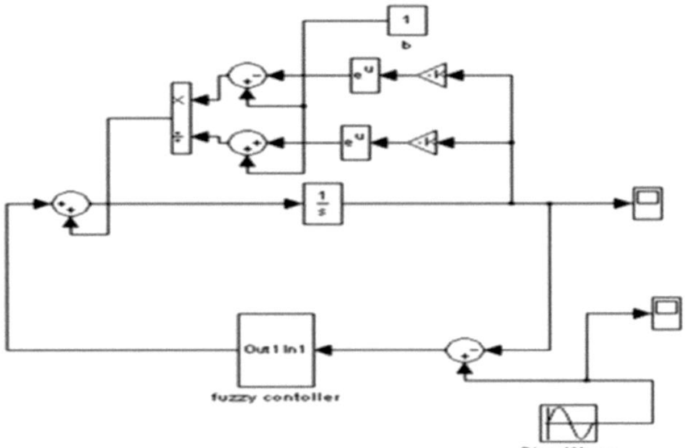

Figure 9. Controller

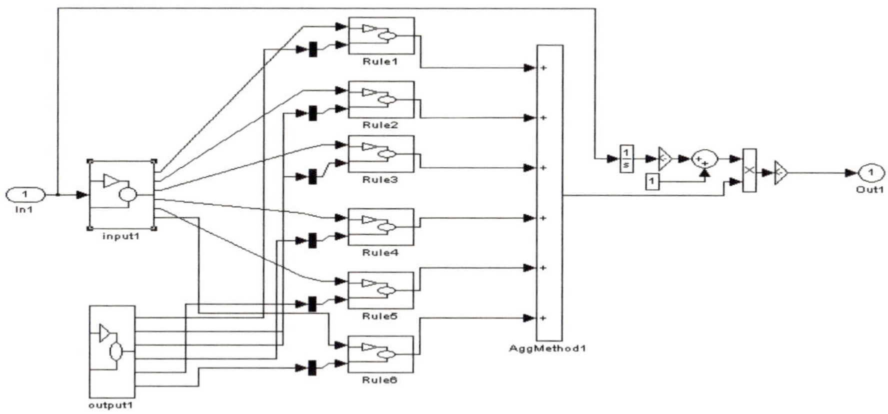

Figure 10. Rules

In order to make out the advantages of the new function, Let $r(t) = \sin t$ the result of controller (seeFig.11) is formed as follows

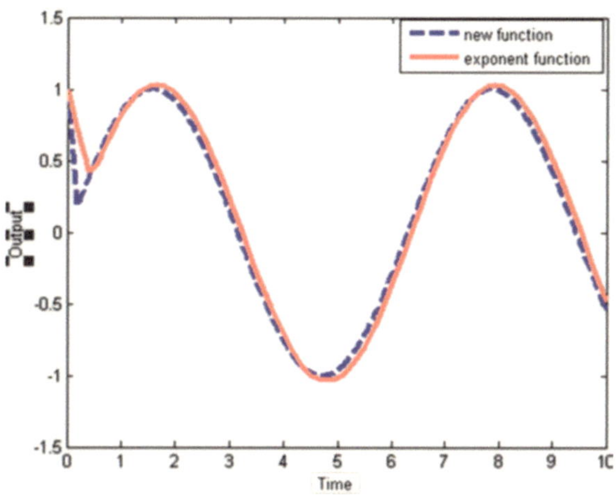

Figure 11. The contrast of control effect

Let

$$r(t) = \begin{cases} 1.5 & 0 \leq t \leq 3 and 6 \leq t \leq 9 \\ 0.5 & etc \end{cases}$$

the result of control (see Fig.12 and Fig.13) is formed as follow

From Fig.12, we learn that there are some errors between aim curve (blue) and real curve (black) because of $\alpha(e(t))$ =1. System cannot immediately regulate control strategy to make e(t)=0. From Fig.13, we can clearly learn that the real curve (black) almost coincide with aim curve (blue). So we say that the variable fuzzy controller is one of the efficient tools for control system. From Fig.11, we can see the difference between the new function and exponential function (conventional function), and the algorithm module with new contraction-expansion factor is applied successfully in Matlab, whose results show that algorithm module is reasonable, adaptive and feasible. In the other hand, the new function can be realized easily by C++ to optimize the controller of complicated nonlinear control system.

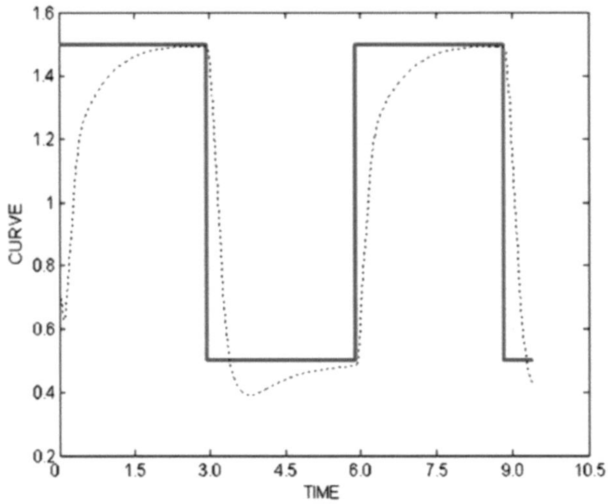

Figure 12. The simulation curves ($\alpha(e(t))=1$)

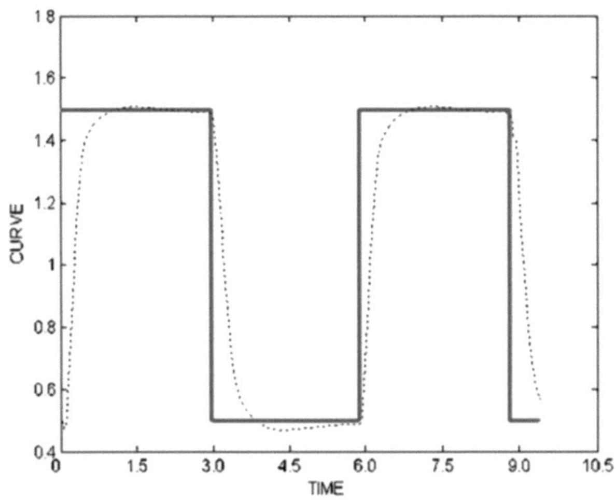

Figure 13. The simulation curves (T=10)

6. Practical application

Refrigerator is one kind of popular home appliance, and it became more and more important to economize the energy. The controller of conventional refrigerator keep anticipative temperature through PTC-relays and compress, but a lot of energy is waste. In this paper the new controller based on variable universe adaptive fuzzy control theory can resolve this problem. The variable universe fuzzy control theory has become more and more important in process control. The idea of variable universe fuzzy control is first proposed in refs, and several types of variable universe adaptive fuzzy controller are discussed in ref.

The compressor, condenser, evaporator,capillary and other electro-equipments compose the refrigeration system which is a close circulatory system. R-600a as refrigeration material from the low-pressure liquid to gaseity in evaporator to make the icebox inside temperature lowed through absorbing the heat. In other words, the control system of refrigeration makes R-600a changed by electric power. The simplified model of the refrigerator (see Fig.14) show as follow:

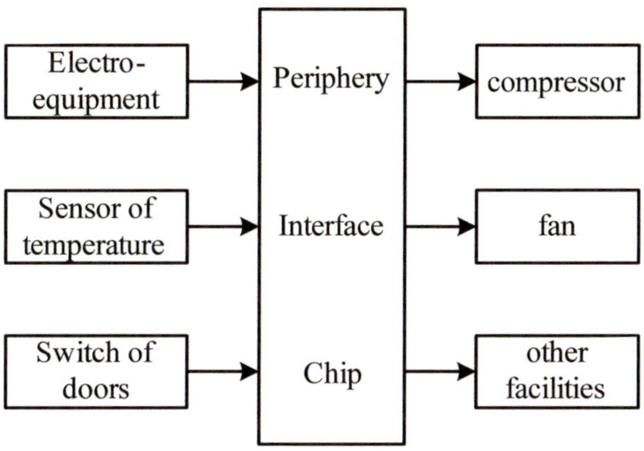

Figure 14. Simplified model of the refrigerator

The popular refrigerator through driving compressor makes the temperature constant, but there are some disadvantages in the control strategy. If there is minuteness temperature warp in system, control system frequent start-up equipments to modulate inside temperature, and a lot of energy will be wasted. In order to solve this problem, we design the new control strategy based on the idea of variable universe fuzzy control.

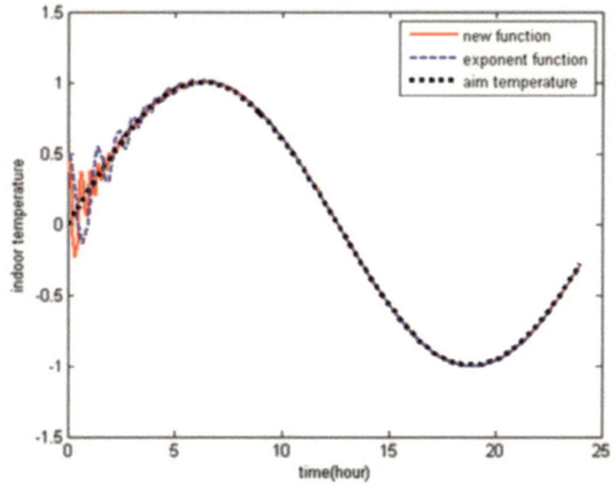

Figure 15. Contrast of controller effect

A refrigerator plant is a complex nonlinear system and may be prone to instability and oscillatory behaviors. The Fig.15 is the contrast of controller effect by Ying learning (red line), exponent function (blue line).In this section, a fuzzy controller is designed and simulated exclusively to control a refrigerator plant with a new-type function of contraction-expansion factor to optimize the controller of temperature is steady.

Using control method to explain medical phenomenon is currently a hot subject of research. The traditional Chinese drug fumigation steaming treat protrusion of protrusion of protrusion of lumbar intervertebral disc with steam generated by boiling medicinal herbs, and this process is a typical non-linear, multivariable, and strong coupling. Experienced nurse and doctor cure patient by their experience. So establish a model of this process can discover more factor of the disease, better treat to protrusion of protrusion of protrusion of lumbar intervertebral disc and reduce of energy consumption.

The traditional Chinese drug fumigation fume or steaming treat diseases with fume in moxibustion or with steam generated by boiling medicinal herbs, and its process is a typical non-linear, multivariable, strong coupling. In addition, its characters are difficult to quantitative analysis. So the period of treatment is only determined by experience of doctors. Therefore, there is theoretical and practical significance in studying of traditional Chinese drug fumigation medical data mining.

The illustration of the traditional Chinese drug fumigation machine is shown in Fig.16. Here, the type of machine is MJD-2003 and it has been used 6 years.

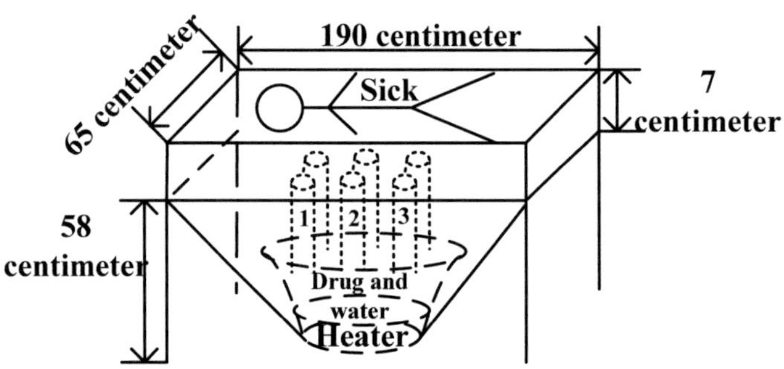

Figure 16. Drug Fumigation Machine

Doctor treats protrusion of Protrusion of protrusion of lumbar intervertebral disc with steam generated by boiling medicinal herbs at this machine.

Fig.17 is the temperature of steam to body by VUF and YL-VUF. YL-VUF is the blue real line, and VUF is the green dash line. In this picture the aim is 40 Celsius Degrees. The temperature decrease when patient's posture is changed. After 10.725 minute, YL-VUF makes the temperature to 40 Celsius Degrees. On the other hand, VUF almost cost 22.568 minute. DFNN and YL-VUF have the similar frame, but YL-VUF using new local space to forecast. So YL-VUF can avoid over heat.

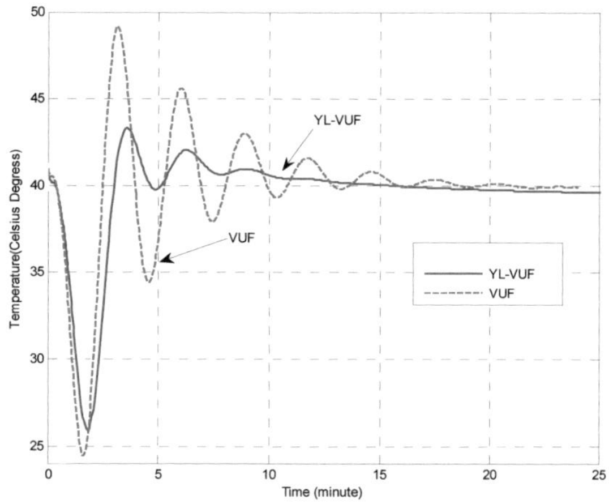

Figure 17. Temperature (YL-VUF and VUF) of steam to body

Author details

Ping Zhang
Lanzhou University of Technology, China

Guodong Gao
University Hospital of Gansu Traditional Chinese Medicine, China

7. References

[1] Aihua Dong. Fuzzy Control Algorithm used in Asynchronous Motor Power Saver. J. Electric Drive. 2009, pp. 49--21

[2] Bin Wang. Fuzzy control algorithm on variable output domain in automotive ACC system. J. Application Research of Computers. 2010,pp. 465--471

[3] Ping zhang. Novel lazy learning variable universe fuzzy controller for temperature system Communications in Computer and Information Science, 2011,Vol58,No4, 364-370

[4] YajunGuo, HuoLong; Ain Shams Engineering Journal Self organizing fuzzy sliding mode controller for the position control of a permanent magnet synchronous motor drive .2090-4479, Volume 2, Issue 2, 2011, Pages 109-118

[5] AdisornThomya, YottanaKhunatorn; Energy Procedia (2011) Design of Control System of Hydrogen and Oxygen Flow Rate for Proton Exchange Membrane Fuel Cell Using Fuzzy Logic Controller .1876-6102, Volume 9, Issue 000, 2011, Pages 186-197

[6] Jabr, H. M.; Lu, D. Design and Implementation of Neuro-Fuzzy Vector Control for Wind-Driven Doubly-Fed Induction Generator.Sustainable Energy, IEEE Transactions on.1949-3029, Volume 2, Issue 4, 2011, Pages 404-413

[7] Mehrjerdi, H.; Saad, M.; Ghommam, J. (2011) Hierarchical Fuzzy Cooperative Control and Path Following for a Team of Mobile Robots.Mechatronics, IEEE/ASME Transactions on.1083-4435, Volume 16, Issue 5, 2011, Pages 907-917

[8] Jayasiri, A.; Mann, G. K. I.; Gosine, R. G.(2011) Behavior Coordination of Mobile Robotics Using Supervisory Control of Fuzzy Discrete Event Systems.Systems, Man, and Cybernetics, Part B, IEEE Transactions on .1083-4419, Volume 41, Issue 5, 2011, Pages 1224-1238

[9] Pan, Y.; Er, M. J.; Huang, D.; Wang, Q.(2011) Adaptive Fuzzy Control With Guaranteed Convergence of Optimal Approximation Error.Fuzzy Systems, IEEE Transactions on .1063-6706, Volume 19, Issue 5, 2011, Pages 807-818

[10] Khanesar, M. A.; Kaynak, O.; Teshnehlab, M.(2011)Direct Model Reference Takagi–Sugeno Fuzzy Control of SISO Nonlinear Systems.Fuzzy Systems, IEEE Transactions on.1063-6706, Volume 19, Issue 5, 2011, Pages 914-924

[11] Navarro, G.; Manic, M.(2011) FuSnap: Fuzzy Control of Logical Volume Snapshot Replication for Disk Arrays.Industrial Electronics, IEEE Transactions on .0278-0046, Volume 58, Issue 9, 2011, Pages 4436-4444

[12] A. A. Niftiyev; C. I. Zeynalov; M. Poormanuchehri (2011) Fuzzy optimal control problem with non-linear functional.Fuzzy Information and Engineering.1616-8658, Volume 3, Issue 3, 2011, Pages 311-320

[13] KarimTamani[a], RedaBoukezzoula[a], GeorgesHabchi[b];(2011) Application of a continuous supervisory fuzzy control on a discrete scheduling of manufacturing systems.Engineering Applications of Artificial Intelligence.0952-1976, Volume 24, Issue 7, 2011, Pages 1162-1173

[14] LaurentVermeiren[a][b][c], Thierry MarieGuerra[a][b][c], HakimLamara[b][c];(2011) Application of practical fuzzy arithmetic to fuzzy internal model control.Engineering Applications of Artificial Intelligence.0952-1976, Volume 24, Issue 6, 2011, Pages 1006-1017

[15] Andon V.Topalov[a], YesimOniz[b], ErdalKayacan[b], OkyayKaynak[b];(2011) Neuro-fuzzy control of antilock braking system using sliding mode incremental learning algorithm.Neurocomputing.0925-2312, Volume 74, Issue 11, 2011, Pages 1883-1893

[16] RubiyahYusof[a][1], Ribhan ZafiraAbdul Rahman[b], MarzukiKhalid[a][1], Mohd FaisalIbrahim[c][2](2011) Optimization of fuzzy model using genetic algorithm for process control application.Journal of the Franklin Institute.0016-0032, Volume 348, Issue 7, 2011, Pages 1717-1737

[17] Wang, Y.; Wang , D.; Chai, T (2011) Extraction and Adaptation of Fuzzy Rules for Friction Modeling and Control Compensation.Fuzzy Systems, IEEE Transactions on.1063-6706, Volume 19, Issue 4, 2011, Pages 682-693

[18] Li, Z.; Cao, X.; Ding , N.(2011) Adaptive Fuzzy Control for Synchronization of Nonlinear Teleoperators With Stochastic Time-Varying Communication Delays.Fuzzy Systems, IEEE Transactions on .1063-6706, Volume 19, Issue 4, 2011, Pages 745-757

[19] M.S. Shahidzadeh;H. Tarzi;M. Dorfeshan (2011) Takagi-Sugeno Fuzzy Control of Adjacent Structures using MR Dampers.Journal of Applied Sciences.1812-5654, Volume 11, Issue 15, 2011, Pages 2816-2822

[20] Zhu, Y.(2011) Fuzzy Optimal Control for Multistage Fuzzy Systems.Systems, Man, and Cybernetics, Part B, IEEE Transactions on .1083-4419, Volume 41, Issue 4, 2011, Pages 964-975

[21] Zhang, Wei;Li, Xue Yong;Li, Li;Lv, Jing Qiao;Chen, Yan Feng;Mao, Xin Hua (2011). Design and Application of Fuzzy Controller .1013-9826 ; 2011;Volume 1076 ;Issue 464 ;Pages 107

[22] Antonio Sala (2009) .On the conservativeness of fuzzy and fuzzy-polynomial control of nonlinear systems .1367-5788 ; 2009;Volume 33 ; Issue 1 ;Pages 48

[23] Zhu, Y. .(2011) .Fuzzy Optimal Control for Multistage Fuzzy Systems .1083-4419 ; 2011;Volume 41 ;Issue 4 ;Pages 964

[24] Sala, Antonio (2009) .On the conservativeness of fuzzy and fuzzy-polynomial control of nonlinear systems .1367-5788 ; 200904; Volume 33 ; Issue 1 ;Pages 48-58

[25] KostasKolomvatsos, StathesHadjiefthymiades; .(2012) . Buyer behavior adaptation based on a fuzzy logic controller and prediction techniques0165-0114, Volume 189, Issue 1, 2012, Pages 30-52

[26] Vahab Nekoukar; Abbas Erfanian .(2011) .An adaptive fuzzy sliding-mode controller design for walking control with functional electrical stimulation: A computer simulation study .1598-6446, Volume 9, Issue 6, 2011, Pages 1124-1135

[27] Xiangjian Chen; Di Li; Yue Bai; Zhijun Xu .(2011) .Modeling and Neuro-Fuzzy adaptive attitude control for Eight-Rotor MAV .International Journal of Control, Automation and Systems

[28] Han HoChoi, Jin-WooJung; .(2011) .Takagi–Sugeno fuzzy speed controller design for a permanent magnet synchronous motor .0957-4158, Volume 21, Issue 8, 2011, Pages 1317-1328

[29] Mehdi Roopaei; Mansoor Zolghadri Jahromi; Bijan Ranjbar-Sahraei; Tsung-Chih Lin Nonlinear Dynamics .(2011) . Synchronization of two different chaotic systems using novel adaptive interval type-2 fuzzy sliding mode control .0924-090X, Volume 66, Issue 4, 2011, Pages 667-680

[30] Yin LeeGoh, Agileswari K.Ramasamy, Farrukh HafizNagi, Aidil Azwin ZainulAbidin; Microelectronics Reliability (2011) DSP based overcurrent relay using fuzzy bang–bang controller .0026-2714, Volume 51, Issue 12, 2011, Pages 2366-2373

[31] Ana Belén Cara; Héctor Pomares; Ignacio Rojas; Zsófia Lendek; Robert Babu?ka Evolving Systems .(2010) Online self-evolving fuzzy controller with global learning capabilities .1868-6478, Volume 1, Issue 4, 2010, Pages 225-239

[32] Mohammad PourmahmoodAghababa; Communications in Nonlinear Science and Numerical Simulation .(2010) Comments on "Fuzzy fractional order sliding mode controller for nonlinear systems" [Commun Nonlinear Sci Numer Simulat 15 (2010) 963–978] .1007-5704, Volume 17, Issue 3, 2012, Pages 1489-1492

[33] Shih-YuLi, Zheng-MingGe; Expert Systems with Applications (2011) .Corrigendum to "Generalized synchronization of chaotic systems with different orders by fuzzy logic constant controller" [Expert Systems with Applications 38 (3) (2011) 2302–2310] .0957-4174, Volume 39, Issue 3, 2012, Pages 3898-3898

[34] Neng-ShengPai, Her-TerngYau, Chao-LinKuo; Expert Systems with Applications (2012) Comments on "Fuzzy logic combining controller design for chaos control of a rod-type plasma torch system" .0957-4174, Volume 39, Issue 2, 2012, Pages 2236-2236

[35] BehnamGanji, Abbas Z.Kouzani; Expert Systems with Applications .(2012) Combined quasi-static backward modeling and look-ahead fuzzy control of vehicles .0957-4174, Volume 39, Issue 1, 2012, Pages 223-233

[36] Ruey-JingLian; Expert Systems with Applications (2012) Design of an enhanced adaptive self-organizing fuzzy sliding-mode controller for robotic systems .0957-4174, Volume 39, Issue 1, 2012, Pages 1545-1554

[37] NordinSaad, M.Arrofiq; Robotics and Computer-Integrated Manufacturing (2012)A PLC-based modified-fuzzy controller for PWM-driven induction motor drive with constant V/Hz ratio control .0736-5845, Volume 28, Issue 2, 2012, Pages 95-112

[38] B.A.A.Omar, A.Y.M.Haikal, F.F.G.Areed, Ain Shams Engineering Journal (2011) Design adaptive neuro-fuzzy speed controller for an electro-mechanical system .2090-4479, Volume 2, Issue 2, 2011, Pages 99-107

Chapter 10

Fuzzy Controllers: A Reliable Component of Smart Sustainable Structural Systems

Maguid H. M. Hassan

Additional information is available at the end of the chapter

http://dx.doi.org/10.5772/48263

1. Introduction

Structural control has been introduced, several decades ago, as one of the basic forms of smart systems [1, 2]. The structural system's performance is enhanced by the presence of a closed loop feedback controller that employs observed data, about the system's responses, in evaluating and applying corrective actions in order to improve its performance. Initially, conventional control theory has been the backbone of such controllers [1, 2]. Yet, the sheer complexity and size of such structural systems, coupled with the time required for solving the control problem and thus evaluating the necessary corrective actions, limited the applications of such concepts. Needless to say, such systems are intended to operate real time during the occurrence of earthquake events, which are usually over in about few minutes at the most. Recently, smart control algorithms have been introduced in an attempt to fill that gap [3, 4].

Fuzzy control is one of the smart control strategies that were employed in structural control recently [5, 6]. Fuzzy controllers employ a set of input control variables, a rule-base and an inference engine to infer proposed actions aiming at the improvement of the system's performance [7]. Several factors are crucial to a successful fuzzy controller design, namely, membership functions of fuzzy variables, rule-base generation and suitable implication functions [7]. Several membership functions were employed in various applications of fuzzy controllers. It is imperative to select the membership functions that best captures the nature of the modeled variables [7]. The generation of a relevant and suitable rule-base is another major concern, several approaches have been employed, such as relying on expertise of human operators as opposed to designing a smart algorithm which would generate the rule-base, such as neural networks. Finally, appropriate implication functions should be carefully selected in order to reflect the proper and expected performance of the designed controller.

Fuzzy control, as a heuristic-based control strategy and given the uncertain nature of the problem in question, would definitely require a reliability assessment and assurance algorithms to reinforce its implementation in such a critical application. Successful reliability evaluation of any given system is performed in consecutive steps that start with creating a comprehensive reliability assessment framework, developing a system model, complete definition of potential failure modes, transformation of such failure modes into limit state equations and finally the calculation of the reliability measures for the component and/or system in question.

In this chapter, the design of fuzzy controllers, tailored for functioning as structural controllers, is outlined together with all necessary definitions of relevant variables, their membership functions, fuzzification and de-fuzzification procedures. The definition of the required inference engine and its underlying rule-base, implication functions and inference mechanisms are also presented. Knowing the importance of reliable performance of such heuristic systems and to ensure their general applicability, a reliability assessment procedure is also outlined to evaluate the reliability of the designed controllers. Finally, other potential applications of fuzzy inference systems are also briefly presented, such applications include, but not limited to, smart abstract deformed shape identification of structural systems under earthquake excitation.

2. Smart sustainable structural systems

2.1. Introduction

Sustainable design entails a range of actions, decisions and procedures that would result in an environmentally friendly structural system. Such a concept has long been ignored in structural engineering and when realized was taken as one that relates to a single dimensional approach which always referred to the use of recyclable materials. Surely, recyclable materials are considered one of the main players in such a design problem, however, structurally speaking this process requires a multi faceted approach that employs higher levels of design decisions and considerations. A sustainable structural system would be one that employs the optimum amount of environmentally friendly construction materials with ensured reliable performance along its expected life time. The keywords here are being recyclable, optimum and reliable. Therefore, when designing a structural system that is expected to withstand uncertain loading conditions, such as earthquake loads, it is more sustainable to design a smart system that is capable of adjusting its own physical and/or engineering characteristics in order to improve its response to such loads, as opposed to a system that is designed to resist loads that it may or may not encounter during its life time. Smart systems, by definition, would result in lighter more optimum systems which definitely would be even more sustainable if they are constructed using a recyclable material, such as structural steel. Even if more invasive materials were used, such as, reinforced concrete, the optimum design coupled with the smart features would result in a more sustainable system. Therefore, it is proposed that if it is possible to design reliable smart structural systems, this would result in a more sustainable structural design.

Smart structural systems are defined as ones that demonstrate the ability to modify their characteristics and/or properties in order to respond favorably to unexpected severe loading conditions [8]. Conventional structural systems are usually designed to resist predefined loading conditions. However, due to the uncertain nature of engineering systems, and the lack of complete and accurate information about some types of highly uncertain loads, such as earthquakes, smart structural systems have emerged as a potential solution for such problems. Instead of designing systems to withstand a single extreme earthquake event that may or may not occur in its lifetime, new designs of smart systems could emerge where the system is capable of responding favorably, in a smart manner, to any type of loading that was not specifically considered at the design stage. The significance of such systems is even further enhanced when modeled systems are unconventional such as historic buildings and/or structures.

As in all engineering endeavors, with a long deep look at god's creations, one can surely develop a lot of smart ideas. For example, if a similarity is drawn between a human trying to balance himself on a shaky table, and a building trying to balance itself on a shaking ground. The first, develops no mathematical models, solves no complicated sets of equations and yet is successfully capable of balancing himself. He simply employs three basic properties of his. First, his sensing capabilities, through his nervous system, which sends messages to his brain, signaling that an adverse effect is about to happen. The brain uses this piece of information and, based on its collection of experiences and reasoning capabilities, develop a balancing solution for the problem. The brain, then, sends specific commands to a set of muscles that are capable of restoring the balance of the human body. The body is balanced throughout a smart procedure that started with data collection about the current state of the body, then, data processing, state identification and problem solving. The final step is action implementation.

If a building is required to balance itself on a shaking ground, in a similar manner, it should employ similar smart procedures. Therefore, for any structural system to behave in a smart manner, it should go through three basic steps. First, it has to realize, somehow, what is going on in terms of adverse effects. Second, it should be able to process this information, i.e., translate that into state identification, and accordingly decide the type of necessary countermeasures. Third, it should have the ability to perform whatever corrective action is required. A structural system, designed as such, should employ three basic components, integrated within its structure, in order to be able to perform the previously mentioned activities.

- First, *Sensors*, which are analogous to the human nervous system, shall be employed in order to measure and register important internal and external information and / or changes.
- Second, *Processors*, which are brain-like units, that are responsible for interpreting the collected data into meaningful state identifications and accordingly necessary corrective actions to be taken.
- Third, *Actuators*, which are elements that maintain the capability of adjusting either the system structural characteristics or its own characteristics in order to respond favorably to external excitation.

According to the type and nature of the employed components, several levels of smart systems could be developed. It should be realized that both the actuators and processors, in a human being, have additional levels of smartness based on their nature. For example, the muscles, i.e., the actuators, exert a variable amount of force depending on the signals sent by the brain. The brain, itself, employs highly adaptive thinking and learning techniques in its reasoning process. Therefore, multiple integrated levels of smart structural systems could be realized according to the type and properties of the components used in its development. As the level of integration increases, the level of smartness of the resulting system increases. Figure 1 shows a model of a smart single-degree-of-freedom system, while Figure 2, shows a smart three-story building. Both figures outline the inter-relations among the additional components that drive the performance of the smart system. It should be noted that multi-degree-of-freedom systems require a more complex processor that incorporates two main components, i.e., a fuzzy state identifier in addition to the fuzzy controller. The state identifier is required to define the deformed shape of the system, thus, guiding the firing sequence of relevant actuators. The following discussion outlines the properties of each of the three basic components in the sake of providing a comprehensive description of the system under consideration.

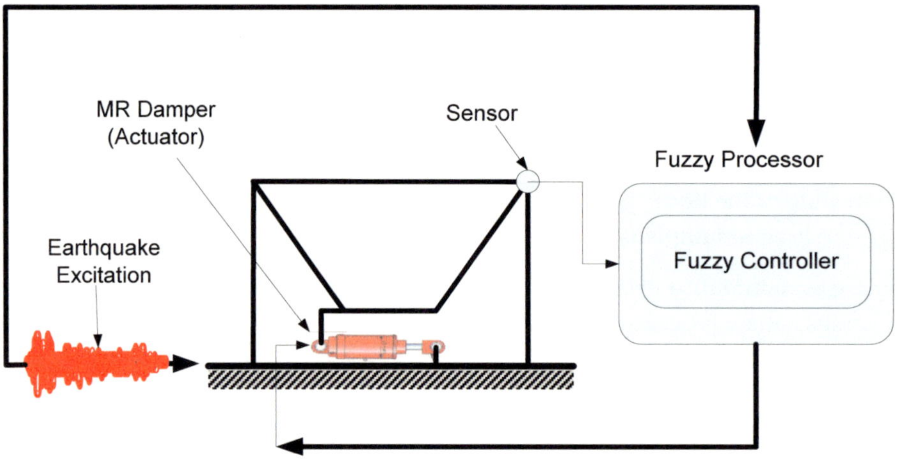

Figure 1. Smart Single-Degree-of-Freedom System

2.2. Sensors

Sensors are the first component of any smart structural system. The system needs to be able to identify any changes occurring to its state in order to perform any corrective action [8]. The monitoring operation could be implemented in two possible modes. The first mode is a continuous monitoring for a select group of parameters, such as displacements, velocities and accelerations. The second mode is a continuous monitoring for a select group of damage indicators such as cracking, fatigue, corrosion or excessive deflections. The smart structural system application, in question, dictates the required mode of monitoring. Currently, such systems are either designed for structural control, or for structural health monitoring applications. The first application requires the first mode of monitoring, while the second application requires the second mode of monitoring.

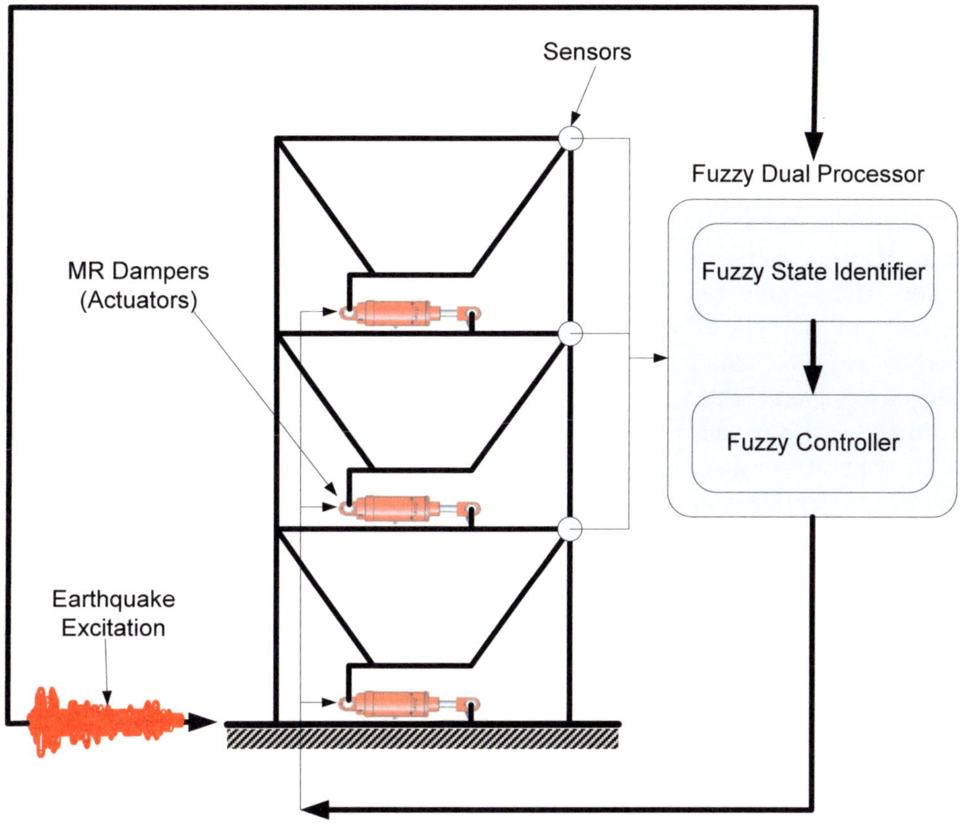

Figure 2. Smart Sustainable Steel Frame

There are several potential sensor technologies that are being used or considered for the smart structural applications in civil engineering. As indicated earlier, a higher level of smartness is attained if smart materials are used as sensors in addition to, or instead of, conventional sensor technologies. Conventional sensor systems are ones that do not posses any smart potential. In other words, such materials are incapable of altering or adjusting their own characteristics in response to external excitation. Their role would be to measure specific state variables and send such records to the processor unit for state identification and corrective action evaluation. Such sensors are very well documented and have been implemented in civil / structural applications for a long time. As an example, Displacement Transducers, Velocity and Acceleration Transducers and Strain Transducers are considered as conventional sensors. Smart sensors, on the other hand, by definition are ones that are capable of altering or adjusting their characteristics in response to external excitation. Such excitation might be temperature, electric current or mechanical movements, piezoelectric ceramics and optical fibers are examples of such smart sensors.

2.3. Processors

Processors are brain-like units that are capable of evaluating the current state of the system, based on the data communicated by the sensors, and proposing corrective actions accordingly [8]. The processor shall be capable of operation in one of two modes. The first mode is system monitoring, where the processor only identifies the state of the system without taking any remedial actions. The second mode is system control, where the processor is called upon to identify the state of the system, evaluate the proper corrective action to be taken and implement the suggested action automatically. It should be pointed out that system control mode, by definition, employs system monitoring mode as a subsequent major component. One of the major factors that would dictate the mode of operation of the processor is the type of application and the state parameter being monitored. For example, RC elements might be supplied with a monitoring system, in order to identify any potential damage to a given element, such as steel corrosion, concrete cracking, excessive deflection, etc. The processor, in this case, is only called upon to identify the occurrence of a certain type of damage. Furthermore, any structural system could be supplied with a control system that is capable of suppressing the vibration and balancing the system under wind and earthquake excitations. Thus, a processor operating at the control mode would be required for such an application.

2.4. Actuators

Actuators act as the muscles of the structural system. Actuator technology is responsible for the development of materials and/or devices that would either apply control forces to the system or add new characteristics to the structure [8]. Actuators do not necessarily apply balancing forces to the structural system. In case smart actuators are utilized, the system adjusts its structural characteristics without any introduction of external forces, which is the current preferred approach.

All applications that employed conventional actuator technologies were in the field of structural control [1, 2]. Structural control is one of the early applications of smart structural systems. There are three potential schemes of structural control, namely, Passive, Active and Semi-Active [1, 2, 4]. Passive control employs energy dissipation components that are designed for predefined limits and possess no adaptive capabilities. Although most of the practical applications of structural control, currently in operation, are of this primitive type, they do not show efficient performance under real conditions. Active Control employs the basic conventional structure of a smart structural system. It comprises sensors, processors and actuators that are, predominantly, of the conventional type [1, 2]. This type of control exerts an external control force that is utilized in balancing the system in response to external loads. Semi-Active control has received increased attention recently as the most practical and state of the art control system [3, 4]. Semi-Active control employs actuators that are, predominantly, of the smart type. Such actuators cannot inject mechanical energy directly to the system, yet, they have the ability to adjust their properties in a way to optimally adjust the response of the system under unforeseen external events. Some of the smart actuators which are currently being explored for application in civil engineering systems are Shape Memory Alloys (SMA), Piezoelectric Ceramics, Electro-Rheological (ER) fluids, and Magneto-Rheological (MR) fluids. MR fluids, which are employed in manufacturing MR dampers, have already reached full-scale applications and showing very promising results in civil engineering applications [3, 4].

3. Fuzzy controllers as processors

Fuzzy controllers are known to employ fuzzy logic and fuzzy set theory in developing their control strategies and evaluating control actions [9, 10, 11, 12, 13]. Fuzzy logic has two primary advantages, as opposed to conventional mathematical algorithms, when employed in control applications. First, it reduces the difficulties of modeling and analysis of extremely complex systems. Second, it is capable of incorporating several qualitative aspects of the human knowledge in the control laws [10, 11, 12, 13]. Fuzzy control is based on the fuzzy set theory which allows for the qualitative, imprecise and/or vague information to be quantitatively included in the evaluation of a representative control action [5, 6, 7, 10, 11, 12, 13]. Such inherent uncertainty would probably be ignored in a conventional mathematical algorithm, thus, rendering inaccurate control forces. Fuzzy set theory utilizes a very important tool in its manipulation procedure, which is the membership function [7]. The membership function, usually takes one of the following forms, i.e., triangular, trapezoidal or Gaussian, in order to evaluate a degree of membership for the element in question. This degree of membership is the major difference between this approach and conventional mathematical methods. Fuzzy control comprises four main components [5, 6, 7, 10, 11, 12, 13];

- Fuzzification: the state variables to be monitored, when measured, have crisp values. These values should be fuzzified, using fuzzy linguistic terms defined by the membership functions of the individual fuzzy sets.
- Rule-Base: is a collection of If-Then rules describing the control laws governing the evaluation of necessary control actions.
- Inference Engine: comprises two main stages, namely, Implication and Aggregation. The implication procedure evaluates a control action from each applicable rule, given a certain input fuzzy value. The Aggregation procedure evaluates a collective control action, i.e., output, by adding all control actions from all applicable rules in a predefined manner.
- Defuzzification: the resulting control action is in a fuzzified form that could not be applied to any actuator device. Thus, this step evaluates an equivalent crisp value for the fuzzy collective control action.

The processor, as identified in smart structural applications could perform two main tasks, the first is state identification, if necessary, while the second is control action evaluation. Figure 1 shows a fuzzy controller without a state identifier, while Figure 2 shows a fuzzy dual processor which comprises a fuzzy state identifier and a fuzzy controller. The fuzzy controller would employ the input variables in addition to the output of the fuzzy state identifier in evaluating the appropriate control action. The following sections outline the implementation of fuzzy control in the development of the controller component of the processor while the fuzzy state identifier is discussed in section 5. The reliability of fuzzy controllers when operating within the smart system is a major concern if such a setup is considered for designing systems that are sustainable as defined above. The reliability framework and assessment procedures for fuzzy processors are discussed in section 4 of this chapter.

3.1. Input variables

Fuzzy controllers usually employ two input variables one is an error measure while the second is a rate of change of that error [7]. In that context, it is usually required of the controller to monitor the performance of the modeled system in order to minimize or even eliminate the error if possible. In case of structural control, this corresponds to the dynamic movement of the controlled system which is generally measured by the velocity of a select set of control points referred to as degrees of freedom [8]. Such degrees of freedom correspond to the floor levels of the framed building shown in Figures 1 & 2 and have assigned sensors to measure their movements. The rate of change of the measured variable, i.e., velocity, would be the acceleration of the control points. Therefore, in structural control applications it is expected to include the velocity and the acceleration of degrees of freedom as input variables to the fuzzy controllers. When dealing with complex systems, having so many degrees of freedom, and in order to attain the objective of reliable, optimum and sustainable systems, it is expected that the control actions would not be required of all actuators, however, a select group of actuators which are identified based on the deformed shape of the controlled building would be fired. Therefore, the input variables to the fuzzy controller should include an additional input variable which classify the current deformed shape of the monitored building. Thus, three dimensional rules would be necessary to drive the inference engine of structural fuzzy controllers. Input variables, as well as, output variables need to be fully defined as part of the design of a fuzzy controller. Such definition would not be complete without the identification of a suitable membership function for each variable.

3.1.1. Membership functions

A major step in defining control variables in fuzzy control applications is the definition of membership functions [7]. Such a task has to be performed in two main underlying steps. The first is the selection of the range of values which the function should cover while the second is the type of membership function to be employed and its relevant parameters. Several membership functions were reported successfully in several fuzzy control applications, such as, triangular, trapezoidal and Gaussian functions [7]. For structural control applications it is expected that either triangular and/or Gaussian membership functions would be suitable for modeling control input and output variables. The proper identification of a representative range of values for properly defining such membership functions should be based on actual results of the modeled system. In order to evaluate the range of values, a structural model of the system under consideration should be created and a time history analysis shall be conducted [14, 15, 16]. The results of such an analysis would generate all potential values of velocities and accelerations of control points. These values could be used in identifying several bands within the expected range, correlate these bands to fuzzy variables and evaluate the required parameters, for each band, of the velocity and/or acceleration [17].

Gaussian Membership Functions, The Gaussian membership function is fully defined by two main parameters, namely, the average value and the standard deviation. Figure 3 outlines a generic Gaussian membership function with the expected form of the function [7, 8]. When modeling input and/or output variables using a Gaussian membership function, the time history of the modeled variable needs to be evaluated using a finite element model of the structural system under consideration. The resulting time history would allow the segmentation of the variable range into several bands with relevant fuzzy labels and suitable standard deviations.

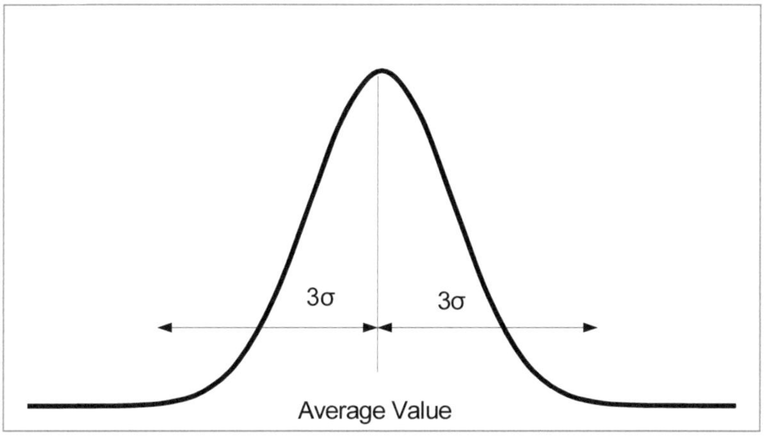

Figure 3. Generic Gaussian Membership Function

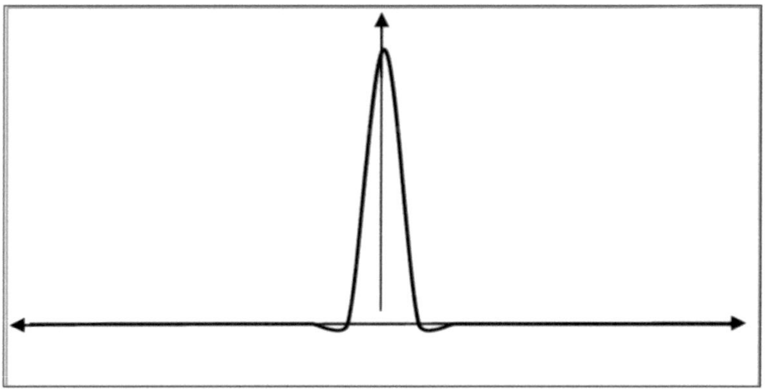

Figure 4. A Singleton Gaussian Fuzzy Variable with Zero Label

For example a fuzzy variable with a zero label would have a zero average value and a very narrow standard deviation to simulate the singleton value of zero as shown in Figure 4. While a negative fuzzy variable would have a negative average value, that is equivalent to the range of values the variable takes as indicated by the time history analysis results, and a suitable standard deviation to model the dispersion about this average value as shown in Figure 5.

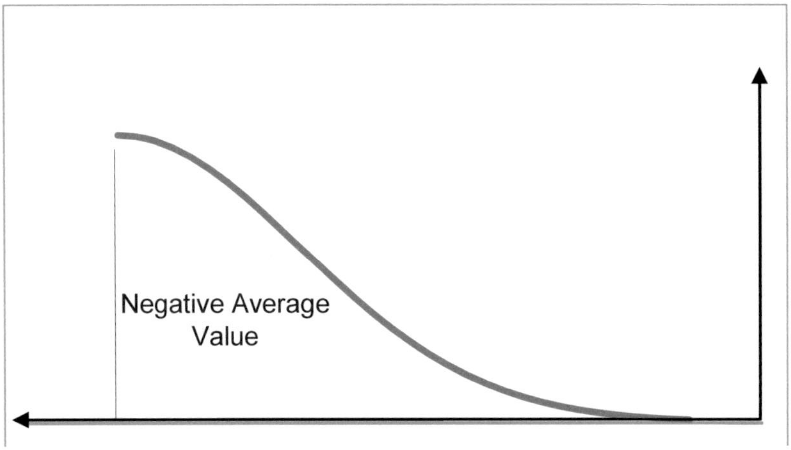

Figure 5. A Gaussian Fuzzy Variable with Negative Label

The standard deviation in the first case was selected to be 0.001 to reflect the narrow range and refelect the singleton nature of the zero label, while the standard deviation in Figure 5 was selected to be 1 to reflect the uncertainty associated with the negative label. Depending on the range of input variables some or all of the memebrship functins could be used in modeling the variable.

Triangular Membership Functions, The triangular membership function is one of the most widely used and successful membership functions in a wide variety of applications [7, 11, 12, 17]. Figure 6 shows a generic triangular membership function where three basic parameters are necessary in order to fully define the function [17]. The parameters are identified as (a, b and c) in Figure 6 where (a) represents the lower bound of the function, (b) defines the average value and (c) defines the upper bound of the membership function. As in the case of Gaussian membership functions, the range of input values would dictate if the whole function is employed or just a portion is only enough to represent the modeled variable. Moreover, the amount of uncertainty incorporated in the function which is measured by the triangular base of the function, i.e., (c-a), is also problem dependant and should be evaluated based on the actual data resulting from the finite element model of the system. If the same variables, modeled with Gaussian membership functions, are modeled using triangular functions, the zero fuzzy label and the negative fuzzy label would be defined as shown in Figure 7

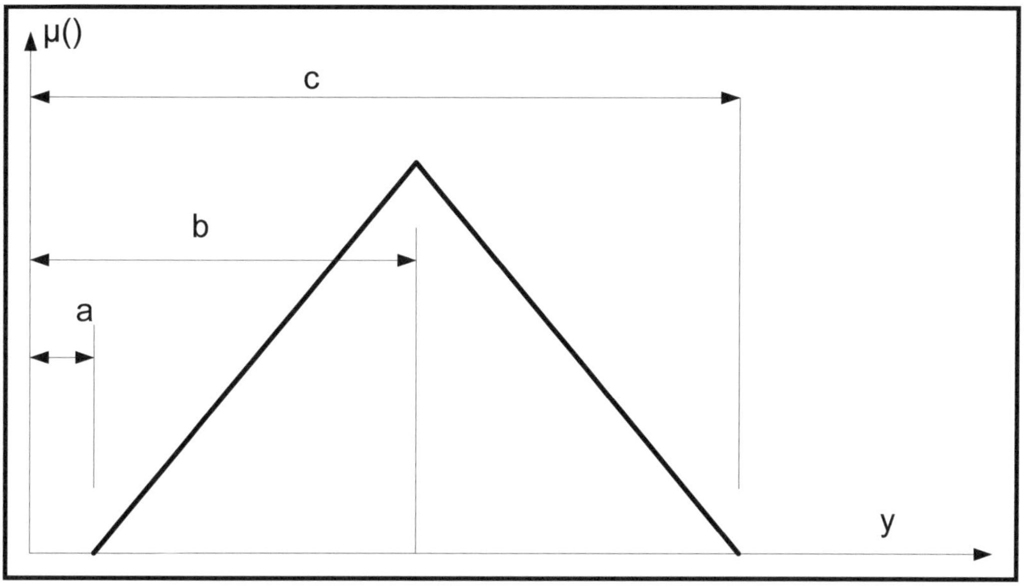

Figure 6. Generic Triangular Membership Function

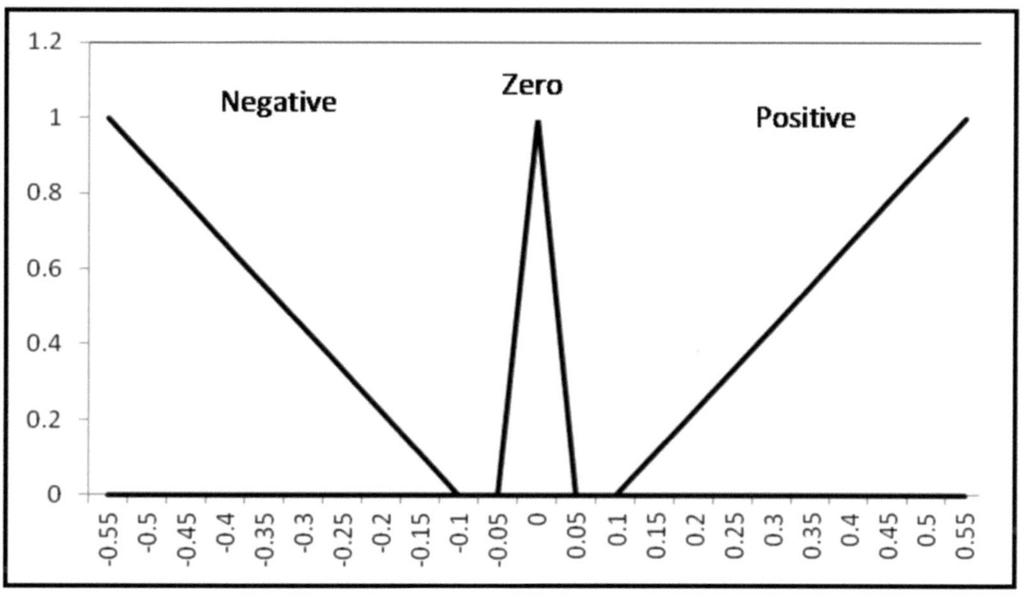

Figure 7. Triangular Fuzzy Variable with Zero, Positive & Negative Labels

The triangular membership functions for variables shown in Figure 7 are defined mathematically as follows:

$$\mu_{NEGATIVE}(x) = \begin{cases} \dfrac{x}{LB} & for\ LB \le x \le 0 \\ 0 & for\ all\ other\ values\ of\ x \end{cases} \tag{1}$$

$$\mu_{ZERO}(x) = \begin{cases} -\dfrac{1}{10^{-6}}\left(-10^{-6} - x\right) & for\ -10^{-6} \le x < 0 \\ \dfrac{1}{10^{-6}}\left(10^{-6} - x\right) & for\ 0 \le x < 10^{-6} \\ 0 & for\ all\ other\ values\ of\ x \end{cases} \tag{2}$$

$$\mu_{POSITIVE}(x) = \begin{cases} \dfrac{x}{UB} & for\ 0 \le x \le UB \\ 0 & for\ all\ other\ values\ of\ x \end{cases} \tag{3}$$

Where, $\mu_{NEGATIVE}(.), \mu_{ZERO}(.)$ & $\mu_{POSITIVE}(.)$= are the membership functions for the three fuzzy states of an input variable, NEGATIVE, ZERO & POSITIVE respectively; LB & UB = are the lower and upper bounds of the interval holding the range of values of the variable, as evaluated by a time history analysis, at any point in time, LB < 0 and UB > 0; and x = is the value of the variable, at any point in time. For the shown membership functions in Figure 7 the bounds of the interval holding the variable range of values is [-0.55, 0.55].

3.2. Inference engine

Fuzzy controllers are built on top of an inference engine which employs a rule-base that summarizes the necessary knowledge for inferring actions and an inference engine which performs the evaluation process based on fuzzy logic [7, 12]. The Inference engine comprises inference functions, inference mechanisms and aggregation functions that would combine the results of relevant fired rules into a single fuzzy output variable. There are several types of inference mechanisms, however, the most widely used in control applications is Mamdani's inference [7, 12]. The nature of the problem at hand and its impact on the evaluation of the overall output variable dictates the choice of the relevant inference mechanism [7, 12]. The details of the inference mechanism are beyond the scope of this chapter, however, the method of developing a representative rule-base is further discussed in this section with examples from structural control applications.

It is first important to identify the structure of the rule before building a rule-base. Rules could be multi-dimensional depending on the nature of the problem. In other words, rules could construct a one-to-one mapping between a single input and a single output, or a many-to-one mapping where several input variables are mapped to a single output variable. The number of inputs necessary to infer an output is obviously a problem dependant factor. In structural control applications it is necessary to include at least two measurable input variables in order to infer realistic output values [12]. Usually these two variables are some measure of error and rate of change of that error. The interpretation of an error term would be different from one application to the next. In case of structural control problems, any variable that would measure the movement of the system as a result of dynamic load effects, e.g., earthquakes, would qualify as an error measure. Therefore, it is reasonable to employ the velocity of predefined degrees of freedom as the error measure while the acceleration, which is the rate of change of the velocity, would be employed as the second input variable [12]. Therefore, structural control applications should at least involve two input variables in their rules. This setup would be enough for s single degree-of-freedom system, as shown in Figure 1, where the movement of a single floor would completely define the deformed shape of the system and thus the necessary action to restore the original shape of the system. In case of multi-degree-of-freedom systems, such as the system shown in Figure 2, a third input variable is necessary in order to provide additional information about the abstract deformed shape of the structural system. The need for that additional variable is reflected in the enhanced fuzzy processor where a fuzzy pattern identifier is integrated with the controller in order to identify the abstract deformed shape of the system [19]. This information is crucial in firing relevant actuators with the proper output value and sequence. Therefore, rules that would drive the operation of a smart sustainable multi-degree-of-freedom structural system are expected to employ three input variables and a single output variable [19].

In reference to a single degree of freedom system, as shown in Figure 1, a sample rule should include two input variables and a single output variable. The input variables are the velocity and acceleration of the floor level, while the output variable is the voltage which is communicated to an MR damper in order to restore the system's un-deformed shape. The rule could be defined as follows:

$$IF\ \dot{D}(t)\ is\ \text{BIG}\ AND\ \ddot{D}(t)\ is\ \text{NEGATIVE SMALL}\ THEN\ V(t)\ is\ \text{SMALL} \tag{4}$$

Where, $\dot{D}(t)$= is the velocity at the floor level at a given point in time (t), $\ddot{D}(t)$= is the acceleration at the floor level at a given point in time (t), V(t) = is the command voltage at a given point in time (t), and BIG, NEGATIVE SMALL and SMALL are fuzzy variables. On the other hand, in reference to the smart system defined in Figure 2, the fuzzy controller would accept the velocity and acceleration of a given degree of freedom in addition to an abstract deformed pattern, as input and produce a voltage value as output. The voltage value is communicated to a specific MR damper, selected based on the abstract deformed shape of the system, which would ultimately result in improving the response of the system under the effect of earthquake excitation. A sample rule, as defined above, could be written as follows:

$$IF\ \dot{D}_1(t)\ is\ \text{BIG}\ AND\ \ddot{D}_1(t)\ is\ \text{NEGATIVE SMALL}\ AND\ P(t)\ is\ 2\ THEN\ V_j(t)\ is\ \text{SMALL} \tag{5}$$

Where, $\dot{D}_i(t)$= is the velocity at ith degree of freedom at a given point in time (t), $\ddot{D}_i(t)$= is the acceleration of the ith degree of freedom at a given point in time (t), P(t) = is the abstract deformed pattern at a given point in time (t), $V_j(t)$ = is the command voltage to the jth damper, at a given point in time (t), BIG, NEGATIVE SMALL and SMALL are fuzzy variables and 2 is a pre-defined abstract pattern, as evaluated by a smart pattern identifier [17, 19, 20].

3.3. Rule-base generation

The heart of a fuzzy controller is its rule-base. The rule-base houses a collection of IF-THEN rules that summarize the knowledge-base that underpins the decisions made by the fuzzy controller [7, 11]. Being a non-parametric heuristic algorithm, fuzzy controllers are built to simulate a human operator's reasoning when facing a similar control situation. In an effort to design smart sustainable structural systems, that are built to be autonomous systems, the developed rule-base should be capable of handling all potential situations that might arise during the system's expected life time. Such controllers should be designed with self learning capabilities such that their initial rule-bases could be amended and expanded as new experiences and/or situations arise. There are currently several applications and toolboxes that allow the automatic extraction of rules of a given problem, knowing the input/output data sets of the problem without the pre-existing knowledge of a model for the system. This approach might be suitable for ill-defined systems. However, in case of structural systems under earthquake excitation, the system behavior is fully defined and could be identified using finite element models under several types of conventional analysis techniques.

Therefore, it is important to start the creation of the rule-base with a set of rules that outlines the basic features of the problem at hand, if an analytical model of the system could be developed. Such rules could be generated using time history analysis results of finite element models of the structural systems under consideration [14, 15, 16]. The rule-base should be designed to incorporate a self-learning mechanism that is capable of expanding the current rule-base with newly generated rules that capture any new situations [11, 12]. There are several platforms that are designed to allow the creation of fuzzy controllers. The most widely used of these is the MATLAB environment with its fuzzy logic toolbox. This toolbox allows the user the ability to design fuzzy inference systems for control applications or any other applications, such as pattern classification. The toolbox has a user interface that allows the extraction of rules given input/output data sets of the modeled system. As mentioned earlier this approach is suitable for systems that are ill-defined and are difficult to model analytically. The MATLAB environment allows the creation of a static fuzzy inference system. In other words, the created rule base is static and will not expand to incorporate newly acquired experiences. Therefore, it is advisable to create an m-file that is capable of extracting new experiences and expanding the initial rule-base as the need arises. This is usually encountered when the system is faced with a set of input variables that do not fire any of the generated rules [11, 12]. The designer should define a mechanism whereby an initial rule, that defines the encountered case, is generated and then fine tuned later using a performance monitoring scheme [11, 12].

4. Reliability assessment of fuzzy controllers

Engineering, by nature, is not an exact science. Engineering systems encounter several sources of uncertainties which render such systems subject to potential failures with certain probabilities. It is rather unrealistic to attempt to design a perfect engineering system with a failure probability of zero [21 22, 23]. Yet, it is crucial to be able to evaluate the failure probability of any designed system and attempt to design such systems with predefined and acceptable probabilities of failure [21, 22, 23]. Such acceptable values would be comparable to other failure probabilities humans are accepting and facing in other daily activities [21, 22, 23]. Non-parametric systems are often heuristic in nature and should be carefully analyzed in order to ensure their safe and reliable performance under all expected loading conditions. Smart structural systems, as outlined earlier, comprise sets of integrated components which provide added functionalities to the system, as opposed to conventional structural systems. Despite the fact that some of these components might have been proven reliable, in other applications, their reliable performance as an integral component of such a system needs validation and confirmation [8, 9].

In order to develop a comprehensive reliability assessment scheme for smart structural systems, a generic reliability assessment framework needs to be defined. The generic framework functions as a blueprint that identifies the reliability assessment procedures and underlying models, functions and measures that are necessary to perform the reliability assessment as per the nature of the problem at hand [8, 9].

Furthermore, it is crucial to develop proper reliability measures and assessment procedures, at two basic levels. First, individual components shall be investigated, given the appropriate failure conditions that are of concern to the application at hand. Second, the overall system, where all underlying components are integrated and aggregated within a predefined limit state format, shall be investigated in order to evaluate an overall reliability of the resulting system. In this chapter, reliability assessment of a fuzzy controller as a component within a smart structural system is explored. The evaluation of an overall reliability of the system, as a whole, is beyond the scope of this chapter and is addressed in other publications [8, 9].

4.1. Reliability assessment framework

The main objective of this task is to outline a generic reliability assessment framework for evaluating the reliability of a fuzzy controller, as an integral component of a smart structural system. Figure 8 shows the reliability assessment framework for the fuzzy controller, when operating within a smart structural system. The framework identifies two main paths which are necessary to conduct any reliability assessment. The first identifies the main components which are involved in evaluating the commanded output of the controller, while the second identifies another set of components which are responsible for evaluating what would be the expected output of the fuzzy controller. The output of both paths, i.e., commanded output (supply) and expected output (demand), are the basic inputs to any reliability assessment procedure [9, 21, 22, 23].

The reliability assessment framework, when identifying the components involved in each of the referred paths, pinpoints several systems that need to be analytically modeled in order to be able to perform the reliability assessment as necessary. Figure 8 recognizes the following models; a structural model, i.e., finite element model of the system, fuzzy controller's model, inverse dynamics model and an inverse actuator's model. All these components need to be defined and their analytical models developed in order to conduct the reliability assessment procedure. It should be pointed out that any system definition needs to be conducted in a format that lends itself to the reliability assessment calculations [8, 9]. Reliability assessments are related to the failure to supply what is initially demanded from the system. Potential failure modes, the identification of which is one of the first steps in the reliability assessment procedure, define situations where the analyzed system fails to supply and/or provide the required and/or demanded output. These potential failure modes are usually better expressed in a limit state format since this format lends itself to further developments in order to fully conduct the reliability assessment calculations. The following sections outline procedures for creating models for relevant components, identifying potential failure modes, presenting such failure modes in a limit state formats and finally conducting the reliability evaluation of a fuzzy controller.

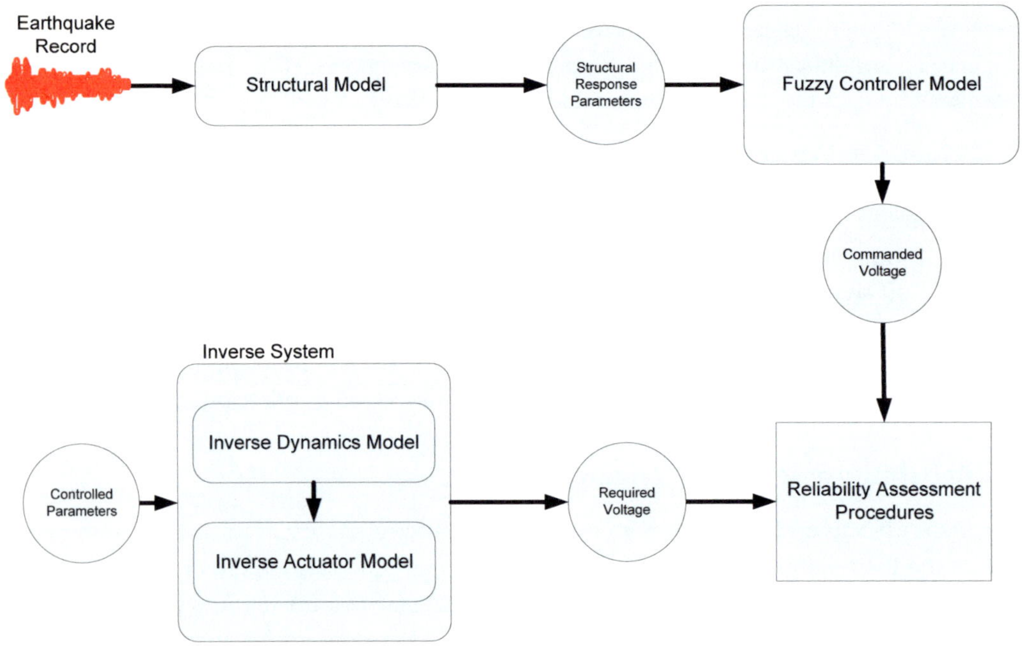

Figure 8. Fuzzy Controller Reliability Assessment Framework

4.2. Analytical models

As indicated earlier, the reliability assessment framework outlines the basic components which are involved in the evaluation of the reliability of the modeled system. The framework, shown in Figure 8, identifies four main components that should be analytically modeled in order to perform the reliability assessment procedure. The first component is a finite element model of the structural system which is necessary in order to evaluate the performance parameters of the system under the effect of an earthquake forcing function. Finite element models of structural systems are very well documented and any structural engineer is capable of creating such models within one of many finite element software packages that are currently available for research and design purposes. The dynamic equation of motion, shown in Eq. 6 outlines the behavior of a single degree of freedom system under the effect of an earthquake forcing function [14, 15, 16]. Given the time history of the applied earthquake, i.e., $\ddot{x}_g(t)$, the solution of the equation shown in Eq. 6 results in the structural performance parameters of the modeled system, i.e., $\ddot{x}(t), \dot{x}(t) \,\&\, x(t)$ [14, 15, 16].

$$m * \ddot{x}(t) + c * \dot{x}(t) + k * x(t) = -m * \ddot{x}_g(t) \tag{6}$$

Where, m = floor mass; c = damping constant; k = system stiffness; $\ddot{x}(t), \dot{x}(t) \,\&\, x(t)$ =are acceleration, velocity and displacement of the floor level, respectively and $\ddot{x}_g(t)$= is the ground acceleration.

The second component is the fuzzy controller model which was discussed in the previous sections. The development of such a model could be performed within a platform that supports fuzzy logic such as MATLAB among others. The development of such a model requires the full definition of input and output variables, including their relevant membership functions, the selection of a suitable inference engine, including inference function, inference mechanism and aggregation function. Finally, this also includes the generation of the rule-base necessary to perform any inference in order to evaluate the output of the controller, given the values of input variables.

The remaining models are relevant to the inverse performance of the system which would start with the controlled structural parameters and back calculate the necessary controller output in order to reach that targeted performance [19, 25]. The inverse system comprise two main components an inverse dynamics model and an inverse actuator model. The inverse dynamics model is simply the dynamic equation of motion which models the behavior of a controlled structural system under the effect of an earthquake loading function. Eq. 6 models the dynamic response of the uncontrolled structural system. Eq. 7, however, includes an additional term that reflects the effect of a control force provided by the fuzzy controller [1, 2]. Eq. 7 should start by introducing a set of required structural parameters, these could be the result of a predefined deformed position which would provide the displacement of the floor level, then by using numerical methods, the accompanying velocity and acceleration could be evaluated and substituted in Eq. 7 to evaluate the required control force.

$$F_{required} = m * \left[\ddot{x}(t) + \ddot{x}_g(t) \right] + c * \dot{x}(t) + k * x(t) \tag{7}$$

Where, m = floor mass; c = damping constant; k = system stiffness; $\ddot{x}(t), \dot{x}(t) \,\&\, x(t)$ = are acceleration, velocity and displacement of the floor level, respectively and $\ddot{x}_g(t)$= is the ground acceleration and $F_{Required}$ = required control force. The identification of such predefined deformed shape would be mostly dependent on the nature of the system in question, its size and its level of importance.

A second inverse model is necessary in order to translate the required control force into a required voltage which is the output of the fuzzy controller. This model should depend on the actuator, which is proposed in the application under consideration. For the proposed system, an MR damper is employed in applying any required corrective actions to enhance the system's response. MR dampers have very well documented models that outline the relationship between the input voltage to the damper and the resulting force, given the damper parameters and response parameters of the controlled system [26, 27]. The modified Buc-Wen model is the most widely used and accepted within the community of smart materials [26, 27]. The outlined model requires input data relating to the response of the system, i.e., displacement (x) and velocity ($\dot{x}$), in addition to the applied voltage (v), in order to evaluate the MR damper force that would be applied to the system [26, 27, 28].

4.3. Potential failure modes

The evaluation of the supplied and demanded fuzzy controller output values is the first step in the reliability assessment calculations. Potential failure modes should be formulated, in order to define situations where the supplied output variable might not satisfy the demanded requirements and thus constitutes a failure condition for the fuzzy controller [9, 19]. The failure modes are formulated in a limit state format in order to lend themselves to the reliability calculations that follow [9, 19]. In order to demonstrate the development of such failure conditions, two potential failure modes are explored for the proposed fuzzy controller. The first is a CRASH failure where the controller fails to produce any voltage signal, i.e., output value, to the MR Damper. The second is a MALFUNCTION failure where the controller produces an inaccurate voltage signal to the MR Damper. The reasons for each failure condition should be explored and all potential situations should be considered in evaluating a representative estimate of the reliability of the system [9, 19, 28].

When evaluating failure conditions all potential situations resulting in such a failure shall be considered and included in the probability of failure to reflect the level of uncertainties involved in the problem [21, 22, 23, 28]. The probability of failure of the controller is, then, evaluated using a Monte-Carlo simulation algorithm where the probability of failure for any given simulation cycle is calculated through the definition of a corresponding limit state as follows [19, 21, 22, 23, 28];

$$LS_1 = \frac{V_{supplied}}{V_{required}} < \lambda_1 \tag{8}$$

Where, LS_1 = is the limit state equation for the first failure mode, $V_{supplied}$ = is the supplied voltage command, $V_{required}$ = is the voltage demand as evaluated by the inverse models and λ_1 = is a cut off limit which defines when the supplied voltage is considered out of range. In case of a CRASH failure there is a single cutoff limit that defines when the controller is considered to have produced an insignificant output. These ranges are problem dependant and should be evaluated based on practical experience and the knowledge of the modeled system's behavior. For the purposes of demonstration if a value of 0.3 is assumed, this means that if the fuzzy controller proposed an output which is less than 30% of the expected value, this controller is considered to have crashed and is not functioning as expected. The reasons for such failure could be due to the lack of relevant rules that handles the set of input values presented to the fuzzy controller. If the rule-base is designed with the ability to expand and learn from experiences, this failure should trigger the creation of additional rules that are capable of handling such a situation [11, 12].

In case of a MALFUNCTION failure, which is defined as an inaccurate controller output, a single limit can't properly define such a failure condition and as a result two limits need to be defined. The limits would define an acceptable range within which the output is expected to fall. If the controller's output is below or above that range, the controller is considered to have malfunctioned [28]. This type of failure is addressed by fine tuning currently existing rules within the rule-base. Therefore, in such a case two limits are necessary in order to fully define the failure condition, i.e., a lower limit and an upper limit. Two underlying failure conditions result and two limit state equations could be written to express this failure as shown in Eqs. 9 [28];

$$LS_{21} = \frac{V_{supplied}}{V_{required}} < \lambda_{21}$$
$$LS_{22} = \frac{V_{supplied}}{V_{required}} > \lambda_{22} \tag{9}$$

Where, LS_{21} and LS_{22} = are the limit state equations for scenarios 1 & 2 of the second failure mode, $V_{supplied}$ = is the supplied voltage command, $V_{required}$ = is the voltage demand as evaluated by the inverse models and λ_{21} and λ_{22} = are lower and upper cut off limits respectively. Such limits are functions of the type of problem and relevant failure modes and resulting practical implications [28]. Monte-Carlo simulatin could be employed in generating values for all random variables which are involved in the problem at hand. Thus, each simulation cycle will result in a value for $V_{supplied}$ and $V_{required}$ and a corresponding evaluation of LS_i. The probability of failure for a given limit state, at any given point in time, is then evaluated using the following equation [9, 19, 21, 22, 23];

$$P_{fi}(t) = \frac{N_{\lambda}}{N} \tag{10}$$

Where, $P_{fi}(t)$ = is the probability of failure of the ith limit state, at any given point in time, N_{λ} = is the number of simulation cycles where the processor output resulted in a failure condition, depending on the failure condition in reference to Eqs. (8) & (9), and N = is the total number of simulation cycles.

The overall probability of failure of the whole processor should be evaluated, taking into consideration all potential failure combinations. This is accomplished by applying a union operator to evaluate the probability of failure of a single limit state with several underlying scenarios, as well as, the overall probability of failure considering all potential limit states.

The probability of failure of both limit states described in Eq. 9 could be evaluated as [19, 21, 22, 23, 24, 28];

$$P_{f21}(t) = \frac{N_{\lambda 21}}{N}$$
$$P_{f22}(t) = \frac{N_{\lambda 22}}{N} \quad (11)$$
$$P_{f2}(t) = P\{LS_{21} \cup LS_{22}\} = P_{f21}(t) + P_{f22}(t) - \left(P_{f21}(t) * P_{f22}(t)\right)$$

Where, $P_{f2}(t)$ = is the probability of failure of condition (2), LS_{21} and LS_{22} = are underlying limit states as defined in Eq. (11), $P_{f21}(t)$ & $P_{f22}(t)$ = are the probabilities of failure of underlying limit states (22 and 21), $N_{\lambda 21}$ and $N_{\lambda 22}$ = are the number of cycles where the processor output resulted in a failure conditions, i.e., $< \lambda_{21}$ and $> \lambda_{22}$ respectively in reference to Eq. 9, and N = is the total number of simulation cycles. In order to evaluate the overall probability of failure of the processor, taking into consideration all potential limit states, this could be defined as [19, 21, 22, 23, 24, 28];

$$P_f(t) = P\{LS_1 \cup LS_2 \cup \ldots \cup LS_i\} = P_{f1}(t) + P_{f2}(t) + \ldots + P_{fi}(t) - \left(P_{f1}(t) * P_{f2}(t) * \ldots * P_{fi}(t)\right) \quad (12)$$

Where, $P_f(t)$ = is the overall probability of failure of the processor, LS_1, LS_2 and LS_i = are potential limit states as defined in Eqs. (8 & 9), $P_{f1}(t)$, $P_{f2}(t)$ and $P_{fi}(t)$ = are relevant probabilities of failure of limit states, as defined in Eqs. (10 & 11). The above calculations are performed at a given point in time T_i, which results in an instantaneous reliability measure $P_f(t)$ for the fuzzy controller. Figure 9, shows a block diagram for the instantaneous reliability calculation procedure, taking into consideration all potential failure modes.

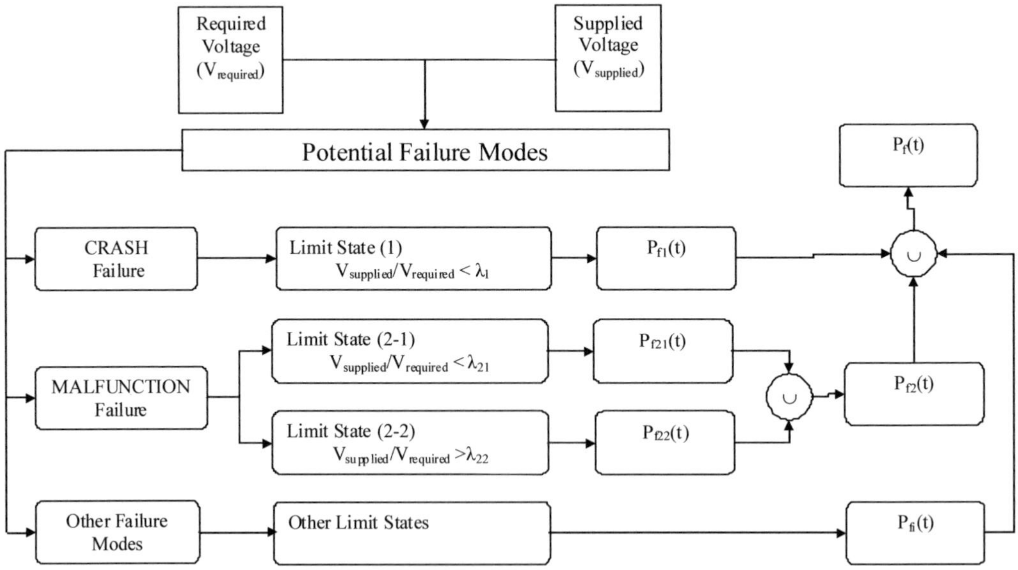

Figure 9. Instantaneous Reliability Evaluation

The resulting probability of failure is an instantaneous probability due to the time dependant nature of the problem under consideration. Therefore, a reliability time history could be developed to reflect the time variation of the controller reliability during operation under the effect of a real earthquake event. Figure 10, shows the step by step calculation procedure for evaluating a reliability time history for the fuzzy controller. Figure 11, shows a sample reliability time history diagram. The time history diagram is helpful in allowing the user to visualize the performance of the controller during a real time event and thus identifying events where the performance was unacceptable. The indentified time step where the controller failed to satisfy its expected performance could help in pinpointing the reasons for such unreliable behavior.

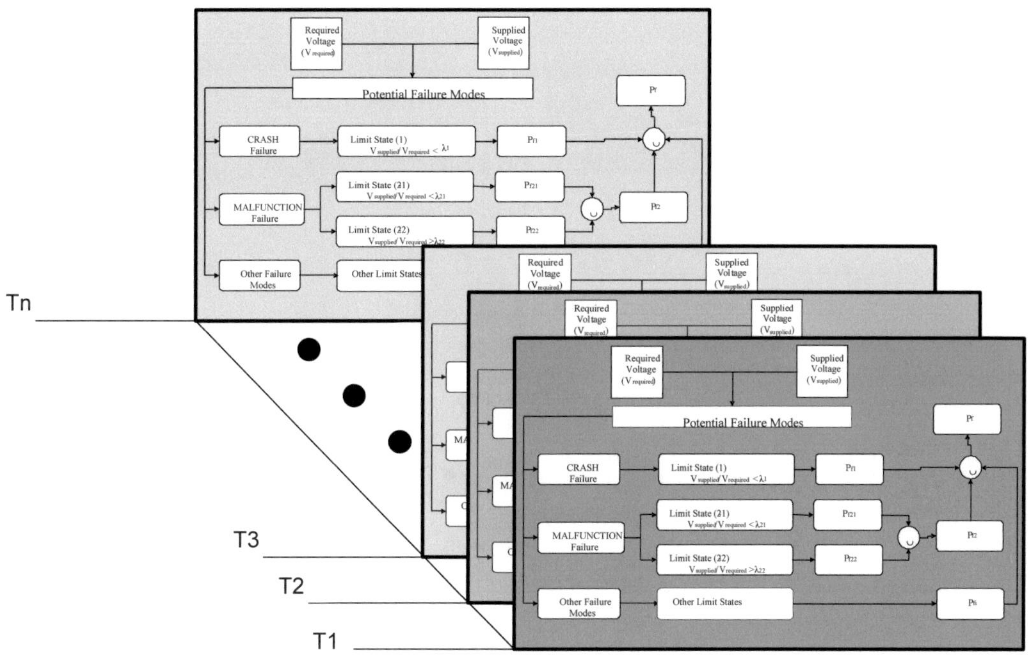

Figure 10. Reliability Time History Evaluation

5. Enhanced fuzzy controllers

5.1. Introduction

In reference to Figure 2, a multi-degree-of-freedom system would require an enhanced fuzzy controller in order to properly suppress any undesirable response of structural systems under earthquake loadings. One of the important enhancements that could be integrated with the controller is a fuzzy pattern identifier [17, 20, 24]. Sustainable Structural systems, as defined above, are bound by three basic characteristics, i.e., recyclable, optimum and reliable. Optimum design of structural systems entails both the minimum amount of material to construct the system itself, in addition to the optimum use of energy resources and any integral elements that are designed to suppress any undesirable responses. By that it is meant the actuators which are integrated within the system. As defined in Figures 1 and 2, these are selected as MR dampers. The designed fuzzy controller should comprise a scheme whereby an optimum firing procedure for such dampers is employed. Such scheme would rely on information relevant to the deformed shape of the system in order to select only those dampers which could significantly affect the response and thus the deformed shape of the system.

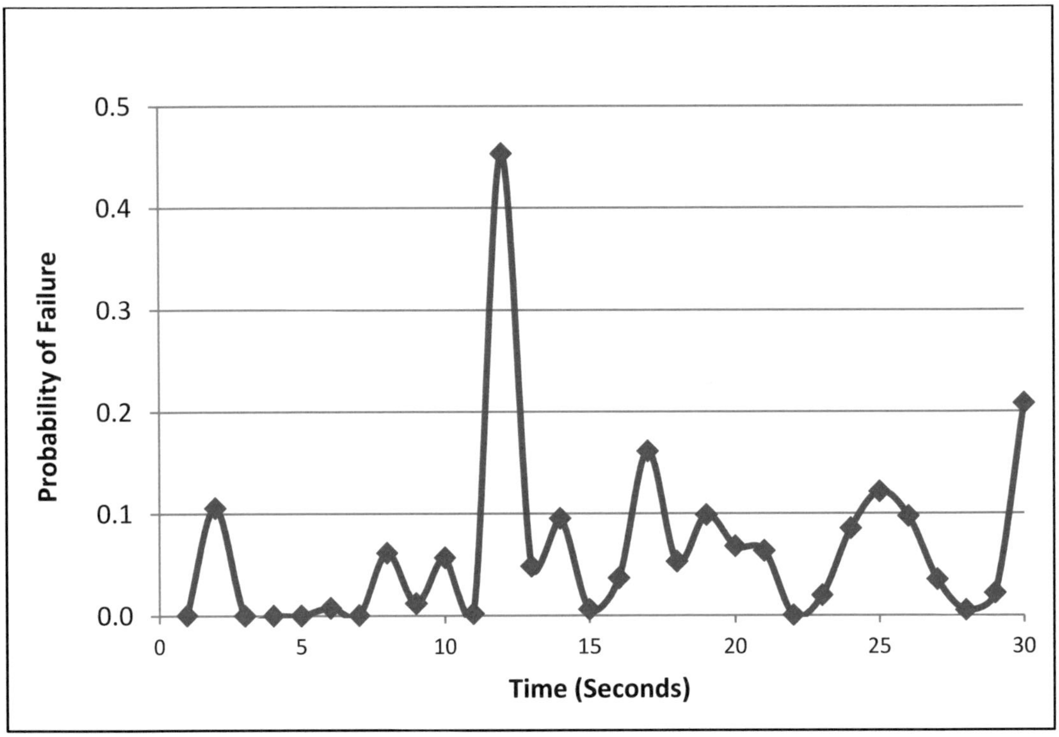

Figure 11. Sample Reliability Time History Diagram

Figure 2 defines an enhanced fuzzy controller where it accepts three input variables instead of only two as discussed earlier. The third variable relates to the abstract deformed shape of the system [17, 20, 24]. This additional piece of information would help in the selection of the firing sequence of the MR dampers not just how much restoring force they are called upon to produce. Thus, the need for an additional smart component, to operate integrally with the fuzzy controller, that is capable of classifying the deformed pattern of the system, given the sensor data relevant to the actual position of control points, i.e., degrees of freedom of the system.

A fuzzy inference system, comprising the same basic components of fuzzy controllers, could be designed in order to perform the required pattern classification task [17, 20, 24]. The fuzzy inference system should employ the gathered sensor data in testing the closeness of the deformed shape of the system to predefined abstract deformed patterns that are relevant to the modeled system. An inference engine built on top of a rule-base that is used to assign the appropriate pattern classification, based on the displacements of individual degrees of freedom, i.e., displacements of individual floors, could be created to drive the fuzzy inference system. The following section outlines the main design of a fuzzy pattern identifier.

5.2. Fuzzy abstract deformed shape identifiers

In order to design a fuzzy inference system that is capable of classifying the deformed pattern of any structural system, a set of potential predefined pattern classifications need to be developed. Such pattern classifications are dependent on the modeled system, its size and its behavior under expected loading conditions. Careful analysis of the modeled system could result in creating such pattern classifications. Figure 12, shows a sample of such potential deformed patterns for a three-degree-of-freedom system. The figure is, by no means, comprehensive, i.e., these are some of the potential deformed patterns a three-degree-of-freedom system could undergo [17, 20, 24].

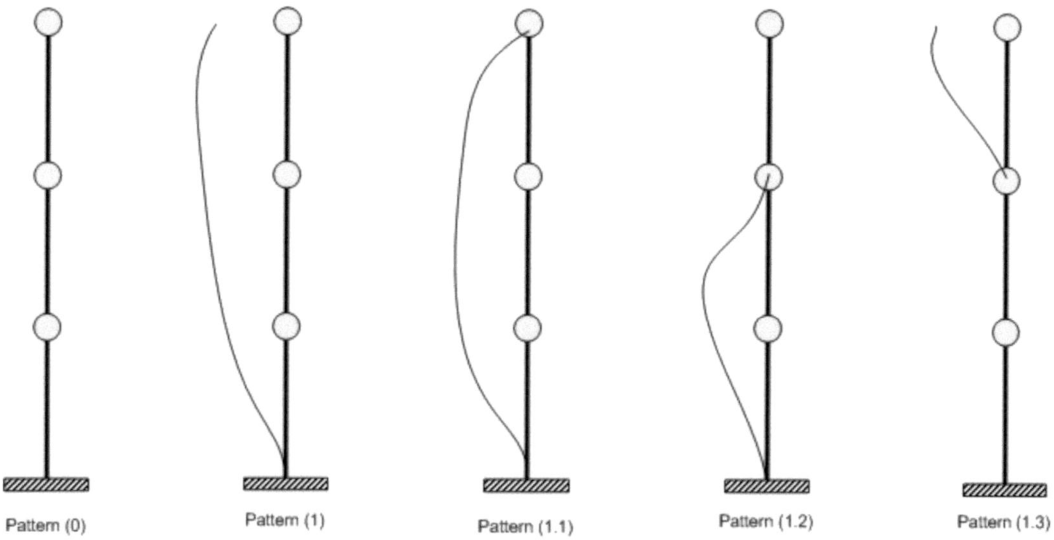

Figure 12. Sample Potential Asbtract Deformed Patterns

Once such pattern classifications are defined, a fuzzy inference system could be designed in order to classify any similar system into one of the predefined patterns. The fuzzy inference system would rely on a relevant rule-base that would accept the input of the individual floor displacements and assign the appropriate pattern classification accordingly. A sample rule could be defined as follows [17, 20, 24]:

$$\begin{aligned} &\text{IF }(\text{LEVEL1 is Positive})\text{ AND }(\text{LEVEL2 is Positive}) \\ &\text{AND }(\text{LEVEL3 is Positive})\text{ THEN }(\text{PATTERN is 1}) \end{aligned} \tag{13}$$

Where, LEVEL1, LEVEL2 & LEVEL3 = are fuzzy variables that define the sensor data of relevant story levels, Positive = is a fuzzy value of positive displacement, PATTERN = is the output variable of the fuzzy inference system, 1 = is a fuzzy singleton that defines the assigned pattern, AND = is the logical operator. In order to ensure the generality of the developed inference system, the pattern classifier should employ a normalized value of the sensor data rather than the actual displacement of the control point. The sensor data is normalized with respect to its maximum input value in order to result in input values within the interval [-1, 1]. In order to classify the abstract shape of a system it is only necessary to identify the relative position of control points with respect to each other rather than their absolute actual position. The normalization function could be defined as follows [17]:

$$L_i^N(t) = \frac{L_i(t)}{\underset{\text{for all t}}{MAX}(L_1(t), L_2(t), L_3(t))} \tag{14}$$

Where, $L_i^N(t)$ = is a normalized sensor output at i[th] degree of freedom at a given point in time; $L_i(t)$ = is the actual sensor output at i[th] degree of freedom at a given point of time; $L_1(t), L_2(t), L_3(t)$ = are the three actual sensor outputs at floor levels 1, 2 and 3 respectively and MAX() = is the maximum operator performed over all time instants of a given earthquake record. Therefore, the rule outlined in Eq. 13 should be rewritten to reflect the normalization function as follows;

IF $L_1^N(t)$ is Positive AND $L_2^N(t)$ is Positive AND $L_3^N(t)$ is Positive THEN PATTERN is 1 (15)

Where, $L_1^N(t)$, $L_2^N(t)$ and $L_3^N(t)$ = are the three normalized sensor outputs which identify the displacement, at each individual story level, at any given point in time; and all other variables are as defined above. The integral structure of the enhanced fuzzy controller results in a dual fuzzy processor where its performance and thus its reliability are dependent on the performance of both components [19]. Referring to Figure 2, it is clear that the fuzzy controller accepts inputs from the fuzzy pattern identifier; therefore, new failure conditions for the dual processor should be developed taking into consideration the possibility of the fuzzy pattern identifier providing inaccurate information to the fuzzy controller and thus causing it to fail [19]. Other failure conditions may arise due to the failure of the pattern identifier to evaluate a pattern, given the data that was provided. All such potential failure conditions should be carefully considered when evaluating the reliability of the dual fuzzy processor [19].

The performance of the fuzzy pattern identifier, as for similar pattern classification algorithms, is usually measured by plotting a linear compliance graph and using its geometrical and statistical information in evaluating the system's performance [17, 20]. Figure 13 shows a sample linear compliance graph. The graph is developed using a plot of the target classifications against the fuzzy pattern identifier classifications then generating a trendline of the plotted data [17]. If the trendline has a zero intercept and has a slope of unity, this implies that the fuzzy pattern identifier has perfectly assigned the proper pattern at all time instances. Therefore, the actual slope of the trendline and how close is the plotted data to that line, both are considered acceptable measures of the performance of the fuzzy pattern identifier and could be used in evaluating its reliability [17].

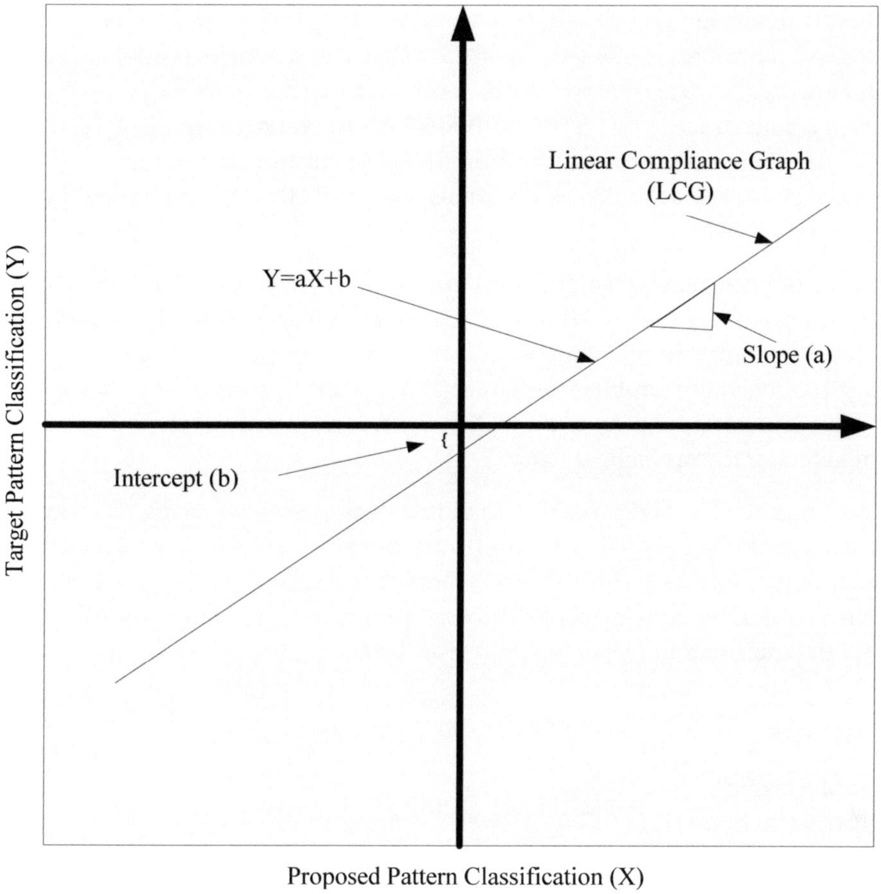

Figure 13. Linear Compliance Graph

6. Conclusions

In this chapter sustainable smart structural systems were presented as those which are constructed of recyclable materials, are optimally designed and demonstrate a reliable performance. As such, systems are equipped with fuzzy controllers that allow the structural systems to adjust their response under the effect of highly uncertain loading conditions, i.e., earthquakes. If such loads were considered in the design process it would have resulted in very heavy designs. Moreover, such earthquakes might not even occur during the expected life time of the designed systems. However, if any of these systems is equipped with smart features that adjust its response under the effect of any unseen loading conditions, it would be much lighter, safe and it should be reliable. In addition, the smart characteristics of such systems would minimize, if not eliminate, the amount of damage and destruction and thus the amount of waste, if failures did take place due to the occurrence of unseen earthquake events.

Smart sustainable structural systems were presented as a simple single-degree-of-freedom system, then, a more complex system was considered. In case of single-degree-of-freedom systems, fuzzy controllers with two input variables and single output variables were discussed. However, in case of more complex systems, the notion of a dual fuzzy processor where a fuzzy pattern identifier feeds additional information to the fuzzy controller was presented. Fuzzy inference systems were discussed in relation to the type of membership functions to be employed in similar applications and the method of generating the necessary rule-bases.

The reliability of such non-parametric systems is of major concern and thus a reliability assessment framework for evaluating the reliability of fuzzy controllers was presented. Potential failure conditions and limit state equations were presented as the basic tool of formulating the reliability problem of a fuzzy controller. The reliability evaluations were performed instantaneously then a reliability time history was created to suit the time dependent nature of the problem at hand.

Finally, the concept of a fuzzy pattern identifier was presented using a fuzzy inference system which would be coupled with the fuzzy controller to form a dual fuzzy processor. Such structure is necessary in case of complex structural systems where the basic information of the dynamics of control points would not be enough to fully define the problem for the controller to formulate proper decisions.

Author details

Maguid H. M. Hassan
British University in Egypt (BUE), Cairo, Egypt

7. References

[1] Soong, T.T. (1990) Active Structural Control, Theory & Practice. New York: John Wiley & Sons Inc.

[2] Connor, J.J. (2003) Introduction to Structural Motion Control. New Jersey: Prentice Hall, Pearson Education.

[3] Spencer Jr., B.F. and Sain, M.K. (1998) Controlling Buildings: A New Frontier in Feedback. Control Systems Magazine, IEEE, Special Issue on Engineering Technology, 17, no. No. 6, pp. 19-35.

[4] Spencer Jr., B.F., and Soong, T.T. (1999) New Applications and Development of Active, Semi-Active and Hybrid Control Techniques for the Seismic and Non-Seismic Vibration in the USA. Proceedings of the Inter. Post-SmiRT Conf. on Seismic Isolation, Passive Energy Dissipation and Active Control of Vibration of Structures, Cheju, Korea.

[5] Casciati, F., Faravelli, L. and Yao, T. (1994) Application of fuzzy logic to active structural control. Proceedings of the Second European Conference on Smart Structures and Materials, pp. 206-209.

[6] Choi, K-M., Cho, S-W., Jung, H-J. and Lee, I-W. (2004) Semi-Active Fuzzy Control for Seismic Response Reduction using Magneto-rheological Dampers. Earthquake Engng. Struct. Dyn., 33, p. 723-736.

[7] Klir, G. J. and Folger T. A. (1988) Fuzzy Sets, Uncertainty, and Information, Prentice Hall, New Jersey.

[8] Hassan, M.H.M. (2006) A System Model for Reliability Assessment of Smart Structural Systems. Structural Engineering & Mechanics, An International Journal (Techno Press) 23, no. 5, pp. 455 - 468.

[9] Hassan, M.H.M. (2005) Reliability Evaluation of Smart Structural Systems. IMECE2005, ASME International Mechanical Engineering Congress & Exposition, November 5-11, Orlando, Florida USA.

[10] Hassan, M.H.M, Ayyub, B.M. and Bernold, L. (1991) Fuzzy-based real-time control of construction activities. in Analysis and Management of Uncertainty: Theory and Applications, Edited by Ayyub, Gupta and Kanal, Elsevier, pp. 331-349

[11] Ayyub, B.M. and Hassan, M.H.M. (1992) Control of Construction Activities: III. Fuzzy-Based Controller. Civil Engineering Systems vol. 9, pp. 275-297.

[12] Hassan, M.H.M. and Ayyub, B.M. (1997) Structural fuzzy control. in Uncertainty Modeling in Vibration, Control and Fuzzy Analysis of Structural Systems, Edited by Ayyub, B.M., Guran, A. and Haldar, A. World Scientific, Chapter 7, pp. 179-231.

[13] Hassan M.H.M. and Ayyub B.M., (1993) A fuzzy controller for construction activities. Fuzzy Sets and Systems, Vol. 5, No. 3, pp. 253-271.

[14] Chopra, A.K. (2007) Dynamics of Structures, Theory and Applications of Earthquake Engineering, Pearson, Prentice Hall, New Jersey.

[15] Paz, M. and Leigh, W. (2004) Structural Dynamics, Theory and Computation, Springer.

[16] Hart, G.C. and Wong, K., (2000) Structural Dynamics for Structural Engineers, John Wiley & Sons. Inc., New York.

[17] Hassan, M.H.M. (2011) FIS Model of an Abstract Shape Identifier for Structural Systems. In Review.

[18] Ang, A.H-S., and Tang, W.H. (2007) Probability Concepts in Engineering Emphasis on Applications to Civil and Enviroenmental Engineering , John Wiley & Sons, Inc., New York.

[19] Hassan, M.H.M. (2012) Reliable Smart Structural Control. 5th European Conference on Structural Control, EACS 2012, Genoa, Italy, June 18-20.

[20] Hassan, M.H.M. (2012) Real-Time Smart Shape Identifiers. 4th International Conference on Smart Materials, Strutcures & Systems, CIMTEC 2012, Montecantini Terme, Italy, June 10-14.

[21] Ditlevsen, O. and Madsen, H.O., (1996) Structural Reliability Methods, John Wiley and Sons, New York.

[22] Haldar, A. and Mahadevan, S., (2000) Probability, Reliability and Statistical Methods in Engineering Design, John Wiley & Sons, INC., New York.

[23] Nowak, A.S., and Collins, K.R. (2000) Reliability of Structures McGraw-Hill, Inc., Boston.

[24] Hassan, M.H.M. (2010) Toward Reliability-Based Design of Smart Pattern Identifiers for Semi Active Control Applications. Fifth World Conference on Structural Control and Monitoring, 5WCSCM 2010, Tokyo, Japan, July 12-14.

[25] Hassan, M.H.M. (2008) A Reliability Assessment Model for MR Damper Components within a Structural Control Scheme. Advances in Science & Technology, Vol. 56, pp 218-224.

[26] Dyke, S. J., Spencer Jr. B. F., Sain, M. K. and Carlson, J. D. (1996) Modeling and Control of Magneto-Rheological Dampers for Seismic Response Reduction. Smart Mater. Struct., 5, p. 565-575.

[27] Spencer Jr., B.F., Dyke, S. J., Sain, M. K. and Carlson, J. D. (1997) Phenomenological Model for Magneto-rheological Dampers. J. Engrg. Mech. 123 (3), p. 230-238.

[28] Hassan, M.H.M. (2008) A Reliability Assessment Model for MR Damper Components within a Structural Control Scheme. Third International Conference Smart Materials, Structures & Systems, Acireale, Sicily, Italy, June 8-13.

Chapter 11

Vehicle Fault Tolerant Control Using a Robust Output Fuzzy Controller Design

M. Chadli and A. El Hajjaji

Additional information is available at the end of the chapter

http://dx.doi.org/10.5772/48262

1. Introduction

Modern life depends increasingly on the availability at all times of services and products provided by technological systems. Many areas, such as communication systems, water supply, power grids, urban transport systems are now completely automated. For such systems, the consequences of faults in component systems can be catastrophic. Reliability of such systems can be increased by ensuring that the faults will not occur, however, this objective unrealistic and often unattainable. In this context, it is very useful to design fault tolerant control systems that are able to tolerate possible faults in such systems to improve reliability and availability. Together with the increasing complexity of engineered systems and rising demands regarding reliability and safety, it is important to develop powerful fault-tolerant control methods.

A number of surveys are discussed various aspects of fault-tolerant control. For example, Stengel (1991) discusses analytical forms of redundancy using artificial intelligence methods. In (Rauch, 1994) a broad overview over basic methodologies based on classical control techniques (pseudo-inverse methods, adaptive approaches ...) is given with several application examples (aircraft, unmanned underwater vehicles). In (Patton, 1997) (Zhang and Jiang, 2003) surveys on fault-tolerant control methods give a broad summary of the field. In the transport domain, to satisfy increasing safety, many new vehicles are equipped with different driver assisted systems such as Traction Control System (TCS) and Electronic Stabilization Program (ESP) to maintain stability and acceptable performances even when some sensors have failed. These systems use a combination of ABS information, yaw rate, wheel speed, lateral acceleration and steer angle to improve the stabilization of the vehicle in dangerous driving situations and then improve the active safety (Kienck and Nielsen, 2000, Dahmani, Chadli and al, 2012).

The most common approach in coping with such a problem is to separate the overall design in two distinct phases. The first phase concerns "Fault Detection and Isolation" (FDI) problem, which consists in designing filters (dynamical systems) able to detect the presence of faults and to isolate them from other faults/disturbances (Isermann, 2001; Ding, Schneider, Ding and Rehm, 2005; Blanke, Kinnaert, Lunze and Staroswiecki, 2003; Gertler, 1998; Oudghiri, Chadli and ElHajjaji, 2007; Oudghiri, Chadli and ElHajjaji, 2008). The second phase usually consists in designing a supervisory unit. This unit reconfigures the control so as to compensate for the effect of the fault and to fulfill performance constraints. In general, the latter phase is carried out by means of a parameterized controller which is suitably updated by the supervisory unit.

Our objective is to develop model-based FTC-scheme for vehicle lateral dynamics. This study is motivated by the practical demands for such monitoring systems that i) automatically and reliably detect and isolate faults from sensors ii) deliver reliable and fault tolerant estimates of the vehicle lateral dynamics and iii) are practically realizable. In this chapter, we propose an observer-based fault tolerant control to detect, identify and accommodate sensor failures. The given method is based on the single failure assumption which states that at most one sensor can fail at any time.

To know the vehicle response, the proposed controller needs to know the yaw rate and the lateral velocity in order to generate the suitable output. If the yaw rate can be directly measurable by a yaw rate sensor (gyroscope), the lateral velocity will have to be estimated using an observer because it is not measurable easily. In this paper, a fuzzy controller is designed by considering the lateral velocity estimated using a nonlinear observer. In the analysis and design, the vehicle lateral will be represented by a switching systems (Chadli and Darouach, 2011) or by a Takagi-Sugeno (T-S) fuzzy model (Takagi and Sugeno, 1985), largely used these last years (Xioodong and Qingling, 2003; Chadli, Maquin and Ragot, 2005; Kirakidis, 2001; Tanaka and Wang, 1998; Chadli and El Hajjaji, 2006; Guerra and al, 2011; Chadli and Guerra, 2012). It is usually referred to as the bicycle model. Moreover, we consider the uncertain Takagi-Sugeno (T-S) fuzzy model to describe the vehicle dynamics in large domains and by the same way to improve the stability of vehicle lateral dynamics (Oudghiri, Chadli and A. ElHajjaji, 2007b; Chadli, ElHajjaji and Oudghiri, 2008). The proposed algorithm is formulated in terms of linear matrix inequalities (LMI) (Boyd and al, 1994) which are easily solvable using classical numerical tools (such as LMI Toolbox for Matlab software).

The subject of this chapter concerns the area of active FTCS for lateral vehicle dynamics that is modeled by uncertain TS fuzzy model. A FDI algorithm based on fuzzy observer is developed and a design method of control law tolerant to some sensors faults is proposed. This chapter is structured as follows. Basic concepts and notions of the FTC field with several general approaches to achieve fault tolerance are described in Sections 2 and 3. In Section 4 applications of control reconfiguration are reviewed briefly. Section 4 describes the vehicle lateral and its representation by uncertain T-S fuzzy model. Section 5 presents the observer-based fault tolerant control strategy with simulations of sensor faults and result analysis. Conclusions are given in Section 6.

Notation: symmetric definite positive matrix P is defined by $P > 0$, the set $\{1,2,..,n\}$ is defined by I_n and symbol * denotes the transpose elements in the symmetric positions.

2. Preliminaries and some definitions

This section introduces concepts and ideas from the field of fault-tolerant control (FTC). Consider the following state space representation of linear systems:

$$\begin{aligned} \dot{x}(t) &= Ax(t) + Bu(t) + B_w w_1(t) \\ y(t) &= Cx(t) + w_2(t) \end{aligned}$$

where $\mathbf{x}(t) \in R^n$ is the state, $\mathbf{y}(t) \in R^r$ is the output, $\mathbf{u}(t) \in R^m$ is the inputs which are measurable, $\mathbf{A} \in R^{n\times n}$ is the state transition matrix, $\mathbf{B} \in R^{n\times m}$ is the input distribution matrix, $\mathbf{C} \in R^{r\times n}$ is the output matrix, $\mathbf{B}_w \in R^{n\times n}$ is the disturbance matrix, and $\mathbf{w_1(t)} \in R^n$ and $\mathbf{w_2(t)} \in R^r$ are the disturbances which are unknowns.

Faults are modelled by changes of system matrices. For example, *Actuator faults* are modelled by modifing input matrix $\mathbf{B}_f$ by scaling columns or setting to zero of columns in case of actuator failure. The *Sensor faults* are modelled by a modified output matrix $\mathbf{C}_f$. This matrix may contain scaled rows due to altered sensor characteristics or zero rows due to failed sensors i.e. the faulty sensor should be switched off. *Plant faults* are modelled by a modified system matrix $\mathbf{A}_f$. In general, when all types of faults present simultaneously, the faulty system model becomes:

$$\begin{aligned} \dot{x}_f(t) &= A_f x_f(t) + B_f u_f(t) + B_w w_1(t) \\ y_f(t) &= C_f x_f(t) + w_2(t) \end{aligned}$$

Notice that in almost works, only one type of fault is assumed to have occurred at a time. A general linear controller *(K)* could be designed as a static or dynamic output feedback controller.

In the following paragraphs, brief definitions of terms common in the fault-tolerant control community are provided (J. Lunze and J. Richter (2006).

Faults. Faults can cause technical systems to malfunction or operate at reduced performance. Reduced service quality is the consequence. Faults may be triggered internally, such as broken power links in a computer or blocked valves in a chemical batch plant, or externally, such as changes in environmental conditions like a temperature drop stopping a chemical reaction.

Faults can be further classified by their location in a block diagram. *Actuator faults* affect only actuation systems, such as pumps, valves, stirrers, switches, motors, brakes. They concern the efficiency of inputs on the system. *Plant faults* affect internal plant components, resulting in changed plant I/O properties, for example clogged pipes or leakages. They concern the system dynamics. *Sensor faults* result in erroneous measurements, such as biased, scaled or simply absent, constant zero readings (Blanke *et al.*, 2003). They concern the measured output of a system.

Failures. Failures contrast faults in the following sense. A fault reduces the system performance. The system can in general still serve its purpose, albeit with reduced functionality and/or performance. After a failure, the system provides no service any more. It cancels service availability completely. Faults and failures can occur both at the component level and at the aggregated system level. Fault-tolerant control aims at preventing component faults, component failures or subsystem faults from becoming system failures (Blanke *et al.*, 2003).

Fault-tolerance. The term *fault-tolerant system* (FTS) will be used to denote a controlled system which can still serve its purpose in spite of the occurrence of faults, at least for some time and to some degree, until the impaired components can be repaired.

Fault-tolerant control (FTC) denotes a framework of methods developed to turn control loops into fault-tolerant systems. The focus is on the design of the automatic control laws. That is, the means to achieve fault-tolerance are specific control design approaches with fault-tolerance in mind. The goal is to keep the loop in operation for as long as possible to minimise the cost of down-time. Shutting down a plant may be expensive due to loss of production, or due to resulting plant damage. The latter can be the case in some chemical reactions. As an example, absence of cooling can cause irreversible solidification of the reactor content of a batch process, which means loss of the reactor.

Fault diagnosis is an area of active research of its own. In most parts of this work, the diagnosis task is taken as a prerequisite already solved, as this work focuses on controller adjustment. When considering the joint properties of diagnosis and controller adjustment or in implicit approaches, diagnosis is covered as well.

3. Classification of fault-tolerant control

There already exist several approaches to achieve fault tolerance for control loops. The classification taken here is illustrated in Figure 1.

The classification can be done according to different criteria. The distinction between *passive* and *active* approaches is explained first, followed by *fault accommodation* and *reconfiguration*.

3.1. Passive and active FTC

Passive fault tolerance is achieved when the loop remains operational in spite of faults *without changing the controller*. If the controller is changed at fault detection time, for instance by controller parameters or even its structure, the approach is called *active*.

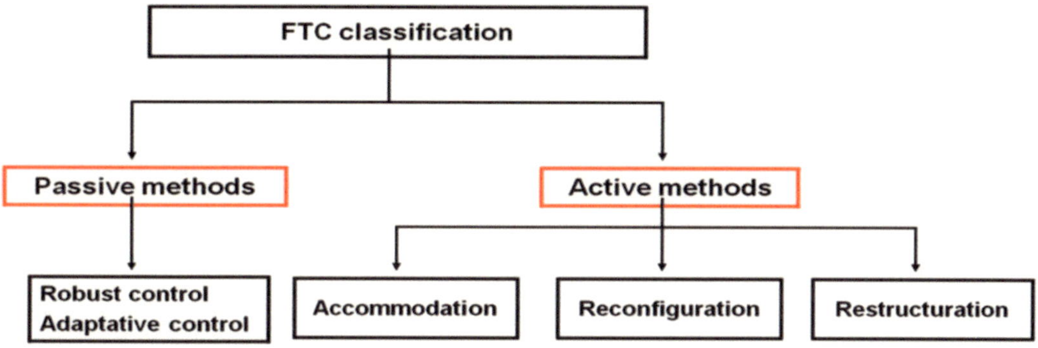

Figure 1. A classification of fault-tolerant control methods

A typical example of a passive approach is robust controller design, a well-established and researched approach to achieve fault tolerance. Typically, faults that can be modelled as plant uncertainties can be well covered by robust design. A large number of publications concerning the achievement of fault tolerance using various robust design techniques exist in the literature.

In robustness approaches, a fixed controller is designed to accommodate a class of anticipated component faults or failures. Most robustness approaches are feasible only for faults representable as parameter drift (see for example Fujita and Shimermura, 1988, Campo and Morari, 1994).

The class of faults covered by robust control is in general more limited in comparison to active approaches. In addition, the necessary trade-off between nominal performance and fault tolerance introduces conservatism.

3.2. Fault accommodation - fault reconfiguration

Fault accommodation denotes the case where the variables measured and manipulated by the controller remain unchanged (Blanke *et al.*, 2003). Only the controller internals (including its dynamic order) may change, but the same measurement and actuation signals as in the nominal case must be used. Adaptive control is an example of an accommodation technique (Ahmed-Zaid *et al.*, 1991; Bodson and Groszkiewicz, 1997).

The approach also has its specific limitations. The most serious one concerns the severity of faults and the speed of adaptation. Only faults representable as slowly changing plant parameters can be well accommodated by adjusting controller parameters. Structural damage is not covered. In addition, adaptive control works well in case of slow plant parameter variations in linear plants with respect to signal variation speed. This assumption is very questionable for faults that occur abruptly and rapidly lead out of the region of valid plant linearisation. Adaptive controllers are generally too slow to compensate abrupt faults.

Switching among a bank of predesigned controllers may be used as an accommodation technique.

Control reconfiguration is an active approach where both the controller and its measured and manipulated variables may change. Reconfiguration allows the structure of the control loop to be changed in response to faults. This goes beyond structural changes inside the controller by including dynamic signal re-routing of inputs and outputs.

4. FTC for vehicle dynamics

4.1. Vehicle model

Vehicle lateral dynamics have been studied since the late 1950's. Segel (Segel, 1956) developed a three-degree-of freedom vehicle model to describe the vehicle directional responses, which includes the yaw, lateral and roll motions. Most of the previous research works on vehicle lateral control have relied on the bicycle model (figure 2) that considers only lateral and yaw motions. It is based on the following assumptions:

- There is no roll, pitch or bounce
- The relative yaw between the vehicle and the road is small
- The steering angle is small
- The tire lateral force varies linearly with the slip angle

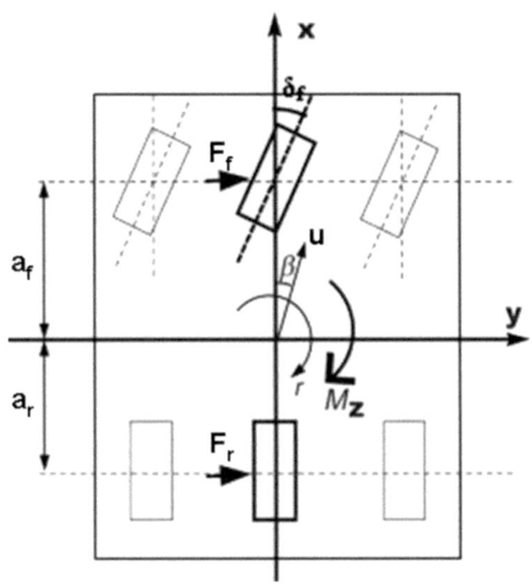

Figure 2. Bicycle model

The following simplified model is obtained:

$$\begin{aligned} m(\dot{v}+ur) &= 2(F_f+F_r) \\ J\dot{r} &= 2(a_fF_f-a_rF_r)+M_z \end{aligned} \tag{1}$$

where u and v ($v=\beta*u$) are components of the vehicle velocity along longitudinal and lateral principle axis of the vehicle body, r is yaw rate, β denotes the side slip angle, m

and J are the mass and the yaw moment of inertia respectively, a_f and a_r are respectively distances of the front and rear axle from the center of gravity, while yaw moment M_z is the control input, which must be determined from the control law, F_r and F_f are rear and front lateral forces respectively. They are described by magic formula (Lin, popov and Mcwilliam, 2004) as

$$\begin{aligned} F_f &= D_f(\mu)\sin\left[C_f(\mu)\tan^{-1}\left\{B_f(\mu)(1 - E_f(\mu))\alpha_f + E_f(\mu)\tan^{-1}(B_f(\mu)\alpha_f)\right\}\right] \\ F_r &= D_r(\mu)\sin\left[C_r(\mu)\tan^{-1}\left\{B_r(\mu)(1 - E_r(\mu))\alpha_r + E_r(\mu)\tan^{-1}(B_r(\mu)\alpha_r)\right\}\right] \end{aligned} \tag{2}$$

Coefficients D_i, C_i, B_i and E_i ($i = f,r$) depend on the tire characteristics, road adhesion coefficient μ and the vehicle operational conditions, α_f and α_r represent tyre slip-angles at the front and rear of the vehicle respectively. Given that

$$\begin{cases} \alpha_f = -\dfrac{v}{u} - \tan^{-1}\left(\dfrac{a_f}{u} r\cos\left(\dfrac{v}{u}\right)\right) + \delta_f \\ \alpha_r = -\dfrac{v}{u} + \tan^{-1}\left(\dfrac{a_r}{u} r\cos\left(\dfrac{v}{u}\right)\right) \end{cases} \tag{3}$$

where δ_f is the front steer angle.

To obtain the TS fuzzy model, we have represented the front and rear lateral forces (2) by the following rules:

$$\text{If } |\alpha_f| \text{ is } M_1 \text{ then } \begin{cases} F_f = C_{f1}(\mu)\alpha_f \\ F_r = C_{r1}(\mu)\alpha_r \end{cases} \tag{4}$$

$$\text{If } |\alpha_f| \text{ is } M_2 \text{ then } \begin{cases} F_f = C_{f2}(\mu)\alpha_f \\ F_r = C_{r2}(\mu)\alpha_r \end{cases} \tag{5}$$

where C_{fi}, C_{ri} represent front and rear lateral tire stiffness, which depend on road adherence μ.

The overall forces are obtained by:

$$\begin{cases} F_f = h_1(|\alpha_f|)\, C_{f1}(\mu)\alpha_f + h_2(|\alpha_f|)\, C_{f2}(\mu)\alpha_f \\ F_r = h_1(|\alpha_f|)\, C_{r1}(\mu)\alpha_r + h_2(|\alpha_f|)\, C_{r2}(\mu)\alpha_r \end{cases} \tag{6}$$

where h_j $(j = 1,2)$ is the jth bell curve membership function of fuzzy set M_j. They satisfy the following constraints

$$\begin{cases} \sum_{i=1}^{2} h_i(|\alpha_f|) = 1 \\ 0 \le h_i(|\alpha_f|) \le 1 \ \forall i = 1,2 \end{cases} \tag{7}$$

The expressions of membership functions h_j $(j = 1,2)$ used are as follows

$$h_i\left(\left|\alpha(t)_f\right|\right) = \frac{\beta_i\left(\left|\alpha_f(t)\right|\right)}{\sum_{i=1}^{2} \beta_i\left(\left|\alpha_f(t)\right|\right)}, i = 1,2 \tag{8}$$

with

$$\beta_i\left(\left|\alpha_f\right|\right) = \frac{1}{\left(1 + \left|\left(\frac{\left|\alpha_f\right| - c_i}{a_i}\right)\right|\right)^{2b_i}} \tag{9}$$

The membership function parameters and consequence of rules are obtained using an identification method based on the Levenberg-Marquadt algorithm (Lee, Lai and Lin, 2003) combined with the least square method, allow to determine parameters of membership functions (a_i, b_i, c_i) and stiffness coefficient values

$$a_1 = 0.5077,\ b_1 = 3.1893,\ c_1 = \text{-}0.4356,\ a_2 = 0.4748,\ b_2 = 5.3907,\ c_2 = 0.5622 \tag{10}$$

$$C_{f1} = 60712.7\ ,\ C_{f2} = 4814\ ,\ C_{r1} = 60088\ ,\ C_{r2} = 3425 \tag{11}$$

Using the above approximation idea of nonlinear lateral forces by TS rules and by considering that

$$\alpha_f \cong \frac{-v - a_f r}{u} + \delta_f\ ,\ \alpha_r \cong \frac{-v + a_r r}{u} \tag{12}$$

nonlinear model (1) can be represented by the following TS fuzzy model:

$$\text{If } |\alpha_f| \text{ is M1 then } \begin{cases} \dot{x} = A_1 x + B_1 M_z + B_{f1}\delta_f \\ y = C_1 x + D_1 \delta_f \end{cases} \tag{13}$$

$$\text{If } |\alpha_f| \text{ is M2 then } \begin{cases} \dot{x} = A_2 x + B_2 M_z + B_{f2}\delta_f \\ y = C_2 x + D_2 \delta_f \end{cases} \tag{14}$$

where $x=(v,r)^T$, $y=(y_1,y_2)^T=(a_y,r)^T$ and

$$A_i=\begin{pmatrix} -2\dfrac{C_{fi}+C_{ri}}{mu} & -2\dfrac{C_{fi}a_f-C_{ri}a_r}{mu^2}-1 \\ -2\dfrac{C_{fi}a_f-C_{ri}a_r}{J} & -2\dfrac{C_{fi}a_f^2+C_{ri}a_r^2}{Ju} \end{pmatrix} \tag{15}$$

$$B_{fi}=\begin{pmatrix} \dfrac{2C_{fi}}{mu} \\ \dfrac{2a_fC_{fi}}{J} \end{pmatrix},\ B_i=B=\begin{pmatrix} 0 \\ \dfrac{1}{J} \end{pmatrix},\ D_i=\begin{pmatrix} 2\dfrac{C_{fi}}{m} \\ 0 \end{pmatrix} \tag{16}$$

$$C_i=\begin{pmatrix} -2\dfrac{C_{fi}+C_{ri}}{mu} & -2\dfrac{C_{fi}a_f-C_{ri}a_r}{mu} \\ 0 & 1 \end{pmatrix} \tag{17}$$

The output vector of system y consist of measurements of lateral acceleration a_y and the yaw rate about center of gravity r

The defuzzified output of this T–S fuzzy system is a weighted sum of individual linear models

$$\begin{cases} \dot{x} &= \sum_{i=1}^{2} h_i(|\alpha_f|)\left(A_ix+B_iM_z+B_{fi}\delta_f\right) \\ y &= \sum_{i=1}^{2} h_i(|\alpha_f|)\left(C_ix+D_i\delta_f\right) \end{cases} \tag{18}$$

From the expressions of front and rear forces (4), (5), we note that stiffness coefficients C_{fi} and C_{ri} are not constant and vary depending on the road adhesion. To take into account these variations, we assume that these coefficients vary as follows:

$$\begin{cases} C_{fi}=C_{fi0}(1+d_if_i) \\ C_{ri}=C_{ri0}(1+d_if_i) \end{cases} \|f_i\|\le 1 \tag{19}$$

where d_i indicates the deviation magnitude of the stiffness coefficient from its nominal value.

After some manipulations, the TS fuzzy model can be written as:

$$\begin{cases} \dot{x}(t) &= \sum_{i=1}^{2} h_i(|\alpha_f|)\left((A_i+\Delta A_i)x(t)+BM_z+\left(B_{fi}+\Delta B_{fi}\right)\delta_f\right) \\ y(t) &= \sum_{i=1}^{2} h_i(|\alpha_f|)\left(C_ix+D_i\delta_f\right) \end{cases} \tag{20}$$

where ΔA_i and ΔB_{fi} represent parametric uncertainties represented as follows

$$\Delta A_i = \mathrm{H}_i \Sigma_i(t) E_{Ai} \tag{21}$$

with $\Sigma_i(t)$ $(i=1,2)$ are matrices uncertain parameters such that $\Sigma_i^T(t)\Sigma_i(t) \le I$, E_i is known real matrix of appropriate dimension that characterizes the structures of uncertainties.

4.2. Output feedback design

a. TS Fuzzy observer structure

Consider the general case of uncertain T-S fuzzy model (Takagi and Sugeno, 1985):

$$\begin{aligned} \dot{x}(t) &= \sum_{i=1}^{q} h_i(z(t))\big((A_i + \Delta A_i)x(t) + (B_i + \Delta B_i)u(t)\big) \\ y(t) &= \sum_{i=1}^{q} h_i(z(t))C_i x(t) \end{aligned} \tag{22}$$

with properties

$$\sum_{i=1}^{q} h_i(z(t)) = 1,\ h_i(z(t)) \ge 0 \quad \forall\, i \in I_q \tag{23}$$

where q is the number of sub-models, $x(t) \in \mathbb{R}^n$ is the state vector, $u(t) \in \mathbb{R}^m$ is the control input vector, $y(t) \in \mathbb{R}^l$ is the output vector, $A_i \in \mathbb{R}^{n.n}, B_i \in \mathbb{R}^{n.m}, C_i \in \mathbb{R}^{l.n}$ are the ith state matrix, the ith input matrix and the ith output matrix respectively. Vector $z(t)$ is the premise variable depending on measurable variables. ΔA_i and ΔB_i, $i \in I_n$ are time-varying matrices representing parametric uncertainties in the plant model. These uncertainties are admissibly norm-bounded and structured, defined as

$$\Delta A_i = \mathrm{H}_i \Sigma_i(t) E_{Ai},\ \Delta B_i = \mathrm{H}_i \Sigma_i(t) E_{Bi} \tag{24}$$

The overall fuzzy observer has the same structure as the TS fuzzy model. It is represented as follows:

$$\begin{cases} \dot{\hat{x}}(t) = \sum_{i=1}^{q} h_i(z(t))\big(A_i\hat{x}(t) + B_i u(t) + G_i\left(y(t) - \hat{y}(t)\right)\big) \\ \hat{y}(t) = \sum_{i=1}^{q} h_i(z(t))C_i\hat{x}(t) \end{cases} \tag{25}$$

where G_i, $i \in I_n$ are the constant observer gains to be determined.

b. TS Fuzzy controller

Like the fuzzy observer, the TS fuzzy controller is represented as follows

$$u(t) = -\sum_{i=1}^{q} h_i(z(t))K_i\hat{x}(t) \tag{26}$$

where $K_i, i \in I_n$ are the constant feedback gains to be determined. We define the error of estimation as

$$e(t) = x(t) - \hat{x}(t) \tag{27}$$

From systems (20), (21) and (22), we have

$$\dot{x}(t) = \sum_{i=1}^{q}\sum_{j=1}^{q} h_i(z)h_j(z)\Big(\big(A_i + \Delta A_i - (B_i + \Delta B_i)K_j\big)x(t) + (B_i + \Delta B_i)K_j e(t)\Big) \tag{28}$$

$$\dot{e}(t) = \sum_{i=1}^{q}\sum_{j=1}^{q} h_i(z)h_j(z)\big(A_i - G_iC_j - \Delta B_iK_j\big)e(t) + \big(\Delta A_i + \Delta B_iK_j\big)x(t) \tag{29}$$

The augmented system can be expressed as:

$$\dot{\tilde{x}}(t) = \sum_{i=1}^{q}\sum_{j=1}^{q} h_i(z)h_j(z)\big(\tilde{A}_{ij} + \Delta\tilde{A}_{ij}\big)\tilde{x}(t) \tag{30}$$

where

$$\tilde{x} = \begin{pmatrix} x \\ e \end{pmatrix},\ \tilde{A}_{ij} = \begin{pmatrix} A_i - B_iK_j & B_iK_j \\ 0 & A_i - G_iC_j \end{pmatrix},\ \Delta\tilde{A}_{ij} = \begin{pmatrix} \Delta A_i - \Delta B_iK_j & \Delta B_iK_j \\ \Delta A_i + \Delta B_iK_j & -\Delta B_iK_j \end{pmatrix} \tag{31}$$

The global asymptotic stability of the TS fuzzy model (25) is summarized in the following theorem:

Theorem 1: If there exist symmetric and positive definite matrices Q and P, some matrices K_i and G_i such that the following LMIs are satisfied $\forall\ (i,j) \in I_q^2, i < j$, then TS fuzzy system (25) is globally asymptotically stable via TS fuzzy controller (21) based on fuzzy observers (20):

$$\begin{pmatrix} \Phi_{ii} & * & * \\ E_{Ai}Q - E_{Bi}M_i & -\left(\varepsilon_{ii}^{-1} + 1\right)^{-1} I & * \\ \mathrm{H}_i^T & 0 & -\left(\varepsilon_{ii} + 1\right)^{-1} I \end{pmatrix} < 0 \tag{32}$$

$$\begin{pmatrix} \Psi_{ij} & * & * & * & * \\ E_{Ai}Q - E_{Bi}M_j & -\left(\varepsilon_{ij}^{-1}+1\right)^{-1} I & * & * & * \\ E_{Aj}Q - E_{Bj}M_i & 0 & -\left(\varepsilon_{ij}^{-1}+1\right)^{-1} I & * & * \\ \mathrm{H}_i^T & 0 & 0 & -\varepsilon_{ij}^{-1} & * \\ \mathrm{H}_j^T & 0 & 0 & 0 & -\varepsilon_{ij}^{-1} \end{pmatrix} < 0 \tag{33}$$

$$\begin{pmatrix} T_{ii} & * & * \\ E_{Bi}K_i & -\left(\varepsilon_{ii}^{-1}+1\right)^{-1} I & * \\ \mathrm{H}_i^T P & 0 & -\left(\varepsilon_{ii}+1\right)^{-1} I \end{pmatrix} < 0 \tag{34}$$

$$\begin{pmatrix} \Theta_{ij} & * & * & * & * \\ E_{Bi}K_j & -\left(\varepsilon_{ij}^{-1}+1\right)^{-1} I & * & * & * \\ E_{Bj}K_i & 0 & -\left(\varepsilon_{ij}^{-1}+1\right)^{-1} I & * & * \\ \left(P\mathrm{H}_i\right)^T & 0 & 0 & -\left(\varepsilon_{ij}+1\right)^{-1} I & * \\ \left(P\mathrm{H}_j\right)^T & 0 & 0 & 0 & -\left(\varepsilon_{ij}+1\right)^{-1} I \end{pmatrix} < 0 \tag{35}$$

with

$$\Phi_{ii} = QA_i^T + A_iQ - M_i^T B_i^T - B_iM_i + I$$

$$\Psi_{ij} = QA_i^T + A_iQ + QA_j^T + A_jQ - M_j^T B_i^T - B_iM_j - M_i^T B_j^T - B_jM_i + D_iD_i^T + D_jD_j^T + 2I$$

$$T_{ii} = A_i^T P + PA_i - C_i^T N_i^T - N_iC_i + K_i^T B_i^T B_iK_i$$

$$\Theta_{ij} = A_i^T P + PA_i + A_j^T P + PA_j - C_i^T N_j^T - N_iC_j - C_j^T N_i^T - N_jC_i + K_i^T B_j^T B_jK_i + K_j^T B_i^T B_iK_j$$

The controller and the observer are defined as follows

$$K_i = M_iQ^{-1} \tag{36}$$

$$G_i = P^{-1}N_i \tag{37}$$

Proof: The proof can be inspired directly from (Chadli & El Hajjaji 2006).

Remarks

In the case of common input matrix B ($B_i = B \ \ \forall i \in I_q$), the above result is simplified. The new stability conditions are given in the following corollary

Corollary 1: If there exist symmetric and positive definite matrices Q and P, some matrices K_i and G_i such that the following LMI are satisfied $\forall\, i \in I_q$, then TS fuzzy system (25) is globally asymptotically stable via TS fuzzy controller (21) based on fuzzy observers (20):

$$\begin{pmatrix} \Phi_{ii} & * & * \\ E_{Ai}Q & -\left(\varepsilon_{ii}^{-1}+1\right)^{-1} I & * \\ H_i^T & 0 & -\varepsilon_{ii}^{-1} I \end{pmatrix} < 0 \tag{38}$$

$$\begin{pmatrix} \mathrm{T}_{ii} & * \\ H_i^T P & -I \end{pmatrix} < 0 \tag{39}$$

with

$$\Phi_{ii} = QA_i^T + A_i Q - M_i^T B^T - BM_i + I$$

$$\mathrm{T}_{ii} = A_i^T P + PA_i - C_i^T N_i^T - N_i C_i + K_i^T B^T B K_i$$

The controller and the observer gains are as defined in (29).

Proof: The result is obtained directly from theorem 1.

Result of corollary 1 derive directly from the TS fuzzy model (15) (with common input matrix $B_i = B, i \in I_2$, and $\delta_f = 0$). This case leads to four constraints to resolve, whereas the result of theorem 1 leads to six constraints, which means less conservatism.

The derived stability conditions are LMI on synthesis variables $P > 0, Q > 0, M_i, N_i$ and scalars $\varepsilon_i > 0$. However the problem to resolve becomes nonlinear in $K_i, i \in I_q$ (inequalities (27)-(28)/(30)-(31)). A method allowing the use of numerical tools to solve these constraints is given in the following.Toresolve the obtained BMI (bilinear matrix inequality) conditions using LMI tools (LMI toolbox of Matlab software for example), we propose to solve synthesis conditions (27) (or (30)) sequentially:

- First, we solve LMIs (25) and (26) in the variables Q, M_i and ε_i,
- Once gains K_i have been calculated from (29a), conditions (28) become linear in P and N_i can be easily resolved using the LMI tool to determine gains L_i from (29b).

5. FTC strategy

It is important to be able to carry out fault detection and isolation before faults have a drastic effect on the system performance. Even in case of system changes, faults should be detected and isolated. Observer based estimator schemes are used to generate residual signals corresponding to the difference between measured and estimated variables (Chen and

Patton, 1999). The residual signals are processed using either deterministic (e.g. using fixed or variable thresholds) (Ding, Schneider, Ding and Rehm, 2005) or stochastic techniques (based upon decision theory) (Chen and Liu, 2000). Here, the first one is used.

The method that we propose is illustrated in figure 2, where it can be seen that the FDI functional block uses two observers, each one is driven by a single sensor output. The failure is detected first, and then the faulty sensor is identified. After that, the state variables are reconstructed from the output of the healthy sensor. The lateral control system enters the degraded mode that guaranteed stability and an acceptable level of performance.

Figure 2 shows the block diagram of the proposed closed system, $\left(a_y \quad r\right)^T$ is the output vector of the system, where a_y denotes the lateral acceleration and r is the yaw rate about the center of gravity. Two observer based controllers are designed, one based on the observer that uses the measurement of lateral acceleration a_y and the other one based on the observer that uses the measurement of yaw rate r .

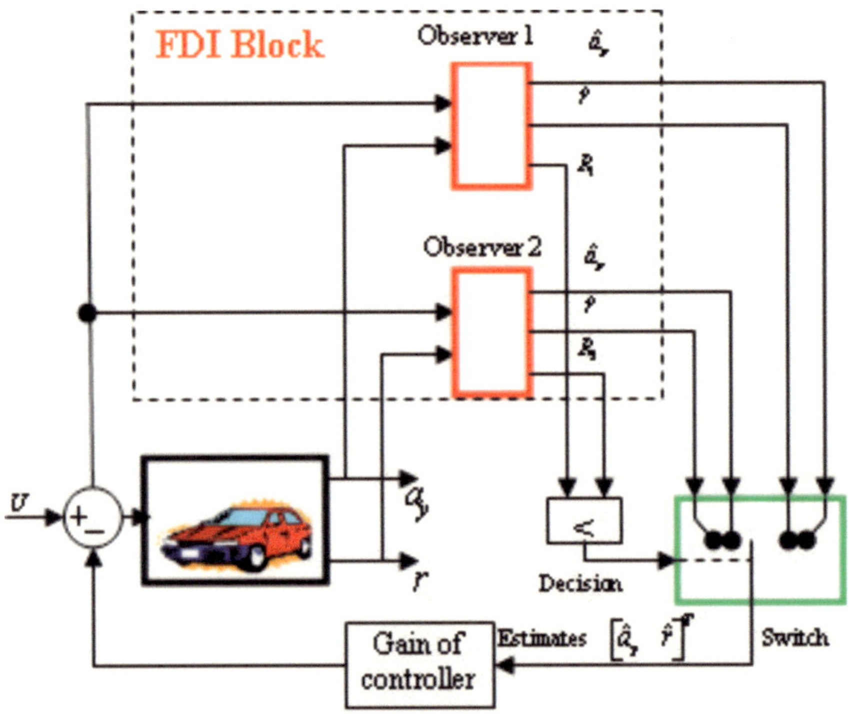

Figure 3. Block diagram of the observer-based FTC

Assumptions

Let $C_i^l(i,l=1,2)$ denote the lth row of matrix C_i (12c.). We assume that $\left(A_i, C_i^l\right)$ are observable, which implies that it is possible to estimate the state through either the first output (a_y) or the second one (r) for the vehicle model (15).

Sensor failures are modeled as additive signals to sensor outputs

$$y = \begin{pmatrix} a_y \\ r \end{pmatrix} = C_i x + D_i \delta_f + Ff \tag{40}$$

where

For failure of sensor 1

$$F = \begin{pmatrix} 1 \\ 0 \end{pmatrix} \tag{41}$$

For failure of sensor 2

$$F = \begin{pmatrix} 0 \\ 1 \end{pmatrix} \tag{42}$$

We also assume that at any time one sensor only fails at the most. This assumption has been implied by the two possible values of F .

Observer-based FDI design

If each $\left(A_i, C_i^l\right) i,l = 1,2$ is observable, then it is possible to construct a TS fuzzy observer for the TS fuzzy model of the vehicle as described in section III.

For observer 1, the state is estimated from the output of the first sensor (a_y). It is given as:

$$\begin{aligned} \dot{\hat{x}}_1(t) &= \sum_{i=1}^{2} \mu_i(|\alpha_f|)\left(A_i \hat{x}_1 + B_{fi}\delta_f + B_i M_z + G_i^1\left(a_y - \hat{a}_{y1}\right)\right) \\ \hat{a}_{y1} &= \sum_{i=1}^{2} \mu_i(|\alpha_f|)\left(C_i^1 \hat{x}_1 + D_i^1 \delta_f\right) \end{aligned} \tag{43}$$

For observer 2, the state is estimated from the output of the second sensor (r). It is given as:

$$\begin{aligned} \dot{\hat{x}}_2 &= \sum_{i=1}^{2} \mu_i(|\alpha_f|)\left(A_i \hat{x}_2 + B_{fi}\delta_f + B_i M_z + G_i^2\left(r - \hat{r}_2\right)\right) \\ \hat{r}_2 &= \sum_{i=1}^{2} \mu_i(|\alpha_f|)\left(C_i^2 \hat{x}_2 + D_i^2 \delta_f\right) \end{aligned} \tag{44}$$

where C_i^l and D_i^l are the lth rows of matrices C_i and D_i (equations 10) respectively and $G_i^l(i,l = 1,2)$ are the constant observer gains to be determined. $\hat{x}_i$, $\hat{a}_{yi}$ and $\hat{r}_i$ are respectively the state estimation, the lateral acceleration estimation and yaw rate estimation with observer i.

The TS fuzzy controller is represented as follows

$$M_z(t) = -\sum_{i=1}^{2} \mu_i(|\alpha_f|) K_i \hat{x}_l(t) \tag{45}$$

with
$l = 1$ If sensor 2 fails
$l = 2$ If sensor 1 fails

We define the residual signals as

$$R_{1,\,ay} = \hat{a}_{y1} - a_y \;\; R_{2,\,ay} = \hat{a}_{y2} - a_y \tag{46}$$

$$R_{1,\,r} = \hat{r}_1 - r \;\; R_{2,\,r} = \hat{r}_2 - r \tag{47}$$

Note that $R_{1,\,ay}$ and $R_{1,\,\mathrm{r}}$ are related to observer 1 and $R_{2,\,ay}$ and $R_{2,\,\mathrm{r}}$ are related to observer 2 with

$$\begin{pmatrix} \hat{a}_{y1} \\ \hat{r}_1 \end{pmatrix} = \sum_{i=1}^{2} h_i(|\alpha_f|)\left(C_i \hat{x}_1 + D_i \delta_f\right) \tag{48}$$

$$\begin{pmatrix} \hat{a}_{y2} \\ \hat{r}_2 \end{pmatrix} = \sum_{i=1}^{2} h_i(|\alpha_f|)\left(C_i \hat{x}_2 + D_i \delta_f\right) \tag{49}$$

The FDI scheme developed in this study follows a classical strategy such as the well-established observer based FDI methods (Isermann, 2001; Huang and Tomizuka, 2005; Oudghiri, Chadli and El Hajjaji, 2007). The residual signals $R_{1,ay}, R_{1,r}, R_{2,ay}, R_{2,r}$ are used for the estimation of the model uncertainties and then, for the construction of model uncertainty indicators. The decision bloc is based on the analysis of these residual signals. Indeed faults are detected and then switching operates according to the following scheme:

Detection: *if* $\max\left(\left\|\mathrm{R}_{1,\mathrm{ay}}, \mathrm{R}_{1,\mathrm{r}}\right\|, \left\|\mathrm{R}_{2,\mathrm{ay}}, \mathrm{R}_{2,\mathrm{r}}\right\|\right) > T_h$ *then* the fault has occurred where T_h the prescribed threshold is and $\|\,.\,\|$ denotes the Euclidian norm at each time instant.

Switching: *if* $\left\|\mathrm{R}_{1,\mathrm{ay}}, \mathrm{R}_{1,\mathrm{r}}\right\| > \left\|\mathrm{R}_{2,\mathrm{ay}}, \mathrm{R}_{2,\mathrm{r}}\right\|$ *then* switch to observer 2. *If not* switch to observer 1.

Since model uncertainties and sensor noise also contribute to nonzero residual signals under the normal operation, threshold T_h must be large enough to avoid false alarms while small enough to avoid missed alarms. In this paper, we do not further discuss the selection of the thresholds.

Simulation results

To show the effectiveness of the proposed FTC based on bank of observer algorithm, we have carried out some simulations using the vehicle model (1) and MATLAB software. In the design, the vehicle parameters considered are given in table 1. To take account of uncertainties, stiffness coefficients C_{fi} and C_{ri} are supposed to be varying depending on road adhesion.

Parameters	I_z Kg.m²	m kg	a_f m	a_r m	U m/s	Nominal stiffness Coefficients (N/rad)			
						C_{f10}	C_{f20}	C_{r10}	C_{r20}
Values	3214	1740	1.04	1.76	20	60712	4812	60088	3455

Table 1.

with the following uncertainties

$$D_1 = D_2 = \begin{pmatrix} 0.4 & 0 \\ 0 & 0.4 \end{pmatrix} \tag{50}$$

We point out that only the yaw rate is directly measurable by a yaw rate sensor (gyroscope), the lateral velocity is unavailable and is estimated using the proposed observer.

By solving the derived stability conditions of theorem 1, the designed controller and observer gains are:

$$K_1 = 10^5\left(\text{-}1.1914 \quad 1.1616\right), K_2 = 10^5\left(\text{-}1.2623 \quad 1.3102\right) \tag{51}$$

$$G_1^1 = \left(\text{-}35.9102 \ \ 6.2245\right)^T, G_2^1 = \left(\text{-}223.2973 \ \ 43.8026\right)^T \tag{52}$$

$$G_1^2 = \left(\text{-}50.7356 \ \ 5.7456\right)^T, G_2^2 = \left(\text{-}28.2271 \ \ 3.0782\right)^T \tag{53}$$

Figure 4 shows the additive signals that represent sensor failures. The first one has been added to sensor 1 output between 2s and 8s, and the second one has been added to sensor 2 output between 10s and 16s.

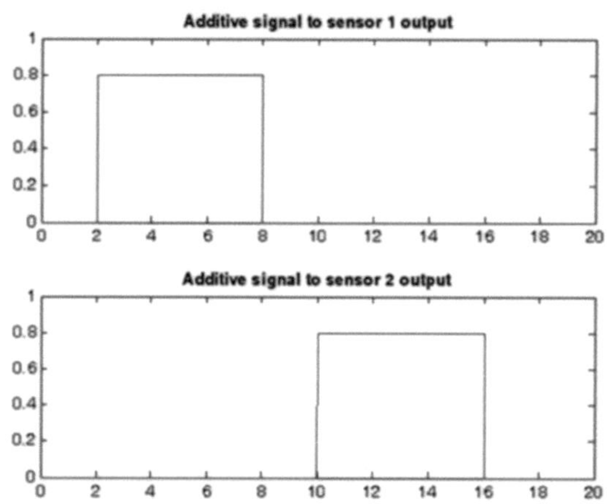

Figure 4. Failure of sensors

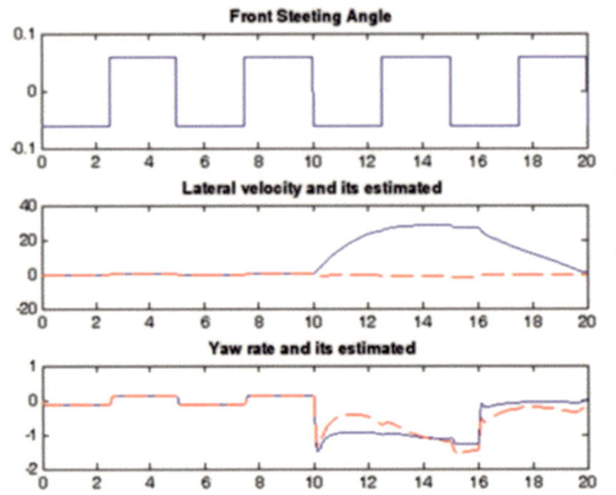

Figure 5. Vehicle sates without FTC strategy

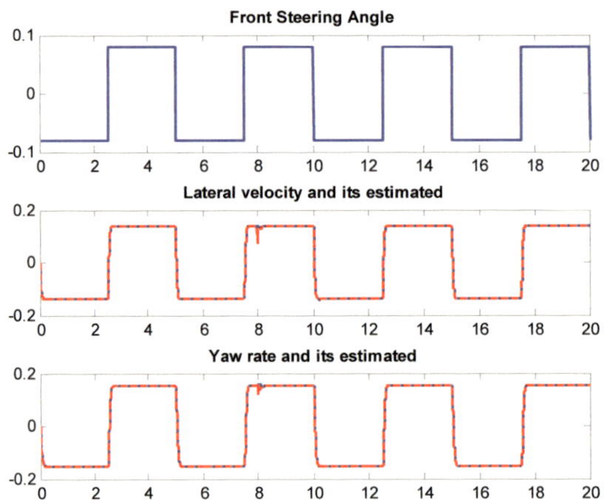

Figure 6. Vehicle sates with FTC strategy

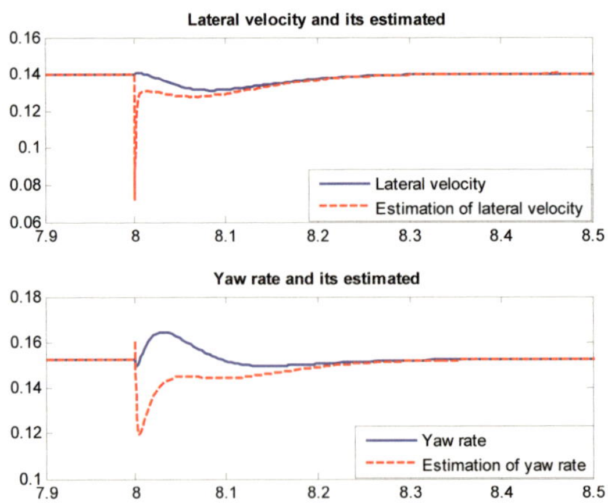

Figure 7. Zooms in of figure 5 at t ≈ 8s

All the simulations are realized on the nonlinear model given in (1) with vehicle speed 20 m/s. The simulation results are given in figures 5 and 6 with and without the FTC strategy. In figure 5 the law control is based on one observer (observer 2) without using the switching bloc. We can see between 10s and 16s that the vehicle lost its performance just after the yaw rate sensor became faulty.

Figure 6 shows vehicle state variables and their estimated signals, when the law control is based on the bank of two observers with the switch bloc. We can note that the vehicle remains stable despite the presence of faults, which shows the effectiveness of the proposed FTC strategy.

The switching from observer 1 to observer 2 is visualized clearly at t ≈ 8s (figure 7). We notice that switching observers is carried out without loss of control of the system state.

The second simulations are realized to show the importance of the proposed FTC method based on an output fuzzy controller, on the stability of the vehicle dynamics. Simulations propose to show the difference between the vehicle dynamics behaviour with TS fuzzy yaw control based on a fuzzy observer (figure 6) and its behaviour with the linear yaw control based on a linear observer (figure 8). Figure 8 clearly shows that the linear control fails to maintain the stability of the vehicle in presence of sensor faults despite a short magnitude of the additive signal ($f = 0.1$) and also a very low front steering angle $\delta_f = 0.001$. Indeed, we can see that by using the proposed fuzzy yaw control based on a fuzzy observer and the algorithm proposed for detection sensors faults, the results are better than these with linear control.

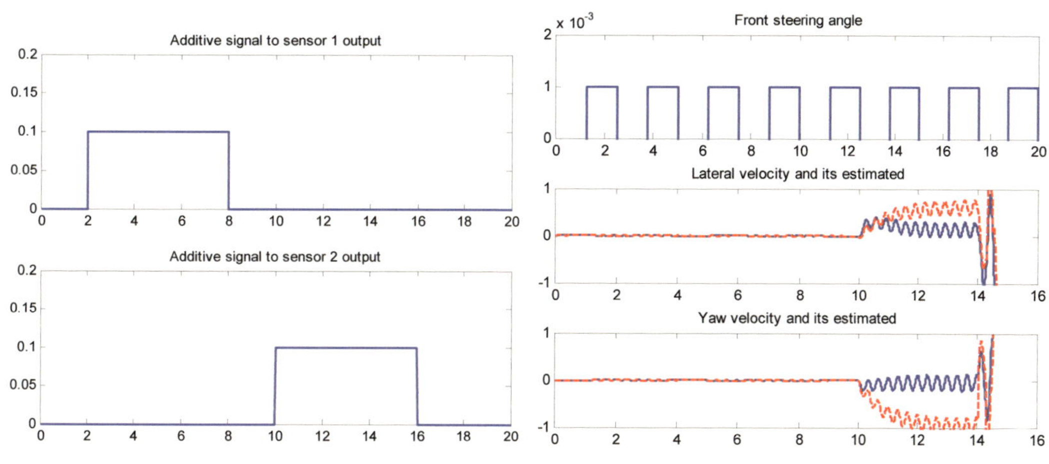

Figure 8. a. Additive signals to sensors output. b. Vehicle states without sensor faults using linear control with road friction coefficient fixed at 0.5

6. Conclusion

Using an algorithm based on a bank of two observers, a fault tolerant control has been presented. The vehicle nonlinear model is first represented by an uncertain Takagi-Sugeno fuzzy model. Then, a robust output feedback controller is designed using LMI terms. Based on the designed robust observer-based controller, a fault tolerant control method is utilized. This method uses a technique based on the switching principle, allowing not only to detect sensor failures but also to adapt the control law in order to compensate the effect of the faults by maintaining the stability of the vehicle and the nominal performances. Simulation results show that the proposed FTC strategy based on robust output TS fuzzy controller are better than these with linear control in spite of a short magnitude of the additive signal and very low front steering angle.

Author details

M. Chadli and A. El Hajjaji
Laboratoire de Modélisation, Information et Système (M.I.S), Amiens, France

7. References

Ahmed-Zaid, F., P. Ioannou, K. Gousman and R. Rooney (1991). Accommodation of failures in the F-16 aircraft using adaptive control. IEEE Control Systems Magazine 11(1), 73–78.

Bauer, H. (1999) 'ESP Electronic Stability Program', Robert Bosch GmgH, Stuttgart.

Blanke, M, Kinnaert, M, Lunze, J. and Staroswiecki, M. (2003) 'Diagnosis and Fault tolerant Control', Springer.

Boyd, S and al. (1994) 'Linear matrix inequalities in systems and control theory', Philadelphia, PA: SIAM.

Bodson, M. and J. E. Groszkiewicz (1997). Multivariable adaptive algorithms for reconfigurable flight control. IEEE Trans. Control Systems Technology 5(2), 217–229.

Chadli, M., Maquin, D and Ragot, J. (2005) 'Stability analysis and design for continuous-time Takagi-Sugeno control systems', International Journal of Fuzzy Systems, Vol. 7, No. 3.

Chadli, M. and El Hajjaji, A. (2006) 'Observer-based robust fuzzy control of nonlinear systems with parametric uncertainties-comment on', Fuzzy Sets and Systems Journal, Vol. 157(9), pp. 1276-1281.

Chadli, M., El hajjaji, A and Oudghiri, M. (2008) 'Robust Output Fuzzy Control for Vehicle Lateral Dynamic Stability Improvement', International Journal of Modelling, Identification and Control. Vol. 3, No. 3, in press.

Chadli, M. and M. Darouach. "Robust admissibility of uncertain switched singular systems". International Journal of Control, Vol. 84, No 10, pp. 1587-1600, 2011.

Chadli, M. and T-M. Guerra. "LMI Solution for Robust Static Output Feedback Control of Takagi-Sugeno Fuzzy Models". IEEE Trans. on Fuzzy Systems. Accepted, 2012.

Campo, P. J. and M. Morari (1994). Achievable closed-loop properties of systems under decentralized control: Conditions involving the steady-state gain. IEEE Trans. Automatic Control 39(5), 932–943.

Chen, R and Liu, J.S. (2000) 'Mixture Kalman Filters', Journal of the Royal Statistical Society (B), Vol. 62, pp493-508.

Chen, J and Patton, R.J. (1999) 'Robust Model Based Fault Diagnosis for Dynamic Systems', Kluwer Academic Publishers, ISBN 0-7923-8411-3.

Dahmani, H., M. Chadli, A. Rabhi, A. El Hajjaji. "Road curvature estimation for vehicle lane departure detection using a robust Takagi-Sugeno fuzzy observer". Vehicle System Dynamics, doi:10.1080/00423114.2011.642806. 2012.

Ding, S.X, Schneider, S, Ding, E.L and Rehm, A. (2005) 'Advanced model-based diagnosis of sensor faults in vehicle dynamics control systems', IFAC, 16th Triennial World Congress, Prague, Czech Republic.

Ding, S.X, Schneider, S, Ding, E.L and Rehm, A. (2005) 'Fault tolerant monitoring of vehicle lateral dynamics stabilizaton systems', Proc. of the 44th IEEE Conference on Decision and Control and European Control Conference ECC'05, Sevilla, Spain, 12.-15.12.

Fujita, M and E. Shimermura (1988). Integrity against arbitrary feedback-loop failure in linear multivariable control systems. Automatica 24(6), 765–772.

Gertler, J.J. (1998) 'Fault Detection and Diagnosis in Engineering Systems', Marcel Dekker Inc.

Guerra T.M., H. Kerkeni, J. Lauber, L. Vermeiren, "An e_cient Lyapunov functionfor discrete TS models : observer design", IEEE Trans. on Fuzzy Systems, 2011.

Huang, J and Tomizuka, M. (2005) 'LTV Controller Design for vehicle lateral control under fault in rear sensors', IEEE/ASME Trans. On Mechatronics, Vol 10, No 1, pp. 1-7.

Isermann, R. (2001) 'Diagnosis methods for electronic controlled vehicles' Vehicle System Dynamics, Vol. 36, No. 2-3, pp. 77–117.

Jiang, J. (1994). Design of reconfigurable control systems using eigenstructure assignments. International Journal of Control 59(2), 395–410.

Kiencke, U and Nielsen, L. (2000) 'Automotive Control Systems', Springer-Verlag.

Lee, C, Lai, W and Lin, Y. (2003) 'A TSK Type Fuzzy neural network systems for dynamic systems identification', In Proceedings of the IEEE-CDC, pp. 4002-4007 Hawaii –USA..

Lin. M, popov, A.A and Mcwilliam, S. (2004) 'Stability and performance studies of driver-vehicle systems with electronic chassis control', Vehicle system dynamics, Vol 41(2), pp.477-486.

Lunze .J, and J. Richter (2006) 'Control Reconfiguration: Surveyof Methods and Open Problems', Bericht Nr. 2006.08, Ruhr-Universität Bochum.

Oudghiri, M, Chadli, M and El Hajjaji, A. (2007) 'Observer-based fault tolerant control for vehicle lateral dynamics', European Control Conference ECC07, Kos, Greece 2-5 July.

Oudghiri, M, Chadli, M and El Hajjaji, A. (2007b) 'Vehicle yaw control using a robust H∞ observer-based fuzzy controller design', 46th IEEE Conference on Decision and Control, New Orleans, LA, USA. December 12-14.

Oudghiri, M, Chadli, M and El Hajjaji, A. (2008) 'Sensors Active Fault Tolerant Control For Vehicle Via Bank of Robust H∞Observers', 17th International Federation of Automatic Control (IFAC) World Congress, Seoul, Korea.

Patton, R. J. (1997). Fault-tolerant control: the 1997 situation. In: Preprints of IFAC Symposium on Fault Detection Supervision and Safety for Technical Processes (R. Patton and J. Chen, Eds.). SAFEPROCESS'97. Kingston upon Hull. pp. 1033–1055.

Rauch, H. E. (1994). Intelligent fault diagnosis and control reconfiguration. IEEE Control Systems Magazine pp. 6–12.

Segel, L. (1956) 'Theoretical Prediction and Experimental Substantiation of the Response of the Automobile to Steering Control', Automobile Division, The Institute of Mechanical Engineers, pp. 26-46.

Stengel, R. F. (1991). Intelligent failure-tolerant control. IEEE Control Systems Magazine pp. 14–23.

Tanaka, K and Wang, O. (1998) 'Fuzzy Regulators and Fuzzy observers: A linear Matrix Inequality Approach', Proceeding of 36 th IEEE CDC, pp. 1315-1320.

Takagi, M and Sugeno M. (1985) 'Fuzzy identification of systems and its application to moddeling and control', IEEE Trans. on Systems Man and Cybernetics-part C, Vol. 15, No. 1, pp. 116-132.

Xioodong and L, Qingling, Z. (2003) 'New approaches to H∞ controller designs based on fuzzy observers for T-S fuzzy systems via LMI', Automatica Vol 39, pp.1571-1582.

Zhang, Y. and J. Jiang (2003). Bibliographical review on reconfigurable fault-tolerant control systems. In: Proceedings of the SAFEPROCESS 2003: 5th Symposium on Fault Detection and Safety for Technical Processes. number M2-C1. IFAC. Washington D.C., USA. pp. 265–276.

Chapter 12

Wheelchair and Virtual Environment Trainer by Intelligent Control

Pedro Ponce, Arturo Molina and Rafael Mendoza

Additional information is available at the end of the chapter

http://dx.doi.org/10.5772/48410

1. Introduction

There are many kinds of diseases and injuries that produce mobility problems. The people affected with any disability must deal with a new lifestyle, specifically people with tetraplegia. According to ICF [1], people with tetraplegia have damages associated to the power of muscles of all limbs, tone of muscles of all limbs, resistance of all muscles of the body and endurance of all muscles of the body. The main objective of this project was to help disabled people to move any member of their body, although this wheelchair can be used for persons with mobility problems, doctors should not recommend it to all patients because it reduces muscle movement, which could lead to muscular dystrophy.

Currently, there is not an efficient system that covers the different needs that a person with quadriplegia could have. Their mobility is reduced by physical injury and, depending on the extent of the damage nursing and family assistance is required. Even though many platforms have been developed to address this problem, there is not an integrated system that allows the patient to move autonomously from one place to another, thus limiting the patient to remain at rest all the time. In previous research projects completed in Canada and in the United States, such as wheelchairs controlled with the tongue [2] and a wheelchair controlled with head and shoulder movements [3]. Those systems provide mobility for the person with any injury in functions related to muscle strength. This work offers a different alternative for the patient and aims to build an autonomous wheelchair that can afford enough motion capacity to transport a person with quadriplegia. Different kinds of controls are provided, so the trajectories required by the patient must be controlled using ocular movements or voice commands, among others.

An existing brand of electric wheelchair was used (the commercial Quickie wheelchair model P222 [4] with a Qtronix controller).

2. Eye movement control system

2.1. General description

The eye control is based on the magnetic dipole generated by the eye movement; therefore a voltage signal is produced allowing us to sense these voltages using clinical electrodes. Those signals, microvolts, come with noise. A biomedical differential amplifier was used to sense the desired signal in the first electronic stage and simple amplification in the second stage. The signals are digitalized and acquired into the computer in the range of volts via data acquisition hardware for further manipulation. Once the signal is filtered and normalized, the main program based on artificial neural networks learns the signals for each eye movement. This allows us to classify the signal, so it can be compared against the next signals acquired. In this manner, the system could detect which kind of movement was made and assign a direction command to the wheelchair.

2.2. Physiological facts

There is a magnetic dipole starting between the retina and cornea that generates differences of voltage around the eye. This voltage ranges from 15 to 200 microvolts depending on the person. The voltage signals also contain noise with the fundamental of a base frequency between 3 and 6 hertz. This voltage can be plotted over time to obtain an electro-oculogram (EOG) [7] which describes the eye movement. Fig. 1 shows a person with the electrodes.

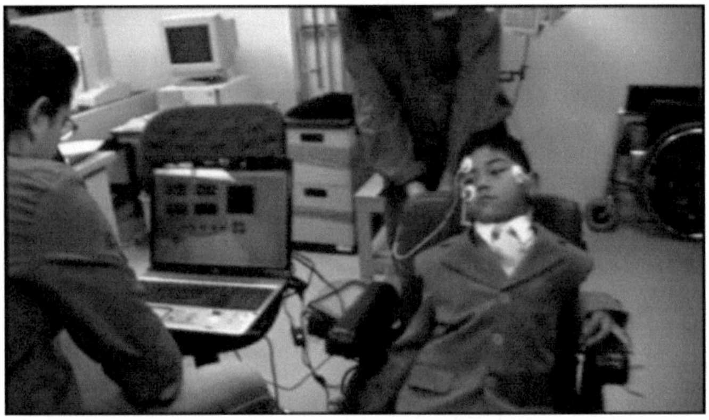

Figure 1. Patient using the EOG and training the signal recognition system.

Prior to digitalizing the signals, an analogical stage of amplifiers, divided in two basic parts, was used. The first p is a differential amplifier AD620 for biomedical applications, a gain of 1000x was calculated using the equation (1):

$$R_G = \frac{49.4k\Omega}{G-1} \tag{1}$$

Where G is the gain of the component and R_G is the resistance. The digitalization of the amplified signal is carried out with the National Instruments DAQ [8] data acquisition hardware.

2.3. EOG LabVIEW Code

This section will present an overview of the program implemented for the EOG Signal acquisition and filtering stages. Fig. 2 shows three icons, the first one (data) represents a local variable which receives the values from the LabVIEW utility used to connect the computer to a DAQ. The second icon represents the filter which is configured as written in part B. The third icon is an output that will display a chart in the front panel in which the user can see the filtered signal in real time.

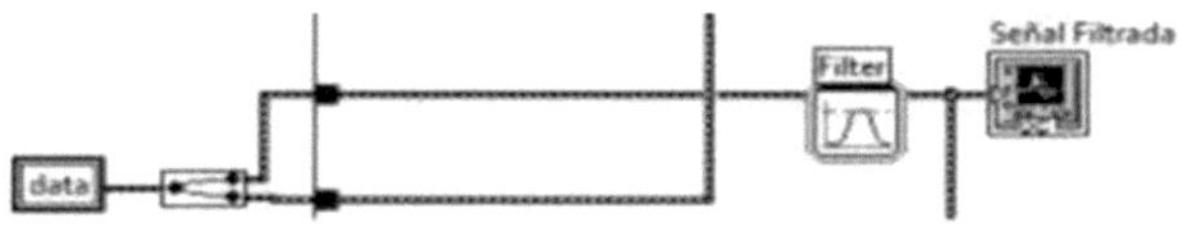

Figure 2. Signal filter

After the signal was filtered, it was to be divided into frames with 400 samples each. This stage is very important because the signals are not all the same length, thus by using the framing process all the signals will have the same length.

Once the length of our data arrays was normalized, the amplitude of the signal had to be normalized as well. After all the aforementioned stages, there will be six normalized arrays, which are then connected to their Neural Network, as shown in Figure 3.

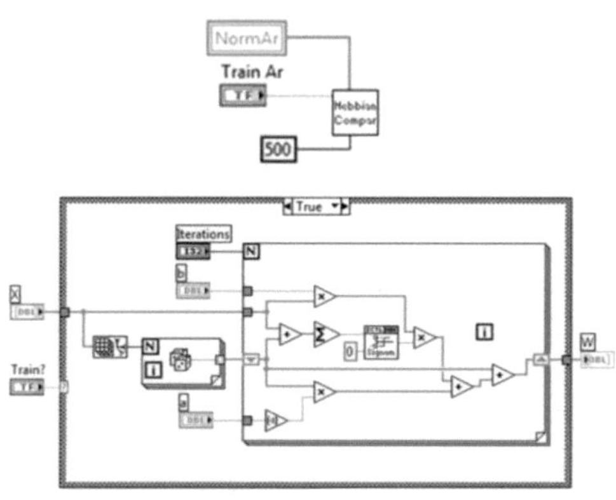

Figure 3. Training System LabVIEW Code

In Figure 3, it can be seen that this section will receive the variables and give the calculated error. In the case of the recognition signals where two different kinds of neural networks, trigonometric neural networks and Hebbian neural networks were tested, both of them gave good results. Figure 3 shows the configuration for the Hebbian Learning. The diagram of the configuration of this kind of network is shown inside the block diagram of Figure 3.

This network will take the point from the incoming signal and will make an approximation of this value and save it into W. If train is false the network will only return the values already saved in W; by doing this "Hebbian Comparison" will calculate the error between the incoming signal and W.

The Front Panel on LabVIEW shown in Figure 4 is the screen that the user will see when training the wheelchair. On the upper half of the screen are all the charts of the EOG (Figure 5) and the upper two charts refer to the filtered signals of both the vertical and the horizontal channels. The lower two charts refer to the length normalized signals. The right-hand chart will show the detected signal. On the lower half of the screen (Figure 6), the user will see all the controls needed to train the system. A main training button will activate and set all the systems in training mode. Then the user will select which signal will be trained. Doing so will open the connection to let only that signal through for its training. Once recognized, the signal will appear in the biggest chart and the user will push the corresponding switch to train the Neural Network. When the user has trained all the movements, the program needs to be set in comparison mode, for this case the user must deactivate the principal training button and put the selector on Blink (Parpadeo). Then the system is ready to receive signals. To avoid problems with natural eye movements, the chair was programmed to be commanded with codes. To get the program into motion mode the user must blink twice, which is why the selector was put on Parpadeo, so that the first signals that go through the system could only be Blink signals. After the system recognizes two Blink signals the chair is ready to receive any other signal. By looking up the chair will move forward, looking left or right will make the chair turn accordingly. The system will stay in motion mode until the user looks down; this command will stop the chair and reset the program to wait for the two blinks. Embedding this code into a higher level of the program will allow the EOG system to communicate with thecontrol program that will receive the Boolean variables for each eye movement direction. Depending on the Boolean variable received on true, the control program will command the chair to move in that direction.

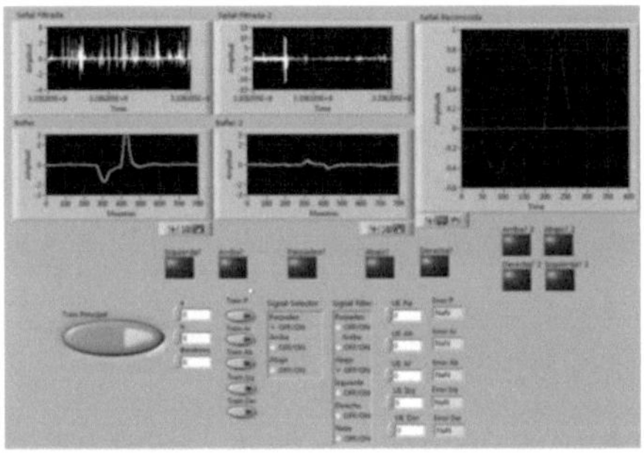

Figure 4. Figure 4. Frontal panel for training signal

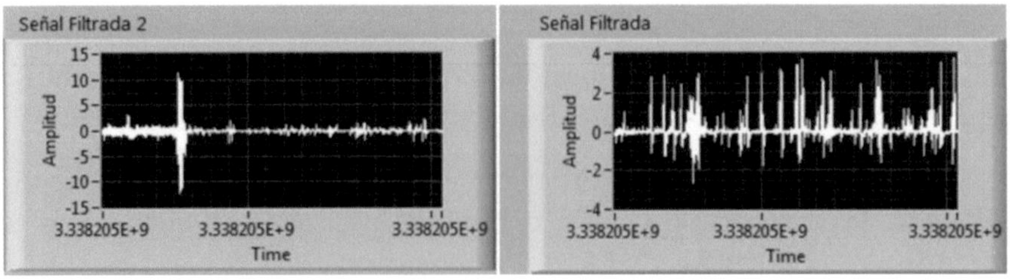

Figure 5. Filtered signal for vertical and horizontal channels

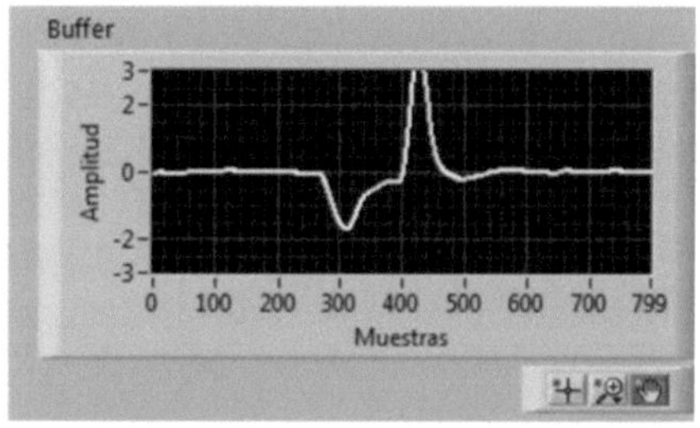

Figure 6. Eye movement

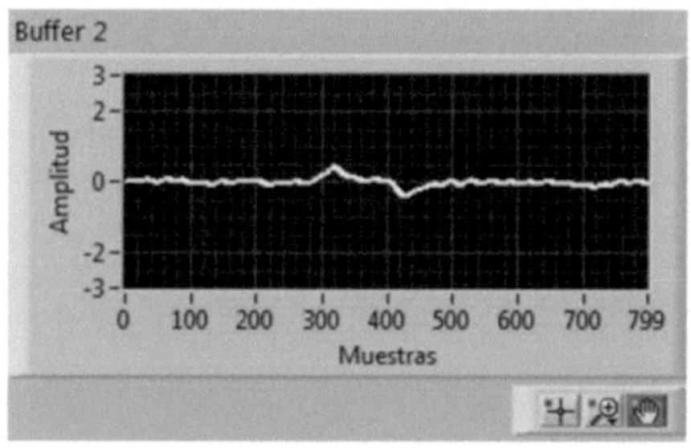

Figure 7. Analog received input from eye movements

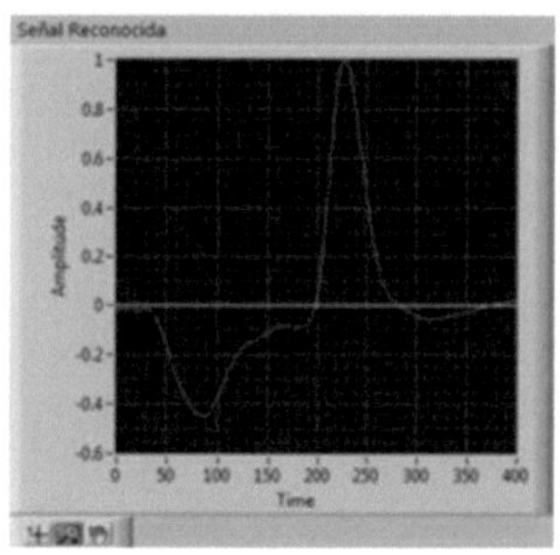

Figure 8. Signal generated when the eye moves up

3. Voice control

The wheelchair in this study is intended to be used by quadriplegic patients; it was programmed to add a voice message system to the chair. This system, will also allow the user to send pre-recorded voice messages by means of the EOG system, as another way to assist the patient. Figure 9 shows the main LabVIEW code.

3.1. EOG and voice message system coupling

In this section of the project, all the EOG system and programming remained the same as in the previous direction control system. But instead of coupling the EOG system to the motor control program, it was coupled it to a very simple program that allows the computer to play pre-recorded messages, such as: I am hungry, I am tired, etc. The messages can be recorded to meet the patients' needs to aid them in their communication with their environment. The EOG program will return a Boolean variable which will then select the message corresponding to the eye movement chosen by the user. The selection will search for the path of the saved pre-recorded message and will then play it.

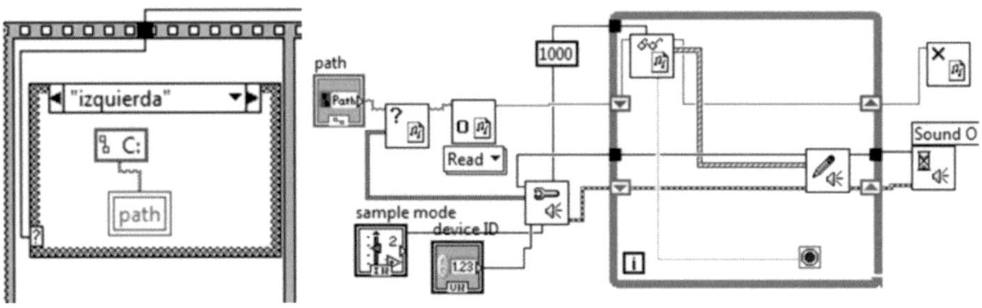

(a) (b)

Figure 9. a.Shows the activated Boolean received into a case structure that selects the path used for opening each file. Figure 9.b.Sound playback.

The second stage shown on Figure.9.b of the structure works by opening a *.wav file, checking for errors and preparing the file to be reproduced, a while structure is used to play the message until the end of the file is reached, then the file is closed and the sequence is over.

3.2. Voice commands

For patients with less severe motion problems, it was decided to implement a Voice Command system. This allows the user to tell the chair in which direction they want to move.

3.3. Basic program

For this section two separate programs were used, Windows Speech Recognition and Speech Test 8.5 by Leo Cordaro (NI DOC-4477). The Speech Test program allows us to modify the phrases that Windows Speech Recognition will recognize. By doing so and coupling Speech Test to our control system, it is possible to control the chair with voice commands.

The input phrases can be modified by accessing the Speech Test 8.5 Vi. By selecting speech (selection box) the connection between both programs can be activated. Then Speech Test 8.5 will receive the variable from Speech Recognition and by connecting it to our control system it is possible to receive the same variable and control the chair.

At first, the user must train the Windows Speech Recognition. This is strongly recommended, because although it can differentiate different people's voices, the system fails continuously if many people use the same trained configuration. On the other hand, the different tests that were performed in a closed space without any source of noise were 100% satisfactory.

This system runs in the same way as the EOG, by saying to the chair *derecho*, the chair will start moving. Saying the words *derecha* or *izquierda* will turn the chair right or left and by saying *atrás* the chair will stop. The Boolean variable is received into our control system the same way as in the EOG.

4. Electric wheelchair navigation system

After the user sends the reference command by voice or eye movement, the electric wheelchair uses fuzzy logic and neural networks for taking over the complete electric wheelchair navigation system.

For transferring the vague fuzzy form of human reasoning to mathematical systems a fuzzy logic system is applied.

The use of IF-THEN rules in fuzzy systems gives us the possibility to easily understand the information modeled by the system. In most of the fuzzy systems the knowledge is obtained from human experts.

Artificial neural networks can learn from experience, but most of the topologies do not allow us to understand the information learnt by the networks. ANN's are incorporated into fuzzy systems to form Neuro-Fuzzy systems which can acquire knowledge automatically by learning algorithms of neural networks. Neuro-Fuzzy systems have the advantage over Fuzzy systems that the acquired knowledge is easy to understand -more meaningful- to humans. Another technique used with Neuro-Fuzzy systems is clustering, which is usually employed to initialize unknown parameters such as the number of fuzzy rules or the number of membership functions for the premise part of the rules. They are also used to create dynamic systems and update the parameters of the system.

4.1. The neuro-fuzzy controller

The position of the wheelchair is taking over by the Neuro- Fuzzy controller, thus it will avoid crashing against static and dynamic obstacles.

The controller takes information from three ultrasonic sensors which measure the distance from the chair to an obstacle located in different positions of the wheelchair, as shown in Figure 10.

The outputs of the Neuro-Fuzzy controller were the voltages sent to a system that generates a PWM to move the electric motors and the directions in which the wheel will turn. The controller is based on trigonometric neural networks and fuzzy cluster means. It follows a Takagi-Sugeno inference method but instead of using polynomials on the defuzzification process it also uses trigonometric neural networks (T-ANNs). The diagram of the neuro-fuzzy controller is shown in Figure 11.

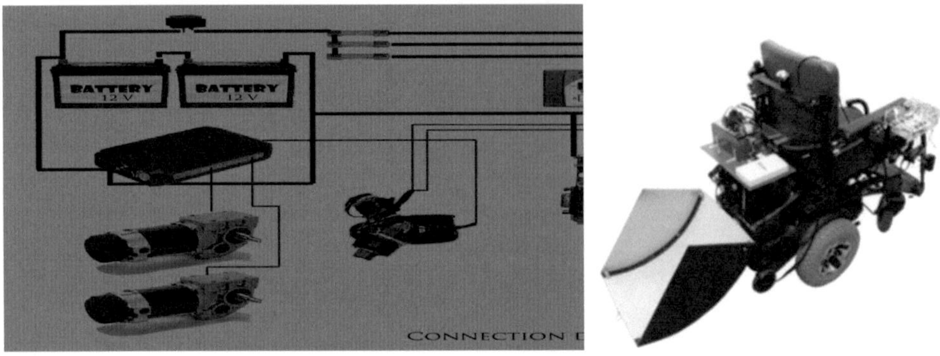

Figure 10. Connection diagram and the electric wheelchair

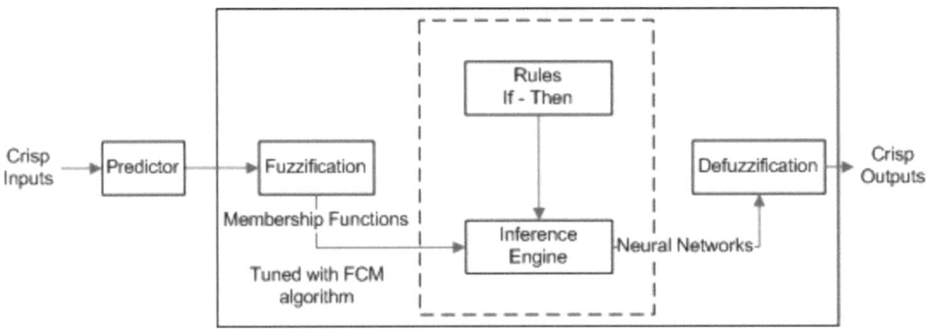

Figure 11. Basic diagram of the Neuro-Fuzzy controller

Theory of Trigonometric Neural Networks

If the function $f(x)$ is periodic and integrable in Lebesgue (continuous and periodic functions (2π) in $[-\pi,\pi]$ or $[0,2\pi]$). It must be written as $f \in C*[-\pi,\pi]$ or just $f \in C*$. The deviation -error- of $f \in C*$ from the Fourier series at the point or from a trigonometric polynomial of order $\leq n$.

$$E_n(f) = \min_{\tau_n} \tag{2}$$

$$\max|f(x) - \tau_n(x)| = \min\|f - \tau_n\|$$

$$0 \leq x \leq 2\pi \tag{3}$$

Using Favard sums of falling in its extreme basic property, give the best approximation for trigonometric polynomials of a class (periodic continuous functions) as follows:

$$\|f'\| = \max_x |f'(x)| \leq 1 \tag{4}$$

Fourier series have been proven to be able to model any periodical signal in [2]. For any given signal $f(x)$ it is said to be periodic if $f(x) = f(x+T)$ where T is the fundamental period of the signal. The signal can be modeled using Fourier series:

$$f(x) \sim \frac{a_0}{2} + \sum_{n=1}^{\infty}\left(a_n \cos(nx) + b_n \sin(nx)\right) = \sum_{n=1}^{\infty} A_k(x) \tag{5}$$

$$a_0 = \frac{1}{T}\int_0^T f(x)dx \tag{6}$$

$$a_n = \frac{1}{T}\int_0^T f(x)\cos(n\omega x)dx \tag{7}$$

$$b_n = \frac{1}{T}\int_0^T f(x)\sin(n\omega x)dx \tag{8}$$

The trigonometric Fourier series consists of the sum of functions multiplied by a coefficient plus a constant, so a neural network can be built based on the previous equations.

The advantages of these neural networks are that the weights of the network can be computed using analytical methods as a linear equation system. The error on the solution decreases when the number of neurons is augmented which corresponds to adding more harmonics according to the Fourier series.

To train the network we need to know the available inputs and outputs. The traditional way to train a network is to assign random values to the weights and then wait for the function to converge using the gradient descendent method. Using this topology the network is trained using the least-squares method fixing a finite number of neurons and arranging the system in a matrix formAx=B. We will use cosines for approximating the function with pair functions and sine in the case of impair functions.

Numerical example of T-ANN's

Figure 12 shows the ICTL and the trigonometric neural networks icons. The trigonometric neural networks inside the ICTL include examples. The front panel and block diagram of the example can be seen in fig. 13. In the block diagram the code is related to training and evaluation of the network. The signals from the eye or voice could be recognized using trigonometric neural networks, as shown in figure 14 in which the example presents a signal approximation.

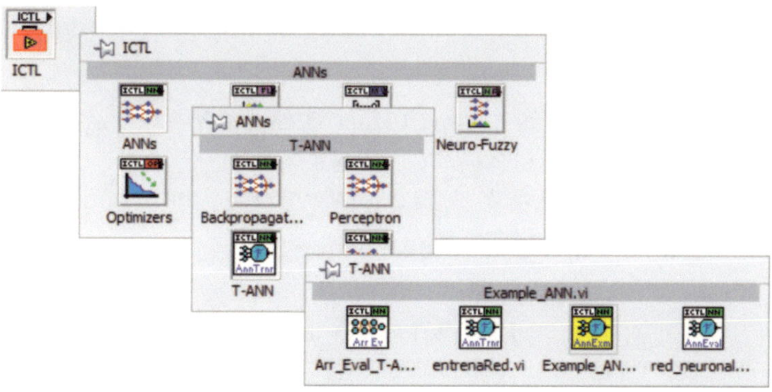

Figure 12. The ICTL showing the Trigonometric Neural Networks icons

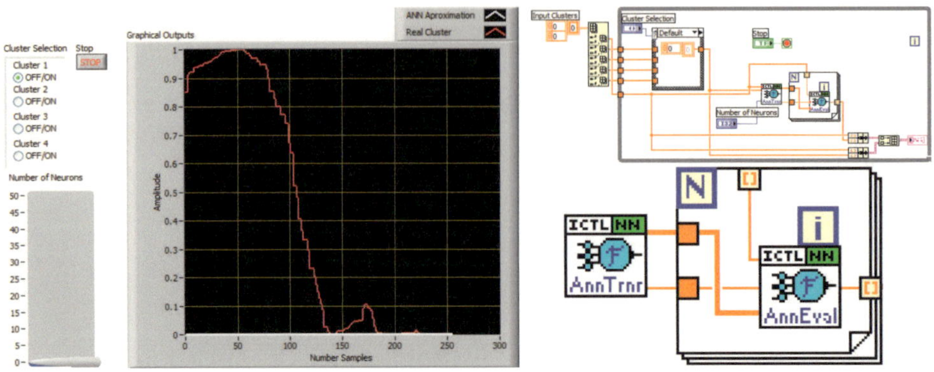

Figure 13. The front panel and block diagram

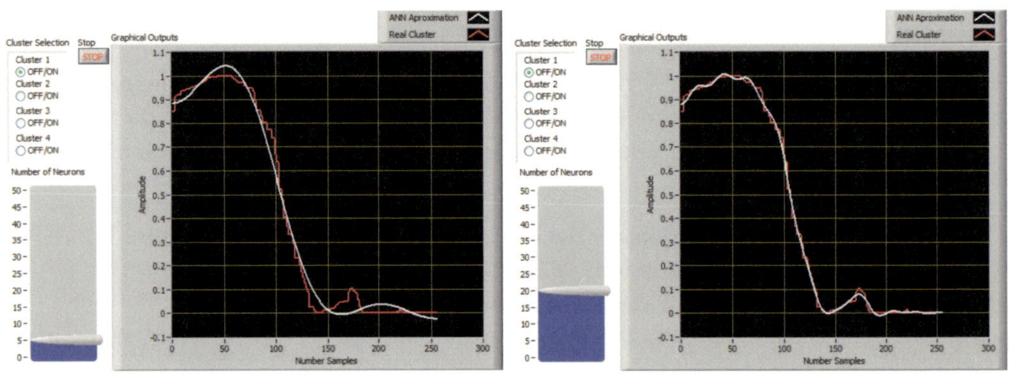

Figure 14. Trigonometric neural network example network using 5 (left) and 20 neurons (right)

Fuzzy Cluster Means

Clustering methods split a set of N elements $X=\{x_1,x_2\ldots,x_n\}$ into a c group denoted $c=\{\mu^1,\mu^2,\ldots\mu^n\}$. Traditional clustering set methods assume that each data vector can belong to one and only one class, though in practice clusters normally overlap, and some data vectors can belong partially to several clusters. Fuzzy set theory provides a natural way to describe this situation by FCM.

The fuzzy partition matrices M, for c classes and N data points were defined by three conditions:$M = \{U \in V_{cN} 1,2,3\}$

- The first condition: $\forall \quad 1 \le i \le c \quad \mu_{ik}[0,1], \quad 1 \le k \le N$
- The second condition: $\sum_{k=1}^{c} \mu_{ik} = 1 \quad \forall \quad 1 \le k \le N$
- The third condition:$\forall \quad 1 \le i \le c \quad 0 < \sum_{k=1}^{c} \mu_{ik} < N$

The FCM optimum criteria function has the following form:

$$J_m(U,V)=\sum_{i=1}^{c}\sum_{k=1}^{N}\mu_{ik}^{m}d_{ik}^{2} \tag{9}$$

Where d_{ik} is an inner product norm defined as:

$$d_{ik}^2 = || x_k - v_i ||_A^2 \tag{10}$$

Where$A$ is a positive definite matrix, m is the weighting exponent $m\epsilon[1,\infty]$.If m and c parameters are fixed and define sets then *(U,V)* may be globally minimal for *Jm(U,V)* only if:

$$\forall \; \begin{matrix} 1 \le i \le c \\ 1 \le k \le N \end{matrix} \quad u_{ik} = \frac{1}{\sum_{j=1}^{c} \left(\frac{|| x_k - v_i ||}{|| x_k - v_j ||} \right)^{\frac{2}{m-1}}} \tag{11}$$

$$\forall \; 1 \le i \le c \quad v_j = \frac{\sum_{k=1}^{N} (u_{ik})^m x_k}{\sum_{k=1}^{N} (u_{ik})^m} \tag{12}$$

FCM Algorithm:

The fuzzy c-means solution can be described as:

1. Fix c and m, set p=0 and initialize $U^{(0)}$
2. Calculate fuzzy centers for each cluster using $V^{(p)}$(12)
3. Update fuzzy partition matrix $U^{(p)}$ for the p-thiteration using (11)
4. If $\|U^p - U^{(p-1)}\| < \epsilon$ then, $j \leftarrow j+1$ and return to the second step

In this algorithm, the parameter m determines the fuzziness of the clusters; if m is large the cluster is fuzzier. For $m \to 1$ FCM the solution becomes the crisp one, and for $m \to \infty$ the solution is as fuzzy as possible. There is no theoretical reference for the selection of m, and usually $m = 2$is chosen. After the shape of the membership functions are fixed, the T-ANN's learn each one of them.

Predictive Method

Sometimes the controller response can be improved by using predictors, which provide future information and allow it to respond in advance. One of the simplest yet most powerful predictors is based on exponential smoothing. A popular approach used is the Holt's method.

Exponential smoothing is computationally simple and fast at the same time, this method can perform well in comparison with other more complex methods. The series used for prediction is considered as a composition of more than one structural component (average and trend) each of which can be individually modeled. We will use series without seasonality in the predictor. This type of series can be expressed as:

$$y(x) = y_{av}(x) + py_{tr}(x) + e(x); p = 0 \tag{13}$$

Where: y(x), $y_{av}(x)$, $y_{tr}(x)$, and $e(x)$ are the data, the average, the trend and the error components individually modeled using exponential smoothing. The p-step ahead of prediction [3] is given by:

$$y * (x + p|k) = y_{av}(x) + py_{tr}(x) \tag{14}$$

The average and the trend components are modeled as:

$$y_{av}(x) = (1-\alpha)y(x) + \alpha\left(y_{av}(x-1) + y_{tr}(k-1)\right) \tag{15}$$

$$y_{tr}(x) = (1-\beta)y_{tr}(x-1) + \beta\left(y_{av}(x) + y_{av}(x-1)\right) \tag{16}$$

Where and are the average and the trend components of the signal. Where $y_{av}(x)$ and $y_{tr}(x)$ are the smoothing coefficients, its values range (0,1). y_{av}andy_{tr} can be initialized as:

$$y_{av}(1) = y(1) \tag{17}$$

$$y_{tr}(1) = \frac{\left(y(1)-y(0)\right)+\left(y(2)-y(1)\right)}{2} \tag{18}$$

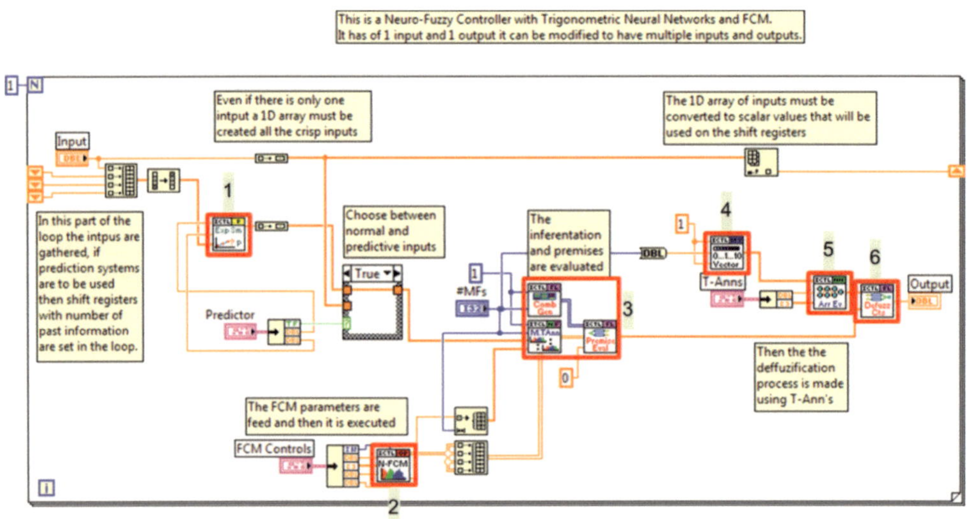

Figure 15. Block diagram of the neuro-fuzzy controller with one input, one output

The execution of the controller depends on several VI's (more information in [4]), which are explained in the following steps:

Step 1. This is a predictor VI based on exponential smoothing; the coefficients alpha and beta must be fed as scalar values. The past and present information must be fed in a 1D array with the newest information in the last element of the array.

Step 2. This VI executes the FCM method; the information of the crisp inputs must be fed as well as the stop conditions for the cycle; the program will return the coefficients of the trigonometric networks, the fundamental frequency and other useful information.

Step 3. These three VI's execute the evaluation of the premises. The first is on the top left generator of the combinations of rules that depends on the number of inputs and membership functions. The second one on the bottom left combines and evaluates the input membership functions. The last one on the right uses the information on the combinations as well as the evaluated membership functions to obtain the premises of the IF-THEN rules.

Step 4. This VI creates a 1D array with the number of rules of the system: where n is the number of rules, it is used on the defuzzification process.

Step 5. This VI evaluates a T-ANN on each of the rules.

Step 6. This VI defuzzifies using the Takagi method with the obtained crisp outputs from the T-ANN.

This version of one input, one output of the controller was modified to have three inputs and four outputs; the block diagram is shown in figure 16.

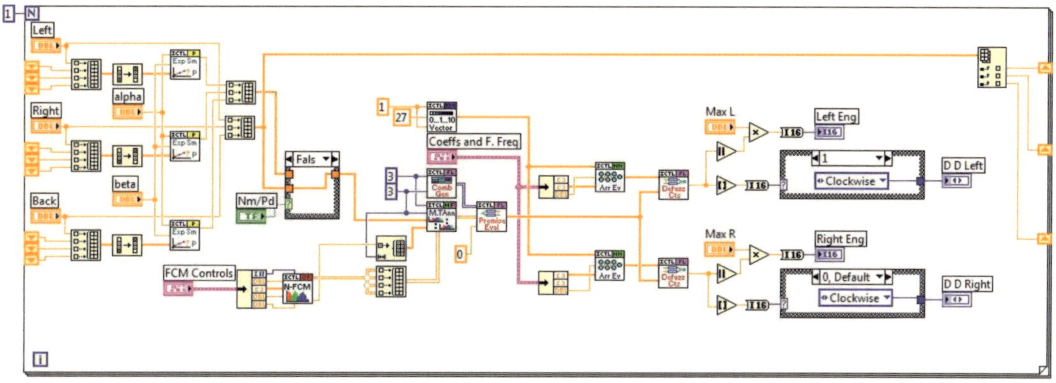

Figure 16. Neuro-Fuzzy controller block diagram

Each input is fuzzified with four membership functions whose form is defined by the FCM algorithm. The crisp distances gathered by the distance sensors are clustered by FCM and then T-ANN's are trained. As can be seen in figure 17, the main shape of the clusters is learnt by the neural networks and no main information is lost.

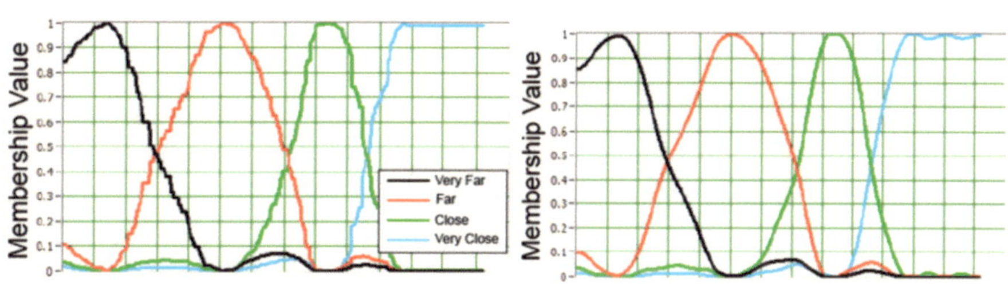

Figure 17. Input membership functions

With three inputs and four membership functions, there is a total of sixty four rules that can be evaluated. These rules are *IF THEN* and have the following form: **IF**x_1 is μ_{in}&x_2 is μ_{in}&x_3 is μ_{in}**THEN***PWM LeftEngine, Direction Left Engine , PWM Right Engine, Direction Right Engine.*

The value of each rule is obtained through the inference method min that consists of evaluating the $\mu_{in's}$ and return the smallest one for each rule. The final system output is obtained by:

$$Output = \frac{\sum_{i=1}^{r}\left[\min\left(\mu_{i1,2,3}\right)NN\left(x_1,x_2,x_3\right)\right]}{\sum_{i=1}^{r}\min\left(\mu_{i1,2,3}\right)} \tag{19}$$

For the direction of the wheel, three states are used: clockwise (1), counterclockwise (-1) and stopped (0). The fuzzy output is rounded to the nearest value and the direction is obtained.

5. Results using the controller

The wheelchair was set on a human sized chessboard and the pieces were set in a maze, presented in Figure 18 with some of the trajectories described by the chair.

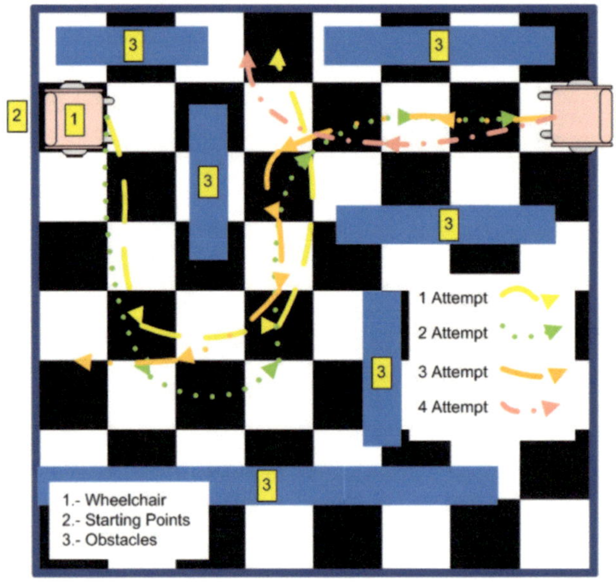

Figure 18. Wheelchair maze and trajectories

The wheelchair always managed to avoid obstacles, but failed to return to the desired direction. It also fails to recognize whether the obstacle is a human being or an object and, thus, have different behaviors to avoid them.

Controller Enhancements

Direction Controller

As can be seen from the previous results, the wheelchair will effectively avoid obstacles but the trajectories that it follows are always different, sometimes it may follow the directions we want but other times it will not. A direction controller can solve this problem, so we need a sensor to obtain feedback from the direction of the wheelchair. A compass could be an option to sense the direction, either the 1490 (digital) or 1525 (analog) from images SI [8]. After the electric wheelchair controller avoids an obstacle the compass sensor will give it information to return to the desired direction, as shown in Figure 19.

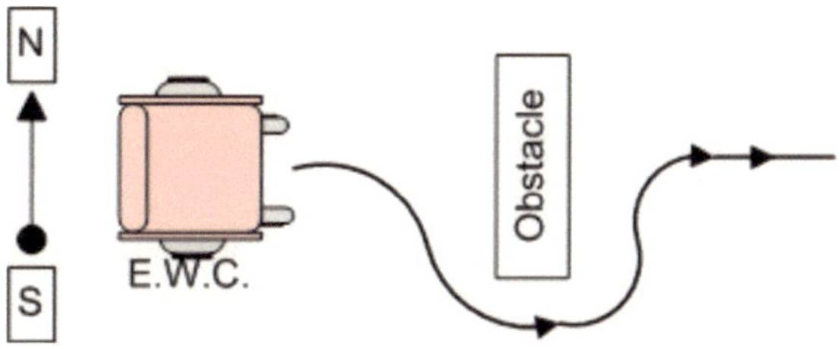

Figure 19. The wheelchair recovering the direction with the Direction Controller.

A fuzzy controller that controls the direction can be used in combination with the obstacle avoidance controller. The directions controller will have as input the difference between the desired and the current direction of the wheelchair. The direction magnitude describes how many degrees the chair will have to turn and the sign indicates if it has to be done in one direction or the other. The output is the PWM and the direction that each wheel has to take in order to compensate.

Three fuzzifiying input membership functions will be used for the degrees and the turning direction, as shown in figure 20. The range for the degrees is [0, 360] degrees and the turning direction is [-180, 180], also in degrees.

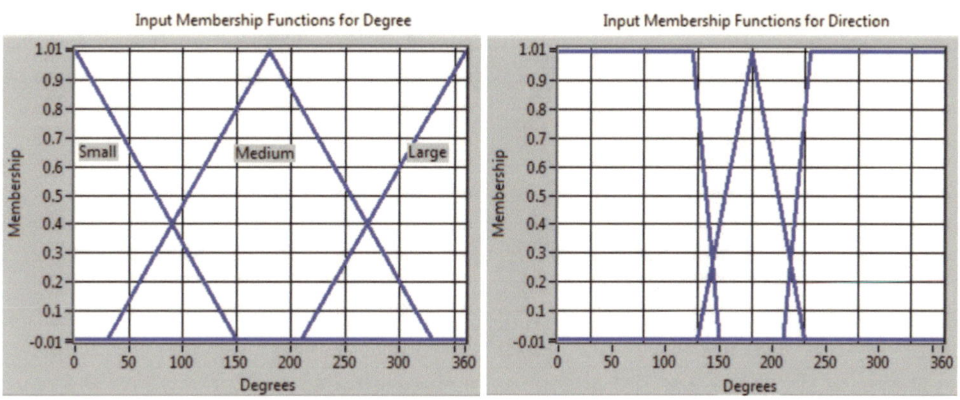

Figure 20. Input membership functions for Degrees and Direction

The form of the rule is the following: **IF** *degree* is A_{in} & direction is B_{in} **THEN** *PWM Left Engine* , *Direction Left Engine* , *PWM Right Engine* , *Direction Right Engine* .

Figure 21 shows the rule base with the nine possible combinations of inputs and outputs. The outputs are obtained with the rule consequences using singletons.

The IF-THEN Rules:

- CCW : Counterclockwise
- CW: Clockwise
- NC: No Change

1. IF Degree is Small & Direction is Left THEN PWMR IS Very Few, PWML IS Very Few, DIRR is CCW, DIRL is CW.

2. IF Degree is Small & Direction is Center THEN PWMR IS Very Few, PWML IS Very Few, DIRR is NC, DIRL is NC.
3. IF Degree is Small & Direction is Right THEN PWMR IS Very Few, PWML IS Very Few, DIRR is CW, DIRL is CCW.
4. IF Degree is Medium & Direction is Left THEN PWMR IS Some, PWML IS Some, DIRR is CCW, DIRL is CW.
5. IF Degree is Medium & Direction is Center THEN PWMR IS Some, PWML IS Some, DIRR is NC, DIRL is NC.
6. IF Degree is Medium & Direction is Right THEN PWMR IS Some, PWML IS Some, DIRR is CW, DIRL is CCW.
7. IF Degree is Large & Direction is Left THEN PWMR IS Very Much, PWML IS Very Much, DIRR is CCW, DIRL is CW.
8. IF Degree is Large & Direction is Center THEN PWMR IS Very Much, PWML IS Very Much, DIRR is NC, DIRL is NC.
9. IF Degree is Large & Direction is Right THEN PWMR IS Very Much, PWML IS Very Much, DIRR is CW, DIRL is CCW.

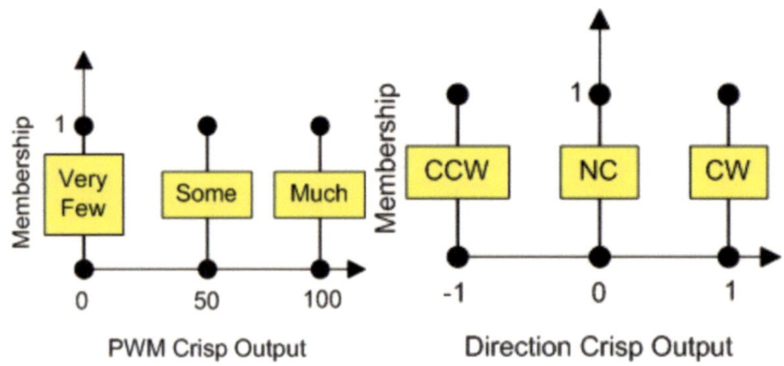

Figure 21. Rule Base and output membership functions for the Direction controller

The surfaces for the PWM and the direction are shown in Figure 22. For both PWM outputs the surface is the same, while for the direction the surfaces change and completely invert from left to right.

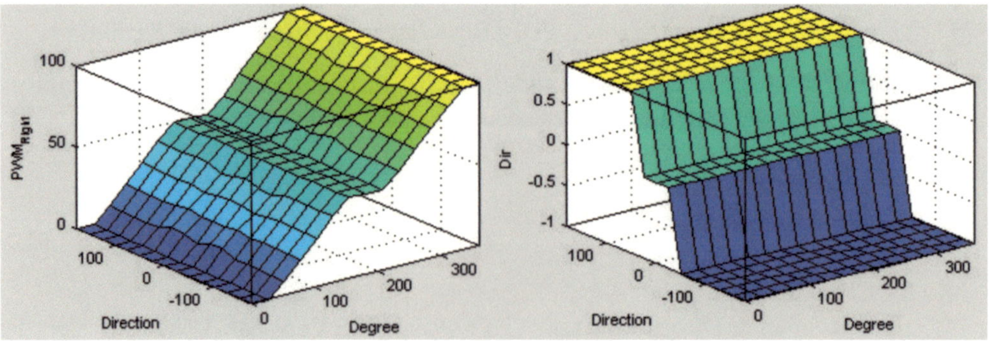

Figure 22. Surfaces for PWM and Direction outputs

This controller will act when the distances recognized by the sensors are Very Far, because the system will have enough space to maneuver and recover the direction that it has to follow, otherwise the obstacle avoidance controller will have the control of the wheelchair.

Obstacle Avoidance Behavior

Cities are not designed to be transited by disabled people, thus one of their main concerns is the paths and obstacles they have to cope with to get from one point to another. Big cities are becoming more and more crowded, so moving around on streets with a wheelchair is a big challenge.

If temperature and simple shape sensors are installed in the wheelchair (Figure 23 shows the proposal) then some kind of behavior can be programmed so the system can differentiate between a human being and a non human being. Additionally the use of a speaker or a horn is needed to ask people to move out of the way of the chair.

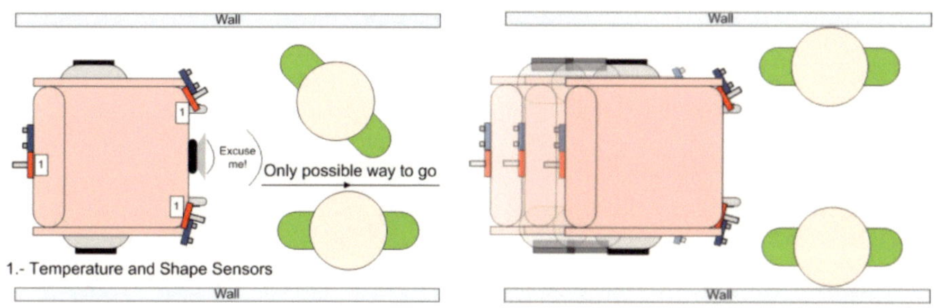

Figure 23. Wheelchair with temperature sensors for obstacle avoidance

The proposed behavior is based on a fuzzy controller which has as input the temperature in centigrade's degrees of the obstacle and as output the time in seconds the wheelchair will be stopped and a message or a horn will be played. It has three triangular fuzzy input membership functions as shown in Figure 24. The output membership functions are two singletons, as can be seen in Figure 25.

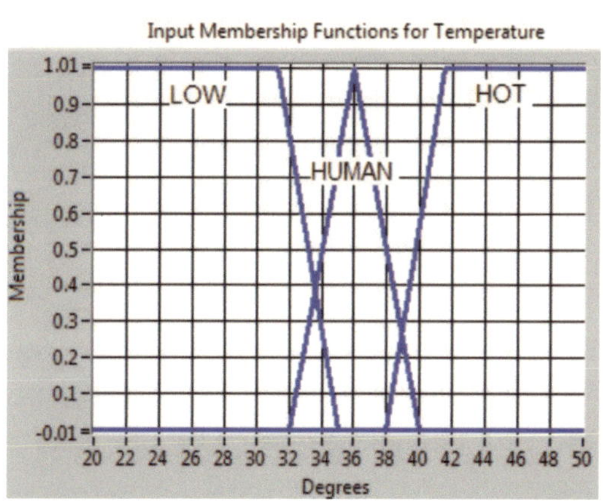

Figure 24. Input membership function for temperature

The IF-THEN Rules:

1. IF Temperature is Low THEN TIME IS Few.
2. IF Temperature is Human THEN TIME IS Much.
3. IF Temperature is Hot THEN TIME IS Few.

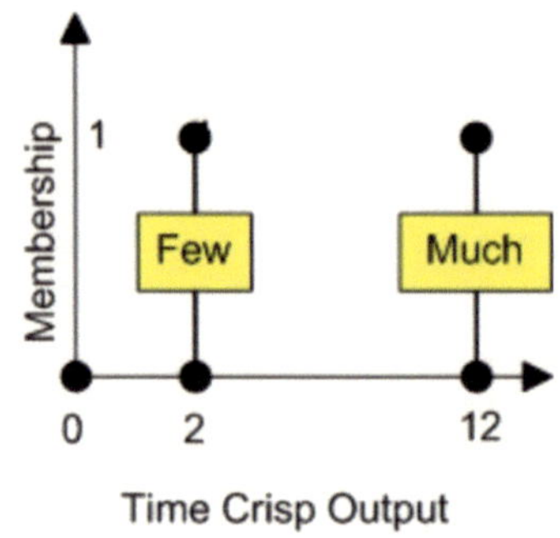

Figure 25. Singleton outputs for the temperature controller

The controller response is shown in Figure 26.

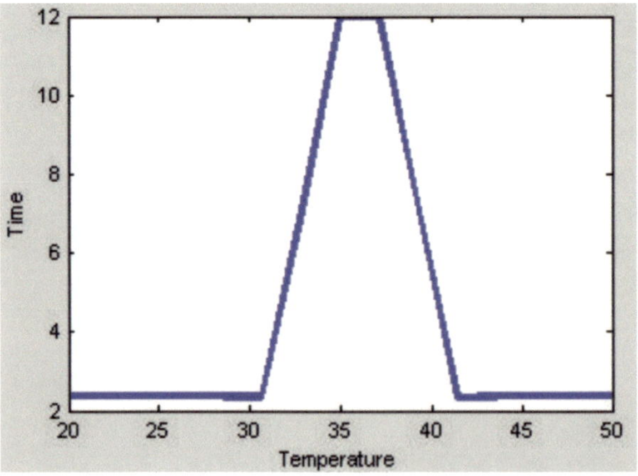

Figure 26. Time controller response

6. Structural design

The full system was built on a Quickie Wheelchair. The full system diagram is shown in Figure 27. Using LabVIEW, three different kinds of controls were programmed:

1. Voice control
2. Eye-movements control
3. Keyboard control

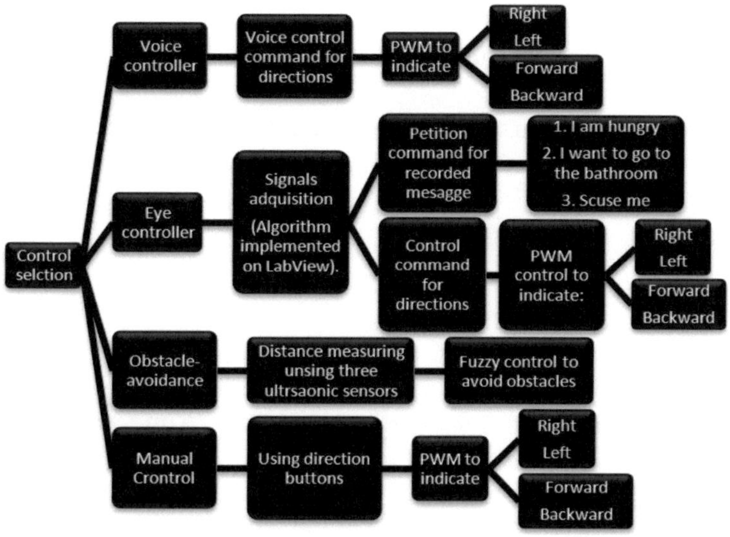

Figure 27. Control structure. The user can select any of the controls depending on his/her needs and the surrounding environment.

The wheelchair is controlled using two coils to generate an electromagnetic field which could be detected by two sensors. Depending on the density of the magnetic field and its intensity, the motors could be controlled to move the wheelchair in any direction. However this solution also requires that both coils should be fixed in place and they cannot be moved with respect to the sensors, so the sensed field will be always the same for one determined configuration. The use of fuzzy logic to design an obstacle-avoidance system and the Hebbian network used to determine the different kinds of eye movements were the tools that helped us to obtain efficient answers. Specific hardware is required to obtain the signals that would be processed with these systems. Each control was programmed on LabVIEW in different files and all of them were included in a LabVIEW project. Each one must be executed separately, so when using the voice controller, the eye controller cannot be used. In future, the obstacle-avoidance system will have higher priority than the eye and voice controllers.

The hardware used is:

1. DAQ: for sensing the different voltage signals produced by the eyes and to set the directions using the manual control. Each one gets values from different ports of a NI USB-6210. In the case of the voltages generated by the eyes, the data acquisition was connected to the analog port and the manual control to the digital input port.
2. CompactRIO: This device was used to generate PWM to the coils allowing us to have control for the different directions. The cRIO model 9014 had the following modules:
   a. a.Two H-bridges: for controlling the PWM.
   b. b.5 V TTL Bidirectional digital I/O Module.
3. BasicStamp[12]: This device is used to acquire the signals detected from three ultrasonic distance sensors.

4. Three ultrasonic sensors that measure distance and are used to help the obstacle-avoidance system. Two of them are placed in front of the wheelchair and one at the back.
5. A laptop to execute the programs and visualize the different commands introduced by the user.

7. Virtual trainning

7.1. Augmented reality

The simulator has a variety of modules that make up the augmented reality of the virtual environment. Augmented reality refers to those aspects that help to represent real physical situations and whose data is printed on screen to help users to understand them.

Distance to close objects

Taking the user's position in the virtual world as the center, a circle with a 5-meters radius is generated; then the distance to all objects within this area is computed with vector operations and the screen displays the distance to the nearest one and its name. For this, a file with specific information about all the objects at the simulator stage is consulted. This information allows the user to gain experience of how to move in small spaces, know the speed of the chair and the time between the moment when the command is indicated and the moment when it is executed (system response time).

Variation of the wheelchair's movement according to the terrain

Depending on the terrain where the patient moves in the virtual world, different physical phenomena are represented. If the terrain's surface is uneven, such as grass or pavement, vibrations are displayed on the screen and there is a change in the traction of the intelligent wheelchair. If the terrain is tilted, the perspective tilts and the corresponding acceleration changes are re-created as shown by the following formula obtained from the analysis of forces in Figure 28.

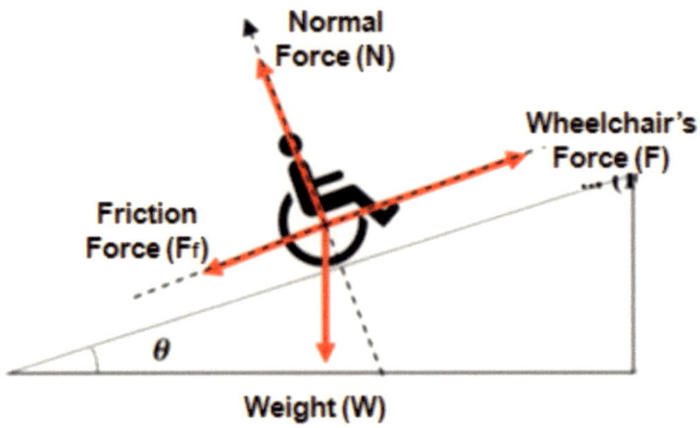

Figure 28. Forces that act upon the user and the intelligent wheelchair while moving on a tilted plane.

$$a = g \cdot \left(sen\theta + \mu_k \cos\theta \right) \tag{20}$$

Where a is the acceleration in the inclined plane, g is gravity, μ_k is the kinetic friction coefficient and θ is the inclination angle.

Static and dynamic obstacles

The 3D virtual trainer presents the dynamic obstacles: pedestrians, animals; and the static obstacles: furniture, walls, etc. that would most likely be seen in the locations in which the patient conducts his/her activities. The simulator offers online recommendations on how to avoid these obstacles or interact with them.

Within the virtual world, sounds and noises, both from dynamic objects and the environment itself, are presented. The user can listen to conversations when he/she is outside: barking, car engines, among others. These sounds vary depending on the patient's position in the virtual world and interaction with certain objects. For example, the volume of dynamic objects (such as people or animals) increases or decreases proportionally according to their distance from the user in the virtual environment.

3D Perspectives

As a way to help users, they can see the virtual world from different perspectives. The first perspective, or first person, presents the objects to the patient as seen from the intelligent wheelchair. This is the most useful because it is how the user will see them in real life. The third-person perspective offers a view of the user's avatar and the objects closest to it, that is, the camera is placed above and behind, five meters in each direction, with a 45° tilt. Thus, the user can see more details of its virtual environment. Finally, a perspective that is independent from the user's movement is offered, making it possible to explore the entire virtual world to get a look at the objects to interact with later.

Statistics: augmented reality

Figure 29. This image shows the virtual trainer along with the augmented reality interface. In the upper left corner, information about the performance of the user is shown: elapsed time, found targets. In the upper right corner there are more statistics such as number of collisions and the name of the nearest object. In the lower area data that can help the user to navigate more properly or about the closest

As mentioned in the description of some other modules of the virtual trainer, the user will be shown at any time information about objects in the simulator: distance to the nearest object, its name and the distance to the nearest target; as well as information about his/her performance: time spent at each level of the simulator and the number of collisions. Likewise, the screen's lower left corner providesinformation on the nearest object, such as extra precautions to consider, material and dimensions, or what would be the best instruction on driving the wheelchair through the location the user is currently at. Also, if relevant, the user is informed about the changes in terrain and sound as well as the change of perspective. These statistics are shown in Figure 29 above.

In this approach, the user is provided with not only a way to learn how to control the intelligent wheelchair, but also a space where he/she can find cultural information about the objects that constitute the virtual world. Likewise, the augmented reality interface facilitates and makes the user's training more pleasant.

7.2. Simulator performance

Due to the intense computing conducted in real time to show the aforementioned statistics and the level of detail present in virtual environments, such as the interior of houses, the implementation of algorithms that provide greater game performance and visual quality is necessary.

In simulators, video games and other interactive media, 3-D models and animations are crucial components. Games like Gears of War and Half-Life 2 would not be as striking if not for the vivid, detailed models and animations. Games within the XNA Framework, which are able to take advantage of the GPU (Graphics Unit Processor) of the Xbox 360 or PC, are not the exception. Many advanced rendering techniques can be exploited through the XNA Framework, such as hardware instancing.

Traditional implementations of 3-D models require a large header on the CPU (Control Unit Processor) and are not efficient or completely instantiated. Many processes are performed in the CPU and each part of the model requires its own call to Draw method and sometimes multiple calls if the model has a large number of polygons. This means, in the XNA framework, that creating a large number of models in the CPU creates a bottleneck.

The aim of this work is to present an alternative to "traditional" techniques to instantiate 3-D models. This technique even makes it possible to render animated models and, depending on its complexity, we can draw more than 45 models with a single call to Draw. Since the Xbox has a powerful graphics card, this is very desirable, and any way the level of processing on the CPU is reduced.

Hardware instancing works by sending two streams of vertexes to the video card, in order to send information about the objects' vertexes (which is called a regular vertex buffer) and information for the instances (position and color) to the GPU simultaneously. The advantage of hardware instancing is that a flag can be used to indicate which data flow (stream) contains information about certain vertexes and instances. Thus, only the original mesh has to be introduced in the data sequence of vertexes and XNA ensures that these data will be repeated for each instance. Thissaves memory and is generally easier to handle, since you can use the original mesh and the only thing needed is a call for each subset. This is because the main bottleneck in the GPU occurs when transformations are made to the pixels, such as the application of textures. With hardware instancing, the common operations for these transformations are not made every time an object is going to be drawn but only a relationship between the data flows through the flags. The arrangement of data streams is shown below in Figure 30.

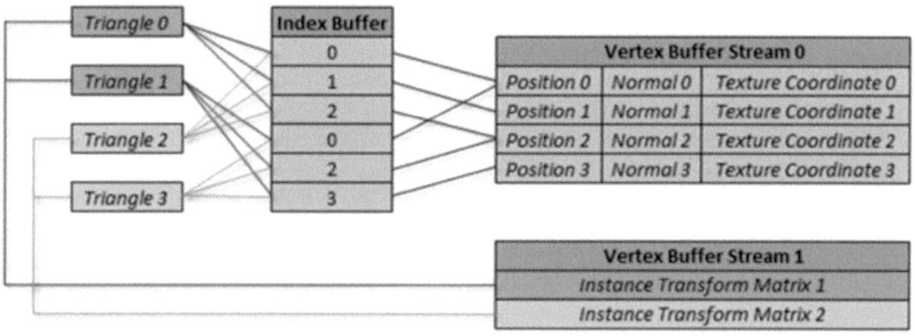

Figure 30. Array of the data sequences of the vertex buffers and their pointers

To accomplish hardware instancing, the following classes, processors and pipelines were used:

- InstancedModelProcessor.- This is the processor that does the heavy work of converting the model's data into vertexes, and giving as output an Instanced Model Content. Basically a cycle goes through the vertexes and assigns them a corresponding texture.
- InstanceSkinnedModelPart.- It is actually a wrapper around the ModelMesh class, with additional functionality to support instancing.

The last point to consider in hardware instancing is that each row of the processed mesh transforms is encoded as a pixel, and because the matrix dimensions are 4x4, 4 pixels represent a transform. Then a texture is assigned to each transformation according to the vertexes that represent them. This form of encoding is depicted in Figure 31.

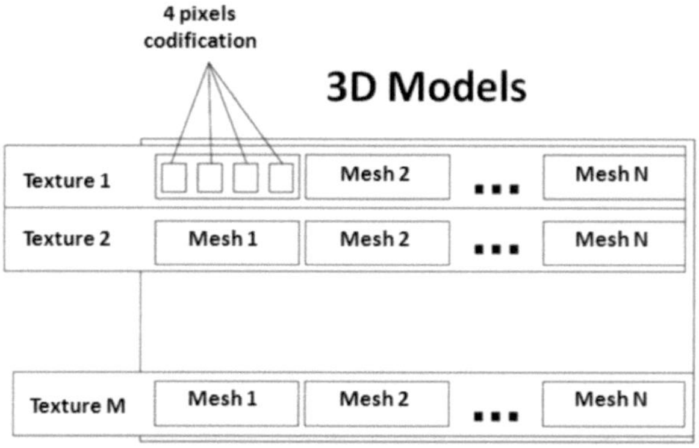

Part I

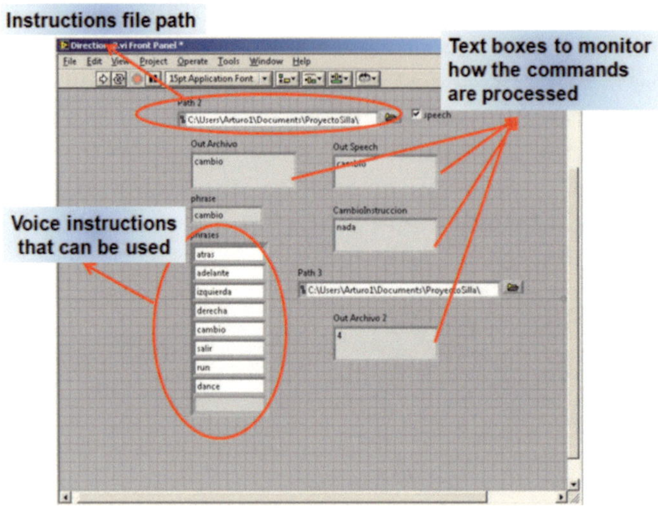

Part II

Figure 31. Encoding of the mesh transforms as in the Hardware Instancing method

7.3. Labview Interface for eye and voice control

The Labview interface that verifies the operation and control of Windows Speech Recognition is shown Figure 20. This window appears in the background of the computer when the game starts if the user wants to verify the voice instructions identified (these commands are recognized only when the Labview program has started). This window appears by means of an object of type Process which calls the Labview file (Virtual Instrument) from XNA.

To communicate with the two applications (Labview and XNA) and control the virtual trainer through the acquired data by Labview, a parallel access to a file which contains the instructions executed by the user in string format was implemented; then these commands are encoded to generate an event in XNA. This part of the project can be improved in order to move the information between the two applications more efficiently and with lower exception handles.

7.4. Web page and data base

In this section the web page of the project where the new simulator's users can register to monitor their activity and performance is explained. The patient's progress is measured through the mentioned statistics, such as number of collisions, instructions used, elapsed time in each level, among other variables. Based on them, a score is set to the user according to the weights assigned to each statistic. This page is also available for the patients' doctors; the page was developed using Microsoft Web Developer 2008.

Once registered, users can log in to access their information as well as that of the other players. Likewise, the user can also share information with other people and send them a message through the web page. This is also a quick means of communication for specialists who care for patients with disabilities and, at the same time, a space where users can share the information not only about the virtual trainer but about their life experiences which can be useful for other users. With this, a community can be created where patients can identify with and help each other.

The screen in Figure 32 shows the storage of users' data through SQL Express Edition. The general table that keeps a record of all the registered patients shows their best time (time in which they completed a level of the simulator), best score, number of games played, as well as their score average.

Similarly, more detailed statistics for each individual user are stored, which can be seen in Figure 33: scores, number of collisions, best time and most used instruction. In this way the patients can monitor their progress and work on the command that is most difficult for them. To help them, the targets that they have to collect in each level of the virtual trainer are placed in such a way as to let the users strengthen the instructions with which they collide the most and lower the percentage of the instruction they most widely use.

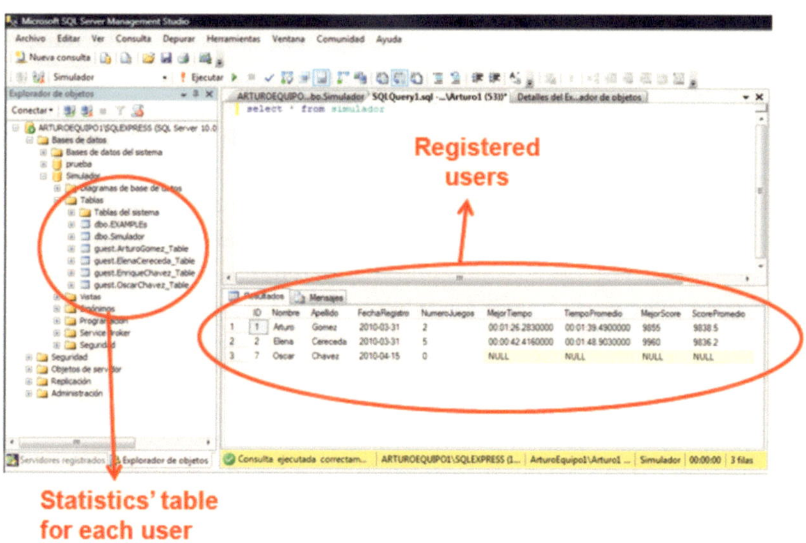

Figure 32. Information kept in the SQL Express data base about the statistics of the registered users

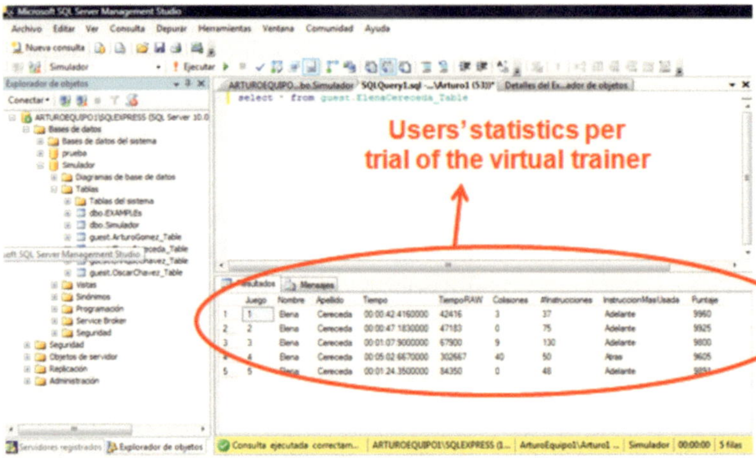

Figure 33. Statistics kept for every user and on which the virtual trainer based the way it distributes the targets among the virtual world to help the patients to strengthen their skills by using the intelligent wheelchair.

All the previous information is transmitted to the database using the libraries System.Data.SqlClient and System.Data.OleDb once a user has completed a level of the virtual trainer. The information consists of the statistics mentioned in section IV.1 and in shown in Figure 5, and some mathematical calculations to obtain averages and keep count.

8. Results

The following results show the controller performance. The voice controller increases the accuracy; if the wheelchair needs to work in a noisy environment, a noise cancelation system has to be included. The results are quite good when the wheelchair works in a normal noise environment, with the average value ranging from 0 to 70 db, and an average value of around 90% is obtained. The EOG recognition system changes the precision value according to the time because the user requires a certain length of time to move the eye in a correct way in order to recognize the signal. At first, the user is not familiarized with the whole system, thus the signal is not well defined and the system has a medium performance. After six weeks, the system increases the precision to around 94 %. Fig 34 shows the results.

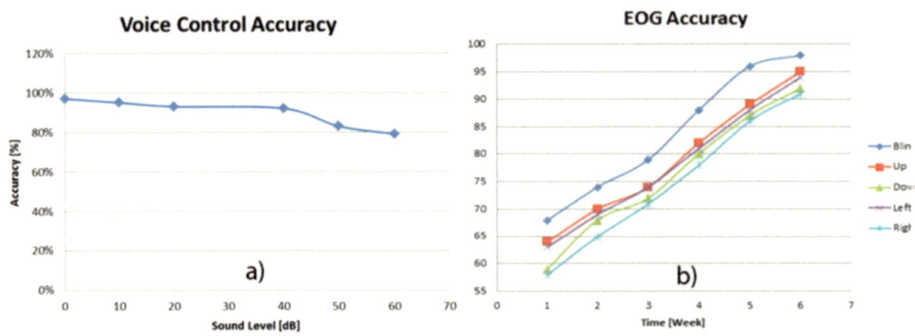

Figure 34. a. Tests on the voice control system response. b. EOG system response.Experimental Results

9. Conclusions

The complete system works well in a laboratory environment. The signals from eye movement and voice commands are translated into actual movements of the chair, allowing people who are disabled and cannot move their hands or even their head to move freely through spaces. There is still not a full version that can run an avoidance system at the same time as the chair is been controlled with eye movement. This should be the next step for further work. As was intended, the four main control systems that give the wheelchair more compatibility and adaptability to patients with different disorders were successfully completed. This allowed the chair to be moved with the eyes for those who cannot speak. Speech recognition was included for people who cannot move and directional buttons (joystick) for any other users. Many problems were presented when trying to interfere with the systems already built by the manufacturer; the use of magnetic inductors is one of the temporal solutions that should be eliminated even though the emulation of the joystick is good and works well. The use of these inductors produces a lot of power loss, thus considerably reducing the in-use time of the batteries. It also generates a small retardation in the use of Windows Vista Speech Recognition software and enters some faults into our system, since it is well known that this user interface is not well developed and sometimes does not recognize what it was expected to do, which is not good enough for a system like ours that requires a quick response to commands. This project demonstrated how intelligent control systems can be applied to improve existing products. The use of intelligent algorithms broadened the possibilities of interpretation and manipulation.

Author details

Pedro Ponce, Arturo Molina and Rafael Mendoza
Escuela de Ingeniería y Arquitectura, Instituto Tecnológico y de Estudios Superiores de Monterrey, Mexico City, Mexico

Acknowledgement

This work is supported by NEDO Japan (New Energy and Industrial Technology Development Organization) project on "Intelligent RT Software Project".

10. References

Book Chapter

[5] P. Ponce and F. D. Ramirez.*Intelligent Control Systems with LabVIEW.*UnitedKingdom, Springer, 2009.

[7] R. Barea, L. Boquete, M. Mazo, E. López and L. M. Bergasa, *Aplicación de electrooculografía para ayuda a minusválidos.*; Alcalá de Henares. Madrid, Spain: Universidad de Alcalá.

[15] F. D. Ramirez and D. Mendez, *Neuro-FuzzyNavigationSystemfor Mobile Robots. Electronics and CommunicationsEngineering Project,* Instituto Tecnologico y de Estudios Superiores de Monterrey Campus Ciudad de México, 2007.

Journal

[1] International classification of functioning, disability and health: ICF. World health Organization, Geneva 2001, 228 págs.
[2] G. Krishnamurthy and M. Ghovanloo, *"Tongue Drive: A Tongue Operated Magnetic sensor Based Wireless Assistive Technology for people with severe Disabilities"*, IEEE Circuits and Systems, 2006. ISCAS 2006.Proceedings. 2006 IEEE International Symposium
[13] P. Ponce, et al. *A Novel Neuro-Fuzzy Controller Based on Both Trigonometric Series and Fuzzy Clusters.*IEEE International Conference an Industrial Technology. India. ICIT, Dec 15-17, 2006, 2006.
[14] P. Ponce, et al. *Neuro-Fuzzy Controller Using LabVIEW.* Paper presented at the Intelligent Systems and Control Conference by IASTED, in Cambridge, MA, Nov. 19 - 21, 2007.

Online Journal

[3] United States Department of Veterans Affairs, " New Head Control for Quadriplegic Patients, 1970," Rehabilitation Research & Development Service, http://www.rehab.research.va.gov/jour/75/12/1/lozach.pdf , (accesed October 21, 2009)
[4] Quickie-Wheelchair.com, "Quickie P222 SE – Wheelchair – Quickie-Wheelchair.com", http://www.quickie-wheelchairs.com/products/Quickie-P222-SE-2974.html, (accesed October 16, 2009)
[6] National Instruments Corporation, "NI LabVIEW – The Software That Powers Virtual Instrumentation – National Instruments", http://www.ni.com/labview/ , (accesed October 16, 2009).
[8] National Instruments Corporation, "NI USB-6210 – National Instruments", http://sine.ni.com/nips/cds/print/p/lang/en/nid/203189 , (accesed October 16, 2009).
[9] National Instruments Corporation, "NI Crio-9014 – National Instruments", http://sine.ni.com/nips/cds/print/p/lang/en/nid/203500 , (accesed October 16, 2009).
[10] National Instruments Corporation, "NI 9505 – National Instruments", http://sine.ni.com/nips/cds/print/p/lang/en/nid/202711 , (accesed October 16, 2009).
[11] Parallax Inc. "BASIC Stamp Discovery Kit – Serial (With USB Adapter and Cable)", http://www.parallax.com/StoreSearchResults/tabid/768/txtSearch/bs2/List/0/SortField/4/ProductID/320/Default.aspx , (accesed October 21, 2009).
[12] XNA libraries, http://msdn.microsoft.com/en-us/aa937791.aspx

A Hybrid of Fuzzy and Fuzzy Self-Tuning PID Controller for Servo Electro-Hydraulic System

Kwanchai Sinthipsomboon, Issaree Hunsacharoonroj, Josept Khedari, Watcharin Po-ngaen and Pornjit Pratumsuwan

Additional information is available at the end of the chapter

http://dx.doi.org/10.5772/48614

1. Introduction

The application of hydraulic actuation to heavy duty equipment reflects the ability of the hydraulic circuit to transmit larger forces and to be easily controlled. It has many distinct advantages such as the response accuracy, self-lubricating and heat transfer properties of the fluid, relative large torques, large torque-to-inertia ratios, high loop gains, relatively high stiffness and small position error. Although the high cost of hydraulic components and power unit, loss of power due to leakage, inflexibility, nonlinear response, and error-prone low power operation tends to limit the use of hydraulic drives, they nevertheless constitute a large subset of all industrial drives and are extensively used in the transportation and manufacturing industries (Merrit, 1976; Rong-Fong Fung *et al*, 1997; Aliyari *et al*, 2007).

The Servo Electro-hydraulic System (SEHS), among others, is perhaps the most important system because it takes the advantages of both the large output power of traditional hydraulic systems and the rapid response of electric systems. However, there are also many challenges in the design of SEHS. For example, they are the highly nonlinear phenomena such as fluid compressibility, the flow/pressure relationship and dead-band due to the internal leakage and hysteresis, and the many uncertainties of hydraulic systems due to linearization. Therefore, it seems to be quite difficult to perform a high precision servo control by using linear control method Rong-Fong Fung *et al*, 1997; Aliyari *et al*, 2007; Pratumsuwan *et al*, 2010).

Classical PID controller is the most popular control tool in many industrial applications because they can improve both the transient response and steady state error of the system at the same time. Moreover, it has simple architecture and conceivable physical intuition of its parameter. Traditionally, the parameters of a classical PID controller, i.e. K_P, K_I, and K_D, are usually fixed during operation. Consequently, such a controller is inefficient for control a system while the system is disturbed by unknown facts, or the surrounding environment of the system is changed (Panichkun & Ngaechroenkul, 2000; Pratumsuwan *et al*, 2010).

Fuzzy control is robust to the system with variation of system dynamics and the system of model free or the system which precise information is not required. It has been successfully used in the complex ill-defined process with better performance than that of a PID controller. Another important advance of fuzzy controller is a short rise time and a small overshoot (Aliyari *et al*, 2007; Panichkun & Ngaechroenkul, 2000). However, PID controller is better able to control and minimize the steady state error of the system. To enhance the controller performance, hybridization of these two controller structures comes to one mind immediately to exploit the beneficial sides of both categories, know as a hybrid of fuzzy and PID controller (Panichkun & Ngaechroenkul, 2000; Pratumsuwan *et al*, 2010).

Nevertheless, a hybrid of fuzzy and PID does not perform well when applied to the SEHS, because when the SEHS parameters changes will require new adjustment of the PID gains. A hybrid of fuzzy and fuzzy self-tuning PID controller is proposed in this paper. The proposed control scheme is separated into two parts, fuzzy controller and fuzzy self-tuning PID controller. Fuzzy controller is used to control systems when the output value of system far away from the target value. Fuzzy self-tuning PID controller is applied when the output value is near the desired value. In terms of adjusting the PID gains tuning using fuzzy as to obtain an optimum value.

2. Servo electro-hydraulic system

The physical model of a nonlinear servo electro-hydraulic system is shown in Figure 1.

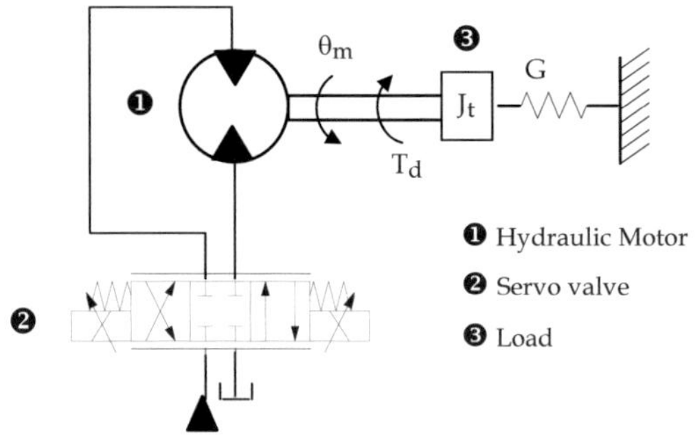

Figure 1. The physical model of a servo electro-hydraulic system.

The inertial-damping with a nonlinear torsional spring system is driven by a hydraulic motor and the rotation motion of the motor is controlled by a servo valve. Higher control input voltage can produce larger valve flow from the servo valve and fast rotation motion of the motor. The entire system equations are described as follows. The servo valve flow equation (1) is described as:

$$Q_L = K_q x_v - K_c P_L \tag{1}$$

where Q_L is the load flow, X_v is the displacement of the spool in the servo valve, K_c is the flow-pressure coefficient, P_L is the load pressure, and K_q is the flow gain which varies at different operating points. K_q is given by

$$K_q = C_d w \sqrt{\frac{(P_S - P_L)\operatorname{sgn}(X_v)}{\rho}} \tag{2}$$

where C_d is the discharge coefficient, w is the area gradient, ρ is the fluid mass density, and P_S is the supply pressure.

The continuity equation to the motor is formulated as

$$Q_L = D_m \dot{\theta}_m + C_l P_L + \frac{V_t}{4\beta_e} \dot{P}_L \tag{3}$$

where D_m is the volumetric displacement, $\dot{\theta}_m$ is the angular velocity of the motor shaft, C_l is the total leakage coefficient of the motor, V_t is the total compressed volume, and β_e is the effective bulk modulus of the system.

Substituting (1) into (3) leads to

$$K_q X_v = D_m \dot{\theta}_m + K_l P_L + \frac{V_t}{4\beta_e} \dot{P}_L \tag{4}$$

where $K_l=K_c+C_l$ is the total leakage coefficient of the hydraulic system.

The torque balance equation for the motor is described as follows:

$$P_L D_m = J_t \ddot{\theta}_m + B_m \dot{\theta}_m + G(\theta_m + G_n \theta_m^3) + T_d \tag{5}$$

where J_t is the total inertial of motor and load, B_m is the viscous damping coefficient of the load, T_d is the disturbance of the system, and $G_n \theta_m^3$ is the nonlinear stiffness of the spring.

From (1) to (5), the hydraulic servomechanism system equation can be described by a state equation as follows:

$$\begin{aligned} \dot{X}_1 &= X_2 \\ \dot{X}_2 &= X_3 \\ \dot{X}_3 &= -\sum_{i=1}^{3} a_i X_i + bU - N(X,t) - d(t) \\ \dot{Z} &= r - X_1 \end{aligned} \tag{6}$$

where

$$X(t)=\left[X_1(t)X_2(t)X_3(t)\right]^T=\left[\theta_m(t)\dot{\theta}_m(t)\ddot{\theta}_m(t)\right]^T$$
$$a_1(t)=\frac{4\beta_e}{V_t}\frac{K_{lt}}{J_t}G$$
$$a_2(t)=\frac{4\beta_e}{V_t}\frac{D_m^2}{J_t}+\frac{4\beta_e}{V_t}\frac{K_{lt}}{J_t}B_m+\frac{G}{J_t}$$
$$a_3(t)=\frac{4\beta_e}{V_t}K_{lt}+\frac{B_m}{J_t}$$
$$b(X)=\frac{4\beta_e}{V_t}\frac{D_m}{J_t}K_qK_V$$

$$N(x,t)=\frac{4\beta_e K_{lt}G_n}{V_tJ_t}GX_1^3+\frac{3G_n}{J_t}GX_1^2X_2$$
$$d(t)=\frac{4\beta_e}{V_t}\frac{K_{lt}}{J_t}T_d+\frac{1}{J_t}T_d$$

in which *N(X,t)* represents the nonlinear terms of the system.

3. System descriptions

We are considering a PC-based speed control of the SEHS that will use either a hybrid fuzzy PID or a hybrid of fuzzy and fuzzy self-tuning PID controller. The motor speed of this system is controlled. In order to construct fair test case for comparing both controllers, the experiments are constructed based on the same hardware elements. The specifications of this system are depicted in Table 1 and Figure 2 respectively.

Figure 2. Experimental Setup.

Elements	Descriptions
Hydraulic Motor	Geometric displacement 19.9 cm^3 Max. Speed 1000 rpm, Max. torque 25Nm Max. pressure drop 100bar Max. oil flow 20l/min
Proportional valve	directly actuated spool valve, grade of filtration 10 μm, nominal flow rate 60l/min (at $\Delta p_N = 6.9$ bar/control edge), nominal current 1600 mA, repeatability < 1%, hysteresis <5%
Pump (supply pressure)	100 bar
Amplifier card	set point values ± 5 VDC, solenoid outputs (PWM signal) 24 V, dither frequency 200 Hz, max power 45W.
Encoder	8 c/t, I(optical shaft encoder)
DAC	Resolution 15 bit DAC, output 0-10V
DAQ Card NI 6221 PCI	analog input resolutions 16 bits (input range ±10V), output resolutions 16 bits (output range ±10V), 833 kS/s (6 μs full-scale settling)
Operating systems & Program	Windows XP, and LabVIEW 8.6

Table 1. Specifications of the SEHS.

4. Controller designs

A closed loop system, whither the reference signal is set manually or automatically, can perform control of motor speed. Figure 3 represents typical of an "Automatic Closed Loop" control system. As shown in the figure, the velocity of a hydraulic motor is controlled by a servo valve. The servo valve solenoid is receiving driving electrical current from an amplifier card, which is generating the driving current based on a control signal supplied by a controller. The controller responsibility is to continuously compare the reference signal and the actual motor speed feedback by the velocity sensor, after consequently generate the adequate control signal.

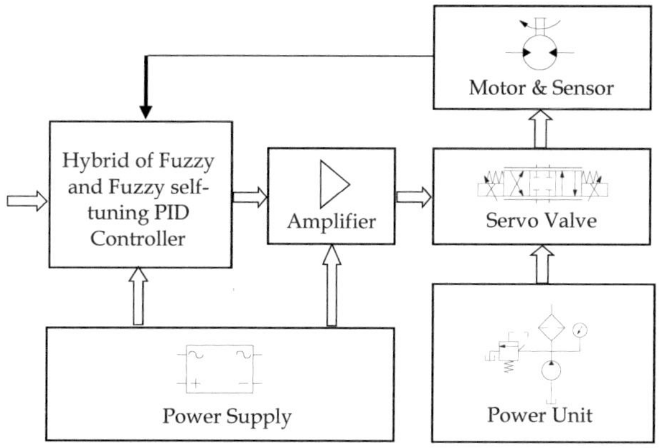

Figure 3. Block diagram of using a hybrid fuzzy and fuzzy self-tuning PID controls the SEHS.

There are various types of control system used in classical control, modern control and intelligent control systems, each having been studied and implemented in many industrial applications. Every control system method has its advantages and disadvantages. Therefore, the trend is to implement hybrid systems consisting of more than one type of control technique.

4.1. PID controller

The PID control method has been widely used in industry during last several decades because of its simplicity. The implementation of PID control, as shown in (7), requires finding suitable values for the gain parameters K_P, K_I, and K_D. To tune these parameters, the model is linearized around different equilibrium points,

$$u(k) = K_P e(k) + K_I \sum_{i=0}^{k} e(i) + K_D \left[e(k) - e(k-1) \right] \tag{7}$$

where $e(k)$ is the error signal.

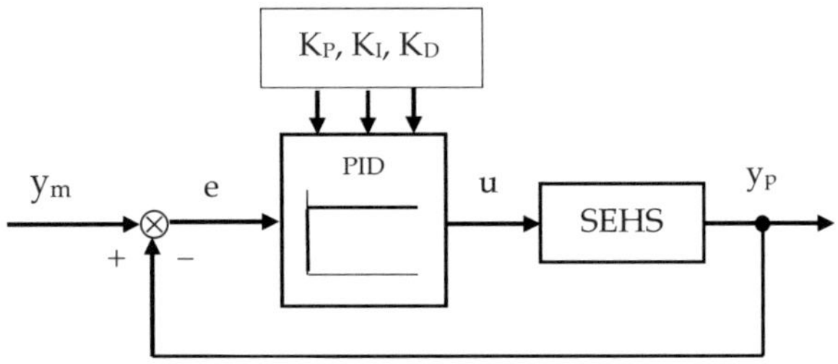

Figure 4. Block diagram of a PID controller.

However, the PID method is not suitable for controlling a system with a large amount of lag, parameter variations, and uncertainty in the model. Thus, PID control cannot accurately control velocity in a SEHS (Rong-Fong Fung *et al*, 1997; Aliyari *et al*, 2007).

4.2. Fuzzy controller

Fuzzy Control (FC) has the advantage that it does not require an accurate mathematical model of the process. It uses a set of artificial rules in a decision-making table and calculates an output based on the table (Aliyari *et al*, 2007; Panichkun & Ngaechroenkul, 2000).

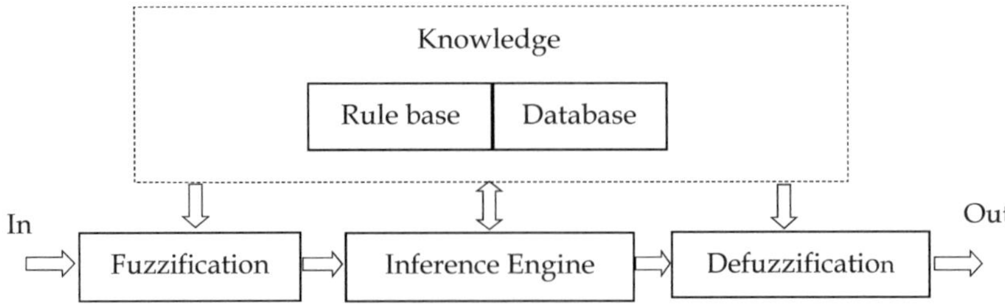

Figure 5. Structure of FC.

Figure 5 & 6 show a schematic diagram of a fuzzy control system. Input variables go through the fuzzification interface and are converted to linguistic variables. Then, a database and rule base holding the decision-making logic are used to infer the fuzzy output. Finally, a defuzzification method converts the fuzzy output into a signal to be sent out.

First, the two input variables must be defined in terms of linguistics. The error *(e)* in velocity is expressed by a number in the interval from -10 to 10. There are five linguistic terms of the error in velocity: negative big (NB), negative (N), zero (Z), positive (P), and positive big (PB). Similarly, the fuzzy set of the error change of the velocity or acceleration *(Δe)* is presented as {NB, N, Z, P, PB} over the interval from -10 to 10V. Finally, the fuzzy set of the output signal is presented as {NB, N, Z, P, PB} over the interval from -5 to 5V.

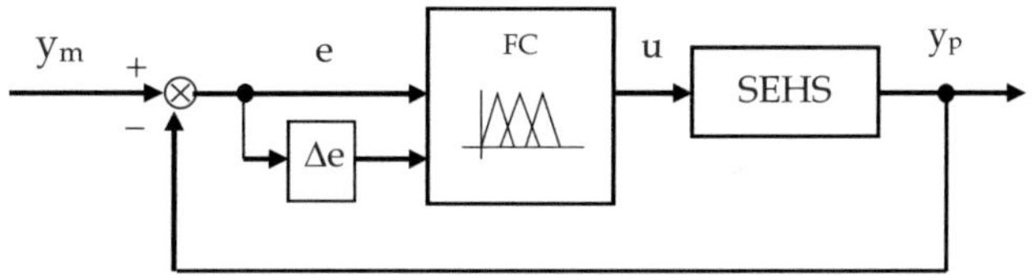

Figure 6. Block digram of a FC.

The knowledge base for a fuzzy controller consists of a rule base and membership functions. It is reasonable to present these linguistic terms by triangular-shape membership functions, as shown in Figure 6. A fuzzy control knowledge base must be developed that uses the linguistic description of the input variable. In this paper, an expert's experience and knowledge method is used to build a rule base (Zhang *et al*, 2004). The rule base consists of a set of linguistic IF-THEN rules containing two antecedences and one consequence, as expressed in the following form:

$$R_{i,j,k} \ : \text{IF} \ \ \mathrm{e} = \mathrm{A_i} \ \ \textit{and} \ \Delta \mathrm{e} = \mathrm{B_j} \ \ \text{THEN} \ \ \mathrm{u} = \mathrm{C_k}, \tag{8}$$

where $1 \le i \le 5$, $1 \le j \le 5$, and $1 \le k \le 5$. The total number of IF-THEN rules is 25 and is represented in matrix form, called a fuzzy rule matrix, as shown in Table 2.

The decision-making output can be obtained using a max-min fuzzy inference where the crisp output is calculated by the center of gravity (COG) method.

e \ Δe	NB	N	Z	P	PB
NB	NB	NB	N	N	Z
N	NB	N	N	Z	P
Z	N	N	Z	P	P
P	N	Z	P	P	PB
PB	Z	P	P	PB	PB

Table 2. Fuzzy Rules of a FC.

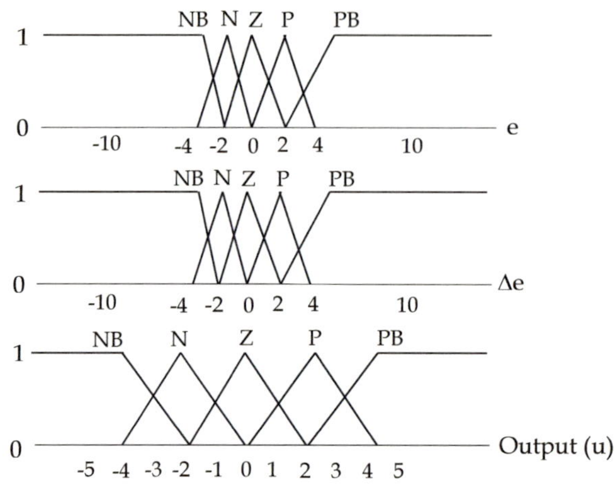

Figure 7. Fuzzy sets of a FC.

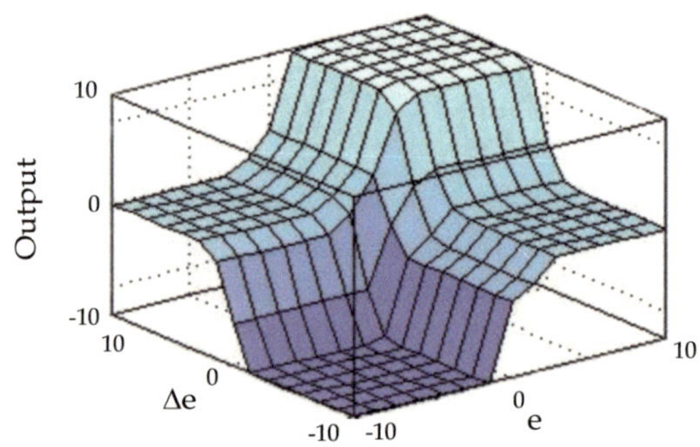

Figure 8. Input-output mapping of a FC.

4.3. Hybrid of fuzzy and PID controller

While conventional PID controllers are sensitive to variations in the system parameters, fuzzy controllers do not need precise information about the system variables in order to be effective. However, PID controllers are better able to control and minimize the steady state error of the system. Hence, a hybrid system, as shown in figure 9, was developed to utilize the advantages of both PID controller and fuzzy controller (Parnichkul & Ngaecharoenkul, 2000; Erenoglu *et al.*, 2006; Pratumsuwan *et al.*, 2009;).

Figure 9 shows a switch between the fuzzy controller and the PID controller, where the position of the switch depends on the error between the actual value and set point value. If the error in velocity reaches a value higher than that of the threshold e_0, the hybrid system applies the fuzzy controller, which has a fast rise time and a small amount of overshoot, to the system in order to correct the velocity with respect to the set point. When the velocity is below the threshold e_0 or close to the set point, the hybrid system shifts control to the PID, which has better accuracy near the set velocity (Parnichkul & Ngaecharoenkul, 2000; Erenoglu *et al.*, 2006; Pratumsuwan *et al.*, 2009;).

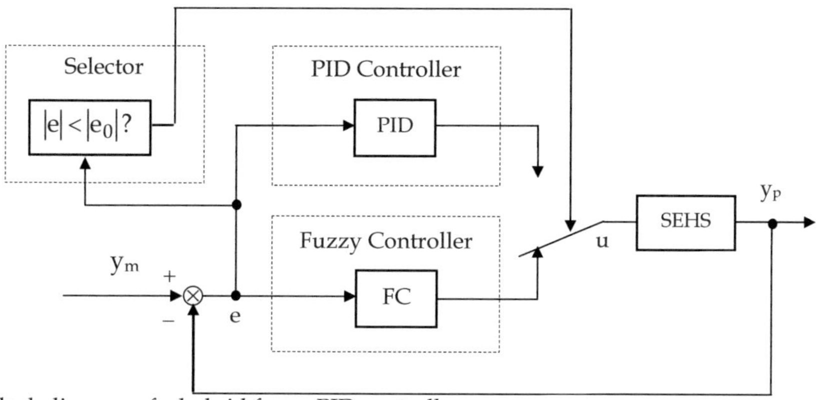

Figure 9. Block diagram of a hybrid fuzzy PID controller.

4.4. Fuzzy self-tuning PID controller

Fuzzy self-tuning PID controller means that the tree parameters K_P, K_I, and K_D of PID controller are tuned by using fuzzy tuner (Zhang *et al*, 2004; Song & Liu, 2010; Zulfatman & Rahmat, 2006; Feng *et al*, 2009). The coefficients of the conventional PID controller are not often property tuned for the nonlinear plant with unpredictable parameter variations. Hence, it is necessary to automatically tune the PID parameters. The structure of the fuzzy self-tuning PID controller is shown in Figure 10. Where e is the error between desired velocity set point and the output, $e\Delta$ is the derivation of error. The PID parameters are tuned by using fuzzy tuner, which provide a nonlinear mapping from e and $e\Delta$ of error to PID parameters.

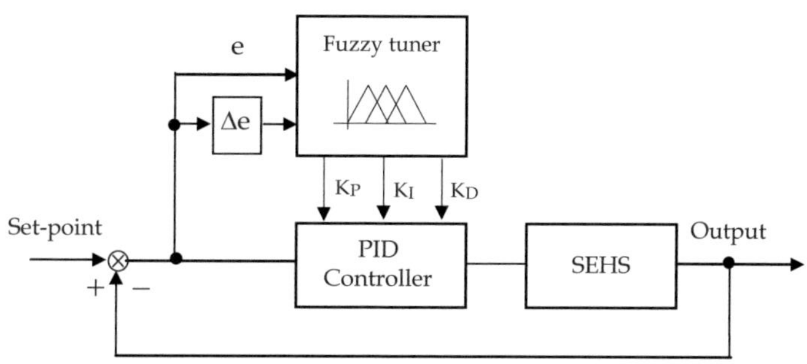

Figure 10. Block diagram of a fuzzy self-tuning PID controller.

Regarding to the fuzzy structure, there are two inputs to fuzzy inference: e and $e\Delta$, and there outputs for each PID controller parameter K'_P, K'_I, and K'_D respectively. Mamdani model is applied as structure of fuzzy inference with some modification to obtain the optimum value for K_P, K_I, and K_D. Suppose the variable ranges of the parameters of PID controller are $[K_{Pmin}, K_{Pmax}]$, $[K_{Imin}, K_{Imax}]$, and $[K_{Dmin}, K_{Dmax}]$ respectively. The range of each parameters was determined based on the experimental on PID controls the SEHS. The range of each parameters are, $K_P \in [8,15]$, $K_I \in [0.003,0.01]$, and $K_D \in [0.0001,0.000001]$. Therefore, they can be calibrated over the interval [0,1] as follows:

$$K'_P = \frac{K_P - K_{P\min}}{K_{P\max} - K_{P\min}} = \frac{K_P - 8}{15 - 8}, K_P = 7K'_P + 8$$

$$K'_I = \frac{K_I - K_{\mathrm{I}min}}{K_{\mathrm{I}max} - K_{\mathrm{I}min}} = \frac{K_I - 0.003}{0.01 - 0.003}, K_I = 0.007K'_I + 0.003$$

$$K'_D = \frac{K_D - K_{D\min}}{K_{D\max} - K_{D\min}} = \frac{K_D - 0.000001}{0.00001 - 0.000001}, K_D = 0.0000009K'_D + 0.000001$$

The membership functions of these inputs fuzzy sets are shown in Figure 8. The linguistic variable levels are assigned as: negative big (NB), negative (N), zero (Z), positive (P), and positive big (PB). Similarly, the fuzzy set of the error change of the velocity or acceleration *(Δe)* is presented as {NB, N, Z, P, PB}. These levels are chosen from the characteristics and specification of the SEHS. The ranges of these inputs are from -10 to 10. Finally, whereas the membership functions of outputs K'_P, K'_I, and K'_D are shown in Fig. 8. The linguistic levels of these outputs are assigned as: negative big (NB), negative (N), zero (Z), positive (P), and positive big (PB) similarly where the ranges from 0 to 1.

	NB	N	Z	P	PB
NB	NB	NB	NB	N	Z
N	NB	N	N	N	Z
Z	NB	N	Z	P	PB
P	Z	P	P	P	PB
PB	Z	P	PB	PB	PB

Table 3. Fuzzy Rules of K_P Gain.

	NB	N	Z	P	PB
NB	PB	PB	PB	N	NB
N	PB	P	P	Z	NB
Z	P	P	Z	N	NB
P	Z	P	N	N	NB
PB	Z	N	NB	NB	NB

Table 4. Fuzzy Rules of K_I Gain.

	NB	N	Z	P	PB
NB	NB	NB	NB	P	PB
N	NB	N	N	Z	PB
Z	N	N	Z	P	PB
P	Z	N	P	P	PB
PB	Z	P	PB	PB	PB

Table 5. Fuzzy Rules of K_D Gain.

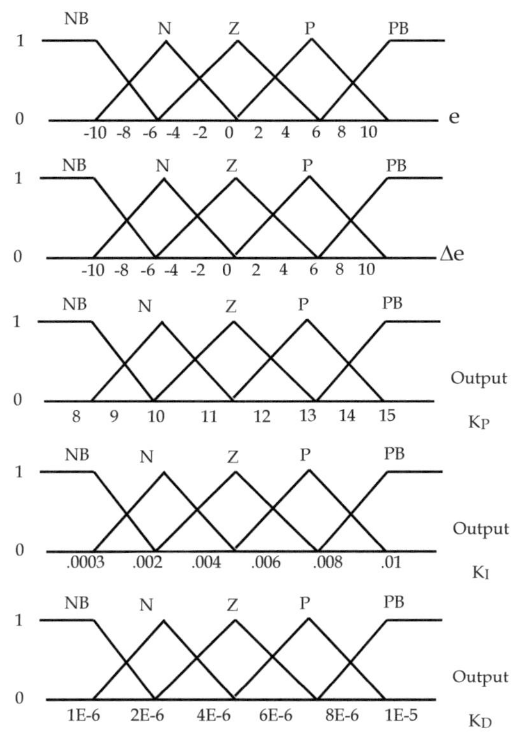

Figure 11. Fuzzy sets of a fuzzy self-tuning PID controller.

4.5. Hybrid of fuzzy and fuzzy self-tuning PID controller

A hybrid of fuzzy and fuzzy self-tuning PID controller, as shown in Figure 12, was developed to combine the advantages of both fuzzy and PID controller together. In addition, the adjustment gain of PID with a fuzzy tuner is included to purposed controller also, which all of these described in section 4.1, 4.2, 4.3, and 4.4.

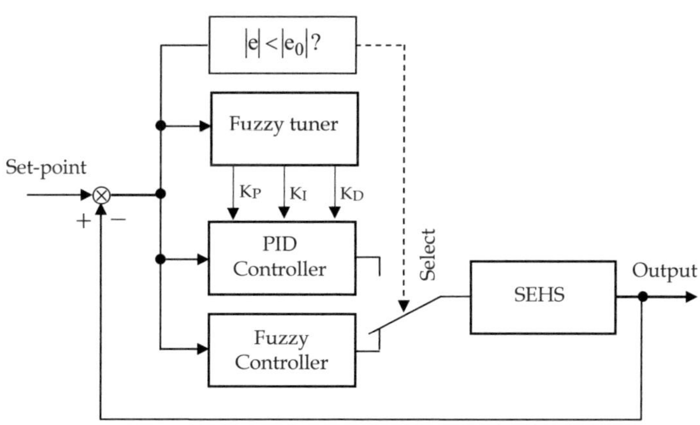

Figure 12. Block diagram of a fuzzy self-tuning PID controller.

5. The experimental results

The effectiveness of the proposed hybrid of fuzzy and fuzzy-tune PID controller is evaluated experimentally with the SEHS and is compared with that of the hybrid fuzzy PID controller which uses the nominal values of the gains obtained by experiment. The control algorithms described in section 4.1, 4.2, 4.3, and 4.4 were hybridized and applied to the SEHS using by LabVIEW program as the development platform and shown in Figure 13.

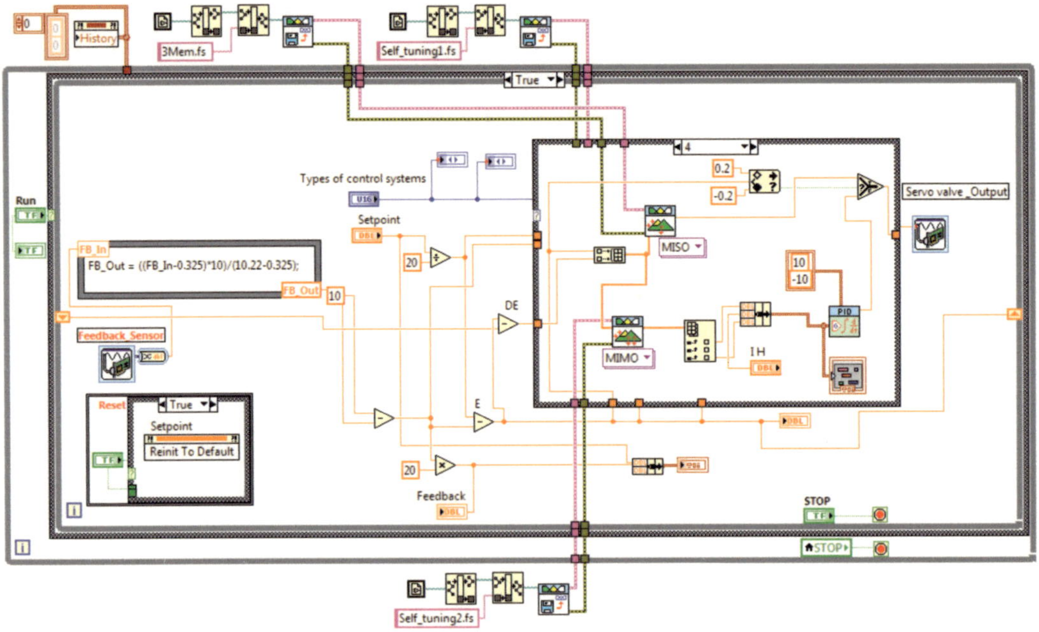

Figure 13. The control algorithms are developed by LabVIEW program.

The proposed of a hybrid of fuzzy and fuzzy self-tuning PID controller is evaluated experimentally with the motor speed control of SEHS and is compared with that of the conventional of a hybrid of fuzzy and PID controller. For the first experiment to observe the response of the SEHS control output of the both controller, which shown in Figure. 14 and Table 6, respectively. Then, change the parameters of the SEHS, because existing experimental set is difficult to change the load so that this change in pressure of the SEHS instead. The change in pressure will make many values, but the parameters of the both controller still use the original setting from the previous first. Figure 14, Table 6, and Figure 15, Table 7 show examples of the responses of the output of the both controller, which resulted from changing the original value of system pressure are 50 bar and 10 bar pressure. However, all these experiments the value of e_0 which is used as a reference in the selection of a controller is set at 0.92 that is the optimum value from experiment.

When the experiment has changed the parameters of the SEHS will find that the hybrid of fuzzy and fuzzy self-tuning PID would lead to a satisfactory response over the hybrid of fuzzy and PID controller. This is because the proposed controller does not require to adjustment the new parameters of PID controller although the parameters of the SEHS will change.

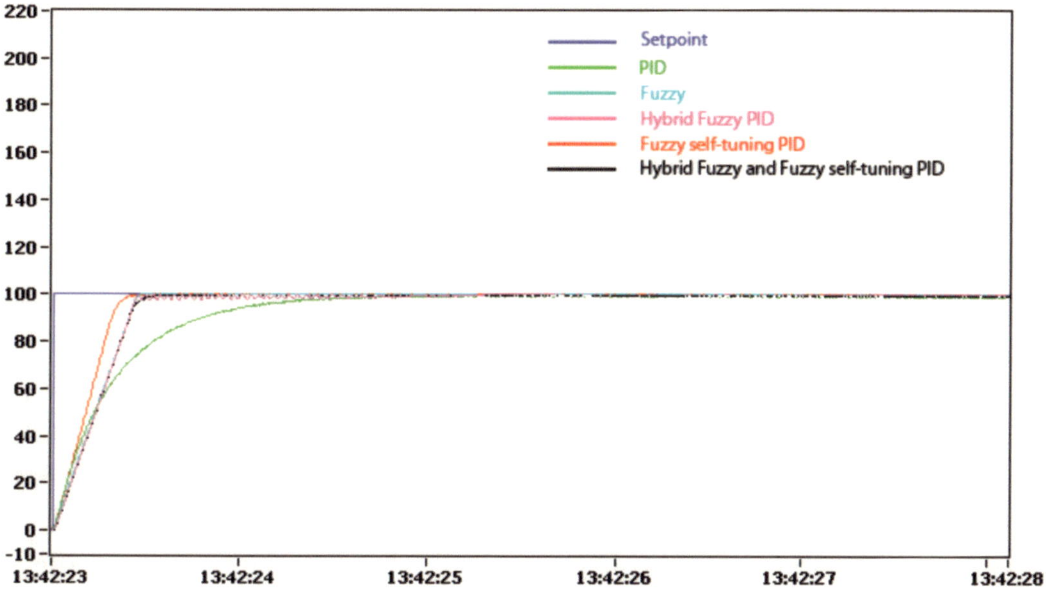

Figure 14. Comparison of the results of the five controls when the pressure was set at 50 bar

Controller	Velocity (rpm)	Results		$P.O.=\frac{M_O}{F_v}\times 100$ % Overshoot	Rise time (T_r)(s)	Time delay (T_d)(s)	Settling Time (T_s)(s)
		Velocity (rpm) Output	Error				
PID	0 -100	99.932	0.003	0	0.675	0.25	2.15
Fuzzy	0 -100	99.919	0.004	0	0.325	0.25	0.5
Hybrid Fuzzy PID	0 -100	99.952	0.002	0	0.325	0.25	2.6
Fuzzy Self-tuning PID	0 -100	99.860	0.006	0	0.25	0.2	0.525
Hybrid Fuzzy and Fuzzy self-tuning PID	0 -100	99.552	0.022	0	0.325	0.2	0.525

Table 6. Comparison of the results of the five controls when the pressure was set at 50 bar.

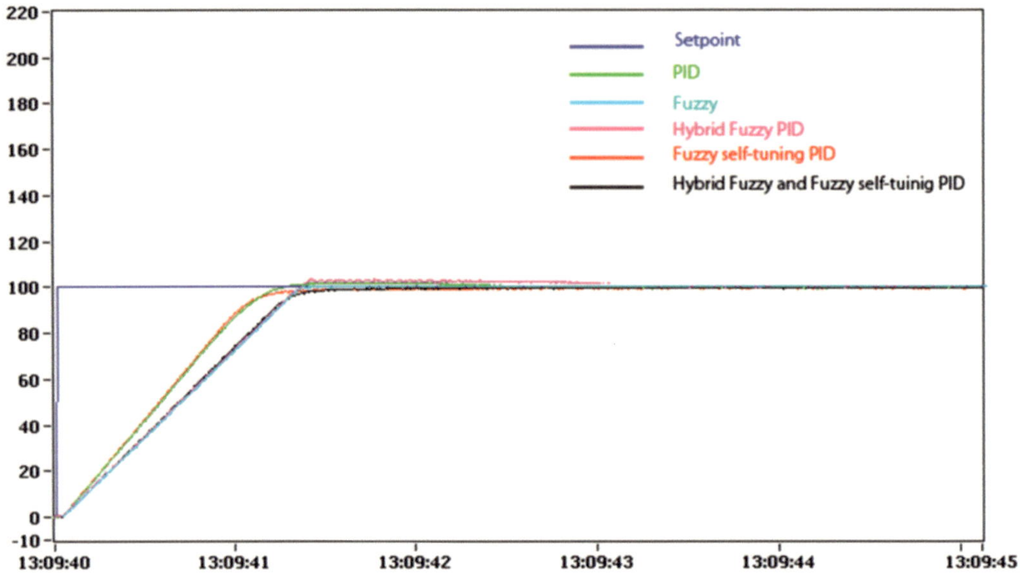

Figure 15. Comparison of the results of the five controls when the pressure was set at 10 bar

Controller	Velocity (rpm)	Results		$P.O.=\frac{M_O}{F_v}\times 100$ % Overshoot	Rise time (T_r)(s)	Time delay (T_d)(s)	Settling Time (T_s)(s)
		Velocity (rpm) Output	Error				
PID	0 -100	99.697	0.015	2.5	0.875	0.55	2.45
Fuzzy	0 -100	99.874	0.006	0	1	0.7	1.7
Hybrid Fuzzy PID	0 -100	99.889	0.001	3	1	0.7	3.05
Fuzzy Self-tuning PID	0 -100	99.513	0.024	0	0.825	0.55	2.6
Hybrid Fuzzy and Fuzzy self-tuning PID	0 -100	99.847	0.007	0	1	0.4	1.8

Table 7. Comparison of the results of the five controls when the pressure was set at 10 bar.

6. Conclusions

The objective of this study, we proposed the hybrid of fuzzy and fuzzy self-tuning PID controller for motor speed control of a SEHS. The proposed control scheme is separated into two parts, fuzzy controller and fuzzy self-tuning PID controller. Fuzzy controller is used to control systems when the output value of system far away from the target value. Fuzzy self-tuning PID controller is applied when the output value is near the desired value. In the terms of adjusting the PID parameters are tuned by using fuzzy tuner as to obtain the optimum value. We demonstrate the performance of control scheme via experiments performed on the motor speed control of the SEHS. The results from the experiments show that the proposed a hybrid of fuzzy and fuzzy self-tuning PID controller has superior performance compared to a hybrid of fuzzy and PID controller. This is because the proposed controller does not require to readjustment the parameters of PID controller although the parameters of the SEHS will change any.

Author details

Kwanchai Sinthipsomboon, Issaree Hunsacharoonroj and Josept Khedari,
Rajamangala University of Technology, Rattanakosin, Thailand

Watcharin Po-ngaen and Pornjit Pratumsuwan
King Mongkut's University of Technology North Bangkok, Thailand

Acknowledgement

The authors would like to thank USE FLO-LINE Co., Ltd. and mechatronics educational research group for their equipments and technical support of this research project.

7. References

Merrit, H.E., "Hydraulic Control System". John Wiley, New York, 1976.

Rong-Fong Fung, Yun-Chen Wang, Rong-Tai Yang, and Hsing-Hsin Huang., "A variable structure control with proportional and integral compensatios for electrohydraulic position servo control system," Mechatronics vol.7, no. 1, 1997, pp. 67-81.

M. Aliyari, Shoorehdeli, M. Teshnehlab, and Aliyari Shoorehdeli., "Velocity control of an electro hydraulic servosystem," IEEE, 2007, pp. 1536-1539.

Parnichkun, M. and C. Ngaecharoenkul., "Hybrid of fuzzy and PID in kinematics of a pneumatic system," Proceeding of the 26th Annual Conference of the IEEE Industrial Electronics Society, Japan, 2000, pp: 1485-1490.

Pornjit Pratumsuwan, Siripun Thongchai, and Surapan Tansriwong., "A Hybrid of Fuzzy and Proportional-Integral-Derivative Controller for Electro-Hydraulic Position Servo System" Energy Research Journal, vol. 1,issue 2, 2010, pp. 62–67.

Jianming Zhang, Ning Wang, and Shuqing Wang., "Developed method of tuning PID controllers with fuzzy rules for integrating processes," Proceeding of the 2004 American control Conference, Massachusetts, 2004, pp. 1109-1114.

Shoujun Song and Weiguo Liu.,"Fuzzy parameters self-tuning PID control of switched reluctance motor based on Simulink/NCD," CIMCA-IAWTIC'06, IEEE, 2006.

Zulfatman and M.F. Rahmat.., "Application of self-tuning fuzzy PID controller on industrial hydraulic actuator using system identification approach," International journal on amart sensing and intelligent system, vol. 2, no. 2, 2009, pp. 246-261.

Bin Feng, Guofang Gong, and Huayong Yang.,"Self-tuning parameter fuzzy PID temperature control in a large hydraulic system," International Conference on Advanced Intelligent Mechatronics, IEEE/ASME,2009, pp.1418-142

Chapter 14

Design and Simulation of Anfis Controller for Virtual-Reality-Built Manipulator

Yousif I. Al Mashhadany

Additional information is available at the end of the chapter

http://dx.doi.org/10.5772/48383

1. Introduction

Fuzzy logic (FL) and artificial neural networks (ANNs), despite their successful use in many challenging control situations, still have drawbacks that limit them to only some applications. Their combined advantages have thus become the subject of much research into ways of overcoming their disadvantages. Neuro-fuzziness is one resulting rapidly emerging field. ANFIS network, proposed by Jang, is one popular neuro-fuzzy system [1-4].

For specific-problem training of an ANFIS network, [1] proposes use of hybrid learning rule, which combines gradient descent technique and least-square estimator (LSE). Being a method of supervised learning, it needs a teaching signal, which can be difficult to provide when the ANFIS network is to be a feedback controller, as the desired control actions that the teaching signal represents are unknown. Literatures have proposed several ANFIS learning methods in which ANFIS is applied as a MIMO controller. Djukanović *et al.*, for example, uses a special ANFIS learning technique called temporal back propagation (TBP); control of a nonlinear MIMO system is by considering both the controller and the plant as a single unit each time step. The method, however, is complex and distinctly computation-heavy [5-9].

Another training approach for ANFIS-controller of nonlinear MIMO systems is inverse learning; the ANFIS network is trained to learn the inverse dynamics of the plant it controls. Its success, however, is crucial on three elements: accurate modeling of the original system (a problem when the system is complex), availability of the system's inverse dynamics (they do not always exist), and appropriate distribution of the training data (could be impossible, given the constraints of the system's dynamics). [10-13] has another training approach besides the ones already mentioned.

Present robot navigation systems demand controllers that can solve complex problems under uncertain and dynamic environments. ANFIS garners interest because it offers the benefits of both neural network (NN) and FL, and removes their individual disadvantages by combining them on their common features. ANN is a new motivation for studies into FL. It can be used as a universal learning paradigm in any smooth parameterized models, including fuzzy inference systems [14-15].

Traditional robot control methods rely on strong mathematical modeling, analysis, and synthesis. Existing approaches suit control of mobile robots operating in unknown environments and performing tasks that require movement in dynamic environments. Operational tasks in unstructured environments such as remote planets and hazardous waste sites, however, are more complex, yet the analytical modeling is inadequate. Many researchers and engineers have tried to solve the navigational problems of mobile robot systems [16-18]. Though fuzzy systems can use knowledge expressed in linguistic rules (and thus could implement expert human knowledge and experience), fuzzy controller lacks a systematic design method. Tuning of membership-function parameters takes time. NN learning techniques can automate the process so development can be hastened and performance improved. The combination of NN and FL has produced neuro-fuzzy controllers and created their present popularity. In real-time autonomous navigation, a robot must be able to sense its environment, interpret the sensed information to obtain knowledge of its position and environment, and plan a route that gets it to the target position from an initial position and with obstacle avoidance and control of its direction and velocity. Ng et al. [19-23] propose a neural-integrated fuzzy controller that integrates FL representation of human knowledge with NN learning to solve nonlinear dynamic control problems. Pham et al. focus on developing intelligent multi-agent robot teams capable of both autonomous action and dynamic-environment collaboration in achieving team objectives. They also propose a neuro-fuzzy adaptive action selection architecture that enables a team of robot agents to achieve adaptive cooperative control of cooperative tasks, track dynamic targets, and push boxes. Crestani et al. defines autonomous navigation in mobile robots as a search process within a navigation environment that contains obstacles and targets, and propose a fuzzy-NN controller that considers navigation direction and navigation velocity as controllable. Rutkowski et al. derived a flexible neuro-fuzzy inference system; their approach increases structural and design flexibility in neuro-fuzzy systems. Hui et al. and Rusu et al. discuss neuro-fuzzy controllers for sensor-based mobile robot navigation. Garbi et al. implemented an adaptive neuro-fuzzy inference system in robotic vehicle navigation [24-26].

Robots are one way to improve industrial automation productivity. Robotic manipulators have been used in routine and dangerous-environment manufacturing jobs. They are highly nonlinear dynamic systems subject to uncertainties. Obtaining accurate dynamic equations for their control laws is thus difficult. Uncertainties in their dynamic models include unknown grasped payloads and unknown frictional coefficients. Adaptive control or model-free intelligent control has been much proposed as able to compensate for those uncertainties [26-28].

Virtual reality (VR) has become important to applications in engineering, medicine, statistics, and other areas where 3D images can aid understanding of system complexity. The interactability of a virtual system can in many applications be enhanced by touch sensing. Haptic feedback can convey to a human user, virtual environment forces. It has become useful in tele-surgery, where a master manipulator guides robotic surgical tools while providing realistic-force feedback to the surgeon. It is already available in many systems under development but these often still are specifically developed research prototypes (i.e., providing specific-force feedbacks and for specific problems) [29, 30].

Kinematics analysis is key to motion control of humanoid manipulators. Its main problems are forward kinematics and inverse kinematics. The inverse kinematics of a 7-DOF manipulator has multiple solutions; obtaining anthropomorphic solutions is thus a problem. Detailed research in it has yet to be found, though works on design, control, and obstacle avoidance in humanoid manipulator exist. In serial manipulators, between forward kinematics and inverse kinematics, solution of the latter is a lot more difficult. Solution methods of inverse kinematics generally are numerical, analytical, or geometric. Numerical method is most widely used, but it cannot obtain all possible solutions. Analytical method can derive all possible solutions but is much more difficult. Geometric method is simple and easy to understand but suits only a few types of manipulators [31, 32].

A human-manipulator skeleton has 7-DOF mechanism; other degrees of freedom of the arm are performed by the tendon. A 7-DOF anthropomorphic arm has been developed; it has the manipulability criterion and uses 3-DOF planar manipulator theory (i.e., the mechanism of the human limb can be modeled by three moving links). 3-DOF planar mechanism is fundamental to an anthropomorphic arm; its evaluation criteria can be used to analyze the arm's operational performance. 3-DOF planar manipulator theory is a supposition that the three link lengths are of the upper arm, the forearm, and the hand, and the three joints are 3-DOF shoulder joint, 1-DOF elbow joint, and 3-DOF wrist joint [33].

This chapter presents the design of an ANFIS controller of a VR manipulator model and simulation of the ANFIS-controlled system's command execution. Simulation results of the 7-DOF human-manipulator show an improved control system. Section II presents the manipulator's kinematic model whereas Section III the structure of the ANFIS controller and its learning methods. Section IV presents the manipulator's VR model, whereas Section V, the simulation of the case study, the system design, and the conclusions.

2. Kinematics of the 7-DOF manipulator

Forward kinematics was used to calculate the racket's posture according to the joint angles. It is quite useful for analysis of the manipulator's workspace and verification of the inverse kinematics. Denoting the shoulder width as D, the upper arm length as L_1, and the lower arm length as L_2, the position of the shoulder is thus $P_1(0, -D, 0)$ and the position of the elbow is P_2 (x_{p2} , y_{p2} , z_{p2}). Denoting the joint angles as q_1 … q_7, the posture of joint i relative to joint i-1 can thus be described by a 4×4 homogeneous matrix ${}^{i-1}T_i$ [34]:

$$\left.\begin{array}{l} {}^0T_1=\begin{bmatrix} cq_1 & 0 & sq_1 & 0 \\ 0 & 1 & 0 & -D \\ -sq_1 & 0 & cq_1 & 0 \\ 0 & 0 & 0 & 1 \end{bmatrix},\ {}^1T_2=\begin{bmatrix} 1 & 0 & 0 & 0 \\ 0 & cq_2 & -sq_2 & 0 \\ 0 & sq_2 & cq_2 & 0 \\ 0 & 0 & 0 & 1 \end{bmatrix},\ {}^2T_3=\begin{bmatrix} cq_3 & -sq_3 & 0 & 0 \\ sq_3 & cq_3 & 0 & 0 \\ 0 & 0 & 1 & 0 \\ 0 & 0 & 0 & 1 \end{bmatrix} \\ {}^3T_4=\begin{bmatrix} 1 & 0 & 0 & 0 \\ 0 & cq_4 & -sq_4 & 0 \\ 0 & sq_4 & cq_4 & 0 \\ 0 & 0 & 0 & 1 \end{bmatrix},\ {}^4T_5=\begin{bmatrix} cq_5 & -sq_5 & 0 & 0 \\ sq_5 & cq_5 & 0 & 0 \\ 0 & 0 & 1 & 0 \\ 0 & 0 & 0 & 1 \end{bmatrix},\ {}^5T_6=\begin{bmatrix} 1 & 0 & 0 & 0 \\ 0 & cq_6 & -sq_6 & 0 \\ 0 & sq_6 & cq_6 & 0 \\ 0 & 0 & 0 & 1 \end{bmatrix},\ {}^6T_7=\begin{bmatrix} cq_7 & 0 & sq_7 & 0 \\ 0 & 1 & 0 & -D \\ -sq_7 & 0 & cq_7 & 0 \\ 0 & 0 & 0 & 1 \end{bmatrix} \end{array}\right\} \quad (1)$$

Where: $sq_i \equiv \sin(q_i)$; $cq_i \equiv \cos(q_i)$

Assuming the position of Joint-7 in the fixed coordinate is P_3 (x_{p3} , y_{p3} , z_{p3}) and its pose as described by RPY (Roll Pitch Yaw) angles is (ϕ, θ, ψ), the posture of Joint-7 can thus be described by a homogenous matrix ${}^0\boldsymbol{T}_7$:

$${}^0T_7=\begin{bmatrix} c\varphi c\theta & c\varphi s\theta s\psi - s\varphi c\psi & c\varphi s\theta c\psi + s\varphi s\psi & x_{p3} \\ s\varphi c\theta & s\varphi s\theta s\psi + c\varphi c\psi & s\varphi s\theta c\psi - c\varphi s\psi & y_{p3} \\ -s\theta & c\theta s\psi & c\theta c\psi & z_{p3} \\ 0 & 0 & 0 & 1 \end{bmatrix} \quad (2)$$

Matrix ${}^0\boldsymbol{T}_7$ also stands for the racket's posture and can be derived also as:

$${}^0T_7={}^0T_1{}^1T_2{}^2T_3{}^3T_4{}^4T_5{}^5T_6{}^6T_7\begin{bmatrix} n_x & o_x & a_x & p_x \\ n_y & o_y & a_y & p_y \\ n_z & o_z & a_z & p_z \\ 0 & 0 & 0 & 1 \end{bmatrix} \quad (3)$$

From (1) and (2), the racket's posture can be calculated as:

$$\left\{\begin{array}{c} \varphi = a\tan 2(n_y, n_x) \\ \theta = a\tan 2(-n_z, c\varphi n_x + s\varphi n_y) \\ \psi = a\tan 2(s\varphi a_x - c\varphi a_y, -s\varphi o_x + c\varphi o_y) \end{array}\right. \quad \& \quad \left.\begin{array}{c} x_{p3}=p_x \\ y_{p3}=p_y \\ z_{p3}=p_z \end{array}\right\} \quad (4)$$

with atan2( ) being the four-quadrant inverse tangent function and (3) the manipulator's forward kinematics. All the commands (e.g., the racket's hitting position and hitting speed) are given by the visual system, in the operation space. They must be transformed into joint space values. Jacobian matrix is used to calculate the joint space speed according to the operation space speed. The mapping relationship between them is [35]:

$$V = J(q)\dot{q} \quad (5)$$

with $\boldsymbol{V}$ being the racket's speed in the operation space and $\dot{q}$ the joint space speed. $\boldsymbol{J}$ is the 6×7 Jacobian matrix and can be derived by differential transformation method. The ith item of $\boldsymbol{J}$ is:

$$J_i = \begin{bmatrix} (p_i \times n_i)_k \\ (p_i \times o_i)_k \\ (p_i \times o_i)_k \\ n_{ik} \\ o_{ik} \\ a_{ik} \end{bmatrix} \tag{6}$$

Where $\boldsymbol{n}_i(n_{ix}, n_{iy}, n_{iz})$, $\boldsymbol{o}_i(o_{ix}, o_{iy}, o_{iz})$, $\boldsymbol{a}_i(a_{ix}, a_{iy}, a_{iz})$ and $\boldsymbol{p}_i(p_{ix}, p_{iy}, p_{iz})$ are the items of matrix ${}^{i-1}T_i$

$${}^{i-1}T_7 = {}^{i-1}T_i \ldots\ldots {}^{6}T_7 = \begin{bmatrix} n_x & o_x & a_x & p_x \\ n_y & o_y & a_y & p_y \\ n_z & o_z & a_z & p_z \\ 0 & 0 & 0 & 1 \end{bmatrix} \tag{7}$$

The parameter k stands for the rotational axis of joint i. For example, if the joint rotates around the x-axis, then k is x. Racket speed $\boldsymbol{V}$ can be calculated by (4) whereas joint space speed $\dot{q}$ cannot be uniquely determined because $\boldsymbol{J}$ is not a square matrix. This problem can be solved by Moore-Penrose method:

$$\dot{q} = J^{+}V \tag{8}$$

with $J^{+} = (J^T J)^{-1} J^T$ being the Moore-Penrose pseudo inverse matrix of $\boldsymbol{J}$.

The inverse kinematics is used to calculate the joint angles according to the racket's posture. The manipulator is redundant, so the elbow's position is not uniquely determined when the racket's posture is given. The motion characteristics of a human arm show the mapping relationships between elbow position and racket posture. In a general configuration of the manipulator (see Fig. 2), any three points on the manipulator's neck, shoulder, elbow, and wrist are not collinear. The position of elbow P_2, whose axis is P_1P_3, is in circle $O^{'}$. The position of the center point $O^{'} = (x_{O^{'}}, y_{O^{'}}, z_{O^{'}})$ and the radius r of the circle are determined by positions P_1 and P_3, and arm length parameters L_1 and L_2. Ω_1 denotes the plane constructed by points P_1, P_2, and P_3, and Ω_2 the plane constructed by points O, P_1, and P_2. α denotes the separation angle between Ω_1 and Ω_2. Once the position of P3 is known, α can uniquely determine P2 elbow position. If the points O, P_1, P_3 are collinear whereas P_1, P_2, P_3 are not, the plane Ω_2 does not exist. Angle α can be defined as the separation angle between Ω_1 and the horizontal plane. Also, if the points P1, P2, P3 are collinear, the plane Ω_1 does not exist and P2 position can be calculated according to positions P_1 and P_3 and arm length parameters L_1 and L_2. Considering the general configuration of the manipulator (see Fig. 2), the inverse kinematics can be solved if angle α and the racket's posture are given. According to the motion characteristics of human arms, the mapping relationship between α and the racket posture can be built offline. Denoting with $\boldsymbol{i}$ (i_1, i_2, i_3) the unit vector pointing from P_3

to P_1, and assuming the angle α to have been calculated by a well-trained ANN model, the circle O' can thus be expressed as [34-36]:

$$\begin{Bmatrix} i_1(x - x_{o'}) + i_2(y - y_{o'}) + i_3(z - z_{o'}) = 0 \\ (x - x_{o'})^2 + (y - y_{o'})^2 + (z - z_{o'})^2 = r^2 \end{Bmatrix} \tag{9}$$

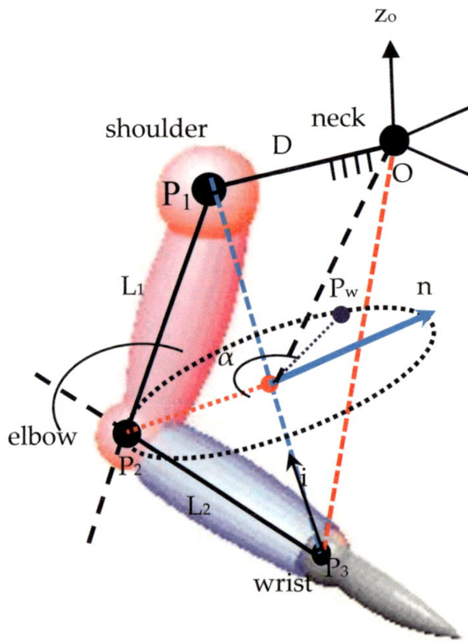

Figure 1. General configuration of the manipulator

The plane Ω2 and the circle O' intersect at two points. One point near the neck is P_w (x_w, y_w, z_w) and angle $\angle P_2O'P_w$ is the separation angle α between Ω_1 and Ω_2. Denoting Ω_2 norm vector as $\boldsymbol{n}$ and position as P_w should satisfy this equation:

$$\overrightarrow{OP_w}.n = 0 \tag{10}$$

P_w position can be calculated from (9) and (10). P_2 position (x_{p2}, y_{p2}, z_{p2}) satisfies this equation:

$$\sqrt{(x_{p2} - x_m)^2 + (y_{p2} - y_m)^2 + (z_{p2} - z_m)^2} = 2r\sin\frac{\alpha}{2} \tag{11}$$

P_2 position can be calculated from (9) and (11). With P_1, P_2, P_3 positions and the cosine theorem, Joint-4 angle can be calculated as:

$$q_4 = \pi - a\cos\left(\frac{L_1^2 + L_2^2 - \left\|\overline{P_1P_3}\right\|^2}{2L_1L_2}\right) \tag{12}$$

With P2 position, this can be obtained:

$$\begin{bmatrix} x_{p2} & y_{p2} & z_{p2} & 1 \end{bmatrix}^T = {}^0T_1{}^1T_2{}^2T_3\begin{bmatrix} 0 & 0 & -L_1 & 1 \end{bmatrix}^T \tag{13}$$

The angles of Joints 1 and 2 can thus be derived as:

$$\left.\begin{aligned} q_1 &= a\tan 2(\frac{-x_{p2}}{cq_2L_1},\frac{-z_{p2}}{cq_2L_1}) + k\pi \qquad (k \in N) \\ q_2 &= a\sin((y_{p2} + D)/L_1) \end{aligned}\right\} \tag{14}$$

With P3 position, this can be obtained:

$$\begin{bmatrix} x_{p3} & y_{p3} & z_{p3} & 1 \end{bmatrix}^T = {}^0T_1{}^1T_2{}^2T_3{}^3T_4\begin{bmatrix} 0 & 0 & -L_2 & 1 \end{bmatrix}^T \tag{15}$$

Joint-3 angle can thus be derived as:

$$\begin{Bmatrix} q_3 = a\tan 2(\dfrac{y_3 + D - sq_2L_1 - sq_2cq_4L_2}{cq_1cq_2sq_4L_2}sq_1sq_2 - \dfrac{x_3 + sq_1cq_2(1+cq_4)L_1}{sq_2cq_1L_1} \\ ,\dfrac{y_3 + D - sq_2L_1}{cq_2sq_4L_2} - \dfrac{sq_2cq_4}{cq_2sq_4}) \end{Bmatrix} \tag{16}$$

From (2),

$$T_5{}^4T_6{}^5T_7^6 = \left[T_1{}^0T_2{}^1T_3{}^2T_4^3\right]^{-1}T_7^6 = T^* \tag{17}$$

The angles of Joints 5-7 can thus be derived as:

$$\left.\begin{aligned} q_5 &= a\tan 2(-T_{13}^*, T_{23}^*) + k\pi \qquad (k \in N) \\ q_6 &= a\tan 2((sq_5T_{13}^* - sq_5T_{23}^*, T_{33}^*) \\ q_7 &= a\tan 2((-cq_5T_{12}^* - sq_5T_{22}^*, cq_5T_{11}^* + sq_5T_{21}^*) \end{aligned}\right\} \tag{18}$$

with T_{ij}^* being the ith row and j^{ij} the column item of T

3. General structures of ANFIS

ANFIS integrates ANN with FIS. The ANFIS analyzed here was a first-order Takagi Sugeno Fuzzy Model. The analysis has four inputs: front obstacle distance (x_1), right obstacle distance (x_2), left obstacle distance (x_3), and target angle (x_4). The output is steering angle. The 'if-then' rules are [26, 37]:

$$\begin{aligned} &Rule: \ IF \ \ x_1 \ \ is \ \ A_j; \ \ x_2 \ \ is \ \ B_k; \ \ x_3 \ \ is \ \ C_m \ \ and \ \ x_4 \ \ is \ \ D_n \\ &THEN \quad F_i = p_ix_1 + r_ix_2 + s_ix_3 + t_ix_4 \end{aligned} \tag{19}$$

Where

$$\begin{array}{l} F_i = p_i x_1 + r_i x_2 + s_i x_3 + t_i x_4 + u_i \quad \text{for steering angle} \\ J=1 \text{ to } q_1;\; k=1 \text{ to } q_2;\; m=1 \text{ to } q_3;\; n=1 \text{ to } q_4;\; \text{and } i=1 \text{ to } q_1 \cdot q_2 \;\; q_3 \cdot q_4 \end{array} \tag{20}$$

A, B, C, and D are the fuzzy membership sets defined for input variables x_1, x_2, x_3, and x_4. q_1, q_2, q_3, and q_4 are the number of membership functions, respectively for the fuzzy systems of inputs x_1, x_2, x_3 and x_4. fi is the linear consequent functions defined in terms of inputs x_1, x_2, x_3, and x_4. q_i, r_i, s_i , ti, and ui are consequent parameters of an ANFIS fuzzy model. Same-layer nodes of an ANFIS model have similar functions. Output signals from the nodes of a preceding layer are input signals to a present layer. The output obtained through the node function will be input signals to the next layer (see Figure 2) [38, 39].

Layer 1: This is the input layer, which defines obstacles as either static or moving and also the tracker robot's target position. It receives signals from x_1, x_2, x_3, and x_4.

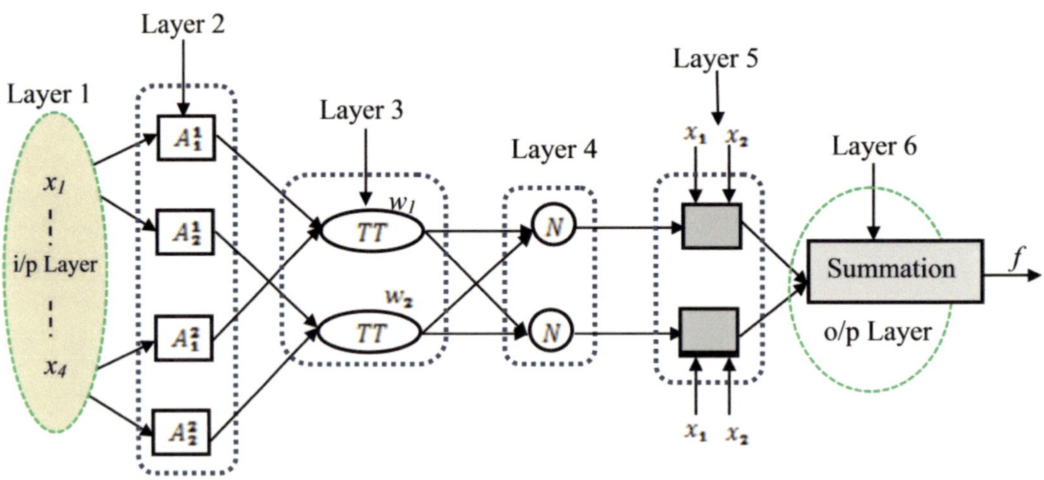

Figure 2. Structure of a six-layer ANFIS

Layer 2: Every node in this layer is an adaptive node (square node) with a particular fuzzy membership function (node function) specifying the degrees to which the inputs satisfy the quantifier. For four inputs, the node outputs are:

$$\begin{array}{llll} L_{2g} = U_{ag}(x) & for & g = 1,\ldots\ldots, q_1 & (for \;\; input \;\; x_1) \\ L_{2g} = U_{Bg}(x) & for & g = q_1 + 1,\ldots\ldots, q_1 + q_2 & (for \;\; input \;\; x_1) \\ L_{2g} = U_{Cg}(x) & for & g = q_1 + q_2 + 1,\ldots\ldots, q_1 + q_2 + q_3 & (for \;\; input \;\; x_1) \\ L_{2g} = U_{Dg}(x) & for & g = q_1 + q_2 + q_3 + 1,\ldots\ldots, q_1 + q_2 + q_3 + q_4 & (for \;\; input \;\; x_1) \end{array} \tag{21}$$

The membership functions considered here for A, B, C, and D are bell-shaped functions and defined as:

$$\left.\begin{aligned}
\mu_{Ag}(x) &= \frac{1}{1+\left\{\left(\frac{x-c_g}{a_g}\right)^2\right\}^{b_g}}; \quad g=1 \quad to \quad q_1 \\
\mu_{Bg}(x) &= \frac{1}{1+\left\{\left(\frac{x-c_g}{a_g}\right)^2\right\}^{b_g}}; \quad g=q_1+1 \quad to \quad q_1+q_2 \\
\mu_{Bg}(x) &= \frac{1}{1+\left\{\left(\frac{x-c_g}{a_g}\right)^2\right\}^{b_g}}; \quad g=q_1+q_2+1 \quad to \quad q_1+q_2+q_3 \\
\mu_{Bg}(x) &= \frac{1}{1+\left\{\left(\frac{x-c_g}{a_g}\right)^2\right\}^{b_g}}; \quad g=q_1+q_2+q_3+1 \quad to \quad q_1+q_2+q_3+q_4
\end{aligned}\right\} \tag{22}$$

with a_g, b_g, and c_g being the parameters for fuzzy membership function. The bell-shaped function changes its pattern with changes to the parameters. This change will give various contours of the bell-shaped function, as needed and in accordance with the data set for the problem considered.

Layer 3: Every node in this layer is a fixed node (circular) labeled 'π'. L_{2i} output is the product of all incoming signals.

$$\begin{aligned}
&L_{3i} = W_i = U_{ag}(x), U_{Bg}(x), U_{Cg}(x), U_{Cg}(x); \\
&For\, i = 1, \ldots, q_1+q_2+q_3+q_4 \quad and \quad g = 1, \ldots, q_1+q_2+q_3+q_4
\end{aligned} \tag{23}$$

Each of the second layer's node output represents the firing strength (degree of fulfillment) of the associated rule. The T-norm operator algebraic product $\{T_{ap}(a,b) = ab\}$ was used to obtain the firing strength (W_i).

Layer 4: Every node in this layer is a fixed node (circular) labeled "N". The output of the ith node is the ratio of the firing strength of the ith rule (W_i) to the sum of the firing strength of all the rules [40].

$$L_{4i} = \overline{W}_i f_i = \frac{W_i}{\sum_{r=1}^{r=q_1 \cdot q_2 \cdot q_3 \cdot q_4} W_r} \tag{24}$$

This output gives a normalized firing strength.

Layer 5: Every node in this layer is an adaptive node (square node) with a node function.

$$L_{5i} = \overline{W}_i f_i = \overline{W}_i (p_i x_1 + r_i x_1 + s_i x_3 + t_i x_4 + u_i) \quad (25)$$

with $\overline{W_i}$ being the normalized firing strength form (output) from Layer-3 and {p_i, r_i, s_i, t_i, u_i} the steering-angle parameter set. Parameters in this layer are consequent.

Layer 6: The single node in this layer is a fixed node (circular) labeled "Σ". It computes the overall output as the summation of all incoming signals.

$$L_{6i} = \sum_{r=1}^{r=q_1 \cdot q_2 \cdot q_3 \cdot q_4} \overline{W}_i f_i = \frac{\sum_{i=1}^{i=q_1 \cdot q_2 \cdot q_3 \cdot q_4} \overline{W}_i f_i}{\sum_{i=1}^{i=q_1 \cdot q_2 \cdot q_3 \cdot q_4} W_i} \quad (26)$$

This work's ANFIS development has six-dimensional space partitions and q_1, q_2, q_3, and q_4 regions. Each region is governed by a fuzzy if-then rule. The first layer is the input layer. The second contains premise or antecedent parameters of the ANFIS and is dedicated to fuzzy sub-space. Consequent parameters of the fifth layer were used to optimize the network. During the forward pass of the hybrid learning algorithm, node outputs go forward until Layer-5 and the consequent parameters are identified by least-square method. In the backward pass, error signals propagate backwards and the premise parameters are updated by gradient descent method [40, 41].

4. VR Modeling of the 7-DOF manipulator

Design requirements for Virtual Reality Modeling Language (VRML) are described in finite processing allocations, autonomy, consistent self-registration, and calculability. VRML design procedure will be presented. Design in VRML depends on the information available to the designer and his imaging of the object. There are two choices for VR design: one is standard configuration such as sphere, cone, cylinder, etc., another is free design by selecting indexed face set button to get many configurations with free rearrangement of points; every real-form design is thus considered to be the latter [42-45], which starts with building parts one by one and comparing the shape's similarity against that of the real manipulator part. Manipulator parts cannot be simulated in VR when the VR library's standard shapes (they are not uniform) are used. Designing thus uses indexed face set in VR. The second choice to be made in design work is very important as it is about connecting all parts to get the final object, and limiting the object's original point. This is the starting point of the design work. The first shape (e.g., the shoulder) is first set, and then the next shape (forearm) is connected to the "children" button. The same procedure is repeated for other parts. Figure 3 presents the full design of the 7-DOF human arm manipulator [46-50].

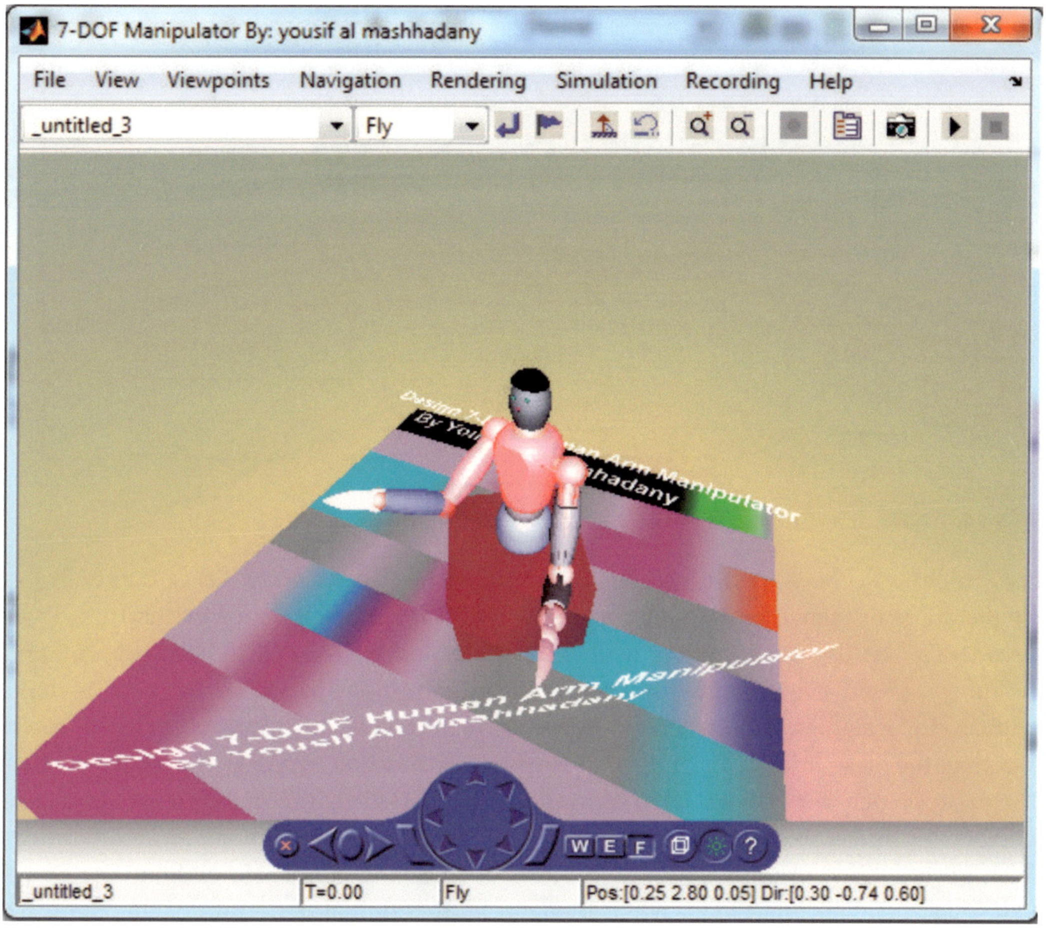

Figure 3. The VR-modeled 7-DOF human-arm manipulator

5. Design of the ANFIS controller for the 7-DOF manipulator

The design work considered many parameters related to the system's real values (see Table 1 for real limits of the joints of a human arm). The joints motor is considered a real DC-motor with a transfer function similar with that in Equation (1).

$$T.F_m(s) = \frac{1}{s^2 + 6s + 8} \tag{27}$$

Figure 4 is a block diagram of the control system. The inputs to the system design have two sets of targets: orientation (θ_{T1}, θ_{T2}, θ_{T3}) and position (T_x, T_y, T_z). In the proposed technique, each joint has its own controller, so in all, seven identical (same structure, same training algorithm) ANFIS controllers were used. Inputs of the training algorithm were the desired joint angle and the actual angle. The desired values were calculated by using analytical solution of the IKP algorithm shown previously. Actual values of the joint angle were obtained by feedback from the virtual model.

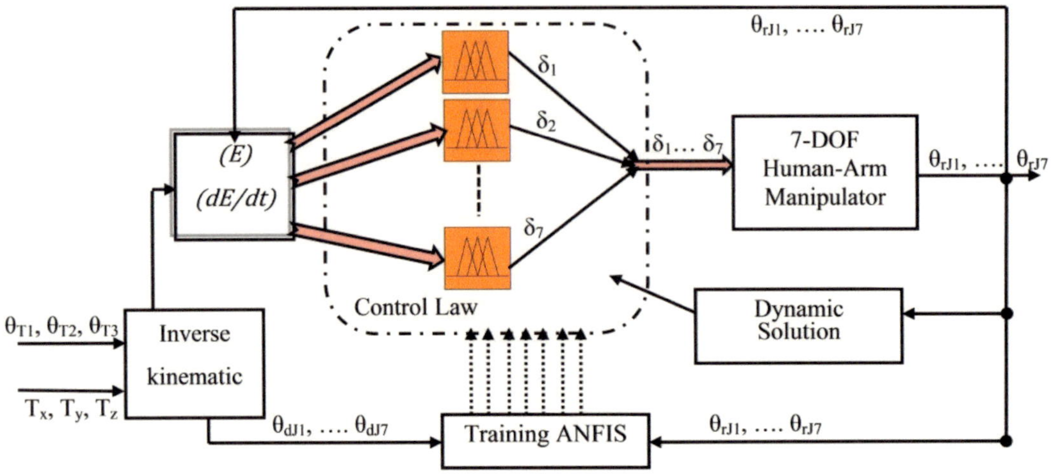

Figure 4. ANFIS control of the 7-DOF human-arm manipulator

The structure of the ANFIS controller was built in Matlab software Ver.2011b, with two inputs, an error signal, and change in the error. The fuzzy inference method used was Mamdani's, because it is intuitive, widely accepted, and well-suited to human input, and, for the proposed control structure, it gives better results than does Sugeno inference method. In designing the controller, types of membership functions were tried before selecting the best: triangular built-in membership function (trimf). The trial-and-error design approach for the ANFIS controller, i.e., selecting the interference type, the membership function type, and the number of this membership function in the hidden layer, gave optimal results: minimum number of rules and simple simulation. The design uses seven parallel-connected ANFIS to compute the optimal deflection of the joints and get the desired angle. Figures (5-7) show the procedure of the Matlab-fuzzy-toolbox-based design.

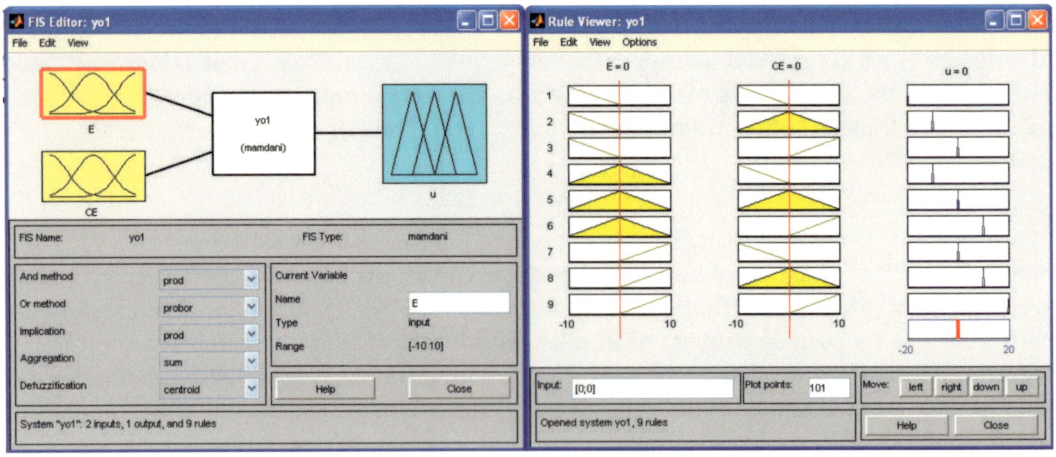

Figure 5. Mamdani's fuzzy inference and the set of rules for training of the ANFIS controller

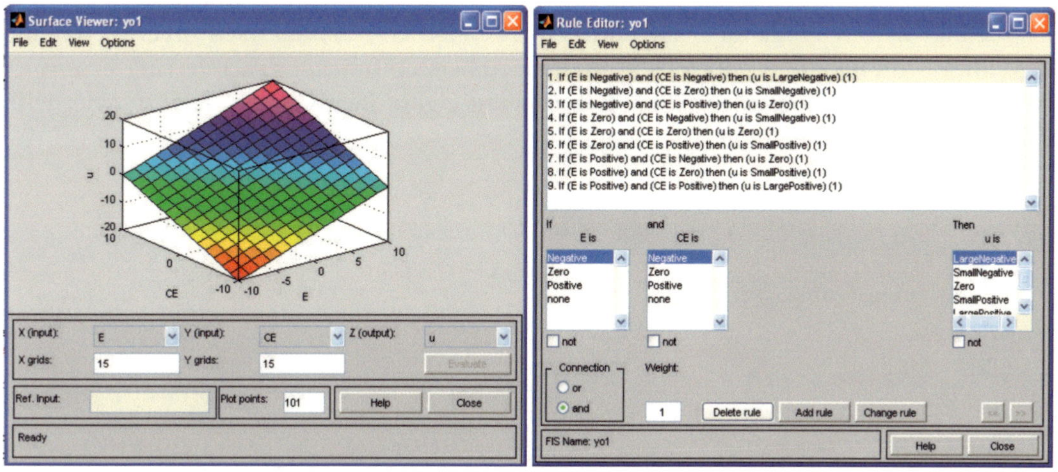

Figure 6. The surface error and the set of rules for training of the ANFIS controller

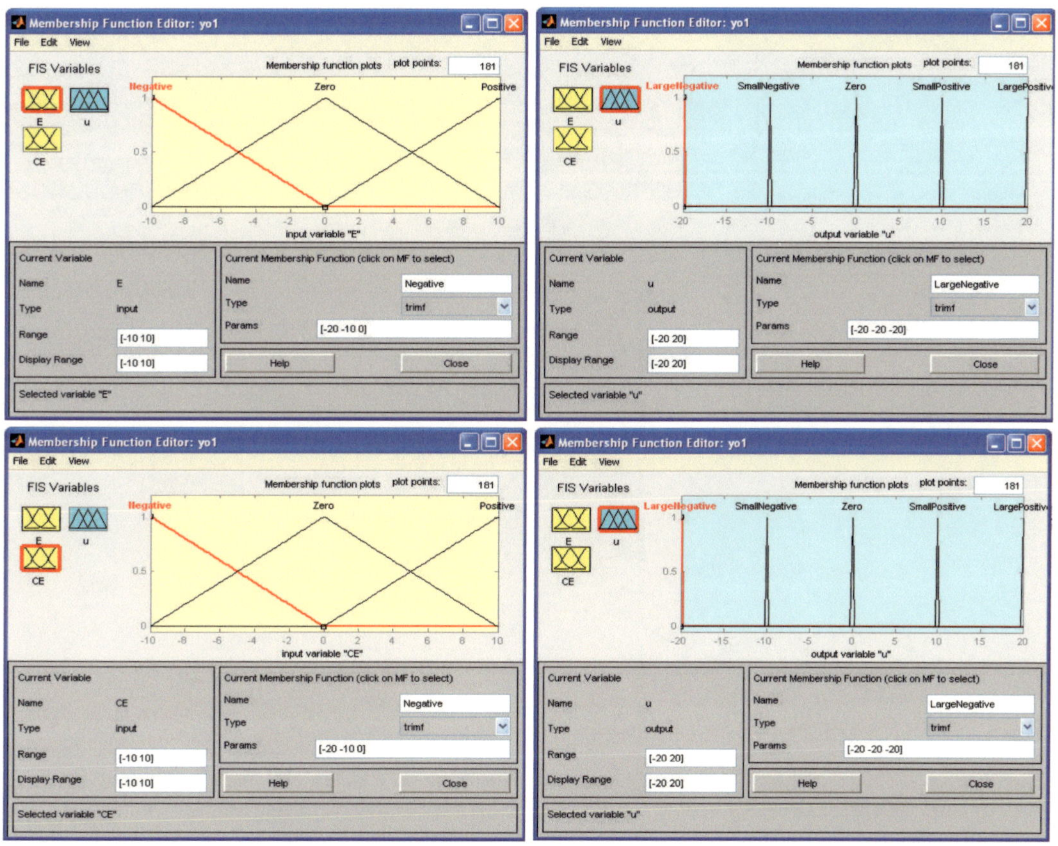

Figure 7. The triangular built-in memberships function with error signal and change in error signal

Figure 8 shows in Matlab Simulink GUI window the internal structure of the ANFIS controller and the training output for the input signal, with the various steps used in instructing the manipulator's movement. The ANFIS training used hybrid training algorithm, with the input nodes (3, 3) to the membership functions each having nine rules (see Figure 5). Epoch length was used in training eighty iterations for each sample, with 0.01s Simulink sampling time.

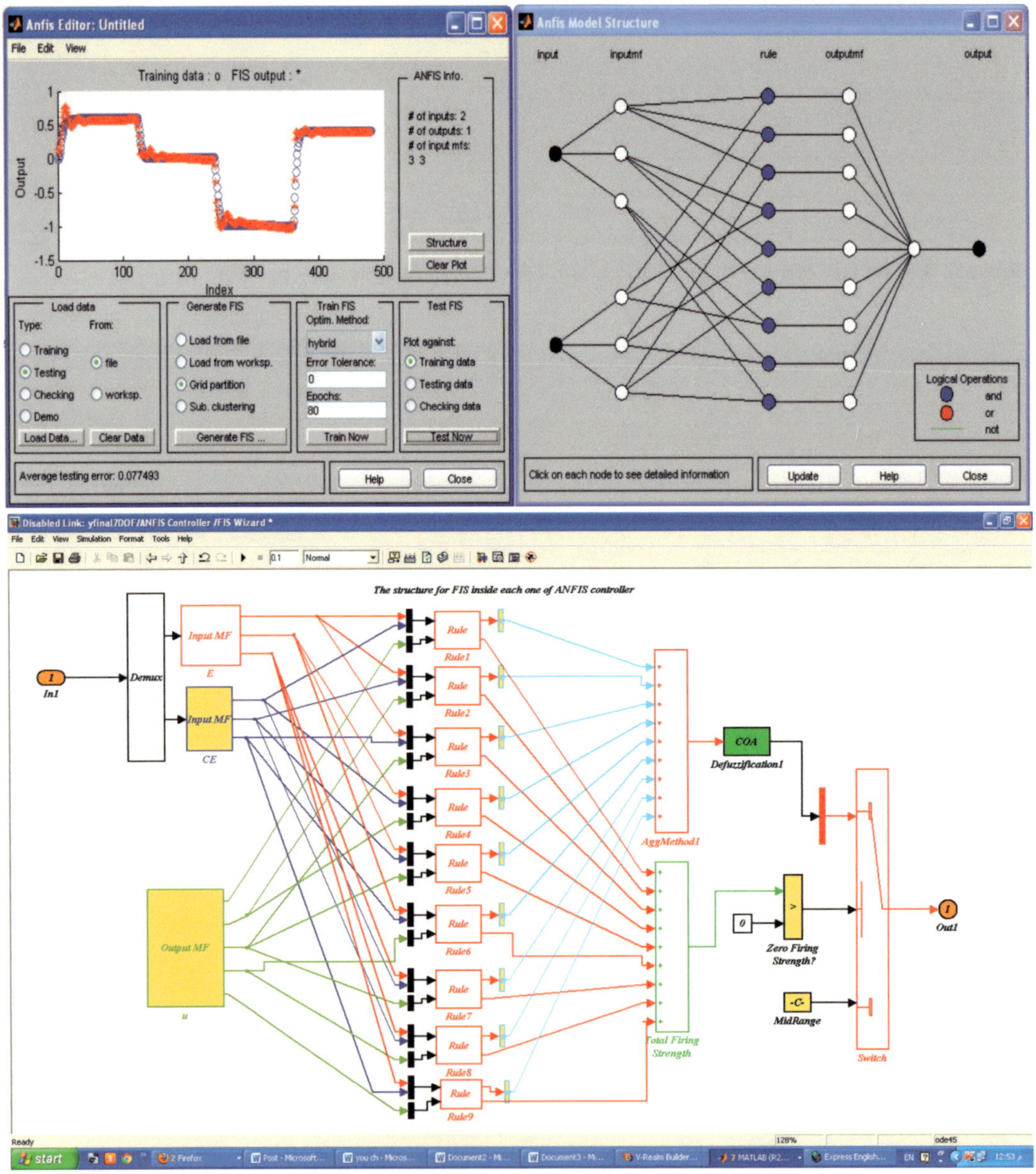

Figure 8. The ANFIS structure in Matlab-Simulink GUI and its training response

6. Simulation results

Figure 9(a) is a block diagram of the simulation done for the ANFIS-controlled manipulator. Seven ANFIS controllers were used, one each for each degree of freedom of the three joints (3 for the shoulder, 1 for the elbow, and 3 for the wrist). The seven were effective in tracking the trajectory desired for the 7-DOF manipulator. The controller's rules base has 9 rules, each determined by fuzzy neural network (FNN). The desired position and orientation were, in simulation entered as input signal, whereas actual positions for the joints were given as feedback from the output signal. Figure 9(b) shows the results of using both ANFIS and PID controllers on the joints and for the ANFIS controller's implementation into the virtual model. Performance of the ANFIS-controlled joint was better than that of the PID-controlled one. The ANFIS controller effected fast response in the manipulator and reduced errors, for various complex trajectories of the manipulator.

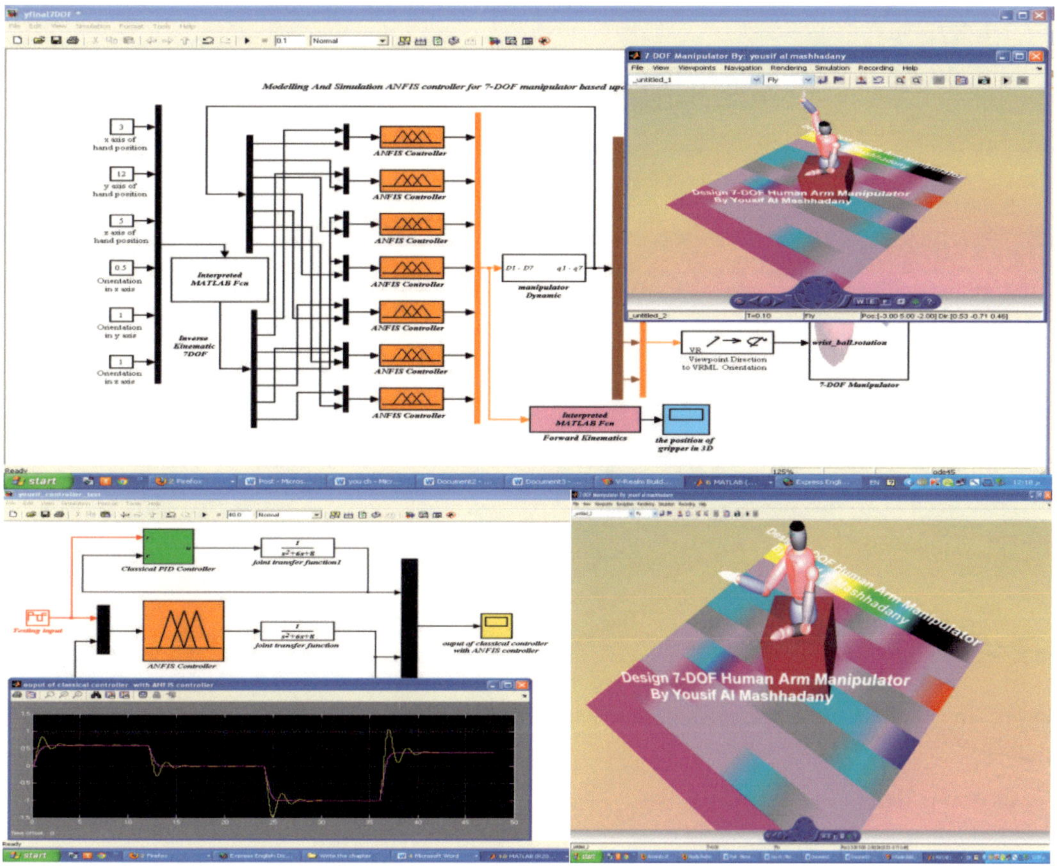

Figure 9. (a, b, c). Simulation of the ANFIS controller for the VR-implemented 7-DOF manipulator

The manipulator's movements used the link between Matlab-Simulink and VR environment. Computation for the order of movement was done in Matlab-Simulink. The order was then sent to the VR model to implement, with considerations for the axes between

Matlab's and VR's to get the real movement (i.e., for general motion: elbow flexion/extension, elbow rotation (supination/pronation), shoulder adduction/abduction, shoulder flexion/extension, shoulder interior/exterior rotation, wrist flexion/extension, wrist ulnar/radial deviation, shoulder horizontal flexion/extension; for special motion: arm reaching towards the head, arm reaching to the right and the head, arm reaching to the left and the head, and arm reaching to the right) (see Figure 10 for examples).

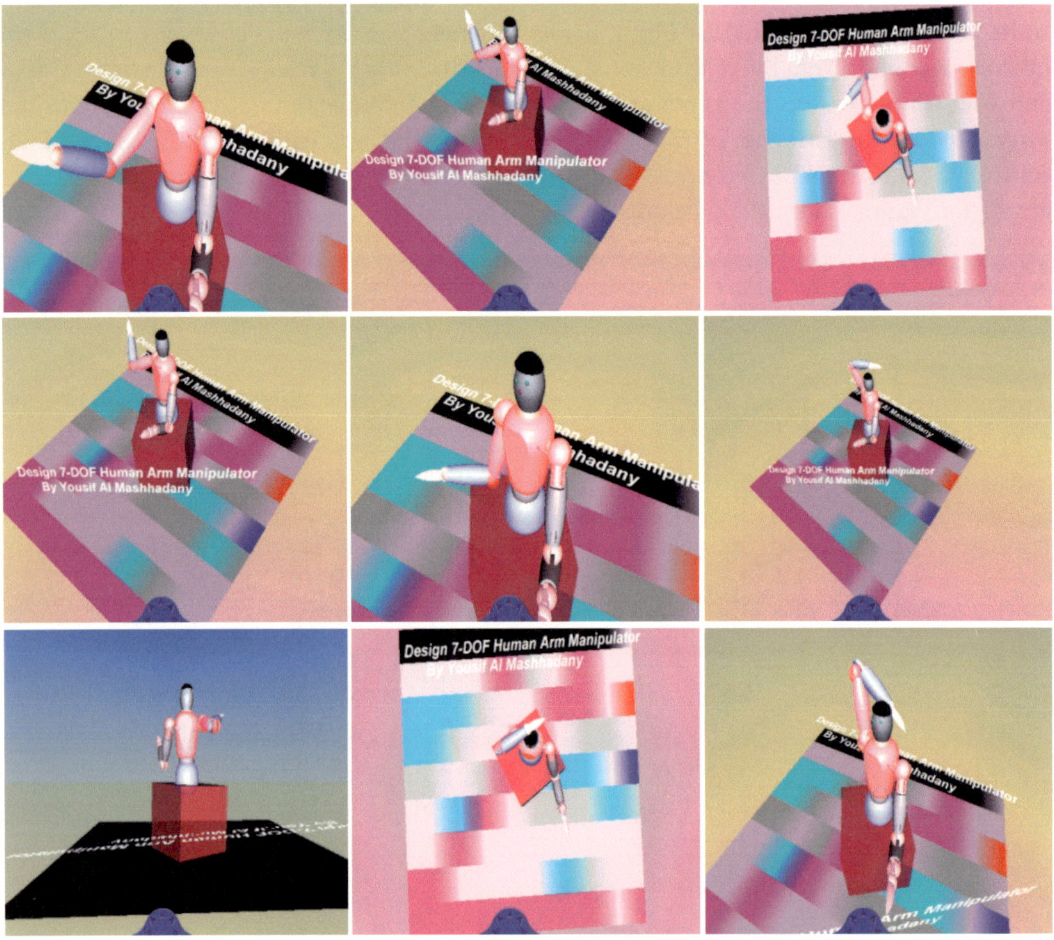

Figure 10. Postures of the ANFIS-controlled 7-DOF manipulator

7. Conclusion

This work aimed to design an ANFIS-based controller that overcomes the general problems of FL and NN in a dynamic system. To obtain excellent manipulator postures, training of the ANFIS controller for all the elements (fuzzy interference, membership function, number of neurons, number of rules) was by trial and error. The controller was compared with classical PID controller, in tracking the speed and the joint angle's accuracy. The simulation results allowed these conclusions to be drawn:

- For any speed, the ANFIS controller has the better transient response and the steadier state response than does a PID controller; even the best-tuned PID controller is unable to perform well in both slow-speed and high-speed ranges.
- With only 9 neurons, 4 layers, and 9 rules, the proposed ANFIS controller is simpler than other adaptive neuro-fuzzy controllers reported by many other researches.
- The ANFIS controller does not require an accurate model of the plant. Its relative simplicity makes it fairly easy to construct and implement. High-level knowledge of system is not needed to build a set of rules for a fuzzy controller or for the identification needed in an NN controller.
- The ANFIS controller was used in both simulation and experiment in trajectory tracking of multiple manipulators. Kinematic analysis of the 7-DOF manipulator produced the calculation for the envelope of similar manipulators.
- VR implementation of the manipulator was able to show the latter's accuracy. The manipulator can be depended on for many high-accuracy applications such as collecting of minute/fragile items.

Author details

Yousif I. Al Mashhadany
Electrical Dept., Al Anbar University, Engineering College, Baghdad, Iraq

Acknowledgement

Special thanks to Ms. Wirani M. Munawir of Verdana Inc. (verdana.inc@live.com) for her editing of the text.

8. References

[1] AWARE M. V, KQTHARI A.G, CHOUBE S.O, (2000), "Application of adaptive neuro-fuzzy controller (ANFIS) for voltage source inverter fed induction motor drive", IEEE Power Electronics and Motion Control Conference, 2000. Proceedings. IPEMC 2000. The Third International 945-939

[2] Choon Y. L, Lee J, (2005)," Multiple Neuro-Adaptive Control of Robot Manipulators Using Visual Cues", IEEE transactions on industrial electronics, Vol. 52, No.1, 320-326.

[3] Hui C, Gangquan S, Yanbin Z, Xikui M, (2007),"A Hybrid Controller of Self-Optimizing Algorithm and ANFIS for Ball Mill Pulverizing System", Proceedings of the IEEE International Conference on Mechatronics and Automation, Harbin, China

[4] Swasti R. K, Sidhartha P, (2010), "ANFIS Approach for TCSC-based Controller Design System Stability Improvement Design for Power" , IEEE ICCCCT-10, 149-154

[5] Prabu D, Surendra K, Rajendra P, (2011), "Advanced Dynamic Path Control of the Three Links SCARA using Adaptive Neuro Fuzzy Inference System", IN BOOK, Robot Manipulators, Trends and Development, InTech, ch 18, ISBN: 978-953-307-073-5. pp. 399-412

[6] Zhiqiang G, Thomas A. T, James G. D, (2000),"A Stable Self-Tuning Fuzzy Logic Control System for Industrial Temperature Regulation", IEEE Industry Applications Conference, Vol 2, 1232-1240

[7] Jeich M, Feng-J. L, (2001), "An ANFIS Controller for the Car-Following Collision Prevention System", IEEE transactions on VEHICULAR TECHNOLOGY, Vol. 50, No. 4, 1106-1113.

[8] Hassanzadeh, S. K, liang G. A, (2002), "Implementation of .I Functional Link Net-ANFIS Controller for a Robot Manipulator", Third International Workshop on Robot Motion and Control, 399-404

[9] Saifizul A. A., Zainon M. Z, Abu Osman N. A, (2006), "An ANFIS Controller for Vision-based Lateral Vehicle Control System", Control, Automation, Robotics and Vision, 2006. ICARCV '06. 9th International Conference on IEEE ICARCV, 1-4.

[10] Ravi S, Balakrishnan P .A, (2010), "Modeling and control of an ANFIS temperature controller for plastic extrusion process", IEEE Communication Control and Computing Technologies, ICCCCT-10, 314-320.

[11] Omar F. L, Samsul B. M. N, Mohammad H. M, (2011), "A Genetically Trained Simplified ANFIS Controller to Control Nonlinear MIMO Systems", International Conference on Electrical, Control and Computer Engineering Pahang, Malaysia, 349-354

[12] Sgg Pedro P. C, Maya R. E, (2004), "Vector Control using ANFIS Controller with Space Vector Modulation", Universities Power Engineering Conference, 2004. UPEC 2004. 39th International, 545-549

[13] Thair S. M, Mohammed H. M, Tang S. H, Sokchoo N, (2008), "ANFIS Controller with Fuzzy Subtractive Clustering Method to Reduce Coupling Effects in Twin Rotor MIMO System (TRMS) with Less Memory and Time Usage", IEEE International Conference on Advanced Computer Control, 19-24

[14] Mohammad A, (2006), "ANFIS Based Soft-Starting and Speed Control of AC Voltage Controller Fed Induction Motor", 0-7803-9525-5/06/6 IEEE Power India Conference.

[15] Srinivasan A, Nigam M. J, (2008), "Adaptive Neuro-Fuzzy Inference System based control of six DOF robot manipulator", Journal of Engineering Science and Technology Review ,106- 111

[16] Sanju S, Sarita R, (2012), "Temperature Control Using Intelligent Techniques", IEEE Second International Conference on Advanced Computing & Communication Technologies, 138-145

[17] Abolfazl H. N, Abolfazl V, Hassan M, (2006), "ANFIS-Based Controller with Fuzzy Supervisory Learning for Speed Control of 4-Switch Inverter Brushless DC Motor Drive", Power Electronics Specialists Conference, PESC '06. 37th IEEE , 1-5

[18] Chitra V, (2010), "ANFIS Based Field Oriented Control for Matrix Converter fed Induction Motor", IEEE international conference on power and energy (PECon2010), Malaysia, 74-78

[19] Muthukumar G. G, Albert V. T. A, (2011), "A DE – ANFIS Hybrid Technique For Adaptive Deadbeat Controller", IEEE 978-1-61284-379-7/11, 1st International Conference on Electrical Energy Systems, 134-139

[20] Yajun Z, Tianyou C, Yue F, Hong N, (2009), "Nonlinear Adaptive Control Method Based on ANFIS and Multiple Models", Joint 48th IEEE Conference on Decision and Control and 28th Chinese Control Conference Shanghai, P.R. China, 1387-1392I

[21] Al-Mashhadany Y. I, (2011), "Modeling and Simulation of Adaptive Neuro-Fuzzy Controller for Chopper-Fed DC Motor Drive", IEEE applied power electronic colloquium (IAPEC), 110-115

[22] Ginarsa M, Soeprijanto A, Purnomo M.H, (2009), "Controlling Chaos Using ANFIS-Based Composite Controller (ANFIS-CC) in Power Systems", Instrumentation, Communications, Information Technology, and Biomedical Engineering (ICICI-BME).
[23] Yajun Z, Tianyou C, Hong W, (2011), "A Nonlinear Control Method Based on ANFIS and Multiple Models for a Class of SISO Nonlinear Systems and Its Application", IEEE TRANSACTIONS ON NEURAL NETWORKS, VOL. 22, NO. 11, 1783-1795
[24] JafarT, AfsharShamsi J, Muhammad A. D, (2012), "A new method for position control of a 2-DOF robot arm using neuro– fuzzy controller", Indian Journal of Science and Technology Vol. 5 No. 3, ISSN: 0974- 6846, 2253-2258
[25] Giuliani P. G, Gamarra R, Francisco J. G, (2007), "Multivalued Adaptive Neuro-Fuzzy Controller for Robot Vehicle", Proceedings on Intelligent Systems and Knowledge Engineering (ISKE).
[26] Singh M. K, Parhi D. R, Pothal J. K, (2009), "ANFIS Approach for Navigation of Mobile Robots", 2009 International Conference on Advances in Recent Technologies in Communication and Computing, 727-731
[27] Ming-Y. S, Ke H. C, Chen Y. C, Juing S. C, Jeng H. L, (2007), "ANFIS based Controller Design for Biped Robots", IEEE Proceedings of International Conference on Mechatronics TuA2-B-1 Kumamoto Japan, 1-6
[28] Widodo B, Achmad J, Djoko P, (2010), Indoor Navigation using Adaptive Neuro Fuzzy Controller for Servant Robot", IEEE Second International Conference on Computer Engineering and Applications, 582-586
[29] Greg R. L, (2011), "Haptic Interactions Using Virtual Manipulator Coupling with Applications to Underactuated Systems", IEEE transactions on robotics, Vol. 27, No. 4, 730-740.
[30] Al-Mashhadany Y. I,(2012), "A Posture of 6-DOF Manipulator By Locally Recurrent Neural Networks (LRNNs) Implement in Virtual Reality", IEEE Symposium on Industrial Electronics and Applications (ISIEA), Penang, Malaysia, 573-578.
[31] Jacob R, Joel C. P, Nathan M, Stephen B, Blake H, (2005), "The Human Arm Kinematics and Dynamics During Daily Activities – Toward a 7 DOF Upper Limb Powered Exoskeleton", This work is supported by NSF Grant #0208468 entitled "Neural Control of an Upper Limb Exoskeleton System" - Jacob Rosen (PI) 0-7803-9177-2/05/ IEEE, 532-539
[32] Erico G, Travis D, (2012), "Robotics Trends for 2012", IEEE Robotic & Automation Msgazine, 1070-9932/12/, 119-123
[33] Shahri M. R. A, Khoshravan H, Naebi A, (2011) " Design ping-pong player robot controller with ANFIS", IEEE Third International Conference on Computational Intelligence, Modelling & Simulation, 165-189
[34] Younkoo J, Yongseon L, Kyunghwan K, Yeh-Sun H, Jong-Oh P, (2001), "A 7 DOF Wearable Robotic Arm Using Pneumatic Actuators", Proceedings of the 32nd ISR(International Symposium on Robotics), 19-21
[35] Tie-jun Z, Jing Y, Ming-yang Z, Da-long T, (2006), "Research on the Kinematics and Dynamics of a 7-DOF Arm of Humanoid Robot", IEEE International Conference on Robotics and Biomimetics , Kunming, China, 1553-1558
[36] Zhang B, Xiong R, WU J, (2011), "Kinematics Analysis of a Novel 7-DOF Humanoid Manipulator for Table Tennis", NSFC-2008AA042601/978-1-4577-0321-8/11/IEEE, 1524-1528

[37] Patricia M, Oscar C, (2005), "Intelligent control of a stepping motor drive using an adaptive neuro–fuzzy inference system", Elsevier Information Sciences 170,133–151 www.elsevier.com/locate/ins

[38] Al-maliki K. H, Wali W.A, Hameed L. J, Turky Y. A, (2011), "Force / Motion Control for Constrained Robot Manipulator Using Adaptive Neural Fuzzy Inference System (ANFIS)", it is available with (the last visit at 12/4/2012) http://www.nauss.edu.sa /En/DigitalLibrary/Researches/Documents/2011/articles_2011_3157.pdf

[39] Oscar C, Patricia M, (2003), "Intelligent adaptive model-based control of robotic dynamic systems with a hybrid fuzzy-neural approach", Elsevier Applied Soft Computing, 363–378

[40] Mukhtiar S, Chandra A, (2012), "Real Time Implementation of ANFIS Control for Renewable Interfacing Inverter in 3P4W Distribution Network", This article has been accepted for publication in a future issue of IEEE journal

[41] Ouamri B, Ahmed Z, (2012), "Adaptive Neuro-fuzzy Inference System Based Control of Puma 600 Robot Manipulator", International Journal of Electrical and Computer Engineering (IJECE) Vol.2, No.1, ISSN: 2088-8708, 90~97

[42] Greg R. L, (2011), "Haptic Interactions Using Virtual Manipulator Coupling with Applications to Underactuated Systems", IEEE transactions on robotics, Vol. 27, No. 4, 730-740.

[43] Zappi M., Maltina R., Cerveri,P, (2010), "Modular micro robotic instruments for transluminal endoscopic robotic surgery: new perspectives", 978-1-4244-7101-0110/IEEE journal, 440-446

[44] Eckhard F, Jürgen R, (2003), "Integrating Robotics and Virtual Reality with Geo-Information Technology: Chances and Perspectives", In L. Bernhard, A. Sliwinski, K. Senkler (Hrsg.): Geodaten- und Geodienste-Infrastrukturen – von der Forschung zur praktischen Anwendung. Beiträge zu den Münsteraner GI-Tagen 2003, Reihe IfGI Prints, Uni Münster, 285-296

[45] Michal J, Michal P, Michal C , Peter Nand O, (2012), "Towards Incremental Development of Human-Agent-Robot Applications using Mixed-Reality Testbeds", This article has been accepted for publication in IEEE Intelligent Systems but has not yet been fully edited. Some content may change prior to final publication.

[46] Ben C, (2009), "Humanoid Robotic Language and Virtual Reality Simulation" in book "Humanoid Robots", InTech ,chapter 1, 1-20

[47] Syed I. A, Nageli V. S, Sangeeta S, Rakshit S, (2012), "Digital Sand Model using Virtual Reality Workbench", IEEE International Conference on Computer Communication and Informatics (ICCCI -2012), Coimbatore, INDIA

[48] Manuela C, Fabio S, Silvio P, (2011), "Virtual Reality to Simulate Visual Tasks for Robotic Systems", IN BOOK In tech, ISBN: 978-953-307-518-1 " Virtual Reality"ch 4,, 71-92

[49] Patton J. L, Dawe G, Scharver C, Mussa-Ivaldi1 F. A, Kenyon R, (2012), "Robotics and Virtual Reality: The Development of a Life-Sized 3-D System for the Rehabilitation of Motor Function" Supported by NIDRR RERC. 0330411Z, NIH 1 R24 HD39627-0, NIH 1 R01- NS35673-01, and the Falk Trust

[50] Rong-wen H, Chia-hui L, (2007),"Development of Fuzzy-based Automatic Vehicle Control System in a Virtual Reality Environment", IEEE International Conference on Emerging Technologies, 10.1109/ICET.2007.4516340, pp 184 – 189.

Chapter 15

Hierarchical Fuzzy Control

Carlos André Guerra Fonseca, Fábio Meneghetti Ugulino de Araújo
and Marconi Câmara Rodrigues

Additional information is available at the end of the chapter

http://dx.doi.org/10.5772/48627

1. Introduction

Growing demands for comfort, reliability, accuracy, energy conservation, safety and economy have fueled interest in proposals that can contribute to facilitate high performance control systems design. In terms of vibrations active control, it may represent, for example, a good relationship between the maximum reduction in vibrations transmission between two systems and the minimum energy expended in order to accomplish this reduction [1].

The use of more than one controller to provide higher performance for complex systems has attracted interest because in each operation condition, their combination can take advantage of each controller's characteristics. To take advantage of controllers' combination, a supervisor can make a hierarchical classification of controllers' signals, according to the identified operational condition.

Advances in artificial intelligence, processing power and data storage, allowed the development of intelligent methods for different characteristics controllers' fusion. The use of intelligent methods allows to the controlled system: adaptability to various operational situations and proper performance, even in the presence of significant uncertainties. Intelligent supervisors are ease to maintain, to reconfigure and could have optimality during its operation according to the learning mechanism.

This chapter describes a methodology for controllers' combination called controllers hierarchical fusion. In this methodology, a supervisor system is used to obtain a single control signal from the control signals generated simultaneously by two or more controllers. A hierarchical controller's example compounded by one robust controller, one fuzzy controller and one fuzzy supervisor is applied for mechanical vibrations isolation and reference tracking using an electromechanical system proposed in [2]. This controller is called hierarchical fuzzy controller (HFC).

This electromechanical system can be used to eliminate vibrations in the camera of unmanned vehicles and also to position this camera. It can also be used in manned vehicles for drivers' seat positioning and to eliminate vibrations on it, as shown in Figure 1.

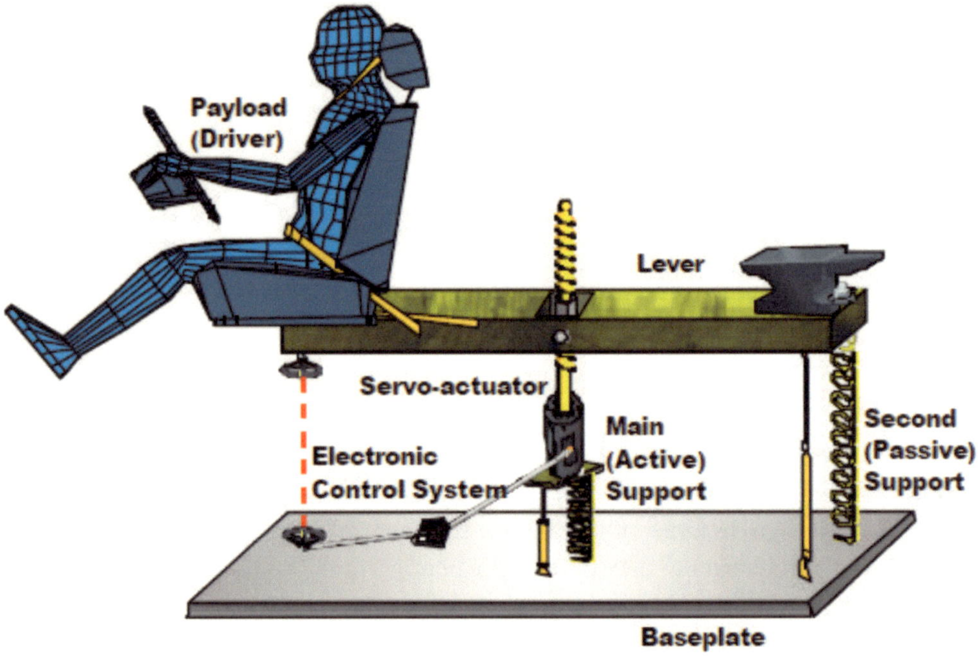

Figure 1. Application example: active suspension system

Digital simulations are employed in two case studies and the results are compared. On the first case study, the fuzzy controller and the fuzzy supervisor are tuned manually. Genetic algorithms (GA) are used on those systems tuning, in the second case study. Genetic algorithms usage facilitates designer's task and allows tuning parameters' optimization.

Next session describes the electromechanical system used and presents its models developed in [1]. The nonlinear model is used to validate the hierarchical fuzzy controller and in its fuzzy components' tuning, while the linearized model is used for robust control design. Performance criteria's are established at the end of this section.

2. Electromechanical system

Figure 2 details the electromechanical system used for vibration suppression and reference tracking. It consists on an l centimeters long bar with J inertia angular moment. It is considered that its mass m_B, is concentrated in its geometric center. This bar works as a lever which is supported in two points by systems with stiffness and damping, given by: k_A, k_B, c_A, c_B. In one extremity of the bar, a mass, m_A, called absorbing mass, is used to make a counterbalance with the payload. The payload is represented by a mass, m_C, on bar's free end. This system part is purely mechanical, being called lever system.

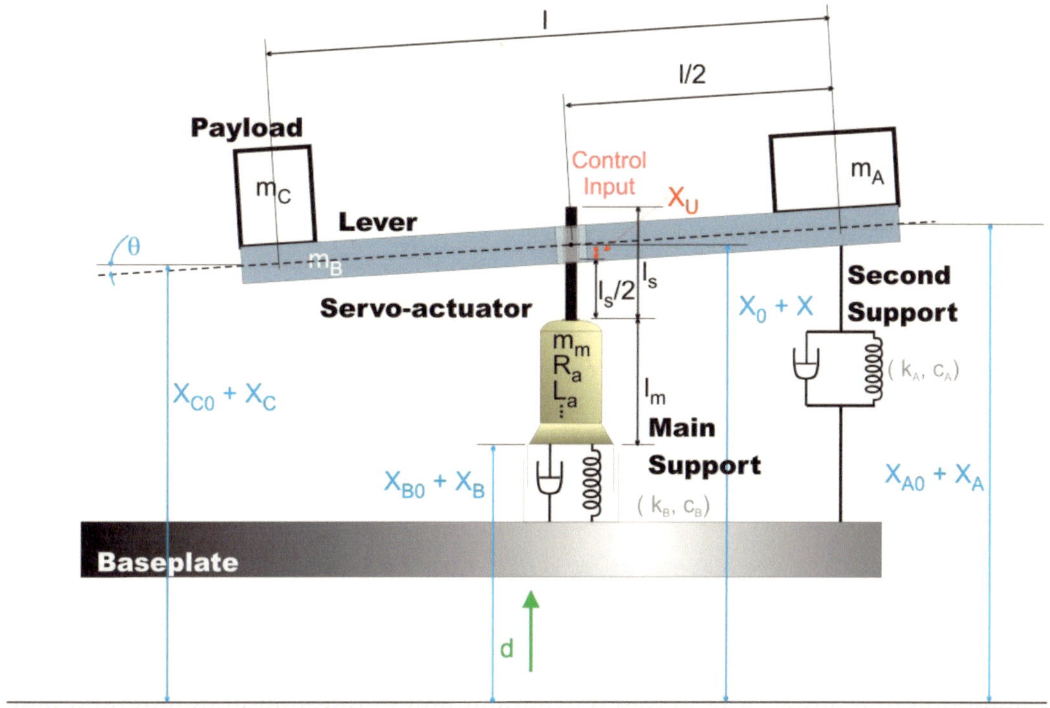

Figure 2. Electromechanical system

The vertical position control of bar's center is made by a servo actuator. This actuator consists of a DC servo motor whose axis is directly coupled to a spindle. The propeller's spindle step is given by L_P. It represents the direct relationship between motor's rotation angle (θ_M) and control's vertical displacement (X_u) imposed to bar's center with reference to the motor position (X_B).

The servo actuator varies the vertical position of bar's center depending on the measured displacements on bar's free end. This is done to isolate the payload from vibrations originated at the base.

A sensor that converts movements into voltage is used to measure vibrations on the payload. Those voltages feed servo motor, thus closing the control loop. Controllers are used to improve control efficiency, reaching thus performance specifications previously determined. This subsystem composed by one (or more) sensors, controllers and a servo-actuator, is called control system.

The nonlinear model used was developed in [1]. For the lever system it was given by:

$$\begin{aligned} \dot{\mathbf{x}} &= \mathbf{f}\left(\mathbf{x}(t), \mathbf{u}(t), t\right) \\ y &= g\left(\mathbf{x}(t), t\right) = q_1 - \frac{l}{2} sen\left(q_2\right) \end{aligned} \qquad (1)$$

Where:

$$\mathbf{x}(t)=\begin{bmatrix} q_1 \\ \dot{q}_1 \\ q_2 \\ \dot{q}_2 \end{bmatrix};\quad \mathbf{u}(t)=\begin{bmatrix} x_u \\ d \end{bmatrix}; \tag{2}$$

And:

$$\mathbf{f}(\mathbf{x}(t),\mathbf{u}(t),t)=\begin{bmatrix} \dot{q}_1 \\ \dfrac{-k_2(T_{11}+T_{12})+k_1\cos(q_2)(T_{21}+T_{22})}{T_D} \\ \dot{q}_2 \\ \dfrac{-m(T_{21}+T_{22})+k_1\cos(q_2)(T_{11}+T_{12})}{T_D} \end{bmatrix} \tag{3}$$

With:

$$k_1=\frac{l}{2}(m_A-m_C) \tag{4}$$

$$k_2=\left(\frac{l}{2}\right)^2(m_A+m_C)+\frac{1}{12}m_B\left(a^2+l^2\right) \tag{5}$$

$$\begin{aligned} T_{11}&=(k_A\delta_A+k_B\delta_B-mg)-\frac{1}{8}k_A\left(8q_1+4l sen(q_2)-8d\right) \\ &-lk_B(q_1-x_U-d)-c_B\left(\dot{q}_1-\dot{x}_U-\dot{d}\right)+k_1\dot{q}_2^2 sen(q_2)+m_m\overline{x}_u \end{aligned} \tag{6}$$

$$\begin{aligned} T_{12}&=-\frac{\frac{1}{16}c_A\left(8q_1+4l sen(q_2)-8d\right)}{4\left(q_1+\frac{l}{2}sen(q_2)-d\right)^2+l^2\left(1-\cos(q_2)\right)^2} \\ &\left[8\left(\dot{q}_1+\frac{l}{2}\dot{q}_2\cos(q_2)-\dot{d}\right)\left(q_1+\frac{l}{2}sen(q_2)-d\right)+2l^2\dot{q}_2 sen(q_2)\left(1-\cos(q_2)\right)\right] \end{aligned} \tag{7}$$

$$T_{21}=\frac{l}{2}(m_A-m_C)g-\frac{1}{8}k_A\left[4\left(q_1+\frac{l}{2}sen(q_2)-d\right)l\cos(q_2)+2l^2\left(1-\cos(q_2)\right)sen(q_2)\right] \tag{8}$$

$$\begin{aligned} T_{22}&=-\frac{\frac{1}{16}c_A\left[4\left(q_1+\frac{l}{2}sen(q_2)-d\right)l\cos(q_2)+2l^2\left(1-\cos(q_2)\right)sen(q_2)\right]}{4\left(q_1+\frac{l}{2}sen(q_2)-d\right)^2+l^2\left(1-\cos(q_2)\right)^2} \\ &\left[8\left(\dot{q}_1+\frac{l}{2}\dot{q}_2\cos(q_2)-\dot{d}\right)\left(q_1+\frac{l}{2}sen(q_2)-d\right)+2l^2\dot{q}_2 sen(q_2)\left(1-\cos(q_2)\right)\right] \end{aligned} \tag{9}$$

$$T_D = -k_2 m + \left(k_1 \cos\left(q_2\right)\right)^2 \tag{10}$$

The equation that describes servo actuator dynamics is given by:

$$\ddot{x}_u + \frac{1}{T_m}\dot{x}_u = \frac{L_P K_m}{T_m} e_a \tag{11}$$

For robust control project it was used the linearized model founded in [1].

$$\begin{bmatrix} \dot{x}_1 \\ \dot{x}_2 \\ \dot{x}_3 \\ \dot{x}_4 \\ \dot{x}_5 \\ \dot{x}_6 \end{bmatrix} = \begin{bmatrix} 0 & 1 & 0 & 0 & 0 & 0 \\ -a_1^{12} & -a_1^{11} & -a_2^{12} & -a_2^{11} & -a_3^{12} & -a_3^{11} \\ 0 & 0 & 0 & 1 & 0 & 0 \\ -a_1^{22} & -a_1^{21} & -a_2^{22} & -a_2^{21} & -a_3^{22} & -a_3^{21} \\ 0 & 0 & 0 & 0 & 0 & 1 \\ 0 & 0 & 0 & 0 & 0 & -a_3^{31} \end{bmatrix} \cdot \begin{bmatrix} x_1 \\ x_2 \\ x_3 \\ x_4 \\ x_5 \\ x_6 \end{bmatrix} + \begin{bmatrix} 0 & \beta_2^{11} \\ \beta_1^{12} & \beta_2^{12} \\ 0 & \beta_2^{21} \\ \beta_1^{22} & \beta_2^{22} \\ 0 & 0 \\ \beta_1^{32} & 0 \end{bmatrix} \cdot \begin{bmatrix} e_a \\ d \end{bmatrix}$$

$$y = x_c = \begin{bmatrix} 1 & 0 & -\frac{l}{2} & 0 & 0 & 0 \end{bmatrix} \cdot \begin{bmatrix} x_1 \\ x_2 \\ x_3 \\ x_4 \\ x_5 \\ x_6 \end{bmatrix} \tag{12}$$

The system states are:

$$x_1 = q_1 = x,\ x_2 = \dot{q}_1 - \beta_2^{11} d = \dot{x} - \beta_2^{11} d,\ x_3 = q_2 = \theta,\ x_4 = \dot{q}_2 - \beta_2^{21} d = \dot{\theta} - \beta_2^{21} d,\ x_5 = \theta_m,\ x_6 = \dot{\theta}_m \tag{13}$$

Where:

$$\begin{gathered} \beta_1^{12} = b_1^{12},\ \beta_1^{22} = b_1^{22},\ \beta_1^{32} = b_1^{32},\ \beta_2^{11} = b_2^{11},\ \beta_2^{21} = b_2^{21},\ \beta_2^{12} = b_2^{12} - a_1^{11} b_2^{11} - a_2^{11} b_2^{21}, \\ \beta_2^{22} = b_2^{22} - a_1^{21} b_2^{11} - a_2^{21} b_2^{21} \end{gathered} \tag{14}$$

The coefficients a_i^{jk} and b_i^{jk} are given by:

$$\begin{gathered} a_1^{11} = -CL_{11},\ a_1^{12} = -CL_{12},\ a_2^{11} = -CL_{13},\ a_2^{12} = -CL_{14},\ a_3^{11} = -L_P CL_{18} + \frac{L_P CL_{17}}{T_m}, \\ a_3^{12} = -L_P CL_{19},\ a_1^{21} = -CL_{21},\ a_1^{22} = -CL_{22},\ a_2^{21} = -CL_{23},\ a_2^{22} = -CL_{24}, \\ a_3^{21} = -L_P CL_{28} + \frac{L_P CL_{27}}{T_m},\ a_3^{22} = -L_P CL_{29},\ a_3^{31} = \frac{1}{T_m} \end{gathered} \tag{15}$$

And:

$$b_1^{12} = \frac{L_P K_m CL_{17}}{T_m},\ b_2^{11} = CL_{15},\ b_2^{12} = CL_{16},\ b_1^{22} = \frac{L_P K_m CL_{27}}{T_m},\ b_2^{21} = CL_{25},\ b_2^{22} = CL_{26}$$
$$b_1^{32} = \frac{K_m}{T_m} \tag{16}$$

Where:

$$CL_{11} = \frac{-k_2\left(-c_a - c_b\right) - \frac{l}{2}k_1 c_a}{-k_2 m + k_1^2} \tag{17}$$

$$CL_{12} = \frac{-k_2\left(-k_a - lk_b\right) - \frac{l}{2}k_1 k_a}{-k_2 m + k_1^2} \tag{18}$$

$$CL_{13} = \frac{\frac{l}{2}k_2 c_a - \left(\frac{l}{2}\right)^2 k_1 c_a}{-k_2 m + k_1^2} \tag{19}$$

$$CL_{14} = \frac{\frac{l}{2}k_2 k_a - \left(\frac{l}{2}\right)^2 k_1 k_a}{-k_2 m + k_1^2} \tag{20}$$

$$CL_{15} = \frac{-k_2\left(c_a + c_b\right) + \frac{l}{2}k_1 c_a}{-k_2 m + k_1^2} \tag{21}$$

$$CL_{16} = \frac{-k_2\left(k_a + lk_b\right) + \frac{l}{2}k_1 k_a}{-k_2 m + k_1^2} \tag{22}$$

$$CL_{17} = \frac{-k_2 m_m}{-k_2 m + k_1^2} \tag{23}$$

$$CL_{18} = \frac{-k_2 c_b}{-k_2 m + k_1^2} \tag{24}$$

$$CL_{19} = \frac{-k_2 l k_b}{-k_2 m + k_1^2} \tag{25}$$

$$CL_{21} = \frac{\frac{l}{2}mc_a + k_1\left(-c_a - c_b\right)}{-k_2 m + k_1^2} \tag{26}$$

$$CL_{22} = \frac{\frac{l}{2}mk_a + k_1\left(-k_a - lk_b\right)}{-k_2m + k_1^2} \tag{27}$$

$$CL_{23} = \frac{\left(\frac{l}{2}\right)^2 mc_a - \frac{l}{2}k_1c_a}{-k_2m + k_1^2} \tag{28}$$

$$CL_{24} = \frac{\left(\frac{l}{2}\right)^2 mk_a - \frac{l}{2}k_1k_a}{-k_2m + k_1^2} \tag{29}$$

$$CL_{25} = \frac{-\frac{l}{2}mc_a + k_1\left(c_a + c_b\right)}{-k_2m + k_1^2} \tag{30}$$

$$CL_{26} = \frac{-\frac{l}{2}mk_a + k_1\left(k_a + lk_b\right)}{-k_2m + k_1^2} \tag{31}$$

$$CL_{27} = \frac{k_1m_m}{-k_2m + k_1^2} \tag{32}$$

$$CL_{28} = \frac{k_1c_b}{-k_2m + k_1^2} \tag{33}$$

$$CL_{29} = \frac{k_1lk_b}{-k_2m + k_1^2} \tag{34}$$

Nonlinear system response to a step reference and for a step disturb was used to determine the performance criteria.

Figure 3 shows the nonlinear system in closed loop, without controllers, step response. This response is characterized by the influence of two vibrations modes: one slower and overdamped and the other faster and oscillating. It practically has no overshoot. The settling time, considering an accommodation range of ± 5% of the reference signal amplitude, is more than 12.5s. The rise time from 0 to100% of the reference signal amplitude is greater than 19s. This large difference between the rise time and the settling time highlights the influence of the overdamped mode [3].

Figure 4 shows the non-controlled system response to a disturbance.

With the reference fixed at zero, when a 0.01m amplitude step disturbance is injected into the system without the controller, its output goes upper than one and a half the amplitude of the injected disturbance. The non-controlled system needs about 12.8s to reject this disturbance on the mentioned condition, considering that the disturbance is sufficiently rejected when the response amplitude is reduced to a range of ± 5% of the injected disturbance amplitude, around zero. Figure 4 shows this response.

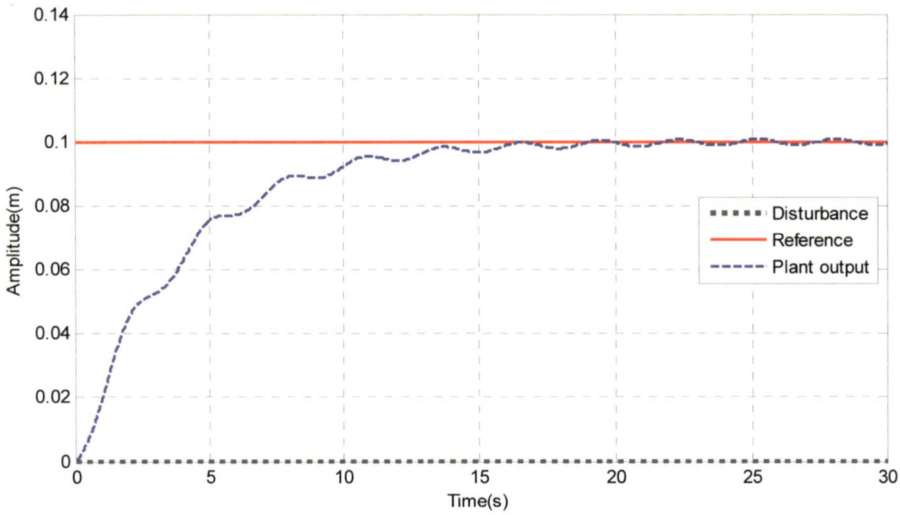

Figure 3. Electromechanical system step response without controllers and disturbance

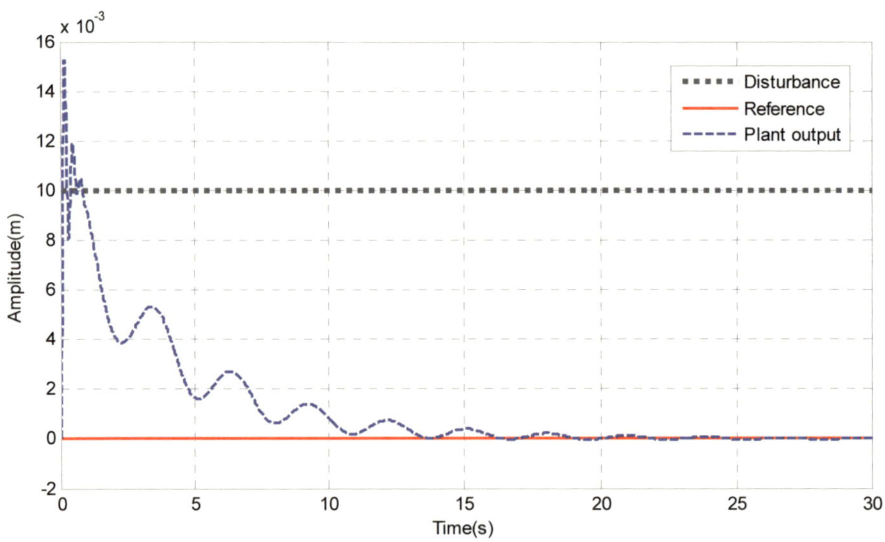

Figure 4. Non-controlled system response to a step disturbance

Thus, the performance specifications that characterize a satisfactory response to the nonlinear system are: A step reference signal must be tracked without regime error; the rise time should be reduced to at most 10% of the time obtained by the non-controlled system;

The settling time should be reduced to at most 20% of the time obtained with the non-controlled system; The overshoot should be less than 10%; The time required for the controlled system to reject a step disturbance, must be reduced by at least 95%; Furthermore, the response signal may not exceed 40% of disturbance's amplitude; Finally, the control signal generated must respect the servo-actuator saturation limits, that, in this case, is ± 15V.

Those specifications were achieved through the use of the hierarchical fuzzy controller. Each controller design aimed to meet some performance specifications. In that way, conflicting specifications were separately addressed, instead of trying, in each project, to get a fit to satisfy conflicting specifications, relaxing those specifications. So the hierarchical fuzzy controller should take the best features of each controller, to meet all the specifications described in this section.

3. Robust control

In vibration control, as well as in several other applications, it is desired that the control system presents robustness to the effects of factors such as: modeling errors, variations in the parameters of the system being controlled, noise and disturbances. There are at least two reasons why the robustness is a desirable feature in the control systems: the need of control systems that operates satisfactorily, even in operating conditions different from the ones considered in the model design; and the possibility to adopt an intentionally simplified project model, to reduce: the time spent in the modeling stage and the resulting controller complexity [4].

Among the main techniques for robust controllers synthesis can be cited: The Linear Quadratic Gaussian / Loop Transfer Recovery (LQG/LTR), H2 and H∞ optimizations, methods based on Lyapunov functions, minmax optimization and Quantitative Feedback Theory (QFT).

The LQG/LTR controller designed in [1] was used to allow a better comparison between the optimized hierarchical fuzzy controller implemented and the non-optimized developed in [1]. Furthermore the LQG/LTR technique has a simple and systematic design procedure, the controller robustness is ensured by this procedure, even in a broad class modeling errors presence and also the number of design parameters is relatively small [5].

This procedure has two steps: initially the target filter loop (TFL) must be projected. It must meet the performance specifications previously established. Once obtained an appropriate TFL, its characteristics are recovered for the transfer function of the loop formed by the controller and the nominal model $\left(G_K(s) \cdot G_N(s)\right)$.

The LTR procedure, initially proposed in [6], suggests that the TFL is achieved through the design of a Linear Quadratic Regulator (LQR) and then recovered by adjusting a Kalman filter. Another way to do it is to set a Kalman filter, to obtain a satisfactory target filter loop, and then project an optimal state feedback, type LQR, to recover the TFL [1].

Given the linearized model in form:

$$\begin{aligned}\dot{\mathbf{x}}(t) &= \mathbf{A}\mathbf{x}(t) + \mathbf{B}\mathbf{u}(t)\\ \mathbf{Y}(t) &= \mathbf{C}\mathbf{x}(t)\end{aligned} \tag{35}$$

The Kalman's filter design begins with the solution of the following algebraic Riccati equation:

$$\mathbf{A\Sigma} + \mathbf{\Sigma A}^T + \mathbf{W\Xi W}^T - \mathbf{\Sigma C}^T\mathbf{\Theta}^{-1}\mathbf{C\Sigma} = 0 \tag{36}$$

In [1] it was used:

$$\mathbf{W} = \mathbf{B}(:,1); \mathbf{\Xi} = \mathbf{I}; \mathbf{\Theta} = \mu\mathbf{I} \tag{37}$$

Where $\mathbf{B}(:,1)$ corresponds to the first column of the B matrix and μ is the project's free parameter. This choice was made because the first attempt to select the W matrix must be the matrix related with the control input [5]. As could be seen in [1], this choice proved satisfactory.

In [1] were also used: $\mu = 10^{-6}$ to obtain the TFL and $\rho = 10^{-12}$ to recover the TFL, resulting in a LQG/LTR robust controller with the following desired characteristics: good speed in test model controlled response accommodation, when tracking a reference, and principally a good rejection of disturbances. Figure 5 illustrates the TFL obtained and recovered for these values of μ and ρ.

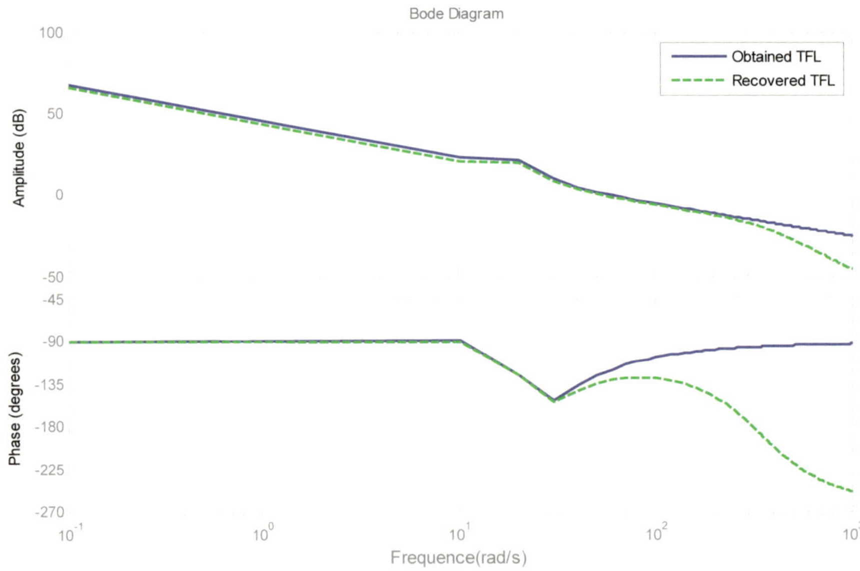

Figure 5. TFL obtained and recovered

As mentioned earlier, this LQG/LTR controller was used to allow a better comparison between the optimized hierarchical fuzzy controller implemented and the non-optimized developed in [1].

With the system controlled only by this robust controller, a step reference with 0.1m amplitude, was tracked without regime error; the rise time from 0 to 100% of the reference, in disturbance absence, was about 0.03s which corresponds to 0.16% of the rise time obtained by the non-controlled system; the settling time for (± 5%) was 0.17s, so, it was reduced to 1.36% of the time obtained with the non-controlled system; the overshoot was 22.4% and the control signal generated to track this reference signal, surpassed the actuator saturation levels. Therefore, with respect to the reference tracking, the controller could not satisfy two performance criteria established, because the overshoot was higher than 10% of the reference signal and some control signals produced, extrapolates the servo actuator saturation levels. Figures 6 and 7 show the system response when controlled only by this LQG/LTR robust controller.

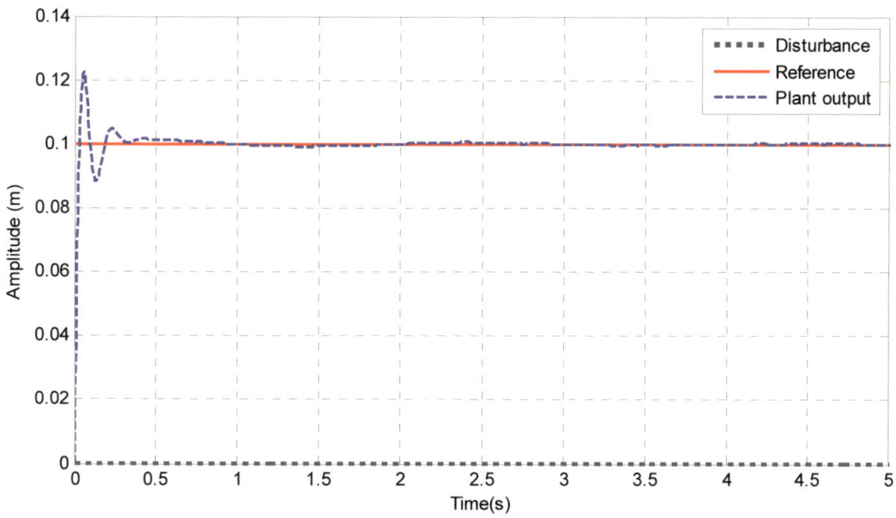

Figure 6. System response on step reference tracking, only with the robust controller, and in disturbances absence

With a null reference, a 0,01m step disturbance was injected in the system. The time required for the system to reject this disturbance using only the robust controller, was approximately 0.17s; what represents a 98.67% time reduction when compared to non-controlled system exposed to the same situation; The response signal maximum amplitude was 17.89% of the disturbance amplitude; the control signal varied within the levels of the servo actuator saturation. So in disturbance rejection, with null reference, the robust controller met all performance requirements described, as could be seen on figures 8 and 9.

It was also evaluated the system response, only with the robust controller, to a square wave reference with 0.1m peak to peak, 0.015Hz frequency and 100s duration. The system tracked this reference without regime error, the rise time and the settling time satisfied the performance specifications, but, again, as was expected, the control signal exceeded the actuator saturation limits and the overshoot exceeded the maximum stated in performance criteria, as could be seen on figures 10 and 11.

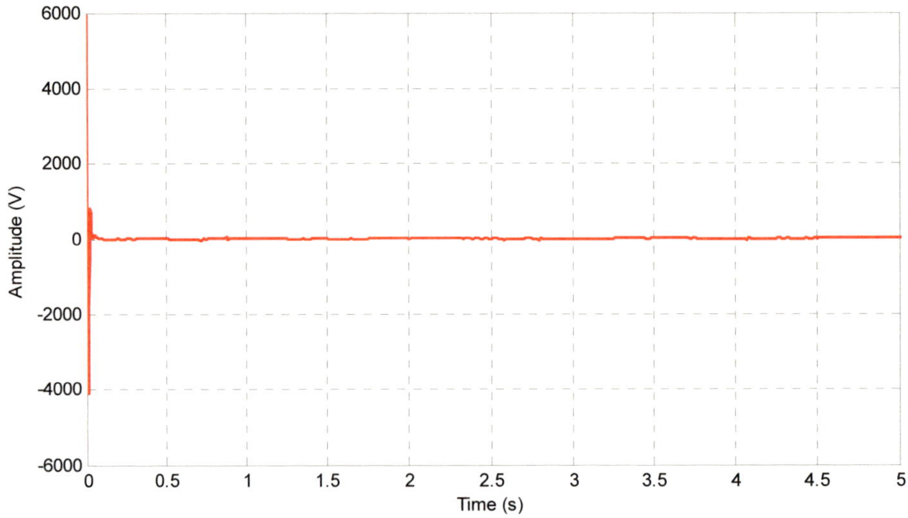

Figure 7. Robust controller signal for a step reference tracking, in disturbances absence

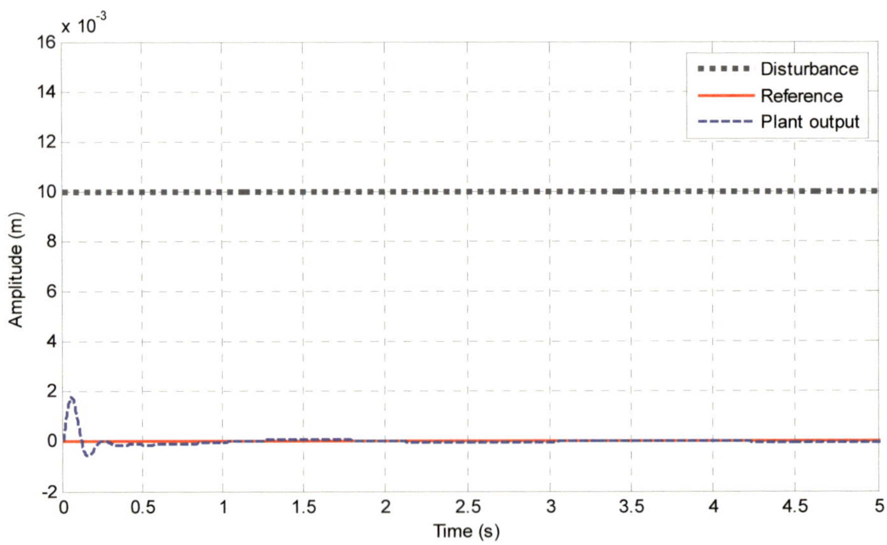

Figure 8. System response on step disturbance rejection, only with the robust controller, and with a null reference

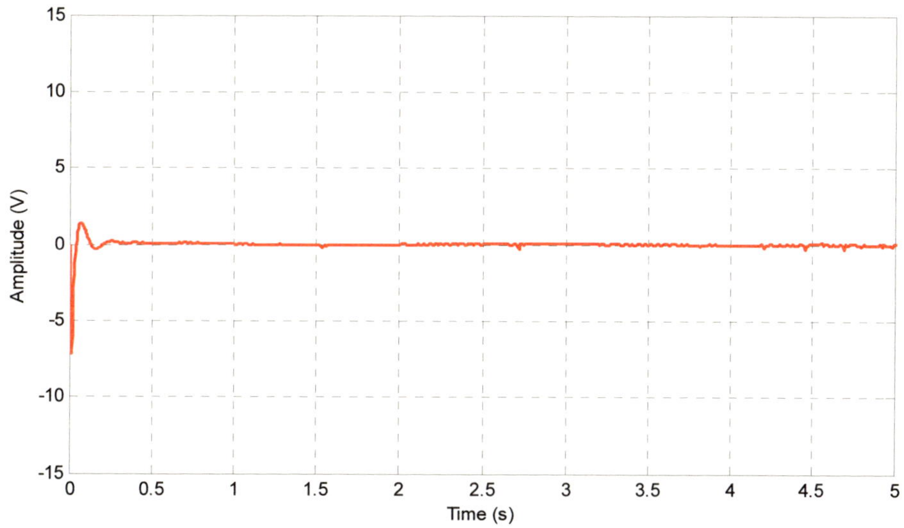

Figure 9. Robust controller signal for a step disturbance rejection, with a null reference

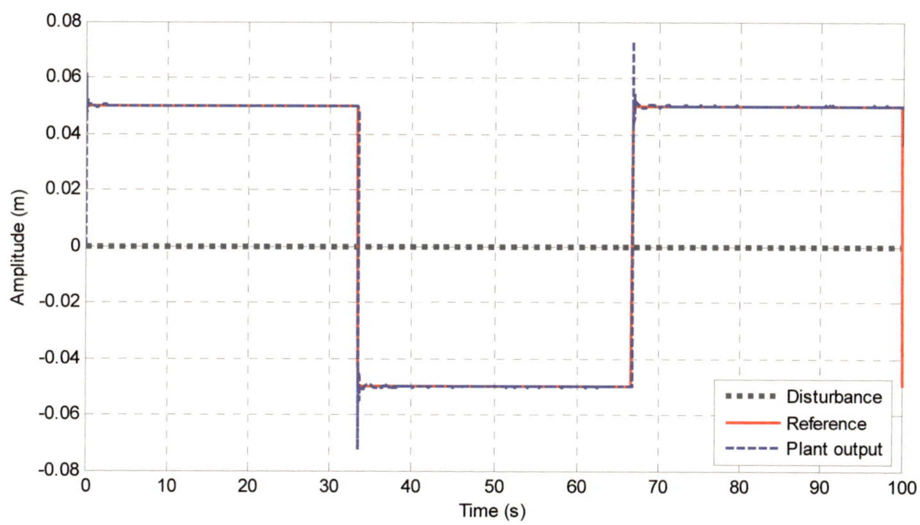

Figure 10. System response on square wave reference tracking, only with the robust controller

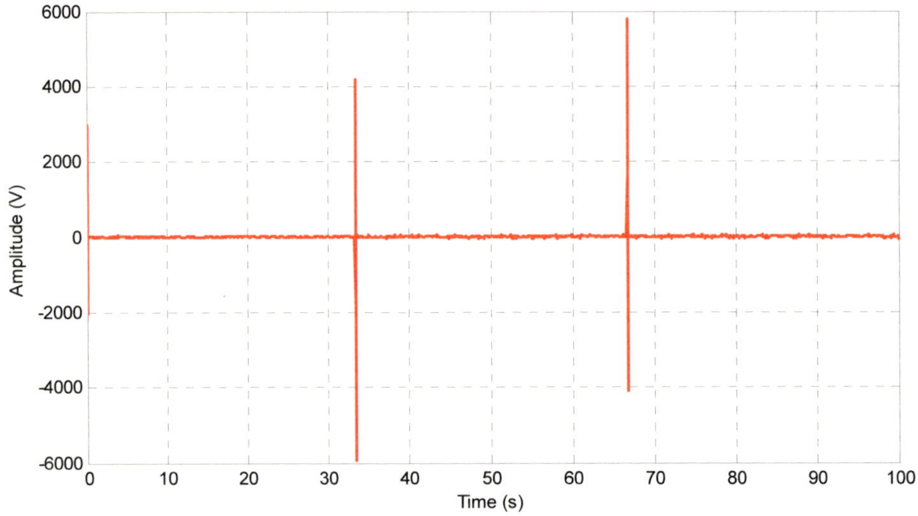

Figure 11. Robust controller signal for a square wave reference tracking, in disturbances absence

Finally, the system, only with the robust controller, was tested on tracking a step reference in the presence of uniformly distributed white noise with 0.02m peak to peak. Figures 12 and 13 show the system response and the control signal applied to the plant in this situation.

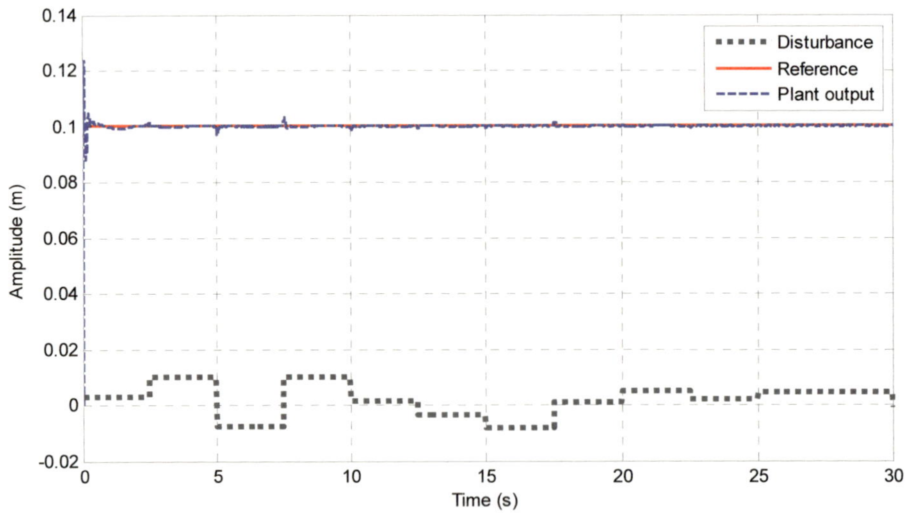

Figure 12. System response on step reference tracking, using only the robust controller, and in uniformly distributed white noise presence

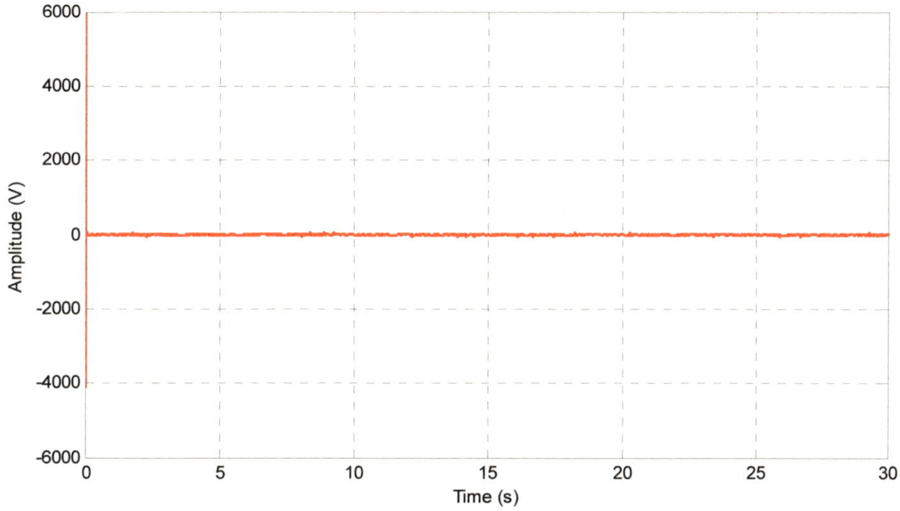

Figure 13. Robust controller signal for a step reference tracking, in uniformly distributed white noise presence

Comparing those results with the first shown, it is concluded that the rise time and the settling time were the same for both situations. In the white noise presence, the system showed a slightly higher overshoot, 23.4%, what is unsatisfactory according to the performance criteria, as well as the control signal applied that extrapolates the actuator saturation limits. So, as expected, in both cases the same performance requirements were not satisfied.

Therefore, those requirements should be met by the fuzzy controller and the supervisor must properly combine those two controllers to meet all performance criteria.

4. Fuzzy control

Fuzzy controllers are those that make use of fuzzy logic, which is based on the fuzzy sets' theory. This theory was developed by Zadeh in 1965 [7], to deal with the vague aspect of information through the mathematical representation of expressions commonly used by humans, also called linguistic variables, which give a not exact value to a variable characteristic of the object under observation.

Fuzzy logic attaches to a statement, not the value 'true' or 'false', but a veracity degree within a numeric range.

Due to its ability to handle uncertainty and imprecision, fuzzy logic has been characterized as one of the current technologies for the successful development of systems to control sophisticated processes, enabling the use of simple controllers to satisfy complex design requirements, even when the model of the system to be controlled has uncertainties [8-14].

The greatest difficulty in creating fuzzy systems is the definition of linguistic terms and rules. One way to solve this problem is to use hybrid approaches as models called neuro-fuzzy. In a neuro-fuzzy system those parameters are learned with the presentation of training pairs (input, desired output) to a neural network whose nodes basically computes intersection and union operators [15-18]. Another hybrid approach that allows the parameters tuning for fuzzy systems, consists in the use of genetic algorithms [19].

A satisfactory definition of the number of membership functions and the degree of overlap between them is fundamental when implementing a fuzzy controller. It directly influences on the next stage, called inference [20].

The inference uses a set of rules that describe the dependence between the linguistic variables of input and output functions. This relationship is usually determined heuristically and consists of two steps: aggregation, when evaluating the 'if' part of each rule, through the operator "and fuzzy," and the composition stage, using the operator "or fuzzy" to considering the different conclusions of the active rules [20, 21].

After the inference from the action to be taken, the classical fuzzy models require a decoding of the linguistic value for the numeric variable output, called defuzzification. This output can represent functions such as adjusting the position of a button, or provide voltage to a particular motor.

The Takagi Sugeno fuzzy controllers do not need a defuzzification step, because they obtain this precise equivalence directly [9, 19]. Therefore they were used to compound the fuzzy hierarchical controller.

For the design and optimization of the fuzzy logic controller it was used the nonlinear model of the physical system, as this model provides a more accurate representation of it.

All available knowledge about the system being controlled is of fundamental importance for the initial stage of designing a fuzzy controller, therefore, knowing the geometrical characteristics, the dynamics and any system particularity, can significantly reduce the project effort [1]. The fuzzy logic controller used has the following structure: Two inputs, which are: the tracking error (the difference between the reference and the system output) and its derivative; an output which is the control signal. For the output variable composition 25 first-order Sugeno functions are used; five linguistic variables were defined for each input variable: Negative Big, Negative Small, Zero, Positive Small and Positive Big; Triangular membership functions were chosen for the input variables; The probabilistic t-norm and t-conorm operators were chosen; The rule base is composed by 25 rules. For each rule there is a Sugeno output function; For the inference procedure, the Sugeno interpolation model was chosen.

The tuning of this fuzzy controller was made by a genetic algorithm. This algorithm is based on the laws of natural selection and evolution. It searches to an optimal solution in the space of solutions given by the designer, using probabilistic rules for combining solutions in order to improve their quality. It is therefore an efficient search strategy that can be used in optimization or classification problems [22-25].

In the fuzzy controller's optimization, each individual is formed by 70 genes. The first 20 genes represent the input membership functions. The 50 subsequent genes describe the coefficients of the Sugeno output functions, t_i and s_i. Those functions are given by:

$$\left[t_i \cdot e + s_i \cdot \frac{de}{dt} + 0\right] \tag{38}$$

Where: e is the error.

With the use of genetic algorithms for tuning of all parameters of fuzzy controller, the designer's task is to limit the search space of GA and find a good setting of its parameters, in order to obtain the desired results.

The determination of the limits of the search spaces for the fuzzy controller optimization was based on the results obtained in [1] and in several tests. The population size, the percentage of mutation and the stopping criteria were also determined from several tests.

To obtain the results that will be shown, a square wave was used as reference, allowing a good fit to the fuzzy controller for several references. The genetic algorithm configuration was: population of 30 individuals, all children were generated by recombination with mutation probability of 5% for each gene; the roulette method was used on selection step. The stopping criteria were: maximum number of iterations equal to 100, repeating the best individual for 25% of the generations' maximum number, maintaining the average fitness of the population for 10% of the generations' maximum number and mean square error of 10^{-5}.

For the evaluation of each individual the control of the nonlinear system using only the fuzzy controller, was simulated during 100s. The evaluation function used for this controller tuning, was:

$$\begin{aligned} f_{ev}(ind.) &= 8t_{r1} + 8t_{r2} + 8t_{r3} + 0{,}9o_{s1} + 0{,}9\left|o_{s2}\right| + 0{,}9o_{s3} + 0{,}7t_{s1} + 0{,}7t_{s2} \\ &+ 0{,}7t_{s3} + 15e_m^{\ 2} + u_{\max} - u_{\min} \end{aligned} \tag{39}$$

Where: the "$t_{ri's}$" are the rise times, the "$o_{si's}$" are the overshoots, the "$t_{si's}$" are the settling times, "e_m" is the average error, "u_{max}" is the maximum positive amplitude of the control signal above actuator's saturation and "u_{min}" is the maximum amplitude of the negative control signal, below actuator's saturation.

Higher weights were given to the mean square error and to the rise times because it was observed that they had a lower representation in the evaluation function, than the settling time and the peaks of the control signals above actuator's saturation. Thus allowing to the genetic algorithm, the search for a tune that provides not only short settling times through low control signals, but also small rise times, and that the system does not presents regime errors. Lower weights were given for the settling times and the overshoots, to allow the search for fuzzy controllers that give the system a higher speed.

Figures 14 and 15, shows the fuzzy controller optimized membership functions.

Two search spaces were defined for output functions' coefficients determination: one from 0 to 100, for the coefficients of the functions associated with rules that involve in its antecedent the linguistic variables negative big or positive big, and another from 0 to 60 to the coefficients of the other functions. The independent terms of output functions were not optimized and were always made equal to zero. The output functions obtained after the tuning can be seen in Table 1.

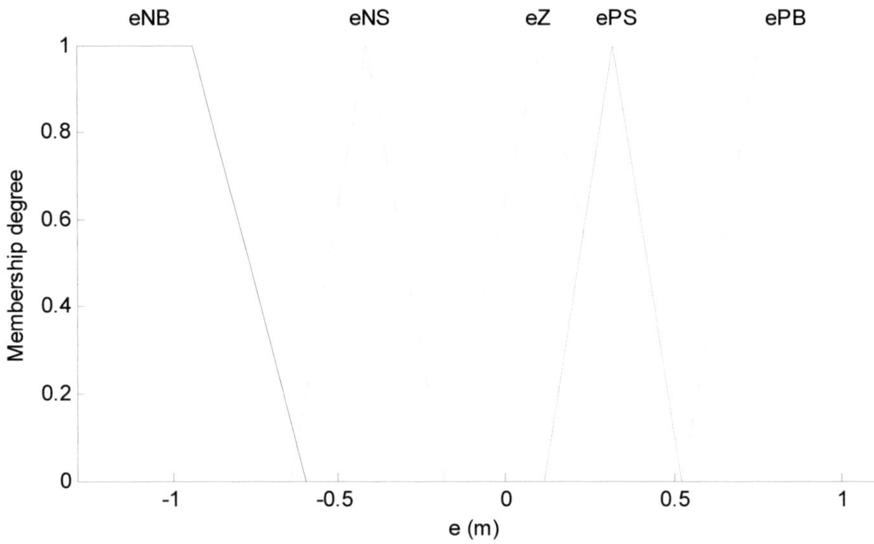

Figure 14. Fuzzy controller optimized membership functions of error input

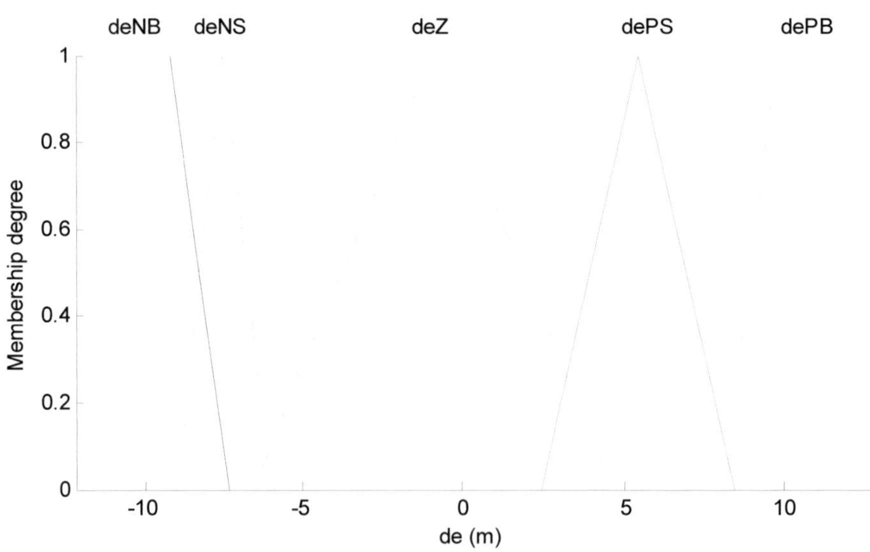

Figure 15. Fuzzy controller optimized membership functions of error derivative input

Function name	Parameters [t s]
S1	[10.93 94.07]
S2	[95.34 3.74]
S3	[25.50 27.17]
S4	[39.12 62.36]
S5	[95.86 94.12]
S6	[28.08 47.32]
S7	[46.76 43.30]
S8	[27.71 13.14]
S9	[42.55 5.52]
S10	[51.22 41.09]
S11	[53.64 5.98]
S12	[31.55 12.47]
S13	[53.31 1.20]
S14	[37.24 16.27]
S15	[33.20 46.69]
S16	[21.36 29.04]
S17	[2.97 23.94]
S18	[11.98 43.12]
S19	[42.94 45.81]
S20	[10.77 27.04]
S21	[75.33 50.81]
S22	[85.35 66.19]
S23	[45.64 50.41]
S24	[58.09 15.50]
S25	[15.18 11.76]

Table 1. Output functions' parameters of the optimized fuzzy controller

Table 2 shows the fuzzy controller rule base.

The control of the electromechanical system made only by the optimized fuzzy controller, presented a poor performance in tracking a 0.1m amplitude step reference, in disturbance absence. The overshoot presented was out of performance specifications (30.60%), and the settling time was almost equal to the uncontrolled system settling time (11.09s). However, the system showed no error at steady state, the rise time was satisfactory, 0.22 s, and the control signal produced was far below the actuator saturation, allowing the use of this controller in the hierarchical control scheme, as a supplier of control signals applicable in situations of great error, where the signals produced by the robust controller extrapolate the servo-actuator saturation. Those results are shown in figures 16 and 17.

		Error				
		eNB	eNS	eZ	ePS	ePB
Error derivative	deNB	S1	S6	S11	S16	S21
	deNS	S2	S7	S12	S17	S22
	deZ	S3	S8	S13	S18	S23
	dePS	S4	S9	S14	S19	S24
	dePB	S5	S10	S15	S20	S25

Table 2. Rule base of fuzzy controller

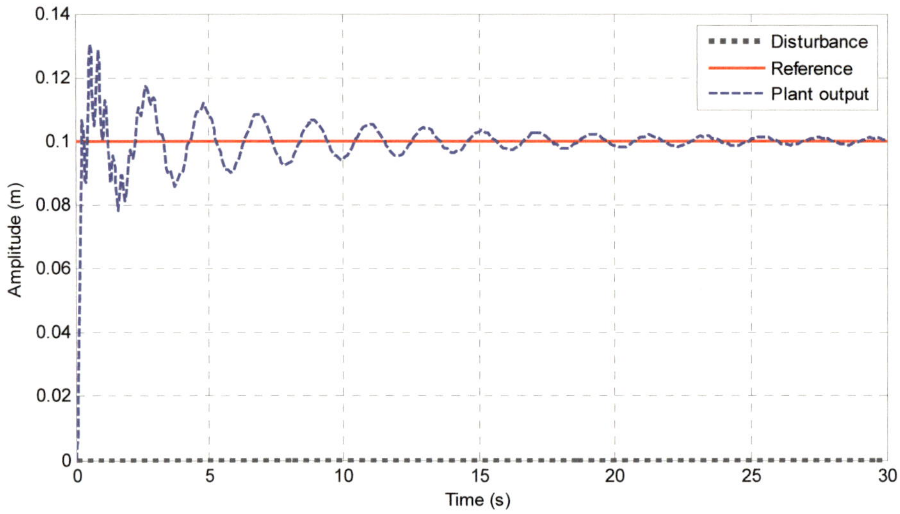

Figure 16. System response on step reference tracking, only with the fuzzy controller, and in disturbances absence

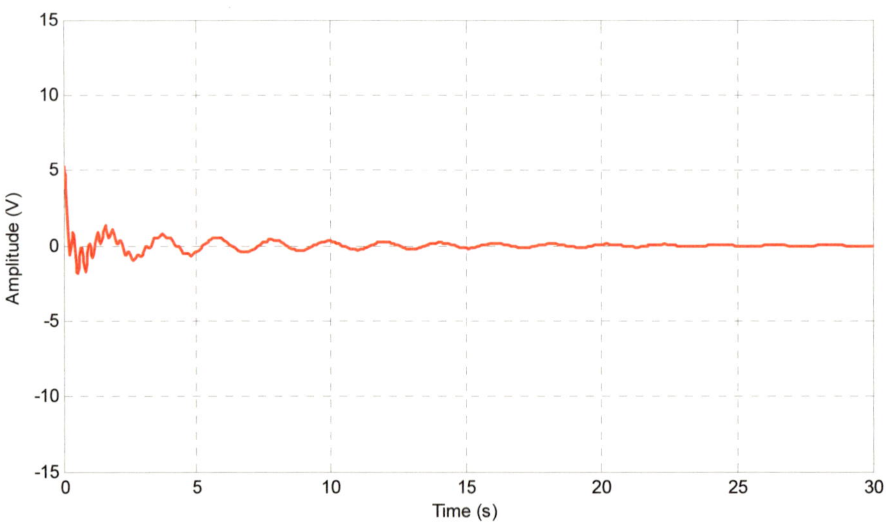

Figure 17. Fuzzy controller signal for a step reference tracking, in disturbances absence

In the rejection of a 0.01m amplitude step disturbance with the null reference, the system response with the fuzzy controller was also unsatisfactory, because its amplitude exceeded in 21% the disturbance amplitude, and it took about 2.01s to reject it, far above the 0.64s, established as a goal. Figures 18 and 19 show the system response and the control signal for this case.

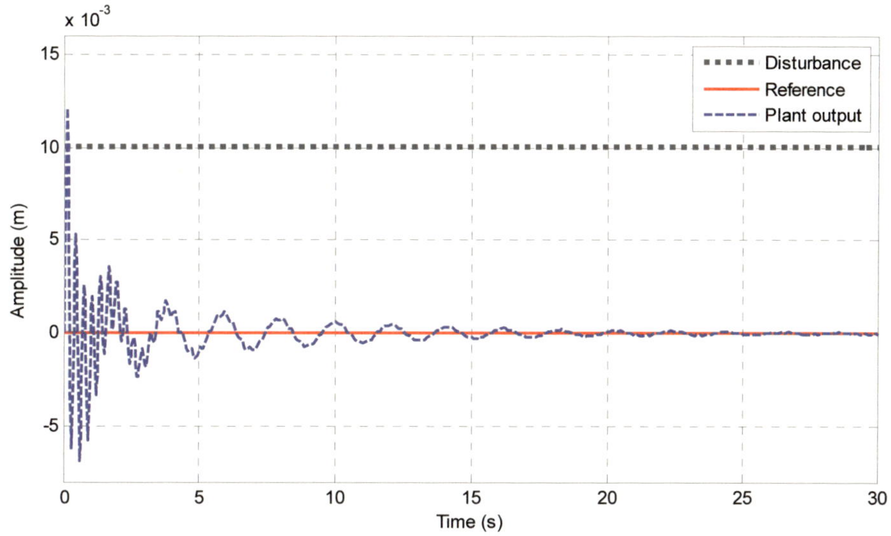

Figure 18. System response on step disturbance rejection, only with the fuzzy controller, and with a null reference

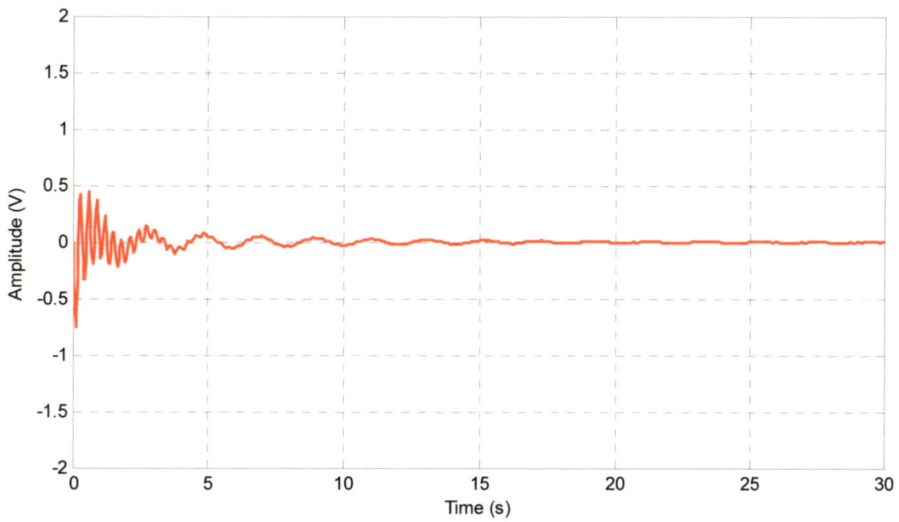

Figure 19. Fuzzy controller signal for a step disturbance rejection, with a null reference

It was also evaluated the system response on a square wave reference tracking in the absence of disturbances and using only the fuzzy controller. As can be seen in figures 20 and 21 the system tracked the reference without regime error, the rise times were acceptable, but the settling times were greater than desirable, moreover, the overshoot and the control signal extrapolated performance specifications. But the fuzzy controller's peak signal was much lower than the robust one.

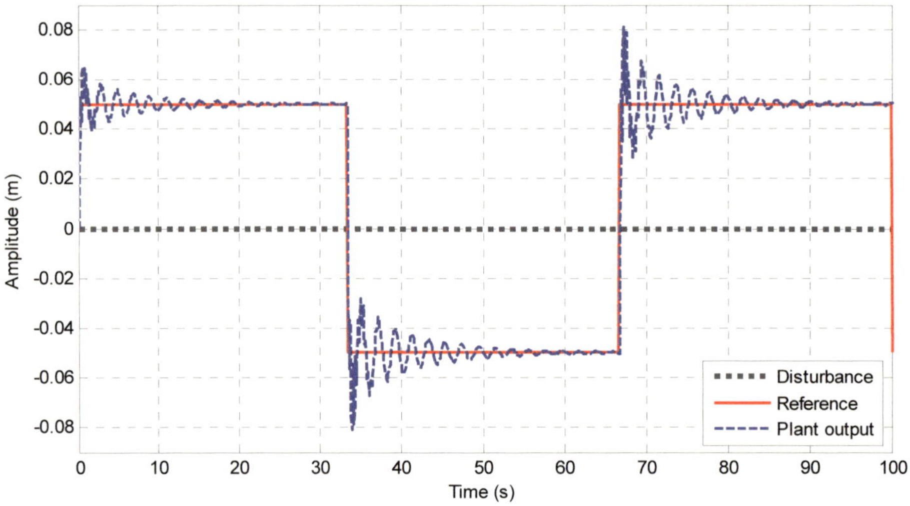

Figure 20. System response on square wave reference tracking, only with the fuzzy controller

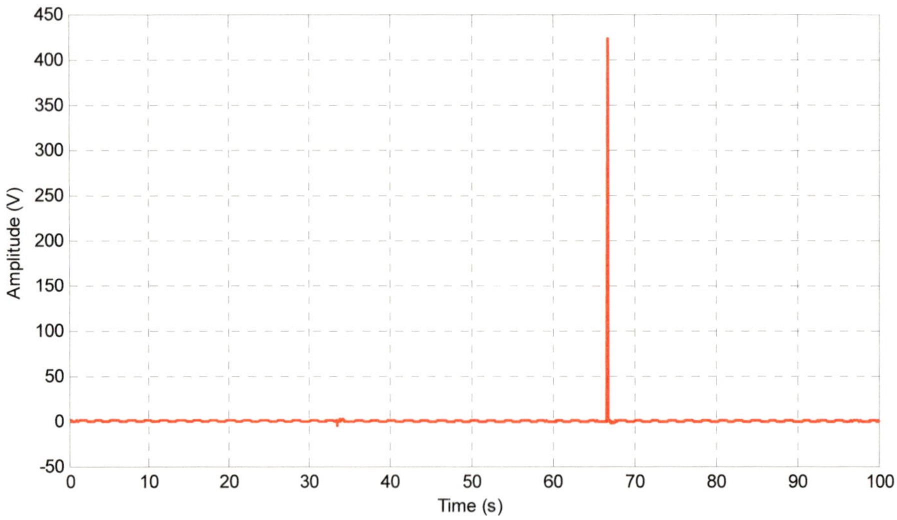

Figure 21. Fuzzy controller signal for a square wave reference tracking, in disturbances absence

From these results, it can be concluded that the function of the fuzzy controller is to bring the plant to a situation that favors the use of the robust controller, avoiding the extrapolation of control signal limits.

5. Fuzzy supervisor

The multiple controllers' fusion seeks to achieve higher performance than those obtained using only one controller.

The supervisor's task is to find an ideal combination of control signals generated by the controllers designed, in such way that this combination compose the control signal which will effectively act on the plant. To do this, the supervisor evaluates the operating condition in each instant, and then determines an importance hierarchy of each control signal. Therefore, in addition to control signals generated by the controllers, the supervisor must also receive information that enables to evaluate the operating condition at all instants, and then, based on this evaluation, the supervisor will sort, hierarchically, the outputs of the controllers, compounding then the control signal that will act on the plant. This hierarchy is the level of importance associated by the supervisor to each controller in every operating condition. It defines the participation of each controller in the control signal that will be applied on the plant.

The fuzzy supervisor used was a Takagi-Sugeno system with: two inputs, which are the same used in the fuzzy controller; 3 linguistic variables (negative, zero and positive), which are represented by trapezoidal membership functions; two output functions, which are zero order functions.

Figure 22 illustrates the architecture used for the control signals fusion via hierarchical fuzzy supervisor.

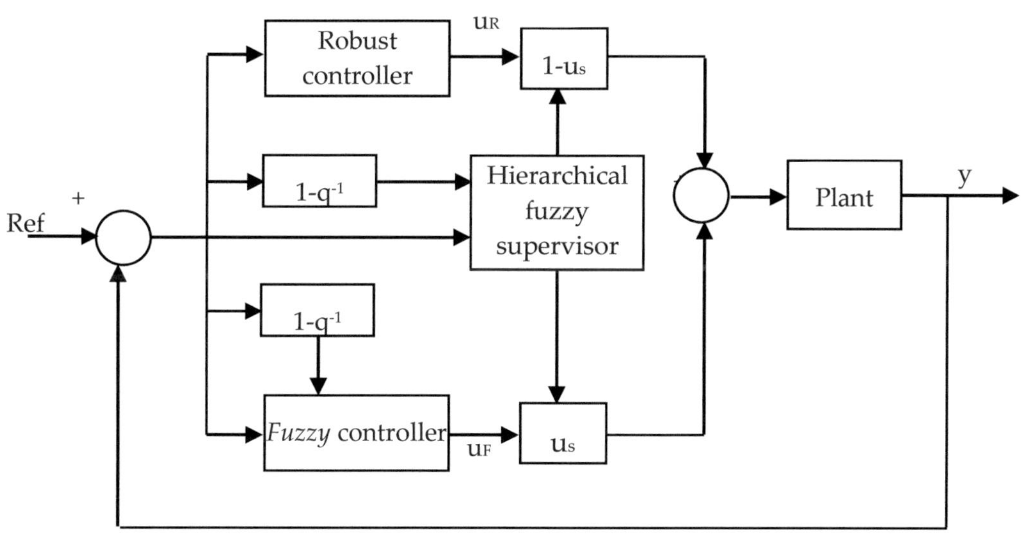

Figure 22. Control scheme using the fuzzy hierarchical controller

From the difference between a reference signal, specified by the operator, and the vertical position of the bar's free end, measured by a sensor, it is produced an error signal. With this error signal, the robust controller determines its control action, trying to correct the vertical position of the bar's free end. The fuzzy controller also provides a control signal in an attempt to eliminate the tracking error; for this, it needs this error signal and its derivative. The control signal which actually will act on the plant will be the weighted sum of signals produced by the controllers. The degree of participation of each control action is determined by the supervisor, which uses as well as the fuzzy controller, the error information and its derivative. According to the control signal, the servo-actuator will provide vertical displacements to bar's center, to correct the tracking error.

The two output functions used are the same presented in [1]. They are described in Table 3.

Function name	Parameters [e(t) de(t)/d(t) 1]x[t s 1]^T
LTR	[0 0 0]
FUZ	[0 0 1]

Table 3. Output functions' parameters of the fuzzy supervisor

So, when supervisor output is null, only the robust controller will actuate on the plant, when supervisor output is equal to one, only the fuzzy controller will actuate, for intermediate outputs a combination of those controllers' signals will be applied on the plant.

The supervisor's input membership functions were tuned by a genetic algorithm using the square wave reference and the two controllers. Its evaluation function is given by:

$$f_{ev}(ind.) = t_{r1} + t_{r2} + t_{r3} + o_{s1} + |o_{s2}| + o_{s3} + t_{s1} + t_{s2} + t_{s3} + e_m^{\ 2}$$
$$+0{,}01u_{\max 1} - 0{,}01u_{\min 1} + 0{,}01u_{\max 2} - 0{,}01u_{\min 2} + 0{,}01u_{\max 3} - 0{,}01u_{\min 3} \quad (40)$$

There was no need to give greater weight to the mean square error and to the rise times, as was done for the tuning of the fuzzy controller, because from some tunings, the settling time and the overshoot became very small. The reduction of all performance descriptors along the supervisor tuning was so high that it was necessary to assign lower weights to control signals peaks above the saturation of the servo actuator, to avoid favoring a performance criterion and neglect others.

Figures 23 and 24, shows the fuzzy supervisor optimized membership functions.

The rule base of the supervisor was not optimized by genetic algorithm. It was the same used in [1], as shown in Table 4.

As mentioned the results obtained with the optimized hierarchical fuzzy controller will be compared with the ones obtained by the non-optimized one (presented in [1]). On tracking a 0.1m amplitude step reference, the optimized hierarchical fuzzy controller has satisfied all performance criteria established and presented a more rapid response than the system controlled by the non-optimized hierarchical fuzzy controller. The rise time from 0 to 100% of the reference was approximately 0.22s, which is half the one obtained in [1]. The overshoot was 3.9% in [1] it was 7%. The settling time for (± 5%) was 0.22s, less than half that was obtained in [1]. The control signal generated by the optimized hierarchical fuzzy controller to track this reference had lower levels than the ones generated by the non-optimized hierarchical fuzzy controller. The optimized hierarchical fuzzy controller has used the fuzzy controller for less time, it is because the optimized fuzzy controller provide a faster response than the designed in [1]. Also the transition between controllers was softer with the optimized system. Figures 25, 26 and 27 shows the results obtained with those two structures on the reference tracking in disturbances absence.

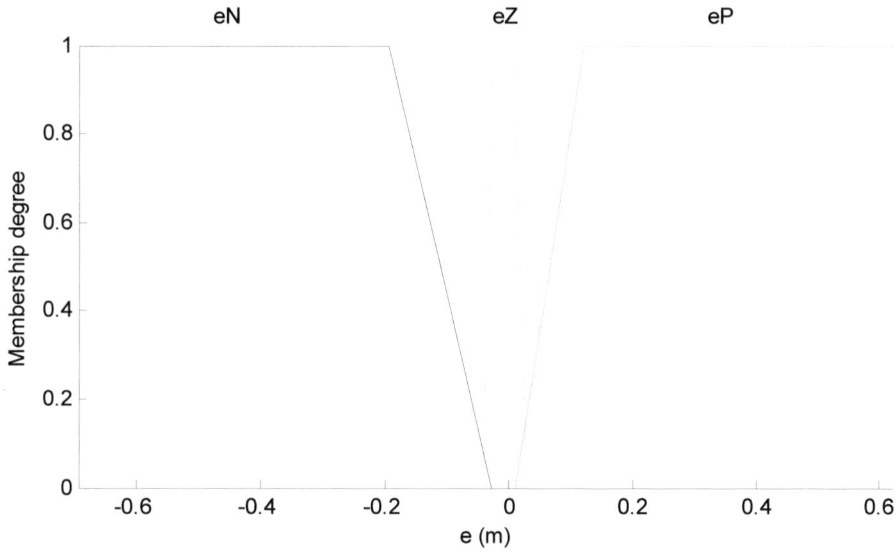

Figure 23. Fuzzy supervisor optimized membership functions of error input

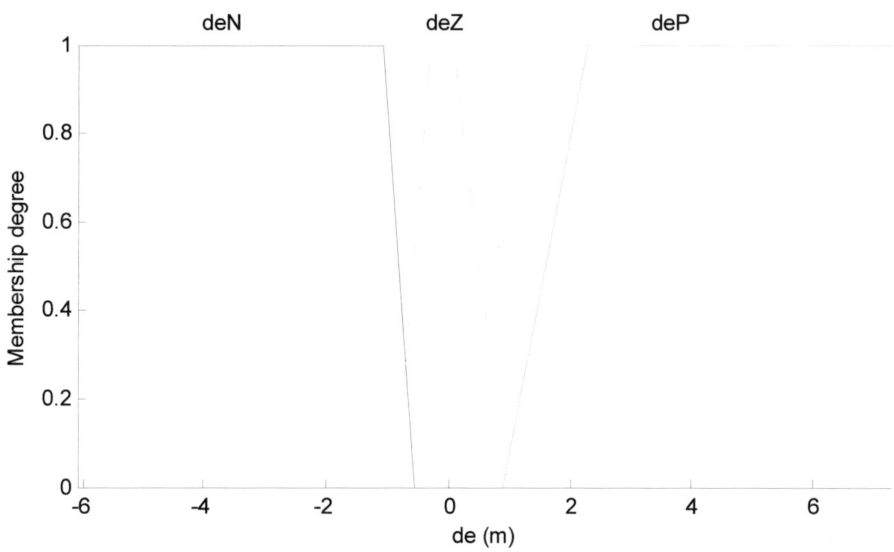

Figure 24. Fuzzy Supervisor optimized membership functions of error derivative input

		e (t)		
		eN	eZ	eP
de(t)/dt	deN	FUZ	FUZ	FUZ
	deZ	FUZ	LTR	FUZ
	deP	FUZ	FUZ	FUZ

Table 4. Rule base of supervisor

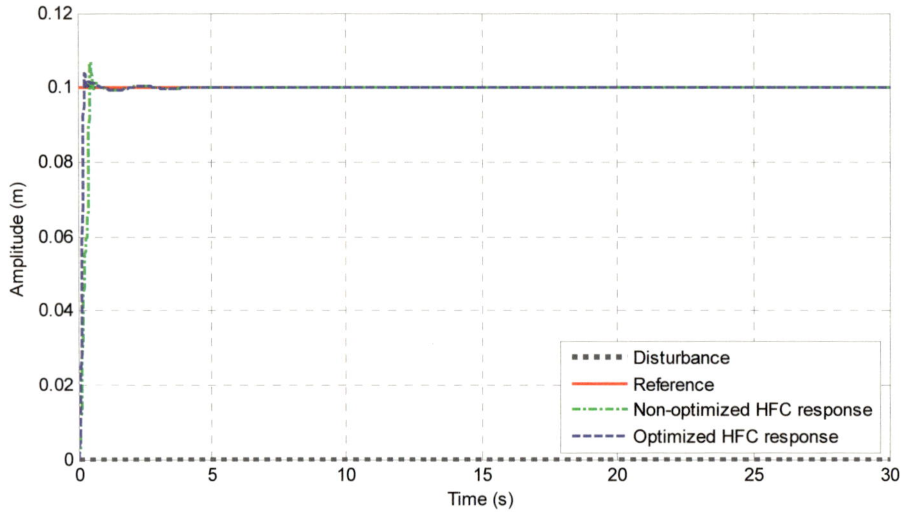

Figure 25. Comparison of the two hierarchical controllers in tracking a step reference

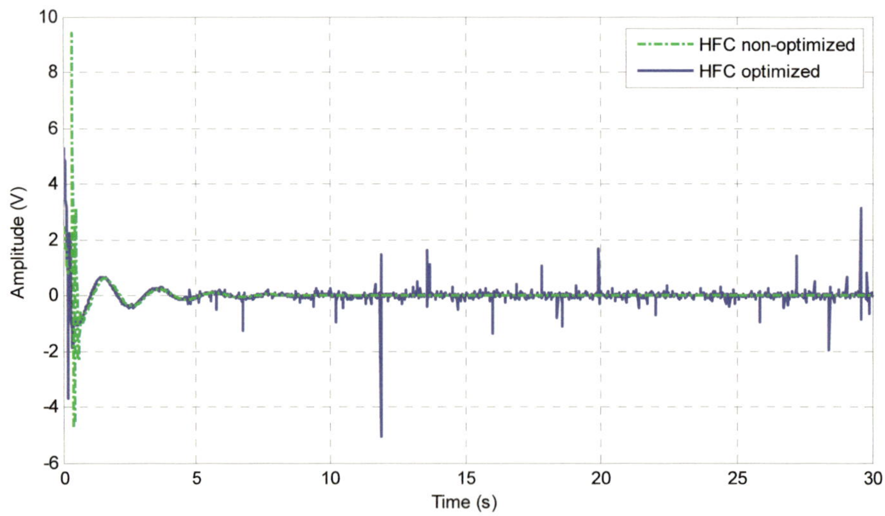

Figure 26. Comparison of control signals generated by the two hierarchical controllers in tracking a step reference

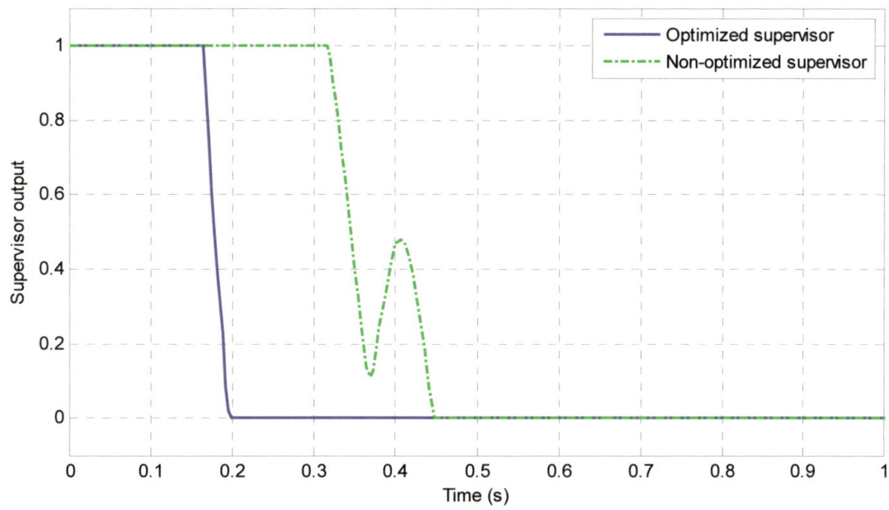

Figure 27. Comparison of signals generated by the two supervisors in tracking a step reference

The performance of the optimized HFC was tested on a step reference tracking, in the presence of white noise with 0.02m peak to peak. Figures 28 and 29 show, again, the best performance of the system controlled by the optimized HFC.

To finalize the comparisons, the system was tested on tracking a square wave reference. As expected, a better performance was obtained using the optimized HFC.

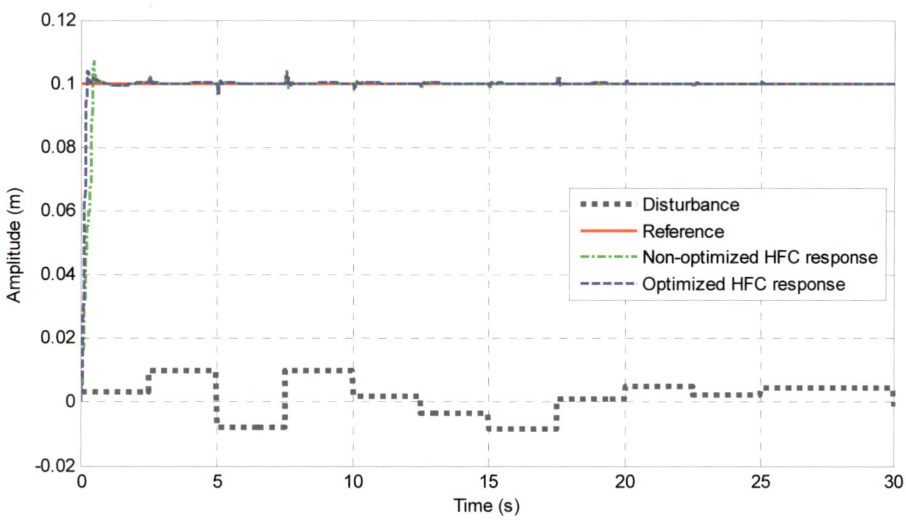

Figure 28. Comparison of the two HFC in tracking a step reference under disturbance

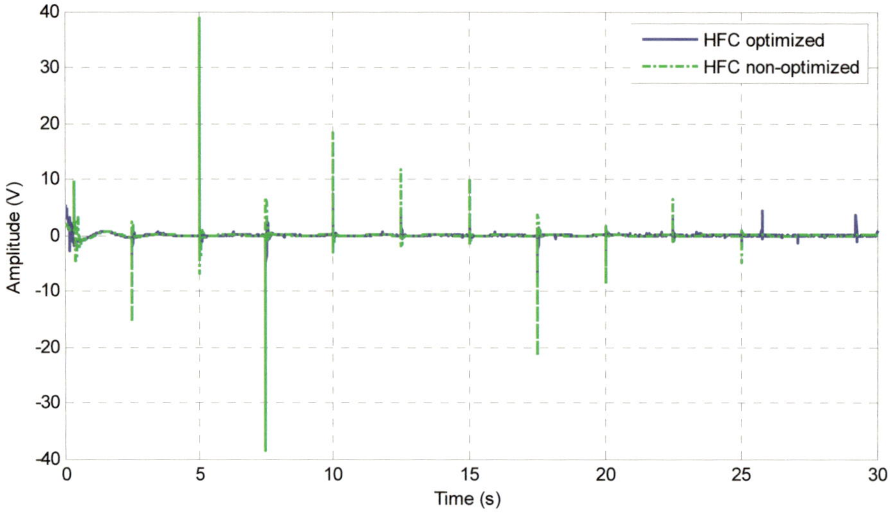

Figure 29. Comparison of control signals generated by the two HFC in tracking a step reference under disturbance

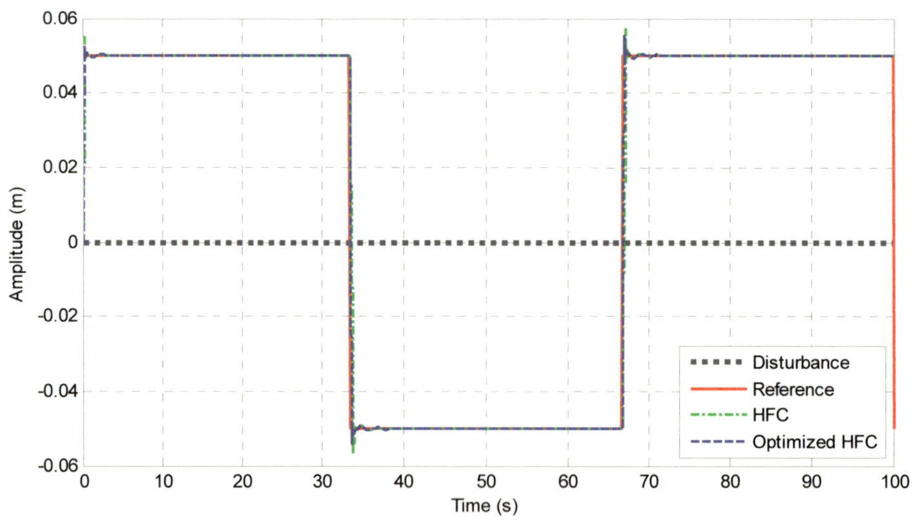

Figure 30. Comparison of the two HFC in tracking a square wave reference

As could be seen on Figure 31, both hierarchical controllers extrapolated the actuator saturation limits, as it was punctual the use of a saturator may not affect the system performance.

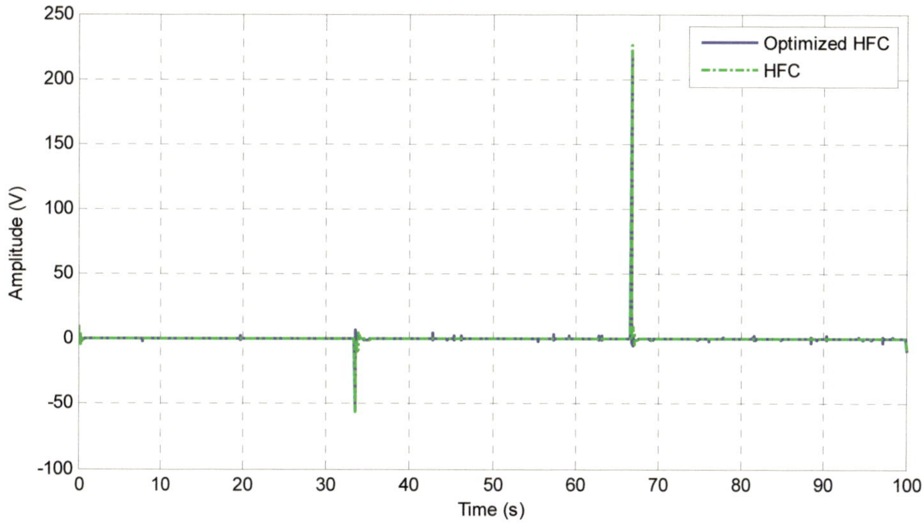

Figure 31. Comparison of control signals generated by the two HFC in tracking a square wave reference

Again the optimized supervisor has used less the fuzzy controller than the non-optimized supervisor.

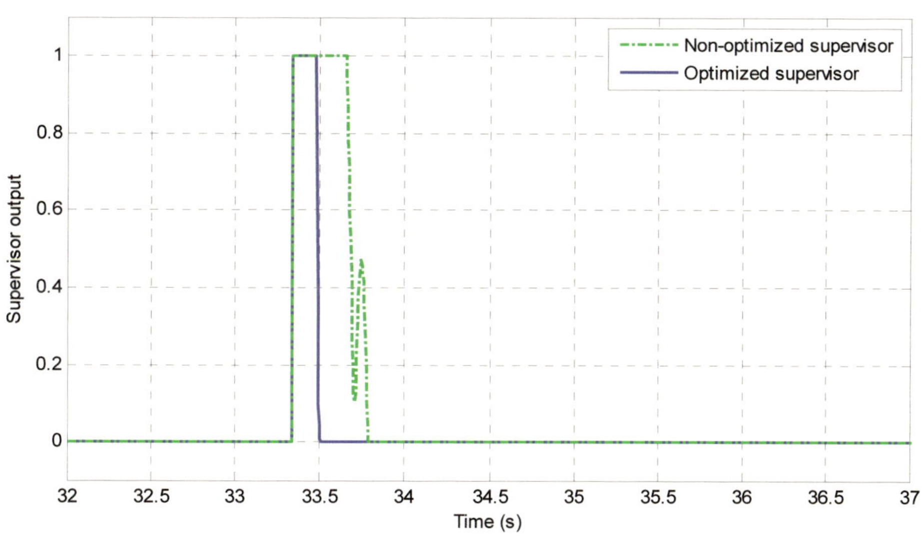

Figure 32. Comparison of signals generated by the two supervisors in tracking a square wave reference

6. Conclusion

One of the main advantages of hierarchical control is to combine different techniques. It allows the supervisor to take the best of each technique.

The results showed the advantages of using genetic algorithms, such as: making automatic tuning of fuzzy components of the HFC, greatly simplifying the design and allowing the obtaining of optimal controllers and supervisors, which is impossible via manual tuning.

As can be seen, the controllers were designed, relaxing some conflicting performance criteria: on the robust controller design the efforts were concentrated to obtain a rapid response and a rapid accommodation, in tracking references and in disturbance rejection, not worrying about the control signal amplitude, for references tracking. In fuzzy controller design the efforts were concentrated to obtain a rapid response and smaller control signals, but no major requirements for rapid accommodation, which had already been achieved by the robust controller; this way all performance requirements were satisfied through the use of the hierarchical fuzzy controller.

With the use of hierarchical control, the controller design becomes simpler because they are more specific, they do not have to meet conflicting performance criteria.

As a suggestion for future projects can be verified: other control techniques for vibration suppression and tracking reference; new ways to optimize the components of HFC; using more controllers in the composition of HFC; other methods for supervisor project; a better configuration of the proposed genetic algorithms.

Author details

Carlos André Guerra Fonseca
Informatics Department, Rio Grande do Norte State University, Natal, Brazil
Computing Engineering and Automation Department, Rio Grande do Norte Federal University, Natal, Brazil

Fábio Meneghetti Ugulino de Araújo
Computing Engineering and Automation Department, Rio Grande do Norte Federal University, Natal, Brazil

Marconi Câmara Rodrigues
Science and Technology School, Rio Grande do Norte Federal University, Natal, Brazil

7. References

[1] Araújo FMU (2002) Automatic Intelligent Controllers with Applications in Mechanical Vibration Isolation [PhD thesis]. Sao Jose dos Campos, Brazil: Aeronautical Technology Institute.

[2] Araújo FMU (1998) Electromechanical System for Vibration Active Control [Master thesis]. Joao Pessoa, Brazil: Paraiba Federal University.

[3] Araújo FMU and Yoneyama T (2001) Modeling and Control of an Electromechanical Device for Vibrations Active Control. Proceedings of the II National Seminar on Control and Automation. pp.15. Salvador, Brazil.

[4] Cruz JJ (1988) Contribution to the Study of Robust Stability for Nonlinear Multivariable Regulators [PhD thesis]. Sao Jose dos Campos, Brazil: National Institute of Space Research.

[5] Cruz JJ (1996) Multivariable Robust Control. Sao Paulo: Publisher from Sao Paulo University.

[6] Doyle JC and Stein G (1981) Multivariable Feedback Design: Concepts for a Classical/Modern Synthesis. IEEE Transactions on Automatic Control, Vol. AC-26, No. 1, pp. 4-16.

[7] Zadeh LA (1965) Fuzzy set. Fuzzy Sets, Information and Control, 8, pp.338-353.

[8] Lee CC (1990) Fuzzy Logic in Control Systems: Fuzzy Logic Controller (Part I). IEEE Transactions on Systems, Man and Cybernetics, 20(2): 404-418.

[9] Driankov D, Hellendoorn H, Reinfrank M (1993) An Introduction to Fuzzy Control. New York: Springer-Verlag. 316 p.

[10] Dutta S (1993) Fuzzy Logic Applications: Technological and Strategic Issues. IEEE Transactions on Engineering Management, 40(3): 237-254.

[11] Karr CL, Gentry EJ (1993) Fuzzy Control of Ph Using Genetic Algorithms. IEEE Transactions on Fuzzy Systems, 1(1): 46-53.

[12] Chiu S, Chand S (1993) Adaptive Traffic Signal Control Using Fuzzy Logic. Proceedings of the 2nd IEEE International Conference on Fuzzy Systems; March 1993; San Francisco, USA. Piscataway: Institute of Electrical and Electronics Engineers.

[13] Castro JL (1995) Fuzzy Logic Controllers are Universal Approximators. IEEE Transactions on Systems, Man and Cybernetics, 25(4): 629-635.

[14] Guerra R, Sandri S, Souza MLO (1997) Autonomous Control of Satellites Altitude Using Fuzzy Logic. In: III Brazilian Symposium on Intelligent Automation, pp.337-342, Vitoria, Brazil.

[15] Kosko B (1992) Neural Networks and Fuzzy System. Englewood Cliffs: Prentice Hall. 449 p.

[16] Wang L, Mendel J M (1992) Generating Fuzzy Rules by Learning from Examples. IEEE Transactions on Systems, Man, and Cybernetics, 22(6): 1414-1427.

[17] Jang JSR (1993) ANFIS: Adaptive-Network-Based Fuzzy Inference System. IEEE Transactions on Systems, Man, and Cybernetics, 23(3): 665-685.

[18] Lin CT (1995) A Neural Fuzzy Control System with Structure and Parameter Learning. Fuzzy Sets and Systems, (70): 183-212.

[19] Sandri AS, Correa C (1999) Fuzzy Logic. In: V Neural Networks School, São José dos Campos, Brazil. pp.c073-c090.

[20] Shaw IS, Simões MG (1999) Fuzzy Control and Modeling. São Paulo: FAPESP, Editora Edgard Blücher LTDA.

[21] Tsoukalas LH, Uhrig RE (1997) Fuzzy and Neural Approaches in Engineering. New York: Publication, John Wiley & Sons.
[22] Fonseca CAG, Araújo FMU, Maitelli AL, Medeiros AV (2003) Genetic Algorithms for Optimization of a Fuzzy Controller for Vibration Suppression. In: VI Brazilian Symposium on Intelligent Automation, pp. 959-963. Bauru, Brazil.
[23] Goldbarg MC and Goldbarg EFG (2005) Evolutionary Computation. In: VIII Neural Networks School. Natal, Brazil.
[24] Holland JH (1970) Robust Algorithms for Adaptation Set in a General Formal Framework. In: IEEE Symposium on Adaptive Processes Decision and Control, 17. Proceedings of the XVII IEEE Symposium on Adaptive Processes Decision and Control.
[25] Holland JH (1975) Adaptation in Natural and Artificial Systems. Ann Arbor: Michigan University Press.

Chapter 16

Enhancing Fuzzy Controllers Using Generalized Orthogonality Principle

Nora Boumella, Juan Carlos Figueroa and Sohail Iqbal

Additional information is available at the end of the chapter

http://dx.doi.org/10.5772/51608

1. Introduction

In the early days, the parameters of the fuzzy logic systems were fixed arbitrary, thus leading to a large number of possibilities for FLSs. In 1992, it has been shown that linguistic rules can be converted into Fuzzy Basis Functions (FBFs), and numerical rules and its associated FBFs must be extracted from numerical data training. Since that time, a multitude of design methods to construct a FLS are proposed. Some of these methods are intensive on data analysis, some are aimed at computational simplicity, some are recursive and others are offline, but all based on the the same idea: *tune the parameters of a FLS using the numerical training data*. Methods for designing FLSs can be classified into two major categories: A first category where shapes and parameters of the antecedent MFs are fixed ahead of time and training data are used for tuning the consequent parameters, and a second category that consists of fixing the shapes of the antecedent and consequent MFs using training data to tune the antecedent and the parameters of the consequent.

Two kinds of FLSs, the Mamdani and the Takagi-Sugeno-Kang (TSK) FLSs are widely used and they are currently adopted by the scientific community. They solely differ in the way the consequent structure is defined. The fact that a TSK FLS does not require a time-consuming defuzzification process makes it far more attractive for most of applications.

In this chapter, we consider the first category to design a TSK FLS basing on alinear method. Our design approach requires a set of input-output numerical data training pairs. Given linguistic rules of the FLS, we expand this FLS as a series of FBFs that are functions of the FLS inputs. We use the input training data to compute these FBFs. Therefore, the system becomes linear in the FLS consequent parameters, and we consider each set of FBFs as a basis vector which is easy to be optimized. Then follows the consequent parameters optimization via a minimizing process of the error vector - *the output training data minus the FBFs vectors weighted by the consequent parameters* - norm. This minimzation can be obtained by applying the *Generalized Orthogonality Principle* (GOP). Optimization process is carefully analyzed in this chapter and its applications in two major areas of concern are demonstrated including robotics and dynamic systems. Firstly, we shall show the improved results with analysis upon the application of GOP in the Fuzzy Logic Controller (FLC) for an inverted pendulum. Secondly, we show how a FLS based on this principle enhances the performance of forecaster for the chaotic time series.

2. Fuzzy Logic Systems (FLS) basic concepts

2.1. Fuzzy sets

A *Fuzzy Set* (FS), $F \in X$ is a set of ordered pairs of a generic element x and its degree, namely *Membership Function* (MF), $\mu_F(x)$. Any FS can be represented as follows:

$$F = \{(x, \mu_F(x)) \,|\forall x \in X\} \tag{1}$$

where the membership degree of x, $\mu_F(x)$, is constrained to be betwwen 0 and 1 for all $x \in X$.

2.2. Mamdani FLS

An FLS is an intuitive and numerical system that maps crisp (deterministic) inputs to a crisp output. It is composed of four elements which are depicted in Figure 1. To completly describe this FLS, we need a mathematical formula that maps the crisp input $\mathbf{x}$ into a crisp output $y = f(\mathbf{x})$, we can obtain this formula by following the signal $\mathbf{x}$ through the fuzzifier to the inference block and into the defuzzifier. We explain, in this section, the working principle of this formula.

2.2.1. Rules

The FLS is associated with a set of *IF-THEN* rules with meaningful linguistic interpretations. The lth rule of a FLS having p inputs $x_1, ..., x_p$ and one output $y \in Y$, *Multiple Input Single Output* (MISO), is expressed as:

$$R^l : \textit{If} \;\; x_1 \;\; \textit{is} \;\; F_1^l \;\; \textit{and}, \ldots, \textit{and} \;\; x_p \;\; \textit{is} \;\; F_p^l \;\; \textit{THEN} \;\; y \;\; \textit{is} \;\; G^l \tag{2}$$

where F_i^l $(i = 1, 2, ..., p)$ are fuzzy antecedent sets wich are represented by their MFs $\mu_{F_i^l}$, and G^l is a consequent set where $l = 1, ..., M$ (M is the number of rules in the FLS).

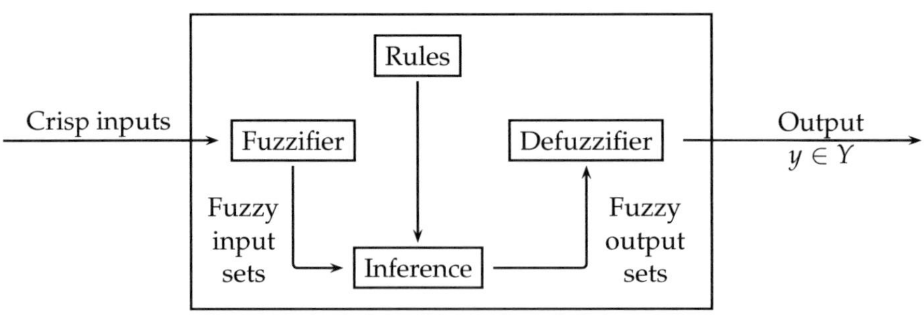

Figure 1. Block diagram of a fuzzy logic system

2.2.2. Fuzzifier

A fuzzifier maps any crisp input $\mathbf{x} = (x_1, ..., x_p)^T \in X_1 \times \cdots \times X_p \equiv \mathbf{X}$ into a fuzzy set $F_{\mathbf{x}}$ in $\mathbf{X}$ [8].

2.2.3. Inference

A fuzzy inference engine combines rules from the fuzzy rule base and gives a mapping from input fuzzy sets in $\mathbf{X}$ to output sets in Y. Each rule is interpreted as a fuzzy implication, i.e., a fuzzy set in $\mathbf{X} \times Y$, and can be expressed as:

$$R^l : F_1^l \times ... \times F_p^l \longrightarrow G^l = A^l \longrightarrow G^l \quad l = 1, ..., M \tag{3}$$

Usually in Mamdani FLS, the implication is replaced by a *t-norm*, i.e. (product or min). Multiple antecedents are connected by a t-norm, so a rule can be expressed by its MF as follows:

$$\begin{aligned} \mu_{R^l}(\mathbf{x}, y) &= \mu_{F_1^l \times F_2^l \times ... \times F_p^l}(x_1, x_2, .., x_p) \bigstar \mu_{G^l}(y) \\ &= \left[T_{i=1}^p \mu_{F_i^l}(x_i) \right] \bigstar \mu_{G^l}(y) \end{aligned} \tag{4}$$

where T and $\bigstar$ are $t-norm$ operators (*product* or *min*). The p-dimensional input to R^l is given by the fuzzy set $A_{\mathbf{x}}$ whose MF is expressed as [8]

$$\mu_{A_{\mathbf{x}}}(\mathbf{x}) = \mu_{X_1}(x_1) \bigstar ... \bigstar \mu_{X_p}(x_p) = T_{i=1}^p \mu_{X_i^l}(x_i) \tag{5}$$

Each rule detemines a fuzzy set B^l in Y which is derived from the sup $-\bigstar$ composition. Then, the MF of this output set is expressed as [8]

$$\mu_{B^l}(y) = \mu_{A_{\mathbf{x}} \circ R^l}(y) = \sup_{\mathbf{x} \in \mathbf{X}} \left[\mu_{A_{\mathbf{x}}}(\mathbf{x}) \bigstar \mu_{R^l}(\mathbf{x}, y) \right] \tag{6}$$

$$\mu_{B^l}(y) = \sup_{\mathbf{x} \in \mathbf{X}} \left[T_{i=1}^p \mu_{X_i}(x_i) \bigstar \left(\left[T_{i=1}^p \mu_{F_i^l}(x_i) \right] \bigstar \mu_{G^l}(y) \right) \right] \tag{7}$$

Finally, the lth rule is expressed as follows

$$\mu_{B^l}(y) = \mu_{G^l}(y) \bigstar \left[T_{i=1}^p \mu_{F_i^l}(x_i) \right] \quad y \in Y \tag{8}$$

2.2.4. Defuzzifier

As we pointed out before, the main idea of a Mamdani FLS is to use crisp inputs to make fuzzy inference and finally find a crisp output which represents the behavior of the FLS. The process of finding a crisp output after fuzzification and inference is called *Deffuzification*. This final step consist on find an operation point given the results of the inference process of the FLS, which results on a fuzzy output set, so we need to use a mathematical method which returns a crisp measure of the behavior of the FLS.

There are many types of defuzzifiers, but we consider in this paper the *Height Defuzzifier* which replaces each rule output fuzzy set by a singleton at the point having maximum membership in that output set, $\overline{y}^l$, then it calculates the centroid of the resultantF set of these singletons. The crisp output of this defuzzifier is expressed as:

$$y(\mathbf{x}) = f(\mathbf{x}) = \frac{\sum_{l=1}^{M} \overline{y}^l \mu_{B^l}(\overline{y}^l)}{\sum_{l=1}^{M} \mu_{B^l}(\overline{y}^l)} \tag{9}$$

where $\overline{y}^l$ is the point having maximum membership in the output set [8].

2.3. Takagi-Sugeno-Kang (TSK) FLS

A TSK FLS is a special FLS which is also characterized by IF-THEN rules, but its consequent is a polynomial. Its output is a crisp value obtained from computing the polynomial output, so it does not need a defuzzification process. The l_{th} rule of a first order type-1 TSK FLS having p inputs $x_1 \in X_1, ..., x_p \in X_p$ and one output $y \in Y$ is expressed as:

$$\begin{aligned} &R^l : \text{IF } x_1 \text{ is } F_1^l \text{ and } x_2 \text{ is } F_2^l \text{ and...and } x_p \text{ is } F_p^l \\ &\text{THEN} \quad y^l(\mathbf{x}) = c_0^l + c_1^l x_1 + ... + c_p^l x_p \end{aligned} \tag{10}$$

where $l = 1, ..., M$, $c_j^l (j = 0, .., p)$ are the consequent parameters, $y^l(\mathbf{x})$ is the output of the lth rule, and F_k^l $(k = 1, ..., p)$ are type-1 antecedent fuzzy sets.

The output of a TSK FLS is obtained by combining the outputs from the M rules in the following form:

$$y_{TSK}(\mathbf{x}) = \frac{\sum_{l=1}^{M} f^l(\mathbf{x}) \left(c_0^l + c_1^l x_1 + ... + c_p^l x_p \right)}{\sum_{l=1}^{M} f^l(\mathbf{x})} \tag{11}$$

where $f^l(\mathbf{x})$ $(l = 1, ..., M)$ are the rule firing levels and they are defined as:

$$f^l(\mathbf{x}) = T_{k=1}^{p} \mu_{F_k^l}(x_k) \tag{12}$$

where T is a $t - norm$ operation, i.e. minimum or product operation (Mendel [8]), and $\mathbf{x}$ is the vector of inputs applied to the TSK FLS.

2.4. Fuzzy basis functions

For Mamdani FLSs, assuming that all consequent MFs are normalized, i.e., $\mu_{G^l}\left(\overline{y}^l\right) = 1$, and using singleton defuzzification, max-product composition and product implication, then the output of the height defuzzifier (9) becomes:

$$y(\mathbf{x}) = f(\mathbf{x}) = \frac{\sum_{l=1}^{M} \overline{y}^l T_{i=1}^{p} \mu_{F_i^l}(x_i)}{\sum_{l=1}^{M} T_{i=1}^{p} \mu_{F_i^l}(x_i)} \tag{13}$$

The FLS in (13) can be expressed as:

$$y(\mathbf{x}) = f(\mathbf{x}) = \sum_{l=1}^{M} \overline{y}^l \phi_l(\mathbf{x}) \tag{14}$$

where $\phi_l(\mathbf{x})$ is called a *Fuzzy Basis Function* (FBF) of the *lth* rule [11], and it is defined as:

$$\phi_l(\mathbf{x}) = \frac{f^l}{\sum_{l=1}^{M} f^l} \qquad l = 1, ..., M \tag{15}$$

where f^l is given in (12).

This linear combination allows us to view an FLS as series expansions of FBFs [11], [1], [4] and [10] which has the capability of providing a mix of both numerical and linguistic information.

2.5. Weighted FBF

The crisp output of the TSK FLS in (11) can be expressed as:

$$y_{TSK}(\mathbf{x}) = \sum_{l=1}^{M} \phi_l(\mathbf{x}) \sum_{k=0}^{p} c_k^l x_k \tag{16}$$

It can also be expressed as:

$$y_{TSK}(\mathbf{x}) = \sum_{l=1}^{M} \sum_{k=0}^{p} \phi_k^l(\mathbf{x}) c_k^l \tag{17}$$

where $\phi_k^l(\mathbf{x})$ is the *kth* Weighted Fuzzy Basis Function (WFBF) of the *lth* rule which is expressed as [2]:

$$\phi_k^l(\mathbf{x}) = x_k \phi_l(\mathbf{x}), \quad l = 1, ..., M; k = 0, ..., p \tag{18}$$

This linear combination allows us to view the FLS as series expansions of WFBFs [2]. The WFBFs have also a capability of providing a combination of both numerical and linguistic information.

3. Orthogonality principle

We explain in this section how we can obtain, graphically, the optimal scalar that minimizes the norm of an error vector [9].Suppose that we have a set of N measurements collected in a N-vector, $\overrightarrow{y}$, gathered for different values collected in another N-vector, $\overrightarrow{\phi}$. The problem is to find :

$$\min_{\theta} \left\| \overrightarrow{y} - \theta \overrightarrow{\phi} \right\| \tag{19}$$

As shown in Figure 2, we can see that the optimal scalar θ that minimizes the norm of the error vector, $\left\| \overrightarrow{e} = \overrightarrow{y} - \theta \overrightarrow{\phi} \right\|$, is obtained when $\overrightarrow{e} \perp \overrightarrow{\phi}$. This can be expressed as follows :

$$\overrightarrow{\phi} \cdot \left(\overrightarrow{y} - \theta \overrightarrow{\phi} \right) = 0 \tag{20}$$

Solving for θ we have:

$$\theta_{opt} = \frac{\overrightarrow{y}^T \overrightarrow{\phi}}{\overrightarrow{\phi}^T \overrightarrow{\phi}} \tag{21}$$

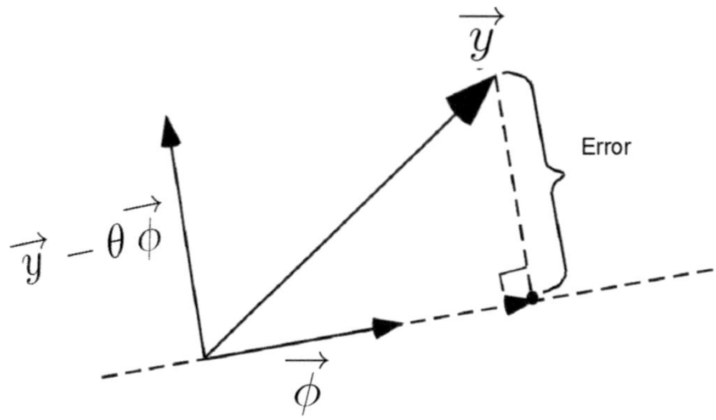

Figure 2. Basic Idea of Orthogonality Principle

4. FLS design based on GOP

GOP is an optimization principle which can be applied to both Mamdani and TSK FLSs. Under the premise of fixed shapes and the parameters of the antecedent MFs over the time, then a training dataset is used to tune the consequent parameters. The consequent parameters are c_k^l $(l = 1, ..., M; k = 0, ..., p)$ in (11) for a TSK FLS, and $\overline{y}^l$ $(l = 1, ..., M)$ in (9) for a Mamdani FLS.

4.1. Mamdani FLS design

Given a collection of N input-output numerical data training pairs

$$\left(\mathbf{x}^{(1)} : y^{(1)}\right), \left(\mathbf{x}^{(2)} : y^{(2)}\right), ..., \left(\mathbf{x}^{(N)} : y^{(N)}\right)$$

where $\mathbf{x}^{(i)}$ and $y^{(i)}$ are respectively the vector input and scalar output of the FLS given by (13). We have to tune the $\overline{y}^l$ $(l = 1, ..., M)$ using these data training. Firstly, we compute the FBFs with training input vectors, then we apply the orthogonality principle on these FBFs and the training output vector.

Equation (14) can be decomposed as follows:

$$\begin{cases} y(\mathbf{x}^{(1)}) = f(\mathbf{x}^{(1)}) = \overline{y}^1\phi_1(\mathbf{x}^{(1)}) + ... + \overline{y}^M\phi_M(\mathbf{x}^{(1)}) \\ y(\mathbf{x}^{(2)}) = f(\mathbf{x}^{(2)}) = \overline{y}^1\phi_1(\mathbf{x}^{(2)}) + ... + \overline{y}^M\phi_M(\mathbf{x}^{(2)}) \\ \vdots \\ y(\mathbf{x}^{(N)}) = f(\mathbf{x}^{(N)}) = \overline{y}^1\phi_1(\mathbf{x}^{(N)}) + ... + \overline{y}^M\phi_M(\mathbf{x}^{(N)}) \end{cases} \tag{22}$$

So we have

$$y(\mathbf{x}^{(i)}) = f(\mathbf{x}^{(i)}) = \sum_{l=1}^{M} \overline{y}^l\phi_l(\mathbf{x}^{(i)}) \quad i = 1, ..., N \tag{23}$$

Now, if each FBF is considered as a basis function, we can compose the following vector:

$$\vec{\phi}_j = \begin{pmatrix} \phi_j(\mathbf{x}^{(1)}) \\ \phi_j(\mathbf{x}^{(2)}) \\ \vdots \\ \phi_j(\mathbf{x}^{(N)}) \end{pmatrix}, \quad j = 1, 2, ..., M \tag{24}$$

where M is the number of rules. We now collect all the N training output data in the same vector $\vec{y}$:

$$\vec{y} = \begin{pmatrix} y(\mathbf{x}^{(1)}) \\ y(\mathbf{x}^{(2)}) \\ \vdots \\ y(\mathbf{x}^{(N)}) \end{pmatrix} \tag{25}$$

and the parameters of the consequent in a vector $\vec{\theta}$:

$$\vec{\theta} = \begin{pmatrix} \overline{y}^1 \\ \overline{y}^2 \\ \vdots \\ \overline{y}^M \end{pmatrix} \tag{26}$$

By considering the N equations, a FLS can be expressed in vector-matrix format as follows:

$$\vec{y} = \mathbf{\Phi} \vec{\theta} \tag{27}$$

where the fuzzy basis function matrix $\mathbf{\Phi}$ is given by:

$$\mathbf{\Phi} = [\vec{\phi}_1, \vec{\phi}_2, ..., \vec{\phi}_M] \tag{28}$$

To find the optimal vector $\vec{\theta}$ and because of fitting with basis sets, we generalize the presented orthogonality principle to a multi-dimensional basis leading to a GOP. The error vector should be perpendicular to all of the basis fuzzy vectors, as shown in Figure 2.

In a matrix form, we obtain:

$$\mathbf{\Phi}^T \cdot \left(\vec{y} - \mathbf{\Phi} \vec{\theta} \right) = 0 \tag{29}$$

Solving for $\vec{\theta}$, we have:

$$\vec{\theta}_{opt} = \begin{pmatrix} \overline{y}^1 \\ \overline{y}^2 \\ \vdots \\ \overline{y}^M \end{pmatrix} = \left[\mathbf{\Phi}^T \mathbf{\Phi} \right]^{-1} \mathbf{\Phi}^T \vec{y}$$

where $\vec{\theta}_{opt}$ is a vector which contains the parameters of the consequent, i.e., $\overline{y}^l$ in (3).

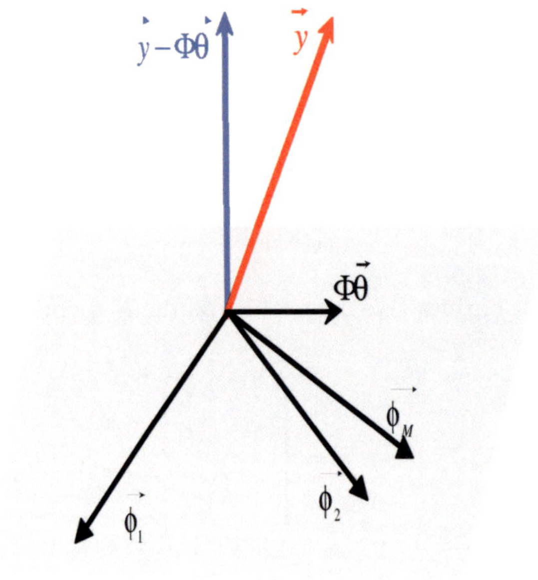

Figure 3. Basic Idea of Generalized Orthogonality Principle. The error vector should be perpendicular to all of the basis fuzzy vectors.

4.2. TSK FLS design

In the same way, the consequent parameters of a TSK FLS are tuned. The design approach is related to the following problem:

Given a collection of N input-output numerical training data pairs:

$$\left(\mathbf{x}^{(1)}:y^{(1)}\right),\left(\mathbf{x}^{(2)}:y^{(2)}\right),\ldots,\left(\mathbf{x}^{(N)}:y^{(N)}\right)$$

where $\mathbf{x}^{(i)}$ is the $(p+1)-$ *dimensional* input vector ($p+1$ inputs with $x_0\equiv 1$) and $y^{(i)}$ is the scalar output of the FLS given by (11). We have to tune the c_k^l $(l=1,...,M;k=0,...,p)$ using these data training.

The WFBF vectors are computed using the training input data, then the GOP is applied to the $(p+1)$ combinations of WFBF vectors and the $(p+1)$ of $N-$*dimensional* training output vector.

Using the elements of the input-output training pairs, the TSK output given in (17), can be rewritten as follows:

$$y_{TSK}(\mathbf{x}^{(i)})=\left\{\begin{array}{c}\begin{bmatrix}\phi_0^1(\mathbf{x}^{(i)})\\ \cdots\\ \phi_p^1(\mathbf{x}^{(i)})\end{bmatrix}^T\begin{bmatrix}c_0^1\\ \vdots\\ c_p^1\end{bmatrix}\\ +\cdots+\\ \begin{bmatrix}\phi_0^M(\mathbf{x}^{(i)})\\ \cdots\\ \phi_p^M(\mathbf{x}^{(i)})\end{bmatrix}^T\begin{bmatrix}c_0^M\\ \vdots\\ c_p^M\end{bmatrix}\end{array}\right. \quad (30)$$

where $\mathbf{x}^{(i)} = \left[1, x_1^{(i)}, ..., x_p^{(i)}\right]^T$. Collecting the N equations we obtain:

$$\overrightarrow{y_{TSK}} = \begin{cases} \begin{bmatrix} \phi_0^1(\mathbf{x}^{(1)}) \cdots \phi_p^1(\mathbf{x}^{(1)}) \\ \ddots \\ \phi_0^1(\mathbf{x}^{(N)}) \cdots \phi_p^1(\mathbf{x}^{(N)}) \end{bmatrix} \begin{bmatrix} c_0^1 \\ \vdots \\ c_p^1 \end{bmatrix} \\ + \cdots + \\ \begin{bmatrix} \phi_0^M(\mathbf{x}^{(1)}) \cdots \phi_p^M(\mathbf{x}^{(1)}) \\ \ddots \\ \phi_0^M(\mathbf{x}^{(N)}) \cdots \phi_p^M(\mathbf{x}^{(N)}) \end{bmatrix} \begin{bmatrix} c_0^M \\ \vdots \\ c_p^M \end{bmatrix} \end{cases} \quad (31)$$

By taking each set of N WFBFs as a Weighted Fuzzy Basis Vector, WFBV:

$$\overrightarrow{\phi_k^l} = \begin{pmatrix} \phi_k^l(\mathbf{x}^{(1)}) \\ \phi_k^l(\mathbf{x}^{(2)}) \\ \vdots \\ \phi_k^l(\mathbf{x}^{(N)}) \end{pmatrix}, \quad \begin{cases} l = 1, ..., M \\ k = 0, ..., p \end{cases} \quad (32)$$

and each set of N outputs as a vector, the output vector can be expressed as follows :

$$\overrightarrow{y_{TSK}} = \begin{cases} \left[\overrightarrow{\phi_0^1} \cdots \overrightarrow{\phi_p^1}\right] \begin{bmatrix} c_0^l \\ \vdots \\ c_p^1 \end{bmatrix} \\ + \cdots + \\ \left[\overrightarrow{\phi_0^M} \cdots \overrightarrow{\phi_p^M}\right] \begin{bmatrix} c_0^M \\ \vdots \\ c_p^M \end{bmatrix} \end{cases} \quad (33)$$

Now we have to tune $p + 1$ parameters for each rule, i.e., M vectors of dimension $(p + 1)$.

$$\overrightarrow{c^l} = \begin{pmatrix} c_0^l \\ \vdots \\ c_p^l \end{pmatrix}, \quad l = 1, ..., M \quad (34)$$

If we define the l_{th} element of Φ_{TSK} as $\Phi_{TSK,l}$, we have:

$$\Phi_{TSK,l} = \left[\overrightarrow{\phi_0^l}, \cdots, \overrightarrow{\phi_p^l}\right], l = 1, .., M \quad (35)$$

the output vector (33) becomes :

$$\overrightarrow{y_{TSK}} = \Phi_{TSK,1}\overrightarrow{c^1} + \cdots + \Phi_{TSK,M}\overrightarrow{c^M} \quad (36)$$

In a matrix form, (36) becomes :

$$\overrightarrow{y_{TSK}} = \Phi_{TSK} \left[\overrightarrow{c^1} \ \ldots \ \overrightarrow{c^M} \right]^T \tag{37}$$

So the *Weighted Basis Function Matrix* (WBFM) Φ can be defined as:

$$\Phi_{TSK} = \left[\Phi_{TSK,1}, \ \ldots, \ \Phi_{TSK,M} \right] \tag{38}$$

The optimal parameters of the consequent conforms a vector, $\overrightarrow{c^l}$ in (34) are obtained when the error vector, $\left(\overrightarrow{y_{TSK}} - \Phi_{TSK} \left[\overrightarrow{c^1} \ \ldots \ \overrightarrow{c^M} \right]^T \right)$, must be perpendicular to all the weighted fuzzy basis vectors, $\overrightarrow{\phi_k^l}$ $(k = 0, \ldots, p$ and $l = 1, \ldots, M)$, which are the columns of the WBFM Φ_{TSK}, as shown in Figure 4.

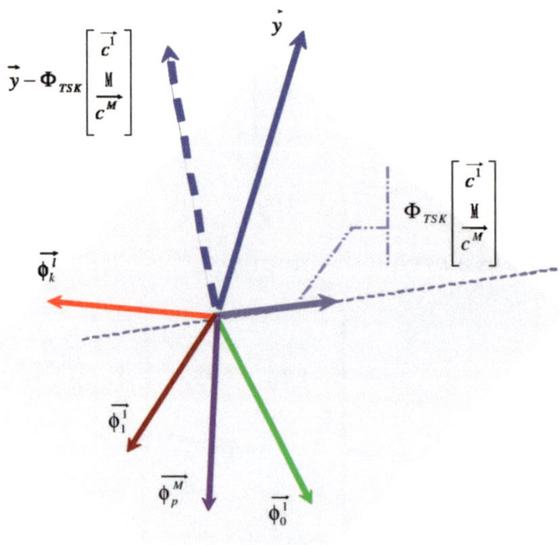

Figure 4. Extended Generalized Orthogonality Principle. The error vector $\overrightarrow{y} - \Phi \left[\overrightarrow{y_C^1} \ \cdots \ \overrightarrow{y_C^M} \right]^T$ should be perpendicular to all the fuzzy basis vectors, $\overrightarrow{\phi_k^l}$

This may be expressed directly in terms of the WBFM Φ as follows:

$$\Phi^T \overrightarrow{y} - \Phi^T \Phi \left[\overrightarrow{y_C^1} \ \cdots \ \overrightarrow{y_C^M} \right]^T = 0 \tag{39}$$

Solving for $\left[\overrightarrow{y_C^1} \ \cdots \ \overrightarrow{y_C^M} \right]^T$ provides the following

$$\left[\overrightarrow{y_C^1} \cdots \overrightarrow{y_C^M} \right]^T_{opt} = \left[\Phi \cdot \Phi^T \right]^{-1} \Phi \overrightarrow{y}$$

5. FLC design for controlling an inverted pendulum on a cart

5.1. Description of the system

Schematic drawing of an *Inverted pendulum On a Cart* (IPOC) system is depicted in Figure 5. where x is the position of the cart, θ is the angle of the pendulum with respect to the vertical direction and $\vec{F}$ is the external acting force in the $x - direction$. In order to keep the pendulum upright, we design a Fuzzy Logic Controller (FLC) using the GOP.

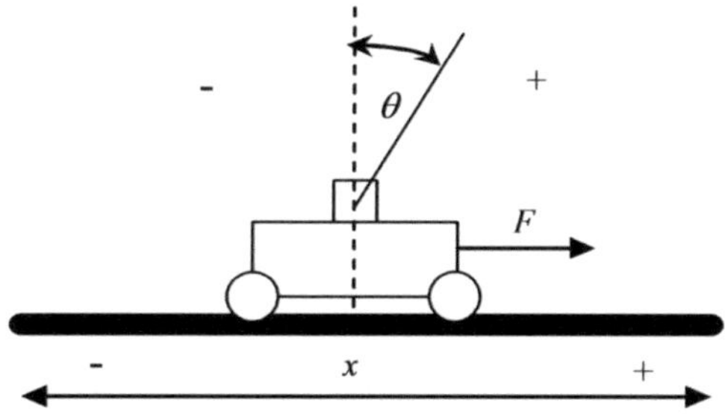

Figure 5. A schematic drawing of the inverted pendulum on a cart

The Lagrange equation for the position of the pendulum, θ, is given by:

$$\left(\frac{ml^2}{4} + J\right)\ddot{\theta} + \frac{ml}{2}(\ddot{x}\cos\theta - g\sin\theta) = 0 \tag{40}$$

The Lagrange equation for the position of the cart, x, is given by:

$$(M_1 + m)\,\ddot{x} + \frac{ml}{2}(\ddot{\theta}\cos\theta - \dot{\theta}^2\sin\theta) = F(t) \tag{41}$$

where J is the moment of inertia of the bar. The masses of the cart and the rod are $M_1 = 2Kg$ and $m = 0.1Kg$, respectively. The rod has a length $l = 0.5m$.

Since the goal of the control system is to keep the pendulum upright the equations can be linearized around $\theta = 0$. We chose $\mathbf{x} = \begin{bmatrix} \theta\ \dot{\theta}\ x\ \dot{x} \end{bmatrix}^T$ as the state vector, where $\dot{\theta}$ is the pendulum angle variation and $\dot{x}$ is the cart position variation. The state representation is given by:

$$\dot{\mathbf{x}} = \begin{bmatrix} 0 & 1\,0\,0 \\ \frac{6}{l(m+4M_1)} & 0\,0\,0 \\ 0 & 0\,0\,1 \\ \frac{-3g\cdot m}{m+4M_1} & 0\,0\,0 \end{bmatrix} \mathbf{x} + \begin{bmatrix} 0 \\ \frac{6}{l(m+4M_1)} \\ 0 \\ \frac{4}{m+4M_1} \end{bmatrix} F(t) \tag{42}$$

$$\mu_{F_i^l}(x_i) = \exp\left[-\frac{1}{2}\left(\frac{x_i - m_{F_i^l}}{\sigma_{F_i^l}}\right)^2\right] \tag{43}$$

5.2. FLC structure and design

We try to keep the pendulum upright regardless the cart's position, i.e., *Pure Angular Position Control System* (PAPCS). Then, the two inputs of the Fuzzy Logic Controller FLC are the angular pendulum position, θ, and its derivative, $\dot{\theta}$, i.e., $\mathbf{x}_1 = [x_1\ x_2] = [\theta\ \dot{\theta}]^T$ and its output is the applied force to the system y =*force*.

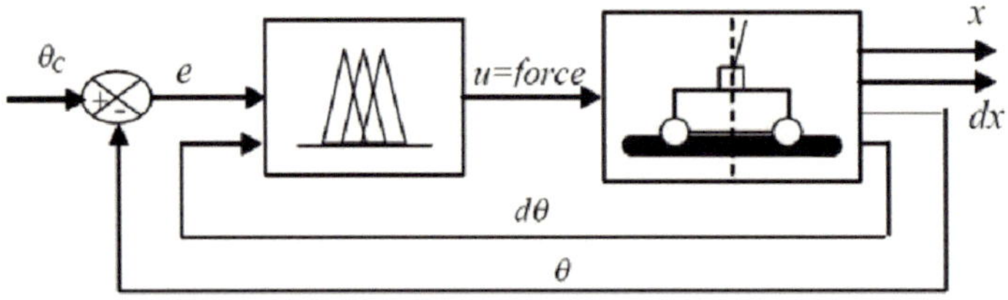

Figure 6. Fuzzy control system of the PAPCS

In this case, we use a Mamdani FLS with four rules. We use gaussian MF to fuzzify the two controller's inputs (44) and triangular MF to fuzzify the controller output.

$$\mu_{F_i^l}(x_i) = \exp\left[-\frac{1}{2}\left(\frac{x_i - m_{F_i^l}}{\sigma_{F_i^l}}\right)^2\right] \tag{44}$$

where $m_{F_i^l}$ and $\sigma_{F_i^l}$ are respectively the centers and standard deviations of these MFs.

The MFs of the antecedents are depicted in Figures 7 and 8.

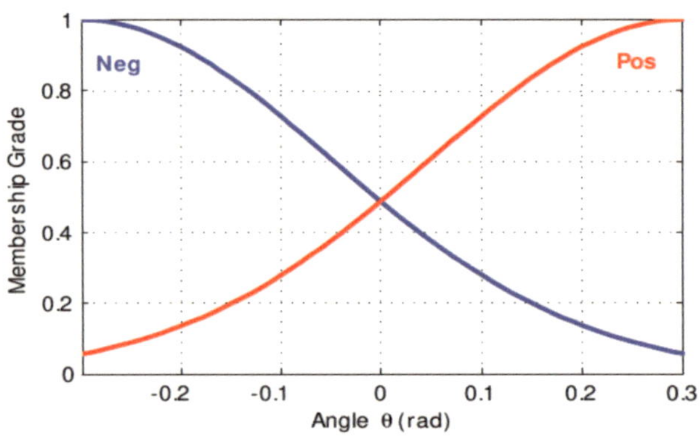

Figure 7. Membership functions for the first controller input θ

Figure 9 shows the 56 data training and the optimal fitting given by the GOP method.

The obtained optimal consequent parameters are

$$\left(\overline{y}^1, \overline{y}^2, \overline{y}^3, \overline{y}^4\right)_{opt} = (-14.3, -14.23, 9.61, 18.96)$$

Figure 10 shows the response of the pendulum system controlled by the designed FLC to a reference $\theta_{ref} = 0$ with its response at the same reference when it is controlled by untuned FLC. The initial state vector is $\mathbf{x}_0 = [\theta_0\ \dot{\theta}_0\ x_0\ \dot{x}_0]^T = [0.1\ 0.2\ 0\ 0]^T$.

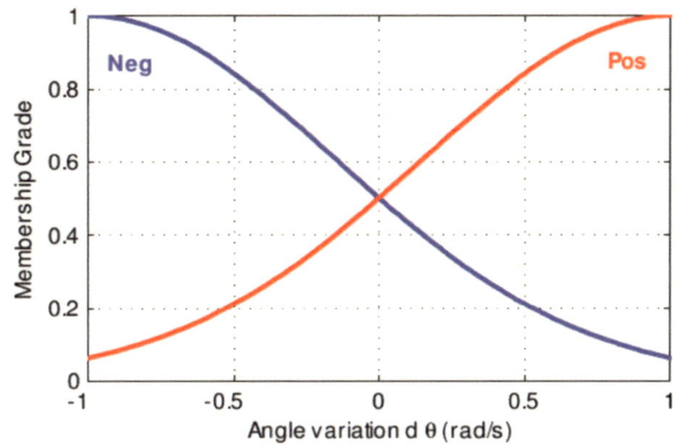

Figure 8. Membership functions for the second crontroller input $\dot{\theta}$

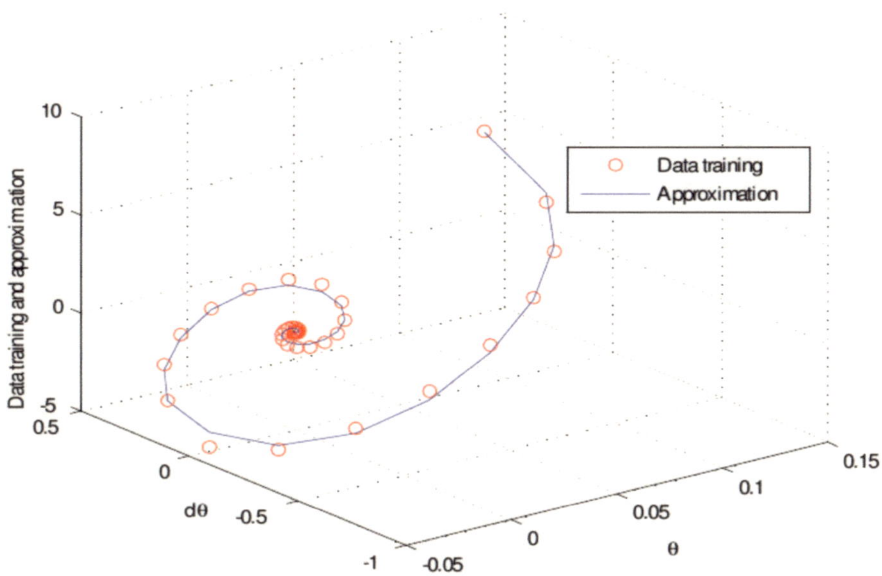

Figure 9. Data training and its approximation based on GOP

We evaluate the proposed design by using its error rate. For quantifying the errors, we use three different performance criteria to analyze the rise time, the oscillation behaviour and the behaviour at the end of transition period. These three criteria are: *Integral of Square Error* ($ISE = \int_0^\infty [e(t)]^2\,dt$), *Integral of the Absolute value of the Error* ($IAE = \int_0^\infty |e(t)|\,dt$) and *Integral of the Time multiplied by Square Error* ($ITSE = \int_0^\infty t\,[e(t)]^2\,dt$)

Table 1 summarizes the obtained values of *ISE*, *IAE* and *ITSE* of PAPCS using FLC, when tuning and no tuning are used.

We notice from this table that the errors obtained when tuning is used are all smaller than those obtained with untuned FLC. Fig. 11, 12, 13 show the different quantified errors.

Figures 10, 11, 12 and 13 show that the system using tuning is less oscillatory, having a rise time and errors at the end of transition period smaller than those obtained by untuned FLC.

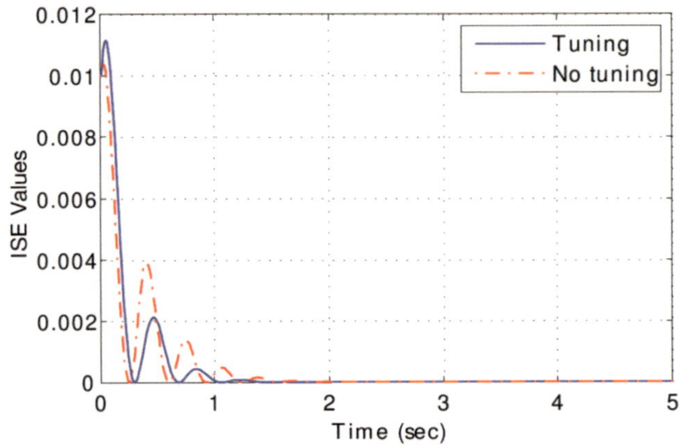

Figure 10. System responses of PAPCS controlled by a tuned and untuned FLC

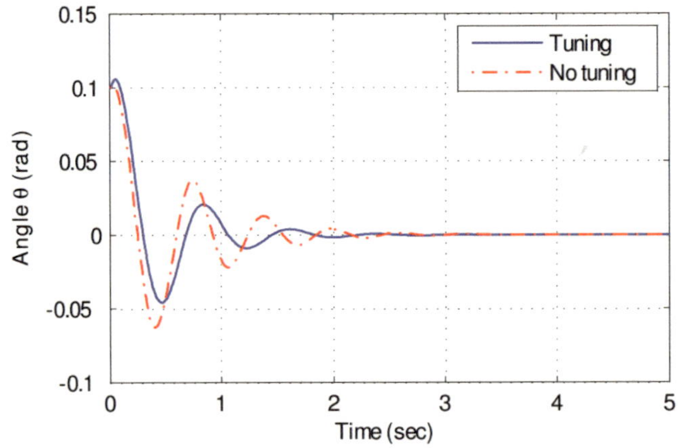

Figure 11. Integral of square error values of the PAPCS of tuned and no tuned consequent parameters. Rise time of the system is shorter for the tuned FLC

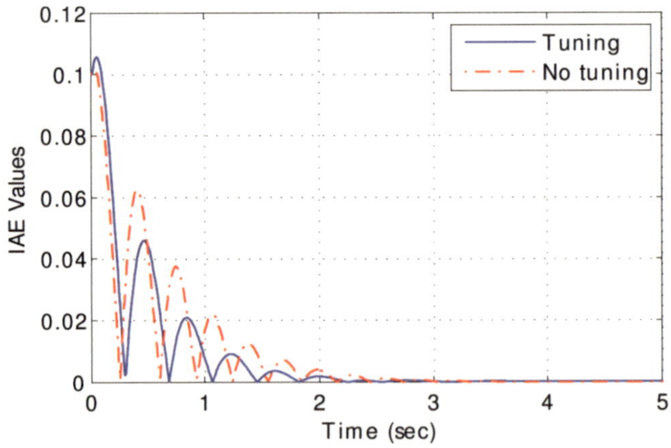

Figure 12. Integral of the absolute value of the error values of PAPCS of tuned and no tuned consequent parameters The system is less oscillatory for the tuned FLC before becoming stable

	No tuning	Tuning
ISE	0.2338	0.2224
IAE	4.7343	4.0403
ITSE	6.7733	4.4278

Table 1. Comparison of performance criteria for of PAPCS using tuned and no tuned FLC.

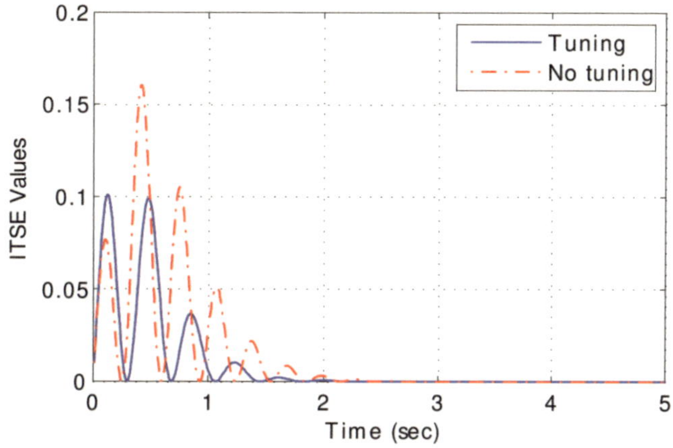

Figure 13. Integral of the time multiplied by square error values of PAPCS of tuned and no tuned consequent parameters. The error at the end of transition period is less important for the tuned FLC

6. FLS design for predicting time series

We apply the GOP to design an FLS which predicts a time series. The FLS has to predict the future value $x(t+6)$ of a Mackey-Glass time series (45) which is volatile. The following four antecedents were used: $x(t-18)$, $x(t-12)$, $x(t-6)$ and $x(t)$, which are known values of the time series ([2], [3]).

$$\frac{dx(t)}{dt} = \frac{0.2x(t-\tau)}{1+x^{10}(t-\tau)} - 0.1x(t) \tag{45}$$

The training data are obtained by simulating (45) for $\tau = 17$. We use the samples $x(1001), \cdots, x(1524)$ to train the IT2 FLS and the samples $x(1501), \cdots, x(2024)$ for testing. We use two Gaussian MFs per antecedent, so we have then 16 rules. The MFs of the antecedents are Gaussian, where its mean and the standard deviation were obtained from the 524 training samples, $x(1001), \cdots, x(1524)$. Table 2 summarizes the consequent parameters per each rule.

Figure 14 displays performance of the FLS in training data, and Figure 15 shows its results on Testing data. Note that the GOP-designed is a better forecaster, since the differences from original data are small in both training and testing data sets.

Some additional analyses should be performed to verify the goodness of fit of the method (See [5], and [6]), but in this case, the proposed GOP has shown good results, so we can recommend its application to real cases. Time series analysis is an useful topic for many decision makers, so the use of optimal and easy-to-be-implemented techniques, as the proposed one has a wide potential.

R^l	c_1	c_2	c_3	c_4	c_5
R^1	−3.58	7.94	−9.17	0.03	0.78
R^2	9.92	−10.9	−0.02	1.29	−7.83
R^3	16.05	7.58	12.40	5.25	−33.96
R^4	8.92	−6.78	−12.22	3.68	−4.13
R^5	1.06	4.64	28.42	−40.17	0.16
R^6	22.57	−33.28	−12.43	17.13	−12.76
R^7	−2.93	−7.65	5.73	−2.91	−1.30
R^8	22.88	26.23	−15.79	−6.19	−0.60
R^9	−3.86	4.36	2.04	0.21	4.77
R^{10}	27.72	−45.35	24.63	7.92	6.26
R^{11}	−0.24	−4.99	30.94	−26.54	6.65
R^{12}	2.36	5.34	−26.93	18.21	−8.03
R^{13}	−30.66	13.37	5.27	3.60	1.43
R^{14}	23.62	−21.97	−3.87	6.04	8.01
R^{15}	3.70	−5.07	0.61	−0.76	8.38
R^{16}	−25.05	11.30	−0.42	1.27	4.64

Table 2. The optimal TSK FLS consequent parameters obtained by GOP design.

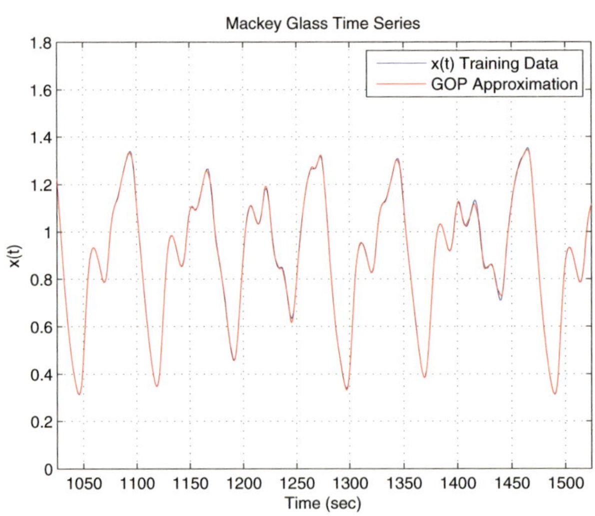

Figure 14. Mackey-Glass time series. The samples $x(1001), \cdots, x(1524)$ are used for designing the FLS forecaster

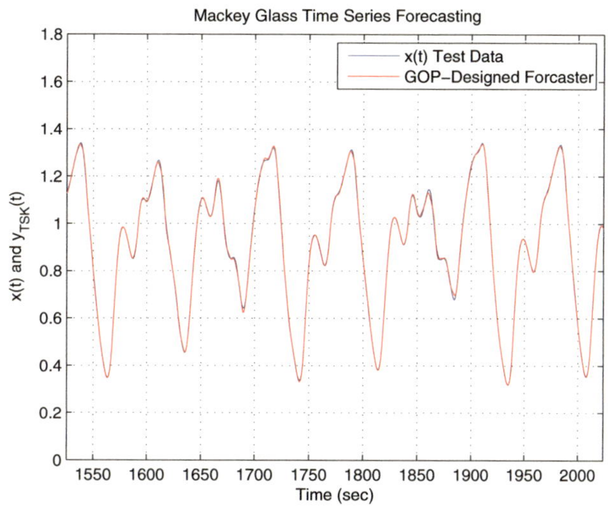

Figure 15. Output of the TSK FLS time-series forecaster. The samples $x(1525), \cdots, x(2024)$ are used for testing the GOP design

7. Concluding remarks

In this chapter we have presented an enhancement method of fuzzy controllers using the generalized orthogonality principle. We applied the method to two different cases: a first one involving control of an inverted pendulum and a second one for fuzzy forecasting. In the first application, numerical rules and their FBFs were extracted from numerical training data. This combination of both linguistic and numerical information simultaneously become FBFs an useful method. Since a specific FLS can be expressed as a linear combination of FBFs, we generalized orthogonality principle on FBFs that results in a better FLS.

In the second study case, we applied the GOP to design a FLS for time series forecasting. The FLS has been applied to a Mackey-Glass time series with better results compared to a non-GOP FLS. The results were validated with simulations.

All the FBFs can be seen as a basis vector, which allows to optimize the parameters of the consequents. This means that the error vectors are orthogonal to these FBFs, resulting in the minimization of the magnitudes of these error vectors, and consequently an optimal FLS.

The proposed method has a wide potential in complex forecasting problems ([5], and [6]). Its application to hardware design problems ([7]) can improve the performance of fuzzy controllers, so its implementation arises as a new field to be covered.

Author details

Nora Boumella
University of Batna, Batna - Algeria

Juan Carlos Figueroa
Universidad Distrital Francisco Jose de Caldas, Bogota - Colombia

Sohail Iqbal
NUST-SEECS, Islamabad - Pakistan

8. References

[1] Berenji, H. & Khedkar, P. [1992]. Learning and tuning fuzzy logic controllers through reinforcements, *IEEE Trans. Neural Networks* 3(1): 724–740.

[2] Boumella, N., Djouani, K. & Boulemden, M. [2011]. On an Interval Type-2 TSK FLS A1-C1 consequent parameters tuning, *in* IEEE (ed.), *Proc. SSCI 2011 T2FUZZ - 2011 IEEE Symposium on Advances in Type-2 Fuzzy Logic Systems*, IEEE, pp. 1–6.

[3] Boumella, N., Djouani, K. & Boulemden, M. [2012]. A robust Interval Type-2 TSK fuzzy logic system design based on chebyshev fitting, *International Journal of Control, Automation, and Systems* 10(4).

[4] Boumella, N., Djouani, K. & Iqbal, S. [2009]. A new design of fuzzy logic controller based on generalized orthogonality principle, *in* IEEE (ed.), *Proc. IEEE International Symposium on Computational Intelligence in Robotics and Automation, CIRA 2009*, IEEE, pp. 497–502.

[5] Figueroa, J. C. [2009]. An evolutive Interval Type-2 TSK fuzzy logic system for volatile time series identification, *2009 Conference on Systems, Man and Cybernetics*, IEEE, pp. 1–6.

[6] Figueroa, J. C., Kalenatic, D. & Lopez, C. A. [2010]. A neuro-evolutive Interval Type-2 TSK fuzzy system for volatile weather forecasting, *Lecture Notes in Computer Science* 6216: 142–149.

[7] Melgarejo, M. & Peña, C. A. [2007]. Implementing Interval Type-2 fuzzy processors I, *Computational Intelligence Magazine* 2(1): Pág. 63–71.

[8] Mendel, J. [2001]. *Uncertain Rule-Based Fuzzy Logic Systems: Introduction and New Directions*, Prentice Hall.

[9] Strang, G. [1988]. *Linear Algebra and its Applications, Third edition*, Brooks/Cole.

[10] Wang, L. [1992]. Fuzzy systems are universal approximators, *in* IEEE (ed.), *Proc. IEEE Int'l. Conf. on Fuzzy Systems, San Diego, CA*, IEEE, pp. 1163–1170.

[11] Wang, L. & Mendel, J. M. [1992]. Fuzzy basis functions, universal approximation, and orthogonal least squares learning, *IEEE Trans. Neural Networks* 3(5): 807–814.

Chapter 17

New Areas in Fuzzy Application

Muhammad M.A.S. Mahmoud

Additional information is available at the end of the chapter

http://dx.doi.org/10.5772/48781

1. Introduction

"The world is not black and white but only shades of gray." In 1965, Zadeh [1] wrote a seminal paper in which he introduced fuzzy sets, sets with un-sharp boundaries. These sets are considered gray areas rather than black and white in contrast to classical sets which form the basis of binary or Boolean logic. Fuzzy set theory and fuzzy logic are convenient tools for handling uncertain, imprecise, or unmodeled data in intelligent decision-making systems. It has also found many applications in the areas of information sciences and control systems.

In this chapter, we shall discuss two important categories of fuzzy logic nonlinear applications: "Control" and "Trending and Prediction". With respect to Fuzzy Control application, among the huge applications that were published under this category, two new applications are selected in this chapter to focus on the Hierarchal Control application with "multi-input" "multi-output" signals, and another application is selected as application of smart electrical grid. However, for Fuzzy Trending and Prediction Application, c-Mean Fuzzy Cluttering technique is discussed as an introduction for Fuzzy trending algorithm, and then two different applications are introduced. The first application discusses very nonlinear problem to predict the rate of accident for labours work in a construction sector, and the second application is to find a fault in complicated electrical network. All these new applications for fuzzy control and fuzzy trending recognition has been found after year 2000.

2. Control

Control is one of the main the application for the fuzzy controller, especially for the applications that can be easily expressed by linguistically. Many machines now in the market are fuzzy machines. Also the fuzzy logic has take place in the DCS's and PLC's as recognized function to build process controllers. In this chapter we shall select three applications as an example for the new application of fuzzy logic in the control.

2.1. Fuzzy control design for gas absorber system

In this section, the chapter shall present the research efforts that have been carried out on the control of gas absorbers/gas reactors. It shall also introduce the new approach to a fuzzy control design for a typical gas absorber system. The approach shall incorporate a linear state-estimation to generate the internal knowledge-base that shall store input-output pairs. This collection of pairs shall be then utilized to build a feedback fuzzy controller for the gas absorber.

2.1.1. Background

A major direction in systems engineering design has been focused on the use of simplified mathematical models to facilitate the design process. This constitutes the so-called model-based system design approach, an overview of the underlying techniques can be found in [2]. Most of the available results have thus far overlooked the operational knowledge of the dynamical system under consideration. On the other hand, a knowledge-based system approach [8] has been suggested to deal with the analysis and design problems of different classes of dynamical systems by incorporating both the simplest available model as well as the best available knowledge about the system. For single physical systems, one of the earlier efforts along this direction has been on the development of an expert learning system; see [4-7] and their references. An alternative approach has been on integrating elements of discrete event systems with differential equations [3].

A third approach has been through the use of fuzzy logic control by successfully applying fuzzy sets and systems theory [9]. In the cases where understood there is no acceptable mathematical model for the plant, fuzzy logic controllers [10] are proved very useful and effective. They are generally base on using qualitative rules of thumb, that is, qualitative control rules in terms of vague and fuzzy sentences. It has been pointed out [11] that fuzzy control systems possess the following features:

Hierarchical ordering of fuzzy rules is used to reduce the size of the inference engine. Real-time implementation, or on-line simulation, of fuzzy controllers can help reduce the burden of large-sized rule sets by fusing sensory data before imputing the system's output to the inference engine.

This section is presenting a new approach to fuzzy control design for a gas absorber system. It provides a new and efficient procedure to construct the inference engine by incorporating a linear state-estimator in generating and storing input-output pairs. This collection of pairs is then utilized to build a feedback fuzzy controller. By fine-tuning of the controller parameters, it is shown that the gas absorber system has always a guaranteed stability. Numerical simulation of a six-order gas absorber is carried out and the obtained results show clearly that the proposed estimator-fuzzy controller scheme yields excellent performance.

2.1.2. A Gas Absorber System

A. Brief Account

Separation processes play an important role in most chemical manufacturing industries. Streams from chemical reactors often contain a number of components; some of these components must be separated from the other components for sale as a final product, or for use in another manufacturing process. A common example of a separation process is gas absorption (also called gas scrubbing, or gas washing) in which a gas mixture is contacted with a liquid (the absorbent or solvent) to selectively dissolve one or more components by mass transfer from the gas to the liquid. Absorption is used to separate gas mixtures; remove impurities, contaminants, pollutants, or catalyst poisons from a gas; or recover valuable chemicals. In general, the species of interest in the gas mixture may be all components, only the component(s) not transferred, or only the component(s) transferred. Absorption is frequently conducted in trayed towers (plate columns), packed columns, spray towers, bubble columns, and centrifugal contactors. A trayed tower is a vertical, cylindrical pressure vessel in which vapor and liquid, which flow counter-currently, are contacted on a series of metal trays or plates; see Fig. 1. Components that enter the bottom of the tower is the gas feed stream are absorbed by the liquid stream, that flows across each tray, over an outlet weir and into a down-comer, so that the gas product stream (leaving the top of the tower) is more pure.

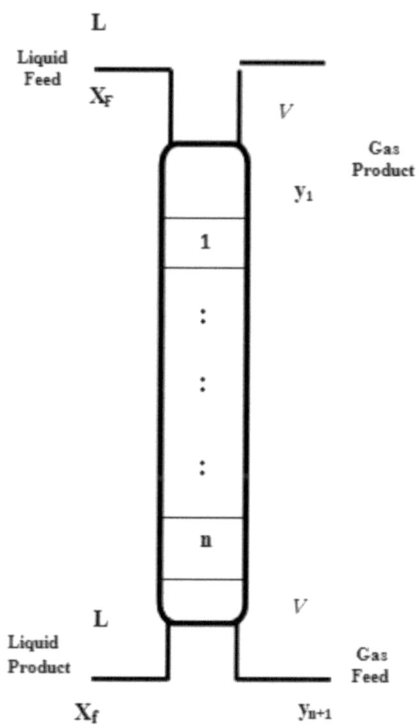

Figure 1. Gas absorption column, n stages

B. Assumptions and definitions

The basic assumptions used are:

A1) The major component of the liquid stream is inert and does not absorb into the gas stream.

A2) The major component of the gas stream is inert and does not absorb into the liquid stream.

A3) Each stage of the process is an equilibrium stage, that is, the vapour leaving a stage is in thermodynamic equilibrium with the liquid on that stage.

A4) The liquid molar holdup is constant.

We now introduce the following variable definitions:

- L = moles inert liquid per time: = liquid molar flow rate.
- V= moles inert vapor per time: = vapor molar flow rate
- M= moles liquid per stage: = liquid molar holdup per stage
- W= moles vapor per stage: = vapor molar holdup per stage
- x_j= moles solute (stage j) per mole inert liquid (stage j)
- y_j= moles solute (stage j) per mole inert vapor (stage j)

C. Dynamic model

The concept of an equilibrium stage is important for the development of a dynamic model of the absorption tower. An equilibrium stage is represented schematically in Fig. 2. The total amount of solute on stage j is the sum of the solute in the liquid phase and the gas phase (that is, $M\,x_j + W\,y_j$). Thus the rate of change of the amount of solute is $d(M\,x_j + W\,y_j)/dt$ and the component material balance around stage j can be expressed as:

$$\begin{aligned} \frac{d(M\,x_j + W y_j)}{dt} &= L\,x_{j-1} + V\,y_{j+1} - L\,x_j - V\,y_j \\ \frac{dM\,x_j}{dt} &\cong L\,x_{j-1} + V\,y_{j+1} - L\,x_j - V\,y_j \end{aligned} \tag{1}$$

where we assumed that in accumulation, liquid is much more dense than vapor. Under assumption A4), then (1) simplifies into:

$$\frac{d\,x_j}{dt} \cong \frac{L}{M}x_{j-1} + \frac{V}{M}y_{j+1} - \frac{L}{M}x_j - \frac{V}{M}y_j \tag{2}$$

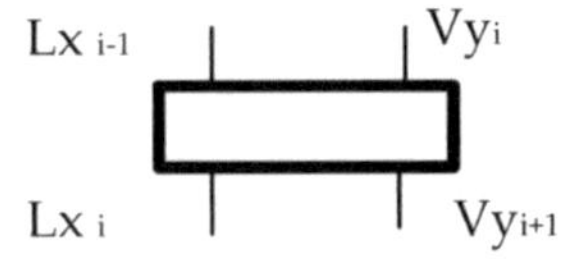

Figure 2. A typical gas absorption stage

Under assumption A3), we let

$$y_j = d\ x_j \tag{3}$$

which expresses a linear relationship between the liquid phase and gas phase compositions at stage j with d being an equilibrium parameter. Using (3) into (2) and arranging we get:

$$\frac{d\,x_j}{dt} = \frac{L}{M} x_{j-1} - \frac{(L+V\,d)}{M} x_j - \frac{V\,d}{M} x_{j+1} \tag{4}$$

For n-stage gas absorber, (4) is valid for j =2,…,n-1. At the extreme stages, we have:

$$\frac{d\,x_1}{dt} = -\frac{(L+V\,d)}{M} x_1 - \frac{V\,d}{M} x_2 + \frac{L}{M} x_f \tag{5}$$

$$\frac{d\,x_n}{dt} = -\frac{(L+V\,d)}{M} x_n + \frac{L}{M} x_{n-1} + \frac{V}{M} y_{n+1} \tag{6}$$

where xf and yn+1 are the known liquid and vapor feed compositions, respectively.

On combining (3), (4),(5) and (6), we reach the state-space model:

$$\dot{x}(t) = A\ x(t) + B\,u(t)\,, \qquad y(t) = C\,x(t) \tag{7}$$

where A an (nxn) system matrix with a triangular structure, B is an (nxm) input matrix and C is an (nxp) output matrix given by:

$$A = \begin{bmatrix} -\frac{L+M}{M} & \frac{Vd}{M} & 0 & 0 & 0\ 0 \cdots & 0 \\ \frac{L}{M} & -\frac{L+Vd}{M} & \frac{Vd}{M} & 0 & 0 \cdots & 0 \\ 0 & \frac{L}{M} & -\frac{L+Vd}{M} & \frac{Vd}{M} & 0 \cdots & 0 \\ 0 & & \ddots & & & 0 \\ \vdots & & & \ddots & & \vdots \\ \vdots & & & & \ddots & \\ 0 & & & & \frac{L}{M} & -\frac{L+Vd}{M} \end{bmatrix} \tag{8}$$

$$B = \begin{bmatrix} \frac{L}{M} & 0 \\ 0 & 0 \\ \vdots & \vdots \\ \vdots & \vdots \\ \vdots & \vdots \\ \vdots & \vdots \\ \vdots & \frac{V}{M} \end{bmatrix} \tag{9}$$

$$C = \begin{bmatrix} 1 & 0 & 0 & 0 & 0 & 0 \\ 0 & 0 & 0 & 0 & 0 & 1 \end{bmatrix} \tag{10}$$

2.1.3. Fuzzy controller design

The design of a fuzzy controller can be implemented by the following steps:

Step1:

Supposed that the output y (t) takes values in the interval $U = [\alpha, \beta] \subset R$. Define 2N+1 fuzzy function A^l in U that are consistent and complete with the triangular membership functions shown in Fig. 3. That is, we use the N fuzzy sets A^1, ---, A^N to cover the negative interval $[\alpha, 0)$, the other N fuzzy sets A^{N+2},---, A^{2N+1} to cover the positive interval $(0, \beta]$, and choose the center x N+1 of fuzzy set A^{N+1} at zero.

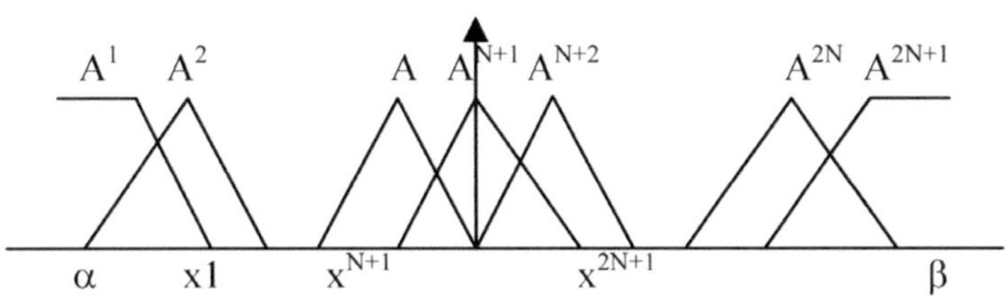

Figure 3. Membership functions for the fuzzy controller.

Step 2:

Consider the following 2N+1 fuzzy IF-THEN rules:

$$\text{IF y is } A^l\text{, THEN u is } B^l \tag{11}$$

Where l = 1, 2, ---, 2N+1, and centers $\overline{y^l}$ of fuzzy set B^l are chosen such that,

$$\overline{y^l} \begin{cases} \leq 0 & \text{for } l=1,\cdots,N \\ =0 & \text{for } l=N+1 \\ \geq 0 & \text{for } l=N+2,\cdots,2N+1 \end{cases} \tag{12}$$

Step 3:

Design the fuzzy controller from the 2N+1 fuzzy IF THEN rules (11) using product inference engine, singleton fuzzifier and center average defuzzifier; that is, the designed fuzzy controller is

$$v=-f(y)=\frac{\sum_{1=1}^{2N+1}\overline{y^1}\mu A^1(y)}{\sum_{1=1}^{2N+1}\mu A^1(y)} \tag{13}$$

Where $\mu A^l(y)$ are shown in Fig. 3 and y^1 satisfy $\overline{y}$ (12).

To estimate the range of the input-output pairs $\{v_i, y_i\}$, full order estimator [2] can be used.

2.1.4. Simulation studies

Consider a gas absorber system with the following parameters: L=80, M=200, V=100 and d=0.5.

Thus,

$$\frac{L+Vd}{M}=-0.65,\frac{L}{M}=0.4,\frac{V\,d}{M}=0.25,\frac{V}{M}=0.5$$

A MATLAB program is written to simulate the gas absorber system. Different positive and negative step input are applied to estimate the outputs. The results of two cases are illustrated in Fig. 4 and Fig. 5. The tracking behaviour of the outputs is shown.

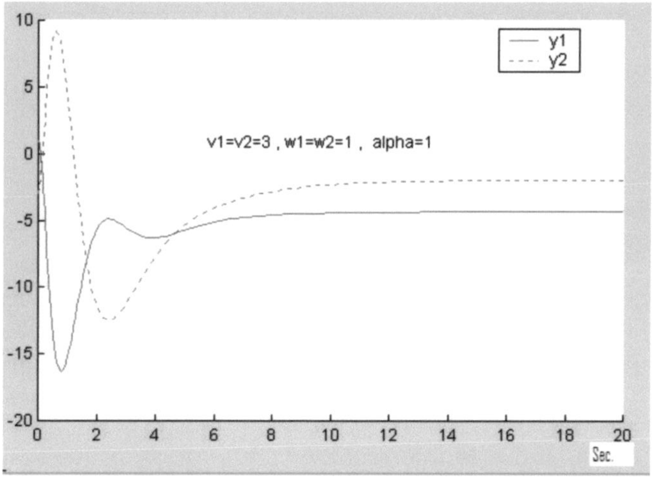

Figure 4. Output response with positive step input signal

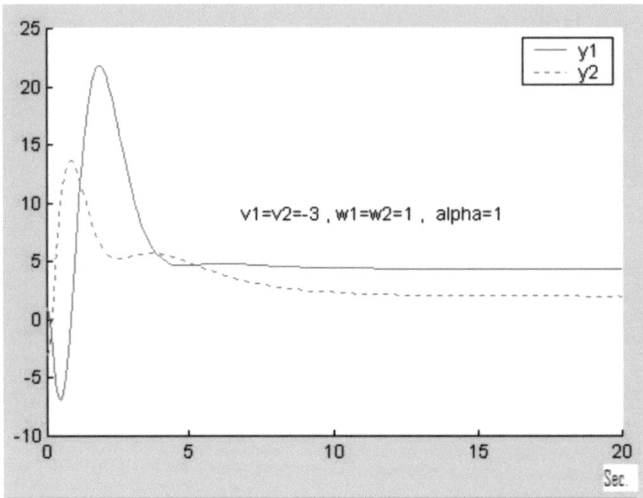

Figure 5. Output response with negative step input signal

From the input-output pair obtained, the behaviour of the system is examined and the ranges of its outputs (controllers' inputs) are predicted. Fig. 6 illustrates a block diagram of the gas absorber and the fuzzy controller array.

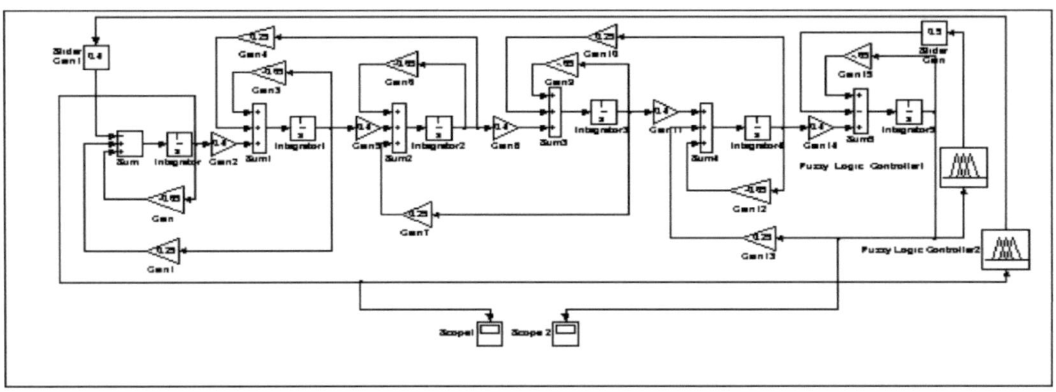

Figure 6. Block Diagram of gas absorber system and the fuzzy controllers

To control the response of the gas absorber, the range of linguistic values of the output of each feedback fuzzy controller is tuned between (– 3) and (3). Comparison between the output response with fuzzy controller (when the number of linguistic values of the controller input – output pair is three) and without controller is illustrated in Fig.7 and Fig.8.

In Fig.7, the controller is tuned to interfere the natural decay of the system. In Fig. 8, the fuzzy controller is adjusted to improve the response of the gas absorber. It is noted that the response of controlled system has less overshoot, less steady state error and faster compared to the uncontrolled system.

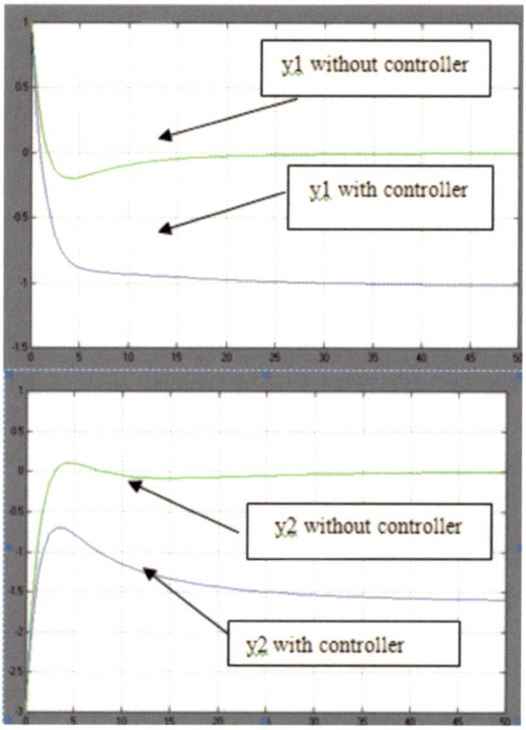

Figure 7. Controller is tuned to interfere the natural decay of the system

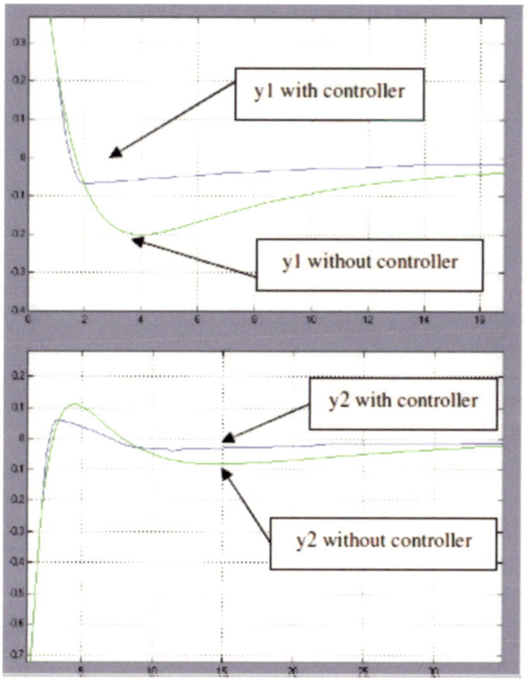

Figure 8. The controller is tuned to improve the response of the system.

2.1.5. Discussion

This section has presented a new and simple fuzzy controller for a gas absorber system to enhance the response of the output. The simulation results have shown that the controller guarantees well-damped behaviour of the controlled gas absorber system.

2.2. Large scale fuzzy controller

In this section, we shall develop a new approach to the control of interconnected system using fuzzy system theory. The approach shall be based on incorporating a group of local estimators on the system level to generate the input-output database. An array of feedback fuzzy controllers shall then be designed to ensure the asymptotic stability of the closed loop system. The developed technique shall be applied to an unstable large-scale system and extensive simulation studies shall be carried out to illustrate the potential of this new approach..

2.2.1. Background

In control engineering research, problems of decentralized control and stabilization of interconnected systems are receiving considerable interest in recent years [14,15] where most of the effort is focused on dealing with the interaction patterns. It is concluded that a systematic approach to deal with the problems of interconnected systems is twofold: first is to base the analysis and design effort on the subsystem level using conventional control methods and second is to deal with interactions effectively. These methods are facilitated, in general, by virtue of several mathematical tools including linearization, delay approximation, decomposition and model reduction. This constitutes the so-called model-based control system approach for which we have seen numerous techniques [16]. Most of the available results have so far overlooked the operational knowledge of the interconnected system under consideration. In [17], a knowledge-based control system approach has been suggested to deal with the analysis and design problems of interconnected systems by incorporating both the simplest available model as well as the best available knowledge about the system. For single physical systems, one of the earlier efforts along this direction has been on the development of an expert learning system [18-19]. An alternative approach has been on integrating elements of discrete event systems with differential equations [20]. A practically-supported third approach has been through the use of fuzzy logic control by successfully applying fuzzy sets and systems theory [21].

For interconnected systems, the foregoing approach motivates the research into intelligent control by combining techniques of control and systems theory with those from artificial intelligence. The main focus should be on integrating a knowledge base, an approximate (humanlike) reasoning and/or a learning process within a hierarchical structure.

Fuzzy logic controllers [23-25] are generally considered applicable to plants that are mathematically poorly understood (there is no acceptable mathematical model for the plant) and where experienced human operators are available for satisfactorily controlling the plant and providing qualitative "rules of thumb" (qualitative control rules in terms of vague and fuzzy sentences).

A concerted effort has been made to formally reduce the size of the fuzzy rule base to make fuzzy control attractive to interconnected systems. Two of the difficulties with the design of any fuzzy control system are:

- The shape of the membership functions.
- The choice of fuzzy rules.

The properties that a fuzzy membership function is used to characterize are usually fuzzy. Therefore, we may use different membership functions to characterize the same description.

Conceptually, there are two approaches to determine a membership function. The first approach is to use the knowledge of human experts. Usually this approach can only give a rough formula of the membership function; fine-tuning is required. In the second approach, data are collected from various sensors to determine the member ship functions. Specifically, the structures of the membership functions are specified first, then fine-tuning of the membership function parameters should be implemented based on the collected data [8].

In this section, we contribute to the further development of intelligent control techniques of interconnected systems. It provides a new approach to fuzzy control design for interconnected system. The approach consists of two stages: In the first stage, a group of local state estimator is constructed to generate the data base of input-output pairs. In the second stage, an array of feedback fuzzy controllers is designed and implemented to ensure the asymptotic satiability of the interconnected system. Simulation studies on a large-scale system with unstable eigenvalus are carried out to illustrate the features and capability of this new approach.

2.2.2. State estimation of interconnected systems

In the sequel, the terms large-scale and interconnected are used interchangeable. The term large scale system (LSS) does not have a unique established meaning, but it covers systems that possess several particular feature, such as multiple subsystem, [14,17] multiple control, multiple objectives, decentralized and/or hierarchical information structures. Any LSS includes many variables but their control is faced by a well-know fact [16] that the states are not always available for measurement and state must be estimated.

Many authors have considered the state estimation of large-scale systems in input decentralized fashion. Here we summarize one convenient algorithm [15]. Let the state model of the ith subsystem described by

$$\dot{x}_i(t) = A_i x_i(t) + B_i u_i(t) + \Sigma^N G_{ij} x_j \tag{14}$$

$$y_i(t) = C_i x_i(t),\ i,j = 1,\ 2,\ \ldots\ldots\ N \tag{15}$$

Where all vectors and matrices are appropriately defined and $g_i(.)$ is the interaction function between the ith subsystem and the rest of the system. It is considered that (C_i, A_i) is completely observable for i = 1, 2, …….. N.

The following algorithm finds the optimal states of a large-scale system based on decentralized estimation and control [17]:

Algorithm 1:

Step 1:

Read the matrices A_i, Bi and select $Q_i \geq 0$ and $R_i > 0$ as weighted matrix.

Step 2:

Solve the following 2N algebraic Riccati equations for H_i, K_i

$$Hi(A^T_i + \alpha I_i) + (A_i + \alpha I_i)H_i - H_i D_i H_i + Q_i = 0 \tag{16}$$

$$Ki(A^T_i + \alpha I_i) + (A_i + \alpha I_i)K_i - K_i S_i K_i + Q_i = 0 \tag{17}$$

Where $D_i = C^T{}_i C_i$, $S_i = B_i R^{-1}{}_i B^T$

Step 3:

Integrate the following set of N simultaneous equation for $e_i(t)$, I = 1, 2 …. N, using the initial condition $e_i(0) = x_i(0)$

$$\begin{pmatrix} \dot{e}_1 \\ \vdots \\ \dot{e}_N \end{pmatrix} = \begin{pmatrix} A_1\text{-}S_1K_1 & \cdots & G_{1N} \\ \vdots & \ddots & \\ G_{N_1} & & A_N\text{-}H_N D_N \end{pmatrix} \begin{pmatrix} e_1 \\ \vdots \\ e_N \end{pmatrix} + \begin{pmatrix} B_1 v_1 \\ \vdots \\ B_N v_N \end{pmatrix} \tag{18}$$

Step 4:

Integrate the following set of n simultaneous equations for x 1(t), i = 1, 2, ….. N

$$\begin{pmatrix} \dot{x}_1 \\ \vdots \\ \dot{x}_N \end{pmatrix} = \begin{pmatrix} A_1\text{-}S_1K_1 & \cdots & G_{1N} & S_1K_1 \cdots & 0 \\ \vdots & & & \ddots & \\ G_{N_1} & & A_N\text{-}S_N I_N & 0 & S_N K_N \end{pmatrix} \begin{pmatrix} x_1 \\ \vdots \\ x_N \end{pmatrix} + \begin{pmatrix} B_1 v_1 \\ \vdots \\ B_N v_N \end{pmatrix} \tag{19}$$

$\dot{x}_N$ G_{N1} A_N - $S_N I_N$ 0 $S_N K_N$ x_N $B_N v_N$

Step 5:

Generate the input-output pairs $\{v_i, \hat{y}_i = c_i \hat{x}_i\}$.

2.2.3. Interconnected system

Assume the following interconnected system of order 10 [17]:

$$A=\begin{pmatrix} -1.5 & -0.3 & -0.25 & 0.1 & 0.5 & r1_{11} & r1_{12} & r1_{13} & r1_{14} & r1_{15} \\ 0.1 & 0 & 0 & -0.2 & 0 & r1_{21} & r1_{22} & r1_{23} & r1_{24} & r1_{25} \\ 0 & 0.2 & -1 & 0 & 0.4 & r1_{31} & r1_{32} & r1_{33} & r1_{34} & r1_{35} \\ 0.6 & -0.1 & -0.25 & -2 & 0 & r1_{41} & r1_{42} & r1_{43} & r1_{44} & r1_{45} \\ 0.4 & 0.2 & 1 & 0.5 & 0.1 & r1_{51} & r1_{52} & r1_{53} & r1_{54} & r1_{55} \\ r2_{11} & r2_{12} & r2_{13} & r2_{14} & r2_{15} & -1.5 & -0.3 & -0.25 & 0.1 & 0.5 \\ r2_{21} & r2_{22} & r2_{23} & r2_{24} & r2_{25} & 0.1 & 0 & 0 & -0.2 & 0 \\ r2_{31} & r2_{32} & r2_{33} & r2_{34} & r2_{35} & 0 & 0.2 & -1 & 0 & 0.4 \\ r2_{41} & r2_{42} & r2_{43} & r2_{44} & r2_{45} & 0.6 & -0.1 & -0.25 & -2 & 0 \\ r2_{51} & r2_{52} & r2_{53} & r2_{54} & r2_{55} & 0.4 & 0.2 & 1 & 0.5 & 0.1 \end{pmatrix} \quad (20)$$

$$B=\begin{pmatrix} 0 & 0 & 0 & 0 \\ 1 & 0 & 0 & 0 \\ 0 & 0 & 0 & 0 \\ 0 & 1 & 0 & 0 \\ 0 & 1 & 0 & 0 \\ 0 & 0 & 0 & 0 \\ 0 & 0 & 1 & 0 \\ 0 & 0 & 0 & 0 \\ 0 & 0 & 0 & 1 \\ 0 & 0 & 0 & 1 \end{pmatrix} \quad (21)$$

$$C=\begin{pmatrix} 1 & 1 & 0 & 0 & 0 & 0 & 0 & 0 & 0 & 0 \\ 0 & 0 & 1 & 0 & 1 & 0 & 0 & 0 & 0 & 0 \\ 0 & 0 & 0 & 0 & 0 & 1 & 1 & 0 & 0 & 0 \\ 0 & 0 & 0 & 0 & 0 & 0 & 1 & 0 & 1 \end{pmatrix} \quad (22)$$

Which is considered to be composed of two-coupled subsystems; each of order 5. The coupling parameters are $r1_{jk}$ and $r2_{jk}$ where j and k take values of 1,2,3,4 and 5. In the sequel, we refer to the structure of the interconnected system model as:

$$\dot{x}=\begin{pmatrix} A11 & \cdots & G12(\underline{r1}) \\ \vdots & \ddots & \\ G21(\underline{r2}) & & A22 \end{pmatrix} x+\begin{pmatrix} B1 \\ \vdots \\ B2 \end{pmatrix} v \quad (23)$$

Where G12(r1) and G21(r2) are the coupling mtrices.

For a typical values [4] of $r1_{15}$=-0.1, $r1_{24}$=0.1, $r1_{42}$=0.2, $r2_{22}$=0.1,$r2_{42}$=0.15,$r2_{51}$=0.11 and allothe values of coupling parameters are zeros, we examined the stability of the system by computing the eigenvalues of matrix A. They are {-1.0915, -1.0641, 0.477 + j0.0206, 0.477 – j0.00206, 0.022 + j0.0544, 0.022 – j0.0544, -1.8709 + j0.1713, -1.8709 – j0.1713, -1.9306 + j0.1413, -

1.9306 – j0.1413}, and it is quite clear that there are four eigenvalues lie in the open right half of the complex plane and thus the interconnected system is unstable. Further, it is easy to check that the interconnected system is both controllable and observable.

2.2.4. Estimation of the system state variables and outputs

A Matlab program is written to implement the computational Algorithm (1) of section 1.2.2 on the interconnected system. Different positive and negative step input are applied to estimate the outputs. The results of two cases are illustrated in Fig. 9 and Fig. 10 It is observed that the outputs tend to track conveniently the input signals.

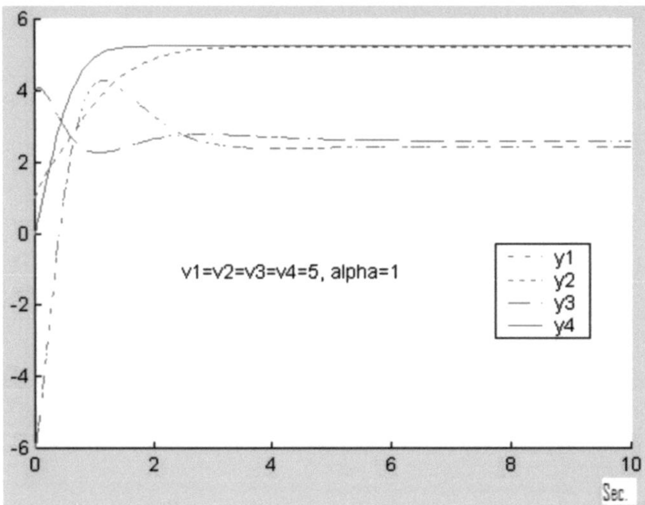

Figure 9. Simulation Results for case 1.

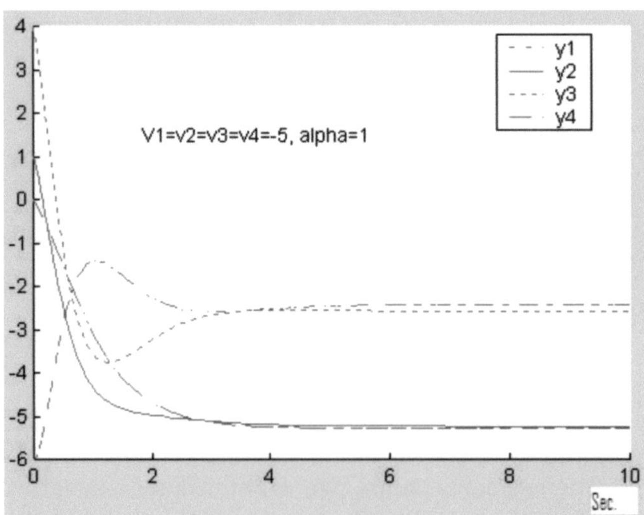

Figure 10. Simulation Results for case 2.

2.2.5. Design of an array of fuzzy controller

We are going to treat the interconnected system at hand as being composed of two identical and coupled subsystems. The control system to be designed is such that each subsystem has its own fuzzy negative feedback controller which its input being the output of the respective subsystem (Fig. 11). Each subsystem fuzzy controller is constructed using two fuzzy systems.

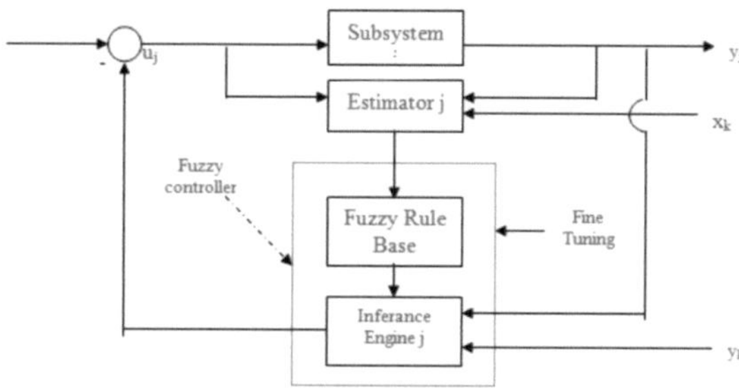

Figure 11. Block diagram of the proposed fuzzy feedback controller array.

In order to build each fuzzy controller, the following steps are implemented:

Step 1:

The range of the inputs to each fuzzy controller $[\alpha_i, \beta_i]$ are driven from the estimated value of the respective subsystem outputs, where i = 1, 2, 3, 4.

Step 2:

2N+1 fuzzy set M^L_i in $[\alpha_i, \beta_i]$ that are normal, consistent and complete with triangular membership functions [24], are defined for each controller, where L = 1, 2--, $2N_i+1$. That is we use N_i fuzzy set M^1_i, ---, $M_i^{N_i}$ to cover the negative internal $[\alpha_I, 0)$, the other N_i fuzzy sets $M_i^{N_i+2}$, ---, $M_i^{2N_i+1}$ to cover the positive internal $(0, \beta]$, and the center of fuzzy set $M_i^{N_i+1}$ at zero.

Step 3:

The following $2N_i+1$ rules are considered

$$\text{IF } y_{ai} \text{ is } M_i^L \text{ or } y_{bi} \text{ is } M_i^L \text{ then u is } K_i^L$$

Where L = 1, 2,---, $2N_i+1$, and a_i, b_i are the input to the fuzzy controller i, and the center y_{ai}^L and y_b^{-L} of the fuzzy set k_i^L are chosen such that

$$y_{ai}^{-L} \text{ and } y_{bi}^{-L} \begin{cases} \leq -0 & \text{for} 1=1,\cdots,N_i \\ =0 & \text{for} 1=N_i+1 \\ \geq 0 & \text{for} 1=N_i+2,\cdots,2N_i+1 \end{cases} \quad (24)$$

Step 4:

Product inference engine, singleton fuzzyfier, and center average defuzzifier are selected to design the fuzzy controller.

2.2.6. Simulation results

The behaviour of the interconnected system outputs after implementing the fuzzy controllers with unity step function input are shown in Fig 12 and Fig: 13. It is clearly evident that the system becomes asymptotically stable by using the negative fuzzy feedback controller array.

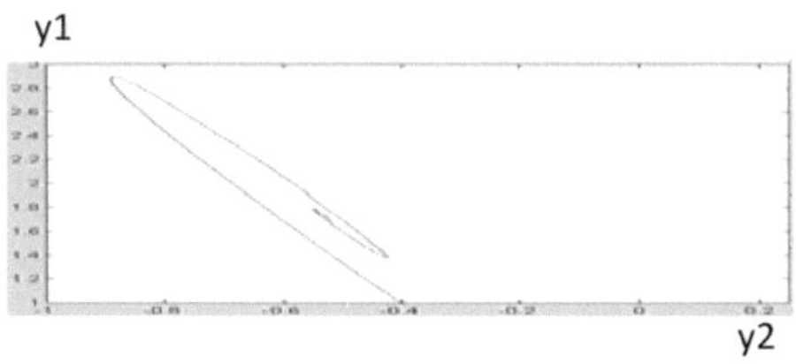

Figure 12. Outputs y1 against y2 y2

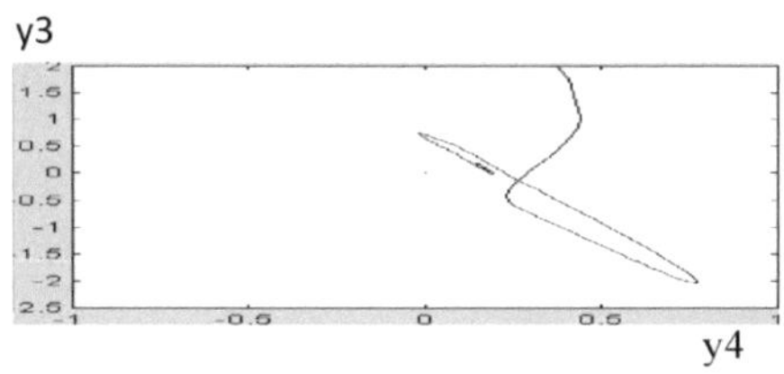

Figure 13. Outputs y3 against y4 y4

2.2.7. Performance of the proposed fuzzy feedback controller array

Now, we examine the effect of coupling matrices on the performance of fuzzy controlled interconnected system. Five additional cases with deferent coupling ranks are implemented. Fine tuning of membership functions was required to adjust their ranges. The following table summarizes the test cases:

Case No.	A11,A2 2Norm	G12 Sparsty	G12 Norm	G21 Sparsty	G21 Norm	System Stability without controller	System Stability with controller
1 (Fig 12, 13)	2.2529	3/25	0.2	3/25	1.8028	Unstable	Stable
2 (Fig. 14, 15)	2.2529	12/25	0.4712	3/25	0.1803	Unstable	Stable
3 (Fig. 16, 17)	2.2529	3/25	.2	12/25	0.5341	Unstable	Stable
4(Fig. 18, 19)	2.2529	1	3.0361	3/25	0.1803	Unstable	Stable
5 (Fig. 20, 21)	2.2529	3/25	.2	1	3.0364	Unstable	Stable
6 (Fig.22, 23)	2.2529	1	3.0361	1	3.0417	Unstable	Stable

Table 1. Results summary for 6 test cases.

The following figures illustrate the above test cases:

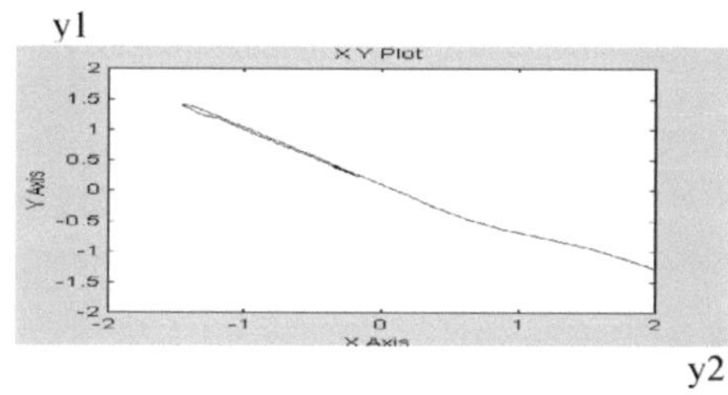

Figure 14. Case 2 Outputs y1 against y2

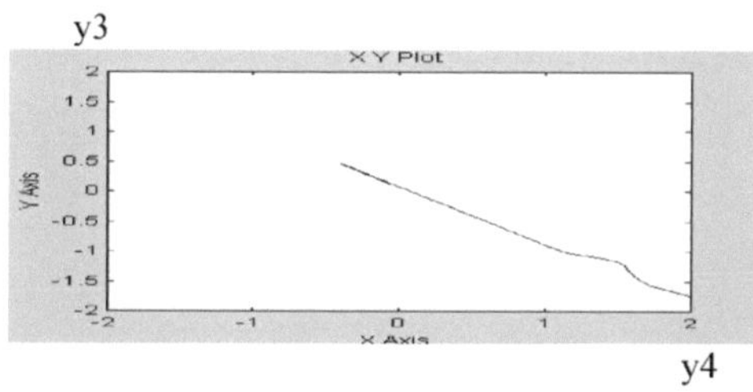

Figure 15. Case 2 Outputs y3 against y4

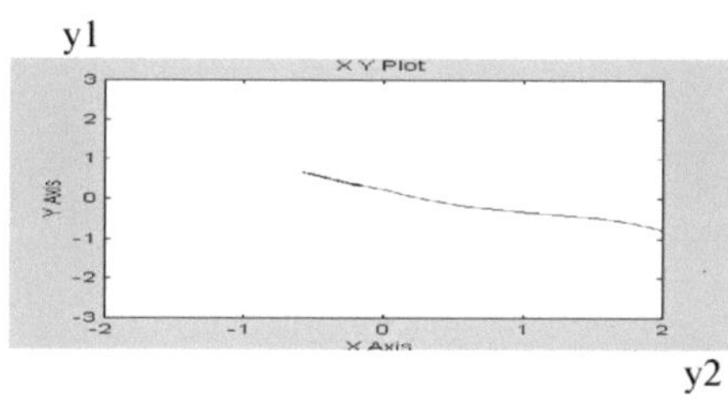

Figure 16. Case 3 Outputs y1 against y2

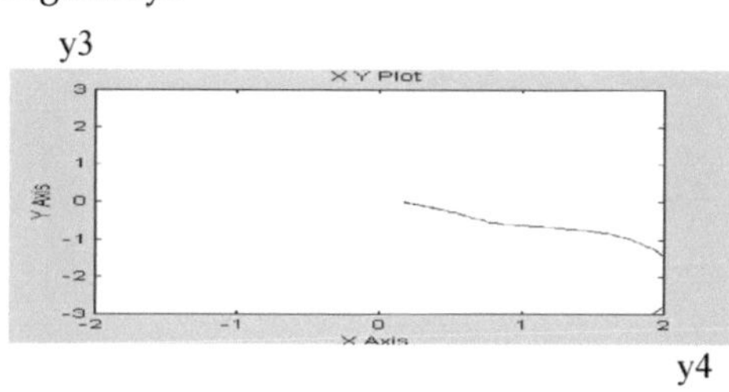

Figure 17. Case 3 Outputs y3 against y4

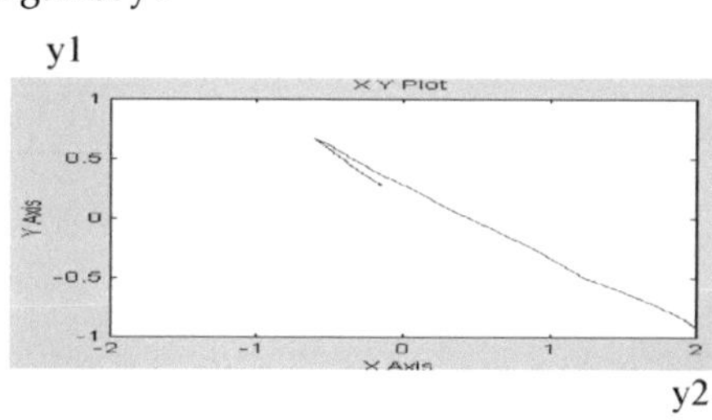

Figure 18. Case 4 Outputs y1 against y2

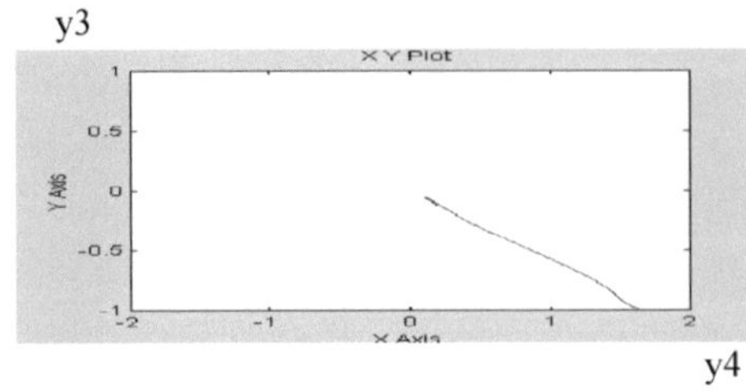

Figure 19. Case 4 Outputs y3 against y4

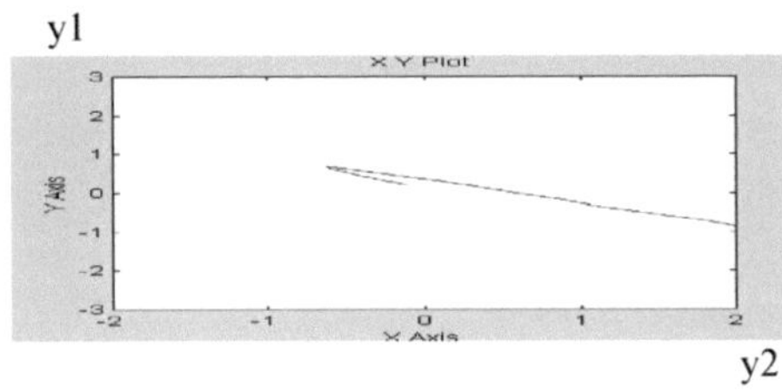

Figure 20. Case 5 Outputs y1 against y2

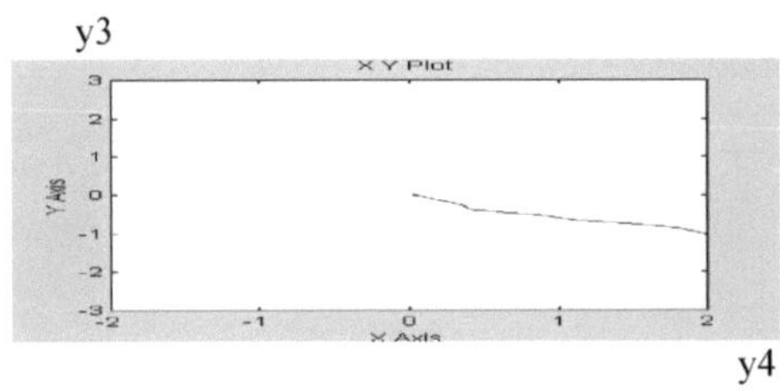

Figure 21. Case 5 Outputs y3 against y4

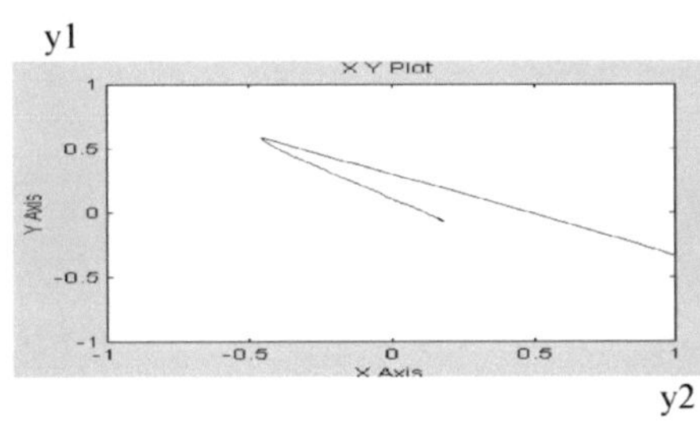

Figure 22. ase 6 Outputs y1 against y2

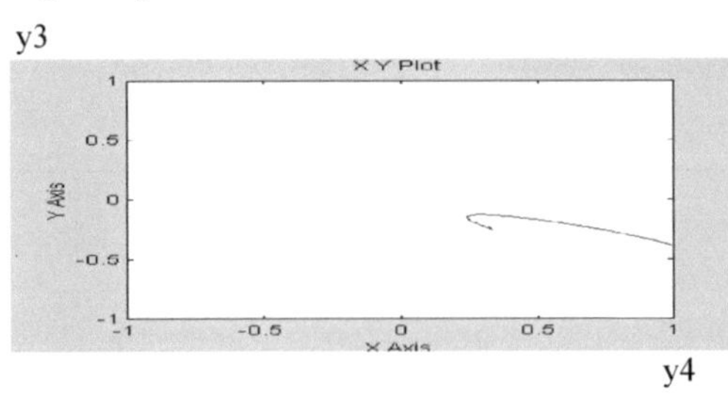

Figure 23. Case 6 Outputs y3 against y4

2.2.8. Discussion

This section has developed a new fuzzy control design approach to interconnected system. It has been shown the approach consists of two stages: In stage 1, a group of local state estimator has been constructed to generate the input-output database. Then an array of feedback controllers has been designed and implemented to guarantee the overall asymptotically system stability. Extensive simulation studies have been performed to support the developed design approach.

2.3. Power factor correction

This section presents the use of fuzzy logic technique to control the reactive power of a load and hence improve the power factor. A shunt compensator is used, which consists of a reactor in series with a phase controlled Thyristor bridge in parallel with a capacitor. The control composed of two independent fuzzy controllers, the Fuzzy Grouse Controller (FGC) and the Fuzzy Fine Controller (FFC). These fuzzy controllers are used to control the firing angle of the Thyristor Bridge until the source power factor reaches a desired value. Simulations for three different practical study cases are presented and the results show how the designed controller is fast and accurate.

2.3.1. Background

Power factor, nowadays, is an important issue. The over increasing utilization of power electronics in all kinds of industry applications and the severe standards requirements are pushing the research toward new solutions to keep the industrial power factor within certain ranges [26].

A mathematical formulation for the optimal reactive power control is discussed in [27]. Also, the optimized Fuzzy logic and digital PID controllers for a single phase power factor correction converter used in online UPS are demonstrated in [28, 29]. Parameters such as input membership functions, output membership functions, inference rules of fuzzy logic controller and proportional gain, integral gain and derivative PID controller are selected and optimized by genetic algorithms. In additional to that, the applications of a hybrid converter are implemented in [30]. The hybrid converter is basically a converter bridge with two GTOs. A control strategy based on learning is proposed. The learning structure is coded into Fuzzy conditional rules to train a neural network in manipulating the converter variables.

The common method of correction is by means of using static capacitors, whether connected in series or parallel. These are installed as a single unit or as a bank, to regulate the voltage and the reactive power flow at the point of connection. In shunt compensation arrangement, a reactor is connected in parallel with conventional capacitor compensation. The shunt reactor current can be varied via a phase-controlled thyristor bridge connected in series with the shunt reactor [31]. Changing the thyristor firing angle varies the amount. of the current flowing through the reactor. Thus, this thyristor controlled reactor acts as a variable reactor

[32]. By varying the firing angle, the total reactive power of the system can be controlled and hence the power factor of the system is improved. The use of fuzzy logic to derive a practical control scheme for a boost rectifier with reactive power factor correction was applied [33]. The control action is primarily derived from a set of linguistic rules used to generate a slow-varying DC signal to determine the PWM ramp function. The proposed technique uses lesser sensing elements than the classical rectifier. A new FACTS controller known as the Bootstrap variable inductance can emulate a variable positive and negative inductance [34]. The bootstrap variable inductance has a variety of FACTS applications such as series compensation of lines, fault current limiting, reactive-power control and load power factor improvement.

Here in this section, we shall focuses on the use of fuzzy logic sets to control the supply power factor. Unlike the conventional capacitive approach for power factor improvement in ac power system, the proposed control scheme has the advantage to avoid complexities associated with the non-linear mathematical modelling of switching converters. The proposed fuzzy logic controlling scheme consists of two controllers. The first controller (FGC) is designed to give the nearest desired value of the firing angle required to compensate for the source reactive power. However, the output correction of this controller is not efficiently accurate and hence, another correction step is needed. Thus, the second controller (FFC) checks the value of the source power factor and improves it above a pre-set desired value. The discussion includes the following:

- Illustration of the proposed control scheme.
- Description of the design steps of the power factor controller.
- Simulation of the proposed technique by testing it for three different study cases.

2.3.2. Fuzzy power factor controller

Figure 24 illustrates the block diagram for a single-phase variable load, with variable lag power factor, supplied by sinusoidal AC power source. Capacitor bank in parallel with inductance, controlled by single-phase full-wave circuit, are connected in parallel to the load in order to govern the total reactive power of the circuit. Fuzzy controller is designed to tune the firing angle of the single-phase full-wave circuit in order to adjust the voltage applied across the Inductance. By this way, the total source reactive power can be minimized to improve the source power factor. For three-phase circuits, one controller is dedicated for each phase. Here, we considered single-phase circuit for simplicity.

The structure of the controller contains two independent fuzzy controllers: Fuzzy Grouse Controller (FGC) and Fuzzy Fine Controller (FFC). FGC input is the load reactive power, the output of this controller gives the nearest value of the desired firing angle, which required to minimize the source power factor. FFC input is the source power factor. The output of FFC corrects the firing angle of the single-phase full-wave controller until the source power factor reaches or exceeds the pre-setted desired value.

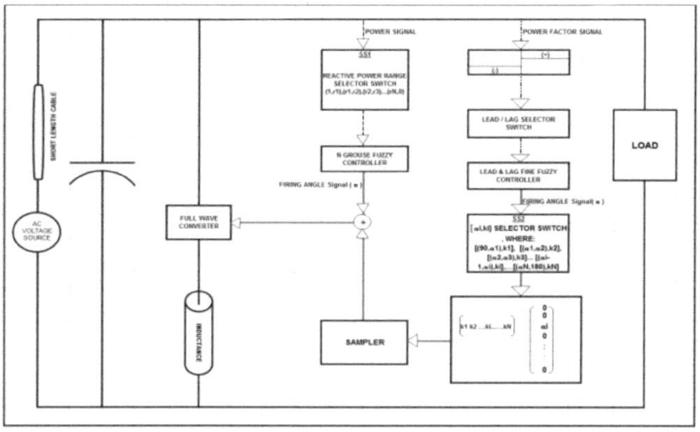

Figure 24. A detailed block diagram of the load, the fuzzy controllers, the source and the control scheme

The following procedures describe the steps of designing the power factor controller:

2.3.2.1. Elements sizing

The sizes of the 'Inductance' and the capacitance bank are selected such that their maximum available reactive power (in VAR) is equal to the maximum load reactive power (MLQ). Since the full source voltage is continuously applied on the capacitance bank (assuming the voltage drop across the short cable is negligible), then capacitance value 'C' of bank can be determined as follows:

$$C = \frac{\text{MLQ}}{2 \times \pi \times f \times \text{V}_{\text{source}}^2} \text{ Farad} \tag{25}$$

Where V_{source} is "source" r.m.s. voltage in Volt and f is "source" frequency in Hz.

However, this is not the case for the inductance since it is connected in series with a full wave controller. The existence of such controller will limit the available maximum reactive consumed by the inductance depending on the firing angle action of the thyristor bridge. Thus, the effect of the single-phase full-wave circuit is considered when determining the size of the inductance.

As listed in [35], the general formulas for the r.m.s value of current (I_{load}) and voltage (V_{load}) across a load, comprises of inductance in series with resistance, controlled by single-phase full-wave circuit. These formulas are given as follows:

$$\text{I}_{Load} = \frac{\sqrt{2 \times V_{source}}}{z} [\frac{1}{\pi} \int_{\pi}^{\beta} \{\sin(\omega\, t - \theta) - \sin(\alpha - \theta) e^{(\text{r}/\text{l})(\alpha/\omega - \text{t})}\} d\omega\, t]^{1/2} \tag{26}$$

$$\text{V}_{\text{Load}} = \frac{\sqrt{2 \times \text{V}_{\text{source}}}}{\text{z}} [\frac{1}{\pi} \int_{\pi}^{\beta} \{\sin(\omega\, \text{t} - \theta) - \sin(\alpha - \theta) \text{e}^{(\text{r}/\text{l})(\alpha/\omega - \text{t})}\} d\omega\, \text{t}]^{1/2} \tag{27}$$

Where:

$\omega = 2\pi f$ radian/second
α = Firing angle
β = Extinction angle (cut-off angle)
$\theta = \tan^{-1}(l/r)$
l = Load Inductance
r = Load Resistance
t = Time
z = Load impedance

Since the conducting angle $\delta = \beta - \alpha$ cannot exceed π, the firing angle α may not be less than θ and the control range of the firing angle is:

$$\pi \geq \alpha \geq \theta \tag{28}$$

For maximum available reactive power consumed by pure inductance MARP where r is ignored in the above equation 24 & 25), the maximum conducting angle is considered. Therefore, the value of the inductance can be calculated from the following equation assuming that $\alpha=\pi/2$ and $\beta=\pi$ (neglecting the impedance of the short Cable and assuming ideal thyristors):

$$\text{MARP} = \left(V_{load}\right) \times \left(I_{load}\right) \tag{29}$$

This MARP value must be equal to the maximum load reactive power MLQ for complete compensation. However, the two equations listed above are nonlinear and difficult to solve. Another simple procedure is needed when determining the size of the inductance L.

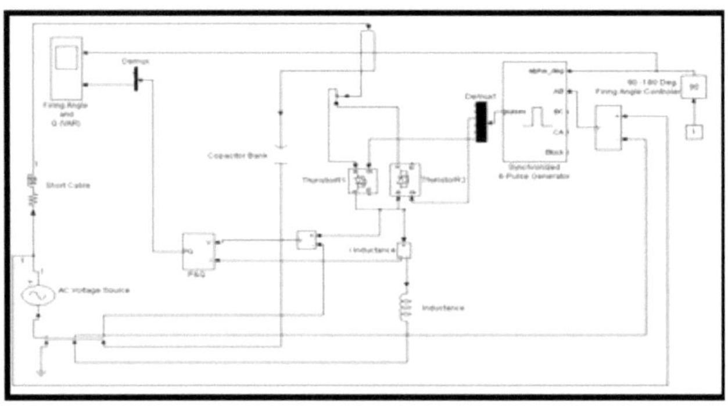

Figure 25. Simulink circuit used to determine and plot the ratio (Q_L/MLQ) verses firing angle (α)in the range from $\pi/2$ to π degree.

Thus, the value of the inductance can be found by a practical and fast method using Simulink tool [26]. Figure 25, illustrates the proposed model that been used. The model consists of an ac power source connected to a reactive power compensator controlled by a thyristor circuit. The procedure to find the value of the inductance L can be summarized by the following steps:

- Select an initial value for the inductance as L = 1 $(\omega^2 C)$
- Run the model and record the source VAR.
- If the source VAR equals zero, then stop the trials. If not, increase slightly the value of the inductance until the source VAR reaches the zero value. Then, this value of the source VAR will determine the desired value of the inductance.

2.3.2.2. Fuzzy Grouse Controller (FGC) design

After using the Simulink model shown in Figure 25, the inductance value is obtained from the iteration. Then, the same model is used again to find the ratio of (Q_L/MLQ) for a range of (α) starting from $\pi/2$ to π degree where (Q_L) is the Inductance reactive power at certain value of (π). This ratio (Q_L/MLQ) verses the firing angle (α) is then plotted. Typical curve is shown in Figure 26.

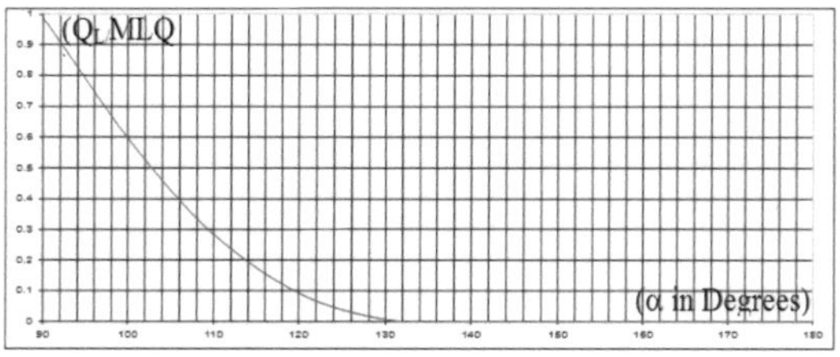

Figure 26. Typical curve for (Q_L/MLQ) verses firing angle (α)

After that, the resultant nonlinear curve is divided to N sections where each nonlinear section is approximated by the nearest linear section. Thus, N Gross Fuzzy controllers (FGC) are built, one FGC for each section, such that the input of each controller is equal to 1-$(Q_{Load}/(MLQ)$, where (Q_{Load}) is the load reactive power. The output of the FGC is the firing angle (α), which results in (Q_L) approximately equal to MLQ minus Q_{Load}. The accuracy of the resultant (Q_L) depends on the curve linearization.

In order to design each FGC, let the full range of the input fuzzy membership function FGCMF(in)[a] for each controller is set to the (Q_L/MLQ) limits of the respective linearzed section, and the range of the output fuzzy membership function FGCMF(out)[b] for each controller is set to the (α) limits of the respective linearzed section. For example, in Case 3 (as will be explained later into details), the first controller is designed to take an action in case of (QL/MLQ) ratio reaches a value between rl=0.95 and 1and, the output firing angle of this controller shall take a value between 90 degree and α_1 = 100 degree. However, the second controller is designed to take an action in case of (QL/MLQ) ratio reaches a value between r2 = 0.175 and rl = 0.950 and, the output firing angle of this controller shall take a value between α_1 = 100 degree and α_2 = 105degree, and so on.

The resultant output of each fuzzy controller can be obtained based on the respective linearzed section using the following functions for fuzzy implication process:

- Mamdany engine.
- Triangle type for Membership functions.
- Product for And.
- Max for Or.

- Proportional for Aggregation.
- Largest of Maximum for Defuzzification.
- Fuzzy rule : IF is $MF(in)^a$ THEN (α) is $MF(out)^b$

where,

a = 1,2, ... F (fuzzy membership function number)
b = F-a+l(fuzzy membership function number)
a and b are fuzzy membership function numbers
F is the number of the fuzzy membership function.

Simulink automatic switching system SS 1 as shown in Figure 24 is designed to check the active range of (Q_L/MLQ) in order to select the proper FGC based on that value of (Q_L/MLQ) ratio.

2.3.2.3. Fuzzy Fine Controller (FFC) design

Since the FGC output is not accurate due to the linearization process, FFC is designed to tune the firing g angle in order to achieve the desired power factor.

Two fuzzy controllers are used along with automatic switching system to select the proper controller based on the power factor type (Lead or Lag), which is determined from the source VAR sign (+ or -) as shown in Figure 24.

The input of each FFC controller is the source power factor (PF) and the output is the corrective firing angle (M), which is required to fine tune the FGC output. Since the power factor value varies between zero and one, then the range of each FPC input membership function $FFCMF(in)^a$ is [0, 1].

The output membership function of each FFC is $FFCMF(out\text{-}Lag)^a$ for lagging input and $FFCMF(out\text{-}Lead)^a$ for leading input and, the magnitude of the firing angle range for the first linearzed section (α_1) is considered as a base to scale the FFC output as given hereinafter with the fact that any other section can be selected as the base. Also, [0, $\Delta\alpha_1$] and [-$\Delta\alpha_1$, 0] are assigned to $FFCMF(out\text{-}Lag)^b$ and $FFCMF(out\text{-}Lead)^b$ respectively. In addition to that, N multiplier factors ($k_N = \Delta\alpha_N,/ \alpha_1$) are used to scale the FFC output in order to match the magnitude of the firing angle range of the respective linearzed section ($\Delta\alpha_N$). By this method, less number of FFC's are used.

Another Simulink automatic switching system SS2 as shown in Figure 24 synchronized with SS 1 is designed to check the active range of (Q_L/MLQ) in order to select the proper multiplier factor (K_N). The fuzzy implication process functions used for FGC design are used for each FFC design as well, but with the following fuzzy rules:

$$\text{IF } (\text{PF}) \text{is FFCMF } (\text{in})^{\text{a}} \text{ THEN} (\alpha_{\Delta}) \text{ is FFCMF } (\text{out Lag})^{\text{a}} \tag{30}$$

$$\text{IF } (\text{PF}) \text{is FFCMF } (\text{in})^{\text{a}} \text{ THEN} (\alpha_{\Delta}) \text{ is FFCMF } (\text{out Lead})^{\text{a}} \tag{31}$$

2.3.2.4. *Discrete control signal design*

Simulink Sum Block is used to add the output of GFC to the output of FFC. Sampler system shown in Figure 24 is designed to convert the resultant analog control signal to discrete signal. The sampling time is selected to be greater than the system time constant. The discrete signal is connected to the input for the synchronized pulse generator to control the thyristor firing angle. Accordingly, the network var and the source power factor are controlled.

2.3.3. *Case study*

The Simulink circuit shown in Figure 24 is used as a base to study three 'test' cases. These cases are assigned to check the capability of the controller to operate within a considerable variation of power factor values at different loading and voltage level.

			Case 1	**Case 2**	**Case 3**
Source Voltage (Volt)			**120**	**480**	**4160**
	Stage 1	P1 (kW)	2	40	40
		Q1(kVAR)	3.197	142.857	142.857
	Stage 2	P2 (kW)	12	200	240
Load Stages		Q2 (kVAR)	12.789	571.429	428.571
	Stage 3	P3(kW)	32	1200	1240
		Q3 (kVAR)	22.38	1000	1000
	Stage 4	P4 (kW)	42	2240	2280
		Q4 (kVAR)	0	0	0
MLQ (MVAR)			0.02238	1	1
F (Number of fuzzy membership functions)			7	7	7
k1			1	1	1
k2			2.8	0.95	0.5
k3			0.44	1	2.3
k4			5.7	4.5	5.3
r1			0.64	0.52	0.95
r2			0.28	0.21	0.2
r3			0.03	0.02	0.04
ALPHA1 (DEGREE)			99	102	100
ALPHA2 (DEGREE)			124	113.5	105
ALPHA3 (DEGREE)			128	125.5	128
N (Number of sections)			4	4	4

Table 2. Circuit data and parameters for the test cases

2.3.4. *Test cases data*

Each test case consists of four load stages. The load stages are selected such that the power factor varies from 0.3 to 1.0 lag. However, for practical cases, the power factor varies between 0.6 to 0.8 and thus the proposed wide range of power factor tested here is to demonstrate the capability of the designed controller. Table 2 summaries the circuit parameters for three voltage levels 120. 480 and 4160 Volts respectively. Figures 27-29 illustrate the linearization process for each case.

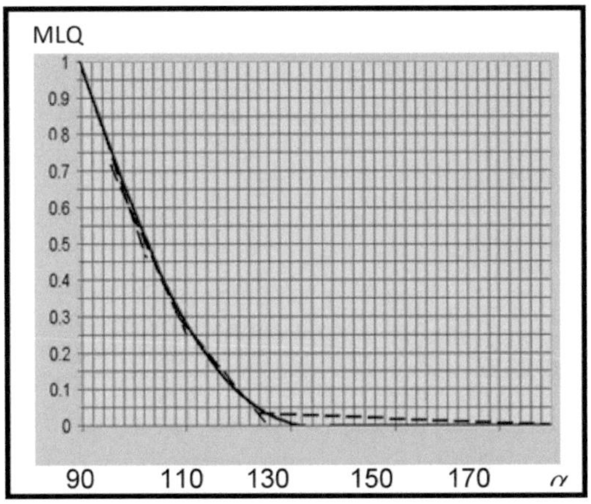

Figure 27. Linearization results for case1.

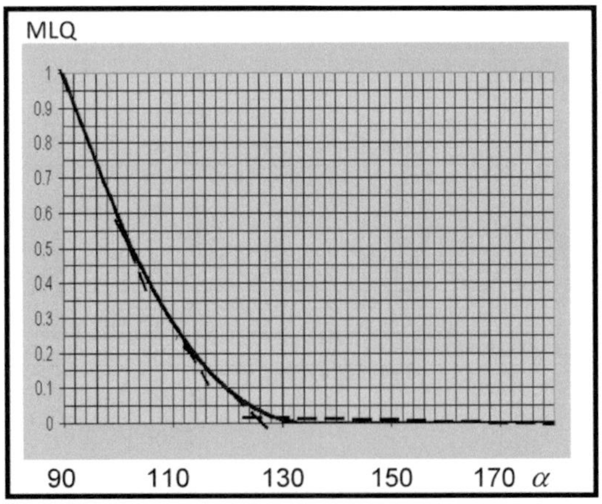

Figure 28. Linearization results for case 2

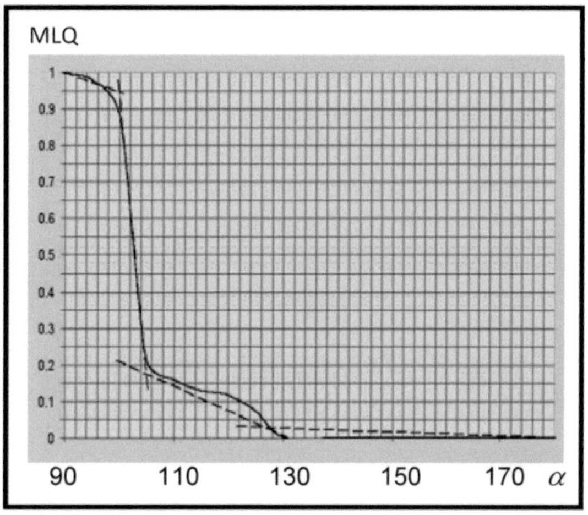

Figure 29. Linearization results for case 3

2.3.5. Results

The controller is adjusted to correct the power factor of the test cases to a value greater than a desired value of 0.97. This value is the pre-set value and it can be any chosen practical value. Figures 30 -32 illustrate the results for cases 1-3 respectively. These figures show the variation of the load active and reactive power with respect to time for each case. The response of the controller during the test period represented by the firing angle is also shown. In addition to that, source and load power factor values are plotted to check the response time of the controller and its accuracy.

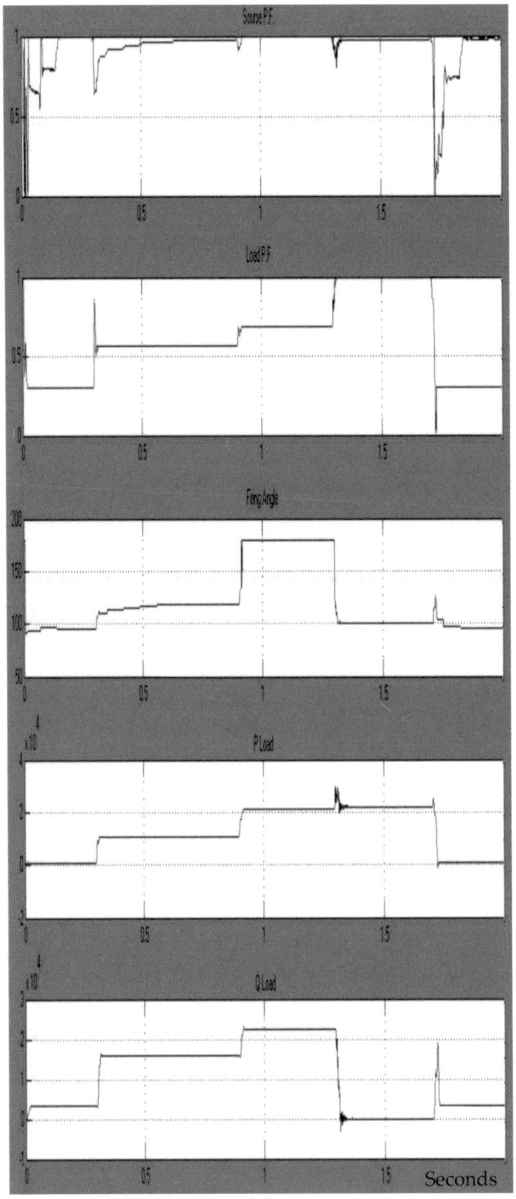

Figure 30. Results of test case 1.

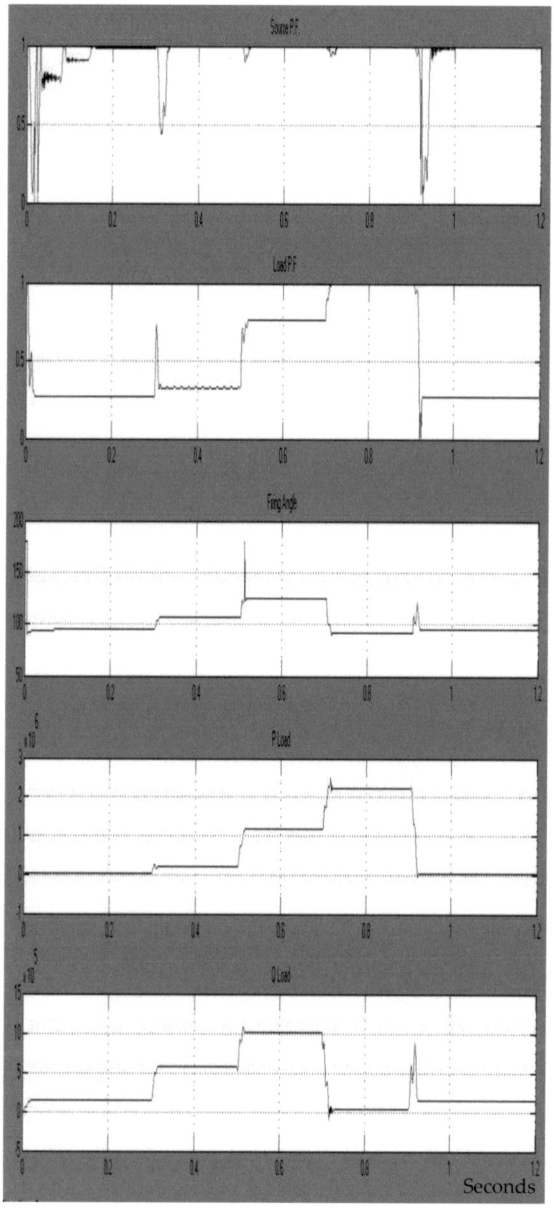

Figure 31. Results of test case 2.

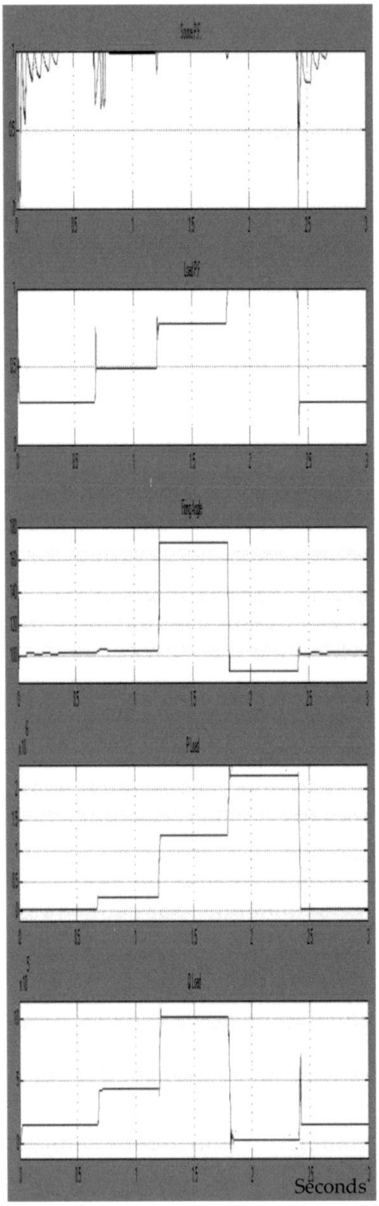

Figure 32. Results of test case 3.

2.3.6. Discussion

The test results for the three cases show clearly how efficient is the controller. Even when the load reactive power is very small at both high and low power factor, the controller was successful in reaching an accurate level. During the stage where the load power factor is greater than 0.97 and, hence no need for capacitor compensation, the controller will check the source power factor at the beginning of that stage and if it drops below 0. 97, it will take an action in order to eliminate the compensation added in the previous stage. That is why the controller took an action as shown in Figure 30 for the fourth load stage of case no. 1 where the source power factor drops below 0.97. However, if the source power factor stays above the pre-set power factor value of 0.97 during the load stage where the load power factor is greater than 0.97, then no action will be taken as shown in Figure 32 for the fourth load stage of case no. 3. The time required for the controller to improve the power factor in all three cases is relatively short compared with practical applications. In real cases, the power factor does remain unchanged for relatively longer time. The maximum time for power factor correction was 0.35 second recorded in test case no.1. Overall, the graphs show that the controller works satisfactory under different load conditions and when there is no need for capacitor compensation.

As mentioned before, power factor correction is really an important issue. The designed controller presented in this section shows an efficient, fast and accurate technique in reactive power control. As seen from the overall structure of the controller, it is applicable for lagging power factor loads. Practically, this is almost true but not always where at rare occasions the power factor of the total load is leading not lagging. This will bring the attention towards generalizing the presented controller such that it will work for both cases. Several issues are also need to be considered in the future such as the dynamics of motors. As known that most connected loads are motors which really necessitate testing this controller under these circumstances. From the test results, it was seen that the speed of the controller depends on the system time constant and hence, a time delay is needed to assure that thc dynamics of the motors reach its equilibrium. Other issues related to Thyristors such as the harmonics are a1so need to be taken care by describing a harmonics filter. In addition to that, protection devices such as relays need to be checked during the controller action. Finally, the work presented was based on a single phase and it can be extended for three phase system.

3. Trending and prediction

Most of the more advanced prediction techniques can be subdivided into two separate tasks. In a first step, the modelling step, the algorithm uses a set of training data to identify a model of a process, from which the training data could have been obtained. In a second step, the simulation step, the algorithm uses the previously identified model to make predictions outside the training data set. The modelling algorithm can either attempt to identify the true structure of the system, from which the training data were obtained, or it can content itself with identifying any process able to explain the training data set. In the former case, we talk about a deep model, whereas models in the latter category are referred to as shallow models.

The identified model can be either a quantitative or a qualitative model. A quantitative model operates on the measurement data directly, whereas a qualitative model first discretizes the measurement data, and then reasons about the discrete classes only. Also the model can be either a parametric model or a nonparametric model. A parametric model maps the knowledge contained in the training data set onto a set of model parameters. During the simulation phase, the training data are no longer needed, since the information contained in them is now stored in the parameter values. A non-parametric model only classifies the training data during the modelling phase, and refers back to these classified training data during the simulation phase.

Fuzzy logic are used now a day in many application for diagnostic, prediction forecast and understanding the behaviour of very nonlinear systems such as marketing, electrical load forecast, work load analysis, technical analysis etc…

In this chapter Section 2.1, we shall introduce an important algorithm for classifying "clustering" the data based on fuzzy logic. Then two new fuzzy trending and prediction application shall be discussed. In Section 2.2 Accident rates Estimation Modelling Based on Human Factors shall be introduces, and in the next section 2.3, Fault Location in Distribution Networks shall be introduced.

3.1. Clustering algorithm and validity criteria

Clustering attempts to assess the relationships among patterns of the data set by organizing the patterns into groups or clusters such that patterns within a cluster are more similar to each other than are patterns belonging to different clusters. Many algorithms for hard and fuzzy clustering have been developed to accomplish this[42]. An intimately related important issue is the cluster validity, which deals with the significance of the structure imposed by a clustering method [43].

For fuzzy sets, the following definitions are recalled from [36]:

a. A fuzzy set in a universe discourse U is characterized by a membership function $\mu_A(x)$ that takes values in the interval [0,1].
b. Let $X=\{x_1,\ldots,x_n\}$ be any set, V_{cn} be the set of real c×n matrices $U=[\mu_{ij}]$, c, i, j be integer numbers with $2 \leq c \leq n$, $1 \leq i \leq c$ and $1 \leq j \leq n$ .Then the fuzzy partition matrix for X is the set $M_{fc} = \{U \in V_{cn} \mid \mu_{ij} \in [0,1]\}$ (32)

Such that

$$\sum_i \mu_{ij} = 1, \forall_j, 1 \leq j \leq n. \tag{33}$$

An α-cut of fuzzy set A is a crisp set $A\alpha$ that contains all the elements in U that have membership value in A greater thanα, that is

$$A_\alpha = \{x \in U \mid \mu_A(x) \geq \alpha\} \tag{34}$$

c. Defuzzification is defined as a mapping from fuzzy set B` in V⊂ R to crisp point $y^* \in V$. Conceptually, the task of the defuzzification is to specify a point in V that best represents the fuzzy set B`.

The following three criteria should be considered in choosing the defuzification method:

- Plausibility: The point y^* should represent B` from an intuitive point of view.
- Computational simplicity.
- Continuity: A small Change in B` should not result in a large change in y^*.

3.1.1. Fuzzy C-Means Clustering Algorithm(FCM)

The fuzzy c-means (FCM) clustering algorithm is the fuzzy equivalent of the nearest hard clustering algorithm [43,44], which minimizes the following objective function with respect to fuzzy membership μ_{ij}, and cluster centroid V_i.

$$J_m = \sum_I^c \sum_j^n (\mu_{ij})^f \mid\mid \left(X_j, V_i \right) \mid\mid^2 \tag{35}$$

where $X = [X_1, \ldots, X_n]^t$ is a vector representing the data, c is the number of clusters, n is the number of data points and f is a fuzziness index (greater than 1)

The FCM algorithm is executed by the following steps:

a. Initialize memberships μ_{ij} of X_j belonging to cluster i such that

$$\sum_j (\mu_{ij}) = 1 \tag{36}$$

b. Compute the fuzzy centroid V_i from i=1 to i=c using

$$V_i = \frac{\sum_j (\mu_{ij})^m \times X_j}{\sum_j (\mu_{ij})^m} \tag{37}$$

c. Update the fuzzy memberships μ_{ij} using

$$\mu_{ij} = \frac{(\mid\mid (X_j, V_i) \mid\mid)^{(-2/(m-1))}}{\sum_j (\mid\mid (X_j, V_i) \mid\mid)^{(-2/(m-1))}} \tag{38}$$

d. Repeat steps 2 and 3 until the value of J_m is no longer decreasing.

The FCM always converges to strict local minimum of Jm starting from an initial guess of μ_{ij}, but different choices of initial μ_{ij} might lead to local minima.

3.1.2. Cluster validity

The quality of a clustering is indicated by how closely the data points are associated to the cluster centers, and it is the membership functions, which measure the level of association or classification. If the value of one of the membership is significantly larger than the others for a particular data point, then that point is identified as being a part of the subset of the data represented by the corresponding cluster center. But, each data point has c memberships; so, it is desirable to summarize the information contained in the memberships by a single number, which indicates how well the data point is classified by the clustering. This can be done in a variety of ways; for example, for the data point X_j with memberships $\{\mu_{ij}, ..., \mu_{cj}\}$, one could use any of the following:

$$\text{Index1} = \sum_i (\mu_{ij})^2 \tag{39}$$

$$\text{Index2} = \sum_i \mu_{ij} \log(\mu_{ij}) \tag{40}$$

$$\text{Index3} = \max_i(\mu_{ij}) \tag{41}$$

$$\text{Index4} = \min_i(\mu_{ij}) / \max_i(\mu_{ij}) \tag{42}$$

In fact, theses four indices of these are used as measure of the quality of clustering and are the basis for the *validity functional, partition coefficient, classification entropy, and proportion exponent*, respectively.

To illustrate the use of validity functional, we shall focus on the partition coefficient technique because of its simplicity. It is based on using $S_j = \Sigma_i (\mu_{ij})^2$ as a measure of how well the jth data point has been classified. This is a reasonable indicator because the closer a data point is to a cluster center, the closer S_j is to 1, the maximum value it could have. Conversely, the further away the kth point is from all the cluster centers the closer the value of S_j is to 1/c, the minimum possible value. The partition coefficient is then the average over the data set of the S_j's. In particular, for a data set $X=\{x_1,\ldots,x_i\}$ and a specific choice of c and m one obtains the output of fuzzy c-means and computes the partition coefficient (PC) by $PC=\Sigma_j(\Sigma_i(\mu_{ij})^2/n$. The closer this value is to one the better the data are classified. So, in theory, one computes PC for the outputs of a variety of values of c and m selects the best clustering as the one corresponding to the highest partition coefficient [44,45].

3.2. Accident rates estimation modeling based on human factors using fuzzy c-mean clustering techniques

Several individual books [37] and projects shed light on worker accident causation. One study on the Bonneville Dam project, reported that seven times the number of work accidents that had occurred on this project were due to unsafe employee actions rather than to unsafe site conditions. In addition, this study found that the negative attitude of the workers toward safety was a major factor in accident occurrence.

In [38]. Many organizations spend a lot of time and effort trying to improve safety. As well as addressing technical and hardware issues, many conduct safety management system audits to discover deviations from the performance standards set in their Health & Safety

Policies. Line management is encouraged to conduct regular inspections of the workplace and employees are trained to behave safely and are given the appropriate protective equipment. The impact of such initiatives could be seen in the overall downward trend in accident statistics from 1990 to 1998/99. After 2000, accident statistics started rising in many UK industrial sectors. In the Quarry Industry, for example, there has been a 60% rise in the number of fatalities.

Another study by Stanford University [39] indicated that risk taking is often a normal part of human psychology. We sometimes drive too fast or take chances we should not. Risk which is taken on the job site, however, can be fatal. This study found that many workers believe that taking unnecessary risks is an accepted part of the job process. This risk acceptance attitude leads to carelessness and accidents. The results of the Stanford study show that workers who are likely to have lost-time accidents share similar characteristics. These workers have a negative attitude toward doing their jobs safely, and they accept unnecessary risk and, therefore, do not work safely. Taking unnecessary risks and adopting a poor safety attitude simply makes workers more prone to accident occurrences. The conclusion of the Stanford study clearly supports the contention that employee actions and attitudes can affect the number and type of workplace accidents. Employers can and do address this attitude of risk taking through safety education, safety rules, and training programs. However, no employer can supervise each employee every minute of the work day.

In [40], the paper focuses on the development and representation of linguistic variables to model risk levels subjectively. These variables are then quantified using fuzzy set theory. In this paper the development of two safety evaluation frameworks, using fuzzy logic approaches for maritime engineering safety based decision support in the concept design stage are presented. An example is used to illustrate and compare the proposed approaches. The paper also suggests that future risk analysis in maritime engineering applications may take full advantages of fuzzy logic approaches to complement existing ones.

The field of fuzzy systems has been making rapid progress over the past decade [36]. There are two kinds of justification for fuzzy systems to be used to achieve our objective:

a. The problem is too complicated for precise description to be obtained, therefore approximation, or fuzziness, must be introduced in order to be a reasonable and net traceable model.
b. As we move into the information era, knowledge is becoming increasingly important and the need for a theory to formulate human knowledge in a systematic manner becomes the norm not the exception.

But as a general principle, a good engineering theory should be capable of making use of all the available information effectively. For many practical systems, important information comes from two sources: one source is from human experts who describe their knowledge about the system in natural languages; the other is sensory measurements or mathematical models that are derived from to physical laws.

An important task, therefore, is to combine these two types of information into system designs. Therefore, the key question is how to transform human knowledge base into a mathematical formula or model. Essentially, what a fuzzy system does is to perform this transformation in a systematic way.

In this part of Section 2, we attempt to use a completely different approach to analyze - accidents. A model shall be developed for data collected from an accident rate questionnaire filled-in by laborers working for a reputable construction company. This questionnaire was designed to include information about human factors, as well as other factors such as work type, managerial factors, training, physical factors and the historical accident rate for each labor during his period of employment in this particular construction company, and his experience during his career life time. The collected data shall be split into a training set for model construction and a test for model verification. The training information shall be classified into a number of groups or clusters, the centroids of these clusters were subsequently used to generate a set of rules to develop a fuzzy engine, which can then predict and forecast the rate of accidents. The test cases shall be used to verify and validate the developed model. Discussion on the results obtained from using fuzzy logic techniques shall be carried out.

3.2.1. Data organization

Construction sites are very dynamic and complex by nature, creating the potential for hazards that change constantly. So, what was safe yesterday may no longer be safe today. Thus, safety precautions should be followed and controlled. Unsafe working conditions and accidents are usually warning signs that something is wrong and has to be rectified.

Different government authorities measure safety at construction sites [41], however co-ordination and sharing of information with each other is still lacking. In addition, the data available on construction site accidents are neither accurate nor complete, due to the absence of a reliable accident reporting and recording system. Incomplete records are due to the poor accident investigation that may be a result of:

- Reluctance of reporters to assert authority.
- Inexperienced and untrained investigators
- Narrow interpretation
- Judgmental behavior.
- Incomplete or erroneous conclusions.
- Delays in accident investigations.

For these reasons we endeavored to avoid the normal way of doing the job, and instead, we focused on the laborer, himself, and his accident rates during his years of work experience as an expert source of data. We have tried to design the questionnaire in such a way as to serve our purpose of analyzing the data, and selected the interview method to get the maximum precise data possible.

3.2.1.1. Questionnaire design

In the design of questionnaire (Appendix) we have selected some certain features of human nature that, we believe, have a great potential on the accident causation in the local market [41]. The first page of the questionnaire concentrated on the personal information of the workers: i.e. 'height', 'weight', 'optical status', 'hearing ability', 'general health', 'education' and 'adherence to safety rules'. In this part we used some linguistic evaluations like 'high', 'low', 'fair', 'good', 'medium' etc., and in some others we have used numerical evaluations like in height, weight, as well as education. Since the objective here is to create a fuzzy model, high accuracy is not important and we considered that the respondents from the same field made the same judgments.

The second page was designed to concentrate on the work information: 'overtime work', 'experience', 'work nature', 'work type', 'hazardous level', 'needs for safety-gears', 'work location' and 'level of boredom'. Again, we have used some linguistic evaluations as well as numerical evaluations. We also concentrated on the managerial factors: 'salary received on time', 'level of training' 'importance' and level of importance placed on safety', with only linguistic evaluations.

The third page was a mix of both external factors: 'noise', 'live with family' and 'communication 'language', and accident history focusing on the number of accidents the laborer has faced during his work in the local construction market, which was the most important data that we needed to develop our model. The severity of accidents has not been taken into account since it is not considered a factor influencing the accident rate.

The cases obtained for this study were collected from three different construction companies selected to represent the local market. We have tried to select the cases from different ranks of the workforce, from higher levels to the lower levels to be able to study the different accident level cases that serve the purpose as well as adding versatility and diversity to this work.

3.2.1.2. The response

From the original cases that we collected on 95 people, we included only 76 cases and excluded 19 cases, which were incomplete. This has produced a very high response rate that reached 82.1%, which is relatively high, especially as the questionnaire is lengthy and a little bit complicated. More cases could have been obtained. However, since the aim of this study was to develop a model for accidents, the number of cases is not set a priority. Rather, the cases are accumulated and the algorithms are stopped when a cluster validity criterion is satisfied thereby yielding the optimum number of clusters.

3.2.1.3. Limitations

Limitations in this study should be noted. One of the limitations is that we did not include any specific information related to the accident consequences. Another limitation is that this study was made only on males and no female cases were studied, which makes it specific only to one sex.

3.2.1.4. The feature matrix

The feature matrix (FM) is the most important part of our work in this section , since by using this matrix we have been able to convert the linguistic variables into numerical variables. Thus, we can deal easily with practical cases and reduce the required operations of processing the output.

The columns of the FM matrix represent the feature variables which we obtained from the questionnaire. The rows of the matrix represent the different cases of laborers that we selected for interviews. Thus, for each case in the matrix we mapped the linguistic meanings into numbers according to weights we have proposed. For example, in case labelled (S1), the feature weight 1 (FW1) represents the rate of accidents per year of experience, which is the actual representation of the accident rates. FW2 represents the ratio between weight and height (specific weight). FW3 represents optical status and FW4 represents hearing ability. These feature weights are scaled on a scale of five from 1 to 5, to represent the linguistic variables. Therefore, 1 means `very bad`, 2 means `bad`, 3 means `medium`, 4 means `good` and 5 means `very good`. All the other variables are dealt in the same way until the matrix was generated. A sample of the feature matrix is shown in Table3.

Feature / Case No	Accidents/ experience	Weight/ Height	Optical status	Hearing Ability	General Health	Adherence to Safety	Education	Overtime work
S1	1/12	71/160	6/18	5	5	4	5	2
S2	5/12	77/ 170	6/60	5	4	3	5	3
S3	1/21	90/175	6/6	4	5	5	5	5
S4	0/8	54/165	6/60	4	5	2	5	20
S5	6/3.5	68/187	6/36	3	4	3	5	0
S6	10/11	85/177	6/6	4	4	3	5	10
S7	2/19	76/173	6/60	4	5	5	5	14
S8	18/25	72/170	6/18	3	4	4	4	4
S9	45/14	80/176	6/6	4	4	3	4	8
S10	3/20	81/174	6/6	4	4	5	4	1

Table 3. Sample of feature matrix illustrates the weight of some features for the first 10 cases

3.2.2. Modelling

In this stage, FCM techniques will be implemented on the feature matrix after normalizing the data, based on column maximum values for ease and as being more indicative, then deciding the optimum number of clusters, by applying cluster validity techniques. The centroides for these optimum clusters are considered perfect models represent the feature matrix.

In order to obtain the models, the following steps have been implemented:

- Each column in the feature matrix is normalized by dividing all the numbers in this column by the maximum number of the absolute values of all the numbers in the said column.
- Cluster validity study is implemented to determine the optimum number of clusters for the normalized data.
- FCM technique is implemented to determine the centroids matrix of the selected number of clusters.

MATLAB fuzzy toolbox has been used to implement the above three steps [46].

3.2.2.1. Clustering results and discussions

The results can be summarized as follows:

a. The optimum number of cluster (twelve) is determined by implementing cluster validity technique. The result is illustrated in Figure 33 which gives the relation between the number of clusters and the corresponding error where:

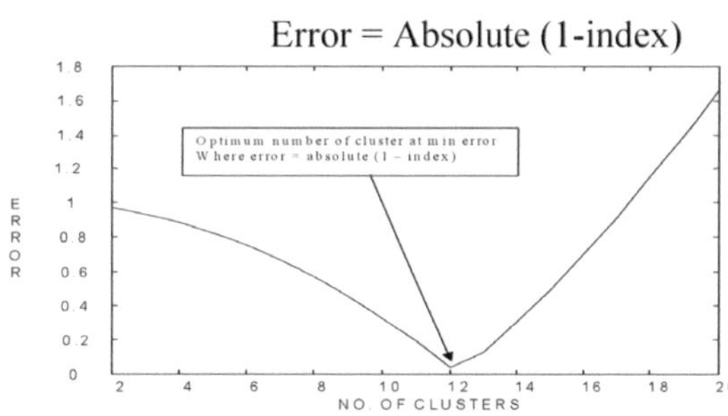

Figure 33. Relation between number of clusters and the corresponding error

b. Table 9 (Appendix) illustrates the centroide matrix for the optimum number of clusters (twelve), where FW(j) stands for feature weight described in Table 10 (Appendix).

3.2.2.2. Scaling of data

In order to reduce the error in the estimation of the membership functions ranges (e.g. the estimated range of FW5 was from 1 to 5, while from centroide matrix the range for the same feature is found to be from 3.750 to 4.9953) each feature vector element is scaled according to the following formula:

$$X_{scaled} = X_i - X_{min} / \left(X_{max} - X_{min}\right) \tag{43}$$

Where:

X_i = Vector element
X_{min} = Min. Vector element
X_{max} = Max. Vector element

3.2.2.3. Model development

By comparing each row of the centroids matrix with the contents of the questionnaire after scaling, one can infer the structure of the respective model, for example maximum and minimum rate of accident as illustrated in Table 11 (Appendix). From structure, following features can be extracted:

a. Labours in this construction company can be classified into 12 models.
b. The expected range of accident rate in company varies from 0.1581 to 2.8894 accidents per year.
c. By comparing the above two extreme models, one can easily discover that receiving salary on time has no effective impact on accident rate.
d. The highest rate of accidents occurs to non-local workers (Live without their family most of the time).
e. The twelve models obtained above shall be utilized later as fuzzy rules representing the this local construction company to predict the rate of accident for any person working on construction field.

3.2.3. Accident rate prediction

Now, fuzzy logic techniques will be implemented using the models obtained in Section 2.2.2, as perfect fuzzy rules, to predict the accident rate for any laborer who works in the construction field. The following flow chart (Figure 34) describes the fuzzy accident prediction system:

The models obtained from the fuzzy c -means the clustering process has been considered as very good and suitable fuzzy rules that govern the relation between the laborers in construction field and the expected annual rate of accident.

The beauty of using this type of clustering is not only to achieve the required models, but also these models are fuzzy, and can be geared in the fuzzy engine.

In order to fuzzify the model variables, a suitable number of Gauss functions (linguistic variable) is selected for each linguistic value so that any rule must fire all the linguistic values and the rules are given as follows [36]:

$$\text{IF}\left(\text{FW1 is mf}_a{}^1\right)\text{ and }\left(\text{FW2 is mf}_b{}^2\right)\text{ and}\ldots\left(\text{FW22 is mf}_v{}^{22}\right)\text{ THEN }\left(\text{FW23 is mf}_w{}^{23}\right) \quad (44)$$

Where,

FW(1to22) : input linguistic variable
FW23 : output linguistic variable
mf $_{a,b\,..w}$: semantic rule
a,b ..w: integer number from 1 to 5

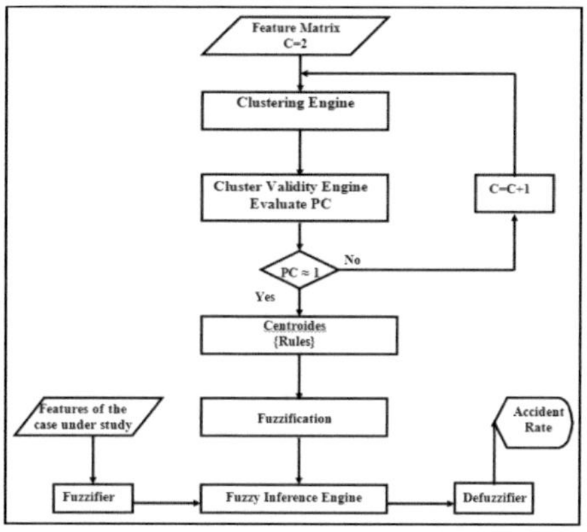

Figure 34. Fuzzy Accident Prediction Flowchart

Mamdani inference engine with centroid defuzzification and proportional aggregation is used in the construction of the fuzzy system. MATLAB Fuzzy Toolbox has been used to implement the required fuzzy prediction system. Eight cases have been tested and the results are given in hereinafter.

3.2.3.1. Relevant results

a. Eight additional random cases have been chosen from a local construction company. Features, actual accident rate and output of fuzzy prediction system for each test case are given in Table 12 (Appendix). The standard deviation between the actual accident rate and the predicted accident rate for each test case is calculated then the average standard deviation is obtained in order to determine the validity of the model. The results are shown as follows in Table 4:

Case Number	Standard Deviation
Case#1	0.3536
Case#2	0.2828
Case#3	0.4243
Case#4	0.7071
Case#5	01414
Case#6	0.1414
Case#7	0.2121
Case#8	0.0318
Average	0.2868

Table 4. Standard deviation results for the test cases

b. In (Appendix), Figure 37 shows the output of the prediction system for a case that fires all the linguistic values at the middle. It is observed from this result that the laborers with `average` personal information, `average` work condition, `average` managerial condition and `average` external effects are exposed to `average` annual accident rate.

c. Figure 38(Appendix) correlates the laborers general health and specific weight with their annual accident rate considering all other factors are `average`. It is clear that the annual accident rate increases with the significant increase of the specific weight and significant poorness of the general health.
d. In Figure 39 (Appendix), the laborers educational level and safety adherence are plotted against their annual accident rate considering all other factors are `average`. It is noticed from this illustration that the laborers with the two educational level extremes are exposed to accidents more than the `average` educational level laborers.
e. Figure 40 (Appendix) correlates the laborers optical status and hearing ability with their annual accident rate considering all other factors to be `average`. It is clear that the annual accident rate increases with the significant poorness of the optical status and hearing ability.
f. From the last plot (Figure 41 - Appendix), it is clear that if the company is not keen on the level of safety, the annual accident rate will be increased, considering all other factors are `average`. In addition, it is noticeable from the figure that the tasks that are considered to be dangerous and need safety-gear are a source of accidents.

3.2.4. Discussion

The main objective of in this example to generate a human model which reflects the interaction between human factors in addition to other factors such as managerial factors, accident information, and work information, using fuzzy clustering techniques. Secondly, to predict annual rate of accident for any sample of workers by applying fuzzy logic techniques. Some of the important results obtained can be summarized as follows:

a. Fuzzy clustering techniques can be used to build a model that characterizes the different features of workers in local construction field against their rate of accidents.
b. The model obtained from clustering is considered as rules to be used in a fuzzy logic engine to predict the rate of accidents for any worker in the construction field.
c. For any specific case, 231 correlations (between any two features and the rate of accidents) can be done via the fuzzy engine.
d. Optimum training to improve the safety attitude for certain laborer with minimum cost can be estimated by analyzing the correlation between the level of training and rate of accident of this particular labourer.
e. By analyzing the correlation between level of safety importance and rate of accidents for the workers in a particular company, the limits of the effective safety improvement can be predicted in order to evaluate the investment in this direction.
f. A similar technique can be applied to a particular company to predict the rate of accident in order to estimate the insurance rate for the people who work in this particular company.
g. Using the accident rate fuzzy prediction techniques companies can select the most suitable workers for any particular task

3.3. Fault location in distribution networks using fuzzy c-mean clustering techniques

In last section of this chapter we shall studies an existing 13.8 kilovolt distribution network which, serves an oil production field spread over an area of approximately sixty kilometers square, in order to locate any fault that may occur anywhere in the network using fuzzy c-mean classification techniques.

In addition, we shall introduce several methods for normalizing data and selecting the optimum number of clusters in order to classify data. Results and conclusion shall be also given to show the feasibility for the using the fuzzy logic to locate the fault location.

3.3.1. Network description

A joint venture oil company possesses two production areas, Area1 and Area2. For each area a power distribution system is provided. The power supply required for the two fields is provided from 130 MVA capacity power generation plant located in Area1. Twenty MW is transmitted to Area2 via 35KM long over head transmission line (OHTL) on wooden poles. Area2 power system also contains two 3.16 MVA stand by generators.

Area2 distribution system consists of three radial overhead transmission lines, 8-10 KM long each, serve submersible oil pumps and other loads scattered in the field (60-kilometer square). These overhead transmission lines have neither differential relays nor sectionalizing fuses. Programmable logic Controller (PLC) is connected to the incomers, outgoings and generators auxiliaries at Area2 power station. This PLC records the running and tripping information for all bus-bar compartments.

Due to the aging of the system, remote area problems and harsh desert weather, repeated faults are experienced in the grid. Because of unavailability of differential relays and/or sectionalizing fuses, it is very difficult and long time is consumed to locate any fault in this network. The problem is reflecting passively on the oil productivity of this important area.

3.3.2. Feature Matrix

In order to measure the features of the faults at 176 nodes of the network; load flow study is implemented to determine the respective power loss for each short circuit case and also short circuit study is carried out to determine the feature vector for each short circuit case.

The results, obtained from the load flow study and the short circuit study, shall be used to form the network ***feature matrix,*** which will be clustered and analyzed hereinafter. The parameters that selected to build the feature matrix are shown in Table 5.

Fuzzy clustering technique shall be used to classify the possible fault locations, which can be near to any node in the network or near to a chosen set of nodes based on the operator experience, into groups. The optimum number of groups (clusters) is computed using validity clustering technique. The remaining 13 cases are used as test cases. Euclidean distance technique is implemented to find out the group of nodes, which the fault may be found near to, for each test case.

Feeder 1	Feeder 2	Feeder 3
Set of nods fed from Feeder 1	Set of nods fed from Feeder 2	Set of nods fed from Feeder 3
Circuit breaker 1 status	Circuit breaker 2 status	Circuit breaker 3 status
Feeder 1 Short circuit Current red from substation	Feeder 2 Short circuit Current red from substation	Feeder 2 Short circuit Current red from substation
Phase Angel A1	Phase Angel A2	Phase Angel A3
Phase Angel B1	Phase Angel B2	Phase Angel B3
Phase Angel C1	Phase Angel C2	Phase Angel C3
Power dip in Feeder 1	Power dip in Feeder 2	Power dip in Feeder 3
VAR dip in Feeder 1	VAR dip in Feeder 2	VAR dip in Feeder 3

Table 5. Summary of the parameters that are selected to build the feature matrix.

Assumptions: The following assumptions are considered:

a. The temperature of the network conductors is assumed constant at seventy degree Celsius.
b. Only symmetrical short circuit is conceded. The same procedures can be implemented for any other type of faults.

Assumption (a) is valid since the transmission lines are short [47]. For assumption (b), the same work can be repeated for all other types of failures.

3.3.3. *Fault location using column maximum normalization*

Now, FCM technique can be implemented after normalizing the data based on column maximum values and deciding the optimum number of clusters. The results shall be analyzed in order to locate any failures may occur in the network.

3.3.3.1. *Calculation procedures*

To detect the fault using FCM technique with column maximum normalization the following steps have been implemented:

a. Each column in the Feature Matrix is normalized by dividing all the numbers in this column by the maximum number of the absolute values of all the numbers in the said column.
b. Cluster validity study is implemented to determine the optimum number of clusters for the normalized data.
c. FCM technique is implemented to determine the fuzzy partition matrix of the selected number of clusters.

d. The norms between each test data and the full data in the chosen cluster is examined, accordingly the corresponding cluster for each test data is decided based on the minimum norm obtained from the said examination.
e. Alpha-cut defuzzification is used with alpha equal to 90% of the average of norms between the cluster center and its data.
f. The nearest node to the fault is checked in order to determine whether it is included in the possible locations or not.

3.3.3.2. Results and discussion

Matlab program is written to implement the above six steps and the results are analyzed and summarized as follows:

a. The optimum number of cluster (twenty five) is determined by implementing cluster validity technique discussed in 2.1. The result is illustrated in Fig 35 which give the relation between the number of clusters and the corresponding error where:

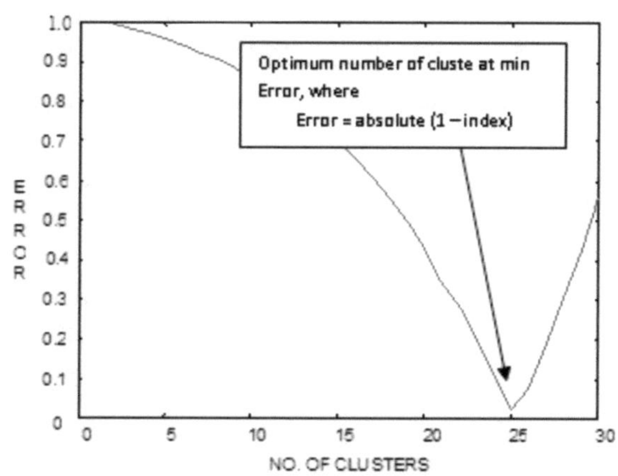

Figure 35. The relation between number of clusters and the corresponding error

b. Table 6 shows the effort saved to locate 13 fault cases. From this table, it can be noticed that:
   - Effort Saving = 1-Ratio between the number of possible locations to the total number of nodes*100%. (45)

Also, we can define the following terms:

- Percentage of successful trials (Ratio of the cases of including the nearest node in the possible locations to the total number of testing cases*100%) = 92%. (46)
- Average effort saving (Summation of the Effort Saving percentages divided by the total number of the cases) =75% (47)

It is important to notice that fuzzy cluster technique failed to locate the fault of test data number 4 due to the lack of information near to this location. However, it is expected that for more available information the performance of this technique will be improved.

TESTING CASE NO.	NUMBER OF POSSIBLE LOCATIONS	NEAREST NODE EXISTS IN THE POSSIBLE LOCATIONS	EFFORT SAVING
1	38	Yes	77%
2	38	Yes	77%
3	23	Yes	86%
4	2	No	0%
5	35	Yes	79%
6	56	Yes	66%
7	23	Yes	86%
8	49	Yes	70%
9	23	Yes	86%
10	17	Yes	90%
11	20	Yes	88%
12	20	Yes	88%
13	17	Yes	90%

Table 6. Effort Saving

3.3.4. Fault location using simple maximum normalization

Here, FCM technique is implemented after normalizing the data based on the maximum value of the data and deciding the optimum number of clusters. Then, the results are analyzed in order to locate any failures may occur in the network.

3.3.4.1. Calculation procedures

To detect the fault using FCM technique with simple maximum normalization, the following steps have been implemented:

a. All the numbers in the feature matrix are normalized by dividing all of them by the maximum number of the absolute values of all the numbers in the matrix.
b. The data are preliminary classified into clusters based on the understanding of the network operation.
c. Cluster validity study is implemented to determine the optimum number of clusters for the selected cluster.
d. FCM technique is implemented to determine the fuzzy partition matrix for the selected number of clusters.
e. The norms between each test data and the full data in the chosen cluster is examined, accordingly the corresponding cluster for each test data is decided based on the minimum norm obtained from the said examination.
f. Alpha-cut defuzzification is used with alpha equal to the average of norms between the cluster center and its data.
g. The nearest node to the fault is checked in order to determine whether it is included in the possible locations or not.

3.3.4.2. Results

Matlab program is written to implement the above six steps and the results are analyzed and summarized as follows:

a. The optimum number of cluster is determined by implementing cluster validity technique and the results are given in Table 7. It is clear from the Table that the optimum number of clusters varies from case to another, which indicates that for any considerable additional of information, cluster validity study should be implemented again to find the new optimum number of clusters.

CASE NUMBER	CASE DISCRIPTION	OPTIMUM NUMBER OF CLUSTERS
1	POWER DIP IN FEEDER #1 AND C.B.1 TRIPS	13
2	POWER DIP IN FEEDER #2 AND C.B.2 TRIPS	15
3	POWER DIP IN FEEDER #3 AND C.B.3 TRIPS	7
4	POWER DIP IN FEEDER #1 AND C.B.1 DOES NOT TRIP	10
5	POWER DIP IN FEEDER #2 AND C.B.2 DOES NOT TRIP	11
6	POWER DIP IN FEEDER #2 AND C.B.2 DOES NOT TRIP	5

Table 7. Shows the optimum number of clusters for each case identified by the operator

b. Figure 36 illustrates the relation between the number of clusters and the corresponding error in case 1, where error is calculated as given in (45).

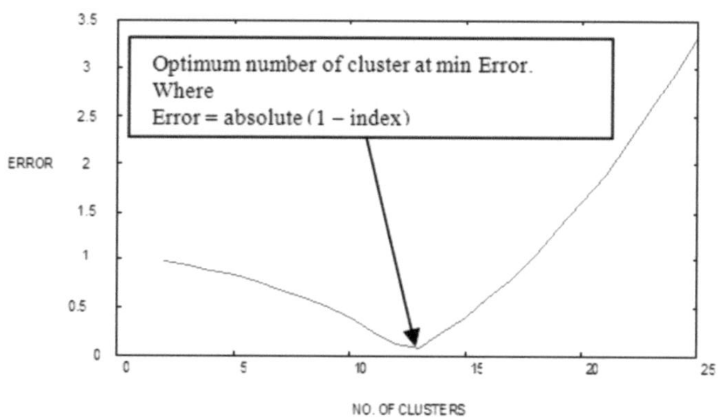

Figure 36. Shows the relation between number of clusters and the corresponding error for case 1

c. Table 8 shows the effort saved to locate 13 fault cases. From the this table , it can be noticed that:

- Effort Saving can be calculated as given in (45)
- Percentage of successful trails = 100%. See (46)
- Average effort saving = 87% See (47)

TESTING CASE NO	NUMBER OF POSSIBLE LOCATIONS	NEAREST NODE EXISTS IN THE POSSIBLE LOCATIONS	EFFORT SAVING
1	21	Yes	87%
2	16	Yes	90%
3	23	Yes	86%
4	21	Yes	87%
5	34	Yes	79%
6	14	Yes	91%
7	33	Yes	80%
8	30	Yes	82%
9	33	Yes	80%
10	5	Yes	97%
11	10	Yes	94%
12	10	Yes	94%
13	9	Yes	94%

Table 8. Effort saved

3.3.5. Discussion

The main objective of was to apply fuzzy c-mean clustering technique to locate any 3-phase fault that may occur at any point on actual power distribution network. Two different normalizing methods have been used to process the feature matrix data. The result obtained can be summarized as follows:

a. Fuzzy clustering technique can be used to investigate the location of faults in networks.
b. Any actual fault can be utilized and be fed back to the database of the clustering system to improve its performance and efficiency.
c. Understanding the network configuration and operation can be utilized to improve the clustering which gives better results.
d. Data matrix comprising the feature vectors should reflect good and adequate description of the network.
e. For any major network's upgrading or change the clustering should be implemented again by using the new data obtained from complete study of the modified network.

4. Summary of the chapter and conclusion

In this chapter we presented five new problems from different application; control, accident analysis, process and electrical network. By using fuzzy logic technique, we succeeded to resolve these problems efficiently. We also introduced different type of normalization of the data. Generating fuzzy rules by either linearization of the curves or by clustering the data were presented as well. Then a method of coloration and prediction of information using the generated fuzzy rules were provided.

Appendix

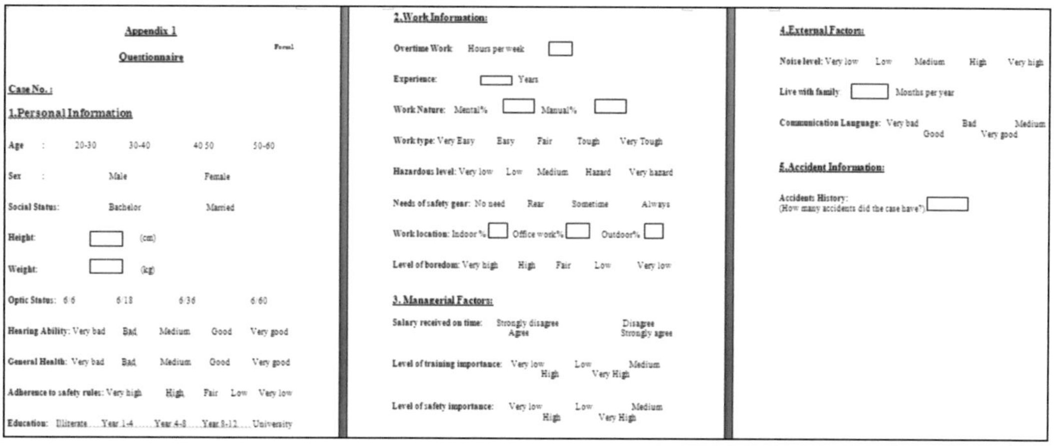
Appendix 1

Questionnaire

Formal

Case No. :

1.Personal Information

Age : 20-30 30-40 40 50 50-60

Sex : Male Female

Social Status: Bachelor Married

Height: (cm)

Weight: (kg)

Optic Status: 6/6 6/18 6/36 6/60

Hearing Ability: Very bad Bad Medium Good Very good

General Health: Very bad Bad Medium Good Very good

Adherence to safety rules: Very high High Fair Low Very low

Education: Illiterate....Year 1-4.....Year 4-8....Year 8-12....University

2.Work Information:

Overtime Work Hours per week

Experience: Years

Work Nature: Mental% Manual%

Work type: Very Easy Easy Fair Tough Very Tough

Hazardous level: Very low Low Medium Hazard Very hazard

Needs of safety gear: No need Rear Sometime Always

Work location: Indoor % Office work% Outdoor%

Level of boredom: Very high High Fair Low Very low

3. Managerial Factors:

Salary received on time: Strongly disagree Disagree Agree Strongly agree

Level of training importance: Very low Low Medium High Very High

Level of safety importance: Very low Low Medium High Very High

4.External Factors:

Noise level: Very low Low Medium High Very high

Live with family Months per year

Communication Language: Very bad Bad Medium Good Very good

5.Accident Information:

Accidents History:
(How many accidents did the case have?)

FW1	FW2	FW3	FW4	FW5	FW6	FW7	FW8	FW9	FW10	FW11	FW12
FW13	FW14	FW15	FW16	FW17	FW18	FW19	FW20	FW21	FW22	FW23	
0.4899	0.4824	0.5548	4.3318	4.3324	3.9963	4.3311	15.6376	46.6328	53.3672	3.3330	3.6684
3.6677	8.3954	19.9348	71.6699	2.6679	2.6683	3.0055	4.0012	3.3330	5.0219	3.0031	
0.3425	0.4881	0.3333	4.9983	4.3328	4.3310	4.6673	0.0000	94.9920	5.0080	3.9983	3.9999
3.3345	23.3133	6.7051	69.9817	2.9999	3.3311	3.3364	4.0020	3.0000	12.0000	3.6656	
0.1581	0.5055	0.7761	4.5545	4.6684	3.9956	4.7782	4.2714	96.6805	3.3195	3.5547	3.7724
3.1099	7.8244	45.6152	46.5605	2.8862	2.3357	3.4470	3.9988	3.6650	11.3039	4.1094	
2.8894	0.4899	0.5016	4.9953	4.9953	2.5048	3.0046	7.4857	2.5093	97.4907	3.9965	4.4954
2.9979	5.0231	14.9297	80.0472	4.4941	2.5000	2.0000	1.5024	3.0034	6.5188	3.0001	
0.3674	0.4435	0.7917	4.7499	4.4997	3.9994	4.2500	8.7491	47.4970	52.5030	3.7497	3.7497
2.7503	21.2531	28.7504	49.9965	3.2497	3.0000	2.7496	3.9992	3.7492	3.3779	3.5003	
0.6164	0.4388	0.8158	4.3160	4.3687	2.7888	3.3152	8.4245	5.0013	94.9987	3.8953	3.8950
3.2638	2.3621	0.0000	97.6379	2.9997	2.7371	2.2635	2.8957	3.4735	4.2838	3.2107	
1.2917	0.4321	0.5000	4.0000	3.7500	3.0000	3.7500	7.5000	27.5000	72.5000	4.0000	3.2500
3.0000	71.2500	10.0000	18.7500	3.2500	2.5000	2.5000	2.5000	3.7500	3.6250	3.0000	
0.3401	0.4600	0.4002	4.3754	4.3744	4.1238	4.8749	3.2411	71.2455	28.7545	3.4994	3.6244
3.2492	6.2440	61.2585	32.4975	2.4996	3.7507	3.0011	3.9998	3.1258	9.3725	4.6244	
0.8238	0.4696	0.2803	4.3322	4.3322	2.3357	4.0000	10.6568	6.7131	93.2869	3.6678	3.6678
2.6680	41.5930	11.7266	46.6804	2.6645	2.6676	2.0000	2.6649	3.6645	4.5258	3.6678	
0.5278	0.4539	0.5997	4.3992	4.2006	3.0011	4.6002	2.8065	62.0051	37.9949	3.0005	3.0005
3.2006	32.9938	43.0014	24.0048	3.4002	3.5998	2.5999	2.6004	2.4002	10.4017	3.8004	
0.2282	0.4517	0.3471	4.7537	4.8743	3.6330	4.8743	3.0413	97.4866	2.5134	3.3767	2.3770
2.3720	4.2728	83.2449	12.4822	2.8797	3.3770	4.1206	3.6233	2.4976	9.4162	4.5074	
1.1461	0.4654	0.8339	4.0001	4.2512	3.2512	3.2468	7.4926	27.4917	72.5083	3.8764	3.7486
3.3742	18.1000	13.1229	68.7771	2.8766	2.6225	3.5013	3.7523	3.5017	5.2219	3.2467	

Table 9. Illustrates the centroide matrix for the optimum number of clusters (twelve),

Feature Weight	Description	Feature Weight	Description
FW1	Accidents/ experience	FW13	Need for Safety Gear
FW2	Weight/Height	FW14	Indoor Work
FW3	Optical status	FW15	Office Work
FW4	Hearing Ability	FW16	Outdoor Work
FW5	General Health	FW17	Level of Boredom
FW6	Adherence to Safety	FW18	Salary on time
FW7	Education	FW19	Level of Training
FW8	Overtime work	FW20	Level of Safety
FW9	Mental work	FW21	Noise level
FW10	Manual work	FW22	live with family
FW11	Work type	FW23	Communication language
FW12	Hazard level		

Table 10. DESCRIPTION of feature weights,

	Personal Factors						**Work Factors**										**Managerial Factors**			**External Factors**		
	Specific weight	Optical status	Hearing ability	General health	Adherence to safety	Education	Overtime work rate	Mental work rate	Manual work rate	Work type	Hazardous level	Needs for safety-gear	Indoor work rate	Office work rate	Outdoor work rate	Level of boredom	Delay on receiving the salary on time	Level of training	Level of safety importance	Level of noise	Live with family	Communication language level
Minimum accident rate 0.1581	high	average high	average	above average	above average	high	low	high	low	fair	above average	average high	low	average	average	low	high	Very high	High	high	9-12 months per year	above average
Maximum accident rate 2.8894.	above average	low	high	good	low	low	average	low	high	tough	high	average low	low	under average	over average	high	high	low	Low	average low	4-6 months per year.	poor

Table 11. Features of the model of Maximum and Minimum accident rate

Feature	Case#1	Case#2	Case#3	Case#4	Case#5	Case#6	Case#7	Case#8
Accidents/ Year experience	2.6	3.2	2.5	2.3	3.1	0	1.1	0.125
Accident rate predicted	2.1	2.8	1.9	1.3	2.9	0.2	1.4	.17
Weight/Height	0.465	.454	.42	.466	.429	.49	.51	.415
Optical status	6/36	6/6	6/6	6/6	6/12	6/60	6/6	6/6
Hearing Ability	Medium	Good	V.Good	Good	Medium	V.Good	V.Good	V.Good
General Health	Good	Good	Good	Good	Good	V.Good	Good	V.Good
Adherence to Safety	Fair	Fair	Fair	V. High	Low	V. High	Fair	V. High
Education	16	9	12	8	5	17	10	19
Overtime work	0	8	2	1	8	0	3	0
Mental work	60	20	50	70	10	100	50	90
Manual work	40	80	50	30	90	0	50	10
Work type	Fait	Tough	Fair	Fair	Fair	V. Easy	Fair	V. Easy
Hazard level	V. High	High	Medium	V. High	High	V. Low	Medium	Low
Need for Safety Gear	Sometime	Sometime	Sometime	Always	Sometime	Rare	Rare	No need
Indoor Work	0	20	30	5	0	0	80	0
Office Work	80	30	40	45	0	100	20	100
Outdoor Work	30	50	30	50	100	0	0	0
Level of Boredom	Medium	High	Medium	Medium	High	Low	High	Medium
Salary on time	Strongly Agree	Agree	Agree	Strongly Agree	Disagree	Strongly Agree	Agree	Strongly Agree
Level of Training importance	Medium	Low	Low	Low	Low	V. High	High	High
Level of Safety Importance	High	Medium	Medium	High	Medium	High	High	V. High
Noise level	High	High	Medium	V. High	Medium	Low	Medium	Low
Live with family	12	12	6	12	0	9	12	12
Communication language	Good	V.Good	Medium	Good	Medium	V. Good	Good	V.Good

Table 12. Result of eight test cases

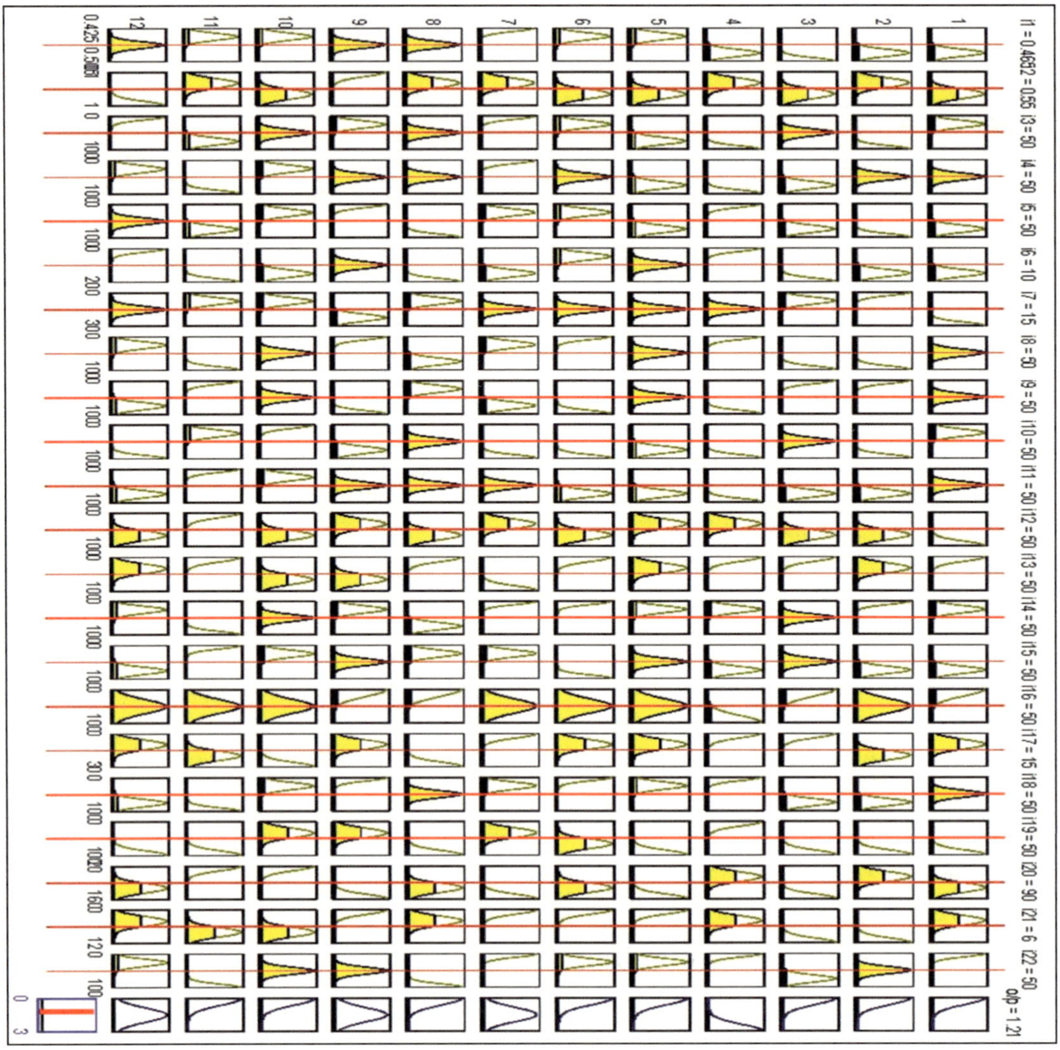

Figure 37. The output of the prediction system for `average` inputs.

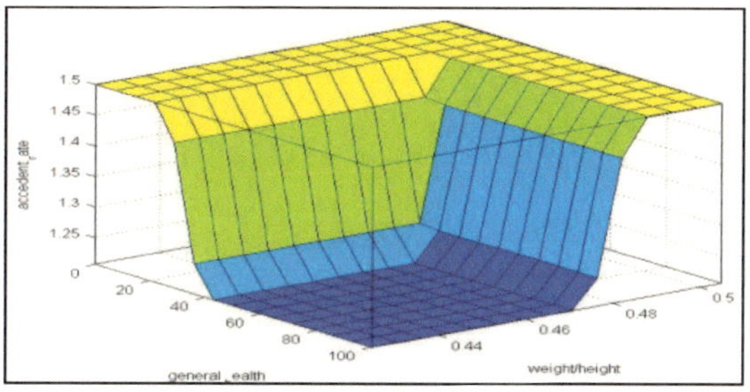

Figure 38. Correlation between weight/height, general health and rate of accident

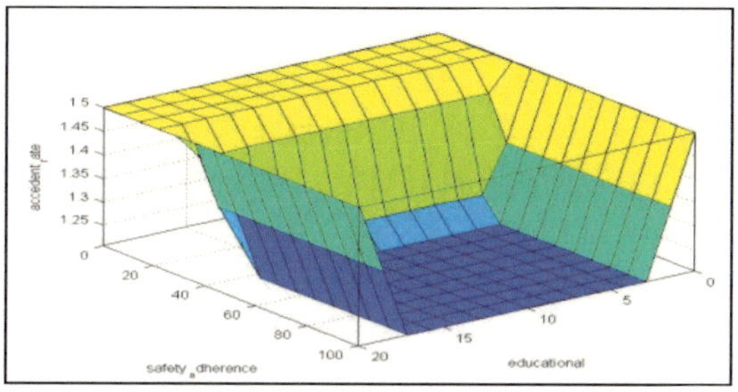

Figure 39. Correlation between education level, safety adherence and rate of accident

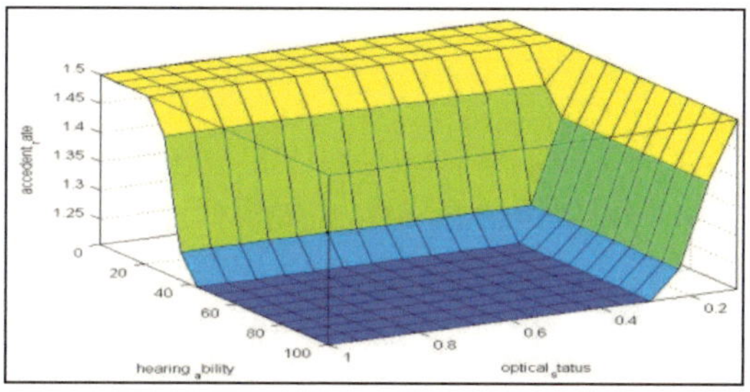

Figure 40. Correlation between optical status, hearing ability and rate of accidents.

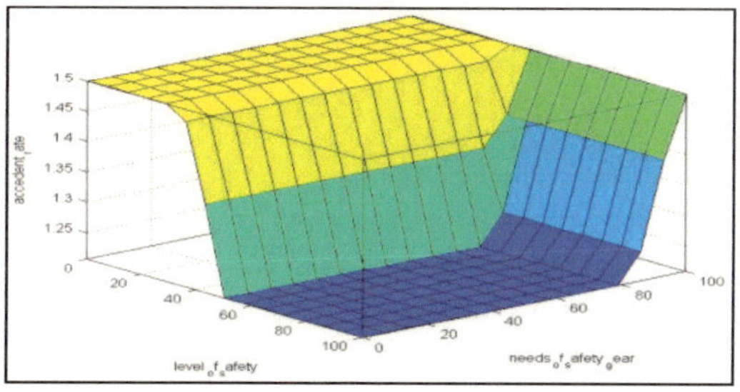

Figure 41. Correlation between level of safety, need of safety-gear and rate of accident.

Author details

Muhammad M.A.S. Mahmoud
Received the B.S. degree in Electrical Engineering from Cairo University and the M.Sc. degree from Kuwait University. PH.D Transilvania University of Brasov, Romania He occupies a position of Senior Engineer at Al Hosn Gas Co. UAE

5. References

[1] Zadeh, L.A., "Fuzzy Sets", Information and Control, Vol. 12, pp. 338-353, 1965.
[2] M. S. Mahmoud, "Computer-Operated Systems Control", Marcel Dekker Inc., New York, 1991.
[3] C. C. Lee, Fuzzy Logic in Control Systems: Fuzzy Logic Controller, Parts I& II", IEEE Systems, Man and Cybernetics, Vol. 20, No.2, March/April 1990, pp.404-435.
[4] M. S. Mahmoud, S.Z. Eid and A .A. Abou-Elseoud, "A Real Time Expert System for Dynamical Processes", IEEE Transactions Systems, Man and Cybernetics, Vol. SMC-19, No. 5, September/October 1989, pp. 1101-1105.
[5] M. S. Mahmoud, S. Kotob, and A. A. Abou-Elseoud, "A Learning Rule- Based Control System", Journal of Information and Decision Technologies, Vol. 18, No. 1, January 1992, pp. 55-66.
[6] M. S. Mahmoud, A. A. Abou-Elseoud and S. Kotob, "Development of Expert Control Systems: A Pattern Classification and Recognition Approach", Journal of Intelligent and Robotic Systems, Vol. 5, No. 2, April 1992, pp.129-146.
[7] L. X. Wang, "A Supervisory Controller for Fuzzy Control Systems that Guarantees Stability", IEEE Trans. Automatic Control, Vol. 39, No. 9, September 1994, pp. 1845-1847.
[8] K. M. Passino, and S. Yurkovick, "Fuzzy Control", Addison Wesley, California, 1998.
[9] Wang, Li-Xin, "A Course In Fuzzy Systems And Control", Prentice-Hall International, Inc. NJ 07458,USA, 1997.
[10] M. Sugeno, and G.T. Kang, Structure Identification of Fuzzy Model, Fuzzy Sets and Systems, 28, 1988, pp. 15-33.
[11] Takagi, and M. Sugeno , "Fuzzy Identification of Systems and its Applications to Modeling and Control", IEEE Trans. On System, Man, and Cybernetics, Vol. 15, 1985 , pp. 116-132.
[12] Jeong-Woo Choi, Seung-Mok Ob, Hyun-Goo Choi, SangBaek Lee, Kwang-Soon Lee and Won-Hong Lee Fuzzy Control of Ethanol Concentration for Emulsan Production in a Fed-Batch Cultivation of Acinetobacter calcoaceticus RAG-I Korean 1. Chern. Eng., 15(3), 310(1998)
[13] Min Oh and II Moon, Framework of Dynamic Simulation for Complex Chemical Processes, Korean J. Chern. Eng., 15(3), 231(1998)
[14] M. S. Mahmoud, M. F. Hassan and M. G. Darwish, "Large Scale Control Systems: Theories and Techniques", Marcel Dekker Inc., New York, 1985.

[15] D. D. Siljak, "Decentralized Control of Complex Systems", Academic Press, Boston, 1991.
[16] M. S. Mahmoud, "Computer-Operated Systems Control", Marcel Dekker Inc., New York, 1991.
[17] M. Jamshidi, "Large Scale Systems: Modeling, Control and Fuzzy Logic", Prentice-Hall, New Jersey, 1997.
[18] M. S. Mahmoud, S.Z. Eid and A .A. Abou-Elseoud, "A Real Time Expert System for Dynamical Processes", IEEE Transactions Systems, Man and Cybernetics, Vol. SMC-19, No. 5, September/October 1989, pp. 1101-1105.
[19] M. S. Mahmoud, S. Kotob, and A. A. Abou-Elseoud, "A Learning Rule-Based Control System", Journal of Information and Decision Technologies, Vol. 18, No. 1, January 1992, pp. 55-66.
[20] M. S. Mahmoud, A. A. Abou-Elseoud and S. Kotob, "Development of Expert Control Systems: A Pattern Classification and Recognition Approach", Journal of Intelligent and Robotic Systems, Vol. 5, No. 2, April 1992, pp. 129-146.
[21] L. X. Wang, "A Supervisory Controller for Fuzzy Control Systems that Guarantees", IEEE Trans. Automatic Control, Vol. 39, No. 9, September 1994, pp. 1845-1847.
[22] K. M. Passino, and S. Yurkovick, "Fuzzy Control", Addison Wesley, California, 1998.
[23] C. C. Lee, "Fuzzy Logic in Control Systems: Fuzzy Logic Controller, Parts I & II", IEEE Systems, Man and Cybernetics, Vol. 20, No. 2, March/April 1990, pp. 404-435.
[24] M. Sugeno, and G.T. Kang, Structure Identification of Fuzzy Model, Fuzzy Sets and Systems, 28, 1988, pp. 15-33.
[25] Takagi, and M. Sugeno , Fuzzy Identification of Systems and its Applications to Modelling and Control, IEEE Trans. On System, Man,and Cybernetics, Vol. 15, 1985 , pp. 116-132
[26] Suciu, C; Liliana; Dafinca; Kansara M Margineanu ,"Switching capacitor fuzzy controller for power factor correction on inductive circuit", Power Electronics Specialist Conference, 31st Annual, 2000, IEEE, vol. 2.pp 773- 777.
[27] K.H . Abdul-Rahman, S.M. Shahidehpour, "Application of Fuzzy sets to optimal reactive power planning with security constrains", TransacTion of Power Systems, 1994, vol. 9, No.2, pp 589-597.
[28] Yu Qin; ShanShan Du, "To design fuzzy and digital controller for a single phase power factor pre-regulator-genetic algorithm approach", Industrial Application Conference, Annual, 1997 IEEE, vol, 2, pp 791-796.
[29] Yu Qin; ShanShan Du, "Control of single phase power factor pre-regulator for on-line uninterruptible power supply using fuzzy logic control inference", Applied power electronics Conference and Exposition, 11th Annual, 1996, vol.2, pp 699- 702.
[30] Borges da Silva, L.E; Ferreira da silva; M; Lambert-Torres, G, "An intelligent hybrid active power factor compensator for power systems,Systems", Man and Cybernetcs, 1995. Intelligentvsystem for the 21st Century, /EEE, vol.2 pp 1367- 1371.
[31] Turan Gonen, "Electrical power distribution system engineering", McGraw-Hill Inc. NY, 1986.

[32] Navd R. Zargari, Yuan Xiao; Bin Wu, "A multilevel thyristor rectifier with improved power faclor", Transaction on Industrial Applications, 1997,vol. 33 pp 1208- 1213.

[33] Chung,H.S .H; Tam,E.P.W; Huni,S.Y.R. "Development of a Fuzzy Logic Controller for boost rectifier with acti ve power factor correction", Power Electronics Specialist Conference, 30th Annual, 1999, IEEE, vol. 1, pp 149- 154.

[34] Mohammed T. Bi na; David C. Hamill , "The Bootstrap Varible Inductance: A New FACTS Control Elemenl".1999,l EEE.

[35] Muhammad Harunur Rash id, "Power Electronics Circuit, Devices and Applications", Prentice Hall Inc, NJ, 1988.

[36] Wang, Li-Xin, "A Course In Fuzzy Systems And Control", Prentice-Hall, N. J., 1997.

[37] ADAMS, J. A. Human factors in engineering. New York, Macmillan Publishing Company, 1989.

[38] Dominic Cooper C.Psychol "Human Factors in Accidents", Institute of Quarrying, North Of England- CoalPro Seminar, Ramside Hall, Durham, UK. 12 March 2002

[39] PEYTON, R. X.. Construction safety practices. New York, Van 1991.

[40] Sii, H.S., Wang, J., Ruxton, T., Yang, J.B., Liu, J. "Fuzzy logic approaches to safety assessment in maritime engineering applications", Journal of Marine Engineering & Technology (A5): 45-58. 2004.

[41] KARTAM, N. A. and BOUZ, R. G.. "Fatalities and Injuries in Kuwaiti Construction Industry", Accident Analysis and Prevention, (30), 805-814, 1991.

[42] A. Kamal, S. M. Eid and M. S. Mahmoud, "Multi-Stage Clustering: An Efficient Technique in Socioeconomic Field Experiments", IEEE Transactions Systems, Man and Cybernetics, Vol. SMC-11, No. 12, December 1981, pp. 779-785.

[43] BEZDEK, J. C. & PAL K. S. "Fuzzy models for pattern recognition". New York: IEEE Press, 1992.

[44] WINDHAM, M. P. "Cluster validity for the fuzzy c-mean clustering algorithm", IEEE Transactions Pattern Analysis and Machine Intelligence, (PAMI-4), 357-363, 1982 .

[45] XUANLI LIISA XIE & GERARDO BENI. "A Validity Measure for Fuzzy Clustering". IEEE Transactions Pattern Analysis and Machine Intelligence, vol. (PAMI-13), no. 8, pp. 841-847, August 1991.

[46] The Mathworks, "Fuzzy Logic Toolbox", Boston,1999.

[47] John J. Granger and William D. Stevenson, Jr., "Power System Analysis", McGraw-Hill, Inc., New York, USA, 1994.

Chapter 18

Fuzzy Control Systems: LMI-Based Design

Morteza Seidi, Marzieh Hajiaghamemar and Bruce Segee

Additional information is available at the end of the chapter

http://dx.doi.org/10.5772/48529

1. Introduction

This chapter describes widespread methods of model-based fuzzy control systems. The subject of this chapter is a systematic framework for the stability and design of nonlinear fuzzy control systems. We are trying to build a bridge between conventional fuzzy control and classic control theory. By building this bridge, the strong well developed tools of classic control could be used in model-based fuzzy control systems

Model-based fuzzy control, with the possibility of guaranteeing the closed loop stability, is an attractive method for control of nonlinear systems. In recent years, many studies have been devoted to the stability analysis of continuous time or discrete time model based fuzzy control systems (Takagi & Sugeno, 1985; Rhee & Won, 2006; Chen et al., 1993; Wang et al., 1996; Zhao et al., 1996; Tanaka & Wang, 2001; Tanaka et al., 2001). Among such methods, the method of Takagi-Sugeno (Takagi & Sugeno, 1985) has found many applications for modelling complex nonlinear systems (Tanaka & Sano, 1994;Tanaka & Kosaki, 1997;Li et al., 1998). The concept of sector nonlinearity (Kawamoto et al., 1992) provided means for exact approximation of nonlinear systems by fuzzy blending of a few locally linearized subsystems. One important advantage of using such a method for control design is that the closed-loop stability analysis, using the Lyapunov method, becomes easier to apply. Various stability conditions have been proposed for such systems (Tanaka &Wang, 2001), (Ting, 2006), where the existence of a common solution to a set of Lyapunov equations is shown to be sufficient for guaranteeing the closed-loop stability. Some relaxed conditions are also proposed in (Kim & Lee, 2000; Ding et al, 2006; Fang et al., 2006, Tanaka & Ikeda, 1998). Parallel Distributed Compensator (PDC) is a generalization of the state feedback controller to the case of nonlinear systems, using the Takagi-Sugeno fuzzy model (Wang et al., 1996). This method is based on partitioning nonlinear system dynamics into a number of linear subsystems, for which state feedback gains are designed and blended in a fuzzy sense. Takagi-Sugeno model and parallel distributed compensation have been used in many applications successfully (Sugeno & Kang, 1986, Lee et al., 2006, Hong & Langari, 2000, Bonissone et al.,

1995). The Linear Matrix Inequality (LMI) technique offers a numerically tractable way to design a PDC controller with objectives such as stability (Wang et al.,1996; Ding et al, 2006; Fang et al., 2006; Tanaka & Sugeno 1992), H∞ control (Lee et al., 2001), H2 control (Lin & Lo, 2003), pole-placement (Jon et al, 1997; Kang & Lee, 1998), and others (Tanaka & Wang, 2001).

2. Takagi-Sugeno fuzzy model

The main idea of the Takagi-Sugeno fuzzy modeling method is to partition the nonlinear system dynamics into several locally linearized subsystems, so that the overall nonlinear behavior of the system can be captured by fuzzy blending of such subsystems. The fuzzy rule associated with the i-th linear subsystem for the continuous fuzzy system and the discrete fuzzy system, can then be defined as

Continuous fuzzy system

$$\text{Rule i :IF } Z_1(t) \text{ is } M_{i1} \ldots \text{ and } Z_l(t) \text{is } M_{il}$$
$$\text{THEN} \quad \begin{cases} \dot{x}(t) = A_i x(t) + B_i u(t) \\ y(t) = C_i x(t) \end{cases} \quad i=1,2,\ldots,r \tag{1}$$

Discrete Fuzzy System

$$\text{Rule i :IF } Z_1(t) \text{ is } M_{i1} \ldots \text{ and } Z_l(t) \text{is } M_{il}$$
$$\text{THEN} \quad \begin{cases} x(t+1) = A_i x(t) + B_i u(t) \\ y(t) = C_i x(t) \end{cases} \quad i=1,2,\ldots,r \tag{2}$$

where, $x(t) \in R^n$ is the state vector, $u(t) \in R^m$ is the input vector, $A_i \in R^{n \times n}$, $B_i \in R^{n \times m}$, $C_i \in R^{q \times n}$; $\{z_1(t), z_2(t), \ldots, z_p(t)\}$ are nonlinear functions of the state variables obtained from the original nonlinear equation, and $M_{ij}(z_i)$ are the degree of membership of $z_i(t)$ in a fuzzy set M_{ij}. Whenever there is no ambiguity, the time argument in *z*(*t*) is dropped. The overall output, using the fuzzy blend of the linear subsystems, will then be as follows:

Continuous fuzzy system

$$\dot{X} = \frac{\sum_{I=1}^{R} w_1(z)\{A_i x(t) + B_i u(t)\}}{\sum_{i=1}^{r} w_i(z)} = \sum_{i=1}^{r} h_1(z)(A_i x(t) + B_i u(t))$$
$$y(t) = \frac{\sum_{i=1}^{r} w_1(z) C_i x(t)}{\sum_{i=1}^{r} w_1(z)} = \sum_{i=1}^{r} h_1(z) C_i x(t) \tag{3}$$

Discrete Fuzzy System

$$
\begin{aligned}
x(t+1) &= \frac{\sum_{i=1}^{r} \omega_i(z(t))\{A_i x(t) + B_i u(t)\}}{\sum_{i=1}^{r} \omega_i(z(t))} \\
&= \sum_{i=1}^{r} h_i(z(t))(A_i x(t) + B_i u(t)) \\
y(t) &= \frac{\sum_{i=1}^{r} \omega_i(z(t)) C_i x(t)}{\sum_{i=1}^{r} \omega_i(z(t))} \\
&= \sum_{i=1}^{r} h_i(z(t)) C_i x(t)
\end{aligned}
\tag{4}
$$

Where

$$
\begin{aligned}
w_1(z) &= \prod_{j=1}^{i} M_{ij}(z_j) \\
h_1(z) &= \frac{w_1(z)}{\sum_{i=1}^{r} w_1(z)}
\end{aligned}
\tag{5}
$$

It is also true, for all t, that

$$
\begin{cases}
\sum_{i=1}^{r} w_1(z) > 0, \\
w_1(z) \geq 0, i = 1, 2, \ldots\ldots, r
\end{cases}
$$

2.1. Building a fuzzy model

There are generally three approaches to build the fuzzy model: "sector nonlinearity," "local approximation," or a combination of the two.

2.1.1. Sector nonlinearity

Figure 1 illustrates the concept of global and local sector nonlinearity. Suppose the original nonlinear system satisfies the sector non-linearity condition (Kawamoto et al., 1992, as cited in Tanaka & Wang, 2001), i.e., the values of nonlinear terms in the state-space equation remain within a sector of hyper-planes passing through the origin. This model guarantees the stability of the original nonlinear system under the control law. A function Φ: R→R is said to be sector [a,c] if for all x∈R, y= Φ(x) lies between $b_1 x$ and $b_2 x$.

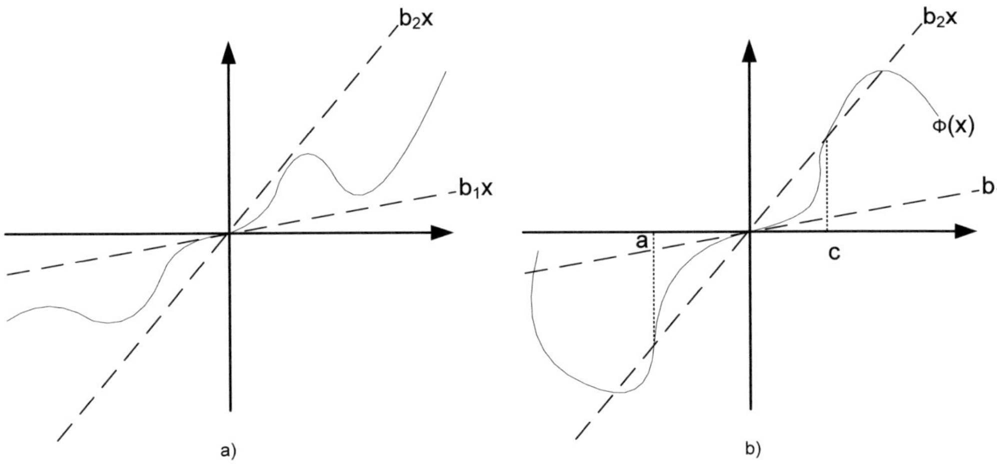

Figure 1. a) Global sector nonlinearity, b) Local sector nonlinearity

Example 1

The well-known nonlinear control benchmark, the ball-and-beam system is commonly used as an illustrative application of various control methods (Wang & Mendel, 1992) depicted in figure 2. Let $x_1(t)$ and $x_2(t)$ denote the position and the velocity of the ball and let $x_3(t)$ and $x_4(t)$ denote the angular position and the angular velocity of the beam Then, the system dynamics can be described by the following state-space equation

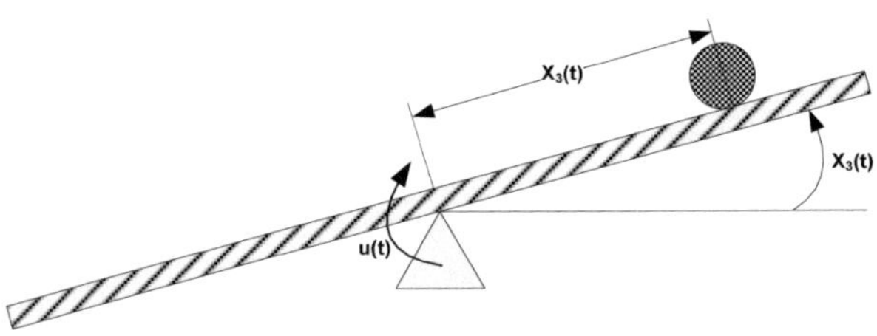

Figure 2. The ball and beam system

$$\dot{x}(t) = f(x(t)) + g(x(t))u(t) \tag{6}$$

Where

$$f(x) = \begin{bmatrix} x_2(t) \\ B(x_1(t)x_4^2(t) - G\sin(x_3(t))) \\ x_4(t) \\ 0 \end{bmatrix} \text{ and } g(x) = \begin{bmatrix} 0 \\ 0 \\ 0 \\ 1 \end{bmatrix}$$

Where $x(t) = \begin{bmatrix} x_1(t) & x_2(t) & x_3(t) & x_4(t) \end{bmatrix}^T$ and u(t) is torque.

$\sin(x_3)$ and $x_1x_4^2$ are nonlinear terms in the state-space equation. We define $z_1 = \sin(x_3)$ and $z_2 = x_1x_4^2$. Assume $x_3 \in \left[-\pi/2 \;\; \pi/2\right]$ and $x_1x_4 \in \left[-d \;\; d\right]$ as the region within which the system will operate. Figure 3 shows that $z_1(t) = \sin(x_3(t))$ and its local sector operating region.The sector [b_1, b_2] consists of two lines b_1x_1 and b_2x_1, where the slopes are $b_1 = 1$ and $b_2 = 2/\pi$. It follows that

$$\left|\frac{2}{\pi}x\right| \le |\sin(x)| \le |x|,$$
$$-dx_4 \le x_1x_4^2 \le dx_4. \quad (7)$$

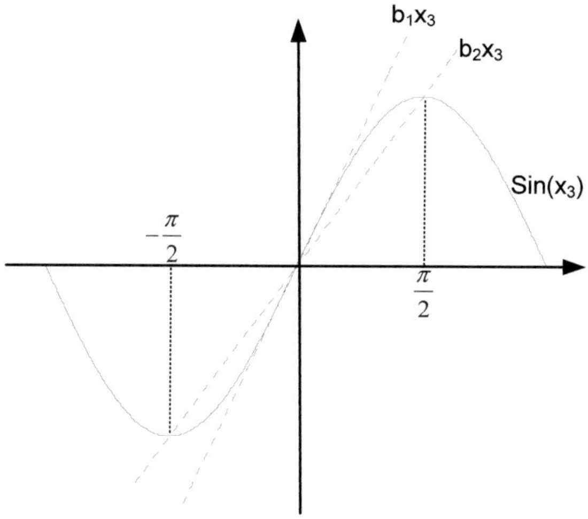

Figure 3. $\sin(x_3(t))$ and its local sector

We present $\sin(x_3(t))$ is represented as follows:

$$z_1 = \sin(x_3(t)) = \left(\sum_{i=1}^{2} M_i(z_1(t))b_i\right)x_3(t) \quad (8)$$

From the property of membership functions $\left[M_1(z_1(t)) + M_2(z_1(t)) = 1\right]$, we can obtain the membership functions

$$M_1(z_1(t)) = \begin{cases} \dfrac{z_1(t) - \left(2/\pi\right)S\sin(z_1(t))}{\left(1 - 2/\pi\right)sin^{-1}(z_1(t))} & z_1(t) \ne 0 \\ 1, & otherwise. \end{cases}$$
$$M_2(z_1(t)) = \begin{cases} \dfrac{sin^{-1}(z_1(t)) - z_1(t)}{\left(1 - 2/\pi\right)sin^{-1}(z_1(t))} & z_1(t) \ne 0 \\ 0, & otherwise. \end{cases} \quad (9)$$

Similarly we obtain membership functions associated with $z_2(t) = x_1(t)x_4(t)$. Assume $\max(z_2(t)) = d = \alpha_1$ and $\min(z_2(t)) = -d = \alpha_2$ we have:

$$z_2(t) = x_1(t)x_4(t) = \left(\sum_{i=1}^{2} N_i\left(z_2(t)\right)b_i\right)\alpha_i \tag{10}$$

$$\begin{aligned} N_1\left(z_2(t)\right) &= \frac{z_2(t)-\alpha_2}{\alpha_1-\alpha_2}, \\ N_2\left(z_2(t)\right) &= \frac{\alpha_1 - z_2(t)}{\alpha_1-\alpha_2}, \end{aligned} \tag{11}$$

The exact TS-fuzzy model-based dynamic system of the ball and beam system can be obtained as following:

$$\begin{bmatrix} \dot{x}_1(t) \\ \dot{x}_2(t) \\ \dot{x}_3(t) \\ \dot{x}_4(t) \end{bmatrix} = \sum_{i=1}^{2}\sum_{j=1}^{2} M_i(z_1(t))N_j(z_2(t)) \times \left(\begin{bmatrix} 0 & 1 & 0 & 0 \\ 0 & 0 & -\mathrm{Gb}_\mathrm{i} & D\alpha_j \\ 0 & 0 & 0 & 1 \\ 0 & 0 & 0 & 0 \end{bmatrix} \begin{bmatrix} x_1(t) \\ x_2(t) \\ x_3(t) \\ x_4(t) \end{bmatrix} + \begin{bmatrix} 0 \\ 0 \\ 0 \\ 1 \end{bmatrix} u(t) \right) \tag{12}$$

The fuzzy model has the following 4 rules:

$$\begin{aligned} &\text{Rule 1: if } z_1(t) \text{ is } M_1 \text{ and } z_2(t) \text{ is } N_1 \\ &\qquad \text{Then } \dot{x}(t) = A_1 x(t) + B_1 u(t), \\ &\text{Rule 2: if } z_1(t) \text{ is } M_1 \text{ and } z_2(t) \text{ is } N_2 \\ &\qquad \text{Then } \dot{x}(t) = A_2 x(t) + B_2 u(t), \\ &\text{Rule 3: if } z_1(t) \text{ is } M_2 \text{ and } z_2(t) \text{ is } N_1 \\ &\qquad \text{Then } \dot{x}(t) = A_3 x(t) + B_3 u(t), \\ &\text{Rule 4: if } z_1(t) \text{ is } M_2 \text{ and } z_2(t) \text{ is } N_2 \\ &\qquad \text{Then } \dot{x}(t) = A_4 x(t) + B_4 u(t) \end{aligned} \tag{13}$$

Where

$$A_1 = \begin{bmatrix} 0 & 1 & 0 & 0 \\ 0 & 0 & -\mathrm{Gb}_1 & D\alpha_1 \\ 0 & 0 & 0 & 1 \\ 0 & 0 & 0 & 0 \end{bmatrix}, A_1 = \begin{bmatrix} 0 & 1 & 0 & 0 \\ 0 & 0 & -\mathrm{Gb}_1 & D\alpha_2 \\ 0 & 0 & 0 & 1 \\ 0 & 0 & 0 & 0 \end{bmatrix},$$

$$A_1 = \begin{bmatrix} 0 & 1 & 0 & 0 \\ 0 & 0 & -\mathrm{Gb}_2 & D\alpha_1 \\ 0 & 0 & 0 & 1 \\ 0 & 0 & 0 & 0 \end{bmatrix}, A_1 = \begin{bmatrix} 0 & 1 & 0 & 0 \\ 0 & 0 & -\mathrm{Gb}_2 & D\alpha_2 \\ 0 & 0 & 0 & 1 \\ 0 & 0 & 0 & 0 \end{bmatrix}$$

$$B_1 = B_2 = B_3 = B_4 = B = \begin{bmatrix} 0 \\ 0 \\ 0 \\ 1 \end{bmatrix}, z_1 = \sin\left(x_3\right) \text{ and } z_2 = x_1 x_4$$

2.1.2. Local approximation

The original system can be partitioned into subsystems by approximation of nonlinear terms about equilibrium points. This approach can have fewer rules and of course less complexity but it cannot guarantee the stability of the original system under the controller. Usually in this approach, construction of a fuzzy membership function requires knowledge of the behavior of the original system and of course different types of membership functions can be selected.

3. Parallel distributed compensation

Parallel distributed compensation (PDC) is a model-based design procedure introduced in (Wang et al,. 1995). Using the Takagi-Sugeno fuzzy model, a fuzzy combination of the stabilizing state feedback gains, $F_i, i = 1,2,...,r$, associated with every linear subsystem is used as the overall state feedback controller. The general structure of the controller is then as

$$\text{If } z_1(t) \text{ is } M_{i1}, \text{and } z_2(t) \text{ is } M_{i2}, ...m, \text{and } z_p(t) \text{ is } M_{ip} \text{ then } u = -F_i x(t), i = 1,2,...,r \quad (14)$$

The output of the controller is represented by

$$u = -\frac{\sum_{i=1}^{r} \omega_i(z) F_i x(t)}{\sum_{i=1}^{r} \omega_i} = -\sum_{i=1}^{r} h_i(z) F_i x(t). \quad (15)$$

The Takagi-Sugeno model and the Parallel Distributed Compensation have the same number of fuzzy rules and use the same membership functions.

4. Stability conditions and control design

4.1. LMI

A variety of problems arising in system and control theory can be reduced to a few standard convex or quasi-convex optimization problems involving linear matrix inequalities (LMIs). Lyapunov published his theory in 1890 and showed that $\frac{d}{dt}x(t) = Ax(t)$ is stable if and only if there exists a positive-definite matrix P such that $A^T P + PA < 0$. The Lypanov inequality, $P > 0$ and $A^T P + PA < 0$ is a form of an LMI.

An LMI has the form

$$F(x) \triangleq F_0 + \sum_{i=1}^{m} x_i F_i > 0, \quad (16)$$

Where $F_i \in R^{n\times n}, i = 0,...,m$ are the given symmetric matrices and $x \in R^m$ is the variable and the inequality symbol shows that $F(x)$ is positive definite (Boyd, 1994).

4.2. Stability conditions

There are a large number of works on stability conditions and control design of fuzzy systems in the literature. A sufficient stability condition for ensuring stability of PDC was derived by Tanaka and Sugeno (Tanaka & Sugeno, 1990; 1992).

By substituting the controller output (15) into the TS model for the continuous fuzzy control (4), we have:

$$\dot{x}(t) = \sum_{i=1}^{r}\sum_{j=1}^{r} h_i(z(t))h_j(z(t))\{A_i - B_iF_j\}x(t) \tag{17}$$

or

$$\begin{aligned}\dot{x}(t) = &\sum_{j=1}^{r} h_i(z(t))h_i(z(t))G_{ii}x(t) \\ &+2\sum_{i=1}^{r}\sum_{i<j} h_i(z(t))h_j(z(t))\left\{\frac{G_{ij}+G_{ji}}{2}\right\}x(t)\end{aligned} \tag{18}$$

where $G_{ij} = A_i - B_iF_j$, Similarly for the discrete fuzzy system we have

$$x(t+1) = \sum_{i=1}^{r}\sum_{j=1}^{r} h_i(z(t))h_j(z(t))\{A_i - B_iF_j\}x(t) \tag{19}$$

or

$$\begin{aligned}\dot{x}(t+1) = &\sum_{j=1}^{r} h_i(z(t))h_i(z(t))G_{ii}x(t) \\ &+2\sum_{i=1}^{r}\sum_{i<j} h_i(z(t))h_j(z(t))\left\{\frac{G_{ij}+G_{ji}}{2}\right\}x(t)\end{aligned} \tag{20}$$

Theorem 1: The equilibrium of the continuous fuzzy system (3) with u(t) = 0 is globally asymptotically stable if there exists a common positive definite matrix P such that

$$A_i^TP + PA_i < 0, \;\; i = 1,2,...,r \tag{21}$$

that is, a common P has to exist for all subsystems.

Theorem 2: The equilibrium of the discrete fuzzy system (4) with u(t) = 0 is globally asymptotically stable i f there exists a common positive definite matrix P such that

$$A_i^TPA_i - P < 0, \;\; i = 1,2,...,r \tag{22}$$

that is, a common P has to exist for all subsystems.

The stability of the closed loop system can be derived by using theorem 1 and 2.

Theorem 3: The equilibrium of the continuous fuzzy control system described by (18) is globally asymptotically stable if there exists a common positive definite matrix P such that

$$\begin{aligned} & G_{ii}^T P + P G_{ii} < 0, \\ & \left(\frac{G_{ij} + G_{ji}}{2} \right)^T P + P \left(\frac{G_{ij} + G_{ji}}{2} \right) \le 0, \end{aligned} \tag{23}$$

$$i < j \text{ s.t. } \mathrm{h_i} \cap h_j \neq \phi \tag{24}$$

Theorem 4: The equilibrium of the discrete fuzzy control system described by (20) is globally asymptotically stable if there exists a common positive definite matrix P such that

$$\begin{aligned} & G_{ii}^T P G_{ii} - P < 0, \\ & \left(\frac{G_{ij} + G_{ji}}{2} \right)^T P \left(\frac{G_{ij} + G_{ji}}{2} \right) - P \le 0, \end{aligned} \tag{25}$$

$$i < j \text{ s.t. } \mathrm{h_i} \cap h_j \neq \phi \tag{26}$$

4.3. Stable controller design

By using the following conditions, the solution of the LMI problem for continuous and discrete fuzzy systems gives us the state feedback gains F_i and the matrix P (if the problem is solvable).

Consider a new variable $X = P^{-1}$ then the stable fuzzy controller design problem is:

Continuous fuzzy system

Find $X > 0$ and M_i , $i = 1,2,\ldots,r$

$$\begin{aligned} & -XA_i^T - A_i X + M_i^T B_i^T + B_i M_i > 0, \\ & -XA_i^T - A_i X - XA_j^T - A_j X \\ & \quad + M_j^T B_i^T + B_i M_j + M_i^T B_j^T + B_j M_i \ge 0. \end{aligned} \tag{27}$$

$$X = P^{-1} \quad i < j \text{ s.t. } \mathrm{h_i} \cap h_j \neq \phi \tag{28}$$

The conditions (27) and (28) gives us a positive definite matrix X and M_i (or that there is no solution). From the solution X and M_i, a common P and the feedback gains can be found as:

$$P = X^{-1},\ F_i = M_i X^{-1} \tag{29}$$

Similarly for a discrete fuzzy system the design problem is

Find $X > 0$ and M_i , $i = 1,2,\ldots,r$

$$\begin{aligned} & X - \left(A_i X - B_i M_i\right)^T X^{-1}\left(A_i X - B_i M_i\right) > 0, \\ & X - \frac{1}{4}X\left(A_i X - B_i M_i + A_j X - B_j M_i\right)^T X^{-1} \\ & \times\left(A_i X - B_i M_j + A_j X - B_j M_i\right)X \geq 0. \end{aligned} \tag{30}$$

4.4. Decay rate

Decay rate is associated with the speed of response. The decay rate fuzzy controller design helps to find feedback gains that provide better setteling time (Tanaka et al,. 1996; 1998a; 1998b).

Continuous fuzzy system: The condition that $\dot{V}\left(x(t)\right) \leq -2\alpha V\left(x(t)\right)$ (Ichikawa et al, 1993, as cited in Tanaka & Wang, 2001) for all $x(t)$ can be written as

$$\begin{aligned} & G_{ii}^T P + P G_{ii} + 2\alpha P < 0 \\ & \left(\frac{G_{ij} + G_{ji}}{2}\right)^T P + P\left(\frac{G_{ij} + G_{ji}}{2}\right) + 2\alpha P \leq 0 \end{aligned} \tag{31}$$

Where

$$G_{ij} = A_i - B_i F_i,\ \alpha > 0 \text{ and } i < j \text{ s.t. } \mathrm{h_i} \cap h_j \neq \phi \tag{32}$$

Therefore, by solving the following generalized eigenvalue minimization problem in X, the largest lower bound on the decay rate that can be found by using a quadratic Lyapunov function:

maximize α subject to

$$\begin{aligned} & X > 0, \\ & -XA_i^T + A_i X + M_i^T B_i^T + B_i M_i - 2\alpha X > 0, \\ & -XA_i^T - A_i X - XA_j^T - A_j X + M_j^T B_j^T + B_i M_j \\ & \qquad + M_i^T B_j^T + B_j M_i - 4\alpha X > 0, \end{aligned} \tag{33}$$

$$i < j \text{ s.t. } h_i \cap h_j \neq \varphi, \text{ where } X = P^{-1},\quad M_i = F_i X. \tag{34}$$

Similarly for a discrete fuzzy system:

The condition that $\Delta V(x(t)) \leq (\alpha^2 - 1)V(x(t))$ (Ichikawa et al, 1993, as cited in Tanaka & Wang, 2001) for all $x(t)$ can be written as

$$G_{ii}^T P G_{ii} - \alpha^2 P < 0,$$
$$\left(\frac{G_{ij}+G_{ji}}{2}\right)^T P \left(\frac{G_{ij}+G_{ji}}{2}\right) - \alpha^2 P \leq 0 \tag{35}$$

$$i < j \text{ s.t. } \mathrm{h_i} \cap h_j \neq \phi \text{ and } \alpha < 1 \tag{36}$$

The generalized eigenvalue minimization can be found in (Tanaka & Wang, 2001).

4.5. Constraint on control

Theorem 5: Assume that the initial condition x(0) is known. The constraint $\|u(t)\|_2 \leq \mu$ is satisfied at all times $t \geq 0$ if the LMIs

$$\begin{bmatrix} 1 & x(0)^T \\ x(0) & X \end{bmatrix} \geq 0$$
$$\begin{bmatrix} X & M_i^T \\ M_i & \mu^2 I \end{bmatrix} \geq 0 \tag{37}$$

Hold, where $X = P^{-1}$ and $M_i = F_i X$.

The above LMI design conditions depend on the initial states. Thus, if the initial states $x(0)$ change, this means that the feedback gains Fi must be again determined. To overcome this disadvantage, modified LMI constraints on the control input have been developed, where $x(0)$ is unknown but the upper bound ϕ of $\|x(t)\|$ is known, i.e., $\|x(t)\| \leq \phi$.

Theorem 6: Assume that $\|x(t)\| \leq \phi$, where x(0) is unknown but the upper bound φ is known. Then,

$$x^T(0) X^{-1} x(0) \leq 1 \text{ if } \phi^2 I \leq X, \tag{38}$$

Where $X = P^{-1}$

Proofs of theorem 1 and 2 are given in (Tanaka & Wang, 2001)

4.6. Performance-oriented parallel distributed compensation

In the modified PDC proposed in (Seidi & Markazi, 2011), unlike the conventional PDC, state feedback gains associated with every linear subsystem, are not assumed fixed. Instead, based on some pre-specified performance criteria, several feedback gains are designed and used for every subsystem. The overall gain associated with each of the subsystems, is then determined by a fuzzy blending of such gains, so that a better closed-loop performance can be achieved. The required membership functions are chosen based on some pre-specified performance indices, for example, a faster response or a smaller control input. In general, the rest of the method for calculating the overall state feedback gain remains similar to the conventional PDC method, as in (14) and (15). Figure 4, depicts the general framework for the proposed method, through which and depending on various performance criteria, different characteristics for the controller can be specified. For example, two different feedback gains could be designed for a typical subsystem; one providing a lower control input with a longer settling time response, and the other a faster response but with a larger control input. The idea is then to select the overall feedback gain for this subsystem as a weighted sum of such gains, where the weights are appropriately adjusted, in a fuzzy sense, during the time evolution of the system response, so that as a whole, a faster response with a lower control input can be achieved. For this purpose, when the magnitude of the control input becomes large, the relative weight of the first feedback gain is increased, so that the magnitude of the control input is kept within the permissible limits. On the other hand, when the control input is well below the permissible limit, the weight of the second feedback gain is increased, for a faster response. The dynamics of the resulting closed-loop control system can be analyzed as follows:

Consider the following Takagi–Sugeno model of the plant

$$\dot{x} = \sum_{i=1}^{r} h_1(z)\{A_i x(t) + B_i u(t)\} \tag{39}$$

The following structure is proposed for the fuzzy controller rules

$$\begin{aligned} &\text{i th rule: If } Z_1(t) \text{ is } M_{i1} \text{ and } Z_2(t) \text{ is } M_{i2}, \ldots\ldots, Z_p(t) \text{ is } M_{ip}, J(t) \text{ is } H_{i1}, \ldots \text{and } J(t) \text{ is } H_{iq} \\ &\text{then } u_i(t) = \left\{ \sum_{n=1}^{q} m_{in}(J(t)) K_{in} \right\} x(t) \end{aligned} \tag{40}$$

Where $i = 1,2,\ldots,r$, q_i is the number of gain coefficients in the ith subsystem, m_{in} is the relevant membership degree for J(t), K_{in} is the nth state feedback gain associated with the ith subsystem, H_{iq} is the n th membership function for J(t), defined in the ith rule. Here $J(t)$ is a term depicting a selected performance index, for instance, if one wants to limit the magnitude of the control signal $u\ (t)$, then $J(t) \equiv |u(t)|$. Where the control input generated by the PDC controller is in the form of

$$\begin{aligned} u(t) &= \sum_{i=1}^{r} h_i(z) u_i(t) = -\left\{ \sum_{n=1}^{r} h_i(z) K_i \right\} x(t) \\ K_i &= \sum_{n=1}^{q} m_{in}(J(t)) K_{in} \end{aligned} \tag{41}$$

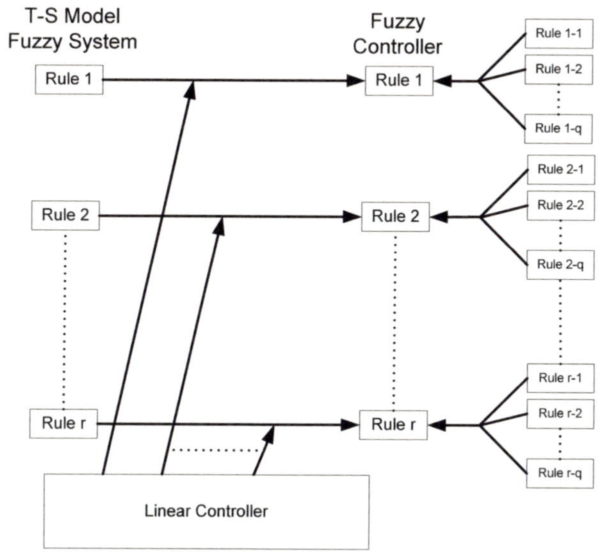

Figure 4. General methodology in the proposed PDC method

Lemma: The fuzzy control system (39), with the control strategy (41) is globally, asymptotically stable, if there exists a common positive definite matrix P such that

$$
\begin{gathered}
G_{iin}^{\ \ T} P + P G_{iin} < 0 \\
\left(\frac{G_{ijn} + G_{jin}}{2} \right)^T P + P \left(\frac{G_{ijn} + G_{jin}}{2} \right) \leq 0
\end{gathered} \tag{42}
$$

where $i < j, \quad h_i \cap h_j \neq \phi, \ G_{ijn} = A_i - B_i K_{jn}$.

Example 2

Consider a single link robot with flexible joint as in Figure 5. This benchmark problem is introduced in (Spong et al., 1987).

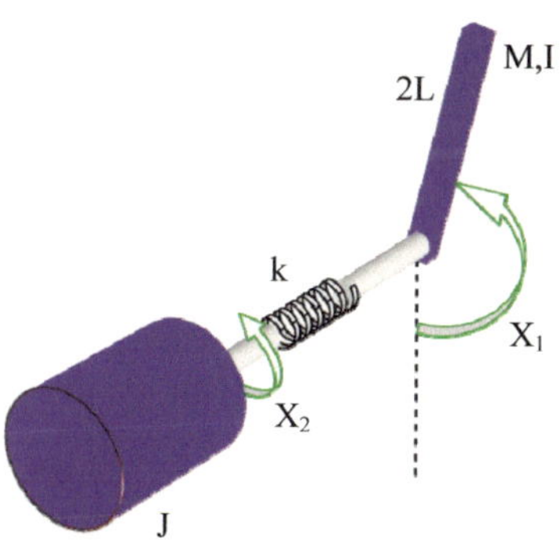

Figure 5. A single link robot with a flexible joint

The state space equations for the system of Figure 4 are

$$\begin{cases} \dot{x}_1 = x_3(t) \\ \dot{x}_2 = x_4(t) \\ \dot{x}_3 = \frac{1}{I}\left(k(x_2(t) - x_1(t)) - mgLsin\left(x_1(t)\right)\right) \\ \dot{x}_4 = \frac{1}{J}\left(u(t) - k(x_2(t) - x_1(t))\right) \end{cases} \tag{43}$$

In order to apply the PDC methodology, the fuzzy Takagi-Sugeno Model is developed first (Seidi & Markazi, 2008). The nonlinear expression $Z = sin\left(x_1(t)\right)$, for $x_1(t) \in [-pi, pi]$, can be expressed as

$$z = \sin\left(x_1(t)\right) = \left(\sum_{i=1}^{2} M_i(z) b_i\right) x_1(t) \tag{44}$$

Where, $b_1 = 1, b_2 = 0$ and, hence, the membership functions for z are obtained as

$$\begin{aligned} M_1(z) &= \begin{cases} \frac{z}{Sin^{-1}z}, & z(t) \neq 0 \\ 1, & \text{Otherwise} \end{cases} \\ M_2(z) &= \begin{cases} \frac{Sin^{-1}z - z}{Sin^{-1}z}, & z(t) \neq 0 \\ 1, & \text{Otherwise} \end{cases} \end{aligned} \tag{45}$$

The resulting fuzzy model would then have the following fuzzy rules:

$$\begin{aligned} &Rule\ 1: \text{If } z(t) \text{is} M_1(z), \text{then } \dot{x}(t) = A_1 x(t) + B_1 u(t) \\ &Rule\ 1: \text{If } z(t) \text{is} M_2(z), \text{then } \dot{x}(t) = A_2 x(t) + B_2 u(t) \end{aligned} \tag{45}$$

Where,

$$A_1 = \begin{bmatrix} 0 & 0 & 1 & 0 \\ 0 & 0 & 0 & 1 \\ \frac{-k - mgLb_1}{I} & \frac{k}{I} & 0 & 0 \\ \frac{k}{J} & -\frac{k}{J} & 0 & 0 \end{bmatrix}, \ A_2 = \begin{bmatrix} 0 & 0 & 1 & 0 \\ 0 & 0 & 0 & 1 \\ \frac{-k - mgLb_2}{I} & \frac{k}{I} & 0 & 0 \\ \frac{k}{J} & -\frac{k}{J} & 0 & 0 \end{bmatrix}, \tag{46}$$

and

$$B_1 = B_2 = B = \left[0,0,0,1\right]^T. \tag{47}$$

Assume $k = 100\ Nm/rad$, $g = 9.8\ m/s^2$ and other parameters are assumed unity then we have

$$A_1 = \begin{bmatrix} 0 & 0 & 1 & 0 \\ 0 & 0 & 0 & 1 \\ -109.8 & 100 & 0 & 0 \\ 100 & -100 & 0 & 0 \end{bmatrix},\ A_2 = \begin{bmatrix} 0 & 0 & 1 & 0 \\ 0 & 0 & 0 & 1 \\ 0 & 100 & 0 & 0 \\ 100 & -100 & 0 & 0 \end{bmatrix},\ B = \begin{bmatrix} 0 \\ 0 \\ 0 \\ 1 \end{bmatrix},$$

$$\begin{aligned} &\text{Control Rule } \mathbf{1}: \\ &\text{If } z(t) \text{ is } M_1(z), \text{then } u(t) = -F_1 x(t) \\ &\text{Control Rule } 2: \\ &\text{If } z(t) \text{ is } M_2(z), \text{then } u(t) = -F_2 x(t) \end{aligned} \tag{48}$$

The final output of the controller is

$$u(t) = -\sum_{i=1}^{2} h_i F_i x(t) = h_1 F_1 x(t) + h_2 F_2 x(t) \tag{49}$$

Case 1: Stable controller design

Using conditions (27) and (28) the stable controller can be obtained by solving below conditions

$$\begin{aligned} &\mathrm{X} > 0 \\ &\left[-\mathrm{X\,A_1} - \mathrm{A_1 X} + \mathrm{M_1}^{\mathrm{T}}\mathrm{B}^{\mathrm{T}} + \mathrm{B\,M_1}\right] > 0, \\ &\left[-\mathrm{X\,A_2} - \mathrm{A_2 X} + \mathrm{M_2}^{\mathrm{T}}\mathrm{B}^{\mathrm{T}} + \mathrm{B\,M_2}\right] > 0, \\ &\left[-\mathrm{X\,A_1}^{\mathrm{T}} - \mathrm{A_1 X} - \mathrm{X\,A_2}^{\mathrm{T}} - \mathrm{A_2 X} + \mathrm{M_2}^{\mathrm{T}}\mathrm{B}^{\mathrm{T}} + \mathrm{B\,M_2} + \mathrm{M_1}^{\mathrm{T}}\mathrm{B}^{\mathrm{T}} + \mathrm{B\,M_1}\right] > 0 \end{aligned} \tag{50}$$

Using the MATLAB LMI Control Toolbox we obtain

$$\begin{aligned} &F_1 = [\text{-}495.76 \quad 668.96 \quad 14.112 \quad 47.388] \\ &F_2 = [\text{-}497.23 \quad 671.34 \quad 14.356 \quad 47.552] \\ &P = \begin{bmatrix} 42.1464 & \text{-}50.7108 & \text{-}1.5337 & \text{-}3.2007 \\ \text{-}50.7108 & 68.9721 & 2.4898 & 4.3456 \\ \text{-}1.5337 & 2.4898 & 0.2554 & 0.1719 \\ \text{-}3.2007 & 4.3456 & 0.1719 & 0.3527 \end{bmatrix} \end{aligned} \tag{51}$$

Figures 6 and 7 show the response of the system and control effort, respectively.

Case 2: The decay rate

Using conditions (31) and (32) the stable controller can be obtained by solving the conditions:

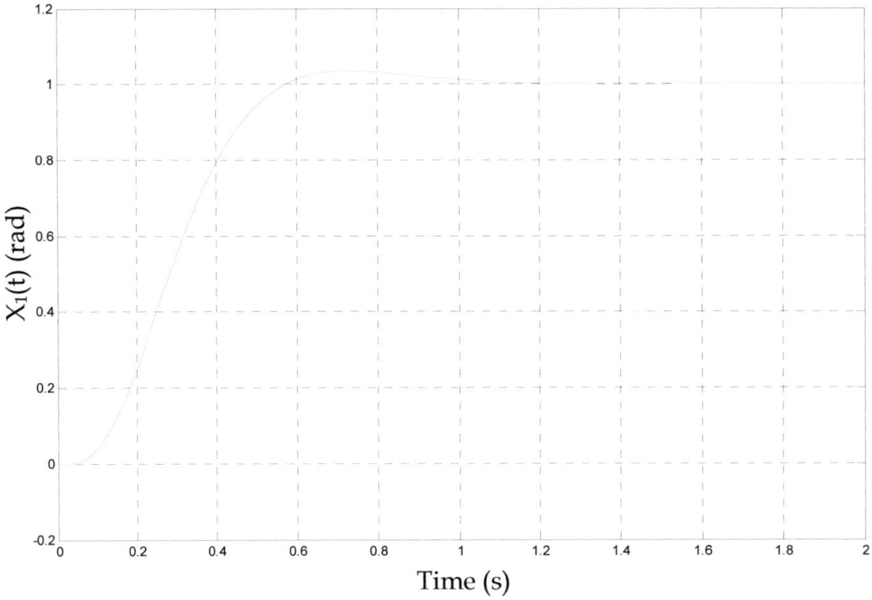

Figure 6. Response of flexible joint robots $x_1(t)$, case 1.

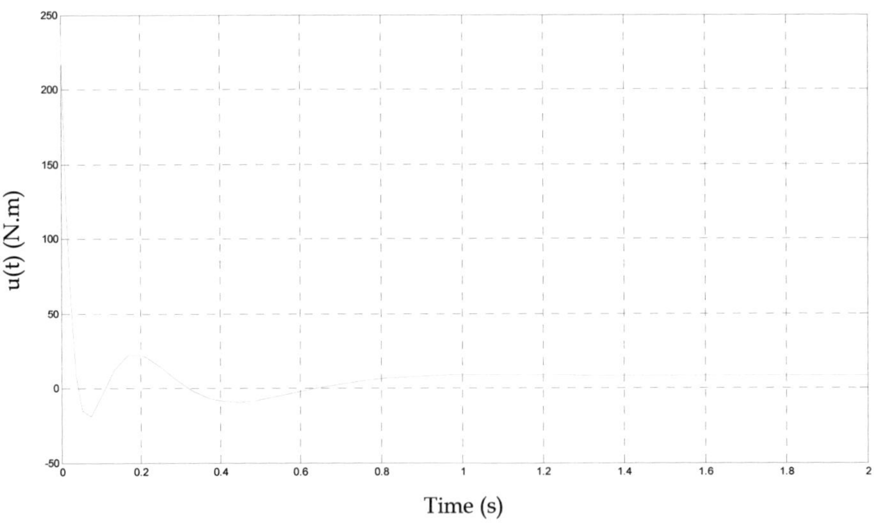

Figure 7. Control input for flexible joint robots, case 1.

$$
\begin{aligned}
&[-X A_1^T - A_1X + M_1^T B^T + B M_1 - 2\alpha X] > 0 \\
&[-X A_2^T - A_2X + M_2^T B^T + B M_2 - 2\alpha X] > 0 \\
&[-X A_1^T - A_1X - X A_2^T - A_2X + M_2^T B^T \\
&+B M_2 + M_1^T B^T + B M_1 - 4\alpha X] > 0
\end{aligned} \tag{52}
$$

Considering $\alpha = 10$ and by using the MATLAB LMI Control Toolbox we obtain:

$$
\begin{aligned}
&F_1 = [4108.8 \quad 6545.2 \quad 1271.3 \quad 127.77] \\
&F_2 = [4066.9 \quad 6502.6 \quad 1261.7 \quad 127.1] \\
&P = \begin{bmatrix} 36.5087 & 24.0140 & 6.2135 & 0.3352 \\ 24.0140 & 30.1341 & 6.3223 & 0.5013 \\ 6.2135 & 6.3223 & 1.4260 & 0.0995 \\ 0.3352 & 0.5013 & 0.0995 & 0.0099 \end{bmatrix}
\end{aligned} \tag{53}
$$

Figures 8 and 9 show the response of the system and control effort, respectively.

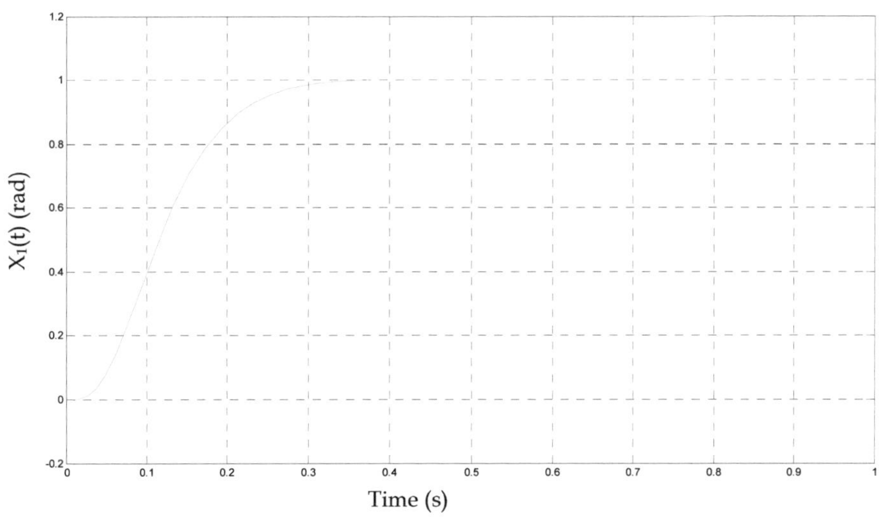

Figure 8. Response of flexible joint robots $x_1(t)$, case 2.

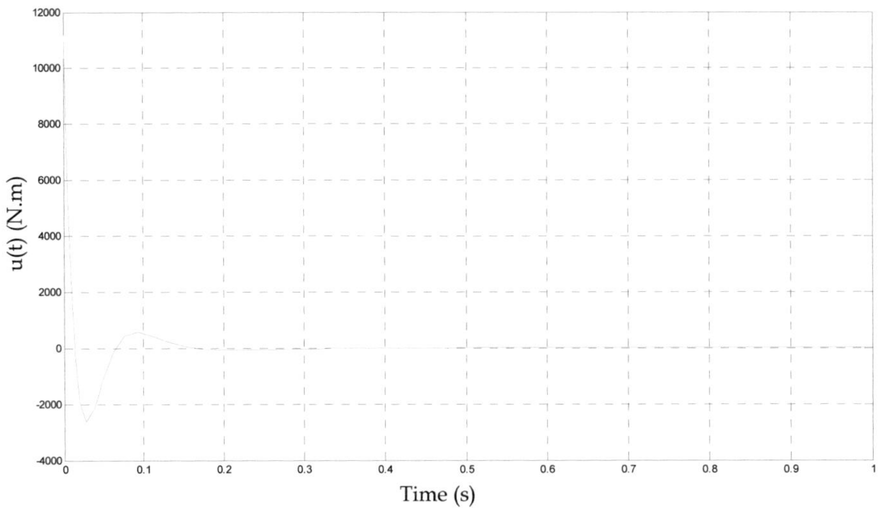

Figure 9. Control input for flexible joint robots, case 2.

Case 3: The decay rate with the constraint on the input

We design a stable fuzzy controller by considering the decay rate and the constraint on the control input. The design problem of the FJR is defined as follows:

Maximize α

$$
\begin{aligned}
& X > 0 \\
& \left[-XA_1^T - A_1X + M_1^TB^T + BM_1 - 2\alpha X\right] > 0 \\
& \left[-XA_2^T - A_2X + M_2^TB^T + BM_2 - 2\alpha X\right] > 0 \\
& \begin{bmatrix} -XA_1^T - A_1X - XA_2^T - A_2X + M_2^TB^T \\ + BM_2 + M_1^TB^T + BM_1 - 4\alpha X \end{bmatrix} > 0 \\
& \begin{bmatrix} X & M_1^T \\ M_1 & \mu^2 I \end{bmatrix} > 0 \\
& \begin{bmatrix} X & M_2^T \\ M_2 & \mu^2 I \end{bmatrix} > 0 \\
& \left[X - \phi^2 I\right] > 0
\end{aligned}
\tag{54}
$$

Where $X = P^{-1}$, $M_i = F_i X$, $\mu = 4600$, $\phi = 1$.

Using the MATLAB LMI toolbox to solve the LMI conditions (50), we can get the positive definite matrix and a set of gains (51), that make the system stable.

$$\alpha = 0.072401$$

$$P=\begin{bmatrix} 0.7301 & 0.32486 & 0.096794 & 0.0034552 \\ 0.32486 & 0.55483 & 0.10616 & 0.010209 \\ 0.096794 & 0.10616 & 0.023049 & 0.0017139 \\ 0.0034552 & 0.010209 & 0.0017139 & 0.00023565 \end{bmatrix}$$

$$F_1=[327.57 \quad 1745 \quad 261.86 \quad 57.475] \tag{55}$$

$$F_2=[356.05 \quad 1739.2 \quad 259.77 \quad 57.5]$$

Figures 10 and 11 show the response of the system and control effort, respectively.

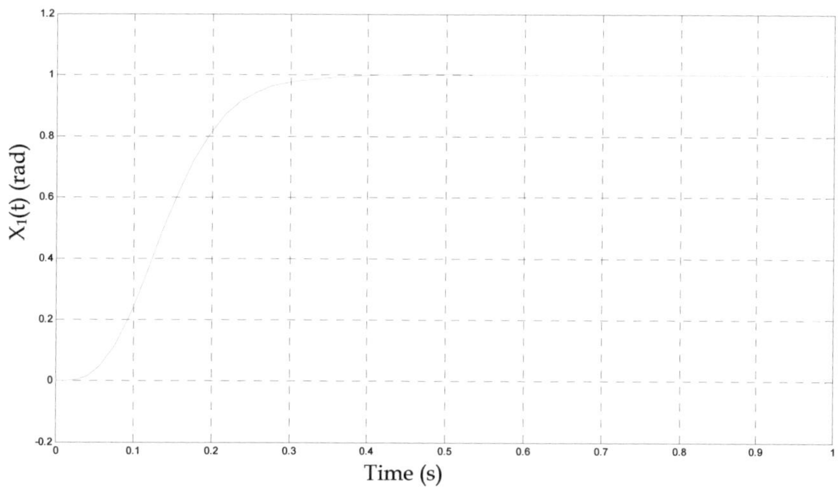

Figure 10. System responses of the single-link flexible joint, case 3.

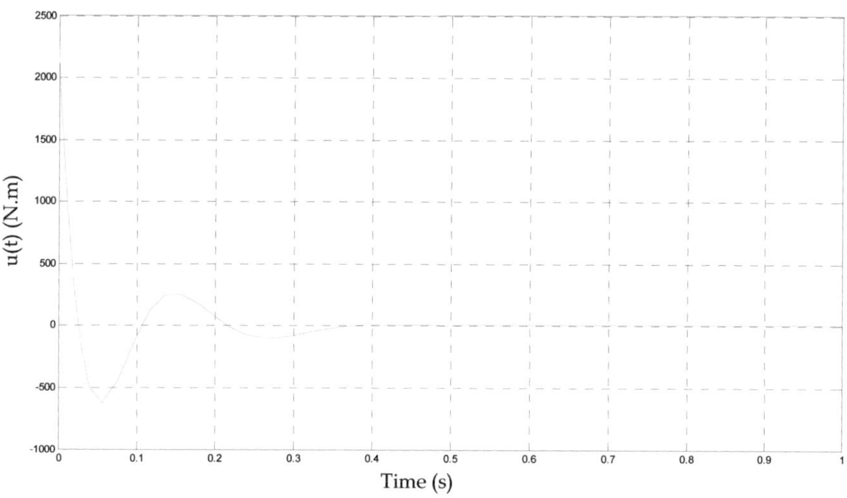

Figure 11. Control input for flexible joint robots, case 3.

Case 4: Performance-oriented parallel distributed compensation

The following stabilizing feedback gains are chosen using the pole placement method, so that K_{11} and K_{21} produce large magnitude inputs for subsystems 1 and 2, respectively, and K_{22} and K_{21} induce low magnitude inputs for those subsystems. In particular,

$$\begin{aligned} K_{11} &= \begin{bmatrix} 6667.2 & 4411.9 & 1052.4 & 92.6 \end{bmatrix} \\ K_{12} &= \begin{bmatrix} -33.321 & 1413.7 & 191.63 & 51.2 \end{bmatrix} \\ K_{21} &= \begin{bmatrix} 6658.7 & 4332.4 & 1025.4 & 91.1 \end{bmatrix} \\ K_{22} &= \begin{bmatrix} 72.3 & 1389.8 & 189.6 & 50.6 \end{bmatrix} \end{aligned} \tag{56}$$

The required simple membership functions are selected as in Figure 12, so that, with a decrease in the corresponding plant input, in subsystems 1 and 2 respectively, the overall feedback gains come closer to K_{11} and K_{21}, and with an increase in the corresponding control input respectively, the overall feedback gains come closer to K_{21} and K_{22}. Now, the fuzzy rules for the controller are constructed as follows:

Rule 1: If $z(t)$ is $M_1(z)$ and $|u(t)|$ is "small" then $u(t) = K_{11}x(t)$

Rule 2: If $z(t)$ is $M_1(z)$and $|u(t)|$ is "large" then $u(t) = K_{12}x(t)$

Rule 3: If $z(t)$ is $M_2(z)$ and $|u(t)|$ is "small" then $u(t) = K_{21}x(t)$

Rule 4: If $z(t)$ is $M_2(z)$ and $|u(t)|$ is "large" then $u(t) = K_{22}x(t)$

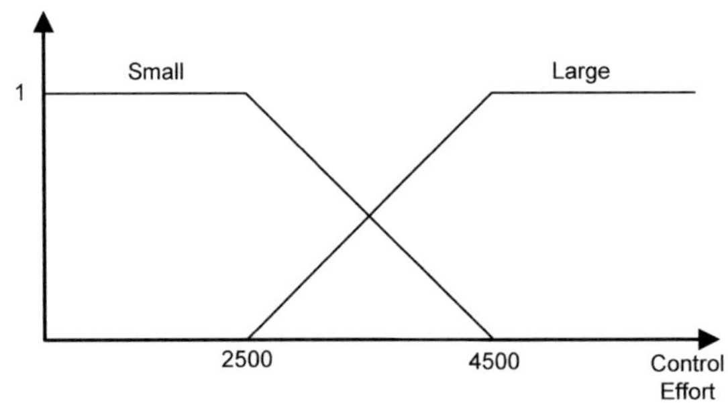

Figure 12. Membership functions for the control effort in the flexible joint robots.

A common positive definite matrix, P, satisfying the stability conditions (42) is obtained by solving the LMI problems:

$$P = 10^4 \times \begin{bmatrix} 121710 & 15858 & 2558.5 & 63.525 \\ 15858 & 8624.4 & 1458.4 & 105.36 \\ 2558.5 & 1458.4 & 702.24 & 42.529 \\ 63.525 & 105.36 & 42.529 & 5.0962 \end{bmatrix}$$

Applying a unit step reference signal for $x_1(t)$, the response history and the corresponding control input are shown in Figures (13) and (14), respectively. Simulation results are investigated for the following three controllers:

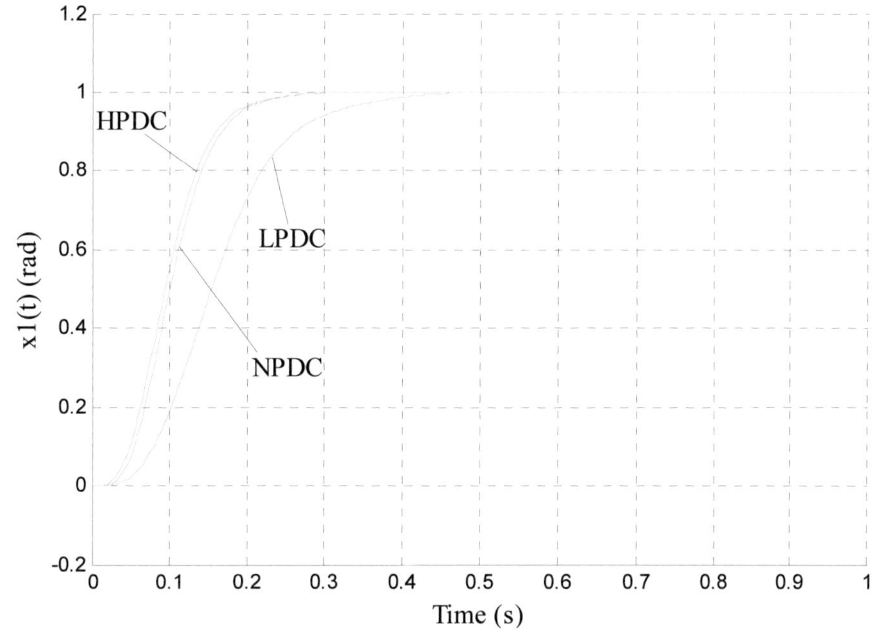

Figure 13. Response of flexible joint robot $x_1(t)$, case 4.

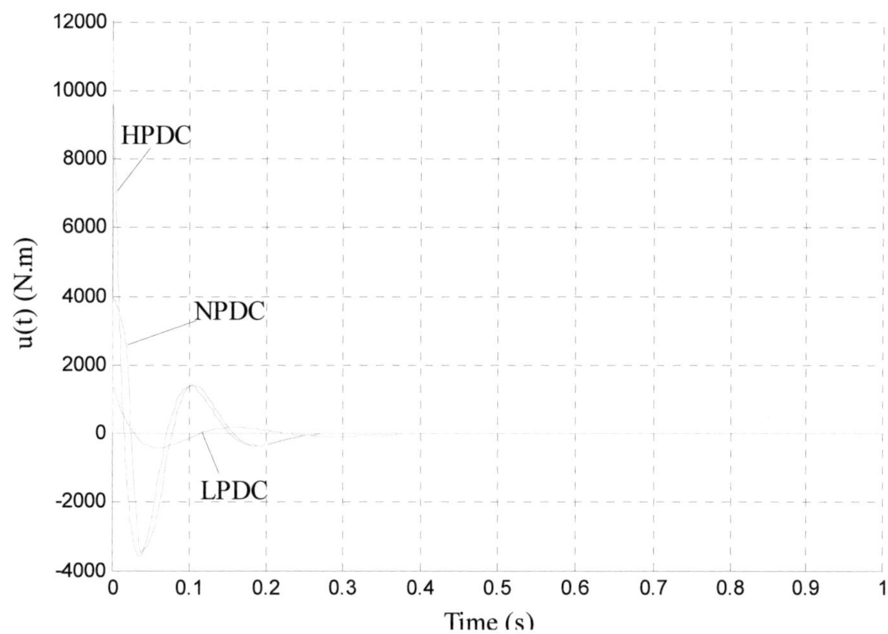

Figure 14. Control input for flexible joint robot, case 4.

1. A PDC controller with feedback gains K_{11} and K_{21} providing a high speed response, and with possible high control inputs (HPDC controller).
2. A PDC controller with feedback gains K_{22} and K_{21} providing a low speed response, and with a lower control input, as compared with the HPDC case (LPDC controller).
3. Proposed modified PDC controller, providing a fast response, yet with an acceptable level of control input (NPDC controller).

It is observed that the new controller provides a settling time similar to the HPDC case, with a much lower magnitude for the control input.

5. Conclusion

This chapter deals with approximation of the nonlinear system using Takagi-Sugeno (T-S) models with linear models as rule consequences and a construction procedure of T-S models. Also, the stability conditions and stabilizing control design of parallel distributed compensation (PDC) are discussed. It is seen that PDC a linear control method can be used to control the nonlinear system. Moreover, the stability analysis and control design problems for both continuous and discrete fuzz control systems can be transformed to linear matrix inequality (LMI) problems and they can be solved efficiently by convex programming techniques for LMIs. Design examples demonstrate the effectiveness of the LMI-based designs.

Author details

Morteza Seidi, Marzieh Hajiaghamemar and Bruce Segee
University of Maine, USA

6. References

Bonissone, P. P., Badami, V., Chaing, K.H., Khedkar, P.S., Marcelle, K. W. & Schutten, M. J. (1995). Industrial applications of fuzzy logic at general electric, *Proceedings of IEEE*, Vol. 83, No.3, (August 2002), p.p. 450-465, ISSN : 0018-9219.

Boyd, S., Ghaoui, L. E. & Feron, Eric & Balakrishnan V. (1994). *Linear Matrix Inequalities in System and Control Theory*, SIAM studies in applied mathematics, ISBN 0-89871-334X.

Chen , C. L., Chen, P. C. & Chen, C. K. (1993). Analysis and design of fuzzy control system, *Fuzzy Sets and Systems,* Vol. 57, No. 2, (July 1993) p.p. 125–140.

Ding, B. C., Sun, H. X. & Yang, P. (2006). Further study on LMI-based relaxed nonquadratic stabilization conditions for nonlinear systems in the Takagi–Sugeno's form, *Automatica,* Vol. 42, No. 3,(March 2006) p.p. 503–508.

Fang, C. H., Liu, Y. S., Kau, S. W., Hong, L. & Lee, C. H. (2006). A new LMI-based approach to relaxed quadratic stabilization of T–S fuzzy control systems, *IEEE Transactions on Fuzzy Systems*, Vol. 14, No. 3, (June 2006), p.p. 386–397, ISSN : 1063-6706.

Hong, S.K. & Langari, R. (2000). Robust fuzzy control of a magnetic bearing system subject to harmonic disturbances, *IEEE Transactions on Control System Technology*, Vol. 8, No. 2, (August 2002), p.p. 366–371, ISSN : 1063-6536.

Ichikawa, A. et al. (1993). *Control Hand Book*, Ohmu Publisher, Tokyo, in Japanese.

Joh, J., Langari, R., Jeung, E. & Chiuig, W. (1997). A new design method for continuous Takagi–Sugeno fuzzy controller with pole-placement constraints: an LMI approach, *Proceedings of IEEE International Conference on Systems, Man, and Cybernetics*, Vol. 3, p.p. 2969–2974, ISBN: 0-7803-4053-1, Orlando, Florida, USA, October 12-15, 1997.

Kawamoto, S., Tada, K., Ishigame A. & Taniguchi, T. (1992). An Approach to Stability Analysis of Second Order Fuzzy Systems, *Proceedings of First IEEE International Conference on Fuzzy Systems*, Vol. 1, pp. 1427-1434, ISBN: 0-7803-0236-2, San Diego, California, USA, March 8-12, 1992.

Kim, E., Lee, H. (2000). New approaches to relaxed quadratic stability conditions of fuzzy control systems, *IEEE Transactions on Fuzzy Systems*, Vol. 8, No. 5, p.p. 523– 534, (August 2002), ISSN : 1063-6706.

Li, J., Niemann, D. & Wang, H. O. (1998).Robust tracking for high-rise/high-speed elevators, *Proceedings of American Control Conference*,Vol.6, p.p. 3445-3449, ISBN: 0-7803-4530-4, Philadelphia, Pennsylvania, USA, June 24-26, 1998.

Lee, H.J., Park, J.B. & Joo, Y.H. (2006). Robust load–frequency control for uncertain nonlinear power systems: a fuzzy logic approach, *Information Sciences*, Vol. 176, No.23, (December 2006), p.p. 3520–3537.

Lee, K.R., Jeung, E.T. & Park, H.B. (2001). Robust fuzzy H_∞ control for uncertain nonlinear systems via state feedback: an LMI approach, *International Journal of Fuzzy Sets and Systems*, Vol. 120, No.1 (May 2001) p.p. 123–134.

Lin, Y.C., & Lo, J.C. (2003). Robust H_2 fuzzy control via dynamic output feedback for discrete-time systems, *Proceedings of IEEE International Conference on Fuzzy Systems*, Vol. 2, p.p. 1384–1388, ISBN: 0-7803-7810-5, May 25-28,2003.

Kang, G. & Lee, W. (1998). Design of TSK fuzzy controller based on TSK fuzzy model using pole-placement, *Proceedings of IEEE International Conference on Fuzzy Systems*, Vol. 1, p.p. 246–251, ISSN : 1098-7584, Anchorage, Alaska, USA, May 4-9, 1998.

Rhee, B. J. & Won, S. (2006). A new Lyapunov function approach for a Takagi–Sugeno fuzzy control system design. *Journal of Fuzzy Sets System*, Vol. 157, No. 9, (May 2006), p.p. 1211–1228.

Seidi, M. & Markazi, A. H. D. (2008). Model-Based Fuzzy Control of Flexible Joint Manipulator: A LMI Approach, *Proceedings of the 5th International IEEE Symposium on Mechatronics and its Applications*, ISBN: 978-1-4244-2033-9, Amman, Jordan, May 27-29, 2008.

Seidi M. & Markazi, A. H. D. (2011). Performance-oriented parallel distributed compensation ,Vol. 348, No. 7, (September 2011), pp. 1231–1244.

Spong, M. W., Khorasani, K. & Kokotovic, P. V. (1987). " An integral manifold approach to the feedback control of flexible joint robots", *IEEE Journal of Robotics and Automation*, Vol.3, No.4, (January 2003), p.p. 291-300, ISSN : 0882-4967,.

Sugeno, M. & Kang , G. T. (1986). Fuzzy Modeling and Control of Multilayer Incinerator, *Journal of Fuzzy Sets Systems*, Vol. 18, No. 3, (April 1986), p.p. 329-345.

Takagi, T., & Sugeno, M. (1985). Fuzzy identification of systems and its applications to modeling and control, *IEEE Transactions on Systems Man and Cybernetics*, Vol. 15, NO.1, (February 1985), p.p.116–132.

Tanaka, K. & Sugeno, M. (1990). Stability Analysis of Fuzzy Systems Using Lyapunov's Direct Method, *Proceedings of the North America Fuzzy Information Processing Society NAFIPS'90*, Vol. 1, pp. 133-136, Toronto, Canada, June 1990.

Tanaka, K. & Sugeno M. (1992). Stability analysis and design of fuzzy control systems, *Journal of Fuzzy Sets and Systems*, Vol.45, No.2, (January 1992), p.p.135–156.

Tanaka, K. & Sano M. (1994). A robust stabilization problem of fuzzy control systems and its applications to backing up control of a truck trailer, *IEEE Transactions on Fuzzy Systems,* Vol. 2, No. 5, (August 2002), p.p. 119-134, ISSN : 1063-6706.

Tanaka, K., Ikeda, T. & Wang, H. O. (1996). Design of fuzzy control systems based on relaxed LMI stability conditions, *Proceedings of 35th IEEE Conference on Decision and Control*, Vol. 1, , pp. 598-603, ISBN: 0-7803-3590-2, Kobe, Japan, December 11-13 1996.

Tanaka, K. & Kosaki, T. (1997). Design of a Stable Fuzzy Controller for an Articulated Vehicle, *IEEE Transactions Systems, Man and Cybernetics*, Vol. 27, No. 3, (August 2002), p.p. 552 – 558, ISSN : 1083-4419.

Tanaka, K., Ikeda, T. & Wang, H. O. (1998). Fuzzy regulator and fuzzy observer: Relaxed stability conditions and LMI-based designs, *IEEE Transactions on Fuzzy Systems,* Vol. 6, No. 2, (August 2002), p.p. 250–265, ISSN : 1063-6706.

Tanaka, K., Taniguchi, T. & Wang, H. O. (1998a). Model-Based Fuzzy Control of TORA System: Fuzzy Regulator and Fuzzy Observer Design via LMIs that Represent Decay Rate, Disturbance Rejection, Robustness, Optimality, *Proceedings of Seventh IEEE International Conference on Fuzzy Systems*, pp. 313-318, Alaska, USA, May 4-9 1998.

Tanaka, K., Ikeda, T., & Wang, H. O. (1998b). Fuzzy Regulators and Fuzzy Observers: relaxed stability conditions and LMI-based designs, *IEEE Transactions on Fuzzy Systems,* Vol. 6, No. 2, (August 2002), pp. 250-265, ISSN : 1063-6706.

Tanaka, K. &Wang, H.O. (2001). Fuzzy Control Systems Design and Analysis: A Linear Matrix Inequality Approach, 1st Edition, Wiley.

Tanaka, K., Hori, T. & Wang, H. O. (2003). A multiple Lyapunov function approach to stabilization of fuzzy control systems, *IEEE Transactions on Fuzzy Systems*, Vol. 11, No. 4, (August 2003), p.p. 582–589, ISSN : 1063-6706.

Ting, C.S. (2006). Stability analysis and design of Takagi–Sugeno fuzzy systems, *Journal of Information Sciences,* Vol. 176, No.19, (October 2006), p.p. 2817-2845.

Wang, H. O., Tanaka, K. & Griffin, M. F. (1995) "Parallel Distributed Compensation of Nonlinear Systems by Takagi-Sugeno Fuzzy Model, *Proceedings of International Joint Conference of the Fourth IEEE International Conference on Fuzzy Systems and The Second International Fuzzy Engineering Symposium*, p.p. 531-538, ISBN: 0-7803-2461-7, Yokohama, Japan, March 20-24, 1995.

Wang, H. O., Tanaka, K. & Griffin M. F. (1996). An approach to fuzzy control of nonlinear systems: Stability and the design issues. *IEEE Transactions on Fuzzy Systems,* Vol. 4, No. 1, (August 2002), p.p. 14–23, ISSN : 1063-6706.

Wang, L. X., & Mendel, J. M. (1992). Fuzzy basis functions, universal approximation, and orthogonal least-squares learning, *IEEE Transactions on Neural Networks,* Vol. 3, No. 5, (August 2002), p.p. 807–814, ISSN : 1045-9227.

Zhao, J., Wertz, V. & Gorez, R. (1996). Fuzzy gain scheduling controllers based on fuzzy models, *Proceedings of The 5th IEEE International Conference on Fuzzy Systems*, Vol. 3, No. 8, p.p. 1670–1676, ISBN: 0-7803-3645-3, New Orleans, Louisiana, USA, September 8-11, 1996.

Chapter 19

New Results on Robust $\mathcal{H}_\infty$ Filter for Uncertain Fuzzy Descriptor Systems

Wudhichai Assawinchaichote*

Additional information is available at the end of the chapter

http://dx.doi.org/10.5772/47142

1. Introduction

The problem of filter design for descriptor systems system has been intensively studied by a number of researchers for the past three decades; see Ref.[1]-[6]. This is due not only to theoretical interest but also to the relevance of this topic in control engineering applications. Descriptor systems or so called singularly perturbed systems are dynamical systems with multiple time-scales. Descriptor systems often occur naturally due to the presence of small "parasitic" parameter, typically small time constants, masses, etc.

The main purpose of the singular perturbation approach to analysis and design is the alleviation of high dimensionality and ill-conditioning resulting from the interaction of slow and fast dynamics modes. The separation of states into slow and fast ones is a nontrivial modelling task demanding insight and ingenuity on the part of the analyst. In state space, such systems are commonly modelled using the mathematical framework of singular perturbations, with a small parameter, say ε, determining the degree of separation between the "slow" and "fast" modes of the system.

In the last few years, many researchers have studied the $\mathcal{H}_\infty$ filter design for a general class of linear descriptor systems. In Ref.[3], the authors have investigated the decomposition solution of $\mathcal{H}_\infty$ filter gain for singularly perturbed systems. The reduced-order $\mathcal{H}_\infty$ optimal filtering for system with slow and fast modes has been considered in Ref.[4]. Although many researchers have studied linear descriptor systems for many years, the $\mathcal{H}_\infty$ filtering design for nonlinear descriptor systems remains as an open research area. This is because, in general, nonlinear singularly perturbed systems can not be easily separated into slow and fast subsystems.

Fuzzy system theory enables us to utilize qualitative, linguistic information about a highly complex nonlinear system to construct a mathematical model for it. Recent studies show

*W. Assawinchaichote is with the Department of Electronic and Telecommnunication Engineering, King Mongkut's University of Technology Thonburi, 126 Prachautits Rd., Bangkok 10140, Thailand.

that a fuzzy linear model can be used to approximate global behaviors of a highly complex nonlinear system; see for example, Ref.[7]-[19]. In this fuzzy linear model, local dynamics in different state space regions are represented by local linear systems. The overall model of the system is obtained by "blending" these linear models through nonlinear fuzzy membership functions. Unlike conventional modelling where a single model is used to describe the global behaviour of a system, the fuzzy modelling is essentially a multi-model approach in which simple sub-models (linear models) are combined to describe the global behaviour of the system.

What we intend to do in this paper is to design a robust $\mathcal{H}_\infty$ filter for a class of nonlinear descriptor systems with nonlinear on both fast and slow variables. First, we approximate this class of nonlinear descriptor systems by a Takagi-Sugeno fuzzy model. Then based on an LMI approach, we develop an $\mathcal{H}_\infty$ filter such that the $\mathcal{L}_2$-gain from an exogenous input to an estimate error is less or equal to a prescribed value. To alleviate the ill-conditioning resulting from the interaction of slow and fast dynamic modes, solutions to the problem are given in terms of linear matrix inequalities which are independent of the singular perturbation ε, when ε is sufficiently small. The proposed approach does not involve the separation of states into slow and fast ones and it can be applied not only to standard, but also to nonstandard nonlinear descriptor systems.

This paper is organized as follows. In Section 2, system descriptions and definitions are presented. In Section 3, based on an LMI approach, we develop a technique for designing a robust $\mathcal{H}_\infty$ filter for the system described in section 2. The validity of this approach is demonstrated by an example from a literature in Section 4. Finally in Section 5, conclusions are given.

2. System descriptions

In this section, we generalize the TS fuzzy system to represent a TS fuzzy descriptor system with parametric uncertainties. As in Ref.[19], we examine a TS fuzzy descriptor system with parametric uncertainties as follows:

$$\begin{aligned} E_\varepsilon \dot{x}(t) &= \textstyle\sum_{i=1}^{r} \mu_i(\nu(t)) \Big[[A_i + \Delta A_i] x(t) + [B_{1_i} + \Delta B_{1_i}] w(t) + [B_{2_i} + \Delta B_{2_i}] u(t) \Big] \\ z(t) &= \textstyle\sum_{i=1}^{r} \mu_i(\nu(t)) \Big[[C_{1_i} + \Delta C_{1_i}] x(t) + [D_{12_i} + \Delta D_{12_i}] u(t) \Big] \\ y(t) &= \textstyle\sum_{i=1}^{r} \mu_i(\nu(t)) \Big[[C_{2_i} + \Delta C_{2_i}] x(t) + [D_{21_i} + \Delta D_{21_i}] w(t) \Big] \end{aligned} \tag{1}$$

where $E_\varepsilon = \begin{bmatrix} I & 0 \\ 0 & \varepsilon I \end{bmatrix}$, $\varepsilon > 0$ is the singular perturbation parameter, $\nu(t) = [\nu_1(t) \ \cdots \ \nu_\vartheta(t)]$ is the premise variable vector that may depend on states in many cases, $\mu_i(\nu(t))$ denotes the normalized time-varying fuzzy weighting functions for each rule (i.e., $\mu_i(\nu(t)) \geq 0$ and $\sum_{i=1}^{r} \mu_i(\nu(t)) = 1$), ϑ is the number of fuzzy sets, $x(t) \in \Re^n$ is the state vector, $u(t) \in \Re^m$ is the input, $w(t) \in \Re^p$ is the disturbance which belongs to $\mathcal{L}_2[0, \infty)$, $y(t) \in \Re^\ell$ is the measurement and $z(t) \in \Re^s$ is the controlled output, the matrices $A_i, B_{1_i}, B_{2_i}, C_{1_i}, C_{2_i}, D_{12_i}$ and D_{21_i} are of appropriate dimensions, and the matrices ΔA_i, ΔB_{1_i}, ΔB_{2_i}, ΔC_{1_i}, ΔC_{2_i}, ΔD_{12_i} and ΔD_{21_i} represent the uncertainties in the system and satisfy the following assumption.

Assumption 1.

$$\Delta A_i = F(x(t),t)H_{1_i},\ \ \Delta B_{1_i} = F(x(t),t)H_{2_i},\ \ \Delta B_{2_i} = F(x(t),t)H_{3_i},$$
$$\Delta C_{1_i} = F(x(t),t)H_{4_i},\ \ \Delta C_{2_i} = F(x(t),t)H_{5_i},\ \ \Delta D_{12_i} = F(x(t),t)H_{6_i}$$
$$and\ \ \Delta D_{21_i} = F(x(t),t)H_{7_i}$$

where H_{j_i}, $j = 1,2,\cdots,7$ are known matrix functions which characterize the structure of the uncertainties. Furthermore, the following inequality holds:

$$\|F(x(t),t)\| \leq \rho \tag{2}$$

for any known positive constant ρ.

Next, let us recall the following definition.

Definition 1. *Suppose γ is a given positive number. A system (1) is said to have an $\mathcal{L}_2$-gain less than or equal to γ if*

$$\int_0^{T_f} \Big(z(t) - \hat{z}(t)\Big)^T \Big(z(t) - \hat{z}(t)\Big)dt \leq \gamma^2 \left[\int_0^{T_f} w^T(t)w(t)dt\right] \tag{3}$$

with $x(0) = 0$, where $(z(t) - \hat{z}(t))$ is the estimated error output, for all $T_f \geq 0$ and $w(t) \in \mathcal{L}_2[0,T_f]$.

3. Robust $\mathcal{H}_\infty$ fuzzy filter design

Without loss of generality, in this section, we assume that $u(t) = 0$. Let us recall the system (1) with $u(t) = 0$ as follows:

$$\begin{aligned} E_\varepsilon \dot{x}(t) &= \textstyle\sum_{i=1}^r \mu_i\Big[[A_i + \Delta A_i]x(t) + [B_{1_i} + \Delta B_{1_i}]w(t)\Big] \\ z(t) &= \textstyle\sum_{i=1}^r \mu_i\Big[[C_{1_i} + \Delta C_{1_i}]x(t)\Big] \\ y(t) &= \textstyle\sum_{i=1}^r \mu_i\Big[[C_{2_i} + \Delta C_{2_i}]x(t) + [D_{21_i} + \Delta D_{21_i}]w(t)\Big]. \end{aligned} \tag{4}$$

We are now aiming to design a full order dynamic $\mathcal{H}_\infty$ fuzzy filter of the form

$$\begin{aligned} E_\varepsilon \dot{\hat{x}}(t) &= \textstyle\sum_{i=1}^r \sum_{j=1}^r \hat{\mu}_i\hat{\mu}_j\Big[\hat{A}_{ij}(\varepsilon)\hat{x}(t) + \hat{B}_i y(t)\Big] \\ \hat{z}(t) &= \textstyle\sum_{i=1}^r \hat{\mu}_i \hat{C}_i \hat{x}(t) \end{aligned} \tag{5}$$

where $\hat{x}(t) \in \Re^n$ is the filter's state vector, $\hat{z} \in \Re^s$ is the estimate of $z(t)$, $\hat{A}_{ij}(\varepsilon)$, $\hat{B}_i$ and $\hat{C}_i$ are parameters of the filter which are to be determined, and $\hat{\mu}_i$ denotes the normalized time-varying fuzzy weighting functions for each rule (i.e., $\hat{\mu}_i \geq 0$ and $\sum_{i=1}^r \hat{\mu}_i = 1$), such that the inequality (3) holds. Clearly, in real control problems, all of the premise variables are not necessarily measurable. In this section, we then consider the designing of the robust $\mathcal{H}_\infty$ fuzzy filter into two cases as follows.

3.1. Case I–$\nu(t)$ is available for feedback

The premise variable of the fuzzy model $\nu(t)$ is available for feedback which implies that μ_i is available for feedback. Thus, we can select our filter that depends on μ_i as follows:

$$\begin{aligned} E_\varepsilon \dot{\hat{x}}(t) &= \sum_{i=1}^r \sum_{j=1}^r \mu_i \mu_j \left[\hat{A}_{ij}(\varepsilon)\hat{x}(t) + \hat{B}_i y(t) \right] \\ \hat{z}(t) &= \sum_{i=1}^r \mu_i \hat{C}_i \hat{x}(t). \end{aligned} \tag{6}$$

Before presenting our next results, the following lemma is recalled.

Lemma 1. *Consider the system (4). Given a prescribed $\mathcal{H}_\infty$ performance $\gamma > 0$ and a positive constant δ, if there exist matrices $X_\varepsilon = X_\varepsilon^T$, $Y_\varepsilon = Y_\varepsilon^T$, $\mathcal{B}_i(\varepsilon)$ and $\mathcal{C}_i(\varepsilon)$, $i = 1, 2, \cdots, r$, satisfying the following ε-dependent linear matrix inequalities:*

$$\begin{bmatrix} X_\varepsilon & I \\ I & Y_\varepsilon \end{bmatrix} > 0 \tag{7}$$

$$X_\varepsilon > 0 \tag{8}$$

$$Y_\varepsilon > 0 \tag{9}$$

$$\Psi_{11_{ii}}(\varepsilon) < 0, \quad i = 1, 2, \cdots, r \tag{10}$$

$$\Psi_{22_{ii}}(\varepsilon) < 0, \quad i = 1, 2, \cdots, r \tag{11}$$

$$\Psi_{11_{ij}}(\varepsilon) + \Psi_{11_{ji}}(\varepsilon) < 0, \quad i < j \le r \tag{12}$$

$$\Psi_{22_{ij}}(\varepsilon) + \Psi_{22_{ji}}(\varepsilon) < 0, \quad i < j \le r \tag{13}$$

where

$$\Psi_{11_{ij}}(\varepsilon) = \begin{pmatrix} \left(E_\varepsilon^{-1} A_i Y_\varepsilon + Y_\varepsilon A_i^T E_\varepsilon^{-1} + \gamma^{-2} E_\varepsilon^{-1} \tilde{B}_{1_i} \tilde{B}_{1_j}^T E_\varepsilon^{-1}\right. & (*)^T \\ \left[Y_\varepsilon \tilde{C}_{1_i}^T + E_\varepsilon^{-1} \mathcal{C}_i^T(\varepsilon) \tilde{D}_{12}^T\right]^T & -I \end{pmatrix} \tag{14}$$

$$\Psi_{22_{ij}}(\varepsilon) = \begin{pmatrix} A_i^T E_\varepsilon^{-1} X_\varepsilon + X_\varepsilon E_\varepsilon^{-1} A_i + \mathcal{B}_i(\varepsilon) C_{2_j} + C_{2_i}^T \mathcal{B}_j^T(\varepsilon) + \tilde{C}_{1_i}^T \tilde{C}_{1_j} & (*)^T \\ \left[X_\varepsilon E_\varepsilon^{-1} \tilde{B}_{1_i} + \mathcal{B}_i(\varepsilon) \tilde{D}_{21_j}\right]^T & -\gamma^2 I \end{pmatrix} \tag{15}$$

with

$$\tilde{B}_{1_i} = \left[\delta I \ I \ 0 \ B_{1_i} \ 0\right],$$

$$\tilde{C}_{1_i} = \left[\tfrac{\gamma\rho}{\delta} H_{1_i}^T \ \tfrac{\gamma\rho}{\delta} H_{5_i}^T \ \sqrt{2}\lambda\rho H_{4_i}^T \ \sqrt{2}\lambda C_{1_i}^T\right]^T,$$

$$\tilde{D}_{12} = \left[0 \ 0 \ 0 \ -\sqrt{2}\lambda I\right]^T,$$

$$\tilde{D}_{21_i} = \left[0 \ 0 \ \delta I \ D_{21_i} \ I\right]$$

$$\text{and } \lambda = \left(1 + \rho^2 \sum_{i=1}^r \sum_{j=1}^r \left[\|H_{2_i}^T H_{2_j}\| + \|H_{7_i}^T H_{7_j}\|\right]\right)^{\frac{1}{2}},$$

then the prescribed $\mathcal{H}_\infty$ performance $\gamma > 0$ is guaranteed. Furthermore, a suitable filter is of the form (6) with

$$\begin{aligned} \hat{A}_{ij}(\varepsilon) &= E_\varepsilon \left[Y_\varepsilon^{-1} - X_\varepsilon\right]^{-1} \mathcal{M}_{ij}(\varepsilon) Y_\varepsilon^{-1} \\ \hat{B}_i &= E_\varepsilon \left[Y_\varepsilon^{-1} - X_\varepsilon\right]^{-1} \mathcal{B}_i(\varepsilon) \\ \hat{C}_i &= \mathcal{C}_i(\varepsilon) E_\varepsilon^{-1} Y_\varepsilon^{-1} \end{aligned} \tag{16}$$

where

$$\mathcal{M}_{ij}(\varepsilon) = -A_i^T E_\varepsilon^{-1} - X_\varepsilon E_\varepsilon^{-1} A_i Y_\varepsilon - \left[Y_\varepsilon^{-1} - X_\varepsilon\right] E_\varepsilon^{-1} \hat{B}_i C_{2_j} Y_\varepsilon - \tilde{C}_{1_i}^T \left[\tilde{C}_{1_j} Y_\varepsilon + \tilde{D}_{12} \hat{C}_j Y_\varepsilon\right]$$
$$-\gamma^{-2} \left\{X_\varepsilon E_\varepsilon^{-1} \tilde{B}_{1_i} + \left[Y_\varepsilon^{-1} - X_\varepsilon\right] E_\varepsilon^{-1} \hat{B}_i \tilde{D}_{21_i}\right\} \tilde{B}_{1_j}^T E_\varepsilon^{-1}.$$

Proof: It can be shown by employing the same technique used in Ref.[18]-[19]. ■

Remark 1. *The LMIs given in Lemma 1 may become ill-conditioned when ε is sufficiently small, which is always the case for the descriptor systems. In general, these ill-conditioned LMIs are very difficult to solve. Thus, to alleviate these ill-conditioned LMIs, we have the following ε-independent well-posed LMI-based sufficient conditions for the uncertain fuzzy descriptor systems to obtain the prescribed $\mathcal{H}_\infty$ performance.* □

Theorem 1. *Consider the system (4). Given a prescribed $\mathcal{H}_\infty$ performance $\gamma > 0$ and a positive constant δ, if there exist matrices X_0, Y_0, $\mathcal{B}_{0_i}$ and $\mathcal{C}_{0_i}$, $i = 1, 2, \cdots, r$, satisfying the following ε-independent linear matrix inequalities:*

$$\begin{bmatrix} X_0 E + D X_0 & I \\ I & Y_0 E + D Y_0 \end{bmatrix} > 0 \quad (17)$$

$$E X_0^T = X_0 E, \;\; X_0^T D = D X_0, \;\; X_0 E + D X_0 > 0 \quad (18)$$

$$E Y_0^T = Y_0 E, \;\; Y_0^T D = D Y_0, \;\; Y_0 E + D Y_0 > 0 \quad (19)$$

$$\Psi_{11_{ii}} < 0, \quad i = 1, 2, \cdots, r \quad (20)$$

$$\Psi_{22_{ii}} < 0, \quad i = 1, 2, \cdots, r \quad (21)$$

$$\Psi_{11_{ij}} + \Psi_{11_{ji}} < 0, \quad i < j \le r \quad (22)$$

$$\Psi_{22_{ij}} + \Psi_{22_{ji}} < 0, \quad i < j \le r \quad (23)$$

where $E = \begin{pmatrix} I & 0 \\ 0 & 0 \end{pmatrix}$, $D = \begin{pmatrix} 0 & 0 \\ 0 & I \end{pmatrix}$,

$$\Psi_{11_{ij}} = \begin{pmatrix} A_i Y_0^T + Y_0 A_i^T + \gamma^{-2} \tilde{B}_{1_i} \tilde{B}_{1_j}^T & (*)^T \\ \left[Y_0 \tilde{C}_{1_i}^T + \mathcal{C}_{0_i}^T \tilde{D}_{12}^T\right]^T & -I \end{pmatrix} \quad (24)$$

$$\Psi_{22_{ij}} = \begin{pmatrix} A_i^T X_0^T + X_0 A_i + \mathcal{B}_{0_i} C_{2_j} + C_{2_i}^T \mathcal{B}_{0_j}^T + \tilde{C}_{1_i}^T \tilde{C}_{1_j} & (*)^T \\ \left[X_0 \tilde{B}_{1_i} + \mathcal{B}_{0_i} \tilde{D}_{21_j}\right]^T & -\gamma^2 I \end{pmatrix} \quad (25)$$

with

$$\tilde{B}_{1_i} = \left[\delta I \;\; I \;\; 0 \;\; B_{1_i} \;\; 0\right],$$
$$\tilde{C}_{1_i} = \left[\tfrac{\gamma\rho}{\delta} H_{1_i}^T \;\; \tfrac{\gamma\rho}{\delta} H_{5_i}^T \;\; \sqrt{2}\lambda\rho H_{4_i}^T \;\; \sqrt{2}\lambda C_{1_i}^T\right]^T,$$
$$\tilde{D}_{12} = \left[0 \;\; 0 \;\; 0 \;\; -\sqrt{2}\lambda I\right]^T,$$
$$\tilde{D}_{21_i} = \left[0 \;\; 0 \;\; \delta I \;\; D_{21_i} \;\; I\right]$$

$$\text{and } \lambda = \left(1 + \rho^2 \sum_{i=1}^{r} \sum_{j=1}^{r} \left[\|H_{2_i}^T H_{2_j}\| + \|H_{7_i}^T H_{7_j}\|\right]\right)^{\frac{1}{2}},$$

then there exists a sufficiently small $\hat{\varepsilon} > 0$ such that for $\varepsilon \in (0, \hat{\varepsilon}]$, the prescribed $\mathcal{H}_\infty$ performance $\gamma > 0$ is guaranteed. Furthermore, a suitable filter is of the form (6) with

$$\begin{aligned} \hat{A}_{ij}(\varepsilon) &= \left[Y_\varepsilon^{-1} - X_\varepsilon\right]^{-1} \mathcal{M}_{0_{ij}}(\varepsilon) Y_\varepsilon^{-1} \\ \hat{B}_i &= \left[Y_0^{-1} - X_0\right]^{-1} \mathcal{B}_{0_i} \\ \hat{C}_i &= \mathcal{C}_{0_i} Y_0^{-1} \end{aligned} \tag{26}$$

where

$$\mathcal{M}_{0_{ij}}(\varepsilon) = -A_i^T - X_\varepsilon A_i Y_\varepsilon - \left[Y_\varepsilon^{-1} - X_\varepsilon\right] \hat{B}_i C_{2_j} Y_\varepsilon - \tilde{C}_{1_i}^T \left[\tilde{C}_{1_j} Y_\varepsilon + \tilde{D}_{12} \hat{C}_j Y_\varepsilon\right]$$
$$-\gamma^{-2} \left\{ X_\varepsilon \tilde{B}_{1_i} + \left[Y_\varepsilon^{-1} - X_\varepsilon\right] \hat{B}_i \tilde{D}_{21_i} \right\} \tilde{B}_{1_j}^T$$

$$X_\varepsilon = \left\{X_0 + \varepsilon \tilde{X}\right\} E_\varepsilon \text{ and } Y_\varepsilon^{-1} = \left\{Y_0^{-1} + \varepsilon N_\varepsilon\right\} E_\varepsilon \tag{27}$$

with $\tilde{X} = D\left(X_0^T - X_0\right)$ *and* $N_\varepsilon = D\left((Y_0^{-1})^T - Y_0^{-1}\right)$.

Proof: Suppose the inequalities (17)-(19) hold, then the matrices X_0 and Y_0 are of the following forms:

$$X_0 = \begin{pmatrix} X_1 & X_2 \\ 0 & X_3 \end{pmatrix} \text{ and } Y_0 = \begin{pmatrix} Y_1 & Y_2 \\ 0 & Y_3 \end{pmatrix}$$

with $X_1 = X_1^T > 0$, $X_3 = X_3^T > 0$, $Y_1 = Y_1^T > 0$ and $Y_3 = Y_3^T > 0$. Substituting X_0 and Y_0 into (27), respectively, we have

$$X_\varepsilon = \left\{X_0 + \varepsilon \tilde{X}\right\} E_\varepsilon = \begin{pmatrix} X_1 & \varepsilon X_2 \\ \varepsilon X_2^T & \varepsilon X_3 \end{pmatrix} \tag{28}$$

$$Y_\varepsilon^{-1} = \left\{Y_0^{-1} + \varepsilon N_\varepsilon\right\} E_\varepsilon = \begin{pmatrix} Y_1^{-1} & -\varepsilon Y^{-1} Y_2 Y_3^{-1} \\ -\varepsilon (Y^{-1} Y_2 Y_3^{-1})^T & \varepsilon Y_3^{-1} \end{pmatrix}. \tag{29}$$

Clearly, $X_\varepsilon = X_\varepsilon^T$, and $Y_\varepsilon^{-1} = (Y_\varepsilon^{-1})^T$. Knowing the fact that the inverse of a symmetric matrix is a symmetric matrix, we learn that Y_ε is a symmetric matrix. Using the matrix inversion lemma, we can see that

$$Y_\varepsilon = E_\varepsilon^{-1} \left\{Y_0 + \varepsilon \tilde{Y}\right\} \tag{30}$$

where $\tilde{Y} = Y_0 N_\varepsilon (I + \varepsilon Y_0 N_\varepsilon)^{-1} Y_0$. Employing the Schur complement, one can show that there exists a sufficiently small $\hat{\varepsilon}$ such that for $\varepsilon \in (0, \hat{\varepsilon}]$, (8)-(9) holds.

Now, we need to show that

$$\begin{pmatrix} X_\varepsilon & I \\ I & Y_\varepsilon \end{pmatrix} > 0. \tag{31}$$

By the Schur complement, it is equivalent to showing that

$$X_\varepsilon - Y_\varepsilon^{-1} > 0. \tag{32}$$

Substituting (28) and (29) into the left hand side of (32), we get

$$\begin{bmatrix} X_1 - Y_1^{-1} & \varepsilon(X_2 + Y_1^{-1}Y_2Y_3^{-1}) \\ \varepsilon(X_2 + Y_1^{-1}Y_2Y_3^{-1})^T & \varepsilon(X_3 - Y_3^{-1}) \end{bmatrix}. \tag{33}$$

The Schur complement of (17) is

$$\begin{bmatrix} X_1 - Y_1^{-1} & 0 \\ 0 & X_3 - Y_3^{-1} \end{bmatrix} > 0. \tag{34}$$

According to (34), we learn that

$$X_1 - Y_1^{-1} > 0 \qquad \text{and} \qquad X_3 - Y_3^{-1} > 0. \tag{35}$$

Using (35) and the Schur complement, it can be shown that there exists a sufficiently small $\hat{\varepsilon} > 0$ such that for $\varepsilon \in (0, \hat{\varepsilon}]$, (7) holds.

Next, employing (28), (29) and (30), the controller's matrices given in (16) can be re-expressed as follows:

$$\begin{aligned} \mathcal{B}_i(\varepsilon) &= \left[Y_0^{-1} - X_0\right]\hat{B}_i + \varepsilon\left[N_\varepsilon - \tilde{X}\right]\hat{B}_i \stackrel{\Delta}{=} \mathcal{B}_{0_i} + \varepsilon\mathcal{B}_{\varepsilon_i} \\ \mathcal{C}_i(\varepsilon) &= \hat{C}_i Y_0^T + \varepsilon\hat{C}_i\tilde{Y}^T \stackrel{\Delta}{=} \mathcal{C}_{0_i} + \varepsilon\mathcal{C}_{\varepsilon_i}. \end{aligned} \tag{36}$$

Substituting (28), (29), (30) and (36) into (14) and (15), and pre-post multiplying by $\begin{pmatrix} E_\varepsilon & 0 \\ 0 & I \end{pmatrix}$, we, respectively, obtain

$$\Psi_{11_{ij}} + \psi_{11_{ij}} \;\; \text{and} \;\; \Psi_{22_{ij}} + \psi_{22_{ij}} \tag{37}$$

where the ε-independent linear matrices $\Psi_{11_{ij}}$ and $\Psi_{22_{ij}}$ are defined in (24) and (25), respectively and the ε-dependent linear matrices are

$$\psi_{11_{ij}} = \varepsilon \begin{pmatrix} A_i\tilde{Y}^T + \tilde{Y}A_i^T & (*)^T \\ \left[\tilde{Y}\tilde{C}_{1_i}^T + C_{\varepsilon_i}^T\tilde{D}_{12_j}^T\right]^T & 0 \end{pmatrix} \tag{38}$$

$$\psi_{22_{ij}} = \varepsilon \begin{pmatrix} A_i^T\tilde{X} + \tilde{X}^T A_i + \mathcal{B}_{\varepsilon_i}C_{2_j} + C_{2_i}^T\mathcal{B}_{\varepsilon_j}^T & (*)^T \\ \left[\tilde{X}\tilde{B}_{1_i} + \mathcal{B}_{\varepsilon_i}\tilde{D}_{21_j}\right]^T & 0 \end{pmatrix}. \tag{39}$$

Note that the ε-dependent linear matrices tend to zero when ε approaches zero.

Employing (20)-(22) and knowing the fact that for any given negative definite matrix $\mathcal{W}$, there exists an $\varepsilon > 0$ such that $\mathcal{W} + \varepsilon I < 0$, one can show that there exists a sufficiently small $\hat{\varepsilon} > 0$ such that for $\varepsilon \in (0, \hat{\varepsilon}]$, (10)-(13) hold. Since (7)-(13) hold, using Lemma 1, the inequality (3) holds. ■

3.2. Case II–$\nu(t)$ is unavailable for feedback

The fuzzy filter is assumed to be the same as the premise variables of the fuzzy system model. This actually means that the premise variables of fuzzy system model are assumed to be measurable. However, in general, it is extremely difficult to derive an accurate fuzzy system model by imposing that all premise variables are measurable. In this subsection, we do not impose that condition, we choose the premise variables of the filter to be different from the premise variables of fuzzy system model of the plant. In here, the premise variables of the filter are selected to be the estimated premise variables of the plant. In the other words, the premise variable of the fuzzy model $\nu(t)$ is unavailable for feedback which implies μ_i is unavailable for feedback. Hence, we cannot select our filter which depends on μ_i. Thus, we select our filter as (5) where $\hat{\mu}_i$ depends on the premise variable of the filter which is different from μ_i. Let us re-express the system (1) in terms of $\hat{\mu}_i$, thus the plant's premise variable becomes the same as the filter's premise variable. By doing so, the result given in the previous case can then be applied here. Note that it can be done by using the same technique as in subsection. After some manipulation, we get

$$\begin{aligned} E_\varepsilon \dot{x}(t) &= \sum_{i=1}^{r} \hat{\mu}_i \Big[[A_i + \Delta\bar{A}_i]x(t) + [B_{1_i} + \Delta\bar{B}_{1_i}]w(t) \\ z(t) &= \sum_{i=1}^{r} \hat{\mu}_i \Big[[C_{1_i} + \Delta\bar{C}_{1_i}]x(t) \Big] \\ y(t) &= \sum_{i=1}^{r} \hat{\mu}_i \Big[[C_{2_i} + \Delta\bar{C}_{2_i}]x(t) + [D_{21_i} + \Delta\bar{D}_{21_i}]w(t) \Big] \end{aligned} \tag{40}$$

where

$$\Delta\bar{A}_i = \bar{F}(x(t),\hat{x}(t),t)\bar{H}_{1_i},\ \Delta\bar{B}_{1_i} = \bar{F}(x(t),\hat{x}(t),t)\bar{H}_{2_i},\ \Delta\bar{B}_{2_i} = \bar{F}(x(t),\hat{x}(t),t)\bar{H}_{3_i},$$

$$\Delta\bar{C}_{1_i} = \bar{F}(x(t),\hat{x}(t),t)\bar{H}_{4_i},\ \Delta\bar{C}_{2_i} = \bar{F}(x(t),\hat{x}(t),t)\bar{H}_{5_i},\ \Delta\bar{D}_{12_i} = \bar{F}(x(t),\hat{x}(t),t)\bar{H}_{6_i}$$
$$\text{and } \Delta\bar{D}_{21_i} = \bar{F}(x(t),\hat{x}(t),t)\bar{H}_{7_i}$$

with

$$\bar{H}_{1_i} = \Big[H_{1_i}^T\ A_1^T \cdots A_r^T\ H_{1_1}^T \cdots H_{1_r}^T\Big]^T,\ \bar{H}_{2_i} = \Big[H_{2_i}^T\ B_{1_1}^T \cdots B_{1_r}^T\ H_{2_1}^T \cdots H_{2_r}^T\Big]^T,$$

$$\bar{H}_{3_i} = \Big[H_{3_i}^T\ B_{2_1}^T \cdots B_{2_r}^T\ H_{3_1}^T \cdots H_{3_r}^T\Big]^T,\ \bar{H}_{4_i} = \Big[H_{4_i}^T\ C_{1_1}^T \cdots C_{1_r}^T\ H_{4_1}^T \cdots H_{4_r}^T\Big]^T,$$

$$\bar{H}_{5_i} = \Big[H_{5_i}^T\ C_{2_1}^T \cdots C_{2_r}^T\ H_{5_1}^T \cdots H_{5_r}^T\Big]^T,\ \bar{H}_{6_i} = \Big[H_{6_i}^T\ D_{12_1}^T \cdots D_{12_r}^T\ H_{6_1}^T \cdots H_{6_r}^T\Big]^T$$

$$\bar{H}_{7_i} = \Big[H_{7_i}^T\ D_{21_1}^T \cdots\ D_{21_r}^T\ H_{7_1}^T \cdots H_{7_r}^T\Big]^T \text{ and}$$

$\bar{F}(x(t),\hat{x}(t),t) = \Big[F(x(t),t)\ \ (\mu_1 - \hat{\mu}_1)\ \ \cdots\ \ (\mu_r - \hat{\mu}_r)\ \ F(x(t),t)(\mu_1 - \hat{\mu}_1)\ \ \cdots\ \ F(x(t),t)(\mu_r - \hat{\mu}_r)\Big]$. Note that $\|\bar{F}(x(t),\hat{x}(t),t)\| \leq \bar{\rho}$ where $\bar{\rho} = \{3\rho^2 + 2\}^{\frac{1}{2}}$. $\bar{\rho}$ is derived by utilizing the concept of vector norm in the basic system control theory and the fact that $\mu_i \geq 0$, $\hat{\mu}_i \geq 0$, $\sum_{i=1}^{r} \mu_i = 1$ and $\sum_{i=1}^{r} \hat{\mu}_i = 1$.

Note that the above technique is basically employed in order to obtain the plant's premise variable to be the same as the filter's premise variable; e.g. [17]. Now, the premise variable of the system is the same as the premise variable of the filter, thus we can apply the result given in Case I. By applying the same technique used in Case I, we have the following theorem.

Theorem 2. *Consider the system (4). Given a prescribed $\mathcal{H}_\infty$ performance $\gamma > 0$ and a positive constant δ, if there exist matrices X_0, Y_0, $\mathcal{B}_{0_i}$ and $\mathcal{C}_{0_i}$, $i = 1, 2, \cdots, r$, satisfying the following ε-independent linear matrix inequalities:*

$$\begin{bmatrix} X_0 E + D X_0 & I \\ I & Y_0 E + D Y_0 \end{bmatrix} > 0 \tag{41}$$

$$E X_0^T = X_0 E, \;\; X_0^T D = D X_0, \;\; X_0 E + D X_0 > 0 \tag{42}$$

$$E Y_0^T = Y_0 E, \;\; Y_0^T D = D Y_0, \;\; Y_0 E + D Y_0 > 0 \tag{43}$$

$$\Psi_{11_{ii}} < 0, \quad i = 1, 2, \cdots, r \tag{44}$$

$$\Psi_{22_{ii}} < 0, \quad i = 1, 2, \cdots, r \tag{45}$$

$$\Psi_{11_{ij}} + \Psi_{11_{ji}} < 0, \quad i < j \leq r \tag{46}$$

$$\Psi_{22_{ij}} + \Psi_{22_{ji}} < 0, \quad i < j \leq r \tag{47}$$

where $E = \begin{pmatrix} I & 0 \\ 0 & 0 \end{pmatrix}$, $D = \begin{pmatrix} 0 & 0 \\ 0 & I \end{pmatrix}$,

$$\Psi_{11_{ij}} = \begin{pmatrix} A_i Y_0^T + Y_0 A_i^T + \gamma^{-2} \tilde{\bar{B}}_{1_i} \tilde{\bar{B}}_{1_j}^T & (*)^T \\ \left[Y_0 \tilde{\bar{C}}_{1_i}^T + \mathcal{C}_{0_i}^T \tilde{\bar{D}}_{12}^T \right]^T & -I \end{pmatrix}$$

$$\Psi_{22_{ij}} = \begin{pmatrix} A_i^T X_0^T + X_0 A_i + \mathcal{B}_{0_i} C_{2_j} + C_{2_i}^T \mathcal{B}_{0_j}^T + \tilde{\bar{C}}_{1_i}^T \tilde{\bar{C}}_{1_j} & (*)^T \\ \left[X_0 \tilde{\bar{B}}_{1_i} + \mathcal{B}_{0_i} \tilde{\bar{D}}_{21_j} \right]^T & -\gamma^2 I \end{pmatrix}$$

with

$$\tilde{\bar{B}}_{1_i} = \left[\delta I \;\; I \;\; 0 \;\; B_{1_i} \;\; 0 \right],$$

$$\tilde{\bar{C}}_{1_i} = \left[\tfrac{\gamma \bar{\rho}}{\delta} \bar{H}_{1_i}^T \;\; \tfrac{\gamma \bar{\rho}}{\delta} \bar{H}_{5_i}^T \;\; \sqrt{2} \bar{\lambda} \bar{\rho} \bar{H}_{4_i}^T \;\; \sqrt{2} \bar{\lambda} C_{1_i}^T \right]^T,$$

$$\tilde{\bar{D}}_{12} = \left[0 \;\; 0 \;\; 0 \;\; -\sqrt{2} \bar{\lambda} I \right]^T,$$

$$\tilde{\bar{D}}_{21_i} = \left[0 \;\; 0 \;\; \delta I \;\; D_{21_i} \;\; I \right]$$

$$\text{and } \bar{\lambda} = \left(1 + \bar{\rho}^2 \sum_{i=1}^{r} \sum_{j=1}^{r} \left[\| \bar{H}_{2_i}^T \bar{H}_{2_j} \| + \| \bar{H}_{7_i}^T \bar{H}_{7_j} \| \right] \right)^{\frac{1}{2}},$$

*then there exists a sufficiently small $\hat{\varepsilon} > 0$ such that for $\varepsilon \in (0, \hat{\varepsilon}]$, the prescribed $\mathcal{H}_\infty$ performance $\gamma > 0$ is guaranteed. Furthermore, a suitable filter is of the form (**??**) with*

$$\begin{aligned} \hat{A}_{ij}(\varepsilon) &= \left[Y_\varepsilon^{-1} - X_\varepsilon \right]^{-1} \mathcal{M}_{0_{ij}}(\varepsilon) Y_\varepsilon^{-1} \\ \hat{B}_i &= \left[Y_0^{-1} - X_0 \right]^{-1} \mathcal{B}_{0_i} \\ \hat{C}_i &= \mathcal{C}_{0_i} Y_0^{-1} \end{aligned} \tag{48}$$

where

$$\begin{aligned} \mathcal{M}_{0_{ij}}(\varepsilon) = &-A_i^T - X_\varepsilon A_i Y_\varepsilon - \left[Y_\varepsilon^{-1} - X_\varepsilon \right] \hat{B}_i C_{2_j} Y_\varepsilon - \tilde{\bar{C}}_{1_i}^T \left[\tilde{\bar{C}}_{1_j} Y_\varepsilon + \tilde{\bar{D}}_{12} \hat{C}_j Y_\varepsilon \right] \\ &-\gamma^{-2} \left\{ X_\varepsilon \tilde{\bar{B}}_{1_i} + \left[Y_\varepsilon^{-1} - X_\varepsilon \right] \hat{B}_i \tilde{\bar{D}}_{21_i} \right\} \tilde{\bar{B}}_{1_i}^T \\ X_\varepsilon = &\left\{ X_0 + \varepsilon \tilde{X} \right\} E_\varepsilon \text{ and } Y_\varepsilon^{-1} = \left\{ Y_0^{-1} + \varepsilon N_\varepsilon \right\} E_\varepsilon \end{aligned}$$

with $\tilde{X} = D\left(X_0^T - X_0 \right)$ *and* $N_\varepsilon = D\left((Y_0^{-1})^T - Y_0^{-1} \right)$.

Proof: It can be shown by employing the same technique used in the proof for Theorem 1. ∎

4. Example

Consider the tunnel diode circuit shown in Figure 1 where the tunnel diode is characterized by

$$i_D(t) = 0.01v_D(t) + 0.05v_D^3(t).$$

Assuming that the inductance, L, is the parasitic parameter and letting $x_1(t) = v_C(t)$ and

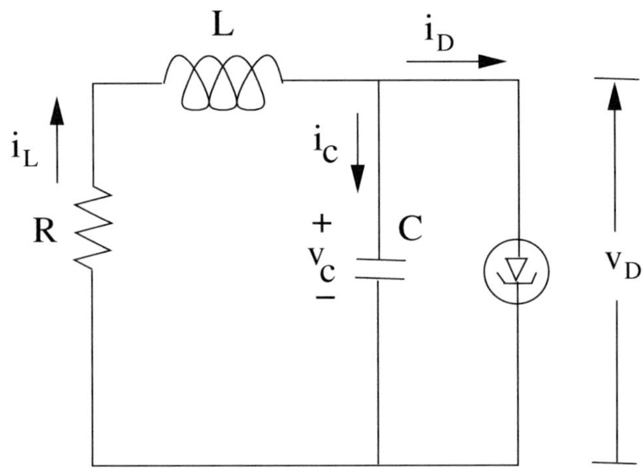

Figure 1. Tunnel diode circuit.

$x_2(t) = i_L(t)$ as the state variables, we have

$$\begin{aligned} C\dot{x}_1(t) &= -0.01x_1(t) - 0.05x_1^3(t) + x_2(t) \\ L\dot{x}_2(t) &= -x_1(t) - Rx_2(t) + 0.1w_2(t) \\ y(t) &= Jx(t) + 0.1w_1(t) \\ z(t) &= \begin{bmatrix} x_1(t) \\ x_2(t) \end{bmatrix} \end{aligned} \quad (49)$$

where $w(t)$ is the disturbance noise input, $y(t)$ is the measurement output, $z(t)$ is the state to be estimated and J is the sensor matrix. Note that the variables $x_1(t)$ and $x_2(t)$ are treated as the deviation variables (variables deviate from the desired trajectories). The parameters of the circuit are $C = 100\ mF$, $R = 10 \pm 10\%\ \Omega$ and $L = \varepsilon\ H$. With these parameters (49) can be rewritten as

$$\begin{aligned} \dot{x}_1(t) &= -0.1x_1(t) + 0.5x_1^3(t) + 10x_2(t) \\ \varepsilon\dot{x}_2(t) &= -x_1(t) - (10 + \Delta R)x_2(t) + 0.1w_2(t) \\ y(t) &= Jx(t) + 0.1w_1(t) \\ z(t) &= \begin{bmatrix} x_1(t) \\ x_2(t) \end{bmatrix}. \end{aligned} \quad (50)$$

For the sake of simplicity, we will use as few rules as possible. Assuming that $|x_1(t)| \leq 3$, the nonlinear network system (50) can be approximated by the following TS fuzzy model:

Plant Rule 1: IF $x_1(t)$ is $M_1(x_1(t))$ THEN

$$\begin{aligned} E_\varepsilon \dot{x}(t) &= [A_1 + \Delta A_1]x(t) + B_{1_1}w(t), \quad x(0) = 0, \\ z(t) &= C_{1_1}x(t), \\ y(t) &= C_{2_1}x(t) + D_{21_1}w(t). \end{aligned}$$

Plant Rule 2: IF $x_1(t)$ is $M_2(x_1(t))$ THEN

$$\begin{aligned} E_\varepsilon \dot{x}(t) &= [A_2 + \Delta A_2]x(t) + B_{1_2}w(t), \quad x(0) = 0, \\ z(t) &= C_{1_2}x(t), \\ y(t) &= C_{2_2}x(t) + D_{21_2}w(t) \end{aligned}$$

where $x(t) = [x_1^T(t) \;\; x_2^T(t)]^T, w(t) = [w_1^T(t) \;\; w_2^T(t)]^T$,

$$A_1 = \begin{bmatrix} -0.1 & 10 \\ -1 & -1 \end{bmatrix}, \quad A_2 = \begin{bmatrix} -4.6 & 10 \\ -1 & -1 \end{bmatrix}, \quad B_{1_1} = B_{1_2} = \begin{bmatrix} 0 & 0 \\ 0 & 0.1 \end{bmatrix},$$

$$C_1 = \begin{bmatrix} 1 & 0 \\ 0 & 1 \end{bmatrix}, \quad C_{2_1} = C_{2_2} = J, \quad D_{21} = \begin{bmatrix} 0.1 & 0 \end{bmatrix},$$

$$\Delta A_1 = F(x(t), t)H_{1_1}, \quad \Delta A_2 = F(x(t), t)H_{1_2} \text{ and } E_\varepsilon = \begin{bmatrix} 1 & 0 \\ 0 & \varepsilon \end{bmatrix}.$$

Now, by assuming that $\|F(x(t), t)\| \leq \rho = 1$ and since the values of R are uncertain but bounded within 10% of their nominal values given in (49), we have

$$H_{1_1} = H_{1_2} = \begin{bmatrix} 0 & 0 \\ 0 & 1 \end{bmatrix}.$$

Note that the plot of the membership function Rules 1 and 2 is the same as in Figure 2. By employing the results given in Lemma 1 and the Matlab LMI solver, it is easy to realize that $\varepsilon < 0.006$ for the fuzzy filter design in Case I and $\varepsilon < 0.008$ for the fuzzy filter design in Case II, the LMIs become ill-conditioned and the Matlab LMI solver yields the error message, "Rank Deficient". *Case I-$v(t)$ are available for feedback*

In this case, $x_1(t) = v(t)$ is assumed to be available for feedback; for instance, $J = [1 \;\; 0]$. This implies that μ_i is available for feedback. Using the LMI optimization algorithm and Theorem 1 with $\varepsilon = 100\ \mu$H, $\gamma = 0.6$ and $\delta = 1$, we obtain the following results:

$$\hat{A}_{11}(\varepsilon) = \begin{bmatrix} -0.0674 & -0.3532 \\ -30.7181 & -4.3834 \end{bmatrix}, \qquad \hat{A}_{12}(\varepsilon) = \begin{bmatrix} -0.0674 & -0.3532 \\ -30.7181 & -4.3834 \end{bmatrix},$$

$$\hat{A}_{21}(\varepsilon) = \begin{bmatrix} -0.0928 & -0.3138 \\ -34.7355 & -3.8964 \end{bmatrix}, \qquad \hat{A}_{22}(\varepsilon) = \begin{bmatrix} -0.0928 & -0.3138 \\ -34.7355 & -3.8964 \end{bmatrix},$$

$$\hat{B}_1 = \begin{bmatrix} 1.5835 \\ 3.2008 \end{bmatrix}, \qquad \hat{B}_2 = \begin{bmatrix} 1.2567 \\ 3.8766 \end{bmatrix},$$

$$\hat{C}_1 = \begin{bmatrix} -1.7640 & -0.8190 \end{bmatrix}, \qquad \hat{C}_2 = \begin{bmatrix} 4.5977 & -0.8190 \end{bmatrix}.$$

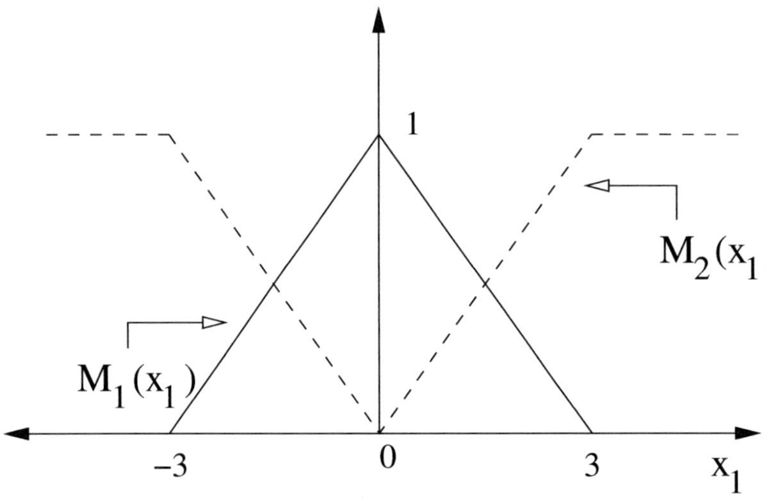

Figure 2. Membership functions for the two fuzzy set.

Hence, the resulting fuzzy filter is

$$E_\varepsilon \dot{\hat{x}}(t) = \sum_{i=1}^{2}\sum_{j=1}^{2} \mu_i \mu_j \hat{A}_{ij}(\varepsilon)\hat{x}(t) + \sum_{i=1}^{2} \mu_i \hat{B}_i y(t)$$

$$\hat{z}(t) = \sum_{i=1}^{2} \mu_i \hat{C}_i \hat{x}(t)$$

where

$$\mu_1 = M_1(x_1(t)) \text{ and } \mu_2 = M_2(x_1(t)).$$

Case II: $v(t)$ are unavailable for feedback

In this case, $x_1(t) = v(t)$ is assumed to be unavailable for feedback; for instance, $J = [0 \;\; 1]$. This implies that μ_i is unavailable for feedback. Using the LMI optimization algorithm and Theorem 2 with $\varepsilon = 100\ \mu$H, $\gamma = 0.6$ and $\delta = 1$, we obtain the following results:

$$\hat{A}_{11}(\varepsilon) = \begin{bmatrix} -2.3050 & -0.4186 \\ -32.3990 & -4.4443 \end{bmatrix}, \qquad \hat{A}_{12}(\varepsilon) = \begin{bmatrix} -2.3050 & -0.4186 \\ -32.3990 & -4.4443 \end{bmatrix},$$

$$\hat{A}_{21}(\varepsilon) = \begin{bmatrix} -2.3549 & -0.3748 \\ -32.4539 & -3.9044 \end{bmatrix}, \qquad \hat{A}_{22}(\varepsilon) = \begin{bmatrix} -2.3549 & -0.3748 \\ -32.4539 & -3.9044 \end{bmatrix},$$

$$\hat{B}_1 = \begin{bmatrix} -0.3053 \\ 3.9938 \end{bmatrix}, \qquad \hat{B}_2 = \begin{bmatrix} -0.3734 \\ 5.1443 \end{bmatrix},$$

$$\hat{C}_1 = \begin{bmatrix} 4.3913 & -0.1406 \end{bmatrix}, \qquad \hat{C}_2 = \begin{bmatrix} 1.9832 & -0.1406 \end{bmatrix}.$$

The resulting fuzzy filter is

$$E_\varepsilon \dot{\hat{x}}(t) = \sum_{i=1}^{2}\sum_{j=1}^{2} \hat{\mu}_i\hat{\mu}_j\hat{A}_{ij}(\varepsilon)\hat{x}(t) + \sum_{i=1}^{2}\hat{\mu}_i\hat{B}_i y(t)$$

$$\hat{z}(t) = \sum_{i=1}^{2}\hat{\mu}_i\hat{C}_i\hat{x}(t)$$

where

$$\hat{\mu}_1 = M_1(\hat{x}_1(t)) \text{ and } \hat{\mu}_2 = M_2(\hat{x}_1(t)).$$

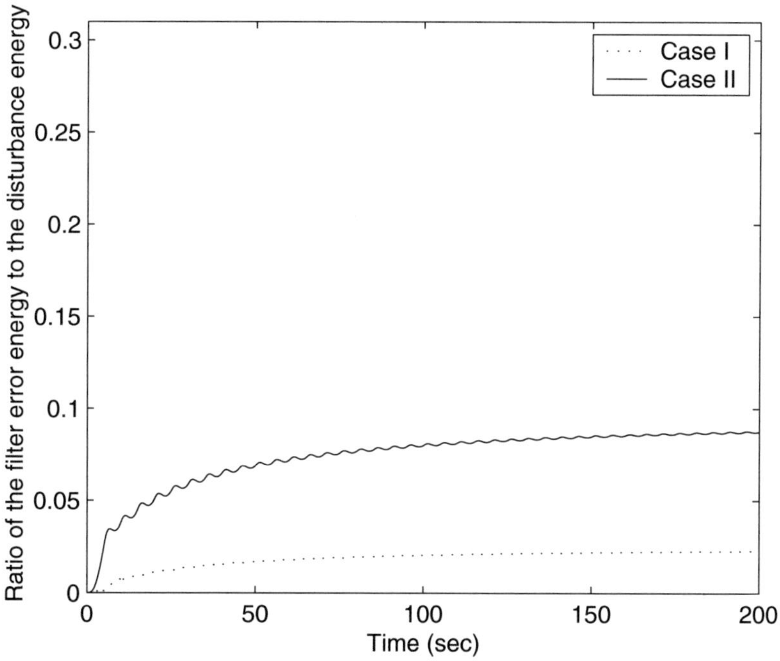

Figure 3. The ratio of the filter error energy to the disturbance noise energy: $\left(\frac{\int_0^{T_f}(z(t)-\hat{z}(t))^T(z(t)-\hat{z}(t))dt}{\int_0^{T_f} w^T(t)w(t)dt}\right)$.

Remark 2. *The ratios of the filter error energy to the disturbance input noise energy are depicted in Figure 3 when* $\varepsilon = 100\ \mu H$. *The disturbance input signal,* $w(t)$, *which was used during the simulation is the rectangular signal (magnitude 0.9 and frequency 0.5 Hz). Figures 4(a) - 4(b), respectively, show the responses of* $x_1(t)$ *and* $x_2(t)$ *in Cases I and II. Table I shows the performance index* γ *with different values of* ε *in Cases I and II. After 50 seconds, the ratio of the filter error energy to the disturbance input noise energy tends to a constant value which is about 0.02 in Case I and 0.08 in Case II. Thus, in Case I where* $\gamma = \sqrt{0.02} = 0.141$ *and in Case II where* $\gamma = \sqrt{0.08} = 0.283$, *both are less than the prescribed value 0.6. From Table 9.1, the maximum value of* ε *that guarantees the* $\mathcal{L}_2$*-gain of the mapping from the exogenous input noise to the filter error energy being less than 0.6 is 0.30 H, i.e.,* $\varepsilon \in (0, 0.30]$ *H in Case I, and 0.25 H, i.e.,* $\varepsilon \in (0, 0.25]$ *H in Case II.* □

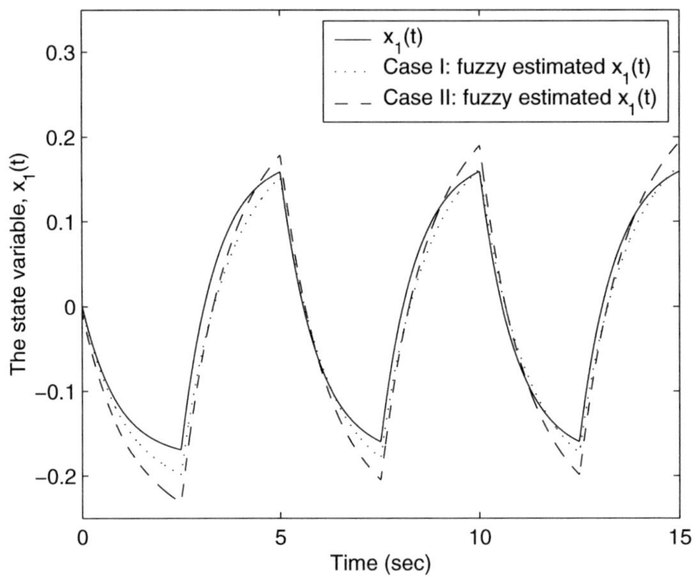

(a) The histories of $x_1(t)$

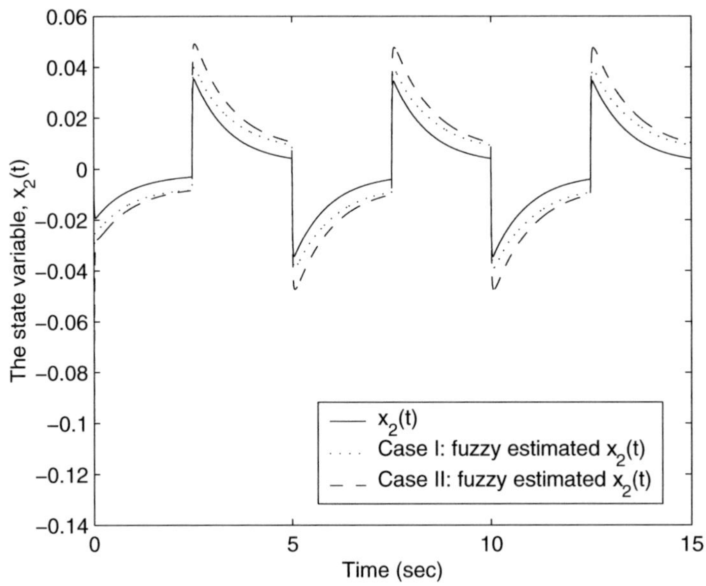

(b) The histories of $x_2(t)$

Figure 4. The histories of the state variables, $x_1(t)$ and $x_2(t)$.

	The performance index γ	
ε	Fuzzy Filter in Case I	Fuzzy Filter in Case II
0.0001	0.141	0.283
0.1	0.316	0.509
0.25	0.479	0.596
0.26	0.500	> 0.6
0.30	0.591	> 0.6
0.31	> 0.6	> 0.6

Table 1. The performance index γ of the system with different values of ε.

5. Conclusion

The problem of designing a robust $\mathcal{H}_\infty$ fuzzy ε-independent filter for a TS fuzzy descriptor system with parametric uncertainties has been considered. Sufficient conditions for the existence of the robust $\mathcal{H}_\infty$ fuzzy filter have been derived in terms of a family of ε-independent LMIs. A numerical simulation example has been also presented to illustrate the theory development.

Author details

Wudhichai Assawinchaichote
Department of Electronic and Telecommunication Engineering at King Mongkut's University of Technology Thonburi, Bangkok, Thailand

6. References

[1] H. K. Khalil, "Feedback control of nonstandard singularly perturbed systems," *IEEE Trans. Automat. Contr.*, vol. 34, pp. 1052–1060, 1989.
[2] Z. Gajic and M. Lim, "A new filtering method for linear singularly perturbed systems," *IEEE Trans. Automat. Contr.*, vol. 39, pp. 1952–1955, 1994.
[3] X. Shen and L. Deng, "Decomposition solution of $\mathcal{H}_\infty$ filter gain in singularly perturbed systems," *Signal Processing*, vol. 55, pp. 313–320, 1996.
[4] M.T. Lim and Z. Gajic, "Reduced-Order $\mathcal{H}_\infty$ optimal filtering for systems with slow and fast modes," *IEEE Trans. Circuits and Systems I*, vol. 47, pp. 250–254, 2000.
[5] P. Shi and V. Dragan, "Asymptotic $\mathcal{H}_\infty$ control of singularly perturbed system with parametric uncertainties," *IEEE Trans. Automat. Contr.*, vol. 44, pp. 1738–1742, 1999.
[6] P. V. Kokotovic, H. K. Khalil, and J. O'Reilly, *Singular Perturbation Methods in Control: Analysis and Design*, London: Academic Press, 1986.
[7] H. O. Wang, K. Tanaka, and M. F. Griffin, "An approach to fuzzy control of nonlinear systems: Stability and design issues," *IEEE Trans. Fuzzy Syst.*, vol. 4, pp. 14–23, 1996.
[8] K. Tanaka, T. Taniguchi, and H. O. Wang, "Fuzzy control based on quadratic performance function - A linear matrix inequality approach," in *Proc. IEEE Conf. Decision and Contr.*, pp. 2914–2919, 1998.

[9] B. S. Chen, C. S. Tseng, and H. J. Uang, "Mixed $\mathcal{H}_2/\mathcal{H}_\infty$ fuzzy output feedback control design for nonlinear dynamic systems: An LMI approach," *IEEE Trans. Fuzzy Syst.*, vol. 8, pp. 249–265, 2000.
[10] L. Xie, M. Fu, and C. E. de Souza, "$\mathcal{H}_\infty$ control and quadratic stabilisation of systems with parameter uncertainty via output feedback," *IEEE Trans. Automat. Contr.*, vol. 37, pp. 1253–1256, 1992.
[11] S. K. Nguang, "Robust nonlinear $\mathcal{H}_\infty$ output feedback control," *IEEE Trans Automat. Contr.*, vol. 41, pp. 1003–1008, 1996.
[12] S. K. Nguang and M. Fu, "Robust nonlinear $\mathcal{H}_\infty$ filtering," *Automatica*, vol. 32, pp. 1195–1199, 1996.
[13] K. Tanaka, T. Ikeda, and H. O. Wang, "Robust stabilization of a class of uncertain nonlinear systems via fuzzy control: Quadratic stabilizability, H_∞ control theory, and linear matrix inequality", *IEEE Trans. Fuzzy Syst.*, vol. 4, pp. 1–13, 1996.
[14] M. Teixeira and S. H. Zak, "Stabilizing controller design for uncertain nonlinear systems using fuzzy models", *IEEE Trans. Fuzzy Syst.*, vol. 7, pp. 133–142, 1999.
[15] S. H. Zak, "Stabilizing fuzzy system models using linear controllers", *IEEE Trans. Fuzzy Syst.*, vol. 7, pp. 236–240, 1999.
[16] L. X. Wang, *A course in fuzzy systems and control.* Englewood Cliffs, NJ: Prentice-Hall, 1997.
[17] S. K. Nguang and P. Shi, "$\mathcal{H}^\infty$ fuzzy output feedback control design for nonlinear systems: An LMI approach ," *IEEE Trans. Fuzzy Syst.*, vol. 11, pp. 331–340, 2003.
[18] S. K. Nguang and W. Assawinchaichote, "$\mathcal{H}_\infty$ filtering for fuzzy dynamic systems with pole placement," *IEEE Trans. Circuits Systs. I*, vol. 50, pp. 1503-1508, 2003.
[19] W.Assawinchaichote and S. K. Nguang, "$\mathcal{H}^\infty$ filtering for nonlinear singularly perturbed systems with pole placement constraints: An LMI approach", *IEEE Trans. Signal Processing*, vol. 52, pp. 579–588, 2004.

Chapter 20

Robust Stabilization for Uncertain Takagi-Sugeno Fuzzy Continuous Model with Time-Delay Based on Razumikhin Theorem

Yassine Manai and Mohamed Benrejeb

Additional information is available at the end of the chapter

http://dx.doi.org/10.5772/48075

1. Introduction

Fuzzy control systems have experienced a big growth of industrial applications in the recent decades, because of their reliability and effectiveness. Many researches are investigated on the Takagi-Sugeno models [1], [2] and [3] last decades. Two classes of Lyapunov functions are used to analysis these systems: quadratic Lyapunov functions and non-quadratic Lyapunov ones which are less conservative than first class. Many researches are investigated with non-quadratic Lyapunov functions [4]-[6], [7].

Recently, Takagi–Sugeno fuzzy model approach has been used to examine nonlinear systems with time-delay, and different methodologies have been proposed for analysis and synthesis of this type of systems [1]-[11], [12]-[13]. Time delay often occurs in many dynamical systems such as biological systems, chemical system, metallurgical processing system and network system. Their existences are frequently a cause of infeasibility and poor performances.

The stability approaches are divided into two classes in term of delay. The fist one tries to develop delay independent stability criteria. The second class depends on the delay size of the time delay, and it called delay dependent stability criteria. Generally, delay dependent class gives less conservative stability criteria than independent ones.

Two classes of Lyapunov-Razumikhin function are used to analysis these systems: quadratic Lyapunov-Razumikhin function and non-quadratic Lyapunov- Razumikhin ones. The use of first class brings much conservativeness in the stability test. In order to reduce the conservatism entailed in the previous results using quadratic function.

As the information about the time derivatives of membership function is considered by the PDC fuzzy controller, it allows the introduction of slack matrices to facilitate the stability analysis. The relationship between the membership function of the fuzzy model and the fuzzy controllers is used to introduce some slack matrix variables. The boundary information of the membership functions is brought to the stability condition and thus offers some relaxed stability conditions [5].

In this chapter, a new stability conditions for time-delay Takagi-Sugeno fuzzy systems by using fuzzy Lyapunov-Razumikhin function are presented. In addition, a new stabilization conditions for Takagi Sugeno time-delay uncertain fuzzy models based on the use of fuzzy Lyapunov function are presented. This criterion is expressed in terms of Linear Matrix Inequalities (LMIs) which can be efficiently solved by using various convex optimization algorithms [8],[9]. The presented methods are less conservative than existing results.

The organization of the chapter is as follows. In section 2, we present the system description and problem formulation and we give some preliminaries which are needed to derive results. Section 3 will be concerned to stability and stabilization analysis for T-S fuzzy systems with Parallel Distributed Controller (PDC). An observer approach design is derived to estimate state variables. Section 5 will be concerned to stabilization analysis for time-delay T-S fuzzy systems based on Razumikhin theorem. Next, a new robust stabilization condition for uncertain system with time delay is given in section 6. Illustrative examples are given in section 7 for a comparison of previous results to demonstrate the advantage of proposed method. Finally section 8 makes conclusion.

Notation: Throughout this chapter, a real symmetric matrix $S > 0$ denotes S being a positive definite matrix. The superscript "T" is used for the transpose of a matrix.

2. System description and preliminaries

Consider an uncertain T-S fuzzy continuous model with time-delay for a nonlinear system as follows:

$$\begin{aligned}&IF\ z_1(t)\ is\ M_{i1}\ and\ldots and\ z_p(t)\ is\ M_{ip}\\ &THEN\quad \begin{cases}\dot{x}(t)=(A_i+\Delta A_i)x(t)+(D_i+\Delta D_i)x(t-\tau_i(t))+(B_i+\Delta B_i)u(t)\\ x(t)=\phi(t), t\in[-\tau,0]\end{cases}\end{aligned} \tag{1}$$

where $M_{ij}\left(i=1,2,\ldots,r, j=1,2,\ldots,p\right)$ is the fuzzy set and r is the number of model rules; $x(t)\in\Re^n$ is the state vector, $u(t)\in\Re^m$ is the input vector, $A_i\in\Re^{n\times n}$, $D_i\in\Re^{n\times n}$, $B_i\in\Re^{n\times m}$, and $z_1(t),\ldots,z_p(t)$ are known premise variables, $\phi(t)$ is a continuous vector-valued initial function on $[-\tau,0]$; the time-delay $\tau(t)$ may be unknown but is assumed to be smooth function of time.. ΔA_i, ΔD_i and ΔB_i are time-varying matrices representing parametric uncertainties in the plant model. These uncertainties are admissibly norm-bounded and structured.

$$0\le\tau(t)\le\tau,\quad \dot{\tau}(t)\le d\prec 1,$$

where $\tau\succ 0$ and d are two scalars.

The final outputs of the fuzzy systems are:

$$\dot{x}(t)=\sum_{i=1}^{r}h_i(z(t))\{(A_i+\Delta A_i)x(t)+(D_i+\Delta D_i)x(t-\tau_i(t))+(B_i+\Delta B_i)u(t)\} \tag{2}$$

$$x(t)=\phi(t),\quad t\in[-\tau,0],$$

where

$$z(t)=[z_1(t)z_2(t)\ldots z_p(t)]$$

$$h_i(z(t))=w_i(z(t))\Big/\sum_{i=1}^{r}w_i(z(t)),\ w_i(z(t))=\prod_{j=1}^{p}M_{ij}(z_j(t))\quad \text{for all } \underline{t}.$$

The term $M_{i1}(z_j(t))$ is the grade of membership of $z_j(t)$ in M_{i1}

Since $\begin{cases}\sum_{i=1}^{r}w_i(z(t))\succ 0\\ w_i(z(t))\geq 0, & i=1,2,\ldots,r\end{cases}$

we have $\begin{cases}\sum_{i=1}^{r}h_i(z(t))=1\\ h_i(z(t))\geq 0, & i=1,2,\ldots,r\end{cases}$ for all t.

The time derivative of premise membership functions is given by:

$$\dot{h}_i(z(t))=\frac{\partial h_i}{\partial z(t)}\cdot\frac{\partial z(t)}{\partial x(t)}\cdot\frac{dx(t)}{dt}=\sum_{l=1}^{s}\upsilon_{il}\xi_{il}\times\frac{dx(t)}{dt}$$

We have the following property:

$$\sum_{k=1}^{r}\dot{h}_k(z(t))=0 \tag{3}$$

Consider a PDC fuzzy controller based on the derivative membership function and given by the equation (4)

$$u(t)=-\sum_{i=1}^{r}h_i(z(t))F_i x(t)-\sum_{m=1}^{r}\dot{h}_m(z(t))K_m x(t) \tag{4}$$

The fuzzy controller design consists to determine the local feedback gains F_i, and K_m in the consequent parts. The state variables are determined by an observer which detailed in next section.

By substituting (4) into (2), the closed-loop fuzzy system without time-delay can be represented as:

$$\dot{x}(t)=\sum_{i=1}^{r}\sum_{j=1}^{r}h_i(z(t))h_j(z(t))\left\{\left[A_{\Delta i}-B_{\Delta i}F_j-\sum_{m=1}^{r}\dot{h}_m(z(t))B_{\Delta i}K_m\right]x(t)+D_{\Delta i}x(t-\tau_i(t))\right\} \tag{5}$$

$$x(t)=\phi(t),\quad t\in[-\tau,0],$$

where $A_{\Delta i}=A_i+\Delta A_i;\ D_{\Delta i}=D_i+\Delta D_i\ \ and\ \ B_{\Delta i}=B_i+\Delta B_i$

The system without uncertainties is given by equation

$$\dot{x}(t)=\sum_{i=1}^{r}\sum_{j=1}^{r}h_i(z(t))h_j(z(t))\left\{\left[A_i-B_iF_j-\sum_{m=1}^{r}\dot{h}_m(z(t))B_iK_m\right]x(t)+D_ix(t-\tau_i(t))\right\} \tag{6}$$

$$x(t)=\phi(t),\quad t\in[-\tau,0],$$

The open-loop system is given by the equation (7),

$$\dot{x}(t)=\sum_{i=1}^{r}h_i(z(t))\left(A_{\Delta i}x(t)+D_{\Delta i}x(t-\tau_i(t))\right) \tag{7}$$

$$x(t)=\phi(t),\ t\in[-\tau,0],$$

Assumption 1

The time derivative of the premises membership function is upper bounded such that $|\dot{h}_k|\le\phi_k$, for $k=1,\ldots,r$, where, $\phi_k, k=1,\ldots,r$ are given positive constants.

Assumption 2

The matrices denote the uncertainties in the system and take the form of

$$\begin{cases}\Delta A_i=D_{a_i}F_{a_i}(t)E_{a_i}\\ \Delta B_i=D_{b_i}F_{b_i}(t)E_{b_i}\end{cases}$$

where $D_{a_i}, D_{b_i}, E_{a_i}$ and E_{b_i} are known constant matrices and $F_{a_i}(t)$and$F_{b_i}(t)$ are unknown matrix functions satisfying :

$$\begin{cases}F_{a_i}^T(t)F_{a_i}(t)\le I,\forall t\\ F_{b_i}^T(t)F_{b_i}(t)\le I,\forall t\end{cases}$$

where I is an appropriately dimensioned identity matrix.

Lemma 1 (Boyd et al. Schur complement [16])

Given constant matrices Ω_1, Ω_2 and Ω_3 with appropriate dimensions, where $\Omega_1 = \Omega_1^T$ and $\Omega_2 = \Omega_2^T$, then

$$\Omega_1 + \Omega_3^T \Omega_2^{-1} \Omega_3 \prec 0$$

if and only if

$$\begin{bmatrix} \Omega_1 & \Omega_3^T \\ * & -\Omega_2 \end{bmatrix} \prec 0 \text{ or } \begin{bmatrix} -\Omega_2 & \Omega_3 \\ * & \Omega_1 \end{bmatrix} \prec 0$$

Lemma 2 (Peterson and Hollot [2])

Let $Q = Q^T, H, E$ and $F(t)$ satisfying $F^T(t)F(t) \leq I$ are appropriately dimensional matrices then the follow-ing inequality

$$Q + HF(t)E + E^T F^T(t) H^T \prec 0$$

is true, if and only if the following inequality holds for any $\lambda \succ 0$

$$Q + \lambda^{-1} H H^T + \lambda E^T E \prec 0$$

Theorem 1 (Razumikhin Theorem)[5]

Suppose $u, v, w : \Re^+ \to \Re^+$ are continuous, non-decreasing functions satisfying $u(s) \succ 0$, $v(s) \succ 0$ and $w(s) \succ 0$ for $s \succ 0$, $u(0) = v(0) = 0$, and v strictly increasing. If there exist a continuous function $V : \Re \times \Re^n \to \Re$ and a continuous non-decreasing function $p(s) \succ s$ for $s \succ 0$ such that

$$u(|x|) \leq V(t,x) \leq v(|x|), \qquad \forall t \in \Re,\ x \in \Re^n, \tag{8}$$

$$\dot{V}(t,x) \leq -w(|x|) \quad \text{if } V(t+\sigma, x(t+\sigma)) \leq p(V(t,x)), \quad \forall \sigma \in [-\tau, 0], \tag{9}$$

then the solution $x \equiv 0$ of (7) is uniformly asymptotically stable.

Lemma 3 [6]

Assume that $a \in \Re^{n_a}$, $b \in \Re^{n_b}$, $N \in \Re^{n_a \times n_b}$ are defined on the interval Ω. Then, for any matrices $X \in \Re^{n_a \times n_a}$, $Y \in \Re^{n_a \times n_b}$ and $Z \in \Re^{n_b \times n_b}$, the following holds:

$$-2\int_{\Omega} a^T(\alpha) N b(\alpha) d\alpha \leq \int_{\Omega} \begin{bmatrix} a(\alpha) \\ b(\alpha) \end{bmatrix}^T \begin{bmatrix} X & Y - N \\ Y^T - N^T & Z \end{bmatrix} \begin{bmatrix} a(\alpha) \\ b(\alpha) \end{bmatrix} d\alpha, \tag{10}$$

where $\begin{bmatrix} X & Y \\ Y^T & Z \end{bmatrix} \geq 0$.

Lemma 4 [9]

The unforced fuzzy time delay system described by **(7)** with u = 0 is uniformly asymptotically stable if there exist matrices $P \succ 0$, $S_i \succ 0$, X_{ai}, X_{di}, Z_{aij}, Z_{dij}, and Y_i, such that the following LMIs hold:

$$\begin{bmatrix} PA_i + A_i^T P + \tau\left(X_{ai} + X_{di}\right) + \left(2\tau + 1\right)P + Y_i + Y_i^T & -PD_i \\ Y_i^T - D_i^T P & -S_i \end{bmatrix} \prec 0 \tag{11}$$

$$S_i \leq P \tag{12}$$

$$A_j^T Z_{aij} A_j \leq P \tag{13}$$

$$D_j^T Z_{dij} D_j \leq P \tag{14}$$

$$\begin{bmatrix} X_{ai} & Y_i \\ Y_i^T & Z_{aij} \end{bmatrix} \geq 0 \tag{15}$$

$$\begin{bmatrix} X_{di} & Y_i \\ Y_i^T & Z_{dij} \end{bmatrix} \geq 0 \tag{16}$$

3. Basic stability and stabilization conditions

In order to design an observer for state variables, this section introduce two theorem developed for continuous TS fuzzy model for open-loop and closed-loop. First, consider the open-loop system without time-delay given by equation(17).

$$\dot{x}(t) = \sum_{i=1}^{r} h_i\left(z(t)\right) A_i x(t) \tag{17}$$

The main approach for T-S fuzzy model stability is given in theorem follows. This approach is based on introduction of ε parameter which influences the stability region.

Theorem 2 [17]

Under assumption 1 and for $0 \leq \varepsilon \leq 1$, the Takagi Sugeno fuzzy system (17) is stable if there exist positive definite symmetric matrices $P_k, k = 1,2,\ldots,r$, matrix $R = R^T$ such that the following LMIs hold.

$$P_k + R \succ 0, \quad k \in \{1,\ldots,r\} \tag{18}$$

$$P_j + \mu R \succ 0, \quad j \in \{1,\ldots,r\} \tag{19}$$

$$\begin{aligned} P_\phi + \frac{1}{2}\Big\{ & A_i^T\left(P_j + \mu R\right) + \left(P_j + \mu R\right)A_i \\ & + A_j^T\left(P_i + \mu R\right) + \left(P_i + \mu R\right)A_j \Big\} \prec 0, \; i \le j \end{aligned} \tag{20}$$

where $i, j = 1,2,\ldots,r$ and $P_\phi = \sum_{k=1}^{r} \phi_k\left(P_k + R\right)$ and $\mu = 1 - \varepsilon$

Proof

The proof of this theorem is given in detailed in article published in [17].

The closed-loop system without time delay is given by equation (21)

$$\dot{x}(t) = \sum_{i=1}^{r} h_i\left(z(t)\right)h_i\left(z(t)\right)G_{ii}x(t) + 2\sum_{i=1}^{r}\sum_{i \prec j} h_i\left(z(t)\right)h_j\left(z(t)\right)\left\{\frac{G_{ij} + G_{ji}}{2}\right\}x(t), \tag{21}$$

where

$$G_{ij} = A_i - B_iF_j \text{ and } G_{ii} = A_i - B_iF_i \,.$$

In this section we define a fuzzy Lyapunov function and then consider stability conditions. A sufficient stability condition, for ensuring stability is given follows.

Theorem 2[18]

Under assumption 1, and assumption 2 and for given $0 \le \varepsilon \le 1$, the Takagi-Sugeno system (21) is stable if there exist positive definite symmetric matrices $P_k, k = 1,2,\ldots,r$, and R, matrices $F_1,\ldots,F_r$ such that the following LMIs hols.

$$P_k + R \succ 0, \quad k \in \{1,\ldots,r\} \tag{22}$$

$$P_j + \mu R \ge 0, \quad j = 1,2,\ldots,r \tag{23}$$

$$\begin{aligned} & P_\phi + \left\{G_{ii}^T\left(P_k + \mu R\right) + \left(P_k + \mu R\right)G_{ii}\right\} \prec 0, \\ & i,k \in \{1,\ldots,r\} \end{aligned} \tag{24}$$

$$\begin{aligned} & \left\{\frac{G_{ij} + G_{ji}}{2}\right\}^T \left(P_k + \mu R\right) + \left(P_k + \mu R\right)\left\{\frac{G_{ij} + G_{ji}}{2}\right\} \prec 0, \\ & \text{for } i,j,k = 1,2,\ldots,r \text{ such that } i \prec j \end{aligned} \tag{25}$$

where

$$G_{ij} = A_i - B_i F_j,\ G_{ii} = A_i - B_i F_i$$

And $P_\phi = \sum_{k=1}^{r} \phi_k \left(P_k + R\right)$

4. Observer design for T-S fuzzy continuous model

In order to determine state variables of system, this section gives a solution by the mean of fuzzy observer design.

A stabilizing observer-based controller can be formulated as follow:

$$\begin{aligned} &\dot{\hat{x}}(t) = \sum_{j=1}^{r} h_i\left(z(t)\right)\left\{A_i \hat{x}(t) + B_i u(t) + L_j\left(C_i \hat{x}(t) - y(t)\right)\right\} \\ &u(t) = \sum_{j=1}^{r} h_j\left(z(t)\right) F_j \hat{x}(t) \end{aligned} \tag{26}$$

The closed-loop fuzzy system can be represented as:

$$\begin{aligned} \dot{x}(t) = &\sum_{i=1}^{r}\sum_{j=1}^{r} h_i\left(z(t)\right) h_j\left(z(t)\right)\left\{\left(A_i - B_i F_j\right) - \sum_{\rho=1}^{r} \dot{h}_\rho\left(z(t)\right)\left(H_\rho + R\right)\right\} x(t) \\ &+ \sum_{i=1}^{r}\sum_{j=1}^{r} h_i\left(z(t)\right) h_j\left(z(t)\right)\left\{B_i F_j + \sum_{\rho=1}^{r} \dot{h}_\rho\left(z(t)\right)\left(H_\rho + R\right)\right\} e(t) \end{aligned} \tag{27}$$

$$\dot{e}(t) = \sum_{i=1}^{r}\sum_{j=1}^{r} h_i\left(z(t)\right) h_j\left(z(t)\right)\left\{A_i - K_i C_j\right\} e(t) \tag{28}$$

The augmented system is represented as follows:

$$\begin{aligned} \dot{x}_a(t) &= \sum_{i=1}^{r}\sum_{j=1}^{r} h_i\left(z(t)\right) h_j\left(z(t)\right) G_{ij} x_a(t) \\ &= \sum_{j=1}^{r} h_i\left(z(t)\right) h_j\left(z(t)\right) G_{ii} x_a(t) + 2\sum_{i=1}^{r}\sum_{i \prec j}^{r} h_i\left(z(t)\right) h_j\left(z(t)\right)\left\{\frac{G_{ij} + G_{ji}}{2}\right\} x_a(t) \end{aligned} \tag{29}$$

where

$$x_a(t) = \begin{bmatrix} x(t) \\ e(t) \end{bmatrix}$$

$$G_{ij} = \begin{bmatrix} A_i - B_i F_j - \sum_{\rho=1}^{r} \dot{h}_\rho B_i \left(H_\rho + R\right) & B_i F_j + \sum_{\rho=1}^{r} \dot{h}_\rho B_i \left(H_\rho + R\right) \\ 0 & A_i - K_i C_j \end{bmatrix}$$

By applying Theorem 2[18] in the augmented system (29) we derive the following Theorem.

Theorem 3

Under assumption 1 and for given $0 \le \mu \le 1$, the Takagi-Sugeno system (29) is stable if there exist positive definite symmetric matrices $P_k, k = 1,2,\ldots,r$, and R, matrices $F_1,\ldots,F_r$ such that the following LMIs hols.

$$P_k + R \succ 0, \quad k \in \{1,\ldots,r\} \tag{30}$$

$$P_j + \mu R \ge 0, \quad j = 1,2,\ldots,r \tag{31}$$

$$\begin{aligned} &P_\phi + \left\{ G_{ii}^T (P_k + \mu R) + (P_k + \mu R) G_{ii} \right\} \prec 0, \\ &i,k \in \{1,\ldots,r\} \end{aligned} \tag{32}$$

$$\begin{aligned} &\left\{ \frac{G_{ij} + G_{ji}}{2} \right\}^T (P_k + \mu R) + (P_k + \mu R) \left\{ \frac{G_{ij} + G_{ji}}{2} \right\} \prec 0, \\ &\text{for } i,j,k = 1,2,\ldots,r \text{ such that } i \prec j \end{aligned} \tag{33}$$

where

$$G_{ij} = \begin{bmatrix} A_i - B_i F_j - \sum_{\rho=1}^{r} \dot{h}_\rho B_i (H_\rho + R) & B_i F_j + \sum_{\rho=1}^{r} \dot{h}_\rho B_i (H_\rho + R) \\ 0 & A_i - K_i C_j \end{bmatrix}$$

And $P_\phi = \sum_{k=1}^{r} \phi_k (P_k + R)$

Proof

The result follows immediately from the Theorem 2[18].

5. Stabilization of continuous T-S Fuzzy model with time-delay

The aim of this section is to prove the asymptotic stability of the time-delay system (6) based on the combination between Lyapunov theory and the Razumikhin theorem [5].

Theorem 4

Under assumption 1 and for given $0 \le \varepsilon \le 1$, the unforced fuzzy time delay system described by (7) with $u = 0$ is uniformly asymptotically stable if there exist matrices $P_k \succ 0, k = 1,2,\ldots,r$, $S_i \succ 0$, X_{aij}, X_{di}, Z_{aij}, Z_{dij}, Y_i, and X, such that the following LMIs hold:

$$\begin{bmatrix} P_\beta + (P_k+\varepsilon X)G_{ij} + G_{ij}^T(P_k+\varepsilon X) \\ +\tau(X_{aij}+X_{di}) + (2\tau+1)(P_k+\varepsilon X) + Y_i + Y_i^T & -(P_k+\varepsilon X)D_i \\ Y_i^T - D_i^T(P_k+\varepsilon X) & -S_i \end{bmatrix} \prec 0 \quad (34)$$

where $P_\beta = \sum_{k=1}^{r} \beta_k (P_k+\varepsilon X)$.

$G_{ij} = A_i - B_i F_j$

$$S_i \le (P_k+\varepsilon X) \quad (35)$$

$$G_{ij}^T Z_{aij} G_{ij} \le (P_k+\varepsilon X) \quad (36)$$

$$D_j^T Z_{dij} D_j \le (P_k+\varepsilon X) \quad (37)$$

$$\begin{bmatrix} X_{aij} & Y_i \\ Y_i^T & Z_{aij} \end{bmatrix} \ge 0 \quad (38)$$

$$\begin{bmatrix} X_{di} & Y_i \\ Y_i^T & Z_{dij} \end{bmatrix} \ge 0 \quad (39)$$

Proof

Let consider the fuzzy Lyapunov function as

$$V(x) = x^T(t) V_k(x) x(t) \quad (40)$$

$$V_k(x) = \sum_{k=1}^{r} h_k (P_k+\varepsilon X)$$

Given the matrix property, clearly,

$$\lambda_{\min}(P_k+\varepsilon X)\|x(t)\|^2 \le x^T(t)(P_k+\varepsilon X)x(t) \le \lambda_{\max}(P_k+\varepsilon X)\|x(t)\|^2,$$

where $\lambda_{\min(\max)}$ denotes the smallest (largest) eigenvalue of the matrix.

Finding the maximum value of $\sum_{k=0}^{r} h_k x^T(t)(P_k+\varepsilon X)x(t)$ is equivalent to determining the maximum value of $\sum_{k=0}^{r} h_k \lambda_{\max}(P_k+\varepsilon X)$.

Finding the minimum value of $\sum_{k=0}^{r} h_k x^T(t)(P_k+\varepsilon X)x(t)$ is equivalent to determining the minimum value of $\sum_{k=0}^{r} h_k \lambda_{\min}(P_k+\varepsilon X)$.

Define

$$\kappa_1 = \min_k \sum_{k=0}^{r} h_k \lambda_{\max}(P_k+\varepsilon X) \text{ for } 0 \le k \le r,$$

$$\kappa_2 = \max_k \sum_{k=0}^{r} h_k \lambda_{\min}(P_k+\varepsilon X) \text{ for } 0 \le k \le r.$$

Then,

$$\kappa_1 \|x(t)\|^2 \le \sum_{k=1}^{r} x^T(t)(P_k+\varepsilon X)x(t) \le \kappa_2 \|x(t)\|^2$$

In the following, we will prove the asymptotic stability of the time-delay system (7) based on the Razumikhin theorem [5].

Since

$$x(t) - x(t-\tau_i(t)) = \int_{t-\tau_i(t)}^{t} \dot{x}(s)ds,$$

The state equation of (7) with $u=0$ can be rewritten as

$$\dot{x}(t) = \sum_{i=1}^{r}\sum_{j=1}^{r} h_i h_j \left[(G_{ij}+D_i)x(t) - D_i \int_{t-\tau_i(t)}^{t} \dot{x}(s)ds \right]$$

where $G_{ij} = A_i - B_i F_j$

The derivative of V along the solutions of the unforced system **(7)** with $u=0$ is thus given by

$$\dot{V} = x^T(t)\sum_{k=1}^{r} \dot{h}_k (P_k+\varepsilon X)x(t) + 2x^T(t)\sum_{i=1}^{r} h_i (P_i+\varepsilon X)\dot{x}(t) = \Upsilon_1(x,t) + \Upsilon_2(x,t) \tag{41}$$

$$\Upsilon_1(x,t) = x^T(t)\sum_{k=1}^{r} \dot{h}_k (P_k+\varepsilon X)x(t)$$

$$\Upsilon_2(x,t) = 2x^T(t)\sum_{k=1}^{r} h_k (P_k+\varepsilon X)\dot{x}(t) = 2x^T(t)\sum_{k=1}^{r} h_k (P_k+\varepsilon X) \times \sum_{i=1}^{r}\sum_{j=1}^{r} h_i h_j \left[(G_{ij}+D_i)x(t) - D_i \int_{t-\tau_i(t)}^{t} \dot{x}(s)ds \right].$$

Then, based on assumption 1, an upper bound of $\Upsilon_1(x,z)$ obtained as:

$$\Upsilon_1(x,z) \le \sum_{k=1}^{r} \beta_k \cdot x(t)^T (P_k+\varepsilon X)x(t) \tag{42}$$

and for $\Upsilon_2(x,t)$ we can written as,

$$\Upsilon_2(x,t)=2\sum_{i=1}^{r}\sum_{j=1}^{r}h_ih_jx^T\sum_{k=1}^{r}h_k(P_k+\varepsilon X)(G_{ij}+D_i)x(t)\ -\sum_{i=1}^{r}\sum_{j=1}^{r}h_ih_j\int_{t-\tau_i(t)}^{t}\left\{2x^T(t)\sum_{k=1}^{r}h_k(P_k+\varepsilon X)D_i\right.$$
$$\left.\times\sum_{\nu=1}^{r}\sum_{\varsigma=1}^{r}h_\nu(s)h_\varsigma(s)\left[G_{\nu\varsigma}x(s)+D_\varsigma x(s-\tau_j(s))\right]ds\right\}$$

$$\Upsilon_2(x,t)=2\sum_{i=1}^{r}\sum_{j=1}^{r}\sum_{k=1}^{r}h_ih_jh_kx^T\{(P_k+\varepsilon X)(G_{ij}+D_i)\}x(t)\ -\sum_{i=1}^{r}\sum_{j=1}^{r}\sum_{k=1}^{r}h_ih_jh_k\int_{t-\tau_i(t)}^{t}\left\{2x^T(t)(P_k+\varepsilon X)D_i\right.$$
$$\left.\times\sum_{\nu=1}^{r}\sum_{\varsigma=1}^{r}h_\nu(s)h_\varsigma(s)\left[G_{\nu\varsigma}x(s)+D_\varsigma x(s-\tau_j(s))\right]ds\right\} \tag{43}$$

Using the bounding method in(10), by setting $a=x(t)$ and $b=G_{ij}x(s)$, we have

$$-\int_{t-\tau_i(t)}^{t}2x^T(t)(P_k+\varepsilon X)D_i\times\sum_{\nu=1}^{r}\sum_{\varsigma=1}^{r}h_\nu(s)h_\varsigma(s)G_{\nu\varsigma}x(s)ds$$
$$\le\tau_i(t)x^T(t)X_{ai}x(t)+2x^T(t)(Y_i-(P_k+\varepsilon X)D_i)\times\int_{t-\tau_i(t)}^{t}\sum_{\nu=1}^{r}\sum_{\varsigma=1}^{r}h_\nu(s)h_\varsigma(s)G_{\nu\varsigma}x(s)ds \tag{44}$$
$$+\int_{t-\tau_i(t)}^{t}\sum_{\nu=1}^{r}\sum_{\varsigma=1}^{r}h_\nu(s)h_\varsigma(s)x^T(s)G_{\nu\varsigma}^TZ_{ai\nu}G_{\nu\varsigma}x(s)ds$$

For any matrices $X_{a\nu},Y_\nu$ and $Z_{ai\nu}$ satisfying

$$\begin{bmatrix}X_{a\nu} & Y_\nu\\ Y_\nu^T & Z_{ai\nu}\end{bmatrix}\ge 0$$

Similarly, it holds that

$$-\int_{t-\tau_i(t)}^{t}2x^T(t)(P_k+\varepsilon X)D_i\sum_{j=1}^{r}h_j(s)D_jx(s-\tau_j(s))ds$$
$$\le\tau_i(t)x^T(t)X_{di}x(t)+2x^T(t)(Y_i-(P_k+\varepsilon X)D_i)\int_{t-\tau_i(t)}^{t}\sum_{j=1}^{r}h_j(s)D_jx(s-\tau_j(s))ds \tag{45}$$
$$+\int_{t-\tau_i(t)}^{t}\sum_{j=1}^{r}h_j(s)x^T(s-\tau_j(s))D_j^TZ_{dij}D_jx(s-\tau_j(s))ds$$

For any matrices X_{di},Y_i and Z_{dij} satisfying

$$\begin{bmatrix} X_{di} & Y_i \\ Y_i^T & Z_{dij} \end{bmatrix} \geq 0$$

Hence, substituting (44) and (45) into (43), we have

$$\begin{aligned}
\dot{V} \leq P_\beta &+ \sum_{i=1}^{r}\sum_{j=1}^{r}\sum_{k=1}^{r} h_i h_j h_k x^T(t)\Big[2(P_k+\varepsilon X)(G_{ij}+D_i)+\tau(X_{ai}+X_{di})\Big]x(t) \\
&+ \sum_{i=1}^{r}\sum_{k=1}^{r} h_i h_k 2x^T(t)\big(Y_i-(P_k+\varepsilon X)D_i\big)\times \int_{t-\tau_i(t)}^{t} \sum_{\nu=1}^{r}\sum_{\varsigma=1}^{r} h_\nu(s)h_\varsigma(s)\Big[G_{\nu\varsigma}x(s)+D_\nu x\big(s-\tau_\nu(s)\big)\Big]ds \\
&+ \sum_{i=1}^{r}\sum_{k=1}^{r} h_i h_k \int_{t-\tau_i(t)}^{t} \sum_{\nu=1}^{r}\sum_{\varsigma=1}^{r} h_\nu(s)h_\varsigma(s)x^T(s)G_{\nu\varsigma}^T Z_{ai\nu} G_{\nu\varsigma}x(s)ds \\
&+ \sum_{i=1}^{r}\sum_{k=1}^{r} h_i h_k \int_{t-\tau_i(t)}^{t} \sum_{j=1}^{r} h_j(s)x^T\big(s-\tau_j(s)\big)D_j^T Z_{dij} D_j x\big(s-\tau_j(s)\big)ds
\end{aligned}$$

$$\begin{aligned}
\leq P_\beta &+ \sum_{i=1}^{r}\sum_{j=1}^{r} h_i h_j x^T(t)\Big[(P_k+\varepsilon X)G_{ij}+G_{ij}^T(P_k+\varepsilon X)+Y_i+Y_i^T+\tau(X_{aij}+X_{di})\Big]x(t) \\
&+ \sum_{i=1}^{r} h_i\Big[x^T(t)\big(Y_i-(P_k+\varepsilon X)D_i\big)S_i^{-1}\big(Y_i-(P_k+\varepsilon X)D_i\big)^T x(t)+x^T\big(t-\tau_i(t)\big)S_i x\big(t-\tau_i(t)\big)\Big] \\
&+ \sum_{i=1}^{r} h_i \times \int_{t-\tau_i(t)}^{t} \sum_{\nu=1}^{r}\sum_{\varsigma=1}^{r} h_\nu(s)h_\varsigma(s)x^T(s)G_{\nu\varsigma}^T Z_{ai\nu} G_{\nu\varsigma}x(s)ds \\
&+ \sum_{i=1}^{r} h_i \int_{t-\tau_i(t)}^{t} \sum_{j=1}^{r} h_j(s)x^T\big(s-\tau_j(s)\big)D_j^T Z_{dij} D_j x\big(s-\tau_j(s)\big)ds
\end{aligned} \qquad (46)$$

Note that, by *Shur* complement, the LMI in (34) implies $L_i(\delta)\prec 0$ for a sufficiently small scalar $\delta \succ 0$, where

$$\begin{aligned}
L_i(\delta) = P_\beta &+ (P_k+\varepsilon X)G_{ij}+G_{ij}^T(P_k+\varepsilon X)+Y_i+Y_i^T+\tau(X_{aij}+X_{di}) \\
&+ \big(Y_i-(P_k+\varepsilon X)D_i\big)S_i^{-1}\big(Y_i-(P_k+\varepsilon X)D_i\big)^T x(t)+(2\tau+1+\tau\delta)(1+\delta)(P_k+\varepsilon X)
\end{aligned}$$

In order to use the *Razumikhin* Theorem, suppose $V\big(x(t+\sigma)\big)\prec(1+\delta)V\big(x(t)\big)$ for $\sigma\in[-\tau,0]$. Then, if the LMIs in (35)–(39) also hold, we have from (46) that

$$\begin{aligned}
\dot{V} \leq &\sum_{i=1}^{r}\sum_{j=1}^{r} h_i h_j x^T(t)\Big[(P_k+\varepsilon X)G_{ij}+G_{ij}^T(P_k+\varepsilon X)+Y_i+Y_i^T+\tau(X_{aij}+X_{di})\Big]x(t) \\
&+ \sum_{i=1}^{r} h_i\Big[x^T(t)\big(Y_i-(P_k+\varepsilon X)D_i\big)S_i^{-1}\big(Y_i-(P_k+\varepsilon X)D_i\big)^T x(t)+x^T(t)(1+\delta)(P_k+\varepsilon X)x(t)\Big] \\
&+ \sum_{i=1}^{r} h_i\tau_i(t)x^T(t)(1+\delta)(P_k+\varepsilon X)x(t)+\sum_{i=1}^{r} h_i \int_{t-\tau_i(t)}^{t} x^T(s)(1+\delta)(P_k+\varepsilon X)x(s)ds
\end{aligned}$$

$$\le \sum_{i=1}^{r} h_i x^T(t)\left[(P_k+\varepsilon X)A_i + A_i^T(P_k+\varepsilon X)+Y_i+Y_i^T+\tau(X_{ai}+X_{di})\right]x(t)$$

$$+\sum_{i=1}^{r} h_i\left[x^T(t)(Y_i-(P_k+\varepsilon X)D_i)S_i^{-1}(Y_i-(P_k+\varepsilon X)D_i)^T x(t)+x^T(t)(1+\delta)(P_k+\varepsilon X)x(t)\right]$$

$$+\tau x^T(t)(1+\delta)(P_k+\varepsilon X)x(t)+\tau x^T(t)(1+\delta)^2(P_k+\varepsilon X)x(t)$$

$$=\sum_{i=1}^{r} h_i x^T(t) L_i(\delta)x(t)$$

$$\prec 0$$

which shows the motion of the unforced system **(7)** with $u = 0$ is uniformly asymptotically stable. This completes the proof.

6. Robust stability condition with PDC controller

Consider the closed-loop system (5). A sufficient robust stability condition for Time-delay system is given follow.

Theorem 5

Under assumption 1, and assumption 2 and for given $0 \le \varepsilon \le 1$, the Takagi-Sugeno system (5) is stable if there exist positive definite symmetric matrices $P_k, k = 1,2,\ldots,r$, and R, matrices $F_1,\ldots,F_r$ such that the following LMIs hols.

$$P_k + R \succ 0, \quad k \in \{1,\ldots,r\} \tag{47}$$

$$P_j + \mu R \ge 0, \quad j = 1,2,\ldots,r \tag{48}$$

$$\begin{bmatrix} \Phi_1 & (P_k+\mu R)D_{ai} & (P_k+\mu R)D_{bi} & (P_k+\mu R)(D_{di}\Delta_{di}E_{di}) \\ * & -\lambda I & 0 & 0 \\ * & * & -\lambda I & 0 \\ * & * & * & 0 \end{bmatrix} \prec 0 \tag{49}$$

$$i,k \in \{1,\ldots,r\}$$

with

$$\Phi_1 = P_\phi + \bar{G}_{ii}^T(P_k+\mu R) + (P_k+\mu R)\bar{G}_{ii} + \lambda(P_k+\mu R)\left[E_{ai}^T E_{ai} + (E_{bi}F_i)^T E_{bi}F_i\right]$$

$$\begin{bmatrix} \Phi_2 & & \\ * & -\lambda I & 0 \\ * & * & -\lambda I \end{bmatrix} \prec 0$$

$$\begin{bmatrix} \Phi_2 & (P_k+\mu R)(D_{ai}+D_{aj}) & (P_k+\mu R)(D_{bi}+D_{bj}) & (P_k+\mu R)(D_{di}\Delta_{di}E_{di}) \\ * & -\lambda I & 0 & 0 \\ * & * & -\lambda I & 0 \\ * & * & * & 0 \end{bmatrix} \prec 0 \quad (50)$$

$i,k \in \{1,\ldots,r\}$

for $i,j,k = 1,2,\ldots,r$ such that $i \prec j$

with

$$\Phi_2 = \left(\frac{\bar{G}_{ij}+\bar{G}_{ji}}{2}\right)^T (P_k+\mu R) + (P_k+\mu R)\left(\frac{\bar{G}_{ij}+\bar{G}_{ji}}{2}\right) + \lambda(P_k+\mu R)\Big[(E_{ai}+E_{aj})^T(E_{ai}+E_{aj})$$
$$+(E_{bi}F_j+E_{bj}F_i)^T(E_{bi}F_j+E_{bj}F_i)^T\Big]$$

where $\bar{G}_{ij} = \left[A_i - B_iF_j - \sum_{m=1}^{r}\dot{h}_m(z(t))B_iK_m\right], G_{ii} = \left[A_i - B_iF_i - \sum_{m=1}^{r}\dot{h}_m(z(t))B_iK_m\right]$, $\mu = 1-\varepsilon$, and

$P_\phi = \sum_{k=1}^{r}\phi_k(P_k+R)$

Proof

Let consider the Lyapunov function in the following form:

$$V(x(t)) = \sum_{k=1}^{r} h_k(z(t)) \cdot V_k(x(t)) \quad (51)$$

with

$$V_k(x(t)) = x^T(t)(P_k+\mu R)x(t), \; k=1,2,\ldots,r$$

where

$$P_k = P_k^T, R = R^T, \; 0 \le \varepsilon \le 1, \mu = 1-\varepsilon, \text{ and } (P_k+\mu R) \ge 0, \quad k=1,2,\ldots,r .$$

The time derivative of $V(x(t))$ with respect to t along the trajectory of the system (21) is given by:

$$\dot{V}(x(t)) = \sum_{k=1}^{r}\dot{h}_k(z(t))V_k(x(t)) + \sum_{k=1}^{r}h_k(z(t))\dot{V}_k(x(t)) \quad (52)$$

The equation (52) can be rewritten as,

$$\dot{V}(x(t)) = x^T(t)\left(\sum_{k=1}^{r}\dot{h}_k(z(t))(P_k+\mu R)\right)x(t) + \dot{x}^T(t)\left(\sum_{k=1}^{r}h_k(z(t))(P_k+\mu R)\right)x(t) + x^T(t)\left(\sum_{k=1}^{r}h_k(z(t))(P_k+\mu R)\right)\dot{x}(t) \tag{53}$$

By substituting (5) into (53), we obtain,

$$\dot{V}(x(t)) = \Upsilon_1(x,z) + \Upsilon_2(x,z) + \Upsilon_3(x,z) \tag{54}$$

where

$$\Upsilon_1(x,z) = x^T(t)\left(\sum_{k=1}^{r}\dot{h}_k(z(t))\cdot(P_k+\mu R)\right)x(t) \tag{55}$$

$$\begin{aligned}
\Upsilon_2(x,z) &= x^T(t)\sum_{k=1}^{r}\sum_{i=1}^{r}h_k(z(t))h_i^2(z(t))\times\left\{\bar{G}_{ii}^T(P_k+\mu R)+(P_k+\mu R)\bar{G}_{ii}\right\}x(t) \\
&+ x^T(t)\sum_{k=1}^{r}\sum_{i=1}^{r}h_k(z(t))h_i^2(z(t))\times\left\{\left(\begin{bmatrix}D_{ai} & D_{bi}\end{bmatrix}\begin{bmatrix}\Delta_{ai} & 0\\ 0 & \Delta_{bi}\end{bmatrix}\begin{bmatrix}E_{ai}\\ -E_{bi}F_i\end{bmatrix}\right)^T(P_k+\mu R)\right. \\
&\left.+(P_k+\mu R)\left(\begin{bmatrix}D_{ai} & D_{bi}\end{bmatrix}\begin{bmatrix}\Delta_{ai} & 0\\ 0 & \Delta_{bi}\end{bmatrix}\begin{bmatrix}E_{ai}\\ -E_{bi}F_i\end{bmatrix}\right)\right\}x(t) \\
&+ x^T(t-\tau_i(t))\sum_{k=1}^{r}\sum_{i=1}^{r}h_i(z(t))h_k(z(t))\left\{(D_{di}\Delta_{di}E_{di})^T(P_k+\mu R)\right\}x(t) \\
&+ x^T(t)\sum_{k=1}^{r}\sum_{i=1}^{r}h_i(z(t))h_k(z(t))(P_k+\mu R)(D_{di}\Delta_{di}E_{di})x(t-\tau_i(t))
\end{aligned} \tag{56}$$

$$\Upsilon_2(x,z) = \sum_{k=1}^{r}\sum_{i=1}^{r}h_k(z(t))h_i^2(z(t))\times\eta^T\Sigma_{ii}\eta$$

where $\eta^T = \begin{bmatrix}x^T(t) & x^T(t-\tau_i(t))\end{bmatrix}$

$$\Sigma_{ii} = \begin{bmatrix}\Pi_1 & (P_k+\mu R)(D_{di}\Delta_{di}E_{di})\\ \left\{(D_{di}\Delta_{di}E_{di})^T(P_k+\mu R)\right\} & 0\end{bmatrix}$$

with $\Pi_1 = \left\{\bar{G}_{ii}^T(P_k+\mu R)+(P_k+\mu R)\bar{G}_{ii}\right\}$

$$+\left\{\left(\begin{bmatrix}D_{ai} & D_{bi}\end{bmatrix}\begin{bmatrix}\Delta_{ai} & 0\\ 0 & \Delta_{bi}\end{bmatrix}\begin{bmatrix}E_{ai}\\ -E_{bi}F_i\end{bmatrix}\right)^T(P_k+\mu R)+(P_k+\mu R)\left(\begin{bmatrix}D_{ai} & D_{bi}\end{bmatrix}\begin{bmatrix}\Delta_{ai} & 0\\ 0 & \Delta_{bi}\end{bmatrix}\begin{bmatrix}E_{ai}\\ -E_{bi}F_i\end{bmatrix}\right)\right\}x(t)$$

where $\bar{G}_{ii} = \left[A_i - B_iF_i - \sum_{m=1}^{r}\dot{h}_m(z(t))B_iK_m\right]$

$$\begin{aligned}
\Upsilon_3(x,z) &= x(t)^T \sum_{k=1}^{r}\sum_{i=1}^{r}\sum_{i\prec j} h_k(z(t))h_i(z(t))h_j(z(t)) \times \left\{ \left[\left(\frac{\bar{G}_{ij}+\bar{G}_{ji}}{2}\right)^T (P_k+\mu R) + (P_k+\mu R)\left(\frac{\bar{G}_{ij}+\bar{G}_{ji}}{2}\right) \right] \right\} x(t) \\
&+ x(t)^T \sum_{k=1}^{r}\sum_{i=1}^{r}\sum_{i\prec j} h_k(z(t))h_i(z(t))h_j(z(t)) \times \left\{ \left(\begin{bmatrix} D_{ai} & D_{bi} \end{bmatrix} \begin{bmatrix} \Delta_{ai} & 0 \\ 0 & \Delta_{bi} \end{bmatrix} \begin{bmatrix} E_{ai} \\ -E_{bi}F_j \end{bmatrix} \right)^T (P_k+\mu R) \right. \\
&\left. + (P_k+\mu R)\left(\begin{bmatrix} D_{ai} & D_{bi} \end{bmatrix} \begin{bmatrix} \Delta_{ai} & 0 \\ 0 & \Delta_{bi} \end{bmatrix} \begin{bmatrix} E_{ai} \\ -E_{bi}F_j \end{bmatrix} \right) \right\} x(t) + x(t)^T \sum_{k=1}^{r}\sum_{i=1}^{r}\sum_{i\prec j} h_k(z(t))h_i(z(t))h_j(z(t)) \\
&\times \left\{ \left(\begin{bmatrix} D_{aj} & D_{bj} \end{bmatrix} \begin{bmatrix} \Delta_{aj} & 0 \\ 0 & \Delta_{bj} \end{bmatrix} \begin{bmatrix} E_{aj} \\ -E_{bj}F_i \end{bmatrix} \right)^T (P_k+\mu R) + (P_k+\mu R)\left(\begin{bmatrix} D_{aj} & D_{bj} \end{bmatrix} \begin{bmatrix} \Delta_{aj} & 0 \\ 0 & \Delta_{bj} \end{bmatrix} \begin{bmatrix} E_{aj} \\ -E_{bj}F_i \end{bmatrix} \right) \right\} x(t) \\
&+ x^T(t-\tau_i(t)) \sum_{k=1}^{r}\sum_{i=1}^{r} h_i(z(t))h_k(z(t)) \left\{ (D_{di}\Delta_{di}E_{di})^T (P_k+\mu R) \right\} x(t) \\
&+ x^T(t) \sum_{k=1}^{r}\sum_{i=1}^{r} h_i(z(t))h_k(z(t)) (P_k+\mu R)(D_{di}\Delta_{di}E_{di}) x(t-\tau_i(t))
\end{aligned} \tag{57}$$

where $\bar{G}_{ij} = \left[A_i - B_iF_j - \sum_{m=1}^{r} \dot{h}_m(z(t)) B_i K_m \right]$

$$\Upsilon_3(x,z) = \sum_{k=1}^{r}\sum_{i=1}^{r}\sum_{i\prec j} h_k(z(t))h_i(z(t))h_j(z(t)) \times \eta^T \Sigma_{ij} \eta$$

where $\eta^T = \begin{bmatrix} x^T(t) & x^T(t-\tau_i(t)) \end{bmatrix}$

$$\Sigma_{ij} = \begin{bmatrix} \Pi_2 & (P_k+\mu R)(D_{di}\Delta_{di}E_{di}) \\ \left\{ (D_{di}\Delta_{di}E_{di})^T (P_k+\mu R) \right\} & 0 \end{bmatrix}$$

with
$$\begin{aligned}
\Pi_2 &= \left\{ \left[\left(\frac{\bar{G}_{ij}+\bar{G}_{ji}}{2}\right)^T (P_k+\mu R) + (P_k+\mu R)\left(\frac{\bar{G}_{ij}+\bar{G}_{ji}}{2}\right) \right] \right\} \\
&+ \left\{ \left(\begin{bmatrix} D_{ai} & D_{bi} \end{bmatrix} \begin{bmatrix} \Delta_{ai} & 0 \\ 0 & \Delta_{bi} \end{bmatrix} \begin{bmatrix} E_{ai} \\ -E_{bi}F_j \end{bmatrix} \right)^T (P_k+\mu R) + (P_k+\mu R)\left(\begin{bmatrix} D_{ai} & D_{bi} \end{bmatrix} \begin{bmatrix} \Delta_{ai} & 0 \\ 0 & \Delta_{bi} \end{bmatrix} \begin{bmatrix} E_{ai} \\ -E_{bi}F_j \end{bmatrix} \right) \right\} \\
&+ \left\{ \left(\begin{bmatrix} D_{aj} & D_{bj} \end{bmatrix} \begin{bmatrix} \Delta_{aj} & 0 \\ 0 & \Delta_{bj} \end{bmatrix} \begin{bmatrix} E_{aj} \\ -E_{bj}F_i \end{bmatrix} \right)^T (P_k+\mu R) + (P_k+\mu R)\left(\begin{bmatrix} D_{aj} & D_{bj} \end{bmatrix} \begin{bmatrix} \Delta_{aj} & 0 \\ 0 & \Delta_{bj} \end{bmatrix} \begin{bmatrix} E_{aj} \\ -E_{bj}F_i \end{bmatrix} \right) \right\}
\end{aligned}$$

Then, based on assumption 1, an upper bound of $\Upsilon_1(x,z)$ obtained as:

$$\Upsilon_1(x,z) \le \sum_{k=1}^{r} \phi_k \cdot x(t)^T (P_k+\mu R) x(t) \tag{58}$$

Based on (3), it follows that $\sum_{k=1}^{r} \dot{h}_k(z(t)) \varepsilon R = \bar{R} = 0$ where R is any symmetric matrix of proper dimension.

Adding $\bar{R}$ to (55), then

$$\Upsilon_1(x,z) \le \sum_{k=1}^{r} \phi_k \cdot x(t)^T (P_k + R) x(t) \tag{59}$$

Then,

$$\dot{V}(x(t)) \le \sum_{k=1}^{r} \phi_k x^T(t)(P_k + R)x(t) + \Upsilon_2(x,z) + \Upsilon_3(x,z)$$

If

$$\begin{bmatrix} H_{11} & (P_k + \mu R) D_{di} \Delta_{di} E_{di} \\ E_{di}^T \Delta_{di}^T D_{di}^T (P_k + \mu R) & 0 \end{bmatrix} \prec 0$$

where $$H_{11} = \sum_{k=1}^{r} \phi_k (P_k + R) + \bar{G}_{ii}^T (P_k + \mu R) + (P_k + \mu R) \bar{G}_{ii}$$

$$+ \left\{ \left(\begin{bmatrix} E_{ai} \\ -E_{bi} F_i \end{bmatrix} \right)^T \left(\begin{bmatrix} D_{ai} & D_{bi} \end{bmatrix} \right)^T (P_k + \mu R) + (P_k + \mu R) \begin{bmatrix} D_{ai} & D_{bi} \end{bmatrix} \begin{bmatrix} \Delta_{ai} & 0 \\ 0 & \Delta_{bi} \end{bmatrix} \begin{bmatrix} E_{ai} \\ -E_{bi} F_i \end{bmatrix} \right\}$$

Then, based on Lemma 2, an upper bound of H_{11} obtained as:

$$\sum_{k=1}^{r} \phi_k (P_k + R) + \bar{G}_{ii}^T (P_k + \mu R) + (P_k + \mu R) \bar{G}_{ii} + \lambda^{-1} (P_k + \mu R) \begin{bmatrix} D_{ai} & D_{bi} \end{bmatrix} \begin{bmatrix} D_{ai}^T \\ D_{bi}^T \end{bmatrix}$$
$$+ \lambda \begin{bmatrix} E_{ai}^T & -(E_{bi} F_i)^T \end{bmatrix} \begin{bmatrix} E_{ai} \\ -E_{bi} F_i \end{bmatrix} (P_k + \mu R) \prec 0$$

by Schur complement, we obtain,

$$\begin{bmatrix} \Phi_1 & (P_k + \mu R) D_{ai} & (P_k + \mu R) D_{bi} \\ * & -\lambda I & 0 \\ * & * & -\lambda I \end{bmatrix} \prec 0$$

with

$$\Phi_1 = P_\phi + \bar{G}_{ii}^T (P_k + \mu R) + (P_k + \mu R) \bar{G}_{ii} + \lambda (P_k + \mu R) \left[E_{ai}^T E_{ai} + (E_{bi} F_i)^T E_{bi} F_i \right]$$

$$\left\{ \left(\frac{\bar{G}_{ij} + \bar{G}_{ji}}{2} \right)^T (P_k + \mu R) + (P_k + \mu R) \left(\frac{\bar{G}_{ij} + \bar{G}_{ji}}{2} \right) \right\} + \left\{ \left(\begin{bmatrix} D_{ai} + D_{aj} & D_{bi} + D_{bj} \end{bmatrix} \begin{bmatrix} \Delta_{ai} + \Delta_{aj} & 0 \\ 0 & \Delta_{bi} + \Delta_{bj} \end{bmatrix} \right. \right.$$
$$\left. \left. \times \begin{bmatrix} E_{ai} + E_{aj} \\ -E_{bi} F_j - E_{bj} F_i \end{bmatrix} \right)^T (P_k + \mu R) + (P_k + \mu R) \times \left(\begin{bmatrix} D_{ai} + D_{aj} & D_{bi} + D_{bj} \end{bmatrix} \begin{bmatrix} \Delta_{ai} + \Delta_{aj} & 0 \\ 0 & \Delta_{bi} + \Delta_{bj} \end{bmatrix} \times \begin{bmatrix} E_{ai} + E_{aj} \\ -E_{bi} F_j - E_{bj} F_i \end{bmatrix} \right) \right\}$$
$$\prec 0$$

Then, based on Lemma 2, an upper bound of $\Upsilon_1(x,z)$ obtained as:

$$\left(\frac{\bar{G}_{ij}+\bar{G}_{ji}}{2}\right)^T(P_k+\mu R)+(P_k+\mu R)\left(\frac{\bar{G}_{ij}+\bar{G}_{ji}}{2}\right)+\lambda^{-1}(P_k+\mu R)\begin{bmatrix} D_{ai}+D_{aj} & D_{bi}+D_{bj}\end{bmatrix}\begin{bmatrix} D_{ai}^T+D^T{}_{aj} \\ D_{bi}^T+D^T{}_{bj}\end{bmatrix}$$
$$+\lambda\begin{bmatrix}\left(E_{ai}+E_{aj}\right)^T & \left(-E_{bi}F_j-E_{bj}F_i\right)^T\end{bmatrix}\times\begin{bmatrix} E_{ai}+E_{aj} \\ -E_{bi}F_j-E_{bj}F_i\end{bmatrix}(P_k+\mu R)\prec 0$$

by Schur complement, we obtain,

$$\begin{bmatrix}\Phi_2 & (P_k+\mu R)(D_{ai}+D_{aj}) & (P_k+\mu R)(D_{bi}+D_{bj}) \\ * & -\lambda I & 0 \\ * & * & -\lambda I\end{bmatrix}\prec 0$$

with

$$\Phi_2=\left(\frac{\bar{G}_{ij}+\bar{G}_{ji}}{2}\right)^T(P_k+\mu R)+(P_k+\mu R)\left(\frac{\bar{G}_{ij}+\bar{G}_{ji}}{2}\right)+\lambda(P_k+\mu R)\Big[\left(E_{ai}+E_{aj}\right)^T\left(E_{ai}+E_{aj}\right)$$
$$+\left(E_{bi}F_j+E_{bj}F_i\right)^T\left(E_{bi}F_j+E_{bj}F_i\right)^T\Big]$$

If (49) and (50) holds, the time derivative of the fuzzy Lyapunov function is negative. Consequently, we have $\dot{V}(x(t))\prec 0$ and the closed loop fuzzy system (5) is stable. This is complete the proof.

7. Numerical examples

Consider the following T-S fuzzy system:

$$\dot{x}(t)=\sum_{i=1}^{r}h_i(z(t))A_i x(t) \tag{60}$$

with: $r=2$

the premise functions are given by:

$$h_1(x_1(t))=\frac{1+\sin x_1(t)}{2};\ h_2(x_1(t))=\frac{1-\sin x_1(t)}{2};\ A_1=\begin{bmatrix}-5 & -4 \\ -1 & -2\end{bmatrix};\ A_2=\begin{bmatrix}-2 & -4 \\ 20 & -2\end{bmatrix};$$

It is assumed that $|x_1(t)|\le\frac{\pi}{2}$. For $\xi_{11}=0, \xi_{12}=0.5,\ \xi_{21}=-0.5$, and $\xi_{22}=0$, we obtain

$$P_1=\begin{bmatrix}37.7864 & 26.8058 \\ 26.8058 & 36.2722\end{bmatrix};\ P_2=\begin{bmatrix}98.5559 & 28.7577 \\ 28.7577 & 22.9286\end{bmatrix};\ R=\begin{bmatrix}-1.2760 & -2.2632 \\ -2.2632 & -0.6389\end{bmatrix}$$

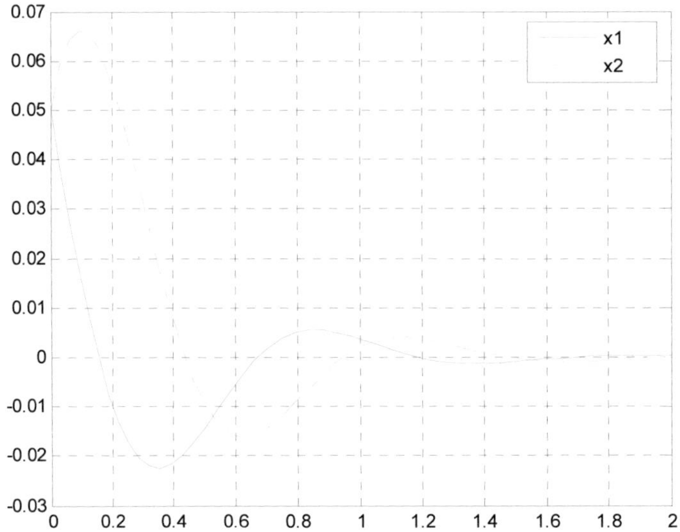

Figure 1. State variables

Figure 3 shows the evolution of the state variables. As can be seen, the conservatism reduction leads to very interesting results regarding fast convergence of this Takagi-Sugeno fuzzy system.

In order to show the improvements of proposed approaches over some existing results, in this section, we present a numerical example, which concern the feasibility of a time delay T-S fuzzy system. Indeed, we compare our fuzzy Lyapunov-Razumikhin approach (Theorem 3.1) with the Lemma 2.2 in [9].

Example 2. Consider the following T-S fuzzy system with u=0:

$$\dot{x}(t)=\sum_{i=1}^{2}h_i(z(t))\{A_ix(t)+D_ix(t-\tau_i(t))\}, \tag{61}$$

with:

$$A_1=\begin{bmatrix}-2.1 & 0.1\\ -0.2 & -0.9\end{bmatrix},\ A_2=\begin{bmatrix}-1.9 & 0\\ -0.2 & -1.1\end{bmatrix},\ D_1=\begin{bmatrix}-1.1 & 0.1\\ -0.8 & -0.9\end{bmatrix},\ D_2=\begin{bmatrix}-0.9 & 0\\ -1.1 & -1.2\end{bmatrix},$$

with the following membership functions :

$$h_1=\sin^2(x_1+0.5);\qquad h_2=\cos^2(x_1+0.5).$$

Assume that $\tau_i(t)=0.5\left|\sin(x_1(t)+x_2(t)+1)\right|$ where $x(t)=[x_1(t),x_2(t)]^T$. Then, $\tau_i(t)\le\tau=0.5$. Table 1. shows that our approach is less conservative than Lemma 2.2. given in [9].

Methods	τ_{max}
Lemma 2.1	0.6308
Theorem 3.1	$+\infty$

Table 1. Comparison results of maximum τ for Example 1

The LMIs in (34)-(39) are feasible by choosing $X_{ai} = X_a$, $X_{di} = X_d$, $Y_i = Y$, $Z_{aij} = Z_a$, $Z_{dij} = Z_d$, and $S_i = S$, $i, j = 1,2$, and for $\tau = 0.5$ a feasible solution is given by

$$P_1 = \begin{bmatrix} 1.5121 & -0.1801 \\ -0.1801 & 1.1057 \end{bmatrix},\ P_2 = \begin{bmatrix} 1.451 & -0.178 \\ -0.178 & 0.883 \end{bmatrix},\ S = \begin{bmatrix} 1.021 & -0.064 \\ -0.064 & 0.664 \end{bmatrix},$$

$$Y = \begin{bmatrix} -0.611 & 0.169 \\ -0.243 & -0.421 \end{bmatrix},\ X_a = \begin{bmatrix} 2.523 & 0.707 \\ 0.707 & 2.155 \end{bmatrix},\ X_d = \begin{bmatrix} 1.448 & 0.094 \\ 0.094 & 2.353 \end{bmatrix},\ Z_a = \begin{bmatrix} 0.201 & -0.087 \\ -0.087 & 0.369 \end{bmatrix},$$

$$Z_d = \begin{bmatrix} 0.849 & -0.227 \\ -0.227 & 0.246 \end{bmatrix},$$

8. Conclusion

This chapter provided new conditions for the stabilization with a PDC controller of Takagi-Sugeno fuzzy systems with time delay in terms of a combination of the Razumikhin theorem and the use of non-quadratic Lyapunov function as Fuzzy Lyapunov function. In addition, the time derivative of membership function is considered by the PDC fuzzy controller in order to facilitate the stability analysis. An approach to design an observer is derived in order to estimate variable states. In addition, a new condition of the stabilization of uncertain system is given in this chapter.

The stabilization condition proposed in this note is less conservative than some of those in the literature, which has been illustrated via examples.

Author details

Yassine Manai and Mohamed Benrejeb
National Engineering School of Tunis, LR-Automatique, Tunis, Tunisia

9. References

[1] T. Takagi, and M. Sugeno, "Fuzzy identification of systems and its application to modeling and control," *IEEE Trans. On System, Man and Cybernetics*, vol 15 (1), pp. 116–132, 1985.

[2] M.A.L. Thathachar, P. Viswanah, "On the Stability of Fuzzy Systems", *IEEE Transactions on Fuzzy Systems*, Vol. 5, N°1, pp. 145 – 151, February 1997.

[3] L. K. Wong, F.H.F. Leung, P.K.S. Tam, "Stability Design of TS Model Based Fuzzy Systems", *Proceedings of the Sixth IEEE International Conference on Fuzzy Systems*, Vol. 1, pp. 83–86, 1997.

[4] C.H. Fang, Y.S. Liu, S.W. Kau, L. Hong, and C.H. Lee, "A New LMI-Based Approach to Relaxed Quadratic Stabilization of T–S Fuzzy Control Systems," *IEEE Transactions on Fuzzy Systems*, Vol. 14, N° 3, pp.386–397, June 2006.

[5] H. K. Lam, F.H. Leung, "Stability Analysis of Fuzzy Model based Control Systems", Hong Kong, Springer 2011.

[6] I. Abdelmalek, N. Golea, and M.L. Hadjili, "A New Fuzzy Lyapunov Approach to Non–Quadratic Stabilization of Takagi-Sugeno Fuzzy Models," *Int. J. Appl. Math. Comput. Sci.*, Vol. 17, No. 1, 39–51, 2007.

[7] L.A. Mozelli, R.M. Palhares, F.O. Souza, and E.M. Mendes, "Reducing conservativeness in recent stability conditions of TS fuzzy systems," *Automatica*, Vol. 45, pp. 1580–1583, 2009.

[8] Y.Y. Cao and P.M. Frank, "Stability analysis and synthesis of nonlinear time-delay systems via Takagi–Sugeno fuzzy models", Fuzzy Sets and systems, Vol. 124 N°2, pp. 213-229, 2001.

[9] C. Lin, Q.G. Wang, T.H. Lee, "Delay-dependent LMI conditions for stability and stabilization of T–S fuzzy systems with bounded time-delay", Fuzzy Sets and Systems, Vol. 157 N°9, pp. 1229-1247, 2006.

[10] C. Lin, Q.G. Wang, and T. H. Lee, "Fuzzy Weighting-dependent approach to H_{∞} filter design for Time-delay fuzzy systems", IEEE Transactions on Signal Processing, Vol. 55 N° 6, 2007.

[11] C. Lin, Q.G. Wang, and T. H. Lee, LMI Approach to Analysis and Control of Takagi–Sugeno Fuzzy Systems with Time Delay, Springer-Verlag, Berlin 2007.

[12] Y.Y. Cao, and P.M. Frank. "Analysis and synthesis of nonlinear time-delay systems via fuzzy control approach". IEEE Transactions on Fuzzy Systems, 8(2), 200-211, 2000.

[13] I Amri, D Soudani, M Benrejeb, "Exponential Stability and Stabilization of Linear Systems with Time Varying Delays",Conf. SSD'09, Djerba, 2009.

[14] K. Tanaka, T. Hori, and H.O. Wang, "A multiple Lyapunov function approach to stabilization of fuzzy control systems," IEEE Transactions on Fuzzy Systems, Vol. 11 N°4, pp. 582–589, 2003.

[15] C.H. Fang, Y.S. Liu, S.W. Kau, L. Hong, and C.H. Lee, "A New LMI-Based Approach to Relaxed Quadratic Stabilization of T–S Fuzzy Control Systems," IEEE Transactions on Fuzzy Systems, Vol. 14, N° 3, pp.386–397, June 2006.

[16] H.O. Wang, K. Tanaka, M. F. Griffin, "An Approach to Fuzzy Control of Nonlinear Systems: Stability and Design Issues", IEEE Transactions On Fuzzy Systems, Vol. 4, N°1, February 1996.

[17] Y. Manai, M. Benrejeb, "Stability for Continuous Takagi-Sugeno Fuzzy System based on Fuzzy Lyapunov Function', Conf. CCCA'11, Hammamet, 2011.

[18] M. Yassine, B. Mohamed, "New Condition of Stabilisation for Continuous Takagi-Sugeno Fuzzy System based on Fuzzy Lyapunov Function", International Journal of Control and Automation, Vol. 4 No. 3, September, 2011.

Chapter 21

A Two-Layered Load and Frequency Controller of a Power System

Mavungu Masiala, Mohsen Ghribi and Azeddine Kaddouri

Additional information is available at the end of the chapter

http://dx.doi.org/10.5772/48404

1. Introduction

Automatic generation control (AGC) or called load frequency control (LFC) has gained a lot of interests in the past 30 decade (Benjamin &. Chan, 1982; Pan & Liaw, 1989; Kothari et al., 1989; Y. Wang et al., 1994; Indulkar & Raj, 1995; Karnavas & Papadopoulos, 2002; Moon et al., 2002; Sherbiny et al., 2003). LFC insures a sufficient and reliable supply of power with good quality. To ensure the quality of the power supply, it is necessary to deal with the control of the generator loads depending on the frequency with a proper LFC design. Therefore, the design of the controller is faced with nonlinear effects due to the physical components of the system, such as governor dead zone and generation rate constraints (GRC) and its complexity and the inherent characteristics of changing loads and parameters. Most actuators used in practice contain static (dead zone) or dynamic (backlash) non-smooth nonlinearities. These actuators are present in most mechanical and hydraulic systems such as servo valves. Their mathematical models are poorly known and limit the static and dynamic performance of feedback control system (Corradini & Orlando,2002). Conventional PI controller has been often used to achieve zero steady state frequency deviation. However, because of the load changing, the operating point of a power system may change very much during a daily cycle (Pan & Liaw, 1989). Therefore, a PI controller which is fixed and optimal when considering one operating point may no longer be suitable with various statuses. On the other hand, it is known that the classical LFC does not yield adequate control performance with consideration of the speed – governor non-smooth nonlinearities and GRC (Karnavas & Papadopoulos, 2002; Moon et al., 2002).

The problem of controlling systems with dead-zone nonlinearity has been addressed in the literature using various approaches some of which are dedicated to power systems. Reference (Tao & Kokotovic, 1994; X.-S. Wang et al., 2004) proposed adaptive schemes with and without dead zone inverse scheme, respectively, to track the error caused by the dead zone effect to zero. In the past decade, fuzzy logic controllers (FLC) have been developed successfully for analysis and control of nonlinear systems (Lee, 1990).

However, it has been sown by (Kim et al., 1994) that usual "Fuzzy PD" controller suffers from poor transient performance and a large steady state error when applied to systems with dead zones. On the other hand, when dealing with complex systems, the single-loop controller may not achieve the control performances and a multilayered controller turns out to be very helpful. The main advantage of the multilevel control lies in the freedom of the design of each layer (Yeh & Li, 2003; Oh & Park, 1998). The layers are designed to target particular objectives, so that design is simpler and performance improved. Motivated by the success of FLC, (Koo, 2001; Rubai, 1991) proposed new adaptive fuzzy controllers with online gain – tuning algorithm.

However, lots of computations are needed to calculate the adaptive control law with and without fuzzy system. To simplify the controller design (Kim et al., 1994) proposed a Two-layered fuzzy logic controller in which a fuzzy pre-compensator and a "fuzzy PD" controller were introduced to control plants with dead zones. Stimulated by ((Kim et al., 1994; L. X. Wang, 1997) designed a 2 layered fuzzy LFC (FLC-FLC) with the dead zone and GRC effects. Reference (Rubai, 1991) proposed a 2 layers fuzzy controller for the transient stability enhancement of the electric power system.

Based on the alternative choices proposed by (L. X. Wang, 1997) and the previous works (Kim et al., 1994; Sherbiny et al., 2003; Rubai, 1991], in this paper we study the case of a two-layer control architecture (FLC-CC) where the pre-compensator layer is constructed from fuzzy systems as a control supervisor and the other layer from the conventional method. In addition, we demonstrate that the proposed scheme exhibits a good transient and steady state performance, and is robust to load variations and system nonlinearities.

This paper is organized as follows. In section 2 we briefly introduce the systems investigated. Section 3 describes the idea underlying the approach and the design procedure of the proposed controller. The simulation plots that illustrate the behaviour of our scheme, taking into account parameters variations, GRC and speed governor dead zone are provided in section 4. Finally, conclusions based on extensive simulation results, recommendations and further research are drawn in section V.

2. Plant model

Power systems can be modeled by their power balance equations, linearized around the operating point. Since power systems are only exposed to small changes in load during their normal operation, a linear model can be used to design LFC. We consider the same single–area non reheat power system model as shown in Fig. 1. The investigated system consists of a speed–governor, a turbine that produces mechanical power, P_g, and the rotating mass (or power system). In steady state, P_g is balanced by the electrical power output, P_e, of the generator. Any imbalance between P_g and P_e produces accelerating power and thereby creates an incremental change in frequency, Δf. All parameters are given Appendix A.

The investigated model consists of a tandem-compound single non reheat turbine. The state space model can be expressed as following:

$$\dot{x}(t) = Ax(t) + BU(t) + F\Delta P_L \quad (1)$$

$$y(t) = Cx(t) \quad (2)$$

where:

$$A = \begin{bmatrix} -1/T_p & K_p/T_p & 0 & 0 \\ 0 & -1/T_t & 1/T_t & 0 \\ -1/RT_g & 0 & -1/T_g & -1/T_g \\ K_i & 0 & 0 & 0 \end{bmatrix} \quad (3)$$

$$B = \begin{bmatrix} 0 & 0 & 1/T_g & 0 \end{bmatrix}^T \quad (4)$$

$$F = \begin{bmatrix} -K_p/T_p & 0 & 0 & 0 \end{bmatrix}^T \quad (5)$$

$$C = [1 \ 0 \ 0 \ 0] \quad (6)$$

The time constant, T_g, in the governor model is quite small and often it is neglected, which means that the governor is assumed to act very fast compared to the change in speed or frequency. This leads to a second order dynamic power system model. But for accuracy and comparison purposes, T_g is considered.

In linear control system theory, it is required that a state feedback controller:

$$\Delta P_C = -Kx(t) \quad (7)$$

Hence, the closed loop eigenvalues become insensitive to variations of the system parameters.

2.1. Model 1: Single-area non reheat power system

Consider the same isolated non reheat power system model reported in (Benjamin &. Chan, 1982; Pan & Liaw, 1989; Y. Wang et al., 1994) as shown in Figure 1, with the system parameters given in appendix A.

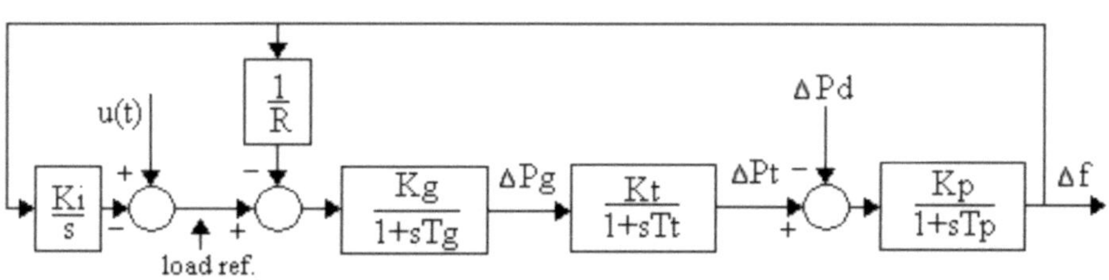

Figure 1. Block diagram of a isolated non reheat power system with supplementary control

Where u(t) denotes the existence of the proportional gain K_P, whereas its absence leads to an integral controller. The above described model has a tandem-compound single non reheat turbine and does not consider the speed-governor dead zone and GRC.

2.2. Model 2: two-areas reheat hydrothermal power system

The linearized mathematical model – 2 (see Fig.2), comprises an interconnection of two areas: single stages reheat thermal system (area 1) and a hydro system (area 2). The system parameters are given in appendix B. Figure 2 shows the small perturbation transfer function model of the hydro thermal system (Sherbiny et al., 2003). The speed governor dead zone and the GRC effects are also included in the model.

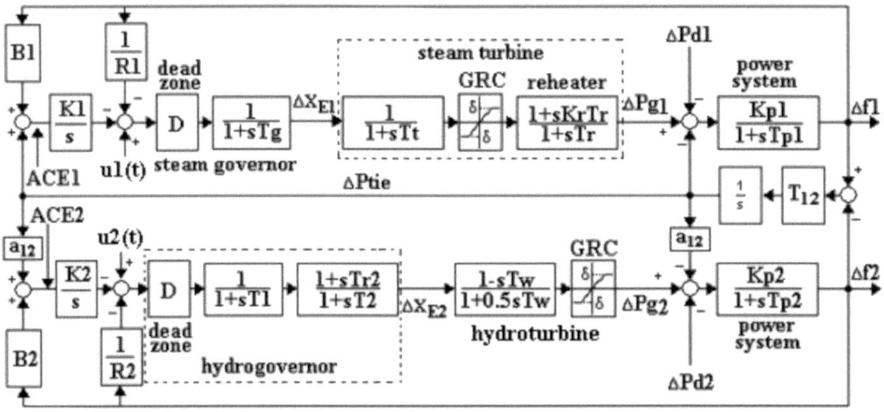

Figure 2. Bloc diagram of two-area reheat hydrothermal system with nonlinearities

3. Design of two layered controller for the system investigated

Considering the system shown in Figures 1, let P(s) represent the plant and D the speed governor actuator with dead zone (not present in Fig. 1). Recall that the supplementary PI control law can be written as following:

$$C_c[e(k), \int e(k)] = K_p e(k) + K_i \int e(k) \tag{8}$$

And in the case of "Fuzzy PD" controller, neglecting the scale factors, we get

$$C_F[e(k), \Delta e(k)] = F[e(k), \Delta e(k)] \tag{9}$$

C_c is a linear function of the error e(k) between the system output y_p(frequency deviation Δf) and the reference input Y_m (load reference ΔP_c) and the integral of the error whereas C_F is a function of the error and the change of error. From the above, we get

$$e(k) = y_m(k) - y_p(k) \quad \text{or} \quad y_p(k) = y_m(k) - e(k) \tag{10}$$

Let us assume that the supplementary control of the system is ensured by a "fuzzy PD" controller of the same type as (Indulkar & Raj, 1995; Karnavas & Papadopoulos, 2002).

3.1. Case 1: No actuator with dead zone

The plant output in this case can be written as

$$y_P(k) = P(s)\ F[e(k), \Delta e(k)] \tag{11}$$

Let $y_m(k) = y_m$. For steady state $\Delta e(k) = 0$ since the system is supposed to have reached the stabilizing time. Therefore, C_F becomes a function of e(k) alone and (11) can be written as following:

$$y_P(k) = K_s\ F[e_{ss}\ , 0] = y_m - e_{ss} \tag{12}$$

where K_s is the system static gain and is given by $K_s = \lim_{s \to 0} P(s)$

By assuming that C_F is well tuned and that the load reference deviation $y_m = \Delta P_c = 0$, (12) becomes:

$$K_s\ F[e_{ss}\ , 0] = -\ e_{ss} \tag{13}$$

Taking into account the feedback negative input sign into the controller (see Fig. 1), it can be verified from the description of Fuzzy PD controller (Indulkar & Raj, 1995; Karnavas & Papadopoulos, 2002). that the law F(. , 0) is an increasing odd function that can satisfy the following condition f(x) = -f(-x), with f(x) = F(. , 0). Therefore, it is clear that the solution to (13) is $e_{ss} = 0$, i.e., the steady state error of the system output is zero, as expected.

3.2. Case 2: Speed governor dead zone is present

The dead zone nonlinearity can be denoted as an operator is written as following:

$$u(k) = D(v(k)) \tag{14}$$

with v(k) as input and u(k) as output. The operator D(v(k)) has been described in detail by (Corradini & Orlando,2002; Tao & Kokotovic, 1994; X.-S. Wang et al., 2004; Oh & Park, 1998; Koo, 2001).The parameters of D(v(k)) are specified by the width 2d of the dead zone and the slop m of the response outside the dead zone. In this case, equation (12) can be written as :

$$y_P(k) = K_s D(v(k))\ F[e(k), 0] = y_m - e(k) \tag{15}$$

The solution to the equation (15) results in the steady state error as follow:

$$K_s D(v(k))\ F[e_{ss}\ , 0] - y_m = -\ e_{ss} \tag{16}$$

From (13) and (16) it can be seen that the steady state error e_{ss} in (16) is no longer zero. This is due to the presence of the dead zone in the speed governor actuator.

It has been demonstrated by (Yeh & Li, 2003) that the steady state error due to the dead zone in the actuator can be eliminated by adding some other constant η to the reference input y_m. We deliberately avoided using explicit knowledge of the value D(v(k)) because its parameters are poorly known or uncertain. Therefore, (16) becomes:

$$K_s D(v(k)) \;\; F[e+\eta \;, 0] - y_m = -e \tag{17}$$

Since PI controller is still the most used controller in power system (Pan & Liaw, 1989; Sherbiny et al., 2003) in our approach we use fuzzy logic rules to determine the appropriate value of η to be added to y_m. In this case, FLC plays the rule of a pre-compensator (supervisor) ensuring that the appropriate value of η is added to e(k) in order to eliminate the steady state error due to the dead zone. The conventional controller, called the stabilizer, present in the system, ensures the stabilization of the system.

The price to pay for changing the existing conventional controller into a FLC, which is proposed by (Sherbiny et al., 2003), would be in the computation. FLC is driven by a set of control rules rather than by two constant proportional and integral gains. As we shall see, the proposed scheme exhibits good transient and steady state behaviour. The proposed control scheme is depicted in Fig. 3 where C_1 is a FLC and C_2 a conventional controller. The feed-forward gain K_1 is normally set to the reciprocal of the K_s and constitutes an additional design parameter.

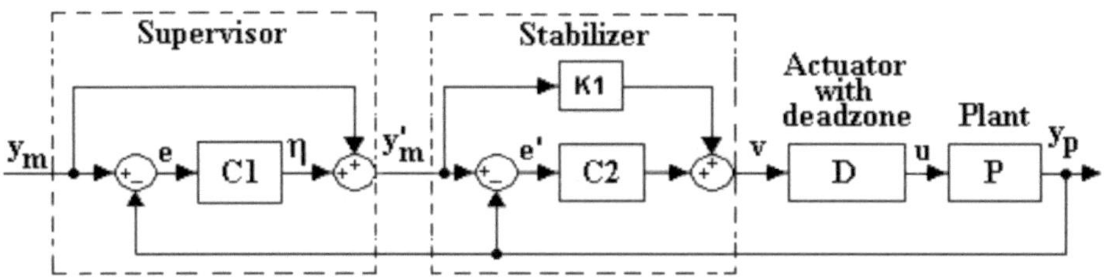

Figure 3. Proposed control structure

4. Design of the supervisor controller

As previously discussed, the first layer of the proposed control structure consists of the fuzzy logic based pre-compensator. The FLC law is based on standard fuzzy logic rules. It is well known that FLC consists of 3 stages, namely fuzzification, control rules inference engine and defuzzification. The reader is refereed to (Lee, 1990; L. X. Wang, 1997) for details on FLC. For LFC the process operator is assumed to respond to error e and change of error Δe (Indulkar & Raj, 1995); defined in (9). Considering the scale factors, (9) becomes as

$$C_F[e(k), \Delta e(k)] = F[n_e \, e(k), n_{\Delta e} \, \Delta e(k)] \tag{18}$$

where n_e and $n_{\Delta e}$ are the error and change of error scale factors respectively.

A label set corresponding to the linguistic variables control input e(k) and Δe(k) with a sampling time of 0.1 sec is as follows: L(e, Δe) = {NB, NM, ZE,PM, PB} where, NB - Negative Big, NM - Negative Medium, ZE – Zero, PM - Positive Medium and PB - Positive Big. The membership functions (MFs) for the control input variables are shown in Fig. 4. The universe of discourse of each control variable is normalised from -1 to 1. The proposed control structure uses the center of gravity defuzzification method to determine the output control as following:

$$C_F[e(k), \Delta e(k)] = n_\eta \frac{\sum_i^m w_i y_i}{\sum_i^m y_i} \quad (19)$$

Where n_η is the output control gain, w_i is the grade of the ith output MF, y_i is the output label for the value contributed by the ith MF, and m is the number of contributions from the rules. The fuzzy output variable is determined by same MFs shown in Fig. 4 and labelled as following L(η) = {NB, NM, ZE, PM, PB}

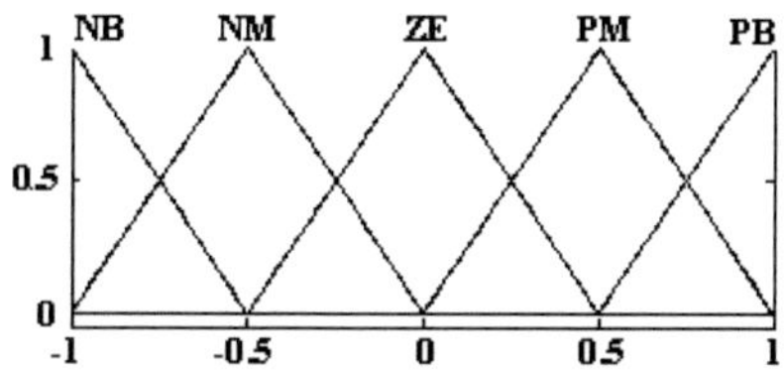

Figure 4. Membership functions of control input/output variables

The associated fuzzy matrices used in this work are given in table 1.

		e(k)				
		NB	NM	ZE	PM	PB
Δe(k)	NB	NB	NB	NB	NM	PM
	NM	NB	NB	NM	ZE	PM
	ZE	NB	NM	ZE	PM	PB
	PM	NM	ZE	PM	PB	PB
	PB	NM	PM	PB	PB	PB

Table 1. Fuzzy logic rules for pre-compensator C1

The performance of the FLC is affected by scaling factors of the inputs/output variables, MFs and the control rules. The selection of the optimum values of these factors is necessary in order to achieve satisfactory response [6]. But for the control system shown in Fig. 3, we can design the FLC without considering stability and use the stabilizer layer to deal with stability related problems.

5. Second layer: Stabilizer

The stabilizing layer consists of a conventional controller which is described in (8) and its design procedure is detailed in (Karnavas & Papadopoulos, 2002). The input to the present layer is the y'_m as shown in Fig. 3.

6. Simulation results

The power systems under investigation are simulated and subjected to different load disturbances in order to validate the effectiveness of the proposed scheme. The nonlinear effects, such as GRC and speed governor dead-zone, are also included in the simulations. The proposed controller (FLC-CC) will be evaluated qualitatively and quantitatively with

A single layer "PD FLC" (FLC) proposed in the first part of the work of (Karnavas & Papadopoulos, 2002) and a single layer conventional control (CC). The reader is referred to (Sherbiny et al., 2003) in order to compare our controller responses with the two-layered fuzzy controller proposed by (Sherbiny et al., 2003). The parameters of our controller for the two investigated models are given in table 2.

		n_e	$n_{\Delta e}$	n_η	K_p	K_i
Model 1		0.25	10.0	0.14	0.425	0.212
Model 2	area 1	10.0	20.0	0.15	4.00	6.00
	area 2	10.0	10.0	0.05	30.0	20.0

Table 2. Proposed controller parameters

6.1. Model 1 (Appendix A)

A step load perturbation of 10% (ΔP_d = 0.1 p.u.) of the nominal loading is considered. Fig 5 shows the simulation results of the frequency deviation Δf response to the step load change. The responses, obtained by the PD Fuzzy and the conventional controller (Karnavas & Papadopoulos, 2002) are also shown for comparison purpose.

Assume that the parameters R, Tg, Tt, Tp, Kp are subjected to a simultaneous changes of +30% from their nominal values. The frequency deviation response of the system is plotted in Fig. 6.

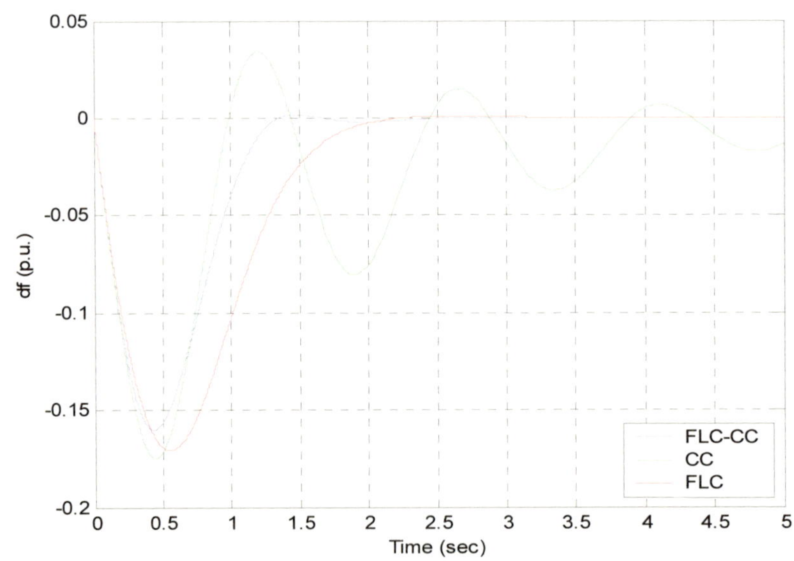

Figure 5. Frequency deviation for a load change of 0.1 p.u.

When GRC is applied to the system, its dynamic responses experience longer transient setting time t_s and larger overshoots OS compare to cases without the GRC. GRC of 3% p.u. MW/min and 10% p.u. MW/min are usually applied to reheat and non reheat turbines, respectively. In addition to GRC, the dead zone effect is also added to the system investigated. A dead zone width of 0.05 p.u. is considered. GRC and dead zone are taken into account by adding limiters to the turbines and an actuator to the speed governor input, respectively. Fig. 7 plots the responses of the system under nonlinear effects and a step load perturbation $\Delta P_d = 0.05$ p.u.

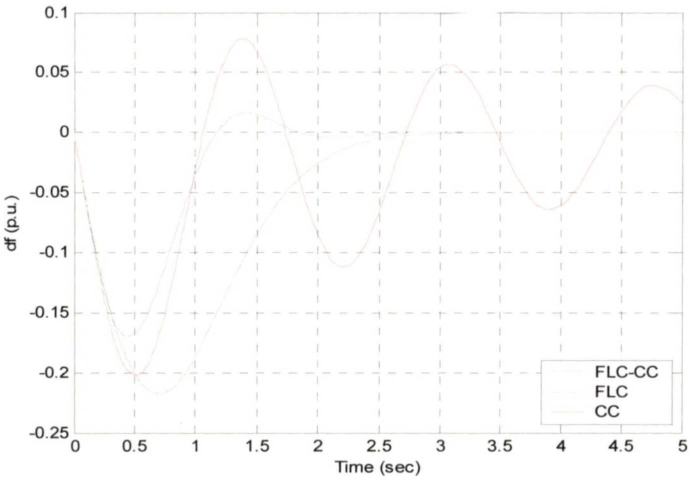

Figure 6. Frequency deviation at parameter changes of +30%

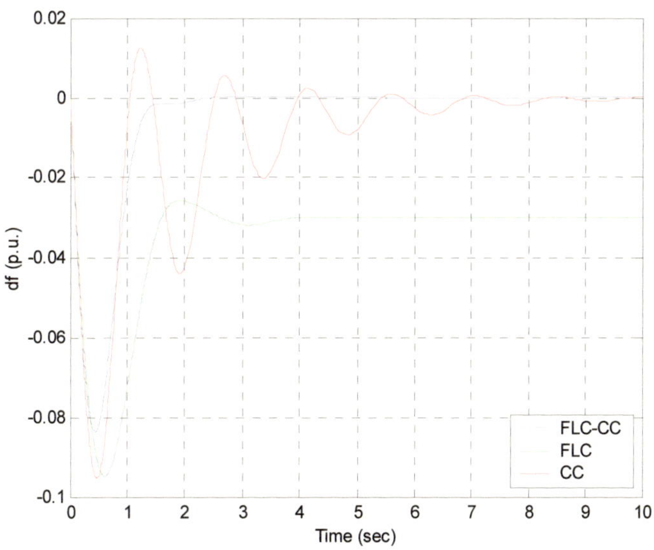

Figure 7. Frequency deviation due to $\Delta P_d = 0.05$ p.u with nonlinear effects

From Figs. 5-7 it can be observed that the proposed controller acts as fast as the FLC-FLC controller with less oscillatory, less undershoot and setting time. In addition the proposed scheme is also robust to load and parameters changes with and without nonlinearities. Fig. 7 shows the system steady state error for the PD FLC as previously predicted.

6.2. Model 2: Appendix (B)

Fig 8-10 show the simulation results of the frequency deviations and the tie line power responses of the two area power system due to a step load perturbation $\Delta P_d = 0.05$ p.u. without non-linear effects. The responses obtained by the conventional controller (CC) are also shown for comparison purpose.

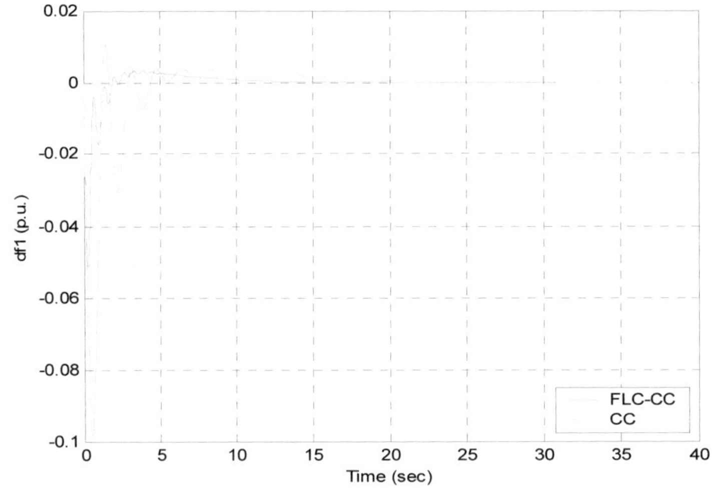

Figure 8. Frequency deviation of area 1 due to $\Delta P_{d1} = 0.05$ p.u.

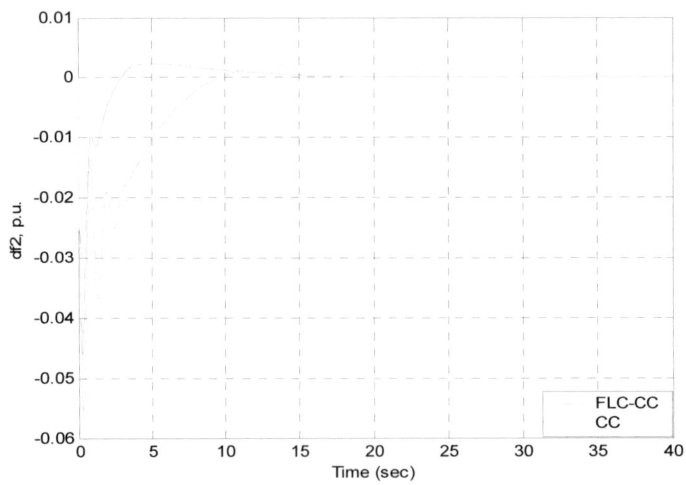

Figure 9. Frequency deviation of area 2 due to $\Delta P_{d2} = 0.05$ p.u

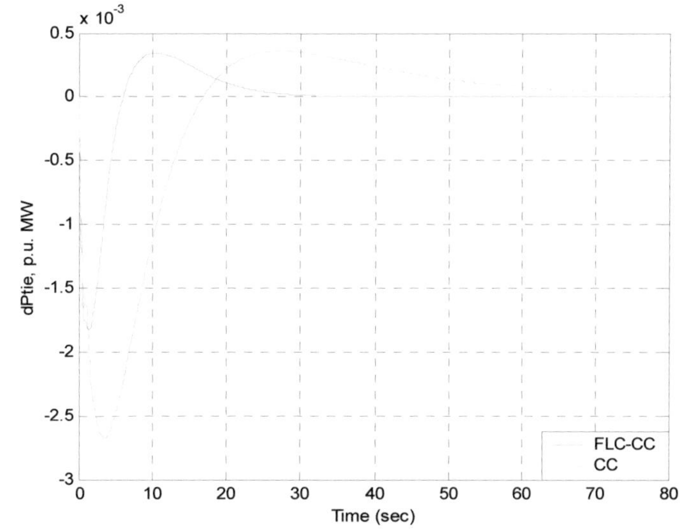

Figure 10. Tie line power deviation response due to ΔP_{d2}

It can be observed from the results obtained in Figs 8-10 that the proposed controller exhibits less oscillations and setting time compare to the conventional controller. Our controller responses are faster with smaller overshoot than the FLC-FLC controller. The reader is referred to (Sherbiny et al., 2003) for comparison.

Now assume that a dead zone width of 0.5 p.u. and GRC effects are considered in both area 1 and 2 simultaneously. Figs 11-13 plot the responses of the system under nonlinear effects.

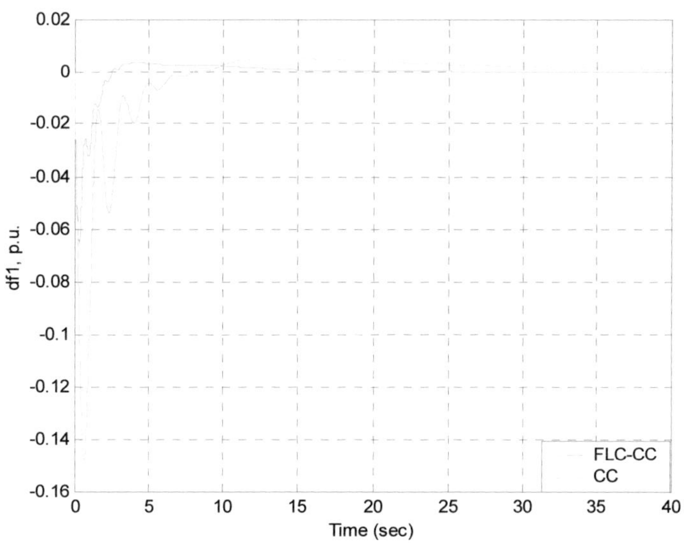

Figure 11. Frequency deviation of area 1 due to $\Delta P_{d1} = 0.05$ p.u. with nonlinear effects

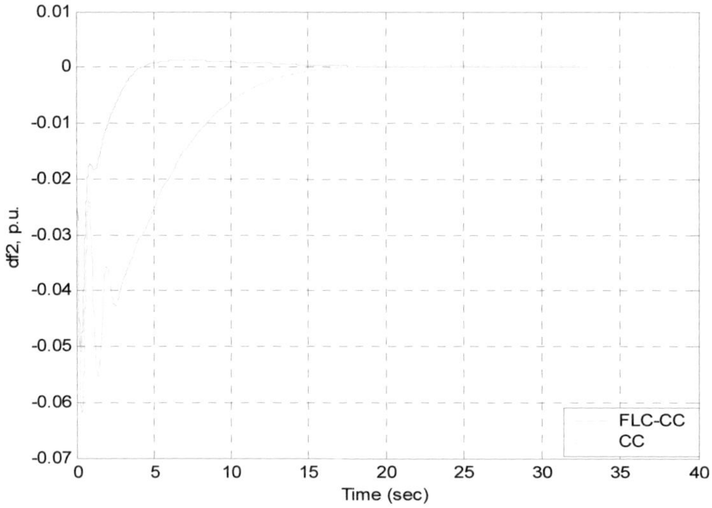

Figure 12. Frequency deviation of area 2 due to $\Delta P_{d2} = 0.05$ p.u. with nonlinear effects

Figures 11-13 demonstrate the robustness of the proposed controller under a large dead zone width and GRC. In addition, it has been possible to reduce the steady state error in the tie line power flow deviations (Fig 10, 13) using the proposed controller while it has been difficult with a single layered FLC proposed by (Indulkar & Raj, 1995).

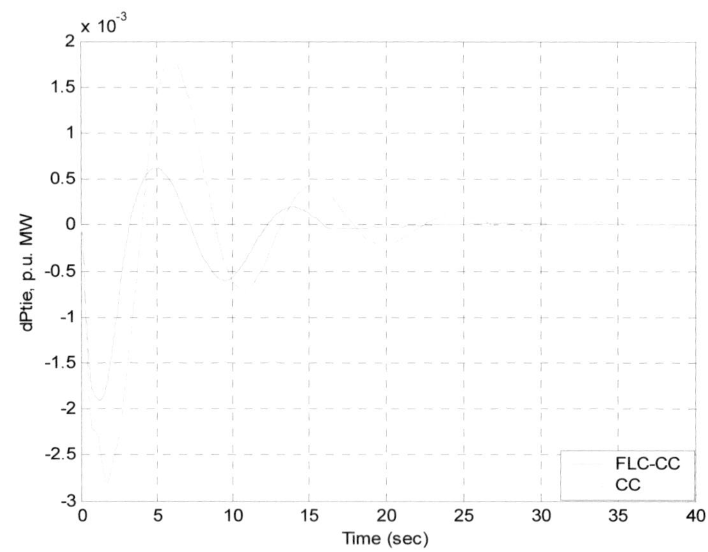

Figure 13. Tie line power deviation response due to $\Delta P_{d2} = 0.05$ p.u.

The performance Evaluation of The proposed controller (FLC-CC) is given by table 3.

		t_s [sec]		OS [p.u.] $\cdot 10^{-3}$		US [p.u.] $\cdot 10^{-3}$	
		w/NE	NE	w/NE	NE	w/NE	NE
ΔP_{tie}	FLC-CC	10	17	0	0	1.2	3
(Δf_1)	FLC-FLC	25	25	2.5	2.5	3.5	3.7
Δf_1	FLC-CC	5	5	0	0.1	45	52
	FLC-FLC	30	32	4.0	5	17	18
Δf_2	FLC-CC	12	10	0	0.1	45	45
	FLC-FLC	30	30	4	4	20	20

Table 3. Performance Evaluation Of The Proposed Controller (FLC-CC)

7. Conclusion

In this paper a two layered controller with a fuzzy pre-compensator is used to damp the power system frequencies and tie line power error oscillation and track their errors to zero. The price to pay for changing a conventional controller into a FLC in order to obtain a two layered controller, where both layers are FLC, would be in the computation. FLC is driven by a set of control rules rather than by two constant proportional and/or integral gains. In our approach, simple tuning of the conventional controller parameters enables the easy and cheap implementation of the proposed controller. Extensive simulations for a single area and an interconnected systems with no reheat, reheat and hydro turbines, taking into account a number of practical aspects such as the loads and parameters disturbances and the nonlinear effects, have verified the validity of our scheme over the conventional controller. Therefore, the proposed controller should be preferred. Further research is based on finding the optimum tuning method for the conventional controller parameters.

Author details

Mavungu Masiala, Mohsen Ghribi* and Azeddine Kaddouri
Greater Research Group, University of Moncton, New-Brunswick, Canada

Appendix A

Nominal Parameters Of A Typical Single-Area Nonreheat Power System (Model – 1):

T_p	- Electric system time constant	=	20,0	[s]
K_p	- Electric system static gain	=	120	[Hz $p.u.MW^{-1}$]
T_t	- Turbine time constant	=	0.30	[s]
T_g	- Governor time constant	=	0.08	[s]
R	- Speed regulation due to governor action	=	2.40	[Hz $p.u.MW^{-1}$]
ΔP_d	- load demand change			[p.u. MW]
ΔP_g	- incremental generation change			[p.u. MW]
ΔX_E	- incremental governor valve position change			
Ki	- integral control gain			
s	- the Laplace operator			

* Corresponding Author

Appendix B

Nominal Parameters Of ATwo-Area Reheat Hydrothermal Power System (Model – 2) :

i	- subscript referring to area	=	1,2
ΔX_{Ei}	- incremental governor valve position change		
K_i	- integral control gain		
T_{12}	- synchronising coefficient		
ΔP_{tie}	- incremental change in tie-line power		[p.u. MW]
ΔP_{gi}	- incremental generation change		[p.u. MW]
ΔP_{di}	- load demand change		[p.u. MW]
P_{ri}	- rated area power		[p.u. MW]
T_r	- reheat time constant	=	10.0 [s]
T_g	- governor time constant	=	0.08 [s]
T_t	- turbine time constant	=	0.30 [s]
R_i	- speed regulation due to governor action	=	2.40 [Hz p.u. MW^{-1}]
B_i	- frequency bias constant	=	0.425 [p.u. MW/Hz]
D_i	- load-frequency constant	=	0.0083 [p.u. MW/Hz]
P_{tie-m}	- maximum tie-line power handling capacity	=	200 [MW]
T_w	- water starting time constant	=	1.0 [s]
T_R	- hydro governor time	=	5.0 [s]
T_1	constants	=	48.7 [s]
T_2		=	0.513 [s]
a_{12}	- rated area power constant	=	$-P_{r1}/P_{r2}$
K_r	- high pressure turbine power fraction	=	0.50

8. References

Benjamin, N.N & Chan, W.C. (1982). *Variable structure control of electric power generation*, IEEE Trans. Power Apparatus and Systems, Vol. PAS-101, No. 2, pp. 376 – 380

Pan C. T., & Liaw, C. M. (1989). *An Adaptive controller for power system load-frequency control*, IEEE Trans. Power Systems, (February 1989), Vol. 4, No. 1, pp. 122 – 128

Kothari, M. L.; Nanda, J.; Kothari, D. P. & Das, D. (1989). *Discrete-mode automatic generation control of a two-area reheat thermal system with new area control error*, IEEE Trans. Power Systems, (May 1989), vol. 4, No. 2, pp. 730 – 738

Wang, Y.; Zhou, Y. R. & Wen C. (1994). *New robust adaptive load-frequency control with system parametric uncertainties*, IEEE Trans. Generation, Transmission and Distribution, (May 1994), Vol. 141, No. 3, pp. 184 – 190

Indulkar, C. S. & Raj B. (1995). *Application of fuzzy controller to automatic generation control*, Electrical Machines and Power Systems, Vol. 23, pp. 209 – 220

Karnavas, Y.L. & Papadopoulos, D.P. (2002). *AGC for autonomous power system using combined intelligent techniques*, Electric Power Systems Research, 62, pp. 225 – 239

Moon, Y-H.; Ryu, H-S.; Lee, J-G.; Song, K-B. & Shin, M-C. (2002). *Extended integral control for load frequency control with the consideration of generation-rate constraints*, Electrical Power and Energy Systems, vol. 24, pp. 263 – 269

Sherbiny, M.K.; El-Saady, G. & Yousef, A.M. (2003). *Efficient fuzzy logic load-frequency controller*, Energy Conversion & Management, Vol. 43, pp. 1853 – 1863

Corradini, M. L. & Orlando, G. (2002). *Robust stabilization of nonlinear uncertain plants with backlash or dead–zone in the actuator*, IEEE Trans. Control Systems Technology, vol. 10, No. 1, pp. 158 – 166

Tao, G. and Kokotovic, P.V. (1994). *Adaptive control of plants with unknown dead–zones*, IEEE Trans. Automatic Control, (January 1994), Vol. 39, No. 1, pp. 59 – 68

Wang, X-S.; Su, C-Y. & Hong H. (2004). *Robust adaptive control of a class of nonlinear systems with unknown dead-zone*, Automatica, vol. 40, pp. 407 – 413

Lee, C. C. (1990). *Fuzzy logic in control systems : Fuzzy logic controller – Part I, II*," IEEE Trans. Systems, Man and Cybernetics, (March-April 1990), Vol. 20, No. 2, pp. 404 – 435

Kim, J-H.; Park, J. H.; Lee, S-W. & Chong, E.K.P. (1994). *A two layered fuzzy logic controller for systems with dead zones*, IEEE Trans. Industrial Electronics, Vol. 41, No. 2, pp. 155–162

Yeh, Z-M. & Li, K-H. *A systematic approach for designing multistage fuzzy control systems*, Fuzzy Sets and Systems, Article in press, pp. 1 – 23, 2003.

Oh, S-Y. & Park, D-J. *Design of new adaptive fuzzy logic controller for nonlinear plants with unknown or time-varying dead zones*, IEEE Trans. Fuzzy Systems, vol. 6, No. 4, pp. 482 – 491, November 1998

Koo, K-M. *Stable adaptive fuzzy controller with time–varying dead–zone*, Fuzzy Sets and Systems, vol. 121, pp. 161 – 168, 2001

Rubai, A. *Transient stability control: A multi-level hierarchical approach*, IEEE Trans. Power Systems, vol. 6, No. 1, pp. 262 – 268, February 1991

Wang, Li-Xi (1997). *A course in fuzzy Systems and control*, Prentice Hall PTR, Upper Saddle River, NJ, pp. 249 – 257

Mamoh, J. A. and K. Tomsovic, K. (1995). *Overview and literature survey of fuzzy set theory in power systems*, IEEE Trans. Power Systems, (August 1995), Vol. 10, no. 3, pp. 1676-1690

Das, D. ; Kothari, M.L.; Kothari, D.P. and Nanda, J., (1991). *Variable structure control strategy to automatic generation control of interconnected reheat thermal system*, IEEE Proceedings on Control Theory and Applications, (November 1991), Vol. 138, no. 6, pp. 579-585

Djukanovic, M. (1995). *Conceptual development of optimal load frequency control using artificial neural networks and fuzzy set theory*, International Journal of Engineering Intelligent Systems for Electrical Engineering & Communication, vol. 3, no. 2. pp. 95-108, 1995.

Ha, Q. P. and Negnevitsky, M., (1997). *Fuzzy tuning in electric power system generation control*, Proceedings of the 4th Conference on APSCOM, (November 1997), vol. 2, no. 450, pp.662-667

Chang, C.S. and Fu, W. (1997). *Area load frequency control using fuzzy gain scheduling of PI controllers*, Electric Power Systems Research, Vol. 42, pp. 145-152

Yesil, E.; Guzelkaya, M. and Ekisin, I. (2004). *Self-tuning fuzzy PID type load and frequency controller*, Energy Conversion and Management, Vol. 45, pp. 377-390

Talaq J. and Al-Basri, F. (1999). *Adaptive fuzzy gain scheduling for load frequency control*, IEEE Trans. Power Systems, (February 1999), Vol. 14, no. 1, pp. 145-150

Li, H.-X., and Gatland, H.B. (1996). *Conventional fuzzy control and its enhancement*, IEEE Trans. Systems, Man and Cybernetics – Part B: Cybernetics, (October 1996), Vol. 26, No. 5, pp. 791-797

Chown, G.A. and Hartman, R.C. (1998). *Design and experiment with a fuzzy controller for automatic generation control (AGC), IEEE Trans. Power Systems,* (Aug. 1998), Vol. 13, pp. 965-970

Fosha, C.E. and Elgerd, O.I. (1970). T*he megawatt frequency control problem: a new approach via optimal control theory,* IEEE *Trans. Power Apparatus and Systems,* (April 1970), Vol. PAS-89 (4), pp. 563–577

Passino, K.M. and Yourkovich, S. (1998), *Fuzzy Control,* Menlo Park, California: Addison Wesley Longman

Chapter 22

Performance Evaluation of PI and Fuzzy Controlled Power Electronic Inverters for Power Quality Improvement

Georgios A. Tsengenes and Georgios A. Adamidis

Additional information is available at the end of the chapter

http://dx.doi.org/10.5772/48394

1. Introduction

In recent years, the increasing use of power electronics in the commercial and industry processes results in harmonics injection and lower power factor to the electric power system [Emanuel A E. (2004)]. Conventionally, in order to overcome these problems, passive R-L-C filters have been used. The use of this kind of filters has several disadvantages. Recently, due to the evolution in modern power electronics, new device called "shunt active power filter (SAPF)" was investigated and recognized as a viable alternative to the passive filters. The principle operation of the SAPF is the generation of the appropriate current harmonics required by the non-linear load.

For the reference currents generation, one of the best known and effective technique is the 'instantaneous reactive power theory' or '*p-q* theory' [Czarnecki L S. (2006)]. In the literature, various modifications of *p-q* theory for the reference currents generation have been proposed [Salmeron P, Herrera R S, Vazquez J R. (2007)], [Kilic T, Milun S, et al. (2007)]. It is a common phenomenon in an electric power system, the grid voltages to be non-ideal [Segui-Chilet S S, Gimeno-Sales F J, et al. (2007)]. In such condition, the *p-q* theory is ineffective. To improve the efficiency of the *p-q* theory various reference currents generation techniques [Kale M, Ozdemir E. (2005)], [Tsengenes G, Adamidis G. (2011)] have been proposed. Except from the reference currents generation method, the current control method plays an important role to the overall system's performance. Plenty of methods have been used in the current control loop [Buso S, Malesani L, et al. (1998)] (e.g. ramp comparison, space vector modulation), one of which is the hysteresis current control. Hysteresis current controller compared to other current control methods has a lot of advantages such as robustness and simplicity [Tsengenes G, Adamidis G. (2010)].

The conventional reference currents generation techniques use a PI controller in order to regulate the dc bus voltage. The tuning of the PI controller requires precise linear mathematical model of the plant, which is very difficult to obtained, and it fails to perform satisfactorily under parameters variations, non-linearities, etc. To overcome these disadvantages, in recent years controllers which use artificial intelligent techniques have been implemented, like fuzzy logic controllers (FLCs) and artificial neural network (ANN) [Saad A, Zellouma L. (2009)], [El-Kholy E E, El-Sabbe, et al. (2006)], [Han ., Khan M M, Yao et al. (2010)], [Skretas S B, Papadopoulos D P (2009)]. The FLC surpasses the conventional PI controller due to its ability to handle non-imparities, its superior perform with a non-accurate mathematical model of the systems, and its robustness. In the literature some papers which implement FLCs in SAPF in order to improve the efficiency of the reference currents generation technique [Han Y, Khan M M, Yao et al. (2010)], [Jain S K, Agrawal P, et al. (2002)] and the current control loop have been reported [Mekri F, Machmoum M. (2010)], [Lin B R, Hoft R G. (1996)].

In this chapter a fuzzy logic controlled SAPF for current harmonics elimination is presented. The control scheme is based on two FLCs, the first one controls the dc bus voltage and the second one controls the output current of the inverter. Furthermore for the reference currents generation a modified version of the *p-q* theory is proposed, in order to improve the performance of the SAPF under non-ideal grid voltages. The performance of the proposed control scheme is evaluated through computer simulations using the software Matlab/Simulink under steady state and transient response. The superiority of the proposed fuzzy logic control scheme over the conventional control scheme is established both in steady state and transient response for current harmonics elimination and dc bus voltage of the SAPF respectively.

At the end a proposal for future investigation is presented. A combination between the fuzzy and the PI control is proposed. The new controller is called "fuzzy-tuned PI controller". The theoretical analysis and some simulation results are illustrated in order to verify the efficiency of the fuzzy-tuned PI controller.

2. Description of the proposed fuzzy control scheme

The main function of the SAPF is the current harmonics elimination and the reactive power compensation of the load. The general block diagram of a grid connected SAPF, as well as the detailed model of the control scheme is illustrated in Fig.1. The Reference currents generation method includes the dc bus voltage control which is the outer control loop. The current control method is the internal control loop which generates the appropriate switching pattern.

2.1. Reference currents generation method

For the reference currents generation a modified version of the *p-q* theory is used. One of the disadvantages of the *p-q* theory is the very poor efficiency of the method under non-ideal grid voltages. In this chapter the generation of three virtual grid voltages is proposed, one per phase as shown in figure 2. These virtual voltages will have the same amplitude as the fundamental harmonic (50 Hz) of the grid voltage, and will be synchronized with zero phase shifting compared with the corresponding grid voltages.

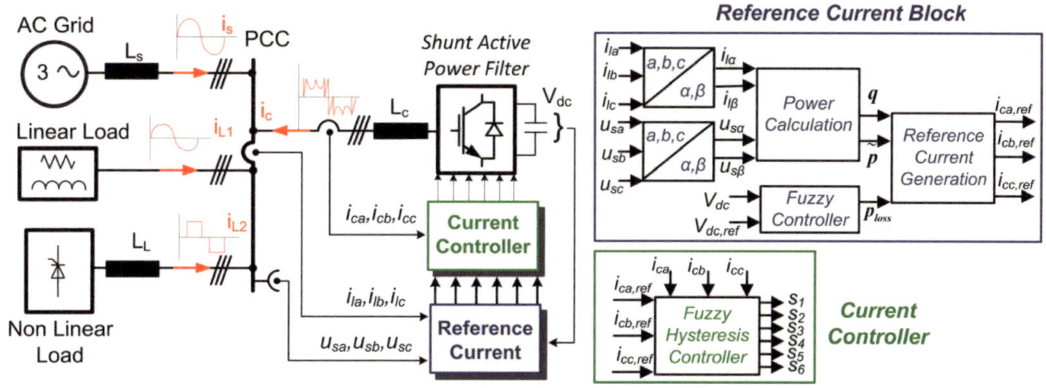

Figure 1. Synoptic diagram of the proposed electric power system and the control system

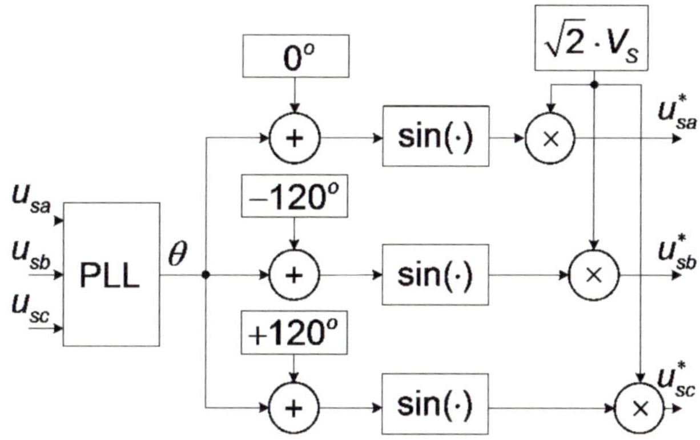

Figure 2. Generation of three virtual grid voltages

Mathematical equations for the virtual grid voltages *a-b-c* reference frame are given by equations (1), (2) and (3).

$$u_{sa}^{*} = \sqrt{2} \cdot V_S \cdot sin(\theta) \tag{1}$$

$$u_{sb}^{*} = \sqrt{2} \cdot V_S \cdot sin(\theta - 120^o) \tag{2}$$

$$u_{sc}^{*} = \sqrt{2} \cdot V_S \cdot sin(\theta + 120^o) \tag{3}$$

Where V_S is the root-mean-square (rms) value of the grid voltage ($V_S = \sqrt{u_{sa}^2 + u_{sb}^2 + u_{sc}^2}$), and θ is the angular frequency of the grid voltages ($\theta = 2 \cdot \pi \cdot f_{grid} = 2 \cdot \pi \cdot 50$).

The modified *p-q* theory, for the reference currents generation, will use the virtual grid voltages $u_{sa}^{*}, u_{sb}^{*}, u_{sc}^{*}$ and not the actual grid voltage. The load currents and the virtual grid voltages are transformed in α-β reference frame according to the transformer matrix of equation (4). The virtual grid voltages and the load current in α-β reference frame are given by equations (5), (6).

$$\left[C\right]_{abc\to\alpha\beta}=\sqrt{\frac{2}{3}}\cdot\begin{bmatrix}1 & -\frac{1}{2} & \frac{1}{2}\\ 0 & \frac{\sqrt{3}}{2} & -\frac{\sqrt{3}}{2}\end{bmatrix} \tag{4}$$

$$\begin{bmatrix}u_{s\alpha}^{*}\\ u_{s\beta}^{*}\end{bmatrix}=\left[C\right]_{abc\to\alpha\beta}\cdot\begin{bmatrix}u_{sb}^{*}\\ u_{sb}^{*}\\ u_{sc}^{*}\end{bmatrix} \tag{5}$$

$$\begin{bmatrix}i_{l\alpha}\\ i_{l\beta}\end{bmatrix}=\left[C\right]_{abc\to\alpha\beta}\cdot\begin{bmatrix}i_{la}\\ i_{lb}\\ i_{lc}\end{bmatrix} \tag{6}$$

The instantaneous active and reactive powers of the electric power system are calculated via the following equation:

$$\begin{bmatrix}p\\ q\end{bmatrix}=\begin{bmatrix}u_{s\alpha}^{*} & u_{s\beta}^{*}\\ -u_{s\beta}^{*} & u_{s\alpha}^{*}\end{bmatrix}\cdot\begin{bmatrix}i_{l\alpha}\\ i_{l\beta}\end{bmatrix} \tag{7}$$

The instantaneous powers p and q are composed from a dc part (¯) and an ac part (˜) corresponding to fundamental and harmonic current respectively. Equation (8) gives the instantaneous active and reactive power respectively.

$$\begin{aligned}p&=\widetilde{p}+\overline{p}\ \text{(a)}\\ q&=\widetilde{q}+\overline{q}\ \text{(b)}\end{aligned} \tag{8}$$

The ac component of the active power is extracted using a low pass filter. Using the *p-q* theory current harmonics are eliminated and the reactive power of the load is compensated. Therefore the reference currents of the SAPF in α-β reference frame are:

$$\begin{bmatrix}i_{c\alpha,ref}\\ i_{c\beta,ref}\end{bmatrix}=\frac{1}{(u_{s\alpha}^{*})^{2}+(u_{s\beta}^{*})^{2}}\cdot\begin{bmatrix}u_{s\alpha}^{*} & -u_{s\beta}^{*}\\ u_{s\beta}^{*} & u_{s\alpha}^{*}\end{bmatrix}\cdot\begin{bmatrix}\widetilde{p}-p_{loss}\\ q\end{bmatrix} \tag{9}$$

Where p_{loss} are related to the inverter operating losses. The grid should cover the p_{loss} in order to keep the capacitor voltage constant. Conventionally p_{loss} are calculated using a dc bus voltage sensor and a PI controller. In order to improve the dynamic performance of

SAPF and reduce the total harmonic distortion (THD_i) of the current a FLC for the dc bus voltage control and a FLC for the current control are implemented. The current controller handles the reference and the actual currents in *a-b-c* reference frame. As a result, the inverse α-β transformation of equation (10) is used in order to transform the reference currents in *a-b-c* reference frame.

$$\begin{bmatrix} i_{ca,ref} \\ i_{cb,ref} \\ i_{cc,ref} \end{bmatrix} = \sqrt{\frac{2}{3}} \cdot \begin{bmatrix} 1 & 0 \\ -\frac{1}{2} & \frac{\sqrt{3}}{2} \\ -\frac{1}{2} & -\frac{\sqrt{3}}{2} \end{bmatrix} \cdot \begin{bmatrix} i_{\alpha,ref} \\ i_{\beta,ref} \end{bmatrix} \tag{10}$$

2.2. Fuzzy logic dc bus voltage controller

For the dc bus voltage control a FLC is implemented. Figure 3 shows the synoptic block diagram of the proposed FLC. As inputs to FLC the error between the sensed and the reference dc bus voltage ($e = V_{dc,ref} - V_{dc}$) and the error variation ($\Delta e = e(k) - e(k-1)$) at k^{th} sampling instant are used. The output of the fuzzy logic controller is considered as the active power losses of the inverter (p_{loss}). The coefficients G_1, G_2 and G_3 are used to adjust the input and output control signals.

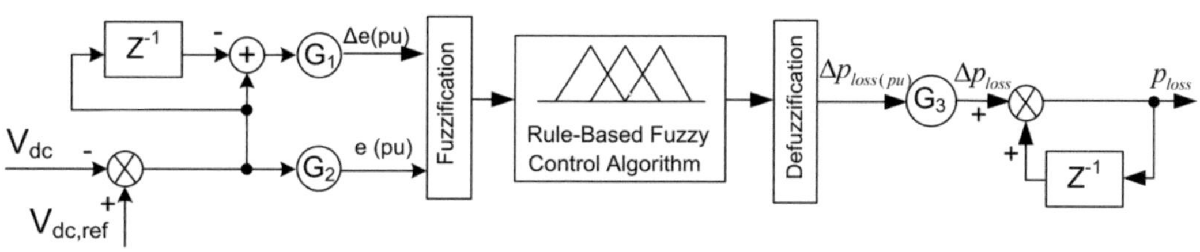

Figure 3. General structure of the fuzzy logic controller for dc bus voltage control

The FLC converts the crisp variables into linguistic variables. To implement this process it uses the following seven fuzzy sets, which are: NL (Negative Large), NM (Negative Medium), NS (Negative Small), Z (Zero), PS (Positive Small), PM (Positive Medium), PL (Positive Large). The fuzzy logic controller characteristics used in this section are:

- Seven fuzzy sets for each input (e, Δe) and output (Δp_{loss}) with triangular and trapezoidal membership functions.
- Fuzzification using continuous universe of discourse.
- Implications using Mamdani's 'min' operator.
- Defuzzification using the 'centroid' method.

Figure 4 shows the normalized triangular and trapezoidal membership functions for the input and output variables. The degree of fuzziness/membership ($\mu_{\delta,tri}(x)$) of the triangular membership function is determined by equation (11.a). The degree of fuzziness ($\mu_{\delta,tra}(x)$) of the trapezoidal membership function is determined by equation (11.b).

$$\mu_{\delta,tri}(x) = \begin{cases} 0 & x < a, x > c \\ \dfrac{x-a}{b-a} & a \le x < b \\ \dfrac{c-x}{c-b} & b \le x \le c \end{cases} \quad \text{(a)}$$
$$\mu_{\delta,tra}(x) = \begin{cases} 0 & x < a, x > d \\ \dfrac{x-a}{b-a} & a \le x \le b \\ 1 & b < x < c \\ \dfrac{d-x}{d-c} & c \le x \le d \end{cases} \quad \text{(b)} \qquad (11)$$

Where x, a, b, c, and d belong to the universe of discourse (X).

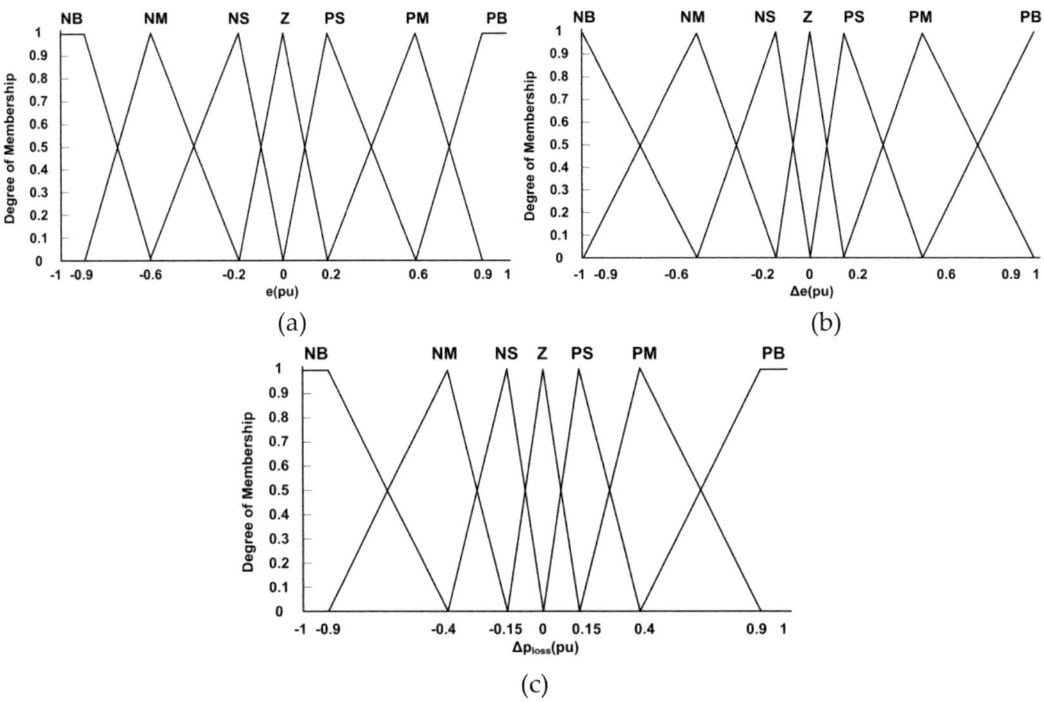

Figure 4. Membership functions for a) input variable e (pu), b) input variable Δe (pu), and c) output variable Δp_{loss} (pu)

Let $\mu_A(x)$ and $\mu_B(x)$ denote the degree of membership of the membership functions $\mu_A(\cdot)$ and $\mu_B(\cdot)$ of the input fuzzy sets A and B, where $x \in X$. Mamdani's logic operator is described as:

$$\phi\left[\mu_A(x), \mu_B(x)\right] = min\left[\mu_A(x), \mu_B(x)\right] = \mu_A(x) \wedge \mu_B(x) \qquad (12)$$

If $\mu_C(x)$ denotes the degree of membership of the membership functions $\mu_C(\cdot)$ of the output fuzzy sets C, where $x \in X$, equation 13 is used.

$$\mu_C(x) = \phi\left[\mu_A(x), \mu_B(x)\right] \cdot \mu_C(\cdot) \tag{13}$$

In the defuzzification procedure the centroid method with a discretized universe of discurse can be expressed as:

$$x_{out} = \frac{\sum_{i=1}^{n} x_i \cdot \mu_{out}(x_i)}{\sum_{i=1}^{n} \mu_{out}(x_i)} \tag{14}$$

Where x_{out} is crisp output value x_i is the output crisp variable and $\mu_{out}(x_i)$ is the degree of membership of the output fuzzy value, and i is the number of output discrete elements in the universe of discourse.

In the design of the fuzzy control algorithm, the knowledge of the systems behavior is very important. This knowledge is put in the form of rules of inference. The rule table which is shown in Table 1 contains 49 rules. The elements of the rule table are obtained from an understanding of the SAPF behavior [Jain S K, Agrawal P, et al. (2002)].

e							
Δe	NB	NM	NS	Z	PS	PM	PB
NB	NB	NB	NB	NB	NM	NS	Z
NM	NB	NB	NB	NM	NS	Z	PS
NS	NB	NB	NM	NS	Z	PS	PM
Z	NB	NM	NS	Z	PS	PM	PB
PS	NM	NS	Z	PS	PM	PB	PB
PM	NS	Z	PS	PM	PB	PB	PB
PB	Z	PS	PM	PB	PB	PB	PB

Table 1. Fuzzy control rule table.

2.3. Fuzzy logic Hysteresis current controller

One of the best known and most effective current control methods is the hysteresis band control technique. Some of its advantages are the simplicity of the construction combined with the excellent dynamic response. Apart from the significant advantages, this method has some drawbacks such as the high THD_i index.

For the reduction of the THD_i index, the implementation of a fuzzy logic hysteresis current controller is proposed. The synoptic diagram of fuzzy logic hysteresis controller for the phase-a is shown in figure 5. The same controller is applied to the other two-phases (b and c). As inputs to FLC the error between the reference current and the sensed current ($e = i_{ca,ref} - i_{ca}$) and the error variation ($\Delta e = e(k) - e(k-1)$) at k^{th} sampling instant are used. The output of the FLC is considered as the amplitude of the current error. The coefficients F_1 and F_2 are used to adjust the input control signals. The saturations blocks are used for limiting the initial error.

The fuzzy logic controller characteristics used in this section are the same as in the previous section (2.2). Figure 6 shows the triangular and trapezoidal membership functions for the input and output variables. The rule table for the hysteresis fuzzy logic controller is the same with Table 1.

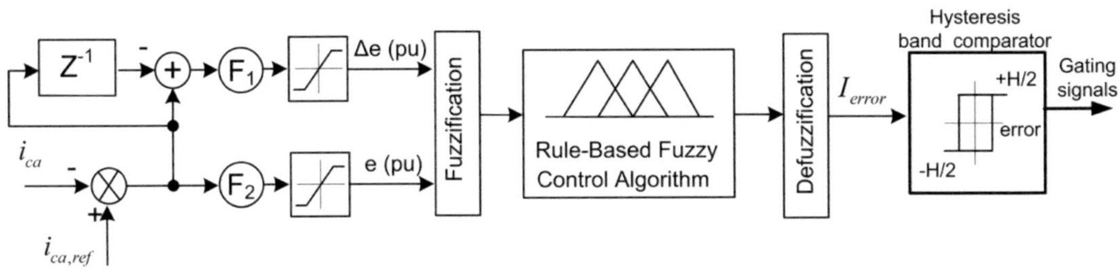

Figure 5. General structure of the hysteresis FLC for the current control loop

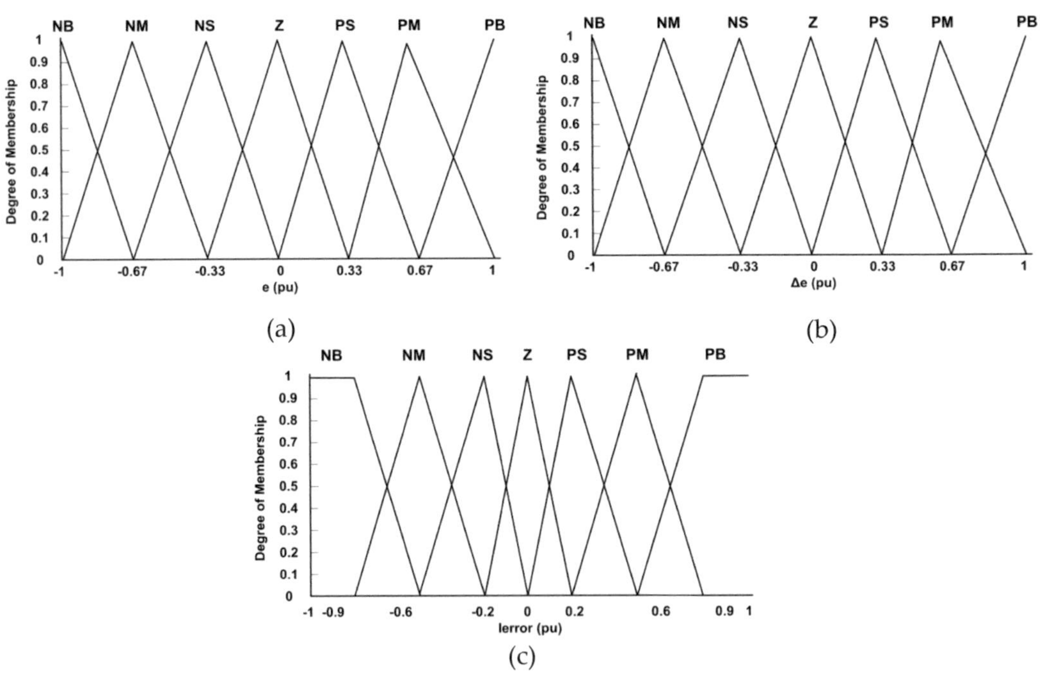

Figure 6. Membership functions for a) input variable e, b) input variable Δe, and b) output variable I_{error}

3. Non-ideal grid voltages

It is a common phenomenon in electric power system the grid voltages to be non-ideal. This problem is particularly important in Greek electric power distribution system, mainly due to the large increase of power electronic devices. In this section the mathematical model of the grid voltages under several non-ideal cases will briefly be presented.

The ideal grid voltages have sinusoidal waveform and can be represented as:

$$\begin{bmatrix} u_{sa} \\ u_{sb} \\ u_{sc} \end{bmatrix} = \sqrt{2} \cdot V_s \cdot \begin{bmatrix} sin(\omega t) \\ sin(\omega t - 120^o) \\ sin(\omega t + -120^o) \end{bmatrix} \tag{15}$$

The ideal grid voltages have only the fundamental frequency component.

When the three-phase grid voltages are unbalanced (u_{su}), the grid voltages can be expressed as positive and negative sequence components as shown in equation (12).

$$\begin{bmatrix} u_{sua} \\ u_{sub} \\ u_{suc} \end{bmatrix} = \begin{bmatrix} u_{sua+} \\ u_{sub+} \\ u_{suc+} \end{bmatrix} + \begin{bmatrix} u_{sua-} \\ u_{sub-} \\ u_{suc-} \end{bmatrix} \tag{16}$$

Where u_{sua+}, u_{sub+}, and u_{suc+} are positive sequence components and u_{sua-}, u_{sub-}, and u_{suc-} are negative sequence components.

It is a very common phenomenon in electric power distribution systems, voltages having non-ideal waveforms, and different levels of harmonics. When the three-phase grid voltages are distorted (u_{sd}), the grid voltages have harmonics components. In this scenario the distorted grid voltage can be represented as:

$$\begin{bmatrix} u_{sda} \\ u_{sdb} \\ u_{sdc} \end{bmatrix} = \begin{bmatrix} u_{sda,f} \\ u_{sdb,f} \\ u_{sdc,f} \end{bmatrix} + \begin{bmatrix} u_{sda,h} \\ u_{sdb,h} \\ u_{sdc,h} \end{bmatrix} \tag{17}$$

Where, $u_{sdb,f}$, and $u_{sdc,f}$ are positive sequence components and , $u_{sdb,h}$, and $u_{sdc,h}$ are harmonics components of the grid voltages.

When the three-phase grid voltages are distorted and unbalanced (u_{du}), the grid voltages contain harmonic components and unbalances. For this case, the distorted and unbalanced three-phase grid voltages are expressed as:

$$\begin{bmatrix} u_{sdua} \\ u_{sdub} \\ u_{sduc} \end{bmatrix} = \begin{bmatrix} u_{sda,f} \\ u_{sdb,f} \\ u_{sdc,f} \end{bmatrix} + \begin{bmatrix} u_{sda,h} \\ u_{sdb,h} \\ u_{sdc,h} \end{bmatrix} + \begin{bmatrix} u_{sua-} \\ u_{sub-} \\ u_{suc-} \end{bmatrix} = \begin{bmatrix} u_{sua+} \\ u_{sub+} \\ u_{suc+} \end{bmatrix} + \begin{bmatrix} u_{sda,h} \\ u_{sdb,h} \\ u_{sdc,h} \end{bmatrix} + \begin{bmatrix} u_{sua-} \\ u_{sub-} \\ u_{suc-} \end{bmatrix} \tag{18}$$

4. Simulation results

In this section the electric power system of figure 1 will be simulated. The simulation will be carried out via Matlab/Simulink. The characteristics of the electric power system are shown in Table 2. Four practical scenarios were examined in which the grid voltages are ideal, unbalanced, distorted and distorted-unbalanced. For the worst case, where the grid voltages are distorted-unbalanced the performance of the electric power system will be analyzed using the conventional and the fuzzy logic control system. The behavior of the PI controller and the FLC will be compared based on the dc bus voltage control.

Besides, the behavior of the conventional hysteresis controller and the hysteresis FLC will be compared based on the inverter output current control. For the comparison of the performance between the conventional control methods and the control methods with fuzzy logic theory the THD_i index in steady state, and the oscillation of the dc bus voltage during the transient response will be considered. Thereafter, the non-linear load will be called "Load_1" and the linear load will be called "Load_2". In all cases the transient response occurs at the same time (t=0.4 sec). It was considered that time t=0.4 sec in the electric power system, additionally to the initial non-linear load (Load_1) a linear load (Load_2) is connected.

Grid voltage (rms)	V_S=230V	Non-linear load	R_1=4Ω	SAPF inductance	L_c=1mH
Grid inductance	L_s=0.1mH	Linear Load	L_2=1mH	dc side capacitor	C_{dc}=3mF
Firing angle	α=10°	Linear Load	R_2=2Ω	dc bus voltage	V_{dc}=1 kV
Non-linear load	L_1=1mH	Non-linear load side impedance			L_L=1mH

Table 2. Parameters of the electric power system.

4.1. Distorted-Unbalanced grid voltages

In this case the grid voltages are considered to be distorted-unbalanced, and they are expressed as:

$$\begin{bmatrix} u_{sda} \\ u_{sdb} \\ u_{sdc} \end{bmatrix} = \sqrt{2} \cdot V_s \cdot \begin{bmatrix} sin(\omega t) \\ sin(\omega t - 120^o) \\ sin(\omega t + -120^o) \end{bmatrix} + 13 \cdot \begin{bmatrix} sin(\omega t) \\ sin(\omega t - 120^o) \\ sin(\omega t + 120^o) \end{bmatrix} + 23 \cdot \begin{bmatrix} sin(5\omega t) \\ sin(5\omega t - 120^o) \\ sin(5\omega t + 120^o) \end{bmatrix} + 8 \cdot \begin{bmatrix} sin(7\omega t) \\ sin(7\omega t - 120^o) \\ sin(7\omega t + 120^o) \end{bmatrix} \quad (19)$$

Figure 7 shows the distorted-unbalanced grid voltages. Figures 8 and 9 show the grid currents (i_{sa}, i_{sb}, i_{sc}) and the reactive power of the grid respectively, without the application of the SAPF. In Table 3 the THD_i index of the grid currents for the loads 'Load_1' and 'Load_1+Load_2' is denoted.

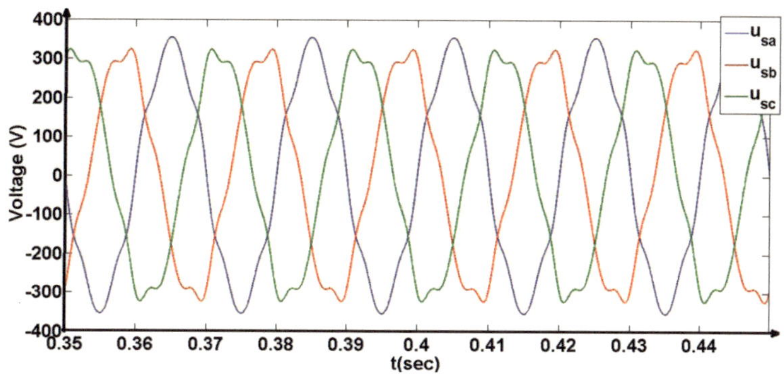

Figure 7. Distorted-unbalanced grid voltages

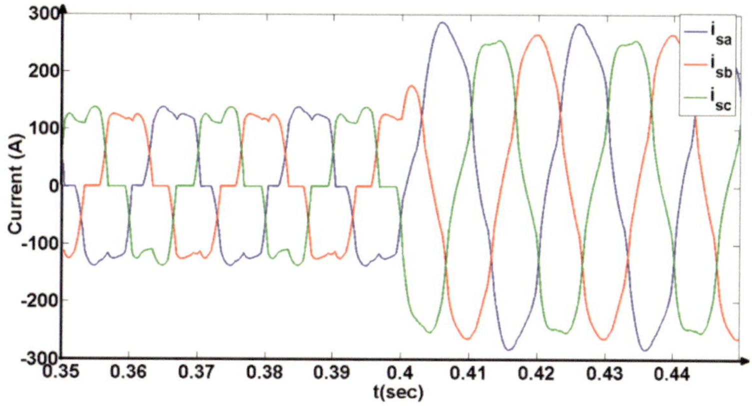

Figure 8. Grid currents without the application of the SAPF

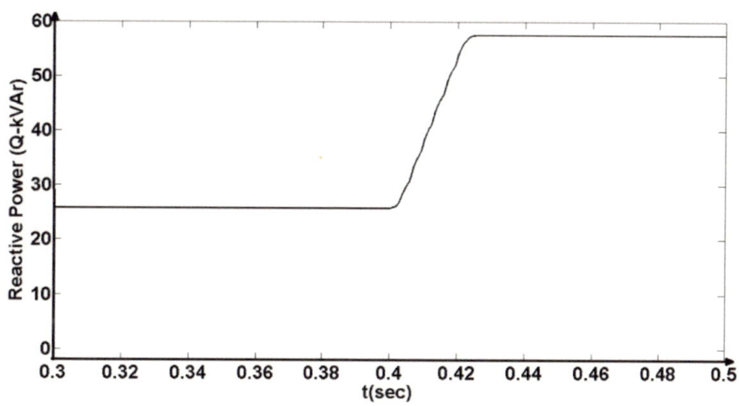

Figure 9. Reactive power of the grid without the SAPF

Phases	*a*	*b*	*c*
THD_i (Load_1)	18.84	26.62	21.92
THD_i (Load_1 + Load_2)	5.61	10.02	5.61

Table 3. Grid current THD_i index.

4.1.1. Conventional controller and fuzzy controller for dc bus voltage control

In this section the control scheme consists of the PI dc bus voltage controller and the hysteresis current controller (called "PI-HYS") will be compared with the control scheme consists of the fuzzy dc bus voltage controller (from section 2.2) and the hysteresis current controller (called "FUZ-HYS"). Figure 10 shows the dc bus voltage transient response at time t=0.4 sec for both control schemes.

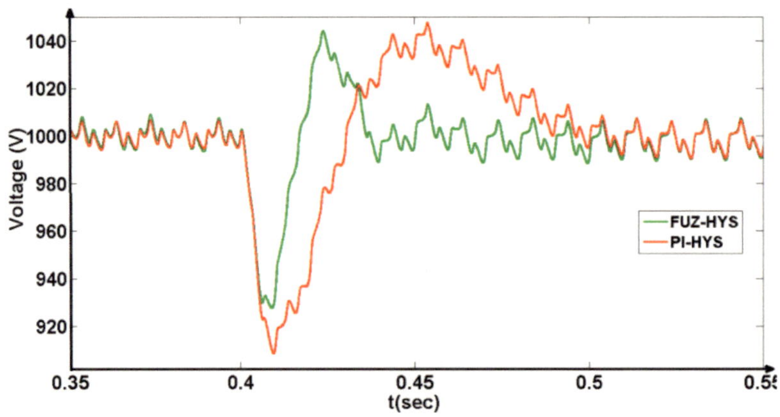

Figure 10. Dc bus voltage response for both control schemes

From figure 10 it is obvious that the dc bus voltage fuzzy logic controller outperforms the conventional PI controller. In particular, it is noted that the oscillation of the dc bus voltage with the application if the fuzzy logic controller is smaller compared to the PI one. Likewise the recovery time until the dc bus voltage returns to steady state is fairly smaller when the FLC is applied. This result has an effect on the time needed by the grid currents to return to steady state operation.

Figures 11 and 12 show the grid currents and the reactive power of the grid when the SAPF connected. Figures 11and 12 illustrate the results for both control schemes. Table 4 shows the THDi index of the grid currents considering the loads 'Load_1' and 'Load_1+Load_2'.

	PI-HYS			FYZ-HYS		
Phases	*a*	*b*	*c*	*a*	*b*	*c*
THDi (Load_1)	4.05	3.81	3.07	4.35	4.12	3.32
THDi (Load_1 + Load_2)	1.83	1.96	1.60	1.86	1.96	1.61

Table 4. Grid current THDi index.

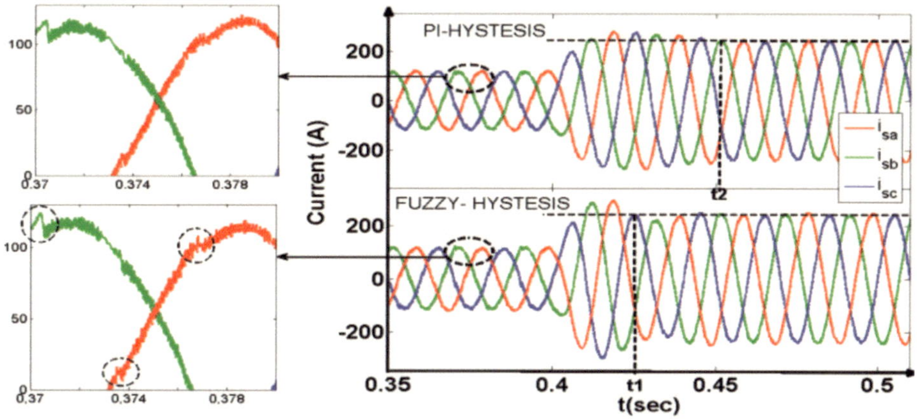

Figure 11. Grid currents with the application of the SAPF, for both control schemes

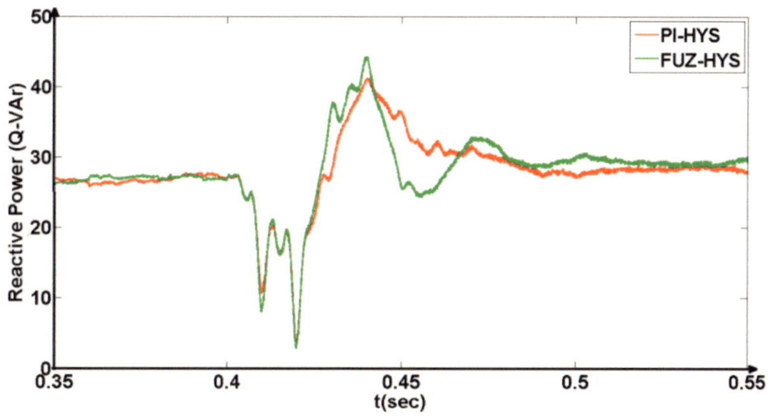

Figure 12. Grid reactive power after the compensation, for both control schemes

From figure 11 it is obvious that the faster response of the dc bus voltage using the fuzzy logic controller has a positive effect on the grid current, as the grid currents return to steady state operation faster (figure 11, time t_1 for FLC, and time t_2 for PI controller). It should be noted that, from figure 11 and Table 4 no significant change in the harmonic distortion of the grid currents in the case of dc bus voltage FLC is observed.

From the simulation results it is observed that the performance of the SAPF is satisfactory in the case where the grid voltages are distorted-unbalanced. This fact is a consequence of the modified version of the *p-q* theory, which was proposed in this chapter. The SAPF successfully eliminates the high order harmonics from the grid currents.

It is also observed that the SAPF compensates the reactive power of the load. As shown in figure 9 the reactive power of the grid without compensation for the 'Load_1' is Q=27 kVAr, then adding the 'Load_2' is increased to Q=58 kVAr. By using the active power filter, reactive power compensation is achieved for both initial and final load (the compensated reactive power of the grid is Q=28 VAr) as shown in figure 12. Comparing the two control schemes, PI-HYS and FYZ-HYS, similar behavior for the reactive power compensation is detected. For both control schemes there is a short transient period during the change of load.

4.1.2. *Conventional dc bus voltage and ac current controller compared with fuzzy controller*

For the reduction of the THDi index of the grid currents, authors propose a control scheme consists of a fuzzy logic dc bus voltage controller together with fuzzy logic hysteresis current controllers (as in section 2.3) (called "FUZ-FYZ HYS").

In this section the control scheme consists of the PI controller for the dc bus voltage control and the hysteresis controller for current control (PI-HYS) will be compared with the control scheme consists of the fuzzy controller for the dc bus voltage control and the fuzzy logic hysteresis controller for current control (FUZ-FUZ HYS). Figure 13 shows the dc bus voltage response at time t=0.4 sec for both control schemes.

From figure 13 it is obvious that the use of fuzzy logic for and ac output current control outperforms the control scheme of PI dc bus voltage control and hysteresis current control. In particular we observe that the oscillation of the dc bus voltage is smaller when the fuzzy logic dc bus voltage control and the fuzzy hysteresis current control is used. Likewise the interval time until the dc bus voltage returns to steady state operation is fairly smaller when the fuzzy logic scheme is applied. Comparing the results of figure 10 with those of figure 10, it is observed that the control schemes of FUZ- HYS and FUZ-FUZ HYS have no significant difference in the control of the dc bus voltage.

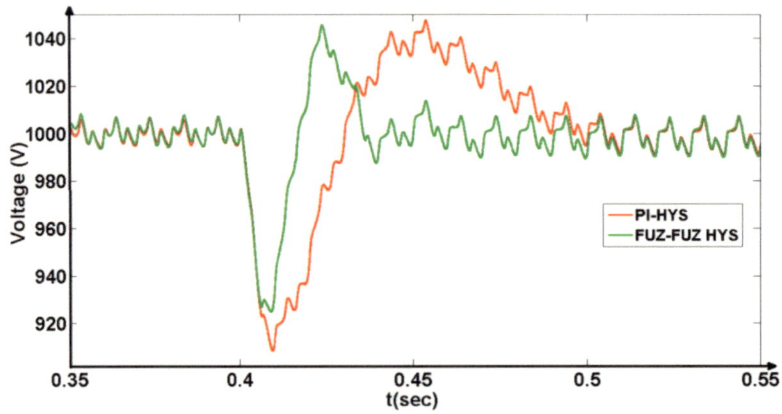

Figure 13. Dc bus voltage response, for both control schemes

Figures 14 and 15 show the grid currents and the reactive power of the grid with the application of the SAPF for both control schemes (PI-HYS and FUZ-FUZ HYS). Table 5 shows the grid currents THDi index for the loads 'Load_1' and 'Load_1+Load_2'.

	PI-HY			FYZ-HYS			FUZ-FYZ HYS		
Phases	*a*	*b*	*c*	*a*	*b*	*c*	*a*	*b*	*c*
THDi (1)	4.05	3.81	3.07	4.35	4.12	3.32	3.37	3.53	3.04
THDi (2)	1.83	1.96	1.60	1.86	1.96	1.61	1.62	1.77	1.57

Table 5. Grid current THDi index.

From figure 14 it is evident that the faster response of the dc bus voltage with the application of the FUZ-FUZ HYS control scheme has a positive effect on the grid current, as they return to steady state operation in smaller interval time (figure 14, time instant t_1 for FUZ-FUZ HYS control scheme, and time instant t_2 for PI-HYS control scheme). It should be noted that, from figure 14 smaller harmonic distortion of the grid currents is observed using the FUZ-FUZ HYS control scheme. In figure 14 some of the points where improvement is observed are highlighted using circles.

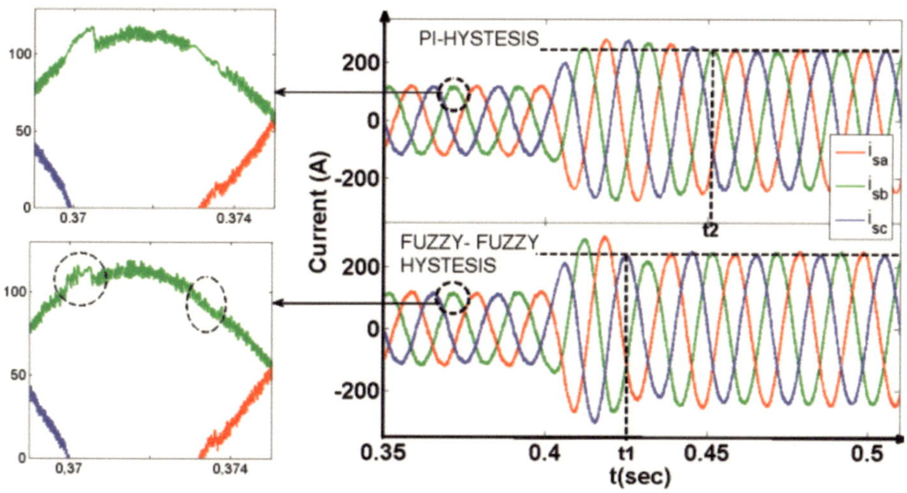

Figure 14. Grid currents with the application of the SAPF, for both control schemes

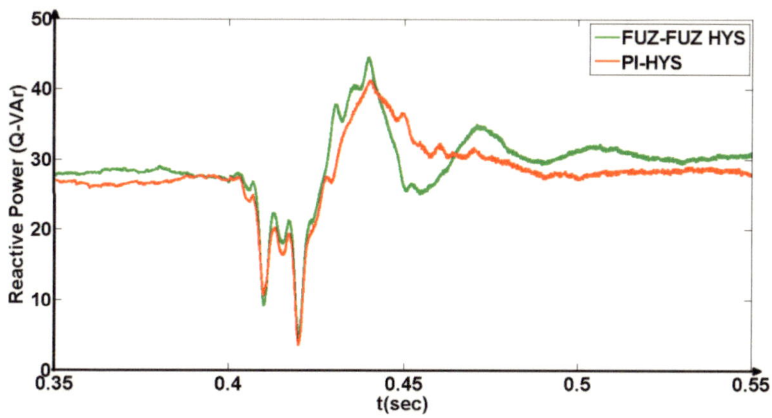

Figure 15. Grid reactive power after the compensation, for both control schemes

From the analysis of the simulation results, the improvement in the THD_i index of the grid current using the FUZ-FUZ HYS control scheme is observed, as shown in Table 5. For phase-a, the improvement in the THD_i index with the FUZ-FUZ HYS control scheme is about 22.5%. For phases-b and -c, the improvement in the THD_i index with the FUZ-FUZ HYS control scheme is about 14.3% and 8.5% respectively. Investigating the electric power system, the unbalances in the THD_i index is the result of the unbalances in the grid voltages.

From the comparison of the PI-HYS and FYZ-FUZ HYS control schemes, similar behavior for the reactive power compensation is observed. For both control schemes there is a short transition period during the load change. As shown in figure 9 the reactive power of the grid considering only the 'Load_1', without compensation for the is Q=27 kVAr, then adding the 'Load_2' the reactive power is increased to Q=58 kVAr. Using the SAPF, reactive power compensation is achieved for both initial and final load (in this case, the reactive power of the grid is approximately Q=29 VAr) as shown in figure 15.

From the simulation results it is observed that considering the above mentioned case the performance of the SAPF is excellent, as well as the performance of the SAPF is not affected by the distorted-unbalanced grid voltages. This fact is a consequence of the modified version of the *p-q* theory.

5. Future research

The fuzzy logic controller outperforms the conventional PI controller due to robustness and the superior transient response. However FLC have some significant disadvantages. The main drawback of the FLC is the requirement of an expert for the design of the membership functions and the fuzzy rules. To overcome this disadvantage, a novel artificial intelligent controller called "fuzzy-tuned PI controller" has been proposed in the literature of automation control [De Carli A, Linguori P, et al. (1994)], [Zhao Z-Y, Tomizuka M, et al. (1993)]. The fuzzy-tuned PI controller in figure 16 is a combination of the fuzzy controller and the PI controller. Using the fuzzy part we can estimate the gains K_p and K_p of the PI controller. Then the PI controller based on these gains outputs the reference signal. The fuzzy-tuned PI controller was initially applied for the speed control of the induction motor drives [Chen Y, Fu b, et al. (2008)] and the dc bus voltage control of the grid connected inverters [Suryanarayana H, Mishra MK (2008)].

No significant work, comparing the performance of the PI and fuzzy-tuned PI controller for the current control of a grid connected inverter, has been reported. In this section the PI and the fuzzy-tuned PI controller are applied to the inner current control loop. The criterion for the comparison of the two controllers are based on the transient response.

5.1. Fuzzy-tuned PI controller analysis for current control

The synoptic block diagram of the proposed fuzzy-tuned PI controller is illustrated in figure 16. As inputs to the fuzzy-tuned PI current controller are the actual and the reference currents. The current controller outputs the appropriate reference signal (reference voltage).

The reference voltage in α-β reference frame will be used by the Space Vector Modulation algorithm for the switching pattern generation.

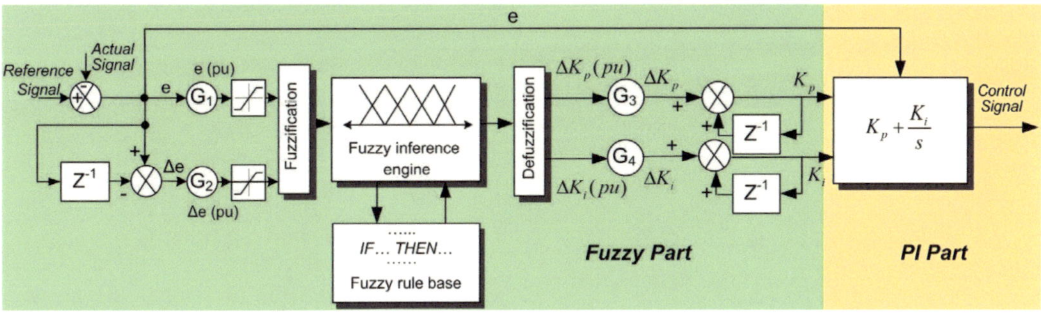

Figure 16. General structure of the fuzzy-tuned PI controller

The operation of the fuzzy-tuned PI controller is based on the use of a FLC for on-line tuning of the gains K_p and K_i of the PI controller, as shown in equation (20). Then the PI controller uses the adjusted gains K_p, K_i and the current error (e) to create the reference output control signals (referencevoltage).

$$\begin{aligned} K_p &= \Delta K_p + K_p(k-1) \\ K_i &= \Delta K_i + K_i(k-1) \end{aligned} \tag{20}$$

As inputs to the fuzzy-tuned PI controller the error $e = i_{c,ref} - i_c$ and the error variation Δe=e(k)-e(k-1) are determined. As outputs from the fuzzy part, the gains ΔK_i (pu) and ΔK_p (pu) of the PI controller, are determined. Using the gains K_i and K_i, the PI controller outputs the reference output voltage of the inverter ($u_{c,ref}$). The scaling factors G_1, G_2, G_3 and G_4 are used to normalize the input and output signals. In figure 17.a seven membership functions are used for each input (NL-Negative Large, NM-Negative Medium, NS-Negative Small, ZE-Zero, PS-Positive Small, PM-Positive Medium, and PL-Positive Large). In figure 17.b two membership functions are used for each output (B for Big and S for Small). For the fuzzy-tuned PI controller the triangular function was used as input and output fuzzy sets.

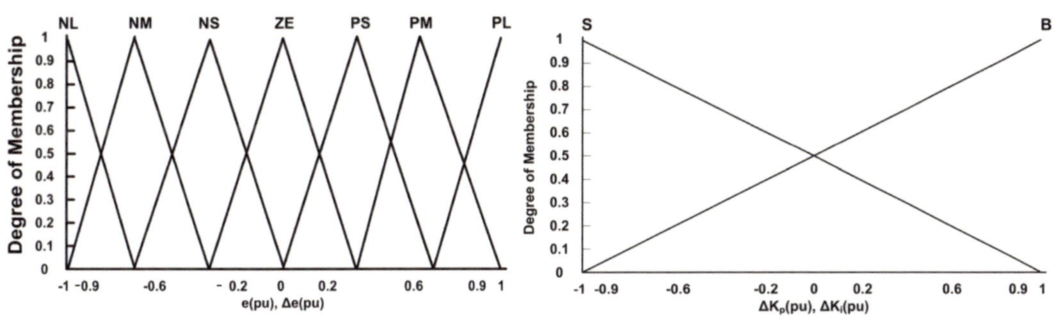

(a) (b)

Figure 17. Membership functions for a) input variables e, Δe, and b) output variables ΔK_i (pu) and ΔK_p (pu)

The fuzzy rules which are shown in Table 6 for the ΔK_P and in Table 7 for the ΔK_i, are determined using the standard form of fuzzy rules: *IF e is* A_i *and* Δe *is* B_j, *THEN* $\Delta K_{P,i}$ *is* C_{ij} *and* $\Delta K_{I,i}$ *is* D_{ij}.

Δe	e						
	NL	NM	NS	ZE	PS	PM	PL
NL	B	B	B	B	B	B	B
NM	S	B	B	B	B	B	S
NS	S	S	B	B	B	S	S
ZE	S	S	S	B	S	S	S
PS	S	S	B	B	B	S	S
PM	S	B	B	B	B	B	S
PL	B	B	B	B	B	B	B

Table 6. Fuzzy control rules table for ΔK_P.

Δe	e						
	NL	NM	NS	ZE	PS	PM	PL
NL	B	B	B	B	B	B	B
NM	B	S	S	S	S	S	B
NS	B	B	S	S	S	B	B
ZE	B	B	B	S	B	B	B
PS	B	B	S	S	S	B	B
PM	B	S	S	S	S	S	B
PL	B	B	B	B	B	B	B

Table 7. Fuzzy control rules table for ΔK_I.

5.2. Comparison between fuzzy-tuned PI controller and the PI controller

In this section the behavior of the two current controllers will be compared based on the dynamic response. At the time instant t=0.4 sec a sudden variation of the output power of the inverter occurs. Figures 18.a and 18.b show the output currents of the inverter in *a-b-c* reference frame for the PI and the fuzzy-tuned PI current controller, respectively.

From figure 18 we can observe that the current error in *a-b-c* reference frame is very big when the PI controller is used (the power of the inverter increases). When the fuzzy-tuned PI controller is applied the error becomes almost zero while the recovery time is smaller compared to the PI. This fact has a direct impact to the output currents, which in the case of fuzzy-tuned PI controller have smoother behavior, while in the case of PI controller have rougher behavior.

From the dynamic response of the electric power system is concluded that the fuzzy-tuned PI controller is best suited for the inner current control loop.

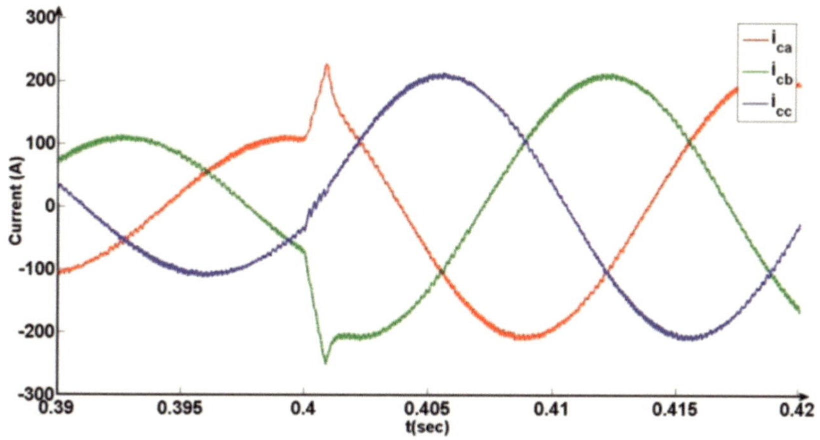

(a)

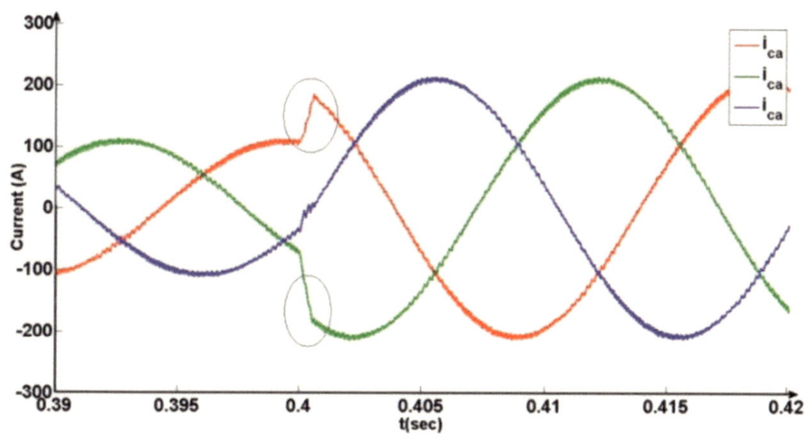

(b)

Figure 18. Current in ac side of the inverter during the dynamic response using the a) PI, and b) fuzzy-tuned PI current controller

6. Conclusion

In this chapter a modified version of the *p-q* theory was proposed, in order to improve the performance of the SAPF in the case of non-ideal grid voltages. For the performance improvement of the control scheme, the fuzzy logic theory was applied. A fuzzy logic controller for the dc bus voltage control was used. From the computer simulations and the analysis of the results, smaller amplitude and duration of the dc bus voltage oscillations during the transient response has been demonstrated. A further investigation of the system was carried out applying fuzzy logic hysteresis controller to control the output current of the inverter. From the investigation of the control system using fuzzy logic controller both for dc bus voltage and inverter output current control, the dc bus voltage during the transient response and the THD_i index of the grid currents are obviously improved.

Furthermore, authors use a combination of the PI and the fuzzy control known as "fuzzy-tuned PI" control. The performance of the inverter in case of the fuzzy-tuned PI control is used on the current control loop was investigated.

Author details

Georgios A. Tsengenes and Georgios A. Adamidis
Department of Electrical and Computer Engineering, Democritus University of Thrace, Greece

7. References

Buso S, Malesani L, Mattavelli P. (1998). Comparison of Current Control Techniques for Active Filter Applications. *IEEE Trans Ind Elect*, Vol.45, No.5, pp.722-729.

Chen Y, Fu b, Li Q (2008). Fuzzy logic based auto-modulation of parameters pi control for active power filter. In: World congress on intelligent control and automation, Chongqing, 2008.

Czarnecki L S. (2006). Instantaneous Reactive Power p-q Theory and Power Properties of Three-Phase System. *IEEE Trans Power Del*, Vol.21, No.1, pp.362-367.

De Carli A, Linguori P, Marroni A (1994). A fuzzy-pi control strategy. *Control Eng Practice*, Vol.2, No.1, pp.147-153.

El-Kholy E E, El-Sabbe, El-Hefnawy, Mharous M H. (2006). Three-phase active power filter based on current controlled voltage source inverter. Int J Electr Power Energy Syst, Vol.28, No.8 , pp.537-547.

Emanuel A E. (2004). Summary of IEEE Standard 1459: Definitions for the Measurement of Electric Power Quantities Under Sinusoidal, Nonsinusoidal, Balanced or Unbalanced Conditions. *IEEE Trans Ind Appl*, Vol.40, No.3, pp.869-876.

Han Y, Khan M M, Yao G, Zhou L-D, Chen C. (2010). A novel harmonic-free power factor corrector based on T-type APF with adaptive linear neural network (ADALINE) control. *Simulat Model Pract Theor*, Vol.16, No.9, pp.1215-1238.

Jain S K, Agrawal P, Gupta H O. (2002). Fuzzy logic controlled shunt active power filter for power quality improving. *IEE Electr Power Appl*, Vol.149, No.5, pp.317-328.

Kale M, Ozdemir E. (2005). Harmonic and reactive power compensation with shunt active power filter under non-ideal mains voltage. *Electr Power Syst Reseach*, Vol.74, No.3 pp.363-370.

Kilic T, Milun S, Petrovic G. (2007). Design and implementation of predictive filtering system for current reference generation of active power filter. Int *Journ of Electr Power Energy Syst*, Vol.29, No.2, pp.106-112.

Lin B R, Hoft R G. (1996). Analysis of power converter control using neural network and rule-based methods. *Electr Power Comp and Systems*, Vol.24, No.7, pp.695-720.

Mekri F, Machmoum M. (2010). A comparative study of voltage controllers for series active power filter. *Electr Power Syst Reseach*, Vol.80, No. , pp.615-626.

Saad A, Zellouma L. (2009). Fuzzy logic controller for three-level shunt active filter compensating harmonics and reactive power. *Electr Power Syst Reseach*, Vol. 79, No.10, pp.1337-1341.

Salmeron P, Herrera R S, Vazquez J R. (2007). A new approach for three-phase compensation based on the instantaneous reactive power theory. *Electr Power Syst Reseach*, Vol.78, No.4, pp.605-617.

Segui-Chilet S S, Gimeno-Sales F J, Orts S, Garcera G, Figueres E, Alcaniz M, Masot R. (2007). Approach to unbalance power active compensation under linear load unbalances and fundamental voltage asymmetries. *Int J Electr Power Energy Syst*, Vol.29, No.7, pp.526-539.

Singh G K, Singh A K, Mitra R. (2007). A simple fuzzy logic based robust active power filter for harmonics minimization under random load variation. *Electr Power Syst Reseach*, Vol.77, No.8 , pp.1101-1111.

Skretas S B, Dimitrios D. P. (2009). Efficient design and simulation of an expandable hybrid (wind–photovoltaic) power system with MPPT and inverter input voltage regulation features in compliance with electric grid requirements. *Electr Power Syst Reseach*, Vol.79, No.9 , pp.1271-1285.

Suryanarayana H, Mishra M K (2008). Fuzzy logic based supervision of dc link pi control in a dstatcom. *In: India conference*, Kanpur

Tsengenes G, Adamidis G. (2010). An Improved Current Control Technique for the Investigation of a Power System with a Shunt Active Filter. *In: International Symposium on Power Electronics, Electrical Drives, Automation and Motion*, Pisa, Italy.

Tsengenes G, Adamidis G. (2011). Investigation of the behavior of a three phase grid-connected photovoltaic system to control active and reactive power. *Elec Power Syst Reser*, Vol. 81, No. 1, pp.177-184, 2011.

Zhao Z-Y, Tomizuka M, Isaka S (1993). Fuzzy gain scheduling of pid controllers. *IEEE Trans Systems Man and Cybern*, Vol.23, No.4, pp. 1392-1398.

Zhou K, Wang D. (2002). Relationship between space-vector modulation and three-phase carrier-based PWM: A comprehensive analysis. *IEEE Trans Ind Electron*, Vol.49, No.1, pp.186-196.

Chapter 23

Discrete-Time Cycle-to-Cycle Fuzzy Logic Control of FES-Induced Swinging Motion

B. S. K. K. Ibrahim, M. O. Tokhi, M. S. Huq and S. C. Gharooni

Additional information is available at the end of the chapter

http://dx.doi.org/10.5772/48488

1. Introduction

Functional electrical stimulation (FES) can be used to restore motor function to individuals with spinal cord injuries (SCI). FES involves artificially inducing a current in specific motor neurons to generate a skeletal muscle contraction. FES induced movement control is a significantly challenging area for researchers. The challenge mainly arises due to muscle response characteristics such as fatigue, time-varying properties and nonlinear dynamics of paralyzed muscles [1]. Another challenge is due to certain motor reflexes such as spasticity. Spasticity is a reflex or uncontrolled response to something that excites the nerve endings and produces muscle contractions. These reflexes are often unpredictable and may impede joint movements [2].

Primarily due to the complexity of the system (nonlinearities, time-variation) practical FES systems are predominantly open-loop where the controller receives no information about the actual state of the system [3]. In its basic form, these systems require continuous user input. Practical success of this open-loop control strategy is still, however, seriously limited due to the fixed nature of the associated parameters. The problem arises especially due to the existing parameter variations (e.g., muscle fatigue), inherent time-variance, and strong nonlinearities present in the neuromuscular-skeletal system or the plant to be controlled. Besides, in such open-loop control approach, the actual movement is not assessed in real time and any mechanism of adapting the stimulation pattern in response to unforeseen circumstances such as external perturbations or muscle spasms is absent [4]. These prominent problems can be resolved by having a suitable closed-loop adaptive control mechanism. Such approach has several advantages over open-loop schemes, including better tracking performance and smaller sensitivity to the modeling errors, parameter variations, and external disturbances [5].

In controlling cyclical movement, one can try to follow pre-set joint angle trajectories. Although the trajectory-based closed-loop control has been developed but it has not been used yet in clinical FES gait because of difficulties in achieving accurate tracking performance [6]. Moreover, in the swing phase of gait, following exact trajectories is unimportant and inefficient, leading to fatigue due to large forces that must be exerted to precisely control the high inertia body segments [3]. For these reasons, cycle-to-cycle control method is expected to be an alternative to trajectory based closed-loop FES control. The cycle-to-cycle control delivers electrical stimulation in the form of open-loop control in each cycle without reference trajectory but it is still closed-loop control. In this control strategy, movement parameters at the end of each cycle are compared as in the desired set point, and the stimulation for the next cycle is adjusted on the basis of the error in the preceding cycle.

In fact, FES induced movements have traditionally been achieved through application of stimulus bursts rather than continuous tracking control. The burst of stimulus signal would drive the joint to its desired orientation through ballistic movement and thus traversing a trajectory defined purely by the physics of the segment combination [5]. The cycle-to-cycle control approach retains this basic mechanism of movement generation through stimulus burst and comes into action when the movement is repetitive or cyclical, through automatic adjustment of the burst parameters to maintain the desired target orientation at each cycle [7]. While the trajectory based closed-loop control for knee joint angle of paraplegic has been criticized for having poor tracking and oscillatory responses and even its inability to reach full knee extension angle [8]. the ability of cycle-to-cycle control approach to realize the target joint orientation has been demonstrated in experimental tests of controlling maximum knee extension angle [9] or hip joint range [7].

Researches as in [7] and [9] investigated a discrete-time proportional-integral-derivative (PID) feedback controller for cycle-to-cycle adaptation of an experimentally initialized stimulation signal with a view to compensate for the fatigue-induced time variation of muscle output. For practical use of cycle-to-cycle control, realization in multi-joint control is crucial, in which problems seen in the PID controller such as drawback in determination of controller parameter values and a lack of capability in compensating muscle fatigue [7] have to be solved. It is difficult to establish the control parameters for these systems since they are not always the same under different circumstances [10]. Therefore, traditional control approaches, such as PID control might not perform satisfactorily if the system to be controlled is of highly nonlinear and uncertain nature [5].

On the other hand, fuzzy logic control (FLC) has long been known for its ability to handle a complex nonlinear system without developing a mathematical model of the system. FLC is the fastest growing soft computing tool in medicine and biomedical engineering [11]. It is being used successfully in an increasing number of application areas in the control community. FLCs are rule-based systems that use fuzzy linguistic variables to model human rule-of-thumb approaches to problem solving, and thus overcoming the limitations that classical expert systems may face because of their inflexible representation of human decision making. The major strength of fuzzy control also lies in the way a nonlinear output mapping of a number of inputs can be specified easily using fuzzy linguistic variables and fuzzy rules [12]. The control signal is computed by rule evaluation called fuzzy inference instead of by mathematical equations. In order to compensate the non-linearity of the musculo-skeletal system responses, the cycle-to-cycle control was implemented using fuzzy controller. Thus FLC with is the preferred option in the current work

This chapter presents the development of strategies for swinging motion control by controlling the amount of stimulation pulsewidth to the quadriceps muscle of the knee joints. The capability of the controller to control knee joint movements is first assessed in computer simulations using a musculo-skeletal knee joint model. The knee joint model developed in Matlab/Simulink, as described in [13], is used to develop an FLC-based cycle-to-cycle control strategy for the knee joint movement. The FLC output is the controlled FES stimulation pulsewidth signal which stimulates the knee extensors providing torque to the knee joint. The swinging movement is performed by only controlling stimulation pulsewidth to the knee extensors to extent the knee and then the knee is left freely to flex in the flexion period. The controllers are then tested through experimental work on a paraplegic in terms of swinging performance and compensation of muscle fatigue and spasticity.

2. Materials and method

2.1. Model of knee joint

The shank-quadriceps dynamics are modelled as the interconnection of passive and active properties of muscle model and the segmental dynamics. The total knee-joint moment is given as [14]:

$$M_{\mathrm{i}} = M_{a} + M_{\mathrm{g}} + M_{\mathrm{s}} + M_{\mathrm{d}} \tag{1}$$

where M_i refers to inertial moment, M_g is gravitational moment, M_a refers to an active knee joint moment produced by electrical stimulation, M_s is the knee joint elastic moment and M_d is the viscous moment representing the passive behaviour of the knee joint. In this research the M_i and M_g are represented by the equations of motion for dynamic model of the lower limb while M_a and M_s+M_d are represented by a fuzzy model as active properties of quadriceps muscle and passive viscoelasticity respectively. A schematic representation of the knee joint model consisting of active properties, passive viscoelasticity and equations of motion of the lower limb is shown in Figure 1. The active joint moment is added with the passive joint moment as an input (torque) to the lower limb model and this will produce the knee angle as the output. The subject participating in this work was a 48 year-old T2&T3 incomplete paraplegic male with 20 years post-injury with height = 173cm and weight = 80kg. Informed consent was obtained from the subject.

A schematic diagram of the lower limb model is shown in Figure 5, where q_2 = shank length, r_1 = position of COM along the shank, r_2 = position of COM along the foot, θ_1 =knee angle and θ_2 =ankle angle. Hence, the dynamics of motion can be represented in the simpler form based on Kane's equations as in [13]. The gravitational (M_g) moment is represented by:-

$$M_g = m_1 g \cos\theta_1 r_1 + m_2 g \cos\theta_1 q_2 \tag{2}$$

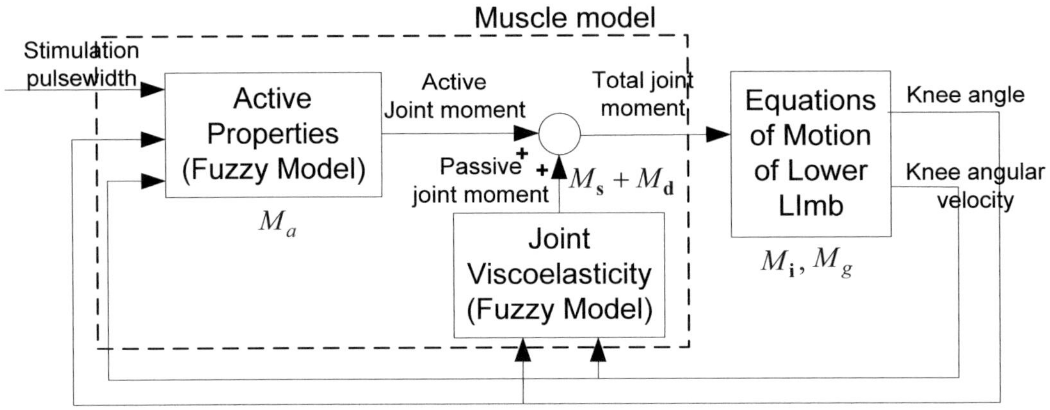

Figure 1. Schematic representation of the knee joint model

The inertial (M_i) moment of the lower limb is represented as follows:-

$$M_i = -m_2 q_2 \dot{\theta}_1^{\,2} r_2 - I_1 \ddot{\theta}_1 - m_1 r_1^{\,2} \ddot{\theta}_1 - m_2 q_2^2 \ddot{\theta}_1 \tag{3}$$

where, m_1 = shank mass, m_2=foot mass, I_1= moment of inertia about COM, $\dot{\theta}_1$ =knee velocity, $\ddot{\theta}_1$ =knee acceleration, g =gravity=9.81 m/s[2].

Anthropometric measurements of length of the lower limb were made and this is shown in Table 1.

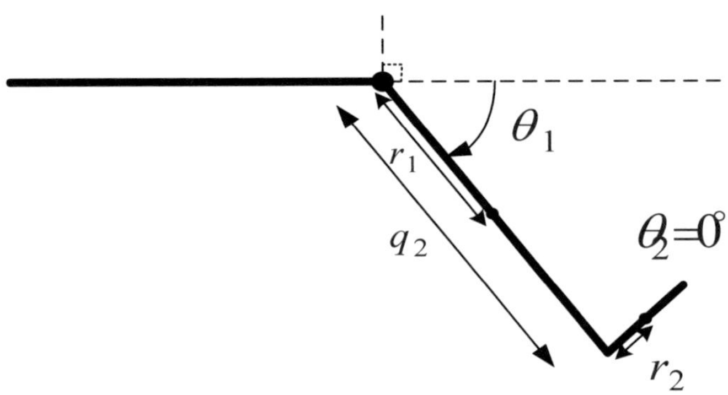

Figure 2. Lower limb model [4]

The knee joint model input is the stimulation pulsewidth as would be delivered in practice by an electrical stimulator. The complete model of knee joint thus developed is utilized as platform for simulation of the system and development of control approaches.

Segment	Length (m)
Shank length	0.426
Foot length	0.068
Approximated position of COM of shank	0.213
Approximated position of COM of soot	0.034

Table 1. Anthropometric data of subject

2.2. Cycle to cycle controller development

Researcher as in [15] highlighted cycle-to-cycle control as a method for using feedback to improve product quality for processes that are inaccessible within a single processing cycle but can be changed between cycles. The same concept has been applied in this study, where only reaching a target joint orientation through ballistic movement is taken into consideration rather than rigorously following a trajectory. The muscle is stimulated by single burst of controlled stimulation pulsewidth for each cycle to induce joint movement reaching the target extension knee angle. Therefore, the method is different from the traditional closed-loop control such as tracking control of desired angle trajectory.

An outline of the discrete-time fuzzy control based cycle-to-cycle control is shown in Figure3. The controlled maximum joint angle of the previous cycle is delivered as feedback signal. Error is defined as difference between the target and measured joint angle. The controller will regulate the duration of stimulation pulsewidth based on the error and previous flexion angle.

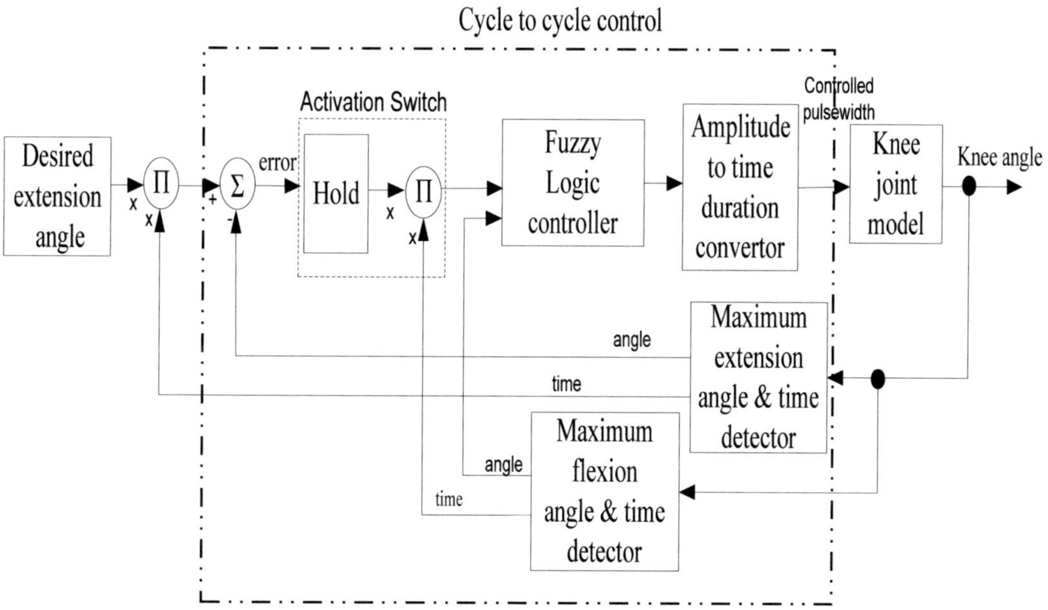

Figure 3. Discrete-time FLC based cycle to cycle control

2.2.1. *Maximum flexion and extension detector*

The maximum flexion time detector will detect the time the angle reaches the peak of knee flexion for each cycle. The maximum extension signal and time detector will detect the peak angle of knee extension and the time the knee angle reaches this point for each cycle. The extension and flexion stages of the knee angle are shown in Figure 4.

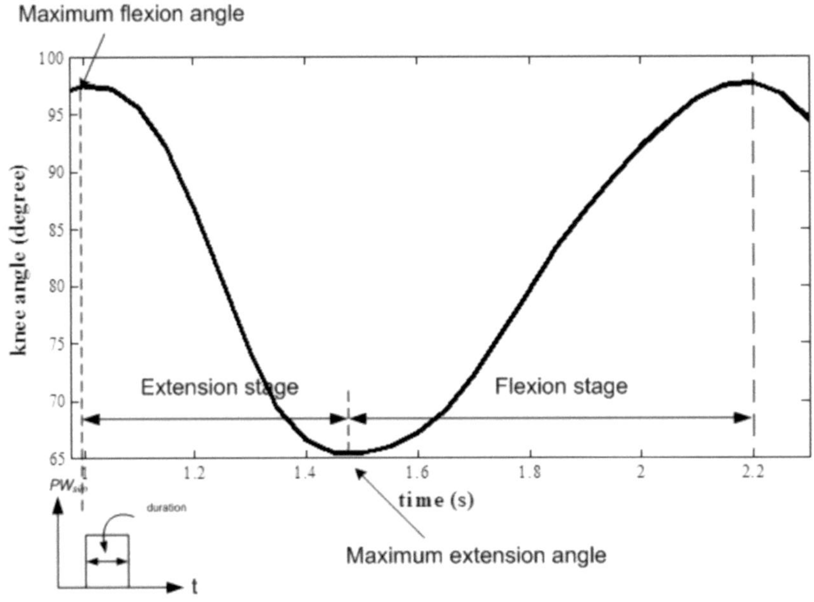

Figure 4. Extension and flexion stages

2.2.2. *Activation switch*

Activation switch consists of hold and multiplier block to be active only when the knee angle reaches maximum flexion. The activation switch will hold the error signal and produce the output whenever it receives a signal from the maximum flexion time detector.

2.2.3. *Amplitude to time duration convertor*

Amplitude to time duration converter is linearly converting the controlled signal (amplitude) from controller to time duration using signal comparator and shifting technique as shown in Figure 6.3. In this technique, first the controlled signal is compared with specific constant values for low to high in the parallel structure. Each comparator compares the controlled signal with the specific constant, if the controlled signal is greater than or equal to the specific constant then a single pulse will pass through the comparator. The first comparator compares the control signal with zero, if there is any signal from controller then the output will be a pulse with 0.05s width. The second comparator compares the control signal with specific constant and shift 0.05s and the next comparator compares and shifts by a further 0.05s. Then the resultant pulse duration for each cycle is obtained by summing up the total pulses passed through the comparators and amplifying the signal with 220μs. The higher the controlled signal the more gates can be passed through and the wider the duration of pulse. Therefore the output of this converter is a single burst of controlled stimulation pulse duration with constant amplitude (220μs) for each cycle.

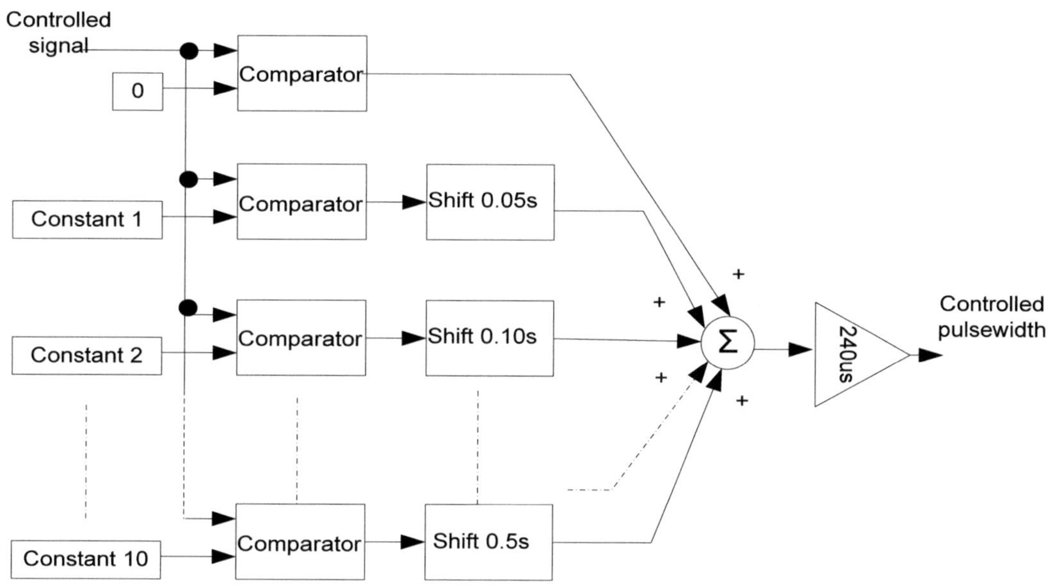

Figure 5. Signal comparator and shifting technique

2.2.4. *Controller objectives*

The FLC-based cycle-to-cycle control was designed to achieve the following objectives:

i. Able to reach full knee extension
ii. Able to reach target extension angle thus maintain a steady swinging motion.
iii. Compensate for muscle fatigue
iv. Compensate for spasticity

2.2.5. *Fuzzy controller design*

Measured output of the controlled musculoskeletal system of the previous cycle is delivered as feedback signal. Proper value of signal is determined and regulated automatically by a Sugeno-type fuzzy controller using control rules as shown in Table 2. Input membership function is expressed as triangle fuzzy sets. Output membership function is expressed as fuzzy singletons. Input of fuzzy controller is aggregated by fuzzy inference using fuzzy rules to produce control action.

The fuzzy rules base directs control action based on error and flexion angle. The error will be higher when the muscle fatigues, in which case the response to a stimulation burst will change. To compensate for this changing system response, the stimulation burst time has to be increased such that shank can reach the desired angle in every cycle. The flexion angle was taken into account to rule out the disturbance due to spasticity. Combination of the information about error and knowledge about flexion angle will be necessary for controller to give an appropriate stimulation pulsewidth in compensation of muscle fatigue and motor reflexes. pulsewidth in compensation of muscle fatigue and motor reflexes.

		Flexion angle					
		Very High	High	Normal	Low	Very Low	Extremely Low
Error	Negative	Low	Low	Low	Low	Zero	Zero
	Zero	Low	Low	Low	Low	Zero	Zero
	Positive Small	Low	Normal	Normal	Very Low	Very Low	Zero
	Positive Medium	Low	Normal	Normal	Normal	Very Low	Zero
	Positive Big	Normal	Normal	Normal	Normal	Normal	Zero

Table 2. Rules of Sugeno-type FLC

3. Results and discussion

This discrete-time fuzzy logic cycle to cycle control technique emphasizes the view to overcome some drawbacks of trajectory based closed-loop FES control such as poor tracking, oscillating response and inability to reach full knee extension angle (Hatwell, 1991). Then the capabilities in compensating for muscle fatigue and spastisity are investigated. The ability of this control approach to realize the target joint orientation is assessed in simulation and experimental test as follows:-

3.1. Controllers' performance in simulation environment

A complete set of non-linear dynamic equations of the knee joint model comprising the passive properties and active properties have been used in the simulations for purposes of controller development. Computer simulations are performed to assess the performance of the designed discrete-time fuzzy logic cycle-to-cycle control approach in generating stimulation burst durations for the desired extension angle. The simulations were carried out within the Matlab/Simulink environment. The muscle model was controlled by changing the pulse width; however the amplitude and the frequency of the stimulation pulses were constant. Here only the knee extensors are controlled by applying regulated stimulation pulsewidth to the quadriceps muscle model.

3.1.1. Full knee extension angle

The test was initiated with stimulation pulse of 240μs amplitude with 0.3s burst duration for the first cycle of swing in gait before activating the controller. FES induced swinging motion was controlled using fuzzy controller to reach full extension angle. The full extension angle that can be achieved by paraplegic was defined as 10°. The computer simulation test was performed with stimulation course of 50 cycles. The first 5 cycles of the controlled swinging leg test of the full extension knee angle are shown in Figure 6.4. As can be seen, using FLC-based cycle-to-cycle control approach the first objective was achieved; to reach the full knee extension. The knee reached full extension at 3rd cycle and was able to maintain the swinging motion without any predefined trajectory.

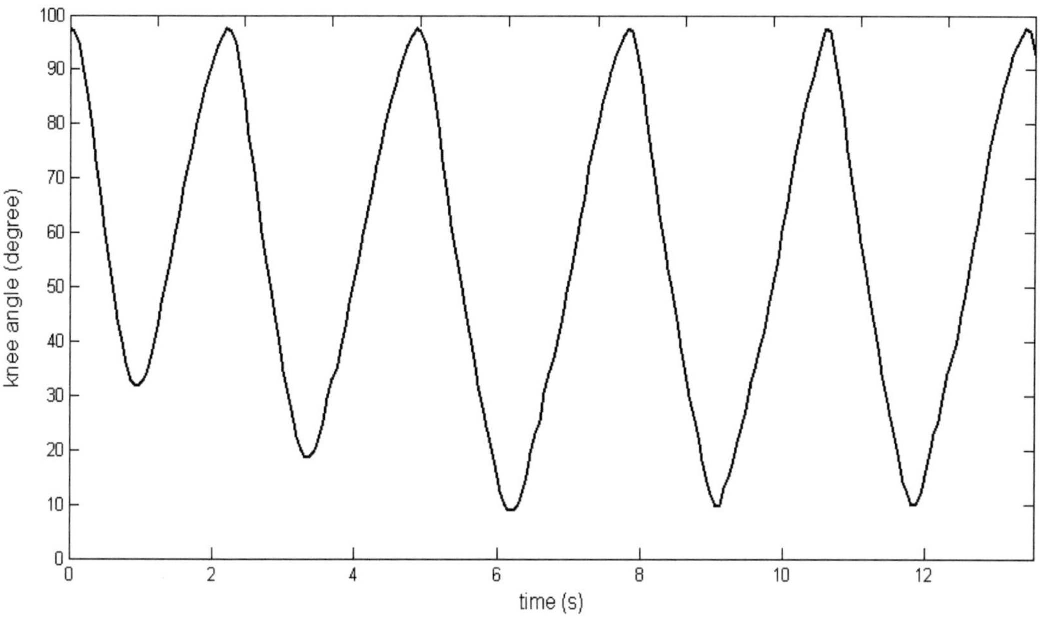

Figure 6. Controlled swinging leg for desired angle at 10° (full extension)

3.1.2. Target extension angle and maintain steady swinging

The desired extension knee angle was set to be at 65° as considered in [16]. The test was initiated with stimulation pulse of 220μs amplitude with 0.25s burst duration for the first cycle before activating the controller.

3.1.2.1. Without presence of musle fatique and voluntary activation

The test is to achieve the target extension angle and thus maintain a steady swing of the shank without presence of musle fatique and voluntary activation. In the each test computer simulation was performed with stimulation course of 50 cycles. The first 10 cycles of the controlled swinging leg test of the knee joint at 65° is shown in Figure 7. As can be seen the cycle-to-cycle control approach can achieve the target extension angle at 3rd and thus maintain a steady swing of the shank. It is noted that the performance of the controller was quite good and acceptable.

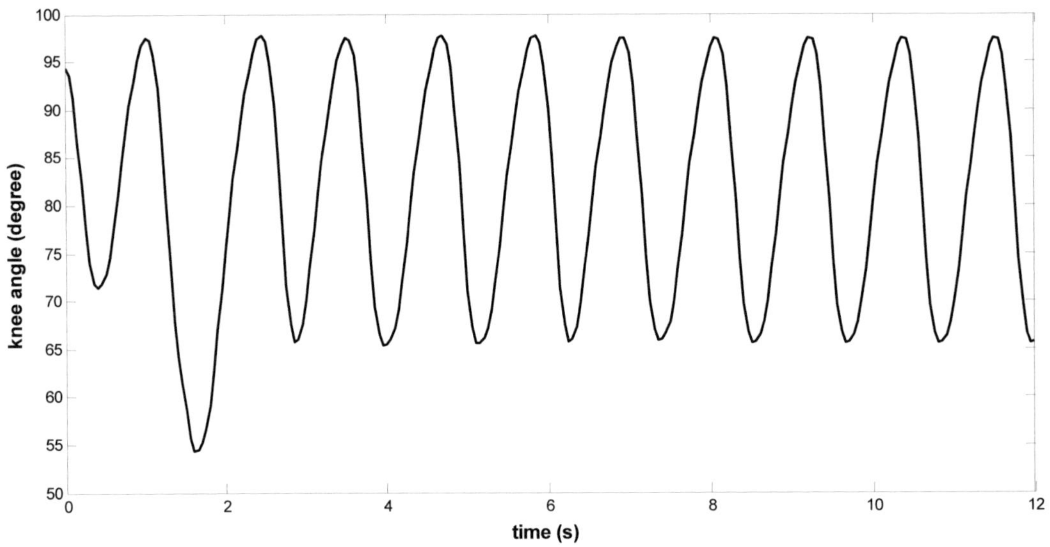

Figure 7. Controlled swinging leg for desired angle at 65° (normal extension)

3.1.2.2. With presence of musle fatique and without presence of voluntary activation

Muscle fatigue is an inevitable pitfall in FES induced control of movements. Fatigue is defined as the inability of a muscle to continue to generate a required force. It limits the duration FES can be effective by drastically reducing the muscle force output. It thus should be considered as an important criterion for FES induced movement control. The fatigue resistance of the control approaches were analyzed based on relative drop in knee extension by simulating the fatigue as in Figure 8. The fatigue simulation was to reduce muscle torque output to the 80% of total torque output at the end of simulation [5]. Figure 6.7 shows the knee joint response obtained using this controller, but with FES torque dropped down to 80% of its normal value. The effect of fatigue can be noted at 3rd cycle, the shank was unable to reach the target angle. Then controller has taken action to overcome this by increasing the stimulation burst time. Then, after 6th cycle the shank reached the target angle thus maintaining the swinging motion. As can be seen the controller performed very well in terms of robustness of the FLC in the presence of muscle fatigue.

3.1.2.3. With presences of musle fatique and spasticity

SCI muscle often exhibits spasticity [17] and may vary with time during cyclical motion [18]. Spasticity is defined as motor disorder characterized by a velocity-dependent increase in tonic stretch reflexes with exaggerated tendon jerks [19]. With regard to FES-approaches for function restoration, spasticity certainly represents a disadvantage especially flexion spasticity [20]. Muscle fatigue (as in previous test) and motor reflex to represent spasticity were simulated to assess the ability of controller to tackle these influences.

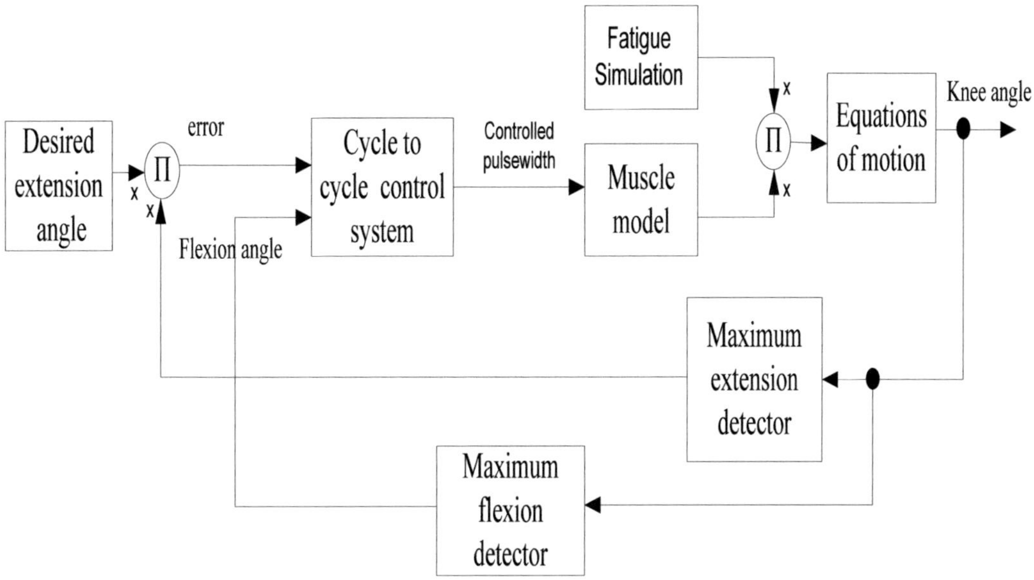

Figure 8. Controller with simulated fatigue

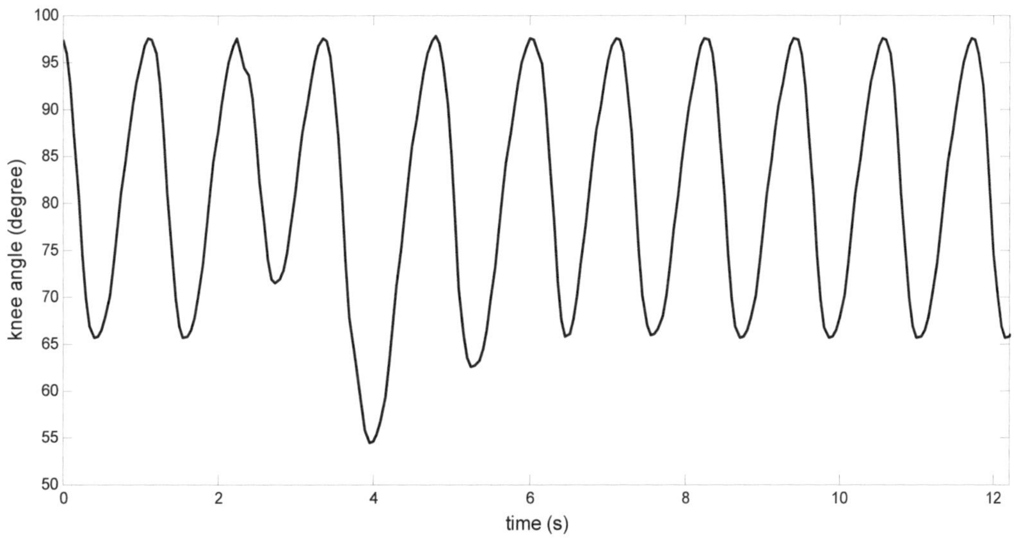

Figure 9. Controlled swinging leg with presence of fatigue

Since in practice spasticity is unpredictable, the motor reflex was simulated by multiplying a random number (between 0.1 to 1) with flexion angle as the second controller's input as in Figure 10. Controller has to compensate for the presence of spasticity in order to maintain swinging motion. Figure 11 shows the knee joint response obtained using this controller with the influence of muscle fatigue and voluntary activation. The presence of spasticity can be noted at 3rd cycle and for almost 5sec, then shank returning back to rest angle. When severe spasticity happens, the controller will stop the stimulation because it may seriously hinder the swinging activity as well as for reason of safety. Once knee angle reaches the rest angle, the controller starts the stimulation. However, as can be seen in Figure 11 muscle spasm is noted leading to muscle fatigue. The controller was able to compensate for the presence of fatigue after few cycles. The controller performed well in terms of robustness of the FLC overcoming the influence of these phenomena after few cycles.

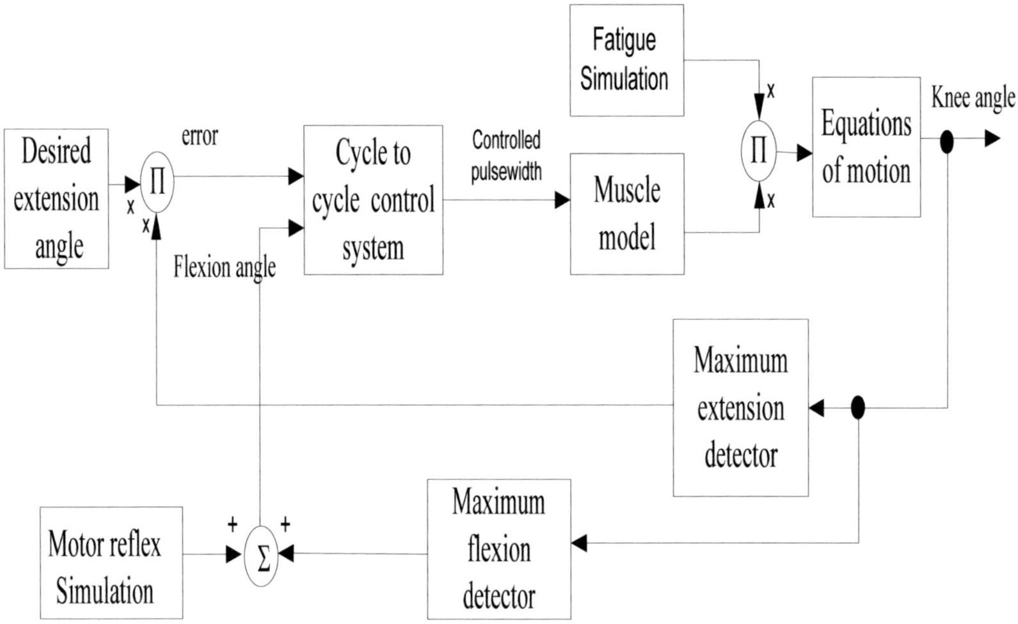

Figure 10. Controller with simulated fatigue and motor reflex

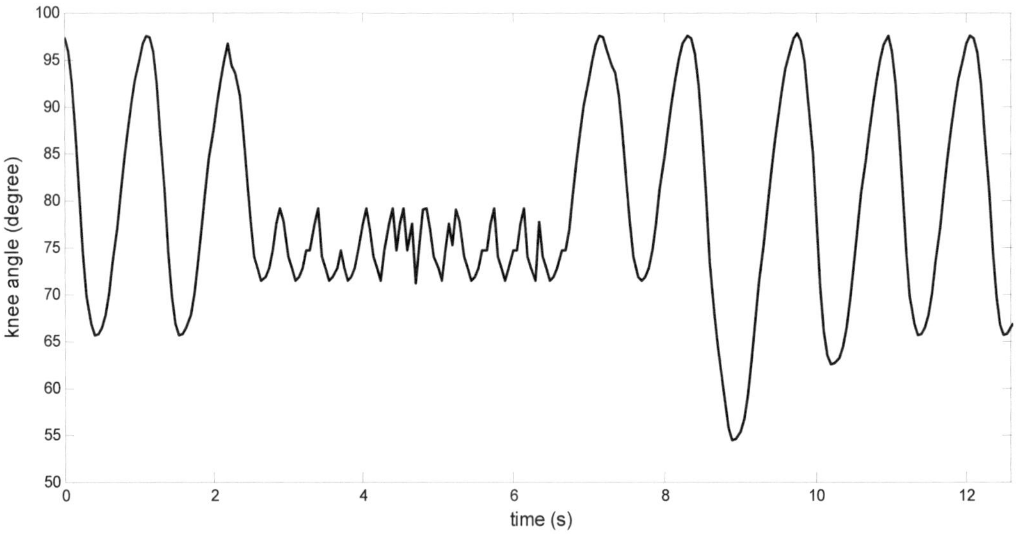

Figure 11. Controlled swinging leg with influence of fatigue and voluntary activation

3.2. Experimental validation of controller

The laboratory apparatus built to study the knee joint control by FES is shown in Figure 12. The subject sat on a chair, which allowed the lower leg to swing freely, while the ankle angle was fixed at 0°. The knee extensors (quadriceps muscle group) were stimulated by a pair of surface electrodes (2"x5"). The cathode was placed on the motor point of rectus femoris and the anode was placed distally at the quadriceps tendon. Knee angle was defined in Figure 2, with when the lower leg was at rest during knee flexion (i.e., 90).

The computer-controlled stimulator system consisted of a personal computer, computer-controlled interface (including analog-to-digital converter), current controlled stimulator and electro-goniometer (see Figure 12). The stimulation pulsewidth is generated by FLC based on the error by comparing the actual extension angle and the desired ones. All these operations were performed in the Matlab/Simulink environment in the computer. The Hasomed stimulator device was connected to PC via USB interface port. The knee joint angle was measured via the Biometric flexible electroganiometer mounted at approximate center of rotation of the knee joint. Stimulation pulsewidth ranged from 0 to 230μs and stimulation current was fixed to 40mA with a biphasic type pulse. The stimulation frequency was set to 25Hz and the knee joint angle sampling time was 0.05s. The experimental validation tests of the discrete-time fuzzy logic cycle to cycle control (based on simulation study) was assessed the capability of the controller to control the swinging motion as desired.

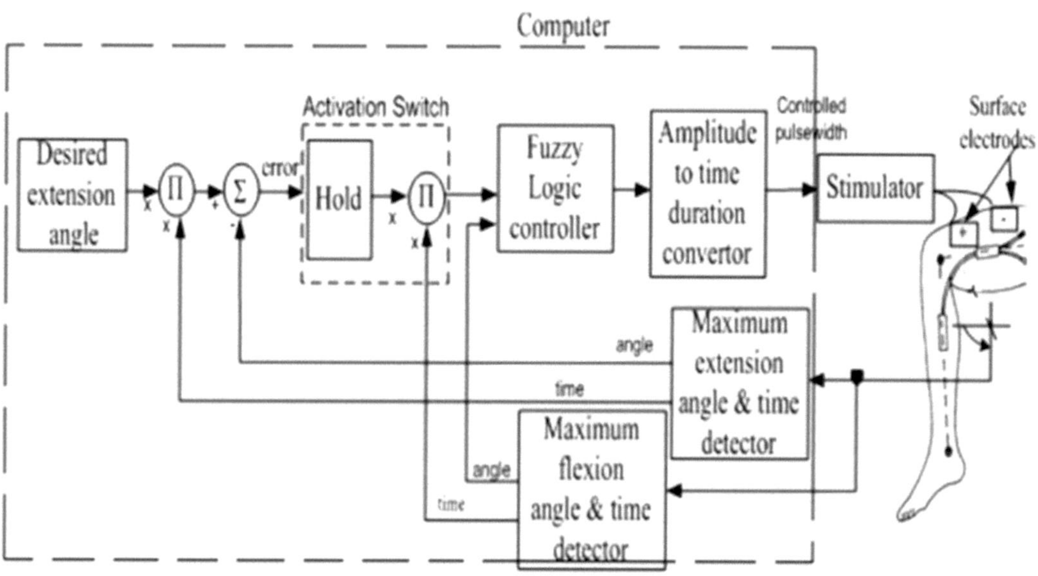

Figure 12. The equipment setup of this study

3.2.1. Full knee extension angle

The test was initiated with stimulation pulse of 240μs amplitude with 0.3s burst duration for the first cycle of swing in gait before activating the controller as in the simulation study.

FES-induced swinging motion was controlled using fuzzy controller to reach full extension angle at 10°. The shank was able to reach full knee extension at 4th cycle as can be seen in Figure 13. The ability of the cycle-to-cycle control approach to reach full knee extension has been demonstrated similar to that in [9].

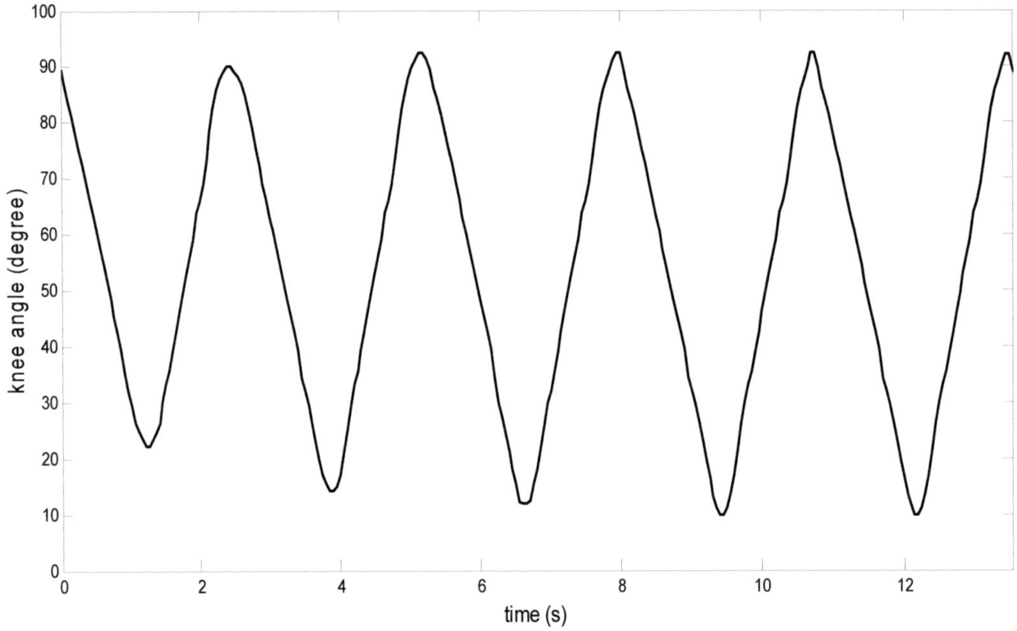

Figure 13. Controlled swinging leg for desired angle at 10° (full extension)

3.2.2. Target extension angle and maintaining steady swinging

The same procedure as in the simulation work was applied with the test initiated with 220μs amplitude with 0.15s burst durations of stimulation pulse. The controller performed in high intense stimulation course of 100 cycles as shown in Figure 14 in order to get influences of muscle fatigue and spasticity. EMG signal via surface electrodes on quadriceps muscle was recorded in this test to monitor EMG activity. The controller was tested in three scenarios, as in the simulations. Few trials were conducted in order to make sure the presence of these three scenarios was on the same stimulation course. An intra-trial interval for 120s was used to reduce the effect of fatigue in the beginning of the stimulation. Finally the best stimulation course with presence of both phenomena; muscle fatigue and spasticity were recorded. The recorded stimulation course was for almost 100 cycles and this was divided into three scenarios as follows:

3.2.2.1. Without presence of musle fatique and voluntary activation

In the first part of test, the controller was validated without fatigue and spasticity by considering only the first 10 cycles of the stimulation course. Before beginning the test, the subject was asked to relax as much as possible. There was no EMG present when the subject was fully relaxed. Figure 14 shows the response of knee angle in the first scenario. The controller was able to perform a steady swinging motion of shank after 5s with ability to extend the knee to the desired extension angle. Hence this controller achieved the main objective; to maintain a steady swinging of the lower limb as desired but the controller needed more time to achieve this.

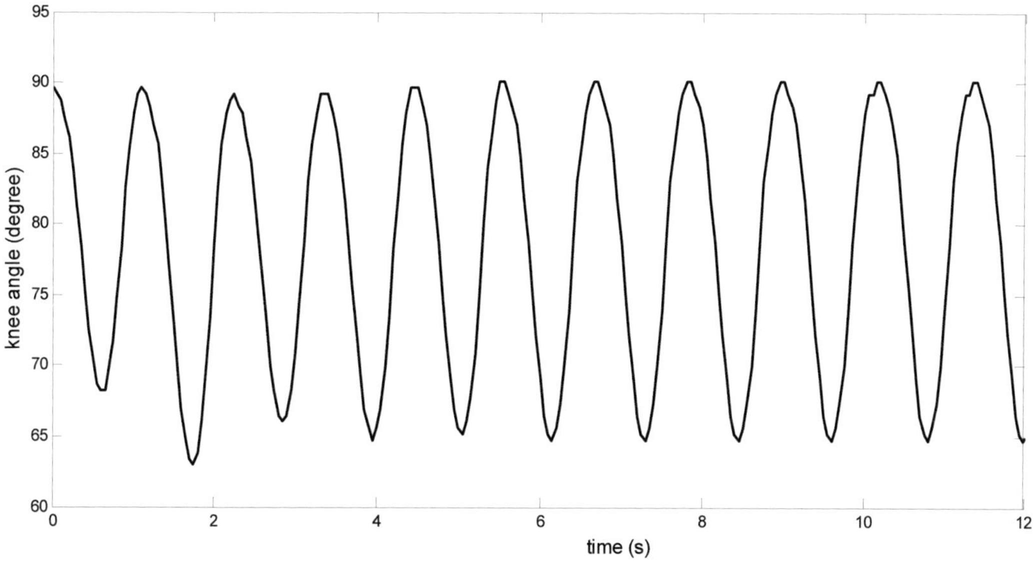

Figure 14. Controlled swinging leg (Experimental work)

3.2.2.2. With presence of musle fatique and without presence of voluntary activation

In the second part of test, the controller was validated when the muscle fatigue happened due to high stimulation intensity. This scenario can be seen by monitoring the reduction in the extension of knee joint. Few cycles of the stimulation course before and after fatigue were considered in this test as shown in Figure 15. It can been seen that at the beginning the knee angle was unable to reach the desired value due to fatigue, and then with the controller action by increasing the stimulation burst time the shank was able move a bit higher. After few cycles the knee angle reached the desired extension angle and swinging motion was maintained. Therefore, this controller achieved the third objective; to maintain a steady swinging of the lower limb as desired in presence of muscle fatigue. Only a small amount of EMG activity was recorded in this scenario.

3.2.2.3. With presence of musle fatique and voluntary activation

In the final validation test, the controller was validated with presence of spasticity and muscle fatigue. This scenario can be seen by monitoring the knee angle at which spasticity stops the natural swing. Furthermore, high EMG activity was apparent throughout the trace. These uncontrolled muscle movements were brought by spasms causing fatigue. Thus, the reduction in the extension of knee joint can be seen after spasm. 15 cycles of the stimulation course before and after spasm were considered in this test as shown in Figure

16. It can be seen that spasticity caused uncontrolled movement. The controller automatically stopped the stimulation due to spasticity. Once there was no motion of the knee, the controller started the stimulation with widest stimulation burst time to compensate for muscle fatigue. After 5s the knee angle reached the desired extension angle and swinging motion was maintained. Therefore, this controller achieved the last objective; to maintain a steady swinging of the lower limb as desired in presence of spasticity and muscle fatigue.

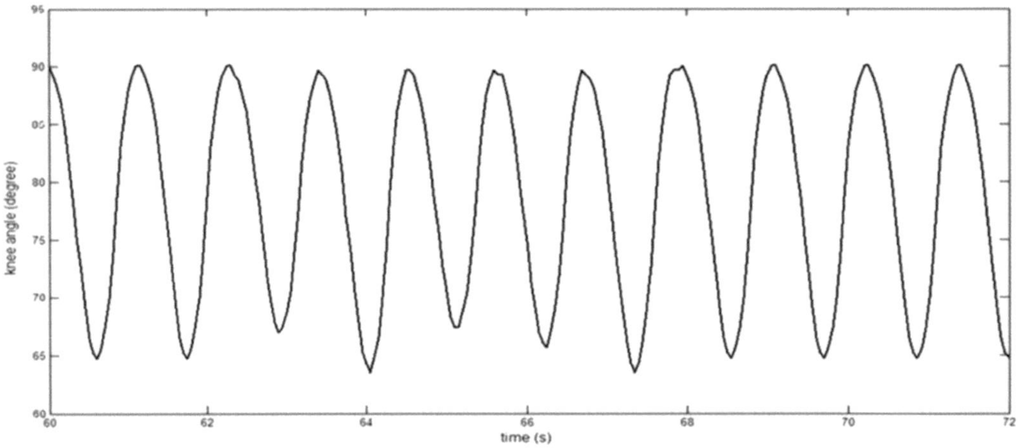

Figure 15. Controlled swinging leg with presence of fatigue (Experimental work)

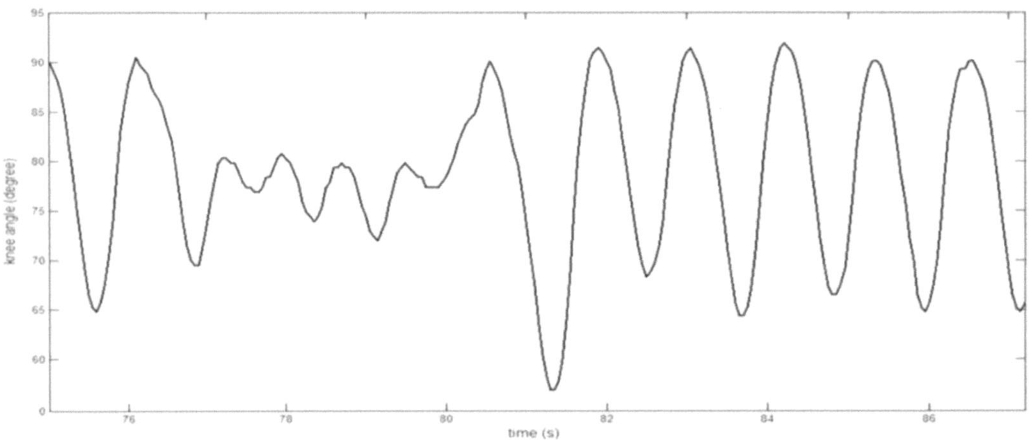

Figure 16. Controlled swinging leg with influence of fatigue and voluntary activation (Experimental work)

4. Conclusion

FES induced movement control is a difficult task due to the highly time-variant and nonlinear nature of the muscle and segmental dynamics. The great merit of a musculoskeletal model of knee joint is to serve for control development. In this study, a new closed-loop control approach using fuzzy logic based cycle-to-cycle control for FES-induced motion control has been proposed. This control technique also emphasizes to overcome some drawbacks of the trajectory based closed-loop FES control. The objectives of this controller have been set to achieve full knee extension angle, to reach target extension angle thus maintain a steady swinging motion and to compensate for muscle fatigue and spasticity. The performance of the controller to achieve these objectives has been assessed through simulation study and validated through experimental work. The controller has been proved to achieve all these objectives. Besides its suitability in generating the target joint orientation, one of the attractions of the cycle-to-cycle control in FES application is the absence of any reference trajectory. Cycle-to-cycle control is easy to implement in practice. Additionally, this method can compensate for non-linearity and time-variance of response of electrically stimulated musculoskeletal system. This controller may be suitable not only for swinging but also for other FES control applications involving movement of cyclical nature.

Author details

B. S. K. K. Ibrahim
Dept of Mechatronics and Robotics, Faculty of Electrical & Electronic Engineering, University Tun Hussein Onn Malaysia, Batu Pahat, Johor, Malaysia

M. O. Tokhi, M. S. Huq and S. C. Gharooni
Department of Automatic Control and System Engineering, University of Sheffield, United Kingdom

Acknowledgement

B.S.K.K.Ibrahim greatly acknowledges the financial supports of Higher Education Ministry of Malaysia and University Tun Hussein Onn, Malaysia.

5. References

[1] M. Levy, J. Mizrahi, and Z. Susak, "Recruitment force and fatigue characteristicsof quadriceps muscles of paraplegics isometrically activated by surface functional electrical stimulation," J. Biomed. Eng., vol. 12, pp. 150–156, 1990.

[2] CL Lynch and MR Popovic Closed-Loop Control for FES: Past Work and Future Directions, 10th Annual Conference of the International FES Society, July 2005 – Montreal, Canada.

[3] P.E. Crago,N. Lan, P. H. Veltink, J.J. Abbas and C.Kantor. New control strategies for neuroprosthetic systems, Journal Rehabilitation Res Device 33(2):158-72,1996.

[4] J. J. Abbas, "Feedback control of coronal plane hip angle in paraplegic subjects using functional neuromuscular stimulation," IEEE Trans. Biomed. Eng., vol. 38, pp. 687–698, 1991.

[5] M.S.Huq, Analysis and control of hybrid orthosis in therapeutic treadmill locomotion for paraplegia, PhD Thesis. The University of Sheffield, Sheffield, UK, 2009.
[6] A. Arifin, T. Watanabe, and N. Hashimiya, (2002). A Test of fuzzy controller for cycle-cycle control of FES-induced hemiplegics gait: Computer simulatilm in single-joint control: Proc. 36th Control of Japanese Soc.& Med. & Bid. Eng., Tohoku Chapter, p.30.
[7] H. M. Franken, P. H. Veltink, R.Tijsmans , H. Nijmeijer, , and H. B. K. Boom, (1993). Identification of passive knee joint and shank dynamics in paraplegics using quadriceps stimulation, IEEE Transactions on Rehabalitation Engineering, vol. 1,pp. 154-164.
[8] M.S. Hatwell, B.J. Oderkerk, C.A. Sacher, and G.F. Inbar,(1991). The development of a model reference adaptive controller to control the knee joint of paraplegics. IEEE Transactions on Automatic Control 36 6, pp. 683–691.
[9] P. H. Veltink. Control of FES-induced cyclical movements of the lower leg. Med Biol Eng Comput 1991 :29:NS8-12.
[10] Y.L. Chen, S.C. Chen, W.L. Chen, C.C. Hsiao, T.S. Kuo and J.S. Lai, Neural network and fuzzy control in FES-assisted locomotion for the hemiplegic, J Med Eng Technol 28 (2004), pp. 32–38.
[11] A. Yardimci, A Survey on Use of Soft Computing Methods in Medicine, Artificial Neural Networks – ICANN 2007,Springer Berlin / Heidelberg, pp. 69-79, 2007.
[12] T.C. Chin, and X. M. Qi, Genetic Algorithms for learning the rule base of fuzzy logic controller. Fuzzy Sets and Systems 97:1, 1998.
[13] B.S. K. K. Ibrahim, M.O. Tokhi M.S. Huq, and S.C. Gharooni, An Approach for Dynamic Characterisation of Passive Viscoelasticity and Estimation of Anthropometric Inertia Parameters of Paraplegic Knee Joint, unpublished.
[14] M. Ferrarin, and A. Pedotti. The relationship between electrical stimulus and joint torque: a dynamic model. IEEE Transactions on Rehabilitation Engineering, vol. 8 (3), pp. 342-352, 2000.
[15] A.K. Rzepniewski, Cycle-to-cycle control of multiple input-multiple output manufacturing processes, Ph.D. Thesis in Mechanical Engineering, Massachusetts Institute of Technology, Cambridge (2005).
[16] Fahey, T.D., Harvey, M., Schroeder, R. and Ferguson, F. (1985) Influence of sex differences and knee joint position on electrical stimulation-modulated strength increases. Medicine Science Sports Exercise 17, 144-147.
[17] Bobet, J. and Stein, R.B. (1998). A simple model of force generation by skeletal muscle during dynamic isometric contractions. IEEE Trans Biomed Eng, 45(8):1010-1016.
[18] Yang, J., F. Fung, J., Edamura, M. et al., (1991). H-reflex modulation during walking in spastic paretic subjects. Canadian Journal of Neurological Sciences 18(4):443–452.
[19] Lance JW. Symposium synopsis. In: Feldmann RG, Young RR, Koella WP, eds.Spasticity: disordered motor control. Chicago: Year Book Medical Publishers, 1980:485–95.
[20] Kralj, A. and Bajd, T, Functional Electrical Stimulation, Standing and Walking After Spinal Cord Injury CRC Press, Boca Raton, FL, 1989.

Chapter 24

Three Types of Fuzzy Controllers Applied in High-Performance Electric Drives for Three-Phase Induction Motors

José Luis Azcue, Alfeu J. Sguarezi Filho and Ernesto Ruppert

Additional information is available at the end of the chapter

http://dx.doi.org/10.5772/48388

1. Introduction

The electric drives are very common in industrial applications because they provide high dynamic performance. Nowadays exist a wide variety of schemes to control the speed, the electromagnetic torque and stator flux of three-phase induction motors. However, control remains a challenging problem for industrial applications of high dynamic performance, because the induction motors exhibit significant nonlinearities. Moreover, many of the parameters vary with the operating conditions. Although the Field Oriented Control (FOC) [16] schemes are attractive, but suffer from a major disadvantage, because they are sensitive to motor parameter variations such as the rotor time constant, and an incorrect flux estimation at low speeds. Another popular scheme for electric drives is the direct torque control (DTC) scheme [15][8], and an another DTC scheme based on space vector modulation (SVM) technique that reduces the torque ripples. This scheme does not need current regulators because its control variables are the electromagnetic torque and the stator flux. In this chapter we use the DTC-SVM scheme to analyze the performance of our proposed fuzzy controllers.

In the last decade, there was an increasing interest in combining artificial intelligent control tools with conventional control techniques. The principal motivations for such a hybrid implementation were that fuzzy logic issues such as uncertainty (or unknown variations in plant parameters and structure) can be dealt with more effectively. Hence improving the robustness of the control system. Conventional controls are very stable and allow various design objectives such as steady state and transient characteristics of a closed loop system. Several [5][6] works contributed to the design of such hybrid control schemes.

However, fuzzy controllers, unlike conventional PI controllers do not necessarily require the accurate mathematic model of the process to be controlled; instead, it uses the experience and knowledge about the controlled process to construct the fuzzy rules base. The fuzzy logic controllers are a good alternative for motor control systems since they are well known for treating with uncertainties and imprecisionï£¡'s. For example, in [1] the PI and fuzzy logic controllers are used to control the load angle, which simplifies the induction motor drive system. In [7], the fuzzy controllers are used to dynamically obtain the reference voltage vector in terms of torque error, stator flux error and stator flux angle. In this case, both torque and stator flux ripples are remarkably reduced. In [10], the fuzzy PI speed controller has a better response for a wide range of motor speed and in [3] a fuzzy self-tuning controller is implemented in order to substitute the unique PI controller, present in the DTC-SVM scheme. In this case, performance measures such as settling time, rise time and ITAE index are lower than the DTC-SVM scheme with PI controller.

The fuzzy inference system can be used to modulate the stator voltage vector applied to the induction motor [18]. In this case, unlike the cases mentioned above, the quantity of available vectors are arbitrarily increased, allowing better performance of the control scheme and lower levels of ripple than the classic DTC. However, it requires the stator current as an additional input, increasing the number of input variables. In this chapter we design and analyze in details three kinds of fuzzy controllers: the PI fuzzy controller (PI-F), the PI-type fuzzy controller (PIF) and the self-tuning PI-type fuzzy controller (STPIF). All of these fuzzy controllers are applied to a direct torque control scheme with space vector modulation technique for three-phase induction motor. In this DTC-SVM scheme, the fuzzy controllers generate corrective control actions based on the real torque trend only while minimizing the torque error.

2. Background

2.1. The three-phase induction motor dynamical equations

By the definitions of the fluxes, currents and voltages space vectors, the dynamical equations of the three-phase induction motor in stationary reference frame can be put into the following mathematical form [17]:

$$\vec{u}_s = R_s\vec{i}_s + \frac{d\vec{\psi}_s}{dt} \tag{1}$$

$$0 = R_r\vec{i}_r + \frac{d\vec{\psi}_r}{dt} - j\omega_r\vec{\psi}_r \tag{2}$$

$$\vec{\psi}_s = L_s\vec{i}_s + L_m\vec{i}_r \tag{3}$$

$$\vec{\psi}_r = L_r\vec{i}_r + L_m\vec{i}_s \tag{4}$$

Where $\vec{u}_s$ is the stator voltage space vector, $\vec{i}_s$ and $\vec{i}_r$ are the stator and rotor current space vectors, respectively, $\vec{\psi}_s$ and $\vec{\psi}_r$ are the stator and rotor flux space vectors, ω_r is the rotor angular speed, R_s and R_r are the stator and rotor resistances, L_s, L_r and L_m are the stator, rotor and mutual inductance respectively.

The electromagnetic torque t_e is expressed in terms of the cross-vectorial product of the stator and the rotor flux space vectors.

$$t_e = \frac{3}{2}P\frac{L_m}{L_r L_s \sigma}\vec{\psi}_r \times \vec{\psi}_s \tag{5}$$

$$t_e = \frac{3}{2}P\frac{L_m}{L_r L_s \sigma}\left|\vec{\psi}_r\right|\left|\vec{\psi}_s\right|\sin(\gamma) \tag{6}$$

Where γ is the load angle between stator and rotor flux space vector, P is a number of pole pairs and $\sigma = 1 - L_m^2/(L_s L_r)$ is the dispersion factor.

The three-phase induction motor model was implemented in MATLAB/Simulink as is shown in [2].

2.2. The principle of direct torque control

In the direct torque control if the sample time is short enough, such that the stator voltage space vector is imposed to the motor keeping the stator flux constant at the reference value. The rotor flux will become constant because it changes slower than the stator flux. The electromagnetic torque (6) can be quickly changed by changing the angle γ in the desired direction. This angle γ can be easily changed when choosing the appropriate stator voltage space vector.

For simplicity, let us assume that the stator phase ohmic drop could be neglected in (1). Therefore $d\vec{\psi}_s/dt = \vec{u}_s$. During a short time Δt, when the voltage space vector is applied it has:

$$\Delta\vec{\psi}_s \approx \vec{u}_s \cdot \Delta t \tag{7}$$

Thus the stator flux space vector moves by $\Delta\vec{\psi}_s$ in the direction of the stator voltage space vector at a speed which is proportional to the magnitude of the stator voltage space vector. By selecting step-by-step the appropriate stator voltage vector, it is possible to change the stator flux in the required direction.

3. Direct torque control scheme with space vector modulation technique

In Fig. 1, we show the block diagram for the DTC-SVM scheme [14] with a Fuzzy Controller, the fuzzy controller will be substitute for the three kind of proposed Fuzzy Controller one for time. The DTC-SVM scheme is an alternative to the classical DTC schemes [15], [8] and [9]. In this one, the load angle γ^* is not prefixed but it is determinate by the Fuzzy Controller. Equation (6) shows that the angle γ^* determines the electromagnetic torque which is necessary to supply the load. The three proposed Fuzzy Controllers determine the load angle using the torque error e and the torque error change Δe. Details about these controllers will be presented in the next section. Figure 1 shows the general block diagram of the DTC-SVM scheme, the inverter, the control signals for three-phase two-level inverter is generated by the DTC-SVM scheme.

3.1. Flux reference calculation

In stationary reference frame, the stator flux reference $\vec{\psi}_s^*$ can be decomposed in two perpendicular components ψ_{ds}^* and ψ_{qs}^*. Therefore, the output of the fuzzy controller γ^* is added to rotor flux angle $\angle\vec{\psi}_r$ in order to estimate the next angle of the stator flux reference.

In this chapter we consider the magnitude of stator flux reference as a constant. Therefore, we can use the relation presented in equation (8) to calculate the stator flux reference vector.

$$\vec{\psi}_s^* = |\vec{\psi}_s^*|\cos(\gamma^* + \angle\vec{\psi}_r) + j|\vec{\psi}_s^*|\sin(\gamma^* + \angle\vec{\psi}_r) \tag{8}$$

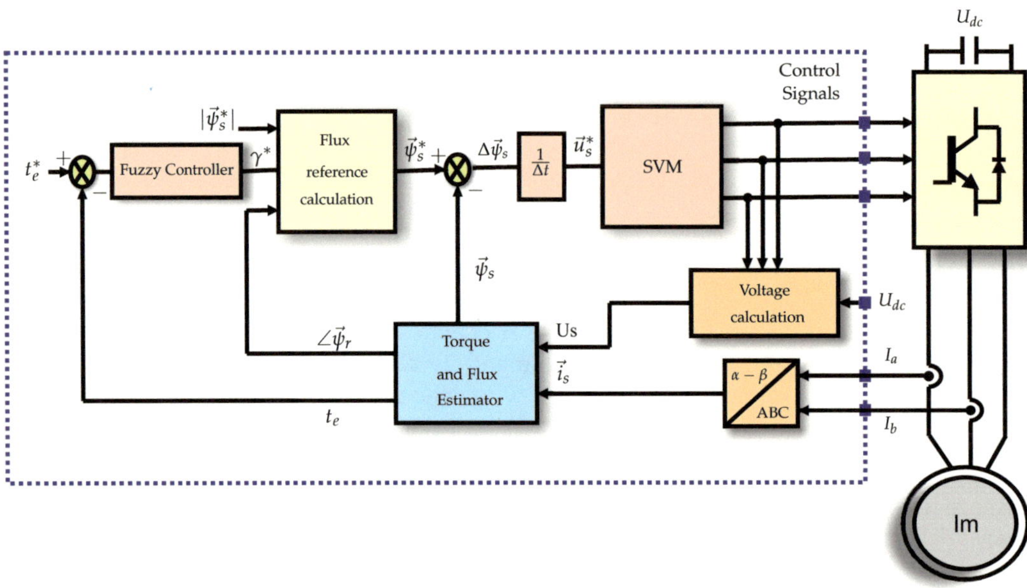

Figure 1. Direct torque control with space vector modulation scheme and fuzzy controller.

Moreover, if we consider the stator voltage $\vec{u}_s$ during a short time Δt, it is possible to reproduce a flux variation $\Delta\vec{\psi}_s$. Notice that the stator flux variation is nearly proportional to the stator voltage space vector as seen in the equation (7).

3.2. Stator voltage calculation

The stator voltage calculation uses the DC link voltage (U_{dc}) and the inverter switch state (S_{Wa}, S_{Wb}, S_{Wc}) of the three-phase two level inverter. The stator voltage vector $\vec{u}_s$ is determined as in [4]:

$$\vec{u}_s = \frac{2}{3}\left[(S_{Wa} - \frac{S_{Wb} + S_{Wc}}{2}) + j\frac{\sqrt{3}}{2}(S_{Wb} - S_{Wc})\right] U_{dc} \tag{9}$$

3.3. Electromagnetic torque and stator flux estimation

As drawn by Fig. 1 the electromagnetic torque and the stator flux estimation depend on the stator voltage and the stator current space vectors,

$$\vec{\psi}_s = \int (\vec{u}_s - R_s \cdot \vec{i}_s)dt \tag{10}$$

The problem with this kind of estimation is that for low speeds the back electromotive force (emf) depends strongly of the stator resistance, to resolve this problem is used the current model to improve the flux estimation as in [13]. The rotor flux $\vec{\psi}_{rdq}$ represented in the rotor flux reference frame is given by:

$$\vec{\psi}_{rdq} = \frac{L_m}{1+sT_r}\vec{i}_{sdq} - j\frac{(\omega_{\psi_r} - \omega_r)T_r}{1+sT_r}\vec{\psi}_{rdq} \tag{11}$$

Notice that $T_r = L_r/R_r$ is the rotor time constant, and $\psi_{rq} = 0$. Substituting this expression in the equation (11) yields:

$$\psi_{rd} = \frac{L_m}{1 + sT_r} i_{sd} \tag{12}$$

In the current model the stator flux is represented by:

$$\vec{\psi}_s^i = \frac{L_m}{L_r}\vec{\psi}_r^i + \frac{L_s L_r - L_m^2}{L_r}\vec{i}_s \tag{13}$$

Where $\vec{\psi}_r^i$ is the rotor flux according to the equation (12). Since the voltage model is based on equation (1), the stator flux in the stationary reference frame is given by

$$\vec{\psi}_s = \frac{1}{s}(\vec{v}_s - R_s\vec{i}_s - \vec{U}_{comp}) \tag{14}$$

With the aim to correct the errors associated with the pure integration and the stator resistance measurement, the voltage model is adapted through the PI controller.

$$\vec{U}_{comp} = (K_p + K_i\frac{1}{s})(\vec{\psi}_s - \vec{\psi}_s^i) \tag{15}$$

The K_p and K_i coefficients are calculated with the recommendation proposed in [13]. The rotor flux $\vec{\psi}_r$ in the stationary reference frame is calculated as:

$$\vec{\psi}_r = \frac{L_r}{L_m}\vec{\psi}_s - \frac{L_s L_r - L_m^2}{L_m}\vec{i}_s \tag{16}$$

The estimator scheme shown in the Fig. 2 works with a good performance in the wide range of speeds.

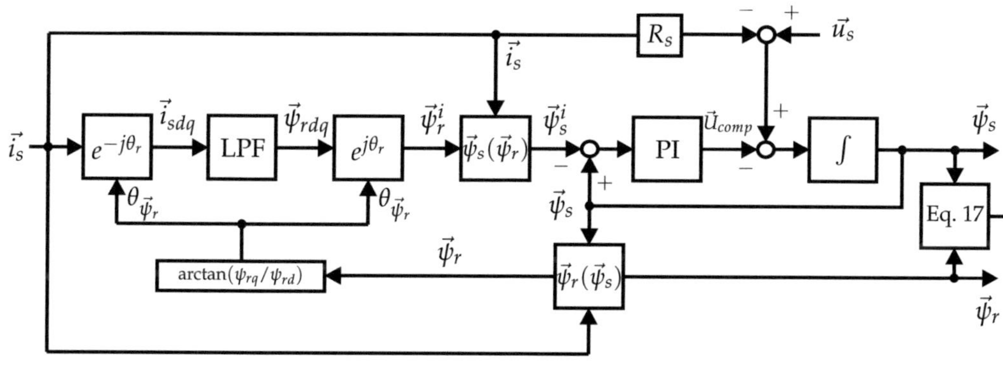

Figure 2. Stator and rotor flux estimator, and electromagnetic torque estimator.

Where LPF means low pass filter. In the other hand, when equations (14) and (16) are replaced in (5) we can estimated the electromagnetic torque t_e as:

$$t_e = \frac{3}{2}P\frac{L_m}{L_r L_s \sigma}\vec{\psi}_r \times \vec{\psi}_s \tag{17}$$

4. Design of fuzzy controllers

4.1. The PI fuzzy controller (PI-F)

The PI fuzzy controller combines two simple fuzzy controllers and a conventional PI controller. Note that fuzzy controllers are responsible for generating the PI parameters dynamically while considering only the torque error variations. The PI-F block diagram is shown in Fig. 3, this controller is composed of two scale factors G_e, $G_{\Delta e}$ at the input. The input for fuzzy controllers are the error (e_N) and error change ($e_{\Delta N}$), and theirs outputs represent the proportional gain K_p and the integral time T_i respectively. These parameters K_p and T_i are adjusted in real time by the fuzzy controllers. The gain K_P is limited to the interval $[K_{p,min}, K_{p,max}]$, which we determined by simulations. For convenience, K_P is normalized in the range between zero and one through the following linear transformation.

$$K_p' = \frac{K_p - K_{p,min}}{K_{p,max} - K_{p,min}} \tag{18}$$

Then, considering that the fuzzy controller output is a normalized value K_p', we obtain K_p by:

$$K_p = (K_{p,min} - K_{p,max})K_p' + K_{p,min} \tag{19}$$

However, for different reference values the range for the proportional gain values is chosen as $[0, K_{p,max}]$,

$$K_p = K_{p,max}K_p' \tag{20}$$

Due to nonlinearities of the system and in order to avoid overshoots for large reference torque r, it is necessary to reduce the proportional gain. We use a gain coefficient $\rho = 1/(1 + 0002 * r)$ that depends on the reference values. In order to achieves real time adjustment for the K_p values. Therefore, $K_{p,max} = \rho K_{p,max0}$ where the value $K_{p,max0} = 1.24$ was obtained through various simulations. Note that both ρ and $K_{p,max}$ decreases as the reference value increases. Consequently, the gain K_p decreases. The PI-F controller receives as input the torque error e and as output the motor load angle γ^*.

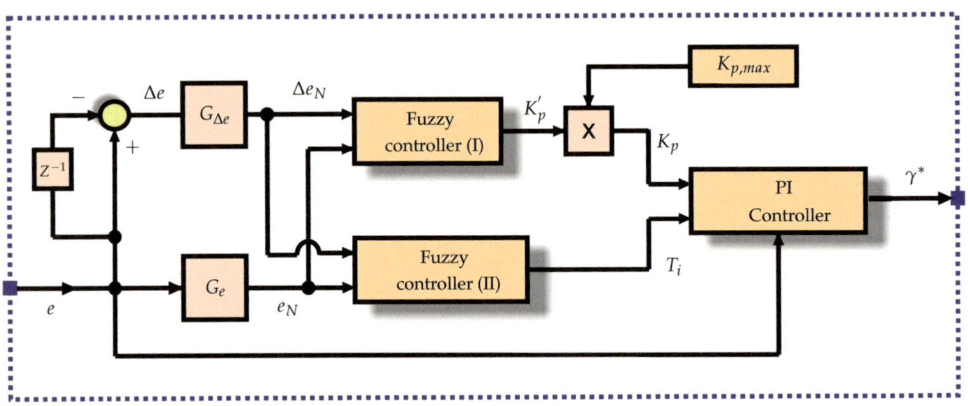

Figure 3. PI Fuzzy Controller block diagram.

4.1.1. Membership Functions (MF)

In the Fig. 3, the first fuzzy controller receives as inputs the errors $e_N, \Delta e_N$, each of them has three fuzzy sets that are defined similarly, being only necessary to describe the fuzzy sets of the first input. The first input e_N has three fuzzy sets whose linguistic terms are N-Negative, ZE-Zero and P-Positive. Each fuzzy set has a membership function associated with it. In our particular case of, these fuzzy sets have trapezoidal and triangular shapes as shown in Fig.4. The universe of discourse of these sets is defined over the closed interval $[-1.5, 1.5]$.

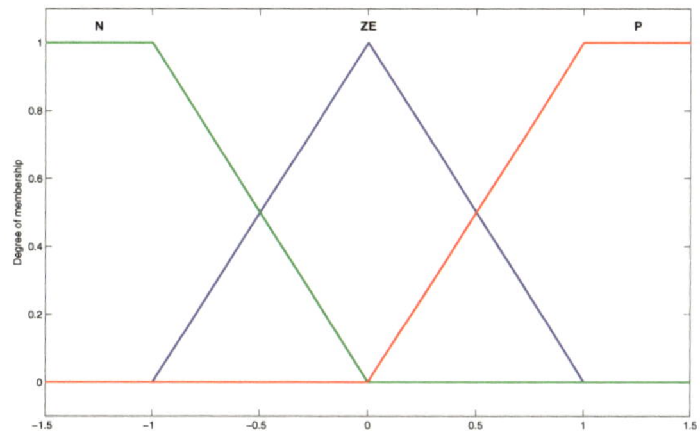

Figure 4. Membership functions for the inputs e_N, Δe_N.

The output has two fuzzy sets whose linguistic values are associated with them are S-small and B-Big, respectively. Both have trapezoidal membership functions as shown in Fig.5. The universe of discourse of the fuzzy sets is defined over the closed interval $[-0.5, 1.5]$. The fuzzy controller uses: triangular norm, Mamdani implication, max-min aggregation method and the center of mass method for defuzzification [11].

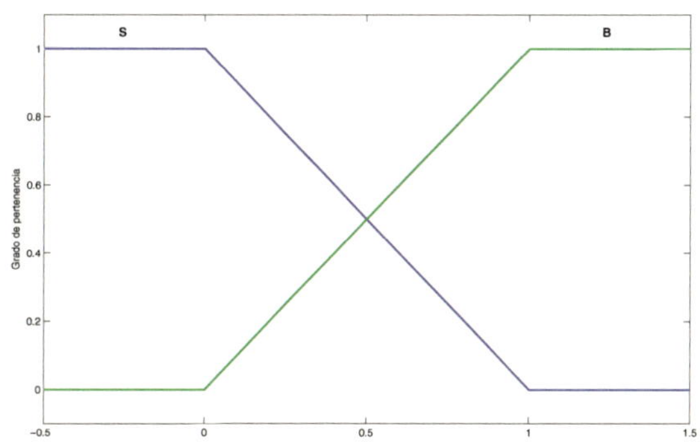

Figure 5. Membership functions for the first fuzzy controller output K_p.

Similarly, the second fuzzy controller has the same fuzzy sets for its two inputs, however, its output is defined by three constant values defined as 1.5, 2 and 3 which linguistic values associated with them are S-Small, M-Medium and B-Big. This controller uses the zero-order Takagi-Sugeno model which simplifies the hardware design and is easy to introduce programmability [19]. The defuzzification method used for this controller is the weighted sum.

4.1.2. Scaling Factors (SF)

The PI-F controller has two scaling factors, G_e and $G_{\Delta e}$ as inputs, while the fuzzy controllers outputs are the gain $K_p^{'}$ and the integral time T_I respectively. From these values we can calculate the parameter $K_I = K_p/T_I$.

The scale factor ensures that both inputs are within the universe of discourse previously defined. The parameters K_p and K_I are the tuned parameters of the PI controller. The inputs are normalized, by:

$$e_N = G_e \cdot e \tag{21}$$

$$\Delta e_N = G_{\Delta e} \cdot \Delta e \tag{22}$$

4.1.3. The rule bases

The rules are based on simulation that we conducted of various control schemes. Fig.6 shows an example for one possible response system. Initially, the error is positive around the point a, and the error change is negative, then is imposed a large control signal in order to obtain a small rise time.

To produce a large signal control, the PI controller should have a large gain K_p and a large integral gain K_I (small integral time T_I), therefore,

$$R_x : \text{ if } e_N \text{ is } S \text{ and } \Delta e_N \text{ is } N \text{ then } K_p \text{ is } G$$

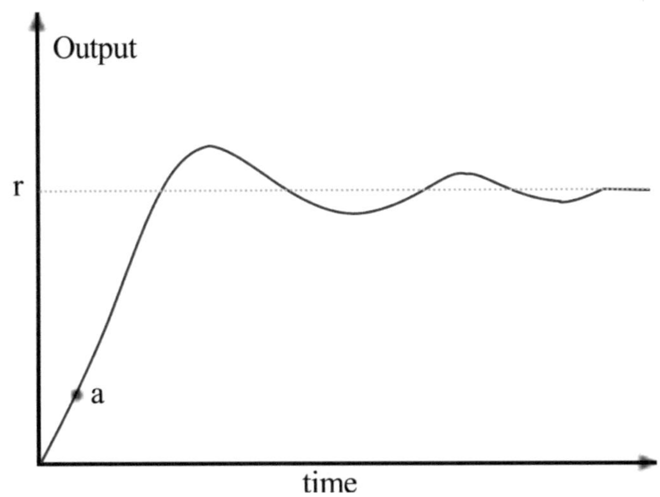

Figure 6. Response system.

The rule base for the first fuzzy controller is in Table 1, also, the rule base for the second fuzzy controller is in Table 2.

Fig. 7 shows the control surface for the first and second fuzzy controllers. This figure clearly shows the non-linear relationship between $(e, \Delta e, K_p)$ and $(e, \Delta e, T_I)$

e_N / Δe_N	N	ZE	P
N	B	B	B
ZE	S	B	S
P	B	B	B

Table 1. Rule base for fuzzy controller (I), output K'_p

e_N / Δe_N	N	ZE	P
N	S	S	S
ZE	B	M	B
P	S	S	S

Table 2. Rule base for fuzzy controller (II), output T_I

4.2. The PI-type fuzzy controller (PIF) and The self-tuning PI-type fuzzy controller (STPIF)

The PI-type fuzzy controller (PIF) is a fuzzy controller inspired by a digital PI controller, which is depicted in Fig. 8. It is composed by two input scale factors "G_e, $G_{\Delta e}$" and one output scale factor "G_{γ^*}". Finally it uses saturation block to limit the output.

This controller has a single input variable, which is the torque error "e" and one output variable which is the motor load angle "γ^*" given by:

$$\gamma^*(k) = \gamma^*(k+1) + \Delta\gamma^*(k) \tag{23}$$

In (23), k is the sampling time and $\Delta\gamma^*(k)$ represents the incremental change of the controller output. We wish to emphasize here that this accumulation (23) of the controller output takes place out of the fuzzy part of the controller and it does not influence the fuzzy rules.

Fig.9 shows the self-tuning PI-type fuzzy controller (STPIF) block diagram, its main difference with the PIF controller is the gain tuning fuzzy controller (GTF) block.

4.2.1. Membership Functions (MF)

The MF for PIF controller are shown in Fig. 10(a). This MF for input variables "e_N, Δe_N" and output variable "$\Delta\gamma^*_N$" are normalized in the closed interval [-1,1].

The MF's for GTF controller are shown in Fig. 10(a) and in Fig. 10(b) for input and output variables respectively. Input variables "e_N, Δe_N" are defined in the closed interval [-1,1] and the output variable "α" is defined in the closed interval [0,1].

Most of the MF variables have triangular shape [Fig. 10] with 50% overlapping neighbor functions, except the extremes which are trapezoidal. The linguistic variables are referred to as: NL-Negative Large, NM-Negative Medium, NS-Negative Small, ZE-Zero, VS-Very Small, S-Small, SL-Small Large and so on as shown in Table 3 and in Table 4.

4.2.2. Scaling factors

The two inputs SF "$G_{\Delta e}$, G_e" and the output SF "G_{γ^*}" can be adjusted dynamically through updating the scaling factor "α". "α" is computed on-line, using a independent fuzzy rule model

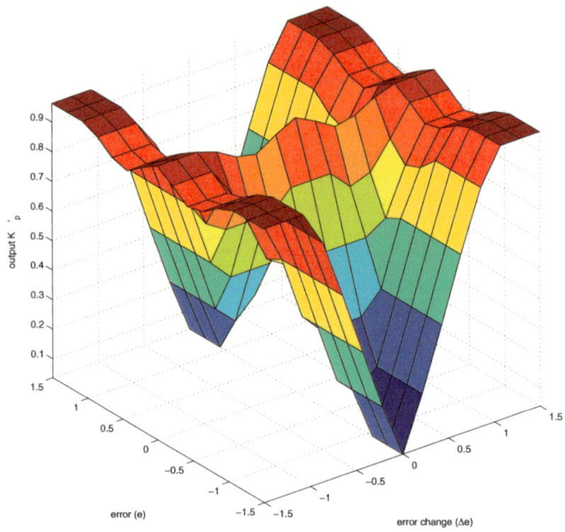

(a) Control surface for fuzzy controller (I), output K_p'.

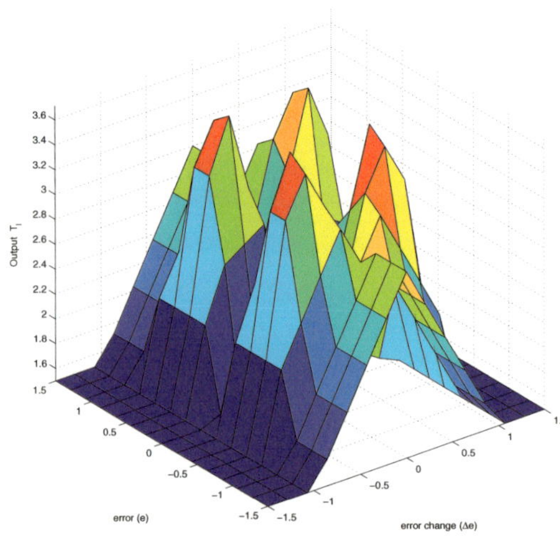

(b) Control surface for fuzzy controller (II), output T_I.

Figure 7. Control surface for: (a) fuzzy controller (I) and (b) fuzzy controller (II)

defined in terms of "e, Δe". The relationship between the SF and the input/output variables of the STPIF controller are shown bellow:

$$e_N = G_e \cdot e \tag{24}$$

$$\Delta e_N = G_{\Delta e} \cdot \Delta e \tag{25}$$

$$\Delta\gamma^* = (\alpha \cdot G_{\gamma^*}) \cdot \Delta\gamma_N^* \tag{26}$$

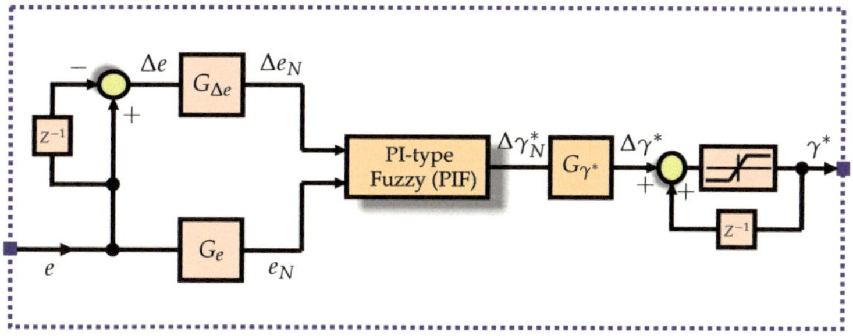

Figure 8. PI-type fuzzy controller.

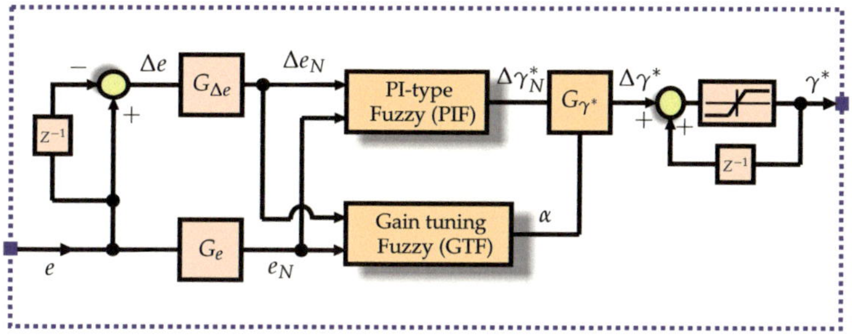

Figure 9. Self-tuning PI-type fuzzy (STPIF) controller.

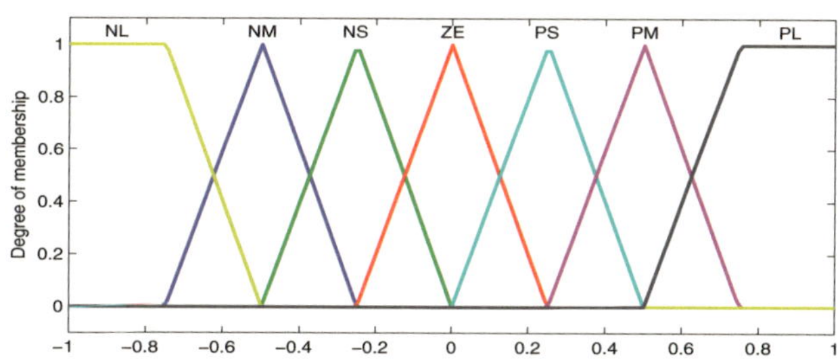

(a) Membership function for e_N, Δe_N and $\Delta\gamma_N^*$.

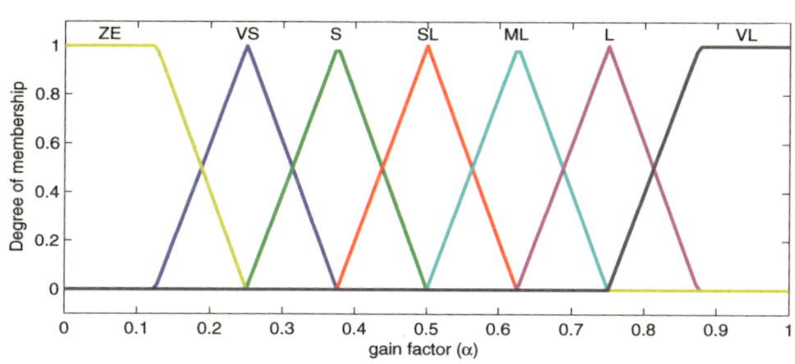

(b) Membership function for α for GTF controller output

Figure 10. Membership functions for: (a) error e_N and change of error Δe_N is the same for PIF and GTF controllers as well as for the output $\Delta\gamma_N^*$ of the PIF controller. (b) the gain updating factor α

4.2.3. The rule bases

The incremental change in the controller output $\Delta\gamma_N^*$ to PIF controller is defined as,

$$R_x : \text{ if } e_N \text{ is } E \text{ and } \Delta e_N \text{ is } \Delta E \text{ then } \Delta\gamma_N^* \text{ is } \Delta\Gamma_N^*$$

Where $E = \Delta E = \Delta\Gamma_N^* = \{NL, NM, NS, ZE, PS, PM, PL\}$. The output α of the GTF controller is determined by the following rules:

$$R_x : \text{ if } e_N \text{ is } E \text{ and } \Delta e_N \text{ is } \Delta E \text{ then } \alpha \text{ is } \chi$$

Where $E = \Delta E = \{NL, NM, NS, ZE, PS, PM, PL\}$ and $\chi = \{ZE, VS, S, SL, ML, L, VL\}$. The rule base for $\Delta\gamma_N^*$ and α are shown in Tab. 3 and Tab. 4 respectively.

Δe_N / e_N	**NL**	**NM**	**NS**	**ZE**	**PS**	**PM**	**PL**
NL	NL	NL	NL	NM	NS	NS	ZE
NM	NL	NM	NM	NM	NS	ZE	PS
NS	NL	NM	NS	NS	ZE	PS	PM
ZE	NL	NM	NS	ZE	PS	PM	PL
PS	NM	NS	ZE	PS	PS	PM	PL
PM	NS	ZE	PS	PM	PM	PM	PL
PL	ZE	PS	PS	PM	PL	PL	PL

Table 3. Fuzzy rules for the computation of $\Delta\gamma_N^*$

Δe_N / e_N	**NL**	**NM**	**NS**	**ZE**	**PS**	**PM**	**PL**
NL	VL	VL	VL	L	SL	S	ZE
NM	VL	VL	L	L	ML	S	VS
NS	VL	ML	L	VL	VS	S	VS
ZE	S	SL	ML	ZE	ML	SL	S
PS	VS	S	VS	VL	L	ML	VL
PM	VS	S	ML	L	L	VL	VL
PL	ZE	S	SL	L	VL	VL	VL

Table 4. Fuzzy rules for the computation of α

4.2.4. Gain tuning fuzzy

The purpose of the GTF controller is update continuous the value of α in every sample time. The output α is necessary to control the percentage of the output SF "G_{γ^*}", and therefore for calculating new "$\Delta\gamma^*$",

$$\Delta\gamma^* = (\alpha \cdot G_{\gamma^*}) \cdot \Delta\gamma_N^* \tag{27}$$

The GTF controller rule base is based on knowledge about the three-phase IM control, using a DTC type control according to the scheme proposed in [14], in order to avoid large overshoot and undershoot, e.g., when "e" and "Δe" have different signs, it means that the estimate torque

"t_e" is approaching to the torque reference "t_e^*", then the output SF "G_{γ^*}" must be reduced to a small value by "α", for instance, if "e" is "PM" and "Δe" is "NM" then "α" is "S".

On the other hand, when "e" and "Δe" have the same sign, it means that the torque estimate "t_e" is moving away from the torque reference "t_e^*", the output SF "G_{γ^*}" must be increased to a large value by "α" in order to avoid that the torque depart from the torque reference, e.g., if "e" is "PM" and "Δe" is "PM" then "α" is "VL".

The nonlinear relationship between "e, Δe, $\Delta\gamma_N^*$" and "e, Δe, α" are shown in Fig. 11.

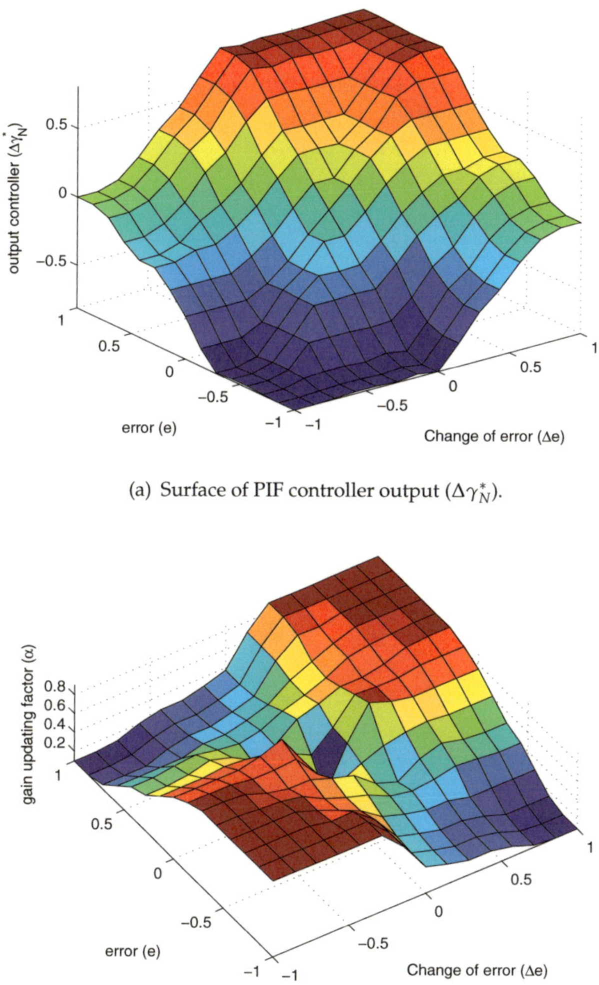

(a) Surface of PIF controller output ($\Delta\gamma_N^*$).

(b) Surface of GTF controller output (α).

Figure 11. Surface of: (a) PIF controller and (b) GTF controller

The inference method used in PIF and GTF controllers is the Mamdani's implication based on max-min aggregation. We use the center of area method for defuzzification.

5. Simulation results

We have conducted our simulation with MATLAB simulation package, which include Simulink block sets and fuzzy logic toolbox. The switching frequency of the pulse width modulation (PWM) inverter was set to be 10kHz, the stator reference flux considered was 0.47 Wb. In order to investigate the effectiveness of the three proposed fuzzy controllers applied in the DTC-SVM scheme we performed several tests.

We used different dynamic operating conditions such as: step change in the motor load (from 0 to 1.0 pu) at 90 percent of rated speed, no-load speed reversion (from 0.5 pu to -0.5 pu) and the application of a specific load torque profile at 90 percent of rated speed. The motor parameters used in the tests are given in Table 5.

Fig. 12, shows the response of the speed and electromagnetic torque when speed reversion for DTC-SVM with PI-F controller is applied. Here, the rotor speed changes its direction at about 1.8 seconds. Fig. 13 shows the stator and rotor current sinusoidal behavior when applying reversion.

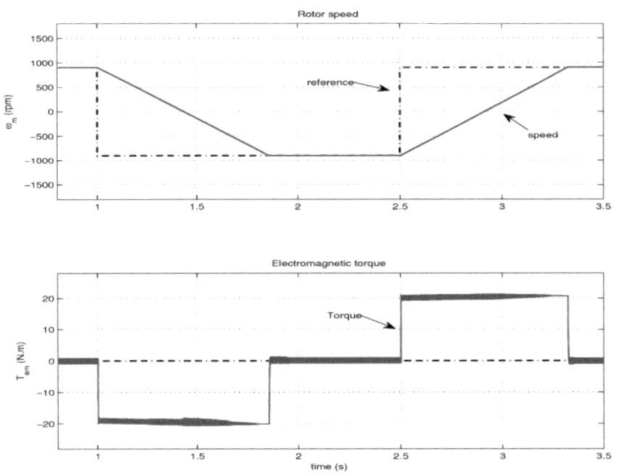

Figure 12. Speed reversion for DTC-SVM with PI-F controller.

Fig. 14 and Fig. 15 show the torque and currents responses respecively, when step change is applied in the motor load for DTC-SVM with the PI-F controller. This speed test was established at 90 percent of rated speed.

In Fig. 16, we demonstrate the speed response when applying a speed reversion for DTC-SVM with PIF controller. In this case the speed of the rotor changes its direction at about 1.4 seconds. Fig. 17 shows the electromagnetic torque behavior when the reversion is applied.

Fig. 18 and Fig. 19 show the response of the electromagnetic torque and phase *a* stator current respectively, when applying a step change in the motor load for DTC-SVM whit PIF controller. In this test the speed of the motor was set to 90 percent of rated speed.

Fig. 20 shows the behaviors of the electromagnetic torque, phase *a* stator current and the motor speed, when applying speed reversion from 0.5 pu to -0.5 pu in the DTC-SVM scheme with STPIF controller. The sinusoidal waveform of the current shows that this control technique also leads to a good current control.

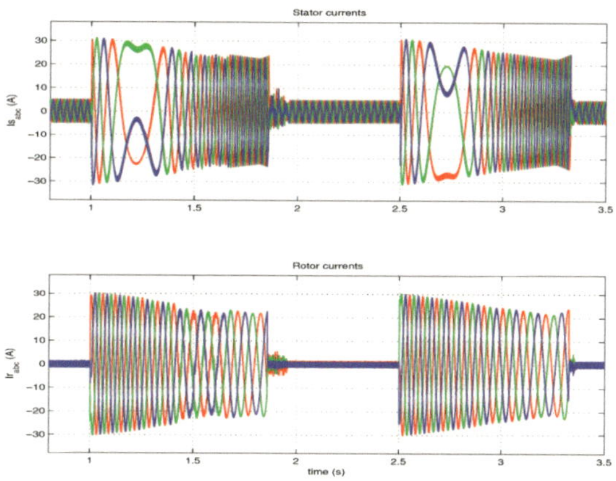

Figure 13. Stator and rotor current for speed reversion for DTC-SVM with PI-F controller.

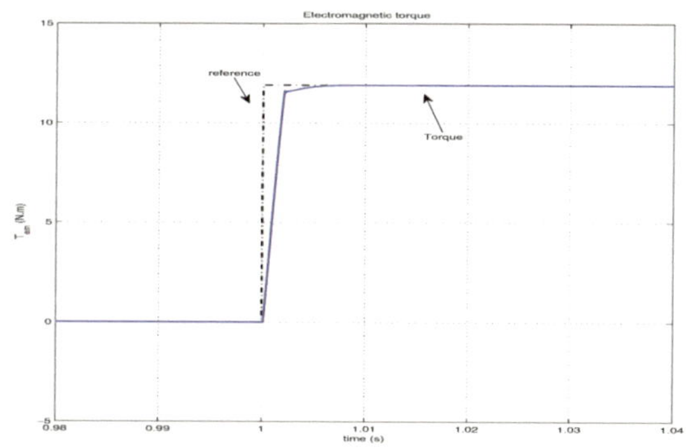

Figure 14. Sudden torque change for DTC-SVM whit PI-F controller

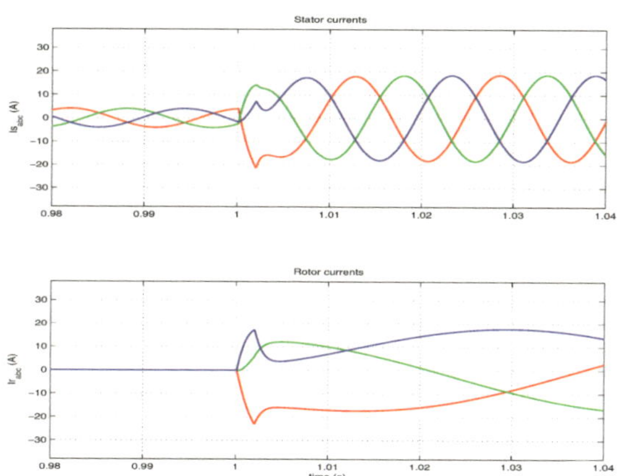

Figure 15. Stator and rotor currents for sudden torque change for DTC-SVM with PI-F controller.

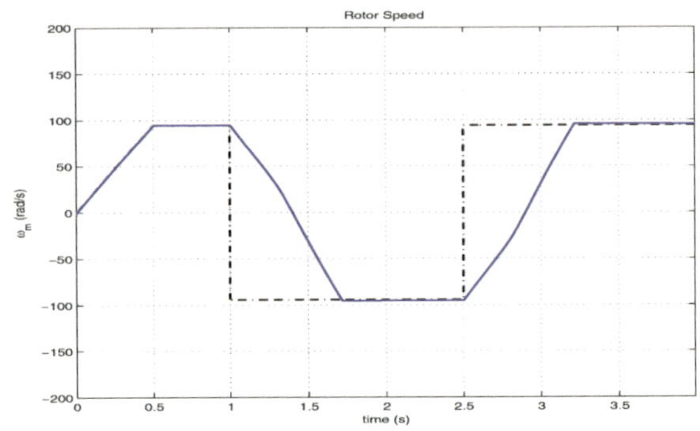

Figure 16. Speed reversion for DTC-SVM with PIF controller.

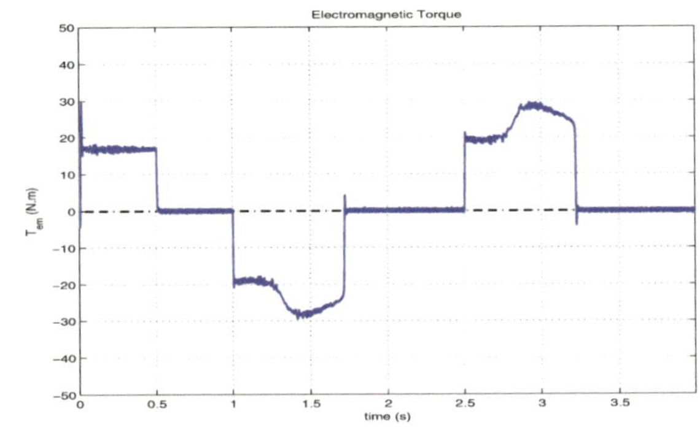

Figure 17. Torque bahavior for speed reversion for DTC-SVM with PIF controller.

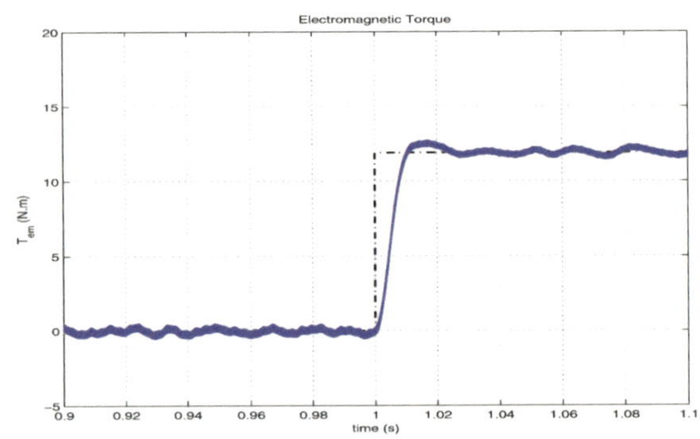

Figure 18. Sudden torque change for DTC-SVM whit PIF controller.

Fig. 21 presents the results when a specific torque profile is imposed to DTC-SVM scheme with STPIF controller. In this case the electromagnetic torque follow the reference.

Fig. 22 illustrates the response of the electromagnetic torque for the DTC-SVM scheme with STPIF controller, when applying step change in the motor load. In this test we used the rise time $t_r = 5.49mS$, the settling time $t_s = 12mS$ and the integral-of-time multiplied by the absolute magnitude of the error index $ITAE = 199.5$.

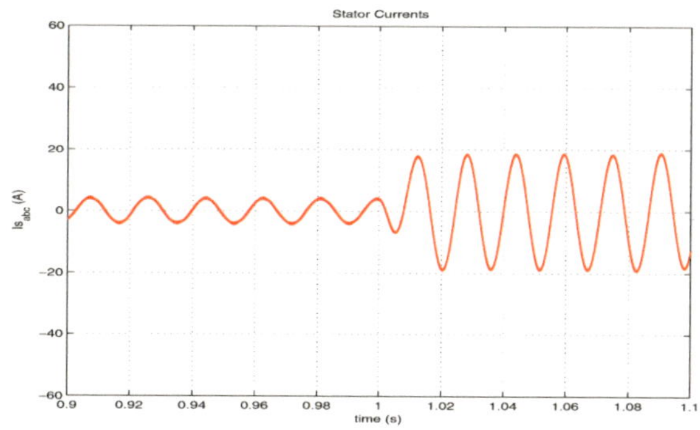

Figure 19. Phase *a* stator current for sudden torque change for DTC-SVM with PIF controller.

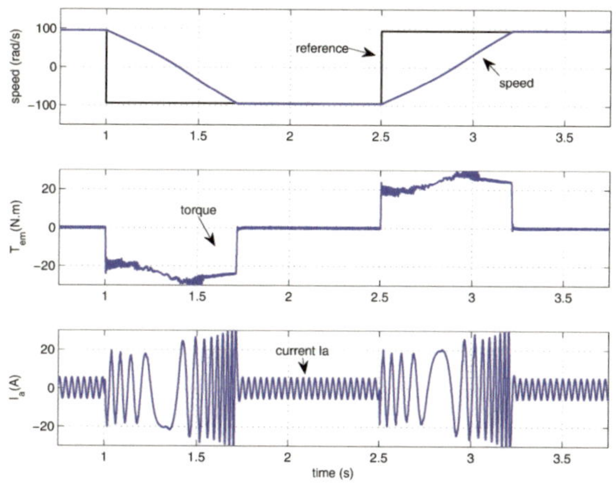

Figure 20. Speed, torque and phase *a* stator current for speed reversion for DTC-SVM with STPIF controller.

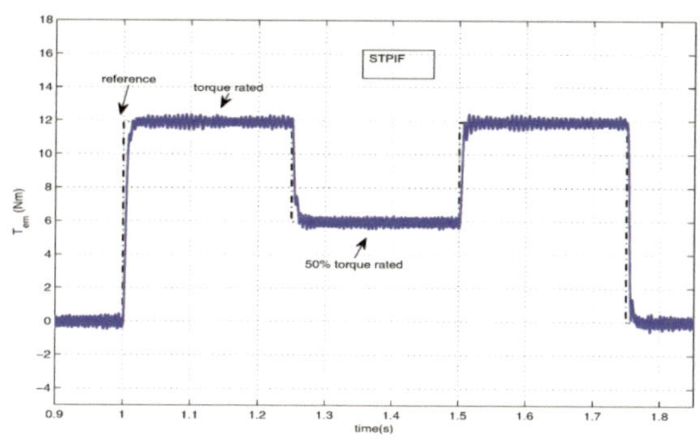

Figure 21. Torque profile for DTC-SVM whit STPIF

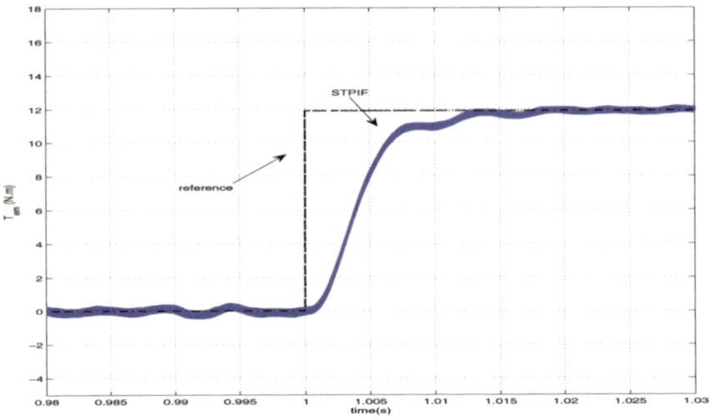

Figure 22. Step change in torque for DTC-SVM scheme with STPIF

Rated voltage (V)	220/60Hz
Rated Power (W)	2238
Rated Torque (Nm)	11.9
Rated Speed (rad/s)	179
$R_s, R_r(\Omega)$	0.435, 0.816
L_{ls}, L_{lr} (H)	0.002, 0.002
L_m (H)	0.0693
$J(K_g m^2)$	0.089
P	2

Table 5. Induction Motor Parameters [12]

6. Conclusion

In this chapter we have presented the DTC-SVM scheme that controls a three-phase IM using three different kinds of fuzzy controllers. These fuzzy controllers were used in order to determinate dynamically and on-line the load angle between stator and rotor flux vectors. Therefore, we determine the electromagnetic torque necessary to supply the motor load. We have conducted simulations with different operating conditions. Our simulation results show that the all proposed fuzzy controllers work appropriately and according to the schemes reported in the literature. However, the STPIF controller achieves a fast torque response and low torque ripple in a wide range of operating conditions such as: sudden change in the command speed and step change of the load.

Acknowledgements

The authors are grateful to FAPESP and CAPES for partially financial support.

Author details

José Luis Azcue and Ernesto Ruppert
School of Electrical and Computer Engineering of University of Campinas, UNICAMP, Department of Energy Control and Systems, Campinas-SP, Brazil

Alfeu J. Sguarezi Filho
CECS/UFABC, Santo André - SP, Brazil

7. References

[1] Abu-Rub, H., Guzinski, J., Krzeminski, Z. & Toliyat, H. [2004]. Advanced control of induction motor based on load angle estimation, *Industrial Electronics, IEEE Transactions on* 51(1): 5 – 14.

[2] Azcue P., J. L. [2010]. *Three-phase induction motor direct torque control using self-tuning pi type fuzzy controller*, Master's thesis, University of Campinas (UNICAMP).

[3] Azcue P., J. & Ruppert, E. [2010]. Three-phase induction motor dtc-svm scheme with self-tuning pi-type fuzzy controller, *Fuzzy Systems and Knowledge Discovery (FSKD), 2010 Seventh International Conference on*, Vol. 2, pp. 757 –762.

[4] Bertoluzzo, M., Buja, G. & Menis, R. [2007]. A direct torque control scheme for induction motor drives using the current model flux estimation, *Diagnostics for Electric Machines, Power Electronics and Drives, 2007. SDEMPED 2007. IEEE International Symposium on* pp. 185 –190.

[5] Cao, S.-G., Rees, N. & Feng, G. [1999]. Analysis and design of fuzzy control systems using dynamic fuzzy-state space models, *Fuzzy Systems, IEEE Transactions on* 7(2): 192 –200.

[6] Chen, C.-L. & Chang, M.-H. [1998]. Optimal design of fuzzy sliding-mode control: A comparative study, *Fuzzy Sets and Systems* 93(1): 37 – 48.
URL: *http://www.sciencedirect.com/science/article/pii/S0165011496002217*

[7] Chen, S., Kai, T., Tsuji, M., Hamasaki, S. & Yamada, E. [2005]. Improvement of dynamic characteristic for sensorless vector-controlled induction motor system with adaptive pi mechanism, *Electrical Machines and Systems, 2005. ICEMS 2005. Proceedings of the Eighth International Conference on*, Vol. 3, pp. 1877 –1881 Vol. 3.

[8] Depenbrock, M. [1988]. Direct self-control (dsc) of inverter-fed induction machine, *Power Electronics, IEEE Transactions on* 3(4): 420–429.

[9] Habetler, T., Profumo, F., Pastorelli, M. & Tolbert, L. [1992]. Direct torque control of induction machines using space vector modulation, *Industry Applications, IEEE Transactions on* 28(5): 1045 –1053.

[10] Koutsogiannis, Z., Adamidis, G. & Fyntanakis, A. [2007]. Direct torque control using space vector modulation and dynamic performance of the drive, via a fuzzy logic controller for speed regulation, *Power Electronics and Applications, 2007 European Conference on* pp. 1 –10.

[11] Kovacic, Z. & Bogdan, S. [2006]. *Fuzzy Controller Design: Theory and Applications*, CRC Press.

[12] Krause, P. C., Wasynczuk, O. & Sudhoff, S. D. [2002]. *Analysis of Electric Machinery and Drive Systems*, IEEE Press.

[13] Lascu, C., Boldea, I. & Blaabjerg, F. [2000]. A modified direct torque control for induction motor sensorless drive, *Industry Applications, IEEE Transactions on* 36(1): 122–130.

[14] Rodriguez, J., Pontt, J., Silva, C., Kouro, S. & Miranda, H. [2004]. A novel direct torque control scheme for induction machines with space vector modulation, *Power Electronics Specialists Conference, 2004. PESC 04. 2004 IEEE 35th Annual*, Vol. 2, pp. 1392 – 1397 Vol.2.

[15] Takahashi, I. & Noguchi, T. [1986]. A new quick-response and high-efficiency control strategy of an induction motor, *Industry Applications, IEEE Transactions on* IA-22(5): 820 –827.

[16] Trzynadlowski, A. M. [1993]. *The Field Orientation Principle in Control of Induction Motors*, springer.

[17] Vas, P. [1998]. *Sensorless Vector and Direct Torque Control*, Oxford University Press. ISBN 0198564651.

[18] Viola, J., Restrepo, J., Guzman, V. & Gimenez, M. [2006]. Direct torque control of induction motors using a fuzzy inference system for reduced ripple torque and current limitation, *Power Electronics and Motion Control Conference, 2006. EPE-PEMC 2006. 12th International*, pp. 1161 –1166.

[19] Yamakawa, T. [1993]. A fuzzy inference engine in nonlinear analog mode and its application to a fuzzy logic control, *Neural Networks, IEEE Transactions on* 4(3): 496 –522.